Mission as Transformation

"Transformation is to enable God's vision of society to be actualised in all relationships, social, economic, and spiritual, so that God's will may be reflected in human society and his love be experienced by all communities, especially the poor."
Vinay Samuel 1999.

Mission as Transformation:
A Theology of the Whole Gospel

Edited by
Vinay Samuel and
Chris Sugden

regnum

Regnum Books International
P.O. Box 70, Oxford, OX2 6HB, UK
17951 Cowan, Irvine, California 92714, USA
P.O. Box 76, Akropong-Akuapem, Ghana
Jose Marmol 1734, 1602 Florida, Buenos Aires, Argentina
Post Bag number 21, Vasant Kunj, New Delhi 110057, India

03 02 01 00 99   7 6 5 4 3 2 1

British Library Cataloguing in Publication Data
A catalogue record for this book is available from the British Library.

ISBN 1-870345-13-4

Typeset by WestKey Ltd., Falmouth, Cornwall
and printed and bound in the USA by
RR Donnelley and Sons, Harrisonburg, VA.

Contents

Callslip Request   12/5/2011 7:53:03 AM

Pick-up Location

Location: stx
Call Number: 2oo Mo784
Copy Info: c.1
User Comments:

Title   Mission as transformatio
Item Barcode:

Patron Category: UBReg
Patron Barcode:

Request Date/Time: 12/2/2011 08 0 4 AM
Request ID:

Part III
Transformation and Praxis: Practical Issues from the Perspective of Wholistic Mission

Introduction

The aim of this book is to bring together in one place material that has been developed since 1983 on the understanding and practice of Mission as Transformation. Mission as Transformation was developed by an international network of evangelicals who were heavily involved in social ministries. Evidence of their action and reflection began to emerge significantly in the seventies. The Chicago Declaration of Evangelical Social Concern (Appendix A) was made by evangelicals in the United States in 1973 in preparation for the Lausanne Congress of 1974. At that Congress, Dr Rene Padilla and Dr Samuel Escobar from Latin America gave public expression to a missiological understanding that focused on the whole gospel for the whole person, in their social, political, economic, cultural and religious contexts. The Lausanne Covenant (Appendix B) in paragraphs 4 and 5 gave expression to the validity of both evangelism and social responsibility as part of Christian mission. This validation provided a very important affirmation for much ministry that evangelicals had been carrying out, especially in the Two-Thirds World, but had to remain silent about in some quarters lest they be misunderstood as weakening their commitment to sharing the gospel. However the paragraph did not specify the relation between evangelism and social action. In addressing this lacuna, a series of consultations took place. Even though the integrative nature of evangelism and social responsibility needed further elaboration, the Lausanne Covenant had legitimised a growing number of evangelical relief and development agencies in the eyes of evangelical constituencies who began providing increasing financial support to them. They grew exponentially in the 1970s. But they lacked a clear biblical basis for understanding of being involved in development. So a process began in 1978 to explore a theology of development. This process overlapped with and took forward the discussions on evangelism and social concern.

At the 1983 Wheaton Conference sponsored by the World Evangelical Fellowship under the title 'I Will Build My Church', the third track of the conference, the Consultation on the Church in Response to Human Need produced a statement on Transformation. Its key paragraph 11 read:

> According to the biblical view of human life, then, transformation is the change from a condition of human existence contrary to God's purposes to one in which people are able to enjoy fulness of life in harmony with God (Jn 10:10; Col 3:8-15; Eph. 4:13). This transformation can only take place through the obedience of individuals and communities to the Gospel of Jesus Christ, whose power changes the lives of men and women by releasing them from the guilt, power and consequences of sin, enabling them to respond with love toward God and towards others (Rom 5:5) and making them 'new creatures in Christ' (2 Cor 5:17).

This statement, encapsulated in part in this paragraph, sought with some success to overcome polarities in the evangelism, social action and development debates that had developed up to that time. Over against the notion that some nations developed others, or were more developed than others, it insisted that all people and communities needed transformation; over against a statement of Christian mission solely in terms of personal transformation it stressed that communities needed to obey the Gospel of Jesus Christ in value transformation; over against the notion that social action would be enough to bring justice it stressed the need to deal with the guilt, power and consequences of sin through the Gospel of Christ; over against the notion that society would be changed by converting individuals to Christ, it stressed that people and communities needed to enjoy fulness of life in harmony with God through obedience to the Gospel.

This statement along with the statement from the Consultation on the Relationship between Evangelism and Social Responsibility in 1982,[1] put to final rest for many evangelicals, especially in the Two-Thirds World the argument between evangelism and social action. The evidence is that there has been no significant disagreement with the 1983 Wheaton Statement on Transformation – the Church in Response to Human Need in evangelical mission circles, and that it has formed the basis of the theological understanding of many of the leading evangelical relief and development agencies. Further statements have been produced since then expressing the implications of such an understanding of mission for evangelism, church state relations, economics, and many practical expressions of Christian care for the 'excluded', children and the disabled.

Since 1983 a new generation has arisen who have been drawn into wholistic Christian mission. They have brought professional skills from their disciplines and been welcomed into the fellowship of those engaging in wholistic mission, without being theologians. This has been a heartening process. But it also has its dangers. The generation that produced the statement on Transformation had to wrestle with the scriptures in searching for the biblical path of obedience in this area. The subsequent question was not whether to be involved in social action but how. As a consequence, theology has taken a back seat to strategic initiatives. Moreover the new generation of professionals voiced no theological disagreement with their evangelical predecessors. But the result is that agencies have less theological literacy in these matters than a decade or so ago. Since the world of development and social involvement is so dominated by secular culture through funding and government policies, it would be very easy for Christian agencies to lose their Christian undergirding and vision as to why and how they are involved in such ministry as part of their gospel obedience and as Christian mission. One reason for bringing this material together in one place is to articulate for a new generation the theological and biblical resources that inform wholistic Christian mission.

Since 1983 a new global community has also joined the wholistic mission movement: the Pentecostal movement. A wit has written that 'while the Roman Catholic Church in Latin America opted for the poor, the poor opted for the Pentecostals'. The growth of the Pentecostal movement among poor communities has been a major feature of mission in the last 20 years. They have made their own journey and their own contribution to the understanding of wholistic mission. In 1998 the Assemblies of God produced their own statement on 'A Pentecostal approach to evangelisation and social concern'. A second reason for bringing this material together is to make this Pentecostal contribution available.

Major changes have also taken place in the world situation since 1983. The Cold War, which had lain behind many of the suspicions of anything which looked like 'socialism', ended in 1989. Since then the globalisation and integration of all systems in the world has increased apace bringing significant challenges for Christian mission. Much mission thinking has been able to address particular aspects of mission, such as politics and population growth. In addressing the changing global context, the implications of Transformation as a theology of mission have been clarified. A third reason for bringing this material together is to show how the new expressions and implications of Transformation have been worked out.

Key Elements in Transformation

As the unpacking has occurred, some key elements in Transformation have emerged. Fundamentally Transformation is the transformation of communities to reflect kingdom values. The recovery of eschatology and the theology of the Kingdom of God was fundamental to the development of the notion of Transformation. A significant section of this book therefore focuses on the biblical foundations of the understanding of the Kingdom of God. The concern for the Kingdom of God and for wholistic mission is fundamentally a Christological concern. Vinay Samuel writes that a wholistic ministry based on kingdom theology of mission

> centred in the rule of Christ over the whole of life, seeks to impact a community with the values of the kingdom and the spiritual challenges of the kingdom. It recognises that enabling people to experience Christ's Lordship is the key to wholistic ministry.

Such a ministry looks at the transformation that emerges in a community which includes the planting of a church. This transformation is particularly important in the realm of culture.

> Cultures are religio-linguistic entities. They provide people with a framework for understanding their reality and a means for integrating the transcendant into daily life....One must look at how the gospel affects the whole of the communities' cultures, in value system, structures and direction. Vinay Samuel, 'A theological perspective' in *Serving with the Poor In Asia* ed Tetsunao Yamamori, Bryant Myers and David Connor (Monrovia: MARC 1995) pp. 146, 147, 157.

Other key elements in Transformation are: an integral relation between evangelism and social change; Mission as witness and journey in the world; Mission in context; Truth, commitment to change and imagination; Theology, Christian mission and understanding are always local; Freedom and power for the poor; Reconciliation and solidarity; Building communities of change. These elements are explored in Vinay Samuel's contribution on Mission as Transformation.

• While the Kingdom of God is one important theological theme undergirding mission as Transformation, other themes are also important. The Pentecostal movement has identified the role of the Spirit in bringing the experience of transformation, especially for the poor. So a section of Part I on Biblical and Theological Foundations explores the theme of the Spirit and Transformation that emerged both in an international dialogue between evangelicals, charismatics and pentecostals, and in the theological understanding of the Assemblies of God.

As the understanding of Transformation was explored in the realm of economics (1990) and environment (1993), the themes of God as creator and humanity as the steward of creation emerged. Thus a theology of evangelicalism which in some of its expressions had focused almost exclusively on the person and work of Christ as the key to understanding and expressing Christian mission, has with the development of the Kingdom of God, the role of the Spirit, and the work of God in creation become more trinitarian.

This collection is arranged in three parts. Part I explores biblical and theological foundations. Part II explores the missiological expressions of Transformation, particularly in relation to the poor, to development, to evangelism and to modernity. Part III entitled 'Transformation and Praxis' examines practical issues from the perspective of wholistic theology. This third part draws on a series of theological consultations and publications developed under the auspices of the International Fellowship of Mission Theologians, its resource and study centre The Oxford Centre for Mission Studies, and its publications arm Regnum Books International, principally through its quarterly journal *Transformation: An International Dialogue on Mission and Ethics*. *Transformation* has tended to act as the journal of record for the materials developed in exploring Transformation theology. Much of this section was developed in consultations involving many authors. The participants from many cultures and continents captured, in jointly authored statements, their deliberations over a week or ten days based on biblical reflection on their experience. This represents a significant way of doing theology in Transformation. First, mission is the mother of theology, and theological and biblical reflection arises out of engagement with the context, experience and questions of mission. Second, theology and biblical study is inherently a cross-cultural and inter-cultural exercise as people from different cultures share their insights on the biblical text. Thirdly theology is a team game, developed as iron sharpens iron wrestling with issues raised by the call to the obedience of faith.

Mission as Transformation: The Future

It is now twenty years since the process began of reflection on evangelical development practice in the light of the Bible, which gave rise to mission as Transformation. Twenty years ago the divide between evangelicals and liberals over mission was still between proclamation and social action. The missiology of Transformation has contributed to evangelicals combining proclamation with social action as part of mission. It is not clear that liberals on their part have combined proclamation with their passionate commitment to social action. Transformation suggests that liberal missiologies are therefore at this point reductionist with regard to orthodox Christian teaching.

The challenges to orthodox Christian mission practice however come at the beginning of a new millenium from a different quarter. In the mid twentieth century, both evangelicals and liberals shared a common intellectual framework of modernity: the commitment to understand a common text (the bible); a commitment to the universality and role of reason in human discussion; a commitment to appropriate authorities, be they intellectual, legislative or ecclesiastical. It mattered to liberals and evangelicals alike what the Bible was interpreted to mean (text), what positions were rationally objective (the common agreement about reason); and what authorities such as university professors or international Christian bodies said (authority).

The world twenty five years later is very different. The intellectual world, certainly in the West, has affirmed the centrality not of any objective criteria for truth, but of the freedom and authority of autonomous self. The economic and political world in the West has also affirmed the priority of the self in the globalisation of economies, the dominance of the market, the retreat from state control of business or economic life. And these policies appear to be highly successful for some. The New York Stock Market reached an all time high. Within that context, the secular world affirms the plurality of lifestyles. There are no moral choices, only lifestyle choices. Liberal Christians affirm the diversity and plurality of choices for Christian lifestyles and maintain their commitment to Christian unity by affirming inclusivity, that all must be equally welcome and have access to lead and teach the church, regardless of how their lifestyle might be evaluated by the former criteria of bible (text), reason, or authority.

In such a context, Christians committed to a mission based on orthodox Christian teaching, can often use old weapons to fight the new war since those weapons proved successful in earlier campaigns. Thus just as evangelicals came to terms with modernity, the academy, and science in the mid-twentieth century, and based their arguments for Christian faith on the reliability of the biblical text, arguments from reason (such as the evidence for the resurrection), and the authority of Christian history and tradition, they found that the intellectual culture was impervious to these arguments. The Bible was still revered, but as a story of human experience of faith, not of God's action; reason was shown to be culturally determined and biased in the favour of white, male, wealthy cultures; and all authorities were suspect since they regularly inhibited the individual's freedom of self-expression and identity. Indeed, modernity had itself undermined orthodoxy. For modernity offered access to a universal truth, accessible to all, rationally and objectively grounded. If such was possible, Christian faith had to comply with that universal truth. As such it was rendered superfluous.

To return to the old weapons is like using bows and arrows to fight tanks.

How then is Christian mission based on orthodoxy to be commended in this new climate? We must first understand the present climate from a biblical perspective. The autonomy of the individual self who claims the right to express their identity in untrammelled freedom and demand the best for themselves in the market is a sophisticated way of speaking of selfishness.

A number of missionary models are available today. There are the AD 2000 models, the Unreached People model, the Church Growth Model, the Power Encounter Model. These are all market based models, based on increasing growth. Their sensitivity to their context is often in doubt. They homogenise their approach, and undermine local creativity.

There are pluralist models. In the increasing globalisation of the world, people recover their identity by focusing beyond the reach of economics to religion and race. There is a great focus on the contextualisation of all expressions of faith, and on indigenous religious expressions as being most authentic. This is not an entirely negative situation. It enables people to recover their uniqueness in their own way. The downside of this model is that no one allows you to hold your identity in peace. It introduces local conflicts.

The Transformation model which we consider in this volume is rooted in the theology of the mission of the Kingdom of God and seeks to express the Lordship of Jesus over every aspect of life, economic, religious, personal, political. It does not give priority to any area of life as an area for mission, but insists that religious change is at the heart of all real change. But this change will be effected whenever people address issues of life directly, rooted in a gospel perspective. The key elements in Transformation are, again: an integral relation between evangelism and social change; Mission as witness and journey in the world; Mission in context; Truth, commitment to change and imagination; Theology, Christian mission and understanding are always local; Freedom and power for the poor; Reconciliation and solidarity; Building communities of change.

Two biblical distinctives are particularly important in the current western cultural climate. The incarnation helps us to take the world and civil society seriously, and engage with the world as church, not just as individual Christians. In contemporary society there is an increasing emphasis on mission as enterprise. The rapid growth of indigenous mission societies in the Two-Thirds World is the expression of the enterprising qualities of indigenous Christians. Mission needs such qualities which are not by definition immoral or unChristian. In India the natural gifts of enterprise helped develop hundreds of mission societies, many of whom practice wholistic mission. The work of one of the oldest of these, the Friends Missionary Prayer Band, has laid the foundation of three new dioceses in the Church of North India. But we need to balance mission as enterprise with mission as sacrifice.

Sacrifice is an important criteria by which to evaluate all mission. That is the climax of the mission of Jesus on the cross. For him, mission was at its heart sacrifice, pain. This was not just the pain of physical suffering. It was the pain of 'erased relationships'. These are possibly the most bitter pains. Physical pain can be tempered by the love, comfort and support of others. To broken relationships there is no physical, or economic or social cure. Mission as sacrifice for Jesus involved the erased relationship with his Father on the cross to restore those broken relationships between humans and God and one another.

This concept is a challenge to the enterprise based and pain avoiding culture. It should be distinguished from the pain and discomfort people are prepared to undergo to secure their own concerns: the hard working risk taking businessperson endures a degree of suffering, but this is not sacrifice for others. Enterprise shaped sacrifice looks Christian, but such suffering is a personal investment. Mission as sacrifice stands in contrast to pain avoiding cultures. In the Kosovo conflict, NATO announced they would not risk one soldier's life, even though the lives of thousands of men, women and children were under threat.

Culture affects the way we do mission. A particular example of this is the current wisdom of much business, which refuses to take risks with low performing organisations. Even Christian Aid and development agencies are developing a taxonomy of only dealing with those organisations that have well developed systems and good results. In one case this led one organisation to cut those organisations they dealt with from 38 to 12 of which only 1 was from Africa.

There are however movements that do accept mission as pain and sacrifice. This concern is passed on through those churches which develop a culture of supporting others; through families who set an example to their children of bearing suffering to assist others. This central focus of mission will save us from the mistakes and prejudices of some of our cultures which will lead us away from the central concerns of God's will for humanity.

The wellspring of mission as sacrifice is not confidence in the present, or the opportunities that are presented in the current world situation through technology, education, wealth or any other advantage. It is confidence derived from the past, and in particular from the experience of God's faithfulness in the past. This experience is testimony of people to God's continuing faithfulness. It must be distinguished from the recounting of the story of faith. The story of faith is a story about human beings and their response. Testimony is witness to the faithfulness of God. Post-modern understandings of the Bible and Christian faith make no distinction between these. The only category is the story of the faith of people, which has no implications as to the truth of what people have faith in. This is a simple point of the philosophy of religion. Orthodox Christian understanding on the other hand claims that the story of Christians in the past and the present is not only or primarily a story of their faith, (for so often in the Bible the story is rather one of faithlessness), it is a story of the faithfulness of God.

As we enter the twenty first century it is clear that there are many areas in which the church needs to continue to develop its praxis and its reflection. Mission as Transformation has yet adequately to address the issues and contexts of poverty such that the church and Christian development agencies can address contexts where people are poor effectively and with confidence. Mission as Transformation needs to address adequately the issue of strengthening civil society so that society as a whole experiences and expresses Christian values of justice and righteousness. Mission as Transformation needs to address economic life to combine growth with equity and the world of religious plurality. The church itself must also continue be transformed in its own self-understanding and management, away from such modernist concepts as Donald Miller describes:

> Enlightenment thought prescribed rationality and scientific empiricism as the basis for all explorations of truth. One result is that religious debates have been relegated to discussing the truth or falsity of beliefs, making religion a 'disembodied' cerebral matter. . . . The clay feet of rationality have been revealed, and postmodern philosophy is questioning the authoritarian character of any claim to universal epistemology or theory of knowledge. . . . New paradigm churches are attempting to reintegrate bodily experience into religious life. Worship is not simply a matter of the head, affirming various creeds or acknowledging normative beliefs. . . . Beliefs are important, especially when anchored in the retelling of biblical stories, but beliefs in themselves are sterile. Religion is a full bodied experience which includes all the receptors- all the senses with the rational mind being only one locus of information about reality. . . . New paradigm Christians see no reason why they should exclude visions and ecstatic experiences from the realm of religious knowledge. (*Reinventing American Protestantism*, Donald Miller, University of California Press, 1997.)

The process of Transformation applies not only to the world around, but to the church in its life and being. The definitive word on Transformation has not been spoken, and probably never will be spoken, for we are all ' being transformed into his likeness with ever-increasing glory, which comes from the Lord who is the Spirit.' (2 Cor 3.18).

The editors hope that this exposition of Transformation theology and wholistic mission proves an important resource for extending God's gracious work of reconciliation in the world.

Part I

Biblical and Theological Foundations

Introduction to Part One

The Kingdom of God is the organising biblical and theological concept of Mission as Transformation. In Part I, the theme of the Kingdom is explored in depth. The first three chapters explore Christology and Mission as Transformation. Chapters four to six focus on 'The Spirit and Transformation', and chapters seven to ten address issues of Eschatology and Transformation.

The Kingdom of God is presented as central to the way Jesus understood himself and his mission. So chapter one is a statement on Christology produced in Bangkok in 1982 by the first Conference of Evangelical Mission Theologians from the Two-Thirds World, the precursor of the International Fellowship of Evangelical Mission Theologians. The Conference focused on Christology and entitled its papers 'Sharing Jesus in the Two-Thirds World'. Orlando Costas gave the keynote address on 'Proclaiming Christ in the Two-Thirds World'. He identified a new focus emerging in the Two-Thirds World on the historical Jesus and the active presence of Christ among the struggles of the poor, the powerless and the oppressed. He was convinced that the whole Gospel was more authentically recovered and expressed in mission with the poor and oppressed peoples of the world and where the agents and bearers of the Gospel were poor themselves. The statement represents an evangelical commitment to developing Christology in context at the heart of mission. It affirms that 'at the heart of Christian mission is our understanding of Jesus Christ, his person and mission' and develops the meaning of Jesus' person and work in each context.

Chapter two draws on materials from the Pentecostal movement. Since 1983 the Pentecostal movement has joined the stream affirming wholistic mission. Pentecostal growth has been among poor communities. They bring their own contribution to the understanding of wholistic mission. In 1988 a dialogue began between evangelicals, charismatics and pentecostals on Social Action. Three consultations took place in 1988, 1990 and finally in 1994. Graham Cray presented a paper at the first on a Theology of the Kingdom, bringing together the understanding of the Kingdom of God in the work of writers such as Rene Padilla and George Eldon Ladd with the insights of the gift of the Spirit as the gift of the new age. The process ended with the adoption of the statement of Kingdom Affirmations and Commitments by the 1994 conference which appears as chapter three. The statement originated with the Te Atatu Bible Fellowship in New Zealand, was built on by an international forum and brought together a biblical understanding of mission that centred on the kingdom with missiological implications.

The Spirit and Transformation

In 1998 key leaders of the Division of Foreign Missions (DFM) of the Assemblies of God produced their own statement on 'A Pentecostal approach to evangelisation and social concern', the 'Brussels Statement', reprinted here as chapter six. Chapter four by Murray Dempster, entitled 'Social Concern in the Context of Jesus' Kingdom Mission and Ministry', and chapter five by Douglas Petersen, 'Pentecostals – who are they?', provided the original theological and missiological statements respectively which informed the Brussels Conference which drew up the 'Brussels Statement' for adoption by the Assemblies of God DFM.

The Kingdom of God and Transformation

A rediscovery of eschatology by evangelicals has lain behind the development of wholistic mission and transformation. The notion that the Kingdom of God would come in its fulness at the return of Jesus, not just to take individuals to heaven, but to bring a new heaven and new earth in which righteousness would be at home and into which the kings of the earth would bring their glory, has acted as an important stimulus to Christian social involvement by evangelicals. Howard Snyder in chapter seven 'Models of the Kingdom: Sorting out the Practical Meaning of God's Reign' traces a number of understandings of the kingdom of God in Christian history, which demonstrate ways in which the transforming effect of the kingdom on the whole of life can either be expressed, or undermined. Peter Kuzmic in chapter eight in 'Eschatology and Ethics: Evangelical Views and Attitudes' traces how various evangelical views on the millennium shape and influence ethical behaviour especially in the field of socio-political engagement. This made an important contribution to the discussions in the Consultation on the Relation between Evangelism and Social Responsibility in 1982. Vinay Samuel and Chris Sugden in chapter nine develop the theme of the implications of eschatology for understanding God's work and purpose for the world in an article entitled 'God's Intention for the World' presented at the Wheaton consultation in 1983 that produced the Transformation statement. In the seventies and eighties some in the evangelical constituency were very hesitant to embrace the theme of the kingdom of God for Christian social involvement. They saw the kingdom as a utopian ideal focused on Church members and inappropriate for guiding Christian behaviour in a mixed society. In chapter ten Chris Sugden's response on 'Kingdom and Creation in Social Ethics' to some of these concerns voiced by Oliver Barclay, onetime general secretary of Inter-Varsity UK, was the fruit of over 10 years of intense discussions.

Taken together, the chapters provide an overview of the biblical and theological foundations for a wholistic mission theology known as Transformation, developed by evangelicals and pentecostals from 1983 to the present.

One

Why a Conference?

In the late seventies a group of theologians and missiologists from around the world were preparing for an important consultation. Some months before their meeting, the coordinator received a letter from one of the European delegates suggesting that it would be quite adequate and less expensive for the participants to exchange written papers and conduct the consultation by correspondence. The coordinator replied that the writer would do far more than present a paper at the consultation. He would discover new brothers in Christ.

Sharing Jesus in the Two-Thirds World[1] is a book from a conference, the First Conference of Evangelical Mission Theologians from the Two-Thirds World, held in Bangkok from March 20–25, 1982. In the keynote address published here, Orlando Costas gives the background to the calling of the conference. But this book seeks to do more than bind together between two covers the papers presented there. For the conference was more than a forum to present papers. It was a creative workshop to facilitate and promote reflection in

'Why a Conference?' in *Sharing Jesus in the Two-Thirds World*, edited by Vinay Samuel and Chris Sugden (Grand Rapids, Eerdmans, 1986).

community. It was a meeting and a fellowship of persons, testing and affirming insights gained from diverse cultural and theological backgrounds to deepen their understanding of Christ.

The product of the conference was thus more than a collection of papers. It was the creation, experience, and development of community. The book tries to capture this dimension by recording the essence and thrust of some of the discussions, which have been edited for conciseness while preserving the speaker's intention. The video and audio cassette tapes of the conference, including a single three-hour video presentation of the highlights (available from PIM Asia, P.O. Box 162, St. Ives, Sydney 2075, Australia) capture this dimension more fully.

Another product of the conference was a sense of unity. The papers and discussions reflect a unity of commitment to Christ and his mission rather than a uniformity of outlook. The concerns of this commitment are outlined in a final chapter which attempts to discern the issues that emerged during the conference.

The purpose of this process was not to produce a catch-all final statement which could be cited as Two-Thirds World mission theology. The focus was more on the process as time was given for presenters to elaborate their views in discussion, and for the group as a whole to reflect at length on the issues raised. There was no pressure to produce an agreed statement. The final document is only by way of a findings report. It marks the spot on the map where evangelical mission theologians from the Two-Thirds World think they are at the moment. It acts as a signpost to direct them in their further action, biblical study, and reflection.

Why Christology?

At the heart of Christian mission is our understanding of Jesus Christ, his person and mission. A fundamental unity emerged of commitment to the full and final authority of the Scriptures and to Jesus Christ as Saviour and Lord, both personally and communally. The conference affirmed its commitment to the uniqueness, preexistence, Lordship, resurrection, atoning death, and second coming of Jesus Christ.

Many participants felt unable to give a definitive evangelical Christology in their context at this point in time. To be true to their situations, they felt that so many new areas were only now being opened up which contribute to formulating such Christologies, that they felt able only to set directions and agendas for the process of discerning the meaning of Jesus Christ of the Scriptures in their context. They could only share with us the milestone they had reached.

From North America, black and hispanic Christians stressed that they do not always define who Jesus is in the same terms white evangelicals use. Black American Christians point out that the image of Jesus Christ first presented to their forbears by white slave masters was couched in the dominant structures of society. The black experience forced black Christians to discover for themselves from the Bible a new image of Jesus to replace one which they considered to be inauthentic.

Indonesian Christians pointed out that the Christian message which they received from Europe was already couched in terms of European intellectual and analytical rationalism and expressed in European cultural forms.

African Christians questioned the adequacy of the European and North American missionary understanding of the gospel. They sought new dimensions in understanding the biblical Christ for their people in interaction with the African concepts of ancestor veneration and sacral kingship.

Two distinct images of Christ emerge from the Korean church. One is of a figure of protest against governmental injustice. This leads some Christians to accept imprisonment as an authentic witness to the image of Christ for their society. Other Christians feel that such confrontation with the government only jeopardizes the church's witness to the authentic image of Christ as Saviour of all men.

The Context of the Conference

The context in which the conference was held was itself informative and illustrative of our world. While the conference was on, a coup took place in Bangladesh and the travel plans of some members to minister there had to be cancelled. At the same time upheavals in Central America made the return of one participant back to his family very uncertain as borders were closed. Within a month of British and Argentinian theologians dialoguing together, their countries would be at war. One paper writer from Africa was detained during his travel. Since he was unable to produce a vaccination certificate relevant to a transit stop of a few hours, he was held up at a second transit point. He was asked for a small bribe to be allowed to continue his journey. Our contributor refused to pay it, and so was turned back. Another African contributor was refused a visa to leave his country. For these reasons of the setting we live in, the African section of the papers is regrettably reduced in size.

Two contributors brought papers from Europe and North America to affirm that whatever previous imbalances may have existed, we cannot redress them in isolation from one another. Our growth in the body of Christ and as the body of Christ depends on each part continuing to contribute its gift and receive from every other part.

One female participant attended the conference but for various reasons no paper was presented by a woman. There are many possible arrangements to avoid sexist bias in written language. But such arrangements seem contrived when used in speech. Since these papers were originally presented in speech, we have kept the reference to 'men' and 'he' where women are clearly included, but hopefully, not suppressed.

We are most grateful to David and Ruth Thorne for their assistance in preparing the manuscript for the press.

The Editors
Bangalore, Christmas 1982

Note

1. The term refers to the two-thirds of the world's population who live in contexts of poverty and powerlessness.

Two

Kingdom Affirmations and Commitments

Preamble

From March 1–5, 1994, 85 Christians from six continents gathered in Malaysia to seek the Spirit's guidance on how an understanding of the Kingdom could help integrate the three streams of world evangelisation, social action, and renewal in the Spirit. After prayer, dialogue, and searching of the Scriptures, we offer these Kingdom affirmations and commitments to the church worldwide because we believe that focussing on the Gospel Jesus himself announced can unite and empower the church today for costly obedience and wholistic mission.

After John was put into prison, Jesus went into Galilee, proclaiming the good news of God. 'The time has come,' he said. 'The Kingdom of God is near. Repent and believe the good news.'[1] Our Lord Jesus commanded His disciples to pray daily, Your Kingdom come, Your will be

'Kingdom Affirmations and Commitments' in *Transformation*, Vol. 11, No. 3, July 1994.

done on earth,[2] and to seek first the Kingdom of God[3] in the totality of their lives. By word and action, in Galilee, Golgotha and the empty tomb, Jesus powerfully and visibly demonstrated God's reign over all of life. That reign is now powerfully present among us and will reach its fulfillment at Christ's return.

Around the world, in many different places and traditions, the theme of the Kingdom has become central in a new way in our time. It has inspired charismatics, pentecostals, evangelical social activists, ecumenical leaders, and people devoted to world evangelisation. Unfortunately, many Christians have yet to discover the full importance of Jesus' good news of the Kingdom. But we believe that developing our theology and mission with particular attention to the way Jesus himself defined his person and work will help to unite the church to offer God's healing to a lost and broken world.

We Confess That All Too Often –

We have obscured our witness to the Kingdom by tearing apart the interrelated tasks of proclamation of the Word and social transformation, and tried to do both without total dependence on the power of the Holy Spirit.

We have ignored the centrality of the Good News of the Kingdom of God in the teaching of Jesus, failing to present the Gospel the way Jesus did.

We have distorted Jesus' Gospel by failing to preach and demonstrate that it always includes Good News for the poor.

We have failed to recognise that love is the definite mark of the Kingdom of God – neglecting to love the Lord with all our heart, soul, strength and mind, and our neighbours as ourselves.

We have diluted Jesus' Gospel by neglecting to proclaim and live its radical challenge to the evil in every culture, society and socio-economic system.

We have disgraced the Gospel by failing to live what Jesus taught.

We have mocked by our proud divisions Jesus' prayer that our visible love for each other would convince the world he came from the Father.

Some have one-sidedly emphasised the individual and personal aspects of the Kingdom of God to the neglect of the corporate and communal, and others have done the reverse.

We have failed to serve our neighbours and witness to the Kingdom in the affairs of government, education, business, economics, trade unions, science, welfare, medicine, the media and the arts.

We have prayed Your Kingdom come and ignored the command to seek it first in our personal and societal lifestyles.

Therefore we repent of our failure to let Christ be King in these areas. We will redress these failures with biblical teaching, small group accountability, robust theological debate and wholistic congregations and ministries that integrate proclamation, social transformation and renewal in the power of the Holy Spirit.

Biblical Foundations

The Lord is a great God and King above all gods.[4] As the Creator, Sustainer, Owner and Ruler of the whole universe God has never given up, nor will God ever give up, his rule over this universe.

God placed the world under the stewardship of women and men made in God's own image.[5] Tragically they rebelled against their Creator, bringing devastation, disorder and evil into the entire created order.[6] Yet God still desired to establish his authority and rule in the lives of persons and societies. Through Israel, his chosen people, God began to reveal the plan of salvation and restoration of creation. The prophets promised that some day the Messiah would come to bring God's actual rule on earth in a new, powerful way. In that day, there would be salvation, justice, and peace – wholeness in all areas of life – for men, women and children.[7]

Jesus the carpenter, son of David and eternal Son of God, fulfilled the prophetic promise and inaugurated the Messianic age by proclaiming and demonstrating the Kingdom of God.[8] As he healed the sick, cast out demons and announced the Good News of the Kingdom, he demonstrated and taught that the reign of God had broken decisively into history in his person and work.[9]

The character of this dawning Kingdom became clear through Jesus' astonishing words and works which followed his anointing by the Holy Spirit. He taught that God freely welcomes all who repent of their sins and seek God's forgiveness. He identified the enemies of God's Kingdom as Satan with his evil forces and all people who join him in opposing God.

Jesus challenged the evils of his society and showed special concern for the poor, weak and marginalised. To those denied human power and dignity, Jesus offered full access to the love and power of God and a dignified place in the human community. He taught that his Kingdom was not a political kingdom of this world that one could install through military power.[10] But he also showed that his Kingdom was becoming visible in this world both in miraculous signs and wonders and in the new community of forgiven sinners – women and men, prostitutes and tax collectors, young and old, rich and poor, educated and uneducated – who were beginning to live the Kingdom principles he taught. In fact, Jesus insisted that the love and unity of his disciples would be so powerfully visible that it would demonstrate that he had come from the Father.

So sweeping was his challenge to the established social order and so unacceptable his claims to be Messiah and only begotten Son of the Father, that the authorities crucified him to prove that his claims were false. On the cross, Jesus atoned for our sins and reconciled us to God as that we could freely enter his new Kingdom as forgiven sinners. His resurrection on the third day confirmed that the Kingdom of God had broken decisively into history. It also showed that Jesus' example of suffering love, self-denial and suffering for righteousness' sake is normative for believers and a central way in which the kingdom brings life in this world.

After his resurrection and return to the Father, Jesus sent the Holy Spirit to equip and empower men and women to live, proclaim and demonstrate the Good News of the Kingdom to the ends of the earth.[11] In different settings and contexts, the first Christians described the Gospel as the Good News of Christ,[12] of God,[13] of salvation,[14] of grace,[15] and of peace.[16] They were not preaching new, divergent Gospels but rather retelling with different words the one story about Jesus, the Galilean teacher who is the expected Messiah, risen Lord and only Saviour, who now offers salvation freely to all who repent, believe, and join his Messianic community. The Risen Lord called the members of that new community to submit their total lives to his Lordship.[17] As the early church did that, society's sinful walls dividing men and women, Jews and Greeks, rich and poor came crashing down. So different was this new community of the King that Paul dared to teach that the very existence of this multi-ethnic, multi-class body of men and women was a central part of the Gospel he proclaimed and a major demonstration of the power of the cross.[18]

The early church's failure and sin underlines the truth that the Kingdom will not be present in its fullness until Christ returns.[19] Meanwhile the battle with Satan and the kingdom of darkness continues to rage. But the resurrection demonstrates that the Risen One will ultimately prevail.[20] At His return, Christ will complete God's plan of restoring the entire created order to wholeness. That ultimate salvation includes not only the resurrection of persons, but the restoration of the groaning creation,[21] and the inauguration of the new Jerusalem filled with the honour and glory of the nations.[22] Then the kingdoms of this world will truly be the Kingdom of our Lord.

The King and His Kingdom

1. We believe that the Kingdom of God and Jesus Christ the King are inseparable.[23]

   Therefore we make the Lord Jesus Christ our central focus. We refuse either to substitute human programmes for the King and his kingdom or to divorce the naming of the King from the doing of his will.

2. We believe that the Kingdom of God becomes evident where people confess the King and do his will.

   Therefore by word and deed we seek to share the Gospel with men, women and children everywhere, inviting them to accept Christ as Saviour and Lord, join his new community, and submit their total lives to his rule.[24]

3. We believe that wherever people do God's will, signs of the kingdom emerge in human society.

   Therefore we will co-operate with all who do God's will in their searching for peace, justice, life and freedom. In so doing we will always witness that the foundation and fulfillment of God's will are found in Jesus the King of the Kingdom.

4. We believe that God, through the Spirit, enabled Jesus to proclaim and demonstrate the Kingdom of God while he was on earth.[25]

   Therefore we encourage women and men to seek the gifts of the Holy Spirit and know the Holy Spirit's empowering as they seek first the Kingdom of God.

5. We believe churches are called to be the visible expressions of Christ's dawning Kingdom.

Therefore we seek to be transformed communities whose loving unity convinces the world that Jesus came from the Father; we seek to be caring communities that demonstrate to our confused world that the divisions of race, gender and class can be overcome in Christ; and we seek, like Jesus, to challenge all that is evil in society, showing special concern for the weak, poor and marginalised.

6. We believe the Bible is the basis for our understanding of God's Kingdom.[26]

Therefore we fully acknowledge the trustworthiness of the Scriptures of the Old and New Testament, confess that Christ is their centre, and seek to interpret all matters of faith and conduct in the light of its teaching under the guidance of the Holy Spirit.

Signs of the Kingdom of God

We believe that the following are significant signs of the presence of the Kingdom of God:

1. The presence of Jesus in the midst of his gathered people.[27]

Therefore we look to the Church to be both a sign of, and a sign-post to, the Kingdom of God as we experience the joy, peace and sense of celebration which Christ's presence brings.

2. The proclamation of the Gospel.[28]

Therefore we will seek to communicate the Gospel as Jesus did by all means, in all places, at all times and encourage all followers of Jesus to do likewise.

3. Conversion and the new birth.[29]

Therefore we will expect to see the Holy Spirit bringing people out of the kingdom of darkness and into the Kingdom of God.

4. The existence of the church, Jesus' new Messianic community, which unites in love young and old, rich and poor and people from all ethnic groups.

Therefore we pray and expect the church to be a faithful, although imperfect picture of Christ's coming Kingdom – a strikingly different community where the world's brokenness and sinful dividing walls are being overcome.

5. Deliverance from the forces of evil.[30]

We take seriously the power of evil in human affairs: in people's personal behaviour, in the godlessness, injustice and inhumanity seen in every culture, and in occult practices.

Therefore we will minister in the name of Jesus to all who are under the influence of the devil, challenging the faulty teachings, world views, unjust social structures, and cultural and cultic practices that oppress men, women and children today.

6. The Holy Spirit working in power.[31]

We expect to see God transforming people, performing miracles and healings today, and sustaining people in their suffering.

Therefore we will seek to be willing vessels through whom the Holy Spirit can demonstrate that the Kingdom of God is amongst us.

7. The fruit of the Holy Spirit in the lives of people.[32]

Therefore we pray earnestly that all who confess and follow Christ be transformed from day to day into His image and likeness from one degree of glory to another.[33]

8. A courageous, joyous bearing of suffering for righteousness' sake.[34]

Therefore, as Jesus suffered, we will not be surprised if suffering comes to us.

Entering the Kingdom of God

1. We believe that persons enter the kingdom of God not by works and human effort but by the unmerited grace of divine forgiveness as they repent of their sins, trust in God's forgiveness accomplished at the cross, believe in Jesus Christ the crucified and risen Lord, and are born again by the Spirit.[35]

Therefore we do all in our power to urge women and men of all races to accept Christ, join his new community and submit every part of their lives to his Lordship.

2. We believe that faithful communication of the Good News of the Kingdom requires costly, incarnational identification with people whatever their need.[36]

Therefore we commit ourselves to forms of kingdom witness that minister to the whole person in his or her context and refuse to isolate proclamation from social involvement.

3. We believe that Jesus both joyfully welcomed all people into the Kingdom and also taught a particular concern for the poor, weak, and oppressed, even warning that it would be hard for the powerful, the wealthy or the influential of this world to enter it.[37]

Therefore we resolve to practice a costly incarnational witness that demonstrates to the poor as clearly as Jesus did that the Gospel is for them and makes clear to the rich and powerful that they cannot accept Jesus' full Gospel without identifying with the poor the way that Jesus did.

The Kingdom of God and the Church

1. We believe that the Church is the community of the King, the Body of Christ, a visible evidence of his presence and God's chosen people to demonstrate the Kingdom in this world.[38]

   Therefore we will resist the constant temptation to conform to the brokenness of surrounding society, seek to renew the Church so that it is a convincing picture of Christ's dawning Kingdom, and mobilise all Christians to be salt and light in their local communities and around the world.

2. We believe that the local congregation has many interrelated tasks – worship, fellowship, nurture, education, proclamation and social engagement.[39]

   Therefore we will seek to develop biblically balanced, Spirit-filled congregations whose inward communal life and outward mission in the world faithfully reflect all that our Lord summoned the church to be and do.

3. We believe the Church transcends all denominational differences, and is made up of women and men from all nations, cultures, ages and walks of life who are being transformed by the power of the Spirit of God.[40]

   Therefore we will seek to demonstrate visibly love and unity in the worldwide body of Christ so that the world may believe that Jesus came from the Father.[41] Furthermore, the worship and life of each local congregation should affirm the heritage of each culture represented in its midst, allowing this diversity to enrich and enhance our service of God. In addition, since no local congregation can embrace all the diversity of the global body of Christ, we will express in our international relationships a partnership that demonstrates our equality in Christ.

4. We believe that Church growth is a normal outcome of seeking first the Kingdom of God.[42]

   Therefore where Christians do this, local congregations will grow and new congregations will be planted and established.

5. We believe that a loving, servant heart towards God and other people is the prime characteristic of being Kingdom people.[43]

   Therefore we seek to demonstrate this in our congregations, communities and all other areas of life.
6. We believe that the Church does not exist for itself but was established by Christ as a witness to the Kingdom of God.[44]

   Therefore in every area of Church life, we will make decisions not in terms of ecclesiastical self-preservation but rather in terms of what promotes the Kingdom.
7. We believe that God delegates authority to women and men in the Church, raises up men and women as leaders at all levels and expects those in such positions to act responsibly and with humility.[45]

   Therefore we encourage those in authority in the Church to model servant leadership, act with integrity, seek accountability, encourage teamwork, and nurture the spiritual gifts of everyone.

Opposition to the Kingdom of God

1. We believe that Satan is opposed to the Kingdom of God and that there is continual and hostile conflict between the Kingdom of God and the kingdom of darkness.[46]

   Therefore, expecting opposition to the establishment of the Kingdom of God in our own lives, in our families, in our local communities and in our world, we will boldly engage in the kind of spiritual warfare taught in the Scriptures.
2. We believe that the apostle Paul's teaching on the fallen principalities and powers refers to supernatural rebellious beings and the distorted social systems and unjust structures of society.[47]

   When Christians name the unrighteousness of social structures, they become a target of these powers which attack through human or demonic means.

   Therefore we combat the fallen powers by prayer, spiritual warfare, careful socio-economic analysis and political engagement. We reject onesided views that claim that we must either pray or do social analysis, either engage in spiritual warfare or political action. We will do all this in the power of the Spirit.
3. We believe that in the cross, Jesus disarmed the principalities and

powers and broke down the dividing walls between groups that they create and reinforce.[48]

Therefore we will seek to ensure that the church is a community which admits no division of race, class or gender thus becoming a central witness to the principalities and powers that their dominion is over.[49]

4. We believe that Satan regularly seeks to seduce God's people to substitute false gospels for the truth Jesus revealed.

Therefore we reject one-sided gospels of wealth, health, self-esteem and salvation through politics. We refuse to replace divine revelation with subjective experience, to substitute personal preferences for divine commandments, and to exchange management skills and marketing techniques for intercessory prayer and dependence on the Holy Spirit.

The Kingdom of God and Society

1. We believe that God now reigns, though often unacknowledged, over every area of life, that God restrains evil and promotes good in society, and that God desires his will to be done on earth as in heaven.

Therefore we seek not only to live as Jesus' new redeemed community in the church, but also to work as responsible citizens influencing social institutions and systems toward the wholeness God intends.

2. We believe that the Kingdom of God transcends, judges and seeks to transform all cultures. It is radically different from, and challenges the fallenness of the status quo in every society.[50]

Therefore, we will, using the standards of the Kingdom of God, affirm the unique strengths and continuing good of each culture, judge every society, and seek to transform distorted cultural values and evil social structures.

3. We believe that God wills human community to be based on stable family life and life-long fidelity between husband and wife. The Kingdom of God calls into being family-like relationships of brother and sister and mother and father and provides a model for church life which assists in building healthy families. The rule of Christ thus brings dignity and sanctity to both the single and married states.[51]

Therefore we will model and support fidelity within a permanent marriage covenant between one man and one woman, and chastity outside of marriage.

4. We believe that God has ordained a variety of institutions in society and that God wills that political rulers recognise their significant but limited role.

Therefore as we pray for all in authority, we will emphasise the importance of non-governmental institutions including church and family and seek the good of the social order by examining carefully what things are best done by government and what things are best done by intermediate institutions. We reject the political fallacy that the government should or can solve all problems, remembering that divine grace and personal conversion are needed to produce the transformed persons and wholesome families that are so essential for a good society. We also reject the view that dismisses government's responsibility to promote the good and seek justice.

5. We believe that the Kingdom of God affects the whole of every person's being.[52]

Therefore we are concerned about physical, cultural, social, spiritual, intellectual and emotional wholeness in human lives.

6. We believe that God is the rightful owner and ruler of this universe, but he has given the care of the earth to men and women.[53]

Therefore we are committed to a wise and responsible stewardship of all creation and we are opposed to all forms of greed and abuse.

7. We believe that an understanding of the Kingdom of God will bring men and women to a deeper appreciation of the peace and justice of God.[54]

Therefore we determine to act justly, search diligently for non-violent approaches, and promote freedom, peace and justice in society.

8. We believe reconciliation is at the heart of the message of the good news of the kingdom and is God's ultimate intention for humanity[55]

Therefore, while recognising that complete reconciliation among persons is impossible without reconciliation with God and thus that violence and hatred will continue until Christ returns, we nevertheless work for that partial reconciliation between hostile cultures, nations, races and ethnic groups that is possible now, knowing that God's will is peace on earth.

9. We believe the Kingdom of God encourages caring and sharing lifestyles as opposed to materialism and individualism.[56]

    Therefore we urge cooperation rather than excessive competition, and oppose the consumerism and materialism of much of society. We are personally committed to living a sacrificial and simpler lifestyle.

The Kingdom of God and the Future

1. We believe that Jesus Christ will return and that it is God's intention to reconcile all things through Christ.[57]

    Therefore we wait expectantly for the time when the full reign of the Kingdom of God will be seen and the whole creation will be healed and restored.

2. We believe that the Kingdom of God is both a present reality and a future expectation. It is both already and not yet fully. We live in the period between the inauguration and consummation of the Kingdom. At that consummation all the kingdoms of this world will come under the reign of Christ.[58]

    Therefore we seek its demonstration here on earth while awaiting its full revelation in the future.

3. We believe that there is an important role for this earth in the future under the rule and reign of Jesus Christ the King.[59]

    Therefore we will value not only the spiritual but also the material and care for the creation as a sign of Christ's coming restoration of all things.

Commitment to the Kingdom of God

1. We believe that commitment to the cause of the Kingdom of God will mean costly discipleship for people in terms of time, possessions, money and abilities.[60]

    Therefore we urge prayerful evaluation of priorities, mutual accountability, and sacrificial obedience and call Christians to evaluate everything they possess in relation to the Kingdom.

2.　We believe that people were created to live within the kingdom of God and that they thrive under its rule.[61]

Therefore, it is living by the principles of the Kingdom of God in the community of the King, that people reach their maximum potential and experience life in all its fullness. Thus the Kingdom of God is not a threat to humanity, but God's wonderful gift.

3.　We believe that the Kingdom of God confers a new identity on everyone who enters it whatever their standing in life. It affirms their ability to contribute to their neighbours.

Therefore we will encourage all members of the Church to see their work as service to God and to discover and exercise the gifts with which God has endowed them.

4.　We believe that the Kingdom of God calls people to devote their talents to the service of the hungry, the stranger, the naked, the sick, the prisoners whom Jesus identified as his brothers and sisters.

Therefore we encourage people to develop their God-given talents in order that they may risk them in the service of the poor, weak and marginalised.

Final Summation

As Christians gathered together from six continents, we affirm that Jesus' Good News of the Kingdom requires that we observe his Kingly rule:

in all things.

Therefore there is no human activity, no region of human endeavour which is beyond God's reign.

at all times.

Therefore we repudiate any distinction between the sacred and the secular which obscures that biblical truth that God is King of all times and places.

in all situations.

Therefore we urge all Christians to seek first the Kingdom of God in the home, in the Church, at work, in study, in their local community, during recreation and in all other activities of their lives as our highest priority in our lives.

as our highest priority in our lives.

Therefore we will not permit anything to distract or deter us from seeking first the Kingdom of God and His righteousness.

It is therefore our consensus and determined resolve, with prayer and the Holy Spirit's enabling, to commit ourselves to the outworking of these affirmations and commitments. It is also our prayer that all who read them will join us in this commitment.

Notes

1. Mark 1:14–15.
2. Matthew 6:10.
3. Luke 12:31; Matthew 6:33.
4. Psalm 95:3.
5. Genesis 1:27–28; Psalm 8:6–8.
6. Genesis 3.
7. Isaiah 9:6–7; Isaiah 65:17–25.
8. Matthew 9:35; Matthew 4:17–24.
9 Matthew 12:27–28.
10. John 18:36.
11. John 14:16–18: Acts 1:8; 1 Corinthians 14:1–5.
12. Phillipians 1:27.
13. Romans 1:1; Romans 15:16.
14. Ephesians 1:13.
15. Acts 20:24–25.
16. Acts 10:36; Ephesians 6:15.
17. Phillipians 3:7–8.
18. Galatians 3:26–28; Ephesians 2:11–3:6.
19. Revelation 11:15; 1 Corinthians 15:20–28.
20. Hebrews 2:14–15; 1 Corinthians 15:20–28.
21. Romans 8:19–21.
22. Revelation 21:22–22:2.
23. John 3:3–18; Mark 10:17–21; Philippians 2:9–11.
24. Matthew 28:18–20.
25. Luke 4:18–19.
26. 2 Timothy 3:16.
27. Matthew 18:28.
28. Mark 1:15.
29. John 3:3,5.
30. Matthew 12:28; Ephesians 6:10–18.
31. Luke 11:20; 1 Corinthians 12:4–11.
32. Galatians 5:19–26.
33. 2 Corinthians 3:18.
34. Matthew 15:1–12; 1 Peter 4:12–16.

35. John 3:3,5; Acts 2:38; Romans 1:17.
36. Matthew 25:31–46.
37. Mark 10:25.
38. Ephesians 1:22–23; Ephesians 3:10.
39. Acts 2:42–47; 1 Corinthians 12; Ephesians 4:7–11; Romans 12:4–8.
40. Galatians 3:28.
41. John 17:21.
42. Acts 2:42–47.
43. Luke 10:25–37; Matthew 20:25–28.
44. John 13:34–35; Ephesians 3:8–10.
45. Hebrews 13:17; 1 Timothy 3; Acts 18:24–26; Romans 16:1,7.
46. Matthew 12:28; Colossians 1:12–13.
47. Colossians 2:8; Ephesians 6:12.
48. Colossians 2:15.
49. Ephesians 3:8–10.
50. Galatians 3:28.
51. Matthew 19:4–6; 1 Corinthians 7.
52. 1 Thessalonians 5:23; Matthew 25:31–40.
53. Psalm 24:1; Genesis 1:28, 2:15; Psalm 8:6–8.
54. Micah 6:8; Romans 14:17.
55. Colossians 1:20; 2 Corinthians 5:18–21.
56. Acts 4:32–35.
57. John 14:3; Colossians 1:19–20.
58. Luke 17:21, 19:11; Revelation 11:15.
59. Romans 8:19–22; Revelation 21:24, 22:2; Zechariah 14:9; Psalm 2:8; Colossians 1:18–20.
60. Mark 8:34–38; Luke 18:22–20; Luke 14:25–33, Philippians 3:7–11.
61. Matthew 6:25–34.

Three

A Theology of the Kingdom

Graham Cray

For the greater part of this century, the central biblical theme of the Kingdom of God has been understood by most evangelicals to mean 'the present inner rule of God . . . in the heart'.[1] The emphasis on the inner and personal nature of the Kingdom was, to a large extent, in response to the usage by Walter Rauschenbusch and others in the 'Social Gospel' movement.[2] More recently evangelical 'social activists' have used the Kingdom as a major part of their theological framework. Of particular historical importance are the 1974 statement on Radical Discipleship, by some of the participants of the Lausanne Congress, and the 'Transformation' document, drawn up at Wheaton 83.[3]

The Kingdom of God was not a central concept for the first decade of the Charismatic Movement. However, it has become so in two distinct forms. Firstly, some strands of the 'house church' or 'restoration' movement have used the term to describe the rule of Christ in the

'A Theology of the Kindgom' by Graham Cray in *Transformation*, Vol. 5, No. 4, October 1988.

church through the 'delegated authorities' whom he appoints as his agents and through whom his authority is exercised. 'The ascended Christ carries out his ongoing ministry in the church through delegated authorities whom he has appointed . . . How Christians relate to these authorities is crucial if they are to receive what Christ is giving through them, and if they are truly to be in the Kingdom of God. A Kingdom person is one who has submitted his life to a delegated authority, and similarly a Kingdom church is one which submits to an apostle and a prophet'.[4]

More significant has been the use of Kingdom theology to provide an understanding of the ministry of signs and wonders, healing and deliverance in relation to evangelism.[5]

So some evangelicals primarily apply Kingdom theology to social action, and others to healing, signs and wonders. These emphases are by no means mutually exclusive and some efforts have been made to integrate them; most significantly in the section on 'Signs of the Kingdom' in the Grand Rapids report on *Evangelism and Social Responsibility*.

However, Peter Wagner's attempt to distinguish between 'Category A' Social Signs and 'Category B' Personal Signs[6] is not exegetically convincing and shows that we still lack a coherent theology which embodies the heart of each constituency's concerns without merely simplistically adding the two agendas together. This paper is offered as a step towards such a theology.

The Kingdom of God is a theological minefield as well as a vast theme, but I have dared to rush in where theologians fear to tread, because I am convinced that this is the necessary way forward for both movements and a vital step towards greater mutual understanding and practical partnership.

'The Kingdom of God is a matter of . . . justice [righteousness], peace and joy in the Holy Spirit' (Romans 14:17). This paper will explore what Jesus meant by the Kingdom, the Biblical understanding of justice/righteousness and its relationship to the Kingdom, and the relationship of the Holy Spirit to the Kingdom of God and its justice.

What Did Jesus Mean?

'Kingdom of God' was a known but not very common expression in the everyday religious language of the time of Jesus. It was 'one, but only one, of Judaism's ways of speaking about the hoped-for new age, the eschatological age when God's rule would be fully realized, his people vindicated, and his enemies judged.'[6a] The basic theological meaning was that of the new age which replaces the old. However, 'Jesus not only made the term the central theme of his proclamation, but in addition, filled it with a new content which is without analogy.'[7] Jeremias lists eighteen different expressions which have no parallel in the Judaism of Jesus' day.[8] Furthermore, 'Jesus would hardly have devoted so many of his parables to explain what he meant by the Kingdom of God, if he understood by it exactly what everyone else did.'[9] The unprecedented aspect of Jesus' understanding of the Kingdom was that the future rule of God was in some sense present now. Instead of the new age replacing the old, it had invaded it without totally displacing it. 'Christ has cleft the future in two, and part of it is already present.'[10] Jesus still saw human history as divided between two ages, but the critical dividing point (*kairos*) was not the final judgement, but his own proclamation and ministry. 'The time has come, the Kingdom of God is near' (Mark 1:15). From the time of Jesus' public ministry until the judgement, the ages are in overlap. The Kingdom is therefore 'the presence of the future' (George Ladd). It still awaits its consummation and thus has to be understood as 'already' and 'not yet'.

The Already

Jesus taught that the Kingdom was in a real sense present. God's Kingdom was his reign over all things, which cannot be limited to his inner reign in the hearts of those who believe. Consequently, in the ministry of Jesus, the sick were healed, the demonized set free, the dead raised, the hungry fed; authority was exercised over nature and leaders in public life were challenged.

Jesus' proclamation concerned 'the reign of God – God who is creator, upholder and consummator of all that is. We are not talking about one sector of human affairs, one aspect of human life, one strand out of the whole fabric of world history; we are talking about the reign and about the sovereignty of God over all that is, and therefore we are talking about the origin, meaning and end of the universe and of all man's history within the history of the universe.'[11]

But in what sense was the universal and final reign of God present? Firstly, it was present in the unique person of Jesus. His proclamation centred upon the necessity of a response to his own person. 'Blessed is the man who does not fall away on account of me' (Luke 7:23). To respond to Jesus was to respond to the Kingdom. It may be true that Jesus largely proclaimed the Kingdom, and the early church largely proclaimed Jesus, but considering the nature of his proclamation and the fact of his resurrection, they could do no other.

However, the breaking in of the Kingdom required not only a unique person (Luke 1:32f.) but a unique power (Luke 3:21–23; 4:14–21). It is now well established that the root meaning of the word 'Kingdom' was *dynamic rule or strength.* 'Within the symbolic world of the gospels, its main thrust is dynamic strength, even active intervention.'[12] The word means *reign*, not *realm*, and refers to actual dynamic power effective in ministry. Thus the Kingdom invades the old age through the person and ministry of Jesus, and that ministry consists both of proclamation of the Kingdom with its accompanying call to follow Jesus, and of the effective demonstration of the power and reality of the Kingdom. Jesus' reply to John the Baptist was: 'Go back and report to John what you have seen and heard: the blind receive sight, the lame walk, those who have leprosy are cured, the deaf hear, the dead are raised, and the Good News is preached to the poor' (Luke 7:22). Such an understanding of the Kingdom as present was a startling surprise to the people of Jesus' day.

The element of surprise continues throughout the gospels. The Kingdom has an ethical quality. It has values. It is an 'upside – down Kingdom' which presents a direct challenge to and reversal of accepted social and religious values. Consequently, to respond to the Kingdom requires not only faith, but repentance (Mark 1:15). John the Baptist as the forerunner of the Kingdom made it clear that the 'fruit in keeping with repentance' (Luke 3:8) involved the sharing of possessions (v. 11) and that public officials should no longer use their position as an opportunity for oppression (Luke 3:11–14).

Similarly, Jesus gave radically new teaching about both wealth and the exercise of power. He drew a direct connection between the Kingdom and the command to love one's neighbour as oneself (Mark 12:23–34). But he defined neighbour as the one in need whom you are able to help, even if that means crossing hostile racial barriers (Luke 10:25–27). Love of neighbour was to be extended to the love of enemies, even the occupying Roman soldier who could force you to carry his pack a mile (Mt. 5:38–48). Neither John nor Jesus considered Jewish birth to be a guarantee of the Kingdom (Luke 3:8, 9; Mt. 21:43).

Membership of the Kingdom required repentance, evidenced by the fruit of the Kingdom. These values were proclaimed by Jesus as part of his public ministry to all outside of the Kingdom and not just as private teaching to those who had responded.

At the heart of Jesus' Kingdom ministry was the proclamation of the Kingdom as Good News to the poor (Luke 4:18; 7:22). In his reply to John the Baptist, the fact that Good News is preached to the poor is of greater significance even than that the dead are raised. In the 'Nazareth Manifesto' the poor are not one of four categories of people to whom Jesus is sent, but the primary category of whom the prisoners, the blind and the oppressed are examples. The word implies the great mass of ordinary people who were economically poor, socially powerless and regarded by such as the Pharisees as outside of God's Kingdom. It is these people whom Jesus makes the primary focus of both his proclamation and the demonstration of the power of the Kingdom. It is in this context that most of the miracles of healing and deliverance take place. The Kingdom becomes Good News to the poor now, not just a promise of Good News in a future life. The sick are given back the possibility of an active role in society, the demonized are set free and restored to normal relationships, cleansed lepers can come back into the community. Those experiencing untimely bereavement have their loved ones and bread-winners restored. Jesus' table fellowship of tax collectors and sinners was the foretaste of their place in the Messianic banquet on the last day. His acceptance of women and little children gave them a special or best part in the Kingdom both present and future.

Jesus' proclamation of the Kingdom, demonstration of the power of the Kingdom, and call to discipleship resulted in the creation of a community. Those who through following Jesus recognized the absolute value of the Kingdom (Mt. 13:44) and who were willing to pay the price of entry (Luke 8:18–30) became closer to Jesus and to one another than any flesh and blood relative (Mt. 12:46–50; Luke 9:57–62). But the proclamation and practice of the Kingdom were divisive (Mt. 10:34–39). They either created faith or provoked opposition. Opposition could be overtly demonic (Mt. 4:1–11) and the overthrow of the demonic was one of the evidences that the Kingdom of God was present (Mt. 12:22–28); or opposition came through an apparently human source (Mark 8:32, 33; Mark 14:1). 'Since the Kingdom of God was all-embracing, the potential for collision was enormous'.[13]

The Kingdom was 'already', in that the all-transforming final reign of God had broken into the present age in and through the person of Jesus, his proclamation and his ministry of power.

The Not Yet

If the proclamation and ministry of the Kingdom of God could provoke vehement opposition, then clearly the Kingdom had not reached its consummation. Jesus used future language as well as present language (e.g. Mt. 20:1–16; 22:1–14; 24 and 25). The Kingdom was present but not with irresistible power. Men could and did reject it. Too much was happening through the ministry of Jesus for men to ignore, but not enough to convince them overwhelmingly. For John the Baptist, the conflict was between what Jesus was doing, the ministry of the Kingdom; and the fact that he, John, was still in prison and the Gentiles had not been judged (Mt. 11:1–16). Evidently this Kingdom had not finally overcome the old age, although it had powerfully assaulted it (Luke 4:31–37; 8:26–39; 10:1–20; 11:21,22; Acts 10:38).

The major element of Jewish expectation which was missing from Jesus' proclamation was that of judgement. In all of his major allusions to the prophet Isaiah, Jesus omits, or stops short of the reference to final judgement (Isaiah 29:18–20; 35:4–6; 61:1,2).

The reason is that this aspect of the Kingdom is future (see e.g. Mt. 25). The already of the Kingdom is the age of grace. All men were to love and forgive their enemies, because God in his kingly power through his servant Jesus was willing to forgive them (Mt. 6:12–15, 18:21–35; Mark 2:1–12). In an age of grace, men must have the right to accept or reject forgiveness. The Kingdom may not be present in overwhelming force.

Jesus' actions could be limited by the lack of response of others (Mark 6:1–6). His words could be misunderstood (Mark 8:1–21), or completely rejected even by his own followers (Mark 8:31–33). The greater part of his teaching about the Kingdom came in the form of parables, which some would understand and some would not (Mark 4:9–12). Likewise Jesus' acts of power were not automatically convincing. Jesus refused to respond to those who demanded overwhelming proof (Luke 11:16; 29–32). His deliverance ministry could be interpreted as being of demonic origin (Luke 11:14, 15); his table fellowship with the disreputable as a contradiction of his claims to divine inspiration (Luke 7:36–39). Jesus' deeds were signs of the Kingdom, in that they were genuine experiences of the transforming power or transformed relationships of the Kingdom, which pointed beyond themselves to the future consummated Kingdom and which challenged faith in the present.

There is an important parallel between Jesus' acts of power and his parables. 'They are both performances of the motif of the new creation, the Kingdom of God intersecting time and history.'[14] The miracles revealed a new power at work in the world. The purpose of the parables was 'to convey a fresh possibility to the hearer, otherwise unknown to his world or his language. As such, the parables also invite the hearer to participate in what is conveyed'.[15] God's power was as much in action in the telling of parables as in the healing of the sick. 'In the parabolic ministry, the mystery of the Kingdom is given performance in a way that is new: it enables the Kingdom to open out to our vision and understanding so that entry to it becomes possible now. Yet whenever this possibility emerges as real, there is the recognition that it has been "given": It is something that has not entered from our own resources, but has been brought about by the invasion of our lives by a new element, the Kingdom of God. It is God's gracious gift to us' (Mt. 13:10–16).[16]

The frequent introduction to parables that 'the Kingdom of God is like . . .' has three clear implications. Firstly, a Kingdom that can be compared to aspects of ordinary life can be lived out in this life. Secondly, the frequent 'twist in the tail' of the parables shows that the Kingdom is 'unlike' the way we are accustomed to live. 'The general tendency of parables is to confound our conventional and comfortable world view.'[17] Thirdly, the Kingdom may not be precisely identified with human systems, concerns or aspirations. It is 'like' rather than 'the same as'.

In the parables, the Kingdom demands a response. They are a call to discipleship. The Kingdom is like a magnet with two poles – divine initiative and human response;[18] but our response can never fully reflect the Kingdom – the 'already' and 'not yet' are both evident.

The element of surprise or mystery is never far away. It does not even stop when people become committed followers of Jesus. Even though the secret of the Kingdom has been given to them and some of the parables explained to them, they frequently still fail to understand; or are challenged or caught out in some new area of discipleship (Mark 4:11; 35–41; 5:30, 31; 6:45–52; 8:14–21; 9:33–31; etc.). They learn to perform the works of the Kingdom and yet sometimes also fail in the attempt (Mark 3:31–15; 9:14–32). There is no time when they appear to have mastered 'the art of the Kingdom'. Rather the Kingdom is the present active rule of God and he, through Jesus, is in the business of mastering them. If the disciples are continually discomfited, the religious and political leaders are the most threatened. The apparent weakness of the present Kingdom culminates in the cross, where, despite Jesus' many acts of spiritual power, the old age appears overwhelmingly strong. Yet through the apparent weakness and foolishness of the cross, redemption and the power of the Kingdom becomes available to all (1 Cor. 1:18–2:5). The act which briefly extinguished his disciples' hopes proves to have been necessary to open repentance and forgiveness of sins to all, a part of God's active reign after all (Luke 24:25–27; Acts 2:23–24). The resurrection was God's confirmation and seal of approval on what his Son had achieved (Luke 24:19–49).

The ministry of the Kingdom is seen predominantly in the weakness of the cross, not just in the power to heal and deliver. Calvary and the empty tomb open the presence of the Kingdom to all, and securely establish an age of grace until the present 'not yet' becomes the 'future already' (1 Cor. 15:20–28).

The Kingdom of God and Justice

In the Old Testament, the quality of a king was assessed in part by his record in administering justice. Justice was not seen as a matter of both sides getting a fair hearing. The king was to be accessible to those who believed they had been dealt with unjustly (2 Sam. 15:1–6; 1 Kings 3:4–28). Furthermore the king was expected to make active intervention on behalf of those who could not secure justice for themselves. Psalm 72 is a prayer for the king to be endowed with justice, with particular reference to defending the afflicted, saving the children of the needy and crushing the oppressor. He will 'deliver the needy who cry out, the afflicted who have no one to help. He will take pity on the weak and needy, and save the needy from death. He will rescue them from oppression and violence, for precious is their blood in his sight' (12–14). In typical prophetic style, Jeremiah condemned the reign of Shallum, son of Josiah, because he had oppressed his countrymen, unlike his father who 'did what was right and just . . . He defended the cause of the poor and needy' (Jeremiah 22:13–17).

Kings were to administer justice in this way, precisely because this reflected the character and deeds of God the King. The Psalmist declares 'Righteousness and justice are the foundation of your throne' (Ps. 89:14). These things form the basic characteristic of God's rule as King. Righteousness and justice form one quality, not two. The Old Testament knows no division between social justice and private morality. The two words (*tsedaqah u mishpat*) are a figure of speech which express one complex idea. Frequently they are used as synonyms in poetic parallelism. Perhaps the best known example – Amos' famous cry, 'Let justice roll down like waters, and righteousness like an everflowing stream' (Ams. 5: 24) – is a prayer for one event, not two.[19] In Psalm 82, the false gods 'defend the unjust and show partiality to the wicked'. If they were gods they would be like the only God, the God of Israel; they would 'defend the cause of the weak and fatherless, maintain the rights of the poor and oppressed, rescue the weak and needy, deliver them from the hand of the wicked' (2–4).

Many other psalms link God's rule with a justice which actively intervenes on behalf of the weak and oppressed (eg. 9:10, 68, 76, 103, 109, 113, 140). The clearest summary is found in Psalm 146: 'he upholds the cause of the oppressed and gives food to the hungry. The Lord sets prisoners free. The Lord gives sight to the blind. The Lord lifts up those who are bowed down. The Lord loves the righteous. The Lord watches over the alien and sustains the fatherless and the widowed, but he frustrates the ways of the wicked. The Lord reigns for ever . . .' (5–10).

The prophets also portrayed God as the one who intervened to bring justice. On occasion, they confronted kings in his name (1 Sam. 2:1–10; Isaiah 3:13–15). However, they also introduce a new note with prophecies of a time when God will appoint a King who will reign in justice for ever (Isaiah 9:6f.; Jeremiah 23:5f.; Micah 5:2–5; Zechariah 9:9, 10).

It is precisely these prophecies which lie behind Gabriel's announcement to Mary about a baby to be called Jesus. 'He will be great and called the son of the Most High. The Lord God will give him the throne of his father David and he will reign over the house of Jacob for ever; his Kingdom will never end' (Luke 1:32, 33). Mary understood the nature of the Old Testament promise. Her hymn of praise and faith declares: 'He has brought down rulers from their thrones and has lifted up the humble, he has filled the hungry with good things, he has sent the rich away empty' (Luke 1:52, 53). God's king will intervene to bring justice. There will be a great reversal.

At his baptism, Jesus heard his Father's voice alluding to Psalm 2, the anointing or coronation psalm, and Isaiah 42 where the servant of the Lord is anointed with the Spirit so that he might 'faithfully bring forth justice' and 'not fail or be discouraged until he has established justice in the earth' (Luke 3:22, Ps. 2:7, Is. 42:1–4).

In the synagogue at Nazareth, Jesus read from Isaiah 61 and announced his ministry as 'to preach Good News to the poor, to proclaim release to the captives and recovery of sight to the blind, to set at liberty those who are oppressed and to proclaim the acceptable year of the Lord' (Luke 4:14–21; Isaiah 61:1–2). Verse 8 of Isaiah 61 gives the reason for all this – 'for I the Lord love justice'. 'The acceptable year of the Lord' is almost certainly a reference to the year of Jubilee, where debts were remitted, slaves freed, and capital in the form of land redistributed. Again, the image of an intervention to restore justice is clear. In Matthew 9, Jesus preaches the Kingdom and heals, having compassion on the crowd, because he sees they are harassed and helpless (33, 36). He saw the crowd as victims of injustice, and powerless to help themselves, as well as needing to come under his leadership.

He linked his healing ministry with ministry to the poor (Mt. 11:5, 6) because he saw both as 'bringing justice' (Mt. 12:15–21, including the full quotation from Isaiah 42:1–4). It is no wonder then that Jesus explicitly linked the Kingdom with justice (Mt. 6:33), and pronounced God's blessing on those who hungered and thirsted for justice, or who are persecuted for the sake of justice (Mt. 5:6–10). In the light of the Kingdom, giving to the needy was no longer a matter of charity but an 'act of justice' (Mt. 6:1). Much of this is entirely lost to readers of the English Bible, because of the false separation made between righteousness and justice, and because *dikaiosunē* is consistently translated 'righteousness' in English translations, whereas in the Septuagint it was as often used to translate 'justice'.

In this context, the Atonement can be understood as the greatest intervention of God's justice, consistent with his character and action as portrayed in the Old Testament. It was an intervention of restorative rather than retributive justice. Only thus can we understand how the cross was both a demonstration of God's justice and also of his mercy in justifying those who have faith in Jesus (Rom. 3:21–26). This is the God of the Kingdom intervening to die for his enemies, to create a people who would be characterized by the love of neighbour and the love of enemy (Rom. 5:6–11; 12:17–21; 13:8–10). It is no wonder that Paul can say that the Kingdom of God is a matter of justice and peace, for both his justice and his Kingdom are his active intervention to restore *shalom*. The agenda of the Kingdom may validly be summed up as the restoration of justice and peace.

The Spirit and the Kingdom

If the agenda of the Kingdom can be defined from one perspective as the restoration of justice, the *dynamic* of the Kingdom is found in the ministry of the Holy Spirit. 'To be moved and motivated by the Spirit of Jesus is to be moved and motivated by an all-absorbing concern for the coming of God's Kingdom.'[20]

In the time of the Judges, God exercised his rule by empowering chosen individuals with his Spirit for the duration of each crisis. Later, the prophets foretold the coming of the Servant of the Lord who would exercise his ministry through the anointing of the Spirit (Isaiah 42:1–14; 61:1–3).

By the time of Jesus, the Jewish two – age view of history held that the gift of the Spirit was one of the decisive marks of the new age – that is to say, of the Kingdom of God (Joel 2:28–32). Jesus was born by the action of the Holy Spirit (Luke 1:35) and thus was the unique person who could bring the Kingdom by sacrificing his perfect life to atone for sin. However, of equal significance was his anointing by the Spirit at his baptism (Luke 3:21–22). The Father's voice alluded to Isaiah 42. Jesus clearly understood his experience at the Jordan as his anointing to fulfil the role of the Servant. Later, he explicitly identified his ministry with the prophecy of Isaiah 61 in the synagogue at Nazareth (Luke 4:16–21).

The significance of this must not be underestimated. The coming of the Spirit on Jesus begins the new age. 'The decisive change in the ages was effected by the Spirit coming down upon Jesus'.[21] The Spirit equipped Jesus for the Messianic ministry of healing and teaching (Acts 10:38). This launched him directly into spiritual warfare because the new age was invading and assaulting the old (Luke 4:1–13; 18–21; 31–36). The fact that Jesus' ministry of deliverance was by authoritative command through the power of the Spirit, rather than by the ritual exorcisms of contemporary Judaism, was specific evidence that the

Kingdom was present (Mt. 12:28). The incident in the synagogue at Nazareth is of particular importance. With his Gentile audience in mind, Luke does not introduce the Jewish theological term 'Kingdom of God' to his audience (Luke 4:43) before allowing the Isaiah 61 passage to give it content. In claiming its fulfilment, Jesus clearly understood both the rational ministry of preaching and the 'non – rational' ministry of healing and deliverance as being manifestations of the Holy Spirit.

Of greatest significance to us is the scope of the ministry for which Jesus was anointed. The shortest definition of the agenda of the Kingdom is found in the Lord's Prayer; to pray 'your Kingdom come' is in effect to pray 'your will be done on earth as it is in heaven' (Mt. 6:10). Luke 4:18, 19 shows us some aspects, at least, of what that will is.[22] Jesus had been anointed to announce publicly the Good News of God's Kingdom to 'the poor'. The Old Testament words for 'poor' covered many kinds of deprivation. Preaching is Good News to the poor only if it announces God's active intervention on their behalf to restore justice. Many of the words in this quotation have a multiple application. Jesus was anointed by the Spirit to preach (*kēruxai*), a word mainly used later in the New Testament for evangelistic preaching. The content of his preaching was freedom or release, a word applicable to the forgiveness of sin or 'release' in a more physical sense. The word for 'prisoners' most commonly referred to prisoners of war. The blind who are to recover their sight clearly include the physically blind (Luke 7:21, 22), but Isaiah also used the term to speak of spiritual blindness.

The 'release' which is promised to the oppressed, as in a previous phrase, can speak of forgiveness or a more physical liberation, but the 'oppressed' without question include those who are physically, politically or economically oppressed. Jesus also released the *demonically* oppressed; this phrase does not come from Isaiah 61, but rather from Isaiah 58:6 where it is found alongside the hungry, the poor wanderer without shelter, and the naked; the context being that of loosing 'the chains of injustice'. The year of the Lord's favour (as mentioned earlier) was the year of Jubilee, which involved a massive restoration of justice and opportunity, each fifty years. The age of the Spirit is to be an age of perpetual Jubilee. However, the anointing of the Spirit is not to bring 'the day of vengeance of our God'. Rather, Jesus is soon reminding his nationalistic audience of the way in which God's favour reached out to Gentiles in the old Covenant (Luke 4:24–30).

In the anointing of the Spirit upon Jesus, we see the inauguration
of an era which is to be characterized by forgiveness of sin, physical
healing, deliverance from demonic oppression, restoration of liberty,
the end of oppression, the initiation of major social and economic
reform, an end to nationalism and hostility, and the availability of
God's favour to all who will respond – although it is especially offered
to the poor as the King intervenes to restore justice (Luke 6:20). All of
this is focused in the person of Jesus and validated in the power of the
Holy Spirit. Although it is possible to identify what modern evangelicals call evangelism, social action, and signs and wonders in this
context, the overriding picture is of an integrated whole, and a promise of power for a ministry which is as broad as the agenda of the
Kingdom itself.

The Kingdom belongs to the Father (Luke 12:32). It was the
Father who sent the Spirit to confirm to Jesus his identity as the only
Son. Jesus experiences the joy of the Spirit when he sees his disciples
exercising the power and authority of the Kingdom and participating in its victory over Satan's Kingdom. However, his greatest joy is
that these same disciples have experienced revelation from the
Father, and know who the Father and his Son really are (Luke
10:1–24).

If 'all flesh' were to have the opportunity of relationship with the
Father and experience of the power of the Spirit, Jesus must first die
on the cross. There could be no Pentecost without Calvary (John
7:37–39; 12:23–33). The cross and the resurrection open the way for
Pentecost; for what Jordan was to Jesus, Pentecost was to the disciples. It was their initiation into the power of the Kingdom; hence
Peter's quotation of the Joel prophecy. Between his resurrection and
ascension, Jesus taught about the Kingdom of God, but promised the
power of the Spirit (Acts 1:1–18), just as, in his earlier ministry, he
taught his disciples to pray 'your kingdom come', and to ask the
Father for the Holy Spirit, the two prayers having the same meaning
(Luke 11:2, 13). The Father gives the Spirit and the Father gives the
Kingdom (Luke 11:13; 12:32). The two gifts are the same. In other
words, 'the Spirit, we might say, is the presentness of the coming
Kingdom, where he is, the Kingdom is, so that to have the Spirit is to
have part and lot in the Kingdom here and now, or to put it another
way – the Spirit is the executive, ambassador, or steward of the Kingdom: his power and authority are those of the King; his operation is
the exercise of kingly rule'.[23]

The same identification of the Spirit with the 'already' of the Kingdom can be found elsewhere in the New Testament. Christ is a title, not a surname. It signifies the one anointed by the Spirit to bring the Kingdom. Christians are those who are 'in Christ', which means to be in union with him and therefore in relation to the Father, and also to share his anointing for the work of the Kingdom. To be converted is to be recruited. To be born of the Spirit is to enter the Kingdom (John 3:5). 'The goal of Biblical conversion is not to save souls apart from history, but to bring the Kingdom of God into the world with explosive force; it begins with individuals, but it is for the sake of the world.'[24]

The term 'Christ' has little meaning for most Gentile Christians, but the term 'Lord' including its political connotations was explicit in communicating the identical content. The Spirit after Pentecost is the personal *representative* of Jesus, the Lord (2 Cor. 3:17). The gifts of the Spirit are tangible manifestations in word and deed of the Lordship of Jesus (1 Cor. 12:3–11). They were not provided merely for the purpose of building the church but are seen in the ministry of Jesus and the early Christians to be the practical equipment to enable Christians to be the vehicles of God's intervening Kingdom in society. Gifts of healing, miracles, knowledge, wisdom, evangelism, helping, hospitality, showing mercy, generous giving and encouragement are the equipment for Kingdom work. 'In exercising spiritual gifts, we are involved in the restoration of God's perfect work in creation. An activity can only be characterized as a spiritual gift when it assists in the restoration of creation and contributes to the restoration of a sick world.'[25]

The Spirit is the first-fruits of the harvest which will be reaped at the end of the age (Romans 8:23). He is the first instalment, the first part of what will be received in full when Christ returns (2 Cor. 1:22; 5:5; Eph. 1:14). He is the present dynamic power of the future age (Hebrews 6:4, 5; Acts 1:8; 1 Cor. 4:4). However, just because he is first – fruits, not final harvest – first instalment, not the fulfilled Kingdom – his ministry through Christians, like his ministry through Jesus, is not automatically convincing, but is a pointer or sign of the Kingdom. His power is experienced in weakness (2 Cor. 4 and 12). He can be resisted (Acts 7:51). The proclamation of the Kingdom can be rejected. At such times he provides joy and comfort in suffering (1 Thess. 1:4–6). Suffering, Kingdom and Spirit often go together in the overlap of the ages (1 Peter 4:12–14; Rev. 1:9, 10). Through the

Spirit we cry 'Abba', but 'Abba' is a Gethsemane word (Romans 8:15; Mark 14:36). To share in the Spirit is to share in suffering, both at the hands of the old age and over what still waits to be done in oneself and in the creation as a whole (Romans 8:16–39). The Spirit is the 'already', the presence of the Kingdom, and part of his ministry is to sustain us in both the hope and pain of waiting for the 'not yet'. To be involved in the ministry of the Kingdom of God requires, above all, submission to the active leadership of the Spirit (Romans 8:14, Acts 8:29, 39, 10:9–20, 44–48, 13:2, 16:7, 20:22–28).

Mission is not a matter of putting in order of priority *evangelism, social action or signs and wonders*, but of an openness to the whole agenda of the Kingdom, including its priority concern for the poor. Such mission requires personal experience of the power and leading of the Holy Spirit. 'I believe that we could ease the tension between "charismatic" and "social" if we understood the depth and breadth of the Holy Spirit's action, and if the theology of the charisms progressed beyond and corrected certain too narrow and restrictive interpretations'.[26] 'The Gospel is Good News concerning the Kingdom, and the Kingdom is God's rule over the totality of life. Every human need therefore can be used by the Spirit of God as a beach-head for the manifestation of his kingly power'.[27]

Challenges and Implications

The Kingdom of God, the Justice of God and the Spirit of God each speak of God's active intervention with effective power to restore a fallen creation to what it was meant to be. 'The Kingdom of God is creation healed'.[28] 'The Kingdom of God is the new order which began in Christ, and which will be completed by him, wherein all relationships will be put right and not only that between God and man, but also those between people, nations, sexes, generations and races, and that between man and nature'[29] (Eph. 1:9, Col. 1:15–20).

It is my view that neither of the renewal movements, that of charismatic experience and that of social action, has adequately reflected the breadth and integration of this agenda, nor fully grasped the power in weakness *offered* by the Spirit to those who will follow his leading. Our vision of the Kingdom has been impaired by our tendency to compartmentalize and argue about the priority of evangelism, signs and wonders, social action, spiritual warfare. All renewal movements become involved in some degree of polemic and self defence, and tend to emphasize their own concerns out of proportion to the whole body of Christian truth. We have not always learned from the experience of the disciples. To be in the Kingdom and have tasted its power is not to have got everything right. We need to rediscover the element of surprise, challenge and ongoing disorientation.

Theology must be lived in ministry and not just conceptualized. It will not be sufficient for us theoretically to add one another's agendas to our own. We need to learn an integrated practice of mission which parallels that of Jesus and the early Christians.

Too sharp a line has often been drawn between altruistic social action and proclamation. All Kingdom ministry is an implicit or explicit call to discipleship. However, that need be neither legalistic nor crude; the greater part of Jesus' proclamation of the Kingdom was through the indirect method of parables rather than confrontational preaching. (For one church's use of parable *re* mission, see *Power to the Powerless* by Laurie Green, published by Marshalls, England, 1987). Story telling needs to go hand in hand with service and acts of mercy.

Similarly, too tight a boundary wall has often been established around the membership of the church. Membership of the church through baptism is clear enough, but Jesus' table fellowship with the excluded and morally unacceptable shows the need to demonstrate the reality of our love and acceptance of them. This too, requires the power of the Holy Spirit and is a genuine foretaste and sign of the Kingdom. 'It is impossible to do full justice to the doctrine of the Kingdom of God if we ignore the charismatic character of it.'[30] The overtly 'supernatural' character of Jesus' ministry of healing, deliverance and mighty works cannot and must not be 'spiritualized' into a general ministry of 'social service and action'.[31] Neither may the ministry of the Spirit be understood as referring only to the overtly supernatural. The power of the Spirit which Jesus experienced was as much for proclamation, and the wisdom for parables, as for signs and wonders; as much for the journey to the cross as for deliverance ministry. The power of the Spirit to sustain those committed to situations of entrenched suffering or oppression is a crucial aspect of Kingdom ministry. At the same time, the gifts of the Spirit must be set free in practice from being predominantly 'in house' ministries for building up the church, to be experienced as a release of God's effective power in the ministry of the Kingdom in the world.

The 'already/not yet' tension of the Kingdom and the Spirit is of central importance to protect us from triumphalism or pessimism. 'Within that tension of the already given and the still to come, all Christians have to live – including charismatic Christians. God gives enough evidence of Christ risen to call to faith, but not enough to compel to acceptance. Again and again the gifts of the Spirit operate and yet they are never at our disposal. There remains something sovereign and elusive about their coming and going. In the realm of healing much happens to authenticate Christ's present will and power to heal the otherwise incurable and yet often, distressingly, enough fails to happen to serve to remind us that we are not yet in the last day, and to leave the mystery of the not yet all around us.'[32] We are to be neither naïvely triumphalistic nor pessimistically hopeless, setting limits of unbelief on what God can do.

The nature of the Kingdom as God's intervention to bring justice to the poor must not be spiritualized to such an extent that *all* are the spiritual poor and all therefore in equal need. Quite clearly the biblical language is used to indicate that some are poor and oppressed *and others are not*. Some are unjustly suffering because of the way others live. Jesus ministered the Kingdom to all, taught the love of enemies, and died to make it possible. However, his teaching and ministry clearly indicate a Kingdom priority for those who are poor in contrast to others. The practice and teaching of Jesus should inform our own mission priorities, and should lead to an increase in the power of God poured out upon us.

It is essential to emphasize the sovereignty of the Spirit. Since Jordan and Pentecost, he has been present in the world in new power. However, he is not at our beck and call – we are at his. The New Testament implies that the 'already and not yet' of the Kingdom is not merely a matter of present and future, but also of divine choice in each context, and of varying degrees of spiritual power. In this sense the coming and presence of the Kingdom is intermittent. In each situation of need, we have nothing to offer (Luke 11:6). In each situation we have to ask for the Spirit and pray for the Kingdom to come. We are continually to allow ourselves to be filled with the Spirit which means to permit the Spirit to take initiatives through us as he wills (Eph. 5:18; Acts 4:8, 31).

Finally, if the presence of the Kingdom is experienced in the ministry of the Spirit, there may be an answer to the long – standing difficulty as to whether the Kingdom of God needs to be understood as restricted to the ministry of the Spirit through Christians. Because the Spirit is sovereign and takes initiatives, the Kingdom is present where he is at work. Some of the parables of Jesus imply the presence of the Kingdom unseen in the ordinary and everyday. On a larger and political stage, if the Spirit in the Old Testament can anoint Cyrus, a pagan King (Isaiah 45) he can equally be at work in the international and local politics of the world today. An understanding of the Kingdom 'must involve some kind of interpretation of what is happening in the world, however provisional, modest and tentative it may be.'[33] It will not be sufficient simply to learn to recognize where the Spirit is active. If he is at large in the world, it is to convict so as to bring about change. Intervention for the Kingdom sometimes requires conviction of sin, justice and judgement (e.g. Acts 24:25). 'Discerning the Kingdom in a situation includes recognizing where God's judgement stands over an enterprise or a relationship.'[34]

Perhaps our greatest need is to develop the faculty of mature discernment and to be open to the gift of distinguishing between spirits. These are corporate activities, and for them our two movements need one another.

Charismatic ministry and social action, evangelism and signs and wonders all must be defined in relation to the Kingdom of God. By definition that Kingdom will always challenge our efforts as partial and inadequate, but the challenge will always be towards a greater integrity and integration in our practice of mission.

Notes

1. Authur P. Johnston, 'The Kingdom in Relation to the Church and the World' in *Word and Deed* ed. Bruce J. Nicholls (Paternoster Press, 1985), p. 128. See in reply René, Padilla, 'The mission of the Church in the light of the Kingdom of God' in *Mission Between the Times* (Eerdmans, 1985).
2. Walter Rauschenbusch, *A Theology for the Social Gospel* (1919).
3. These and other relevant documents are published in *Texts on Evangelical Social Ethics 1974–1983*, 3 Vols., *ed.* René Padilla and Chris Sugden (Grove Books Ltd., 1985–6).
4. Nigel Wright, *The Radical Kingdom* (Kingsway Publications, 1986), p. 84. Chs. 5 and 6 give an excellent critique of this interpretation. For a history of the U.K. house church movement, *see Restoring the Kingdom* by Andrew Walker (Hodder & Stoughton, 1985).
5. See *Power Evangelism* by John Wimber with Kevin Springer (Hodder & Stoughton, 1985) and *Come, Holy Spirit* by Bishop David Pytches (Hodder & Stoughton, 1985), ch. 2.

6. Peter Wagner, *Church Growth and the Whole Gospel* (Harper and Row, 1981), p. 16.
6a. J.D.G. Dunn, *Jesus and the Spirit* (SCM Press, 1975), p. 47.
7. Joachim Jeremias, *New Testament Theology*, Vol. 1 (SCM Press, 1971), p. 35.
8. *Ibid.*, pp. 32–34.
9. G.B. Caird, *The Language and Imagery of the Bible* (Duckworth, 1980).
10. David Bosch, 'Evangelism and Social Transformation' in *The Church in Response to Human Need*, ed. Tom Sine (MARC, 1983).
11. Lesslie Newbigin, *The Open Secret* (SPCK, 1978), p. 32.
12. Bruce Chilten and J.I.H. McDonald, *Jesus and the Ethics of the Kingdom* (SPCK, 1987), p. 48.
13. *Ibid.*, p. 105.
14. *Ibid.*, p. 62.
15. *Ibid.*, p. 15.
16. *Ibid.*, p. 67.
17. *Ibid.*, p. 65.
18. *Ibid.*, p. 24.
19. For this section I am particularly indebted to Perry B. Yoder, *Shalom, The Bible's Word for Salvation, Justice and Peace* (Faith and Life Press, 1987), in particular Chapter 3. See also Waldron Scott, *Bring Forth Justice* (Eerdmans, 1980), p. 49, and Miranda, *Marx and the Bible* (Orbis, 1974), p. 93.
20. Albert Nolan, quoted in *Cry Justice*, ed. John de Gruchy (Collins, 1986).
21. J.D.G. Dunn, *Baptism in the Spirit* (SCM Press, 1970), p. 26.
22. For this section, I am particularly indebted to Peter Lee, *Poor Man, Rich Man – the priorities of Jesus and the agenda of the Church* (Hodder & Stoughton, 1986), chapter 2.
23. One ancient variant of the Lord's Prayer in Luke 11:2 reads: 'Let thy Holy Spirit come upon us and cleanse us' instead of 'Let thy kingdom come'. J.D.G. Dunn, 'Spirit and Kingdom', *Expository Times* Vol. 82 (1970–71), pp. 34–40.
24. Jim Wallis, *The Call to Conversion* (Harper and Row, 1981), p. 8.
25. Arnold Bittlinger, *Gifts and Graces* (Hodder & Stoughton, 1967).
26. Leon, Cardinal Suenens, in Cardinal Suenens and Dom Helder Camara, *Charismatic Renewal and Social Action – a dialogue* (DLT, 1979), p. 39.
27. René Padilla, *op. cit.*, p. 198.
28. Hans Küng, *On Being a Christian* (Collins, 1976), p. 231.
29. J. Verkuyl, quoted in Orlando Costas, *The Integrity of Mission* (Harper and Row, 1979), p. 7.
30. Michael Harper, *The Healings of Jesus* (Hodder & Stoughton), p. 166.
31. René Padilla, *op. cit.*
32. Thomas Smail, *Reflected Glory* (Hodder & Stoughton), p. 124.
33. Lesslie Newbigin, *op. cit.*, p. 41.
34. J.D.G. Dunn, *The Kingdom of God and North – East England* (SCM Press, 1986), p. 11.

Four

A Theology of the Kingdom – A Pentecostal Contribution

Murray Dempster

My challenge is to write a biblical basis for social concern that reso-
nates with contemporary Pentecostal church mission and ministry in
its global expression and that integrates social ministry with the
church's historic commitment to evangelization.[1]

When the modern Pentecostal movement burst on to the scene
at the turn of the twentieth century, the participants were marked by
a sense of global consciousness. Writing in 1925, but quoting his
own magazine article from 1906, Frank Bartleman's eyewitness
interpretation of the Asuza Street Revival reflects this typical connection between Spirit baptism and the empowerment of the Pentecostal
church for global evangelization.

'Social Concern in the Context of Jesus' kingdom, mission and ministry' by
Murray Dempster in *Transformation*, Vol. 16, No. 2, April 1999.

Pentecost has come to Los Angeles, the American Jerusalem. Every sect, creed and doctrine under Heaven is found in Los Angeles.... All nations are represented, as at Jerusalem. Thousands are here from all over the Union and from many parts of the world, sent of God for 'Pentecost'. These will scatter the fire to the ends of the earth. Missionary zeal is at white heat. The 'gifts' of the Spirit are being given, the church's panoply restored. Surely we are in the days of restoration, the 'last days' wonderful and glorious days... The revival will be a world-wide one, without doubt.[2]

Despite the American centricity of this characterization, L. Grant McClung, Jr., Church of God missiologist, identifies the missiological significance of this Pentecostal interpretation of the twentieth century outpouring of the Spirit, when he notes that, '[e]arly pentecostals were characterized by an "urgent missiology" that caused them to seek immediate world evangelization in light of their conviction of the imminent return of Christ.' McClung concludes, 'Eschatological urgency is at the heart of understanding the missionary fervour of early Pentecostalism'.[3] And the experiential force driving that eschatological urgency was the baptism in the Holy Spirit interpreted within the narrative structure of Acts 2.

That eschatological fervour in the span of nearly one century has produced a movement estimated by some to have close to 500 million adherents worldwide.[4] Global mobility has brought church leaders exposure to the world's political ills, economic woes, social problems and structural injustices. Responding to human need within a global context with its various cultural matrixes has generated a staggering proliferation of social programmes in all sectors of the Pentecostal movement, including the Assemblies of God.[5] In one sense this development should not be surprising because from the beginning of the movement, church leaders established orphanages, hospices, rescue homes, and lepersariums out of compassionate concern for the homeless and the outcasts of society. In another sense, the proliferation is surprising because the expansion of social programmes includes those that are designed to change the unjust social conditions which perpetuate human ills such as poverty and hunger. These programmes aimed at social service and social change testify to an awakened social conscience that has been stimulated by the dire human needs and the devastating living conditions of those to whom Pentecostals often proclaim the 'good news' of the gospel. Pentecostal church leaders, it seems, have learned the truth of the bumper sticker: Think globally, act locally.

Despite this growth of helpful programmes, all is not well within the church and its leadership. Church leaders are not yet sure-footed nor united theologically in justifying Christian social concern as part of the church's mission. A cogent illustration of the ambivalence among Pentecostal leadership towards the theological validity of the church's social ministry can be found by comparing the two editorial statements in the AG mission magazine, *Mountain Movers*, appearing only three months apart from each other.[6]

Mixed signals were sent about the theological significance of the church's social involvement. Two different overriding concerns seemed to be at the heart of the divergent points of view expressed in these statements. On one side of the coin is the concern that ministry emphases on redressing unjust social conditions and promoting human material welfare may undermine, even though unintentionally, the church's evangelistic mandate. On the other side of the coin is the concern that the church may be tempted to use its social programmes as a means to coerce the hungry and the needy to make a public decision for salvation. Both these concerns are certainly valid ones. But in addressing these concerns, those who emphasize evangelism and those who champion social concern are often polarized into opposing camps, creating, as a consequence, a fragmented approach in many of the church's missional programmes.

In checkmating the first concern, for example, evangelism is typically elevated to 'the priority task' of the church; social service and social action, by implication, are thereby demoted to secondary, or perhaps tertiary, tasks of the church. In providing a rejoinder to the other concern of manufacturing 'rice Christians', the church's ministry to the poor, the sick and the hungry is often moralized as right in its own terms independent of its evangelistic potential; social service and social action, by implication, are viewed as possessing no essential relationship to the proclamation of Jesus Christ providing a saving way of life.

An analogous development within evangelical churches stimulated theologian Orlando E. Costas to charge that evangelicals were perpetuating a house divided against itself. Always the prophet, Costas declared that the controversy over whether 'missional programmes should include teaching and preaching the gospel or engaging in the sociopolitical liberation of the weak and the oppressed, or both is as useless a debate as it is a senseless and satanic waste of time, energies and resources.'[7] Such compartmentalized thinking about the church's ministry, in Costas' judgment, invariably leads to preaching a truncated gospel and needs to be conceptually overhauled by a biblically-based understanding of church mission. 'The true test of mission', Costas wrote, 'is not whether we proclaim, make disciples or engage in social, economic and political liberation, but whether we are capable of integrating all three in a comprehensive, dynamic and consistent witness.' 'We need to pray', he admonished, 'that the Lord will liberate us not only from this stagnant situation, but that he may liberate us for wholeness and integrity in mission.'[8]

Costas' call to his fellow evangelicals is one that Pentecostals need to overhear. All programmatic expressions of the church – whether designed to evangelize those who need salvation, or to nurture its own congregational life, or to reach out in service to the hurting and oppressed – need to be rooted in, and give expression to, the church's mission. Mission is the benchmark for the determination of ministry. Only when the church's multiple and diverse ministry programmes are authentically related to church mission will there be integrity and wholeness in the church's witness to the world on behalf of Jesus Christ. And, theological reflection on this connection between ministry and mission needs to be thoroughly grounded in Scripture.

For Pentecostals, the Pentecost narrative of Acts is the natural place to begin formulating the rudimentary principles in a biblically based theology of church mission aimed at the integration of evangelism and social concern.[9] I will accomplish this task in four moves. First, I will connect the Acts 2 narrative to the kingdom mission and ministry of Jesus. Second, I will investigate the theological dimensions of Jesus' kingdom mission and ministry which bear on his ethic and his social concern. Third, I will characterize the ethical dimensions of Jesus' kingdom theology which depicts what life looks like when people respond to God's reign. Finally, I will take a look at how Jesus acts out his social concern when he encounters five burning moral issues of his day – the treatment of aliens; the exploitation of women; the economic exploitation of the oppressed; underemployment and unemployment; and, the dignity of children.

Church Mission: The Connection of The Spirit and The Kingdom

As implied earlier in my introductory comments, theological reflection on church mission by early Pentecostals started with the conviction that the New Testament church was called into existence and empowered for evangelistic witness throughout the world by the coming of the Holy Spirit on the day of Pentecost (Acts 1:8, 2:1–4). Because the outpouring of the Spirit signalled 'the last days' before the return of Jesus Christ, the church's mission of world evangelism was eschatological in character, carried out 'between the times' of Jesus' life, death and resurrection and of his triumphant return to bring history to its apocalyptic conclusion (Acts 2:5f.). The coming of the Holy Spirit and the eschatological hope in the return of Jesus Christ, according to Pentecostal interpretation, were the two experiential realities that inspired and shaped church mission in Acts, and which, in turn, energized the twentieth-century Pentecostal movement with a zeal for global evangelization.

This conceptual connection derived from Acts between church mission, the empowerment of the Holy Spirit and the eschatological hope in Jesus Christ's return provides a theological vantage point from which to develop a biblically-based integrated understanding of evangelism and social concern for today's church. While utilizing this conceptual pattern of traditional Pentecostal thinking, the content of current biblical scholarship on the Acts, particularly the groundbreaking work of Professor Roger S. Stronstad, of Western Pentecostal Bible College in Vancouver, Canada, can help us to interpret Luke's own theological vision more accurately. Based on Stronstad's work, it is possible to demonstrate that Luke linked church mission to the coming of the Spirit at Pentecost and antecedently to the proclamation of the kingdom of God in Jesus' ministry. This Pentecost/kingdom linkage that undergirds Luke's theology of church mission comes to light when Stronstad's claim is acknowledged that Luke's gospel and Luke's Acts constitute two volumes of a single theological treatise.[10]

Stronstad characterized Luke's theology as 'charismatic' in order to highlight the point that Luke used the theme of the Holy Spirit to bind Luke-Acts together as one story in two volumes. The gospel focused on the activity of the Holy Spirit in the story of Jesus; the Acts focused on the activity of the Holy Spirit in the early church. At the beginning of Jesus' ministry, the Holy Spirit came upon him and anointed him for his mission. He proclaimed his message, performed his ministry, and accomplished his mission as the 'charismatic' Christ. At the beginning of the early church's ministry, the Holy Spirit came upon the disciples and empowered them for their mission. They accomplished their mission and performed their ministry as members of the 'charismatic' church. Given this literary and theological continuity of Luke-Acts, Stronstad argued that the outpouring of the Holy Spirit on the church at Pentecost had an essential relationship, in Luke's own theological view, with the prior descent of the Holy Spirit on Jesus at his baptism.[11] Against the backdrop of Luke's portrayal of Jesus as the 'charismatic' Christ in his gospel, Stronstad identified the following didactic purpose for Luke in his portrayal of the coming of the Holy Spirit on the day of Pentecost:

The Pentecost narrative is the story of the transfer of the charismatic spirit from Jesus to the disciples. In other words, having become the exclusive bearer of the Holy Spirit at His baptism, Jesus becomes the giver of the Spirit at Pentecost . . . By this transfer of the Spirit, the disciples become the heirs and successors to the earthly charismatic ministry of Jesus; that is, because Jesus has poured out the charismatic Spirit upon them the disciples will continue to do and teach those things which Jesus began to do and teach (Acts 1:1).[12]

The concept of 'the transfer of the Spirit' from Stronstad's quote needs to be unpacked because of its potential to clarify the eschatological character of Luke's theology of church mission. Transference of the Spirit meant the transference of Jesus' own mission and ministry to the church. At the Pentecost festival, the same Holy Spirit that had earlier anointed and empowered Jesus of Nazareth was outpoured to call out and empower the disciples to form the church in order to perpetuate Jesus' mission, ministry and message. Consequently, Luke made clear in his prologue in the Acts that the church continued to do and teach those things which Jesus began to do and teach (Acts 1:1). The eschatological concept of the kingdom of God was the focal point of all those things that Jesus began to do and teach. As Professor Gordon Fee emphasized in *Called & Empowered: Global Mission in Pentecostal Perspective*, 'the universal witness of the synoptic tradition is that the absolutely central theme of Jesus' mission and message was "the good news of the kingdom of God".'[13] When the Holy Spirit came upon Jesus, he was anointed to proclaim the gospel of the kingdom of God and to inaugurate God's right to reign through his ministry. When the Holy Spirit came upon the early church, the disciples were empowered to continue Jesus' mission and ministry of proclaiming the good news of the kingdom of God.[14] The apostolic proclamation did so, however, in the form of announcing God's reign 'in Christ'.[15]

Luke-Acts makes clear that the mission and ministry of the church is to replicate the mission and ministry of Jesus through the power of the Holy Spirit. To comprehend the mission and ministry of the Spirit-empowered Church in Acts, then, requires an understanding of what Jesus meant when he adopted the kingdom of God as the core theological concept to portray his mission and ministry.

Jesus' Mission: Inaugurating The Kingdom of God

Jesus' mission, ministry and message were self-consciously under-stood by him as inaugurating the kingdom of God.[16] A convenient way to unpack what Jesus meant by the kingdom of God is to use Mark's little outline in 1:14–15 when Jesus started his public ministry: '. . . Jesus went into Galilee, proclaiming the gospel, saying, "The time is fulfilled, the kingdom of God is at hand, repent and believe the good news".' First, we note that Jesus announced the kingdom of God with this phrase . . .

A. 'The Time is Fulfilled . . .'

By introducing his announcement of the kingdom of God with the phrase, 'The time is fulfilled', Jesus emphasized three points. First, by saying 'the time is fulfilled' Jesus linked the kingdom of God with the prophetic expectation of 'The day of the Lord'. After Solomon's reign and the subsequent split of the kingdom, the ten tribes of the north were taken captive by Assyria, and Judah was conquered by Babylon. The prophets presaged a time when God would bring his people back to Zion and restore their land. This hope for a restored and unified Israel centered in the Davidic covenant. God would deliver his people from their oppressors and God's people would be ruled by a King from the seed of Jesse in the lineage of David. The prophets referred to this divine intervention as 'that day' or 'the day of the Lord'. This prophetic expectation fostered the bedrock conviction that God would establish his rule within history.

Second, by saying 'the time is fulfilled' Jesus associated the king-dom of God with the Jewish apocalyptic movement which became highly influential in the intertestimental period. When it became obvi-ous that mere human contrivance and the hand of history were not sufficient to liberate God's people from their oppressors, the hope for

This age	The day of the Lord	The age to come
Rome rules		God rules
Oppression of God's people		Liberation of God's people
		Demons are exorcized
Demon possession	eschaton	and banished
Hunger and poverty		Abundance (esch. Banquet)
Sickness	Kingdom of God	Healing and health

a return to Zion and occupancy of the land centred in God's direct intervention through a deliverer, the Son of Man. The Jewish apocalyptics emphasized that the Son of Man would descend from heaven with power to crush the devil and to demolish the corrupt social, political and economic order of oppression. The apocalyptics aimed to stir up a hope for a reversal in the order of life when 'this age' would end and 'the age to come' would begin. The Jewish apocalyptic movement divided history between 'this age' and 'the age to come'. The dividing line between these two ages was the day of Yahweh.

This age would be brought to a cataclysmic end by the Son of Man. History would end in the apocalyptic destruction of the demonically oppressive social order. For the apocalyptics, the day of the Lord was the age to come beyond history when God would establish his eternal kingdom. Jesus used this apocalyptic framework of history to communicate his message of the kingdom of God and to underscore the truth that God's kingdom could not be established by historical developments but required supernatural divine intervention. Even so, Jesus broke with the apocalyptics by proclaiming that the reversal in the order of life would happen within history just as the Old Testament prophets had said.

Third, by saying 'the time is fulfilled' Jesus clearly identified the kingdom of God as an eschatological reality. Eschatology is related to the end time. Eschaton is the Greek word for the time of the end. When Jesus proclaimed that the kingdom of God was an eschatological reality, he was declaring that the kingdom of God belonged to the category of time rather than a geographical reality that belonged to the category of space. The kingdom of God was the time of God's blessing . . . the kingdom of God was the time of God's reign.

George Eldon Ladd in his book *Jesus and the Kingdom* illustrates the difference between the kingdom being a spatial realm which identified the geographical boundaries of a King's domain and the time when a King has the authority to reign. Ladd uses the following sentence to illustrate the distinction: 'During the kingdom of George III, the Americans revolted from the kingdom of England'. 'During the kingdom of George III' means 'during the time of George the Third's reign'; 'the Americans revolted from the kingdom of England' means 'the Americans revolted from the geographical space of England, or the domain of England, or the realm of England'.[17] In Luke 19:11–15 Jesus made a similar conceptual distinction in order to identify the kingdom of God explicitly with the time of God's reign. The text reads:

> [11]As they were listening to this, he went on to tell a parable, because they supposed that the kingdom of God was to appear immediately. [12]So he said, 'A nobleman went to a distant country to get royal power for himself and then return. [13]He summoned ten of his slaves, and gave them ten pounds, and said to them, "Do business with these until I come back". [14]But the citizens of his country hated him and sent a delegation after him, saying, "We do not want this man to rule over us". [15]When he returned, having received royal power, he ordered these slaves, to whom he had given money, to be summoned so that he might find out what they had gained by trading.' (But note what happened to the delegation that tried to undercut the nobleman's appointment as King – scan down to verse 27) [27]'But as for these enemies of mine who did not want me to be king over them – bring them here and slaughter them in my presence.'

We need to note both the context and the historical background of this parable. The context is the march to Jerusalem and the supposition that the realm of the kingdom of God would emanate from Zion. The background was a piece of contemporary history with which his disciples would have been familiar. After the death of King Herod, his two sons clamoured for the throne. One of the brothers Archelais went to Rome for confirmation hearings and appointment as King of Judea. A delegation followed him to protest his appointment and to petition the Emperor to appoint the younger brother who the delegates believed would make a more beneficent ruler. But despite the protest Archelais was appointed. When he returned back to Judea as King one of his first acts was to slaughter those who tried to undercut his appointment.

But the point of analogy is clear: when Archelais 'received the kingdom' he did not receive the geographical space called Judea. That remained under Rome's domain. The realm still belonged to Caesar. But Archelais did acquire the authority to reign as King over Judea.

In this parable, Jesus clearly identified the kingdom of God that he was inaugurating through his ministry with the time of God's reign. His mission was to demonstrate through his ministry that God was establishing his authority to reign in human history.

In summary, by saying that 'the time was fulfilled' Jesus identified the kingdom of God with the prophetic expectation of the day of Yahweh, with the time of the reversal in the order of life which could only be started by supernatural intervention and with the time of God's eschatological reign. After this introductory phrase, Jesus declared . . .

B. *'The Kingdom of God is at Hand . . .'*

In one sense Jesus seems to say that the kingdom is at hand and therefore the time of God's reign still belongs to the future. In another sense Jesus seems to say that the kingdom of God is at hand and therefore the time of God's reign is about to begin with his ministry. There is sufficient textual support to suggest that Jesus held to both of these assertions.

At least three groups of texts suggest the kingdom of God was in the future for Jesus. One set of texts makes it clear that for Jesus the reversal in the order of life was still in the future. For example: Jesus said in Matthew 8:11–12 that his disciples will sit at table with Abraham, Isaac and Jacob implying clearly that the eschatological banquet was still in the future. In the blasphemy sayings of Matthew 12:32 Jesus said, 'If you blaspheme the son, you shall be forgiven, but if you blaspheme against the Holy Spirit it shall not be forgiven you either in this age or in the age to come', clearly implying that the age to come for Jesus himself was still in the future. Another group of future texts are the Son of Man sayings. The Son of Man sayings always identify the kingdom of God as coming in the future with great power and glory. The watchfulness sayings are a third group of texts in which Jesus admonishes his disciples to watch and wait for the coming kingdom. The watchfulness sayings see the hour of the kingdom yet in the future.

In contrast, at least four groups of texts suggest the kingdom of God was present for Jesus. One group of texts chronicles Jesus' view that the reversal in the order of life was already present. For example: in the kingdom manifesto of Luke 4:18–19 Jesus entered the synagogue and read from the servant songs of Isaiah:

The spirit of the Lord is upon me because he has anointed me
to preach the good news to the poor
to proclaim release to the captive
to recover the sight of the blind
to set at liberty the oppressed
to proclaim the year of the Lord's favour.

He then rolled up the scroll, gave it back to the attendant and sat down as the custom was to preach the sermon. But what they heard did not correspond to custom. He said, 'Today this Scripture has been fulfilled in your hearing'.

Two things stand out in the narrative. First, he broke with the sequence of the lectionary reading because he scrolled through until he found the servant songs of Isaiah 61. Second, he identified his ministry explicitly with the reversal in the order of life.

Similarly in John's imprisonment narrative Jesus cited his proclamation of the good news to the poor and his healing miracles as 'signs' that the reversal in the order of life had already started. When John was in prison awaiting execution, he sent his disciples to Jesus, asking, 'Are you he or do we look for another?' As John's messengers approached, Luke reported that Jesus gave sight to the blind and healed many from their 'infirmities and plagues and evil spirits' (7:21). Jesus then instructed John's emissaries:

'Go and tell John what you have seen and heard: the blind see, the lame walk, lepers are cleansed, the deaf hear, the dead are raised up, and the poor have the gospel preached to them'.

Jesus viewed his ministry of healing, his miracles and his bringing good news to the poor as 'signs' that the kingdom of God has already broken into the present and the reversal in the order of life had already begun.

A second group of texts suggest the kingdom of God was already present because Jesus declared that the old age of the law was already giving way to the new age of kingdom. For example in the Sermon on the Mount he says repeatedly in working through the moral commandments of the Decalogue: 'You have heard it said', . . . 'but I say unto you' . . . The ethic of the old age was no longer normative but had already been superseded by the new order of life resident in God's reign.

A third group of texts shows that the eschatological banquet was already celebrated by Jesus. His table fellowship with sinners was a major controversy with the Jewish religious establishment. On one occasion, recorded in Mark 2:18 and following, both the Pharisees and John's disciples came asking why they fasted while Jesus' disciples did not. Jesus responded that 'while the bridegroom is present the attendants of the bridegroom do not fast, do they'. Well, Jesus said, the bridegroom is here so we are celebrating the eschatological banquet. Then he said, you do not sew a new patch on old clothes, put new wine in old containers, and the chapter ends with Jesus and his disciples plucking heads of grain on the sabbath. These four symbols are the symbols of the day of the Lord – the wedding, new clothes, new wine, bread of the harvest – because they are all times of joy associated with God's blessing and new beginnings.

The casting out of demons was also presented as evidence by Jesus that his ministry had inaugurated God's right to reign in history. For example, in Luke 11:20 Jesus declared, 'If I by the finger of God cast out demons, then the kingdom of God has come upon you'. This statement is part of the Beelzebub narrative in which Jesus was accused of casting out demons by the chief ruler of demons. Jesus retorted that a house divided against itself cannot stand. Jesus said he was able to cast out demons because he had pilfered the strong man's house. The strong man prevails until a stronger one comes. Jesus declared that he was the stronger one who bound the strong man in his house. And now he was able to take the strong man's spoils by a flick of his finger. 'If I by the finger of God cast out demons, then the kingdom of God has come upon you.'

From this textual evidence it seems clear that the kingdom of God was present for Jesus and it seems just as clear that the kingdom of God was future for Jesus. The kingdom of God, according to Jesus, was both a present reality and a future reality. The kingdom of God was 'already' present but 'not yet' fully consummated in the transformation of a new heaven and a new earth. For Jesus the kingdom of God was 'now' and 'not yet'. This 'already/not yet' character of God's reign is made more clear when we consider the response Jesus called for in his announcement.

C. '. . . Repent and Believe The Good News'

In the face of the good news of the gospel, Jesus declared that repentance and belief are a person's greatest joy. The radical changes that attend repentance and belief in response to God's reign was elaborated on by Jesus in Matthew 11:12 and its Lukan parallel in 16:16. Matthew 11:12,13 reads: 'From the days of John the Baptist until now the kingdom of heaven has suffered violence, and the violent take it by force. For all the prophets and the law prophesied until John came.' Luke 16:16 reads: the law and the prophets were in effect until John came; since then the good news of the kingdom is preached, and everyone enters it by force. Or, everyone presses one's way into it. Or, everyone enters it with radical changes.

The meaning of this text is connected to the apocalyptic view of history used by Jesus to frame his kingdom teaching here: this age – the eschaton – the age to come. The tendency is to think along this line:

This age	Eschaton	The age to come
The law and	God's salvation	The 'time' of the
the prophets	John	kingdom of God

→→→→→→→→→→→→→→→→→→→→→→→→→→→→→→→→→→→→→→

But the text does not imply such a chronological sequence of time. It says that the law and the prophets were until John, since then the kingdom of God has been advancing or proclaimed as coming. So the following chart represents the perspective of Jesus:

This age	Eschaton	The age to come
The law and	God's salvation	The 'time' of the
the prophets	John	kingdom of God

→→→→→→→→→→→→→→→→←←←←←←←←←←←←←←←←←←

Jesus declared that it was not that the present historical moment was moving into the future of God's reign. Rather, it was the reign of God that belonged to the future that was moving into the present. The imagery that Jesus used was that the future eschatological kingdom was pressing against the time line of this age. It was the kairos moment – a new era was dawning. The time was fulfilled, the kingdom of God was breaking into the present moment.

And, Jesus said, as the kingdom pressed into this age, people could press against it and already experience the transforming power of God's messianic salvation. It was like new wine placed in old wineskins; it begins to bleed through the leather and just a bead of the new wine of the age to come is powerful enough to unstop a deaf ear or dumb tongue or to restore sight or to cure a leper or to gladden the heart of the poor. It is God's day of salvation. In George Ladd's fine phrase, Jesus declared the kingdom of God as 'the presence of the future'.[18]

And when people press into God's kingdom, God's gracious reign is powerful enough to overthrow the old self-centred kingdom. To experience God's reign is to come under divine management. God's gracious rule overmasters and violates the self's right to rule. And in that transforming moment of radical changes God's future reign becomes the centre of human loyalty. To come under God's reign is to become part of an eschatological people – a people of God who live in the present age by the future kingdom 'not yet' consummated. Within this theological context, the ethical teachings of Jesus are designed to create a people who provide a visible witness in the present age of what the future will look like.

Jesus' Ethic: Describing What Life Looks Like When People Respond to God's Reign

In making an inextricable link between theology and ethics, Jesus reflects the structure of ethical thinking found in the Old Testament. In formulating his moral judgments about individual behaviours and social practices Jesus will draw on many Old Testament concepts: the affirmation that human beings are God's image bearers, the moral significance of the law and its fulfilment in real life, the prophetic spirit that aspires for justice in human affairs, the importance of covenant in creating the social bonds for an ordered society, and the jubilee reversal with the forgiveness of the debt and the debtor to name only a few. When Jesus enunciates the connection between theology and ethics, however, he is adopting the basic structure of thinking ethically found throughout the Old Testament: ethical thinking in the Old Testament was theocentric in nature. The Old Testament narrates the story of the Jewish people as God's people – their identity as a people is centred in God. Ideally, their whole way of life provided a witness to their understanding of who God was and what his will required.[19]

In his comprehensive study on this subject, Professor Walter C. Kaiser writes, 'The character, will, word and work of God supply the determining principle and central organizing tenet of Old Testament ethics'.[20] From this God-centred orientation, a fundamental moral axiom came to dominate Israel's life: Who God is in his character and what God reveals about himself in his mighty acts define what is right. Ethical reflection takes place properly in a theological context. To determine what is morally good requires the prior theological determination of who God is in his character and what God does in his conduct. God and the good are inextricably linked together.

Here is the bottom line implication of this theocentric approach to ethics and its application to everyday life: every theological statement describing God's character and conduct simultaneously is a moral imperative prescribing who God's people ought to be and what they ought to do: as God is in his character, so God's people ought to be in their character; and, as God acts in his conduct, so God's people ought to act in their conduct. T. B. Maston in his classic study of biblical ethics claims that this principle of the imitatio Dei – the imitation of God – is 'the nearest thing we have in biblical ethics to one unifying theme or motif'.[21] This God-centred foundation for ethical thinking and moral life is carried from the Old Testament into the New, and especially is this theological character of ethics enunciated by Jesus. Jesus' theology both defined and justified his ethical principles.

The ethical teachings of Jesus are found scattered throughout the synoptic gospels. The greatest body of his ethical teachings, however, is conveniently found in one section of Matthew's gospel commonly called the Sermon on the Mount, a designation first assigned to Matthew 5, 6 and 7 by St. Augustine. No fewer than twelve different ways of interpreting the Sermon in the 4th and 5th chapters of his book *Understanding the Sermon on the Mount* are identified by Harvey McArthur. In fact, McArthur humorously suggests after reviewing these twelve different interpretations that he should have entitled the section 'Versions and evasions of the Sermon on the Mount' for all but one mode of interpretation avoid the absolute claims of the sermon for the followers of Jesus today.[22]

The critical work of Joachim Jeremias in his book, *The Sermon on the Mount*, connects the ethics of Jesus explicitly to the kingdom theology of Jesus. Noting that the sermon was constructed by Matthew as 'an early Christian catechism' for Jewish Christians the ethical content presupposes that the hearers were Christians already: 'It was preceded by the proclamation of the gospel; and it was preceded by conversion, by being overpowered by the Good News'. Thus, for Jeremias, the sermon 'is spoken to men and women who have already received forgiveness, who have found the pearl of great price, who have been invited to the wedding, who through their faith in Jesus belong to the new creation, to the new world of God'. Jeremias concludes: 'the Sermon on the Mount is not law but gospel'. Jeremias argues that in order to make the distinction clear, one should avoid terms like 'Christian morality' and speak instead of 'lived faith' for 'then it is clearly stated that the gift of God precedes his demands'.[23]

By placing the ethics of the sermon within the double historical context of Jesus' original proclamation of the kingdom of God and the catechetical context of Matthew it becomes clear that the sermon portrays the 'repentance' and the 'righteousness' which belong to the kingdom. It describes what human life looks like when people come under the gracious rule of God. Those who enter the kingdom receive God's benediction as his blessed ones and experience the reversal in the order of life becoming salt and light. God's blessed ones do not live by the old law of retaliation, but by turning the cheek, giving a cloak and going the second mile; by loving both neighbour and enemy; by making the spoken word a moral bond; by respecting the bodily integrity of others; by offering reconciliation to wrongdoers, by praying the 'our Father', fasting, and giving alms to the poor, by trusting that God's righteous verdict will make all things right; by following the way of wisdom in hearing Jesus proclamation of the kingdom come and acting on it so the house will stand in the day of eschatological testing. Jeremias's point needs to be underscored; the ethics of Jesus gathered in the sermon and found elsewhere through the gospels are not so much prescriptions of law as they are descriptions of grace, that is, the ethics define what life looks like under the gracious rule of God.[24]

Accordingly, the moral imperatives of Jesus' ethic need to be interpreted in the context of the theological indicatives that define the nature of God's rule. For the sake of illustration alone, one of Jesus' moral imperatives will be selected and analysed. Naturally other principles could be treated similarly. Jesus' admonition to love one's neighbours and one's enemies is transformed from a perfectionist ideal into a kingdom life principle by this theological indicative/moral imperative logic: when God reigns he loves everyone, so God's people who live under his reign ought to love everyone. When they do so they witness that they are God's people who belong to him. The moral imperative, 'love your enemies', made it clear that all neighbours are included in the geography of love. As Professor Larry Rasmussen from Union Theological Seminary observes: 'If the enemy is included, no one is excluded, since the enemy is the one most likely to be an exception'.[25] Further, all enemies – personal antagonists, legal adversaries, economic competitors, national foes – are brought under the umbrella of love's obligation. No category of enemy is excluded. Given love's unconditional character and global scope, 'the commandment to love our enemies censures love that is mere social solidarity'.[26] Family ties, class standing, national interests, cultural values and religious identity can no longer confine the boundaries where the law of love is normative.

Because love of enemies requires the positive content of boundless neighbour-love associated with love of God, and because love of enemies breaks with the powerful conventional patterns of reciprocity that govern the old age, Professor Allen Verhey flatly states, and correctly so I believe, that 'to welcome this saying is to welcome the coming kingdom'.[27] Verhey's assertion gets to the theological heart of the moral issue. In the theological indicative, we proclaim unabashedly that God loves everyone without exception. Where God reigns, we categorically affirm that love is the moral bond that structures the way of life. But the moral imperative implicit in that declaration should not be glossed over lightly. To enter the kingdom and come under God's rule is to be incorporated into the new order of life in which love is normative. Such unconditional love reflective of God's own moral character, however, runs against the grain of human nature, and as a consequence, it is experienced as an 'ought'. Experiencing the 'ought' of unconditional love, therefore, is both the gift of the kingdom demonstrating its presence and the call to realized discipleship. The call echoing from the 'ought' is to translate the truth of God's unconditional love into a human deed which makes that love visible in the real world. The empowerment of the Holy Spirit and the agency of human will make possible such love-embodying actions that witness to God's reign. Put within this organizational structure, the moral imperative is binding if indeed the theological indicative is true that God does love everyone, even those who have enmity against him.

The ethics of Jesus can and will only be practiced if it is a behavioural expression of God's overmastering rule in the believer and the community of faith. The ethics presuppose that his hearers had 'entered' the kingdom by experiencing the joy of repentance and the humility of child-like trust. Rather than being expressions of 'law', the ethics of Jesus are a part of the 'gospel'. Jeremias makes this point so cogently:

To each of the sayings belongs the message: the old aeon is passing away. Through the proclamation of the gospel and through discipleship you are transferred into the new aeon of God. And now you should know that this is what life is like when you belong to the new aeon of God . . . This is what a lived faith is like. This is what the life of those who stand in the salvation-time of God is like, of those who are freed from the power of Satan and in whom the wonder of discipleship is consummated.[28]

Contextualized within this theological framework, the ethical teachings of Jesus are designed to portray what life looks like when humans respond to the good news. Therefore, 'Jesus' ethics is neither a call to repentance in light of an immanent kingdom nor a blueprint for bringing about the perfect society on earth'. Instead, as Ron Farmer correctly emphasizes, 'Jesus' ethics is a response ethic', describing 'the proper response of people who have experienced the saving activity of God'.[29] Within Jesus' response ethic, ethical reflection is structured by this fundamental axiom: 'God is acting in all actions upon you, so respond to all actions upon you as to respond to his action'.[30]

In his ethical teachings, Jesus revealed the moral principles by which the actions of God's people could give God's redemptive action a visible form in the concrete world of everyday life. To that investigation we now turn in observing Jesus practice his ethical principles in concrete cases involving expressions of social concern.

Jesus and Real Life: Expressing Social Concern in The Context of His Mission, Ministry and Message

If theology and ethics are linked together in the Jewish tradition reflected in the Old Testament, so is the move between moral principle and its specification in concrete action. The moral codes of the Old Testament demonstrate how the law plays itself out in the every day life of the Jewish people. Biblical scholars sometimes distinguish this difference with the terms apodectic law and casuistic law.[31] Apodectic law is categorical and begs of no exceptions: It says you shall not do 'X'. Casuistic law is hypothetical asking the question, 'Suppose that . . .' or 'What if . . .'. Apodectic law says: You shall not murder (Ex. 20:13). Casuistic law inquires: 'Suppose that' or 'what if' two men are brawling and accidentally bump into a pregnant woman and she miscarries. Has the commandment not to murder been broken? Answer: if the child dies and the mother lives, a fine shall be imposed;

if both the child and the mother die, the law of retaliation shall come into effect, an eye for an eye, a life for a life (Ex. 21:22–25).

Jesus thought in these apodectic/casuistic distinctions as the gospel texts make clear. The triadic interaction between theology, ethics, and real life cases was part and parcel of the way he kept fidelity with his mission, ministry and message. It was in his real life where his social concern found expression in tangible terms. Five cases from his everyday life will illustrate how the kingdom theology he proclaimed and the kingdom ethic he taught played themselves out when he made choices or took sides on a socially or politically significant issue.

A. Case 1: The Treatment of Aliens

In the case of the treatment of aliens, Jesus used the principle of love of neighbour. The narrative is the parable of the good Samaritan and is found in Luke 10:25–37. A lawyer asked Jesus for the 'first' or the 'greatest' one of the commandments. Jesus answered with the so-called double commandment of love, clearly communicating his conviction that love of God and love of neighbour are inextricably bound together. There can be no authentic love of God without love of neighbour. Conversely, love of neighbour is the tangible moral expression of love of God. Jesus took the love of God from Deuteronomy 6:4, 5 and the love of neighbour from Leviticus 19:18 and put them together as a unified commandment.

So the lawyer asked, 'Who is my neighbour?' to clarify who was included within the circle of his moral responsibility. He wanted to know where the limits of love could be drawn. The lawyer's question lured Jesus into a rabbinical debate over to whom the neighbour referred in Leviticus 19:18, 'Love your neighbour as yourself', the text that Jesus had just quoted as part of the twin commandment. The position that came into ascendancy in later Judaism was that neighbour, in Leviticus 19:18, referred to members of the covenant community. The law of love was limited, applying only to Israelites and full proselytes. Even so, there were others who championed the removal of limits. Noting that the case commentary that followed Leviticus 19:18 alluded to responsibility for strangers dwelling in the land, rabbis on the other side of the controversy argued that the stranger, or resident alien, was included in the scope of the commandment.[32] Within the context of this rabbinical dispute, Jesus says, 'Suppose that . . . a certain man . . .'. A certain man connotes someone specific but no one in particular.

In telling his parabolic story within this context Jesus ironically reversed the social roles and expectations of the main characters: the priest, the Levite and the Samaritan. The Samaritans included some Israelites who had assimilated into Assyrian Gentile culture after they were conquered by the Assyrians. Samaria was the capital of Assyria and those Jews who had assimilated into the Gentile culture since their conquest by the Assyrians were called 'Samaritans'. The 'Samaritan' Jews were not recognized as true Jews by those Jews who returned from the Babylonian exile. Samaritans were considered 'unclean' bastard Jews and were treated with disdain. In contrast, the priests and the Levites were highly respected members of the Jewish community. With the rabbinical debate in full swing over whether or not aliens should be regarded as neighbours, Jesus intentionally cast the villain into the role of a hero and turned the heroes into the villains in order to add a bite to his story. The 'alien' Samaritan identified with the victim on the side of the road who needed help; the Jewish priest and Levite, who likewise saw the man who was robbed, beaten and left half dead, passed by on the other side, forsaking the victim to suffer his own fate.

The Samaritan, feeling compassion for the brutalized man, involved himself in the life of the needy person. He provided the form of assistance that matched the victim's need and alleviated his suffering. He cleaned and bandaged his wounds, transported him on his own beast, found shelter for him at the nearest inn, and paid for his food and treatment. Upon his departure, he personally guaranteed to pay the cost for any necessary future convalescent care. The Samaritan acted on behalf of the highest good of the needy person, demonstrating that love may begin in feelings of compassion but ends up in 'active and concrete involvement on behalf of those who suffer'.[33]

After Jesus tells the story he turns the question back on the lawyer. And he turns the question itself on its head. 'Who is my neighbour?' was the starting question of the lawyer to Jesus. 'Which of these three proved neighbour to the man who fell among thieves?' was the concluding question of Jesus to the lawyer. The lawyer sought to define the neighbour starting with himself as the point of reference. After telling the story of the priest, Levite and Samaritan, Jesus turned the question on its head, 'Who proved to be a neighbour to the victim?' The victim in need became the reference point for the definition of who was a neighbour to him. By shifting the subject of the question,

Jesus told the story from the viewpoint of the person who was mugged and robbed. The lawyer, in final analysis, did not get to define which neighbours are to be loved and which are not. The victimized person on the roadside actually defined who acted like a neighbour by identifying the one who loved him. Indeed, the 'alien' was a 'neighbour' to the victim in distress. And Jesus made the lawyer himself say it, the 'alien' Samaritan showed mercy – the alien proved himself to be a neighbour. The victim who received love defined who was a neighbour. But love is not the only moral principle in the new order of God's reign. So is the principle of justice, a principle that Jesus enunciated in another hot rabbinical dispute in his time over divorce and remarriage.

B. Case 2: The Exploitation of Women

Jesus' use of the principle of justice in judging justifiable cases of divorce and remarriage is found in Matthew 19:3–9 and its parallel in Mark 10:2–12. Once again his ethical instruction took place in the context of a test question designed to push him into siding with one rabbinical school of thought over another. The debate concerned the lawful reasons permitted by the Mosaic bill of divorcement for which a man could divorce his wife. The bill of divorcement is found as part of the Deuteronomic moral code in Deuteronomy 24:1–4. The rabbinical school of Shammai held that only the sin of sexual unchastity provided a sufficient ground for divorce, while the rabbinical school of Hillel held that any displeasing or indecent behavior on the wife's part justified the husband divorcing his wife.[34] When the question was posed to Jesus whether or not any cause is lawful, Jesus responded back, according to Mark's gospel, 'What did Moses command you?' (v. 3). The Pharisees cited the Mosaic legal code requiring a certificate of divorce. This ordinance, according to Jesus, was not an expression of God's will, but was permitted as a historical concession to human sinfulness (v. 5). Instead, Jesus emphasized the creation story as the basis for his claim that God intended marriage to be a permanent and monogamous bond between a husband and a wife (vs. 6–9).

By shifting away from the argument of how stringent or lax the divorce law should be and focusing instead on the divine intent for marriage portrayed in the creation story, Jesus put his own unique twist on the rabbinical dispute. Divorce, in Jesus' view, called into question the permanent bond of marriage. The 'transgression' involved in the practice of divorce, therefore, was not determined solely by reference to legal grounds as the rabbinical dispute suggested but by reference to the fidelity that one owed to one's spouse. The issue was a moral one not a legal one. Based on the belief that faithfulness between husband and wife was a constituent element in marriage, Jesus carried his logic to its conclusion: divorce was tantamount to adultery (Mk. 10:10–11).

That divorce was equivalent to adultery would have struck a discordant note with Jesus' Jewish audience, and as Professor Wolfgang Schrage has noted, when Jesus added that the adultery was 'against her', his male contemporaries in particular would have been dumbfounded. Professor Schrage explains:

> This would be a provocative statement to a Jewish audience, because the Jewish notion of marriage, defined solely from the perspective of the husband, treats the wife as property and includes marriage under property law. A man's wife is his property, acquired through the payment of the brideprice. . . . Jesus' prohibition of divorce grants protection to the wife, who had virtually no legal standing; this protection goes far beyond the legal institution of divorce, which at least gives the woman the right to remarry. If the original prohibition of divorce was addressed only to the husband, Jesus was taking the side of the wife, who had no legal protection. Jesus' 'strict interpretation of marriage' is therefore the appropriate contemporary expression of the protection and respect proper to a woman, who had no standing in Jewish marital law.[35]

Walter Rauschenbusch, in his *Social Principles of Jesus*, in a vein similar to Schrage, stressed that Jesus demanded more protection for a woman in his divorce teachings because within that culture she was at the mercy of a man for her economic and social well-being. Rauschenbusch amusingly added that, according to Matthew 19:10, Jesus' own disciples upon distilling this major point from his teaching 'ruefully remarked that such a strengthening of the bond did not add to the attractiveness of marriage – for the male'.[36] What needs to be made explicit from these exegetical insights provided by Rauschenbusch and Schrage is that Jesus grounded his moral demand that women should not be treated as chattel in the theological affirmation of God's creation of humanity. Jesus quoted Genesis 1:27 in overturning the normative understanding of the Mosaic divorce law: 'But from the beginning of creation, "God made them male and female" ' (Mk. 10:6).

Jesus made his viewpoint uncompromisingly clear. Because men and women were created in God's own image, Jesus had to break with both rabbinical traditions and take the side of justice against the exploitation of women. Women should not be dehumanized by an oppressive divorce law, even when quotations from Moses are evoked to legitimate the institution and the social practices associated with it. A social institution – even though existing under the cover of law – that permitted woman to be demeaned and trivialized as subservient objects of male domination was debunked by Jesus. As God's image-bearers, Jesus unhesitatingly stated, women and men both deserved fidelity in the marriage relationship – that was their just due, anything less was marked by the same kind of betrayal that is always present in adultery.

But creation in God's image not only provides a fundamental principle of justice which promotes the fair and equitable treatment between men and women in the institution of marriage; creation in God's image is also used by Jesus to foster respect for all persons in our third case.

C. Case 3: Payment of The Poll-Tax

In the poll-tax narrative, found in Mark 12:13–17, Jesus once again emphasized the value of human beings based on their status of being the bearers of God's image. On this occasion he used the concept to enunciate the moral principle of respect for persons. In the poll-tax narrative, Jesus was asked by the Pharisees and Herodians to take sides on a burning issue in the political ethics of Judaism. The question was whether the imperial tax, and the paying of it, was right or wrong. Adding to the generalized sense of the exploitive nature of taxes, the violent measures that were often used to collect them was also causing disenchantment to spread. In particular, the head tax surfaced feelings of oppression because it tangibly symbolized dependence on Rome. Within this context, Jesus stated forthrightly that he knew the test question was asked to trap him, and then he requested a coin. When he received the denarius he asked his detractors to look at it and tell him whose 'image and inscription' was on it. 'Caesar's', they responded. 'Render to Caesar the things that are Caesar's, and to God the things that are God's', Jesus retorted. Professor Wolfgang Schrage correctly contends that proper interpretation of this saying depends largely on knowing what 'image and inscription' was on the coin. Noting that a denarius was a Roman silver coin which visibly represented Roman power and supremacy,

Schrage provides the following description of the sacral character of the 'image and inscription':

Its obverse depicted the emperor with a laurel wreath symbolizing his divinity; the reverse depicted his mother seated on a divine throne as the earthly incarnation of heavenly peace. The reference to the emperor's apotheosis in the inscription made it no less offensive than the portrait: the obverse read 'Emperor Tiberius, venerated son of the venerated God', and the reverse 'High Priest'.[37]

Knowledge of the 'image and inscription' pictured on the coin make clear how wrongheaded is the dualistic view which contends that Jesus taught that God and the emperor, each within his own realm, had autonomy and absolute authority.

Against the backdrop of the depiction of the sacral emperor, Schrage rightly emphasized that 'Jesus' saying effectively secularizes civil authority and removes it from the realm of ideology'.[38] Jesus' saying not only desacralized the Roman state but set specific boundaries around its legitimate sphere of authority. Taxes belonged in the sphere of Rome's legitimate authority. Why? Because Caesar made the coin, it bore his image, and therefore 'belonged' to him. But not without proper delimitation, according to Jesus, because some things 'belonged' to God. The incontestable parallelism of verse 17 makes the unstated premise of what indeed did belong to God the most provocative 'truth' in the pronouncement saying. If the tax rightfully belonged to Caesar because the coin was made in his image, then what belonged to God was that which was made in his image. Only one thing was made in God's own image and that was humankind. Taxes belonged to Caesar, said Jesus, human beings belonged to God. The implications are pictured in the coin and structured in argument. By desacralizing and delimiting Caesar's power, Jesus refused to give Caesar an autonomous sphere even in terms of taxation. If taxation dehumanized, exploited and oppressed people, then Caesar was usurping his authority by robbing God of what rightfully belonged to him. People deserved a tax system that treated them with respect because people are God's image-bearers and God wills that those who belong to him should be treated with dignity.

D. Case 4: the underemployed, the unemployed and the poor

In this parable of the good employer in Matthew 20:1–15, Jesus emphasized that God's reign is governed by the principle of generosity when the staples of life are involved. The plot centred around the identical wages that a landowner paid to workers who were hired at different times of the day. When the first labourers were hired at daybreak from the gathering place of the unemployed, they agreed on a wage of a denarius for the day. Apparently, in order to get the job done by the end of the day, the owner returned to the market-place to hire more workers at the third, sixth, ninth and the last hour before nightfall. At each of these times, he said, 'Whatever is right, I will give you'. When the day was done, the foreman paid the labourers who worked for the last hour the same denarius he paid those who had worked since daybreak. Those farmworkers who had toiled long through the heat of the day felt wronged because all the labourers were paid equally without regard to who merited more or less. Upon hearing their complaints, the employer responded:

> 'Friend, I am doing you no wrong; did you not agree with me for a denarius? Take what belongs to you, and go; I choose to give to this last as I give to you. Am I not allowed to do what I choose with what belongs to me? Or do you begrudge my generosity?' (vs. 13–15).

As Joachim Jeremias points out, in this parable Jesus provided the following defense against his critic's censorious murmuring over his association with the outcasts, including his table fellowship with tax-collectors and sinners:

> 'Do you begrudge my generosity?' God acts like that householder who sympathized with the unemployed and their families. That is the way he acts now. He gives tax-collectors and sinners a share, all undeserved, in his salvation. So, too, he will deal with them on the last day. That, says Jesus, is what he is like; and because he is like that, so am I, as I am acting under his orders and in his stead. Are you going to grumble at God's goodness? That is the core of Jesus' vindication of the gospel: see what God is like – all goodness.[39]

Two worlds were thrown into sharp contrast by Jesus in this parable. In the old order, human justice is achieved by making sure people get what they are due according to calculations of comparative merits. From this perspective, the all-day labourers had a legitimate gripe. In the new eschatological order, discriminations of justice based on merit are fulfilled and brought under the expansive calculus of God's generosity. From this perspective, everyone received 'what was right' from God's generous bounty whether it was merited or not. Real human needs, rather than differences of human merit, was the reference point of God's justice. Deprivation was no more right for the last-hour workers than it was right for the first-hour workers. God is so good, said Jesus, that he compensates generously in order that none is deprived and, as a consequence, real justice reigns. Only a spirit of generosity in ministering to the economically disenfranchised can adequately witness to the kind of justice inherent in God's reign.

E. Case 5: The Dignity of Children

In the various 'child' narratives, Jesus identifies with the 'least' as the hallmark of the kingdom. Where God reigns, promotion of human dignity is established as a moral principle, especially for those who are viewed as non-persons who do not count in the human equation. In Mark 10:13–15 – the 'blessing of the children' narrative – the disciples scolded the parents who were bringing their children to Jesus for a blessing. Jesus became 'indignant', or literally translated, he was boiling inside. What he said to his disciples, therefore, should not be heard as a polite reprimand, but expressive of his deep feelings of anger: 'Let the children come to me and do not hinder them; for to such belongs the kingdom of God' (v. 14). Becoming like a child in this context, according to Allan Boesak, President of the World Alliance of Reformed Churches, has little do with the romantic notions of the child's simplicity, purity or innocence. 'Rather', Dr. Boesak noted, 'the child stood more or less on a par with those who counted for nothing, those peripheral to the real world, the good life; they were the "little people" who could claim no status at all'. The point Jesus made emphatically to his disciples was that where God reigns the unimportant and powerless ones who possess no status at all are the recipients of the eschatological blessing of the kingdom.[40]

Jesus' fury with his disciples and their failure to grasp this kingdom principle is explained by the fact that Jesus had earlier emphasized this teaching to them in the context of their discussion about who was the greatest in the kingdom. Jesus, in response to their dialogue, picked up a child in his arms, and said, 'Whoever receives one such child in my name receives me . . .' (Mk. 9:37). By such a visible object lesson Jesus made it abundantly clear that the greatest in the kingdom was the one who received and gave service to the least.[41] Bruce Chilton and J. I. H. McDonald, in their volume *Jesus and the Ethics of the*

Kingdom, suggest that the main point that Jesus emphasized in this incident was his own identification with the least: 'One must "receive" such a paidion as if he were Jesus himself . . . Jesus identifies with those of lowest status: to serve them is to serve him'.[42]

As we reflect on the interface between Jesus' theology, ethics and moral actions in the context of our work together as church leaders in formulating a declaration of social concern to support our actual practice of social ministry, we need to remind ourselves that our practices and actions are but behavioural expressions of our theology and ethics. Practices and actions that embody love, justice, respect of persons, generosity, and the promotion of human dignity constitute the normative moral structure in a Christian ethic reflective of God's kingly rule. Where God reigns, a society is formed in which brothers and sisters enjoy an affirmative community, strangers are incorporated into the circle of neighbour love, peace is made with enemies, injustices are rectified, the poor experience solidarity with the human family and the creation, generous sharing results in the just satisfaction of human needs in which no one suffers deprivation and all persons are entitled to respect, are to be treated with dignity and are deserving of justice because they share the status of God's image-bearers. Living out this Christian social ethic in the full view of the world provides a tangible witness to the truth that God's future kingdom of love, justice, respect, generosity, and human dignity has already broken into human history in Jesus Christ and continues in the world through the power of the Holy Spirit. A Christian social ethic takes the lofty theological confession that God's reign was inaugurated in the ministry of Jesus and translates that gospel story into the very pedestrian world of everyday life. Bruce Birch and Larry Rasmussen ask this telling question after they have developed their conception of a biblically-based Christian ethic: Who owns this ethic? Who is responsible to live by its imperatives? Birch and Rasmussen argue that it is the Christian community which birthed the Christian ethic and has the responsibility to live it out as a witness of what the life of God's people looks like. For Birch and Rasmussen, the basic ethical question facing the Christian community is this one: 'What character and conduct is in keeping with who we are as a people of God?'[43] Birch and Rasmussen are right. It is through the concrete character and conduct of its own community that the Christian church has the joy of bearing an authentic, Spirit-empowered witness to what life will look like in God's future reign.

Notes

1. For an analysis of the rise of social concern within the Pentecostal movement which I had the privilege of compiling and editing, see the special theme issue of *Transformation: An International Evangelical Dialogue on Mission and Ethics* 11 (January/March 1994) which focused on 'Church mission and social concern: the changing global face of classical Pentecostalism'.

2. Frank Bartleman, *Another Wave Rolls In!*, John G. Myers, ed. (Northridge, CA: Voice Publications, 1970), pp. 64, 65. This book was formerly published in 1925 as *What Really Happened at 'Azusa Street?'* Bartleman is quoting himself from an article that he wrote in *Way of Faith*, August 1, 1906. Miss Minnie Abrams, missionary to India, uses the same Jerusalem to the ends of the earth centrifugal logic in order to identify the reason for Holy Spirit baptism: 'What are you seeking the baptism in the Holy Ghost for? Is it for your own enjoyment? Is it that you may have this wonderful experience of ecstasy and joy, and live constantly in the joy of the Lord. Ah no, that is not it. We want power to witness to the death and resurrection of our Lord Jesus Christ throughout all the earth, beginning at Jerusalem, so that souls will come under the power of repentance, and believe on the Lord Jesus Christ and be saved . . . Let us not forget that it is the salvation of souls that he wants. Power to witness!' 'The object of the baptism in the Holy Spirit', *The Latter Rain Evangel* 3 (May 1911), pp. 8–9.

3. L. Grant McClung, Jr., 'Missiology', in *Dictionary of Pentecostal and Charismatic Movements*, Stanley M. Burgess and Gary B. McGee, eds. (Grand Rapids, MI: Zondervan Publishing House, 1988), p. 607. Hereafter the dictionary will be cited as *DPCM*.

4. The estimation of growth of the Pentecostal movement on a global scale is reported by David B. Barrett in every January issue of the *International Bulletin of Missionary Research* (*IBMR*). Walter J. Hollenweger, the acknowledged Dean of Pentecostal studies, in his recent book *Pentecostalism: Origins and Developments Worldwide* (Peabody, MA: Hendrickson Publishers, 1997), expresses his belief that the movement's growth rate is unprecedented in the historical development of Christianity: '. . . the stupendous growth of Pentecostalism/Charismatism/Independentism from zero to almost 500 million in less than a century, a growth which is unique in church history not excluding the early centuries of the church' (1).

5. My presidential address, 'Christian social concern in Pentecostal perspective,' presented at the Twenty First Annual Meeting of the Society for Pentecostal Studies in November of 1991, highlighted the various ministries of social concern in three of the largest Pentecostal denominations – the Church of God (Cleveland, Tennessee), the Church of God in Christ, and the Assemblies of God. The expansion of social ministry documented in the presentation represented nothing short of a proliferation of social programmes among Pentecostals. The theological portion of the address which sought to provide a theological rationale for such ministry was

subsequently published with the title, 'Christian social concern in Pentecostal perspective: reformulating Pentecostal eschatology,' *Journal of Pentecostal Theology* 2 (April 1993), pp. 51–64.

6. Editorial, 'Sidetracked!', *Mountain Movers* 31 (March 1989), p. 3, and J. Philip Hogan, 'Because Jesus Did', *Mountain Movers* 31 (June 1989), pp. 10–11.

7. Orlando E. Costas, *The Integrity of Mission: The Inner Life and Outreach of the Church* (San Francisco, CA: Harper and Row, Publishers, 1979), p. 75.

8. ibid.

9. For a more comprehensive theological treatment on this topic than the primarily exegetical presentation that follows, please see my chapter, 'Evangelism, social concern, and the kingdom of God', in *Called & Empowered: Global Mission in Pentecostal Perspective*, Murray W. Dempster, Byron D. Klaus, and Douglas Petersen, eds. (Peabody, MA: Hendrickson Publishers, 1991), pp. 22–43.

10. Roger Stronstad, *The Charismatic Theology of St. Luke* (Peabody, MA: Hendrickson Publishers, Inc., 1984), pp. 2–5. The 'Pentecost/kingdom' terminology as a shorthand label to convey the historical continuity of the coming of the Holy Spirit in Luke's Acts with the kingdom of God as the essentializing concept that Jesus used to identify his mission in Luke's gospel and the other synoptic gospels is borrowed from Frank D. Macchia, *Spirituality and Social Liberation: The Message of the Blumhardts in the Light of Wuerttemberg Pietism, with Implications for Pentecostal Theology* (D. Theol. Dissertation: University of Basel: 1989), pp. 296–304.

11. Stronstad, *Charismatic Theology*, pp. 33–62.

12. ibid., p. 49.

13. Gordon D. Fee, 'The kingdom of God and the church's global mission,' in *Called & Empowered: Global Mission in Pentecostal Perspective*, Murray W. Dempster, Byron D. Klaus, Douglas Petersen, eds. (Peabody, MA: Hendrickson Publishers, 1991), p. 8.

14. Paul A. Pomerville's pioneering work on Pentecostal missiology, *The Third Force in Missions* (Peabody, MA: Hendrickson Publishers, 1985), was the first major publication that suggested the revamping of Pentecostal mission theology by reference to a theology of the kingdom interpretive framework of 'salvation history'. His treatment, however, did not incorporate the Pentecost/kingdom association with its implications for integrating evangelization with social concern in advocating a wholistic understanding of the gospel. Even so, the argument of this article is indebted to the original thesis first enunciated by Pomerville.

15. Peter Kuzmic observes that the apostolic proclamation translated the messianic language of the kingdom of God into a 'dynamic equivalent' more suited to the broader audience of the early church's preaching which included both Jews and Gentiles. 'Thus the apostolic "to know Christ" became equivalent of the synoptic "entry into the ".' ' of God,' *DPCM*, pp. 525–6. Paul Pomerville also emphasizes this shift in terminology but views the change in language as part of a pivotal transition in salvation history

that was initiated by the coming of the Holy Spirit in power at Pentecost. *Third Force*, pp. 148–57.

16. The content of this section is particularly indebted to Gordon D. Fee, 'The kingdom of God and the church's global mission,' in *Called & Empowered*, pp. 7–21, and reflects many of the exegetical insights and conclusions made by George Eldon Ladd, *Jesus and the Kingdom: The Eschatology of Biblical Realism* (Waco, TX: Word Books, 1964). For an excellent international statement on Kingdom 'affirmations and commitments' that connects kingdom theology with social transformation see *Transformation: An International Dialogue on Mission and Ethics* 11 (July/September 1994), pp. 2–11, 33. (pp. 11–25 of this volume. Eds)

17. See especially the chapter, 'The kingdom: reign or realm?' in Ladd, *Jesus and the* , pp. 118–44.

18. George Eldon Ladd, *The Presence of the Future* (Grand Rapids, MI: Wm. B. Eerdmans Publishing Co., 1974).

19. These morally significant Old Testament concepts are developed more fully in my article, 'Pentecostal social concern and the biblical mandate of social justice', *PNEUMA: The Journal of the Society for Pentecostal Studies* 9 (Fall 1987), pp. 129–153.

20. Walter C. Kaiser, *Toward Old Testament Ethics* (Grand Rapids MI: Zondervan Publishing House, 1983), p. 38.

21. T. B. Maston, *Biblical Ethics* (Waco, TX: Word Books, 1967), p. 282.

22. Harvey K. McArthur, *Understanding the Sermon on the Mount* (New York, NY: Harper & Row, 1960).

23. Joachim Jeremias, *The Sermon on the Mount*, No. 2 in the Facet books Biblical Series (Philadelphia: Fortress Press, 1963), pp. 23, 30–31.

24. ibid., pp. 30–31.

25. Larry L. Rasmussen, 'Creation, church and Christian responsibility' in *Tending the Garden: Essays in the Gospel and the Earth*, ed. By Wesley Granberg-Michaelson (Grand Rapids, MI: Wm. B. Eerdmans Publishing Co., 1987), p. 188.

26. Wolfgang Schrage, *The Ethics of the New Testament*, trans by David E. Green (Philadelphia, PA: Fortress press, 1988), p. 78.

27. Allen Verhey, *The Great Reversal: Ethics and the New Testament* (Grand Rapids, MI: Wm. B. Eerdmans Publishing Co., 1984), p. 25.

28. Jeremias, *Sermon*, pp. 30–31.

29. Ron Farmer, 'The kingdom of God in the gospel of Matthew', in *The Kingdom of God in 20th-Century Interpretation*, ed. Wendell Willis (Peabody, MA: Hendrickson Publishers, 1987), p. 127.

30. This axiom is taken from H. Richard Niebuhr who first outlined the features of a response ethic in *The Responsible Self* (New York, NY: Harper and Row, 1963), p. 126.

31. See, for example, T. B. Maston, *Biblical Ethics*, pp. 10, 22, 34–35, 146.

32. Schrage, *Ethics of the New Testament*, pp. 73, 74.

33. ibid, p. 78.

34. For a discussion of the rabbinical dispute between Hillel and Shammai over the grounds for divorce, see William Lillie, *Studies in New Testament Ethics* (Edinburgh and London: Oliver and Boyd, 1961), pp. 118–25.
35. Schrage, *Ethics of the New Testament*, pp. 95, 97. The quotation that Schrage cited is from Herbert Braun, *Jesus* (Stuttgart: Kreuz, 1969), p. 103. English translation: *Jesus of Nazareth* (Philadelphia, PA: Fortress Press, 1979).
36. Walter Rauschenbusch, *The Social Principles of Jesus* (New York and London: Association Press, 1916), p. 85.
37. Schrage, *Ethics of the New Testament*, p. 113. Schrage drew this information from the research of Ethelbert Stauffer, *Christ and the Caesars* (London: SCM Press, 1955), pp. 133–4; 135–6.
38. Schrage, *Ethics of the New Testament*, p. 113.
39. Joachim Jeremias, *Rediscovering the Parables*, trans. By S. H. Hooks and Frank Clarke (New York, NY: Charles Scribner's Sons, 1966), p. 111.
40. Allan Boesak, 'The eye of the needle', *International Review of Mission* 72 (January 1983), p. 8.
41. This theme of 'the least' can be seen in the identity sayings of Matthew 25:31–46. Sherman W. Gray, 'The least of my brothers, Matthew 25:31–46. A history of interpretation', *SBL Dissertation Series* 114 (Atlanta Scholars Press, 1989), provides an exhaustive treatment of the history of interpretation of Matthew 25:31–46 from the patristic period to the modern era. He has been understood at different times to refer to the Jewish people (as a whole or as a particular group such as the apostles or Christian witnesses) or to humanity in general. After providing a historical overview of the interpretation of the identity dialogue, Gray concluded that 'the most noticeable characteristic of twentieth-century exegesis of Matt. 25:31–46 is its universalism' (p. 347).
42. Bruce Chilton and J. I. H. McDonald, *Jesus and the Ethics of the Kingdom* (Grand Rapids, MI: Wm. B. Eerdmans Publishing Co., 1987), p. 82.
43. Bruce C. Birch and Larry L. Rasmussen, *Bible and Ethics in the Christian Life, Revised and Expanded Edition* (Minneapolis, MN: Augsburg Press, 1989), pp. 189–202. The quote is from p. 19.

Five

Pentecostals: Who Are They?

Douglas Petersen

Introduction

The spread of pentecostalism, expanding to over 400 million world-wide, most significantly throughout Latin America, is an important socio-religious development that has seldom been examined from the participants' own perspectives.[1] In the past, competent scholars, generally social scientists, who assessed this phenomenon, utilized methodologies which were usually inferential and functionalist.[2] These scholarly works had generally been undertaken without adequate definitions, data and perspective regarding the groups' size, distribution, infrastructure, resources, and most importantly with insufficient understanding of the ethos of pentecostal experience. However, since 1990 with the benchmark publication of David Martin's, *Tongues of Fire*, earlier accounts to the contrary,

'Pentecostals – Who are they?', Doug Petersen in *Transformation*, Vol. 15, No. 2, April 1998.

pentecostalism is being recognized not as the product of exogenous influences nor the result of anomic forces, but as an autochthonous, largely spontaneous religious and social movement.[3]

In spite of these recent analyses, many of the pentecostal nuances – if not major concerns of pentecostals – are lost to scholars working from outside the movement because of a lack of understanding of how participants evaluate their own activities. And only recently have pentecostal scholars provided sturdy academic research in an attempt to interpret their own movement.[4] Further, it must be recognized that an interpretive consensus on the nature of pentecostalism does not exist even from within the movement.[5] Because of the limited scholarly treatment to date, the movement's inherent pragmatism, and as well, its deep regional, ethnic and theological diversities, a coherent articulation of pentecostalism is uneven at best. Any attempt to define pentecostals according to a specific confession of faith is a challenging task. Stereotyped and categorized, pentecostals have been considered fundamentalists.[6] The litmus test of pentecostalism, however, is not confessional but experiential. But, no matter the theological interpretations and differences, it is accurate to say in general that pentecostals hold a basis for theological thinking and action which springs from a transforming spiritual experience, and a subsequent sense of empowerment derived from an intense transcendent presence of the divine.

Certainly, the modern day pentecostal movement did not emerge as a group particularly concerned with theological concepts. Instead, from their inception pentecostals have had the sense that they had been called to be 'doers' of the word. They viewed the outpouring of the Holy Spirit as the source of empowerment needed to generate a gospel witness to 'the uttermost parts of the earth' in the 'last days' prior to the soon return of Jesus Christ. Their 'on fire' ministry passion produced missionaries, pastors and evangelists rather than theologians. The belief that God's miraculous actions in the Scriptures are continuous and normative throughout history, and until the present, have influenced much of pentecostal thought.[7]

For pentecostals the emphasis has been on the process of living out the truth rather than on doctrine alone.[8] Walter J. Hollenweger is on target in his observation that a description of pentecostal theology cannot start with only its doctrinal concepts.[9] Likewise, Eugene Nida has correctly noted that the theological descriptions of doctrines, though important, are not as crucial for pentecostals as they are in other evangelical/protestant churches. Pentecostals have always emphasized experiential Christianity as the way to validate the authenticity of their doctrinal confession. Doctrinal concepts such as redemption and atonement are explained not so much in technical terms as they are in interpreting one's personal relationship with God which produces a radical transformation of life.[10] Pentecostal churches are intent on demonstrating how their fundamental doctrines work their way out practically in the lives of the people. When appraising this experiential-certifying pentecostal approach to doctrine, it is important to recognize the characteristic commonalities of pentecostal faith that provide the necessary motivation and reward to sustain the indi-vidual members' high level of commitment.

For the purposes of this paper, there are five areas that seem to me fruitful to pursue, albeit in a cursory manner, that are foundational to the majority of pentecostals in the Two-Thirds World.[11] For most pentecostals, these dimensions appear to include: first, a time of crisis or vulnerability resulting in conversion; second, acceptance into a church life with accompanying emotional support and opportunity for participation; third, a subjective experience of Spirit-baptism with a sense of the presence of a transcendent God, followed by 'the signs' – most notably tongues and healings – that accompany these intense post-conversion experiences; fourth, satisfaction and the emotional security that derives from the groups' moralistic demands of personal holiness; and fifth, a dynamic tension between the present and the future, demonstrated in most facets of their practice, which enables pentecostals to overcome the restrictive internal and external conditions because their eyes are ever fixed on the future. These five elements can be identified in diverse pentecostal groups, in their collective beliefs and practices, as well as in the spiritual and social formation of individual members.[12] What follows is an account of these assumptions, desires, and expectations.

Conversion and Transformation

Historically, pentecostals have been characterized as the 'church of the poor'. The modernization process has tended to break up the traditional social structures, including the extended family, the village community, and the patrón system that formerly provided the masses with a stable worldview and a supportive social system. This state of vulnerability is the contextual backdrop for the introduction of pentecostalism in most regions of the two-thirds world.

The call to conversion, nonetheless, is not the path of escapism chosen as a way to cope with what appears to be insurmountable problems. Acquaintance with their unwillingness to accept passively their lot in life in the face of personal accounts of enduring hardship and ostracism indicates persons of unusual determination and commitment willing to take considerable risk. The risks taken may be accompanied with significant cost.[13] Conversion often results in the believer's exclusion from their community, a forfeiting of communal social benefits, as well as the rejection of family.[14] The conversion process requires deliberation, assertiveness, and presumably, strength of character. To the extent that this description holds true, pentecostals are not simply responding to changing circumstances because of factors which block hope for material or social fulfillment, but may well be a group of resilient individuals prepared to break away from tradition in order to participate in something novel and revolutionary. The change in their lives as a result of conversion is observable, often dramatic, radical, and real.

When a person decides to convert, their testimony almost invariably follows the pattern of contrast between their old life 'in the world' and their new life 'in Christ'. Once they were 'lost' and now they are 'found'. They have opted to choose between two alternatives – this 'world' or for God. Juan Sepúlveda, a Chilean pentecostal pastor and scholar, observes that when a convert testifies that 'they cease to be of this world', they do not mean that they have opted out of the world, because for pentecostals there are always two worlds – 'two worlds of life, two ways of living. . . . in a pentecostal testimony, a "world" is not an objective category such as society or history. It is strictly a way of life: "world", then is "my life" before accepting a "new life" through conversion.'[15] The goal of conversion can be nothing less than the creation of a new creature and a call to discipleship. Converts almost immediately after conversion, often within a few days, may be seen publicly sharing their testimony of new found faith with their family and friends as well as in the parks, plazas, buses – anywhere and to anyone who will listen.[16]

Eugene Nida observes that though pentecostal preaching is often criticized for its lack of theological content, it is, nonetheless, preaching directed to the needs of the people. It challenges people to make a crisis decision; it is person-centered and it is the *kerygmatic* proclamation. Such power of preaching, avers Nida, provides a personal participation and a psychological identification that cannot be equalled in the traditional churches.[17] In anthropological terminology this convert is a change agent or a 'culture broker', the independent, the entrepreneurial, the aspiring, in short, the taker of initiative. Costa Rican pastor Eric Lennox, in his Sunday morning sermon, vividly describing the initiative, risks and costs of publicly sharing one's conversion experience strikes the same note:

> They say we are the people of *aleluyas* – of tambourines; that we clap our hands and tremble. Do you have the courage to go to work, to the university, plaza or the *colegio* and declare without shame that 'Jesus Christ is Lord?'
>
> Your friends will deny you, your family may forsake you . . . if they accuse you, it is for the gospel, it is for Jesus Christ – say, 'Glory to God!' Many die for a few acres of land, others for gold or silver but we are willing to die for the gospel! Your faith will take you into the fire.[18]

Unquestionably, pentecostals in general have displayed tenacity, persistence, inner strength and determination in the process of establishing their influence, especially as they are regularly thrust into positions that require the assumption of leadership, rationalization of conduct and creativity in confronting the church's problems. The word 'audacious' has sometimes been applied to them. Perhaps the term 'boldness', used by St Luke in the Acts of the Apostles, is more appropriate.

The conversion experience is critical for the establishment of a solid basis for the development of the pentecostal community. Pentecostals have grown especially among popular society. Conversion provides pentecostals with a hope for the future. They hold aspirations for themselves and their families. They see opportunities that remain obscure to the masses who share their circumstances. Because of their conversion, pentecostals believe that the Holy Spirit enables a believer to translate creed into conduct, faith into practice, and doctrine into daily living. In a society where few alternatives exist, Christian converts, comprised largely of ethnic minorities, rural groups, peasants dispossessed of their land, urban immigrants, the young, women and recent foreign immigrants, have channelled their aspirations and creative energies for change not only individually but also corporately into the formation of a significant religious movement.

Church life

Everett Wilson correctly notes that general approaches taken to the study of pentecostalism have tended to neglect one of the most characteristic features of the movement, that is the formation of congregations.[19] The strength of the movement is achieved at the level of the local congregation, where small groups of congregates regularly have not only organized themselves into stable, often growing associations, but have invariably acquired land, support a pastor and have undertaken social programmes.

Citywide crusades held in huge stadiums are often the prevailing stereotypes of pentecostal evangelism or portrayals of revivalists which misdirect the attention of readers from the grassroots, individual dynamics of a movement to the highly visible personalities of the mass media. While the latter reflect the enthusiasm of the masses, these charismatic personalities are hardly capable of generating the interest that sustains their influence. In contrast to this more sensational aspect, the vast majority of evangelism and growth, however, results from Bible studies (*campos blancos*) which begin in the home of a church member.[20] *Campos blancos* are usually initiated by the pastor of the 'mother church', whenever there are two or three church families living in close proximity to each other. The services are fashioned after the style of a home Bible study. People demonstrating leadership ability, under the mentorship of the pastor, are given the opportunity to develop their gifts as leaders of the group. There is a time for praise and worship, sharing testimony, reading, and studying the Bible. Neighbours are invited to attend. As soon as the group grows to approximately a dozen families, the 'mother church' will begin the process of organizing the *campo blanco* into an official congregation. A *campo blanco* is considered strong enough to be independent of the 'mother church' when there is a pastor in place, the church is self-supporting, self-governing, and has secured a piece of property in order to construct a church building. The vast majority of church expansion within the Assemblies of God, for example, follows this pattern.

Converts to pentecostal churches typically find themselves involved in a great deal of structured activity. Beyond the opportunity for expression, neophytes have demands imposed upon them that not only affect their time and resources, but also strongly encourage the development of communication and organizational skills. Recognition of one's leadership and other contributions to the survival and growth of the congregation become circular, as all members are encouraged to invest increasingly in the 'work' and assume still greater responsibility for its development. Leadership, at all levels, is encouraged by an informal apprenticeship programme. Immediately upon conversion the new believers, regardless of social class or economic standing, are given something to do. Responsibility for the cleaning of the church, ushering or leading the song service along with street and personal evangelism are tasks that are assumed to be carried out by all. The apprenticeship system which begins with fulfilling the daily needs of the local congregation quickly expands, especially for those who demonstrate gifts, into teaching a Sunday School class, preaching during the week-night services, and for the most apt, the opportunity arises to 'pastor' a *campo blanco*. Bible school training, informally given by the pastor or presented through the local Bible institute, quickly follows as an equipping complement for the new worker.

Within a relatively short time a new believer has been able to be involved in a myriad of leadership opportunities and likewise to receive training, albeit not always adequate, in order to provide the basic orientation to develop successfully as a leader. Norberto Saracco recognizes that pentecostal leadership training produces a minister who is a natural expression of the group. Rather than being 'a prefabricated model imposed on the church because of intellectual qualifications of his privileged status', unlike so many of his counterparts in the mainline churches, the young leader is permitted to develop within and consequently authentically represent the social and economic context of the group to which he serves.[21] The most capable will, after appropriate seasoning, and with the blessing of the mentoring pastor, be allowed to pastor their own congregation and receive ordination.[22] Their right to gain access to the ministry is based upon their enthusiasm, commitment and capability to establish and develop a congregation. The emerging pentecostal leader produced by this informal apprenticeship system is 'contextual and indigenous' with the qualifications necessary to minister on the popular level.[23] Everett Wilson aptly describes the apprenticeship process as a 'A ladder of career opportunity [which] could take a capable member of a congregation from the position of deacon or *obrero* (lay pastor) to the elected position of a pastor, to that of a presbyter of several churches, to an executive position representing several dozen churches, and to one of several elected national positions.'[24]

Pentecostal congregations, formed by these aspiring members, characteristically are small in size, generally with an average attendance of 80–90 people and an even smaller nucleus of believers who are responsible for the inner operations of the group.[25] The church building is usually located on a small lot, not centrally placed, and often in some stage of construction. It is normal for a congregation to begin construction on their *templo* with minimal resources, proceeding to build as they are able. The completion of the building could, and usually does, take several years. In all, the Assemblies of God in Latin America, including Brazil, with an aggregate of 17,422,758 members and adherents, consists of as many as 12,828 organized churches and an additional 97,846 preaching points totalling at least 110,674 groups.[26]

It would be difficult to overemphasize the importance of property ownership that inheres in these churches. Members submit to the discipline of the group, accept rigid standards of conduct, regularly tithe or otherwise systematically support the programme, exhibit a high degree of loyalty, and freely exercise their rights to express themselves regarding policies. Few members of the popular levels have such an opportunity for expression and recognition, and having acquired a place in their local groups they hold tenaciously to their benefits.

Pentecostal pastors endeavour to incorporate new communicants immediately into active participants in society. Millions of peasants leave their traditional societies in rural areas and migrate to the cities in the hope of attaining a better life for them and their families. In a bus trip of five hours they could make a cultural leap of 500 years! Within a few days, they discover to their dismay, that they are simply unable to negotiate the literacy-centered communication system of the bustling cities. As a consequence, the move to the cities by rural peasants means that the cities are surrounded by homeless squatters with little hope to assimilate into an urban way of life.

Pentecostal church and pastoral practice is directed toward this mushrooming class of the urban poor almost immediately and is clearly depicted in the familiarity of the following story:

> I came to San José, from Guanacaste [province in Costa Rica] with hopes of making a better life for myself and my family. I had saved a little bit of money with hopes that it would last until I could find work. Unfortunately, I could not read or write. It was not long before my savings were gone and we were forced to move into *Los Guido* [a slum dwelling on the

outskirts of the city]. Our home was made up of cardboard and zinc. During the rains our 'house' would fill up to our ankles with water. I could find work only as a *peón* (day labourer) and there was seldom adequate money to buy food for my family much less clothes or the opportunity to buy school uniforms or school supplies for our children. Our situation was desperate.

One evening as I left our little shack I heard singing from a small church – a building with just a dirt floor, roof and a lean-to type wall on one side and the other sides of the building were open to the air – that had just begun to hold services in this community. Out of interest I entered the service. I enjoyed the testimonies and especially the music. After the service was over the pastor, as well as several other people, came to greet me. The following day the pastor came to our house and told us about how the Lord could change our lives. He told us that his church was opening a school and all the children in the community would be able to attend.

I felt drawn in my spirit to this small group of people that showed such joy and compassion. The Lord has changed my life and now I am grateful that I have the opportunity to be a part of this church.[27]

With the breakup of the patron-client relationship of the traditional hacienda and the breakdown of the extended family, some observers have purported to find large numbers of Latin Americans vulnerable to pentecostalism because they offer surrogates for the associations they have lost.[28] It is precisely this tendency to group formation that distinguishes pentecostals from most historic protestant denominations, even though in their early origins they may have had similar characteristics to those one finds today in pentecostal groups.[29]

The church building itself plays an important role in the group's operation. To social elements of the lower and aspiring lower middle sectors, the building provides a location where members find security and recognition. Congregations hold services virtually every night,[30] creating a literal sanctuary for the entire family as commonly different age or gender groupings (youth, women, men) assume the responsibilities of a given meeting. Thus, people who may have little hope of owning real estate contribute to the purchase and maintenance of a substantial physical asset. The emotional support of a pentecostal congregation consequently goes beyond the fervour of an expressive religious service. It is grounded in the ownership of property and the conferred status of membership.

Such benefits also impose demands on the membership. While lower-class pentecostals may enjoy a number of benefits generally not available to their non-pentecostal counterparts, they also assume responsibilities, which the latter may be reluctant to accept. Thus membership in a congregation may differ substantially from other kinds of voluntary organizations which, presumably, could provide the same advantages to their members.

The rapid spread of pentecostalism in popular culture quite obviously has much to do with its relevance to the aspirations and frustrations of the adherents. Rather than viewing the movement as the result of foreign-induced proselytism, it should be recognized as a grass-roots organization which arises in response to the unsatisfied demands of the common people for a more secure, fulfilled existence.[31]

The Baptism of The Holy Spirit, Speaking in Tongues, and Divine Healing

Most scholars agree that the two most prominent features of the movement – tongues and healing – are considered the universal religious phenomena among pentecostals of all stripes.[32] According to psychological theory both involve the 'invasion and control of the individual', with tongues providing a sense of mystical release through ecstasy, and healing offering personal wholeness and well being. This explanation, though not hostile to pentecostal beliefs and practices, is hardly adequate. The following description focusing on the spiritual phenomenon of the 'baptism of the Holy Spirit with speaking in tongues' demonstrates the more profound and tangible features.

The Baptism of The Holy Spirit With Speaking in Tongues

Evaluations of pentecostalism that focus on the vivid and the emotional may neglect to appreciate the importance which the personal experience of Spirit baptism and speaking in tongues has to the participants. In a society that systematically denies them access to basic human rights and marginalizes them to huge slums and shantytowns, the pentecostals, through the impetus of their spiritual experience, react in practical terms. The feelings of power, praise, and wholeness are interpreted theologically into the concrete realities of spiritual and social liberation, dignity and equality, and a sense of divine empowerment. Their vibrant faith, in a surge of irrepressible courage and hope, rejects thoughts of flight into a mystical world. Pentecostal reality is not a passive escape from the context, but on the contrary, the creation of a new existence. In a world where most people have been left to fashion for themselves, within the resources of their own experience, satisfactory responses to insecurity, rejection and injustice, it is impossible to overestimate the function that tongues symbolize. The distinguishing feature of pentecostalism seems to lie in this experience of transcendency. There should be little doubt as to why followers are encouraged to 'be filled with the baptism of the Holy Spirit with the sign of speaking in tongues'.[33]

Beyond simply endorsing such doctrines as Spirit baptism and the exercise of tongues, pentecostalism provides opportunities for the members to receive and participate in the experience. Typically in the format of the worship service,[34] in most pentecostal churches, there is a time when believers are invited to the front of the church where they wait on the Lord for a supernatural enduement of power. The believer is encouraged to experience the reality of the 'baptism of the Holy Spirit' (with speaking in tongues).[35] The believer is urged to speak in tongues, not only during an initial peak experience, but also on a sustained basis through times of prayer in corporate worship, daily devotionals, Bible reading and personal prayer.

The participant is taught that 'baptism of the Holy Spirit' provides a 'first step' into spiritual blessing. Such an experience will result, one is told by the pastor or other church leader, in victory over sin and complete transformation of life. Those 'tarrying' for the experience are taught that old habits and vices will be purged away, and a new enthusiasm will permeate their testimony. Such a peak experience is expected to affect profoundly the seeker. This unique experience in one's life is convincing evidence that he or she has a real and direct contact with God. The power and symbolism of the verbal expression embodied in the experience is exceptional. Following this dynamic, Frank Macchia underscores the profound richness of the dialogue between the individual and God when he notes that 'tongues allow the poor, uneducated, and illiterate among the people of God to have an equal voice with the educated and literate'.[36] Lay people are liberated to preach, sing, speak in tongues and participate in the same kinds of peak experiences as their pastoral leadership.[37] The parishioner is capable of interpreting and even promoting a religious experience on common ground with any other. Pentecostals believe that the baptism of the Holy

Spirit will uniquely empower them to witness to others the reality of God's saving grace. The power of the experience is to be demonstrated in all of their actions.[38] They must become not only participants, but 'doers' as well. Eugene Stockwell is undeniably correct when he states that the 'baptism of the Spirit' focuses on individual experience. There is a tendency within some pentecostal groups to understand the experience of Spirit baptism to be demonstrated by only physical manifestations such as speaking in tongues. Consequently, Spirit baptism, rather than equipping the believer for supernatural empowerment on behalf of others, becomes an obsession in one's concern for more and more personal and extraordinary experiences. When pentecostals utilize their experience with the Spirit for only personal and individual edification, and neglect the community responsibilities that should accompany this phenomenon, they on the one hand, misuse the reason for receiving the gift of the Spirit, and on the other hand, forfeit the opportunity for effective evangelism and acts of compassion. Christopher Rowland is right when he criticizes those pentecostals who are only interested in Spirit baptism for reasons of 'miraculous interventions and escapism offered by tongues of ecstasy'.[39]

However, in spite of valid concerns, it is too rigid to understand the pentecostal experience, as Stockwell suggests, as exclusively individual and that 'community and collective experience is generally omitted from important consideration'. On the contrary, the impact of the pentecostal experience plays a significant role within the structure of the community. The outpouring of the Spirit upon their lives compels them, they would testify, to practice all 'that Jesus said and did'. Certainly, their horizons would include individual considerations and desires, but similar to the miraculous corporate activities in the book of Acts, and because of a miracle of the Spirit, gender, racial, and economic distinctives, characteristic of their own contemporary contexts, must be overcome within their believing community.[40] Of importance for pentecostals, therefore, is not only the emotional euphoria produced by tongues, even though that spontaneity and freedom are significant, but also a ministry of passion marked by a divine empowerment demonstrated supernaturally in real life. Authentic pentecostal doctrine and practice finds fulfilment in the formation of a community of believers who take their authority from the Word of God and respond by providing an integral pastoral action made possible by the gift of the Spirit.

Expression of gratitude for supernatural empowerment is best illustrated in their worship. The pentecostal experience personally has happened to the seekers and they must know and participate in what they are speaking about. Pentecostal worship and especially music go beyond merely permitting expression; they are inseparable partners, along with tongues, in spiritual communication. The participant's sense of being empowered by the Holy Spirit is often expressed in music and singing that is boisterous, strident, provocative and insistent. Testimonial lyrics emphasize boldness, aggressive evangelism, and personal conviction. The repetitive use of phrases and expressions treat themes that are essential to the pentecostal beliefs and practices. Analysis of these songs and choruses especially points out the frequency with which they confirm self-worth, the adequacy of divine grace and the accessibility of divine power.[41]

Although pentecostal worship, often loud, prolonged, vigorous and repetitive may appear to be largely spontaneous, excessive emotional displays and individual expressions are usually restricted in public services. Outbursts that are unusual (even for pentecostals) may, however, be tolerated in given settings like retreats or other intimate meetings where emotional extremes are not especially disruptive. While at times their activities may appear to non-pentecostals as irreverence and uninhibited emotionalism, in practice, pentecostals tend to find a level of emotion consistent with their own experience and expectations.[42] For the participants, the experience of receiving the baptism of the Holy Spirit provides such a profound sense of personal confirmation and freedom that vocal expression, particularly in corporate worship, is foundational.

Pentecostals have little hesitation in testifying to and expounding upon an experience that sounds confusing and mystical to the outsider. Though there may be considerable differences in the explanations given, the claim of 'enduement of power' to live a holy life, proclaim with power the gospel, and participate in supernatural deeds, will be central to most.

Divine Healing

Stereotypes of pentecostals as 'otherworldly', pathological or fanatical obscure the second 'feature' (along with tongues) of the movement's strength. As much as pentecostals are allegedly considered 'other-worldly', their message is essentially one of immediate help. Healing, a mark of personal worth and power, is not deferred and is not considered essentially spiritual, but rather remarkably down-to-earth, gratifying and practical. Though pentecostals

certainly understand divine healing as an indication of divine presence, an indication of inner grace, spiritual transcendence and
symbolic of future restoration, most importantly, healing has immediate practical results. It is, along with tongues, a credential of the
practitioner's New Testament apostolic power. For them, in the context of healing, power shifts from symbolic promise to fulfilment,
from the purely spiritual to the demonstrable.

The tragic reality of the deterioration of public health care has left
millions of people in the two-thirds world with little possibility of
receiving medical care. Sickness in the new economic models
becomes an everyday experience for large sectors of the population.
Similar to the times of Jesus, people are like sheep without a shepherd, but also and in the same breath – without a healer/a doctor. In
many pentecostal churches, for the depressed, malnourished, and the
diseased, divine healing is offered as the only available option for
medical care.

Belief in divine intervention and an assurance that prayer can alter
circumstances give personal confidence often lacking in traditional cultures which are considered generally to be inclined to fatalism. There is
a new sense of personal worth and access to the group's collective tangible and intangible resources. Identification with a group that verifies
such occurrences becomes the basis for recognition of God's empowerment. Healings and other putative demonstrations of divine favour in
such a context are taken at face value. Two-Thirds World pentecostals
make little distinction between God's providence and sovereignty or
His acts of healing or miracle. The consequences of such confidence in
immediate access to divine power, for whatever reason, are easily
extended to every area of life. A pentecostal worldview that does not
make a division between 'miracles' of providence, 'natural healing' or
'supernatural healing' forms an important plank in the base for the
euphoric confidence that sustains pentecostals. The healing testimonies
of pentecostals should be interpreted in the framework of a theology
that subjectively meshes 'methods' with results. The healing may be
sudden or gradual, supernatural or natural! God is the One who is
actively in charge of all events.

The written account, circulated as a miracle testimonial, clearly
illustrates the acceptance of whatever 'method' God uses. Though it
would appear from the evidence available that Joseph was 'healed'
through successful medical treatment, it is apparent that pentecostals
are unconcerned with the process.

Joseph Poveda Céspedes is an elementary student enrolled in the *Escuela Cristiana de las Asambleas de Dios* in Torremolinos [a suburb-slum area in San Jos,, Costa Rica]. Joseph was diagnosed with a serious bone problem, particularly in his spine and hip. This illness forced Joseph to have a childhood different from other children his age – he could not run, jump or play with his classmates. Joseph's health steadily worsened. By doctor's orders he was completely immobilized in a body cast for 90 long days to avoid fractures and to enable the painful medical treatment to be successful.

When the doctors did everything humanly possible to make Joseph a normal child the entire *Escuela Cristiana* united together to make something supernatural possible. The teachers and students, especially his classmates, began to pray for a miracle. Simultaneously something was happening in the lives of Joseph's parents because they had never seen such love demonstrated towards their family and their son. So many teachers and students came to their home to see Joseph and pray with him that before long they were converted at the same church that was such a church of prayer, praise and hope for Joseph.

In spite of the prayers and the preaching of the Word of God that Joseph received he still required difficult operations, that far from weakened his faith, but strengthened his confidence that God, in his time, would perform a miracle in his bones. Everything had a purpose because his parents and other members of his family were converted; the time clock of God worked perfectly and God was miraculously glorified. Joseph is now completely healed! Today Joseph is doing well in his studies and his teacher, Carmen Lía Pérez, confirms that Joseph is running and jumping and glorifying God together with his parents who attend the church located beside the *Escuela Cristiana.*[43]

The testimonial healing of Sara Rodríguez, provided by the same pentecostal group, though far more dramatic and 'supernatural' in nature, granted similar reason to rejoice as did the miracle with Joseph. Certainly, pentecostals are fortified by the experience of a documented healing, but the documentation for them would not be a critical factor.

Sara, a third-grade student, became ill while attending the *Escuela Cristiana de los Cuadros* (a marginal housing community in Costa Rica). Her teacher noticed that Sara was gradually growing weaker – soon she could not attend school. Alarmed, her teacher spoke with Sara's mother and convinced her to take the child to the hospital.

There x-rays revealed that a parasite had infected Sara's liver. It had already destroyed a large portion of the organ, and the doctors said there was little they could do. Sara would undoubtedly die.

When her teachers and friends at school heard of the diagnosis, they began to pray for a miracle! Sara herself announced to her mother, 'Dios me va a sanar' ('God is going to heal me').

Within days, Sara began to feel better. When our nurse took her back to the hospital, new x-rays showed that she had a healthy, intact liver, and the parasite was gone!

A healthy Sara came back to school; her mother accepted Christ as Saviour and began attending church with her daughter.

The verifiable healing of Sara Rodríguez provides a dramatic depiction of a miracle that serves to undergird and sustain a family as well as an entire group of pentecostal believers. These two testimonies provide insight into the ethos of the experience of healing and make the connections between miracle, conversion and church life imminently clear.

Pentecostal reaction when God does not respond miraculously

That pentecostals claim to experience the power of the miraculous in almost every aspect of their daily life is obvious. However, pentecostals, though anticipating the miraculous, theologically interpret the silence of God when He chooses not to intervene as his right to sovereignty. There are countless times when God does not miraculously heal, and the ardent prayer is not answered. God is silent. Dramatic illustrations of the inactivity of God in response to prayers for miraculous interventions can be seen in the reaction of pentecostals in Peru to the terrorist activities of the Maoist-guerrilla group 'The Shining Path' (*Sendero Luminoso*). The goal of the *Sendero Luminoso* is to intimidate and terrorize the civilian population through sabotage, kidnappings, bombings and murder. The terrorists will often enter a village to kill all of the men who refuse to follow them, burn the houses and the crops, leaving the women and children to starve to death.

Evangelical pastors and lay people have been specific targets for the *Sendero Luminoso*. Pastor Lucas Muñoz, a pastor and former superintendent of the *Asambleas de Dios* in Peru, explains the personal attacks upon pentecostals as a consequence of their faith. 'You must understand that these groups [*Sendero Luminoso*] are atheists and very militant in their beliefs. We have found that they are antagonistic towards the *Asambleas de Dios* because we continue to testify of Jesus Christ, and we are simply not afraid to die'.[44] The testimony

of Pastor Elizabeth López demonstrates the faith that Peruvian
pentecostals exhibit in the midst of the persecution.

> On a Saturday night at about 9:00 pm we had between 600–800 people in
> the church for the evening service. The service was just concluding when
> the *Sendero Luminoso* came and threw sticks of dynamite into the church.
> After the explosion there were more than 300 people hurt. . . . The truth is
> it was difficult to go back [to church] wondering if it would happen again,
> and if it did would I live through it. But I went back because I knew the
> Lord wanted me there.[45]

The Peruvian pastors and lay people are given a simple choice by
the terrorists. They must either deny their faith in Jesus Christ or
suffer the consequences. Pastor Isaac Díaz defied the warnings of the
Sendero Luminoso to cease his preaching. One Sunday they came and
found him preaching. They told him, 'You have not obeyed us, now
you are going to die'. Pastor Díaz responded that he preferred to die
and be with Christ rather than to stop preaching. Without a struggle
or a fight they took him outside the building, the congregation knelt
to pray and Pastor Díaz was shot down and killed in the street.[46]

The stories abound, some of miraculous divine intervention, but
many others of God's apparent silence. Since 1980 more than 945 pastors and lay people of the *Asambleas de Dios* have died for the sake of
the gospel. In that same time period of intense persecution, the
Asambleas de Dios has more than doubled its membership.[47]

Pentecostals have understood that God's non-intervention in
response to their prayers is also an opportunity to testify to the faithfulness of God in their lives despite all opposition. Pentecostal Christians regularly testify, 'How can I deny the Lord who has bought me
with His blood'. It is evident that the persecution suffered by pentecostals has not hindered their growth. Such persecution may well be a
significant impetus for authentic evangelism and radical conversion
because of the high cost of active discipleship.

Although the apparent failure of pentecostals to receive a desirable
answer to their prayers (for healing, employment of the resolution of
conflicts, for example) may appear as a major problem, with accompanying disappointment not unlike unfulfilled prophecies of a
personal nature, the pentecostal is not simply manipulating the deity;
he or she is maintaining a dialogue which may progress even without
concrete results to one's prayers.

Practicality and effectiveness are characteristic of these pentecostal groups, who more often appear pragmatic than mystical or passively withdrawn. Although the desire for control of their lives may be expressed in other ways, including political expression,[48] concern with physical healing and similar personal and immediate exercise of power has been a reason to which the growth of the movement has been frequently attributed. Tangible indications of power, consequently, figure largely in their beliefs and practices. Healings, the resolution of unpleasant circumstances, the availability of employment or resources may all be taken as indications of divine favour, or are sometimes simply the inner strength to endure difficulties.

While pentecostal belief in an immanence of God, which would appear to cross acceptable boundaries for most evangelicals – characterized best by their practices of speaking in tongues and divine healing – requires more interpretation than it has received, there is little reason to doubt the sincerity of such testimonies or the wide-ranging effects. 'The theme of power, belief in one's access to power, accounts of supernatural intervention and the fear of another's' power,' Wilson describes as 'all familiar parts of the emotional and cultural life of [popular groups].' Far from offering alternative, 'nonscientific' explanations of natural and social phenomena, Wilson continues, 'Pentecostals simply use the idiom to which they and their communities are accustomed.'[49] Pentecostalism, Wilson argues, is not effective because it introduces such considerations, but rather because it addresses the real-life historical situation with an effective power.[50] And that effective power, often evidenced most visibly in tongues and healings (though by no means limited to), when placed in motion may aptly enable a clearer understanding of how pentecostals do theology.

Tongues and Healing: Two Ingredients of a Pentecostal Hermeneutic

I offer the following observations on a 'pentecostal hermeneutic' with a keen sense that they are very tentative. I would hope, as I have suggested elsewhere, that they would serve to encourage others to do even more constructive work.[51] In spite of the obvious risks, however, pentecostals must formulate a reflective theological explanation that gives credence and conforms to their dynamic life and experience. In so far as these contributions are authentic, most would agree that pentecostal experience is informed not only by the personal event of salvation, but by a 'charismatic experience that is unique to pentecostals'.[52] Pentecostals contend that the biblical text cannot be fully understood apart from personally experiencing the events that the Bible describes. God does miracles today, and the believer is empowered to participate as God's agent by way of the baptism in the Holy Spirit.[53] Pentecostals regularly share with each other the concerns of life and look to supernatural intervention to resolve seemingly impossible problems. The day-to-day health, financial, relational, and morale needs become the objects of prayer and, when they are satisfactorily resolved, the subjects of testimonies that attribute any improvement to divine intervention.

It is in this vein that pentecostals include personal experience in their theological process. They are willing to admit that their understanding of Scripture is formed, in part, by what they have experienced; that does not elevate experience above the text. It should simply be understood as an expression of Christianity, which emphasizes and appreciates the personal and experiential dimension of a relationship with God. Pentecostals rather unabashedly admit they reflect upon their own experiences as they study the text. They have found a certain 'praxis of faith' related to their social, personal, and spiritual condition. Their actions are based upon two foci: a biblical word and an experiential action motivated by the power of the Spirit. They can enact, or put to work, their faith experience nurtured by the constant reading of the Bible, but at the same time, tested by the 'efficacy' of what they do in their everyday life. The relationship between the two is a kind of ellipse in which each focus relates to the other and only as the two are taken together can the totality be understood. A pentecostal hermeneutic, different from a hermeneutic developed in a purely exegetical fashion, consequently is developed by how the interaction of the two foci behave in the actual life of the pentecostal community.[54] The difference between pentecostals and others may be that they use life experience in interrelation to the biblical text with awareness and admission of the fact, and with the belief that their life experience is an appropriate step, a legitimate route of action in constructing their hermeneutic.

Holiness

While the more spectacular display of tongues and miracles may command more attention, pentecostalism (as well as some other evangelical groups) perhaps is distinguished most by its moralism. The pentecostal view of reality, invested as it is with a pervasive sense of the sacred, imposes moral sanctions on their adherents; a participant's life must be characterized by holy living. Bryan Roberts, in a study of Guatemalan churches observed that 'as they [pentecostals] see it, a person's Christian quality . . . is certified by changes which occur in his moral life, rather than by his doctrinal loyalties'.[55] Rather rigid rules of conduct tend to separate adherents from the easy going, permissive attitude toward marital infidelity, gambling, excessive drinking and misrepresentation found often in popular culture. Practical norms and rules provide coherence and assurance to one's behaviour, and illuminate a 'signpost' to the authenticity of the dramatic and radical nature of conversion. Such demands, beyond a demonstration of moral life, have a pedagogic importance, particularly when they guide people clearly out of harmful patterns of behaviour.

Participation in pentecostal meetings is specifically intended to influence conduct, notably a concrete realization of the group's values. The emotional experience of a pentecostal service increases motivations to live a holy life beyond simply a sense of obligation to comply with a sense of spiritual dimensions. Pentecostals appear to draw from their beliefs and experiences in their spiritual sensitivity to invoke an aspiration and commitment to produce high levels of selfless, enthusiastic practice of moral living. Given the somewhat democratic features of the pentecostal groups' organization, however, these sanctions are largely reduced to peer pressure, threat of expulsion and are necessarily internalized by most of the membership.[56]

While the groups may appear to be a largely undifferentiated group adhering to similar standards, members themselves are viewed as being spiritually mature or immature, committed or superficial. After an initial declaration of commitment (usually evidenced by a change of attitude or lifestyle), the convert may progressively be permitted or encouraged to fill functions within the church programme. Depending on demonstrated integrity, perseverance and transparency of motive, the person may gradually be recognized as a leader, with corresponding respect within the group. People who fail in various ways to show such commitment, though perhaps finding a measure of acceptance, will also discover that the path to leadership will likely be commensurate with the amount of confidence one has engendered among his or her peers.

While certain standards of conduct often appear to be arbitrarily defined, they are hardly out of character with the purposes of the group. Honesty, loyalty, reliability and compassion, for example, are respected ideally by virtually everyone even when they are not practiced. In large measure they are features of many traditional popular cultures that are respected and even venerated. Consequently, the undistinguished member of the greater community who asserts himself by assuming a disciplined personal life, may be highly respected, even by persons who dislike the implied criticism of such conduct. Thus, pentecostals, in large part found among the popular groups, often find a begrudging acceptance in public life.

In spite of the pentecostals' emphasis upon corrective discipline, some observers have correctly detected a 'revolving door process' among certain pentecostals.[57] Undoubtedly many initial converts have failed to go beyond an initial statement of faith. Moreover, those persons who do make a statement of faith, but exhibit little interest in being compliant with the stringent requirements of moral life, will soon abandon the congregation altogether. Nominality is not a status encouraged within the churches. It is prudent to note that any analysis of pentecostal growth, or of 'losses' because of the 'revolving door', should be based on net rather than absolute increases. The adherents who submit themselves to the demanding expectations of the pentecostal community are likely to harbour deep commitments to the exigent and intimate life of the church. The robust growth of many congregations suggests that the life of the church is probably best measured by the proportion of highly committed individuals rather than by the proportion of neophytes whose faith may fail to develop in keeping with the groups' beliefs.

Eschatology

An attempt to understand pentecostal practice doctrinally is particularly open to misunderstanding in the area of eschatology. Doctrinal categories that do not take into account the dynamics of pentecostal experience and real life will inevitably be misunderstood in the function they play. As already mentioned, theology comes into play as a rationale for the experience, but it is not so intrinsically connected with the experience itself. The teaching of eschatology in pentecostal churches vividly demonstrates this reality. The majority of pentecostals have traditionally taught a premillennenial eschatology that in more fundamentalistic congregations would place great import on the future and have little to say about the present.[58] Juan Sepúlveda observes that it is precisely the penchant that scholars have, in their study of pentecostalism, to place emphasis solely on doctrine, without observing practice, which creates 'the impression that pentecostalism proposes an other-worldly salvation', when often quite the contrary is the case.[59] Similarly, sociologist Andrés Opazo Bernales, assumes that because the pentecostal churches have a fervent, apocalyptic message they 'naturally do not take interest in earthly things', the typical observation given by most appraisers of the movement.[60] NACLA, a journal reporting on Latin American affairs, demonstrated this same misunderstanding when they categorized pentecostals as merely a church of 'hallelujahs' which systematically ignored the real and physical poverty of Latin America's marginalized masses. They accused pentecostals of presenting a message damaging to Latin American life because the message ignored the present and offered only eternal hopes for the future which NACLA categorized as simply 'pie in the sky for the sweet by and by'.[61] Even sympathetic evangelical scholars like Emilio Núñez and William Taylor erroneously assume that 'they [pentecostals] have not been so concerned with life on this planet; and that is understandable if we remember the socio-economic strata from which most of these believers have come – the lower ranks'.[62]

However, pentecostals are exceptionally optimistic about both their present and future existence. Their theological conviction – that the God who performed mighty works in the New Testament continues to act in miraculous ways through the empowerment of the Holy Spirit – provides the great majority of pentecostal believers with a sense of hope for the present.[63] Certainly they have been uprooted from their social contexts, seen their worldview, values and social norms break down – they have been alienated from traditional society.[64] These 'nonpersons' are exceedingly familiar with unnecessary death, illness, unemployment, prejudice, repression, war, and perhaps even torture. But it is within this context that they receive the testimony of the Word and are converted. In this context of tragedy it is quite clear that the eschatological certainty of eternal life gives freedom to risk one's present life. The pentecostals' personal relationship with a caring and compassionate God encourages them also to celebrate their experience of transformation in the present within a community of mutual love and respect. A personal identity emerges and the nonperson achieves personhood. Such personal realization could not merely envision the promise of history as something ambiguously encased in the indefinite future to be reached only as 'pie in the sky in the sweet by and by'. Eschatology, with its foreshadowing of the future, could not be absent in its permeation of the present.[65] Pentecostals, who live under the shadow of death, but now with newly found dignity and discovered personhood, do not live their lives only with an eye on heaven, but their whole experience is overshadowed by the reality that the eschatological promise of the future has already began to push its way into the present. Clearly, the church is not a waiting room for heaven where the believers are huddled together waiting for the eschatological end. Rather they are interested in appropriating the power of their pentecostal experience to the fullest possible measure in the present.[66]

Pentecostal congregations, quite unlike a group with a mind only on heavenly things, are highly involved in alleviating pain and suffering in the physical realm. They establish programmes and institutions, for example, which reach out to the women and children who have been doubly marginalized – first, because they are from the ranks of the poor and secondly, precisely because they are women and children. Literacy programmes for adults – offered so that believers can read the Bible for themselves, schools for children and adolescents, rehabilitation programmes for alcoholics and drug addicts as well as a multitude of other active expressions of social concern have been established.[67] If their experience is, on the one hand, intensely personal, spiritual, eternal and mystical; on the other hand then, it is unquestionably corporate, practical, and committed to alleviating the pain of real life situations with much-needed compassion.[68]

The demonstration that pentecostal eschatology is not solely otherworldly is implicitly illustrated in each of the other theological themes and practices that have been described in this essay. The conversion experience not only prepares them for 'eternal life', but it gives them dignity, worth and personhood in this life. The experience of the baptism of the Holy Spirit is sought after precisely so that the believer may receive empowerment for the present. Such empowerment is utilized in prayer not only for evangelization or healings in the present, but also for miraculous answers to prayer in the finding of employment, physical protection, and other such physical needs as are represented in the family or in the community. Moral life is an expected characteristic in the present because one wants to be 'ready' at any moment for an eschatological end.

A Summary

Pentecostal movements have grown differently as well as rapidly. Most pentecostal groups, located within popular society, tend to incorporate the common features identified in the paper. However, they adjust to them in various ways. An important feature of these movements is their capacity for continual growth development and change as they adapt to internal and external circumstances. Springing from a variety of situations, the fertile soil of contemporary crisis and change has led to a broad range of conduct, including those that reflect the different aspirations of ethnic groups, those built largely on diverse regions of social classes, and those that accommodate diverse doctrinal, polity and denominational emphases. Pentecostalism quickly became reproducible and was easily networked among popular groups. Not a few observers of the movement have noted the irony of sectarianism so particularistic that it became generic – ecumenical.

Pentecostalism showed itself to be a movement capable of generating an experiential spirituality and a pragmatic and practical temperament among its adherents. Conversion, the act that is central to all experience, produces such a radical and verifiable change in a person, apparent to others, that the convert is known as a 'new creature'. The call to conversion is a call to discipleship that demands active participation in the community. Pentecostals' emphasis on the divine inbreaking of the Spirit into everyday life is characterized by the experience of the baptism of the Spirit with speaking in tongues and divine healing. Tongues, with its essential universality, suggests the inclusiveness of all the participants in the common experience of Spirit baptism. The pentecostal experience diffuses ecclesiastical authority giving recognition to virtually anyone who could produce a following. Divine healing, a tangible symbol of God's intervention, provides both the individual as well as the collective community with a sense of empowerment over the uncertainties of life.

Pentecostalism, by its democratization of religious life, its promise of physical and social healing, its compassion for the socially alienated and its insistence that all human ills were at root a consequence of moral evil, addresses the concerns of the disinherited, frustrated and assertive persons who in large part make up the movement. Despite the various and diverse aspects of pentecostalism, the tendency to adapt theological concepts to actual contexts, besides contributing importantly to its survival and growth, gives the various groups a progressive and dynamic posture. While institutional evolution is apparent in many ways, theological contextualization is an interesting aspect of pentecostal versatility.

Pentecostalism provides not only new opportunities for expression that are regularly denied the poor and disadvantaged, but also the moral support necessary for standing up to adversity and claiming one's rightful place in society. Pentecostalism in these social and secular arenas presents a positive contribution to the resolution of difficulties for large numbers of people. By developing self-esteem within the impoverished, by providing them hope and by arming them with skills applicable to the larger social system, pentecostalism is enabling participants to take part in the achievement of the larger social struggles for a better life and a more secure future. Ultimately, by empowering people who were previously denied a voice, the pentecostal movement in the two-thirds world has acquired a revolutionary potential.[69]

Selected Bibliography

Aguilar, Edwin Eloy *et al.*, 'Protestantism in El Salvador: conventional wisdom versus survey evidence', *Latin American Research Review* 28 (1993), pp. 127–8.

Anderson, Gordon, 'Pentecostal hermeneutics', *Paraclete: A Journal of Pentecostal Studies* 28 (Spring 1994), pp. 18–19.

Bastian, Jean-Pierre, 'The metamorphosis of Latin American protestant groups: a sociohistorical perspective', *Latin American Research Review* 28 (1993), pp. 33–61.

Bernales, Andrés Opazo, 'El movimiento protestante en ~Centroam,rica: una aproximación cuantitativa', in *Protestanismo y Procesos Sociales en Centroamérica*, ed. Luis Samandú (San José, Costa Rica: Editorial Universitaria Centroaméricana, 1991).

Comblin, José, *The Holy Spirit and Liberation* (Maryknoll, NY: Orbis Books, 1989).

Cox, Harvey, *Fire From Heaven: The Rise of Pentecostal Spirituality and the Reshaping of Religion in the Twenty-first Century* (Reading, MA: Addison-Wesley, 1995).

Cleary, Edward L. and Hannah W. Stewart-Gambino, eds., *Power, Politics, and Pentecostals in Latin America* (Boulder, CO: Westview Press, 1996).

Dempster, Murray W., Douglas Petersen, Byron Klaus, eds., *Called and Empowered: Global Mission in Pentecostal Perspective* (Peabody, MA: Hendrickson Publishers, 1991).

Dempster, Murray W., 'The church's moral witness: a study of glossolalia in Luke's theology of Acts' *Paraclete: A Journal of Pentecostal Studies* 23 (Winter 1989), pp. 1–7.

—, 'Soundings in the moral significance of glossolalia', *Paper Presented at the Annual Meeting of the Society for Pentecostal Studies*, (1983).

Freston, Paul, 'The protestant eruption into modern Brazilian politics', *Journal Contemporary Religion* II (1996).

Greenway, Roger S., 'Protestant missionary activity in Latin America', in *Coming of Age: Protestantism in Contemporary Latin America* (Lanham, MD: University Press of America, 1994).

Hollenweger, Walter J., 'The religion of the poor is not a poor religion', *The Expository Times* 87 (May 1976), p. 228.

—, *The Pentecostals* (Minneapolis, MN: Augsberg Publishing House, 1972).

Huntington, Deborah, 'The prophet motive', *NACLA Report on the Americas* 18 (January/February 1984), pp. 2–11.

Lalive d'Epinay, Christian, *Haven of the Masses: A Study of the Pentecostal Movement in Chile* (London: Lutterworth, 1969).

Macchia, Frank, 'The struggle of global witness: shifting paradigms in pentecostal theology', in *The Globalization of Pentecostalism* (Oxford, UK: Regnum Books International, forthcoming, 1998).

—, 'Sighs too deep for words: toward a theology of glossolalia', *Journal of Pentecostal Theology* 1 (1992), pp. 42–73.

Martin, David, *Tongues of Fire: The Explosion of Protestantism in Latin America* (Cambridge, MA: Basil Blackwell, Inc., 1990).

Moltmann, Jürgen, *Pentecostal Movements as an Ecumenical Challenge* (London: SCM Press, 1996).

Nida, Eugene, 'The indigenous churches in Latin America', *Practical Anthropology* 8 (May-June 1961), pp. 97–105.

Núñez, Emilio and William Taylor, *Crisis in Latin America: An Evangelical Perspective* (Chicago: Moody Press, 1989).

Douglas Petersen, 'Alienation' and 'Anomie', *The Evangelical Dictionary of World Missions* (Moreau, Scott A. ed. Grand Rapids: Baker Books, forthcoming, 1998).

—, 'Called and empowered', *Enrichment: A Journal for Pentecostal Ministry* (Winter 1998, forthcoming).

—, 'Toward a Latin American theological political ethic', *Transformation* 14 (January/March 1997), pp. 30–3.

—, *Not by Might Nor by Power: A Pentecostal Theology of Social Concern in Latin America* (Oxford, UK: Regnum Books International, 1996).

—, 'The formation of popular, national, autonomous pentecostal churches in Central America', in *PNUEMA: The Journal of the Society for Pentecostal Studies* 16 (Spring 1994), pp. 23–48.

Roberts, Bryan, 'Protestant groups and coping with urban life in Guatemala', *American Journal of Sociology* 73 (1968), p. 767.

Rowland, Christopher, *Radical Christianity: A Rereading of Recovery* (Maryknoll, NY: Orbis Books, 1988).

Saracco, J. Norberto, 'Type of ministry adopted by Latin American pentecostal churches', *International Review of Mission* 66 (January 1977), pp. 66–7.

Sepúlveda, Juan, 'Reflections on the pentecostal contribution to the mission of the church in Latin America', *The Journal of Pentecostal Theology* 1 (October 1992), pp. 101–2.

—, 'Pentecostalism as popular religiosity', *International ~Review of Mission* 72 (July 1983), pp. 324–32.

Sheppard, Gerald, 'Pentecostals and the hermeneutics of dispensationalism: the anatomy of an uneasy relationship', *PNEUMA: The Journal of The Society for Pentecostal Studies* 6 (Fall 1984).

Schultze, Quentin J., 'TV religion as pagan-American missions', *Transformation: An International Evangelical Dialogue on Mission and Ethics* 9 (October/ December 1992), p. 2.

Stockwell, Eugene, 'Editorial: responses to the Spirit; pt. 2: charismatics', *International Review of Mission* 75 (April 1986), pp. 113–57.

Wilson, Everett, 'Dynamics of Latin American pentecostalism', in *Coming of Age: Protestantism in Contemporary Latin America*, ed. Daniel R. Miller (Lanham, MD: University Press of America, 1994).

—, 'Latin American pentecostalism: challenging the stereotypes of pentecostal passivity', *Transformation: An International Evangelical Dialogue on Mission and Ethics* 11 (January/March 1994), p. 20.

Yung, Hwa, *Mangoes or Bananas? The Quest for an Authentic Asian Christian Theology* (Oxford, UK: Regnum Books International, 1997).

Notes

1. This paper focuses largely on the phenomenon of pentecostalism in Latin America. Latin American pentecostalism, the largest expression of pentecostalism in the world, provides an excellent microcosm, given its immense inroads among popular culture, from which to view the whole. Further, the majority of research available has been done among Latin American pentecostals.

2. Christian Lalive d'Epinay, *Haven of the Masses: A Study of the Pentecostal Movement in Chile* (London: Lutterworth, 1969), and Emilio Willems, *Followers of the New Faith* (Nashville: Vanderbilt University Press, 1967).

3. Martin elaborates his basic thesis that pentecostalism is explained best as a process of forming 'alternative societies' (p. 285), 'new cells', an 'enclosed haven', a 'fraternity', a 'social capsule', (p. 284), 'free social space', 'local empowerment' (p. 280), all of which provide a staging area where adherents may prepare to take on the world. David Martin, *Tongues of Fire* (Oxford, UK: Basil Blackwell, 1991) pp. 280–285. Other important recent

publications include David Stoll, *Is Latin America Turning Protestant?* (Berkeley: University of California Press, 1990); Edward L. Cleary and Hannah W. Stewart-Gambino, eds., *Power, Politics, and Pentecostals in Latin America* (Boulder, CO: Westview Press, 1996); and Harvey Cox, *Fire From Heaven: The Rise of Pentecostal Spirituality and the Reshaping of Religion in the Twenty-first Century* (Reading, MA: Addison-Wesley, 1995).

4. To mention some of the most important of them in Latin American pentecostal research: Juan Sepúlveda, Norberto Saracco, Bernardo Campos, Manuel Gaxiola-Gaxiola, and Everett Wilson. All scholars doing research on pentecostals are indebted to Walter Hollenweger and his numerous works beginning with his classic *The Pentecostals* (Minneapolis, MN: Augsberg Publishing House, 1972).

5. Even efforts to place pentecostals into distinctive groups is difficult. Though attempts have been made, an adequate taxonomy of 'pentecostalisms' has yet to be done. In sweeping strokes, however, pentecostals are usually divided into broad categories. Classical pentecostals, groups that have an existence of at least several decades, and whose total membership accounts for the greatest proportion of pentecostals in Latin America. They were designated 'classical' during the 1970s to distinguish them from the 'charismatic' pentecostals in the Roman Catholic Church and the 'neo-pentecostals' in the mainline protestant churches. It is important to note that in Latin America, at least, the term neo-pentecostal often refers to a middle-class group, whose congregations may be quite large, and has direct ties to a corresponding body in the United States. According to Vinson Synan, 'By 1980 the classical pentecostals had grown to be the largest and fastest-growing family of protestant Christians in the world. . . . In 1987 David Barrett estimated the world constituency of the classical pentecostal churches at 146,906,306.' H. Vinson Synan, 'Classical pentecostalism', *Dictionary of Pentecostal and Charismatic Movements* (DPCM), eds. Stanley M. Burgess and Gary B. McGee (Grand Rapids: Zondervan Publishing Company, 1988), pp. 219–222. Unquestionably, these general categories cloud the unique richness and distinctiveness of the many groups comprised within each classification. However, for the purposes of this paper the generic term 'pentecostals' will have to suffice. A discussion of several attempts to provide a taxonomy for Latin American pentecostals, as well as a contrast and comparison of pentecostals within the larger framework of protestants and evangelicals may be found in *Not By Might*, pp. 41–67.

See David Martin, *Tongues of Fire*; Barbara Boudewinjse, Andre Droogers, and Frans Kamsteeg, eds., *Algo m s que opio: una lectura antropológica del pentecostalismo latinoamericano y caribeño* (San José, Costa Rica: Editorial DEI, 1991); David Stoll, 'A protestant reformation in Latin America?' *Christian Century*, 17 January 1990, pp. 44–48; Jean-Pierre Bastian, 'The metamorphosis of Latin American protestant groups: a sociohistorical perspective,' *Latin American Research Review* 2 (1993): pp. 33–61.

6. The term 'fundamentalist' is used in a way to identify the American 'evangelical' Christian movement that emerged from the fundamentalist-modernist struggle of the early part of the twentieth century and which subsequently broadened its agenda to include the engagement of Christian faith with American politics and social life. For a watershed work that facilitated this movement from fundamentalism to evangelicalism, see Carl F. H. Henry, *The Uneasy Conscience of Modern Fundamentalism* (Grand Rapids, MI: Wm. B. Eerdmans Publishing Co., 1947). Pentecostals were rejected by the fundamentalists until at least the 1940s. In 1928 a resolution was formulated by the World's Christian Fundamentalist Association. This resolution, cited by H. Vinson Synan, 'Fundamentalism', *DPCM*, p. 326, disavowed pentecostals. Billy Graham and the neo-evangelicals recognized pentecostals in the 1940s over the objections of the fundamentalist right wing. For the role of Billy Graham and the neo-evangelicals, see Cecil M. Robeck, Jr., 'National Association of Evangelicals', *DPCM*, pp. 634–636.

7. Murray Dempster, Byron Klaus, and Doug Petersen, eds., *Called and Empowered: Global Mission in Pentecostal Perspective* (Peabody, MA: Hendrickson Publishers, 1991), pp. 3–5.

8. Jürgen Moltmann has used a similar approach in his recently published *Pentecostal Movements as an Ecumenical Challenge* (London: SCM Press, 1996).

9. Walter J. Hollenweger, 'The religion of the poor is not a poor religion', *The Expository Times* 87 (May 1976), p. 228.

10. Eugene Nida, 'The indigenous churches in Latin America', *Practical Anthropology* 8 (May – June 1961), p. 105.

11. Throughout, I will use the term 'popular' to refer to cultures or societies comprised of a mosaic, including urban and rural poor, ethnic minorities, peasants, small business people, etc.

12. These themes are presented, with modifications, from Douglas Petersen, *Not By Might Nor By Power: A Pentecostal Theology of Social Concern in Latin America* (Oxford, UK: Regnum Books International, 1996), pp. 81–113.

13. A new convert remarked that her mother-in-law, a staunch Catholic, would prefer that her son become a drug addict or a criminal rather than convert to pentecostalism. Ironically some of the most devout practitioners of pentecostalism confess that before their conversion they were ardent Catholics who held utmost disdain for pentecostals because they considered them to be a fanatical sect. Such statements are typical of what one can hear in the 'testimony time' during the worship service.

14. José Comblin, a Catholic liberation theologian, candidly admits that pentecostals have been looked down upon prejudicially by the 'higher churches' predominately because they are part of lower-class society. 'Pentecostal churches', he writes, 'are denigrated by their class. . . . They have been accused of being alienated, removed from the world, conservative, but a more sympathetic examination would show these accusations to be exaggerated and even baseless.' Jos, Comblin, *The Holy Spirit and Liberation* (Maryknoll, NY: Orbis Books, 1989), pp. 8–9.

15. Juan Sepúlveda, 'Pentecostalism as Popular Religiosity', *International Review of Mission* 78 (January 1989), p. 82.

16. Ibid.

17. Nida, 'Indigenous Churches in Latin America', p. 102.

18. Eric Lennox is the associate pastor of 'Oasis de Esperanza' an Assemblies of God congregation in San José, Costa Rica. Excerpts were taken from his sermon by the author on May 23, 1993. Such preaching is typical of sermons that the author has heard hundreds of times.

19. Everett Wilson, 'Dynamics of Latin American pentecostalism', in *Coming of Age: Protestantism in Contemporary Latin America*, ed. Daniel R. Miller (Lanham. MD: University Press of America, 1994), p. 100.

20. There are significant similarities, and differences, between *campos blancos* and ecclesial base communities. For a review of the literature, see *Not By Might*, p. 90.

21. Norberto Saracco, 'Type of ministry adopted by Latin American pentecostal churches', *International Review of Mission*, 66 (January 1997), pp. 66–67.

22. Nida observes that this typical apprenticeship system utilized by pentecostals, in addition to providing leadership training, solves two difficult problems that traditional congregations unsuccessfully confront. Firstly, pentecostal ministers can support themselves without any outside help simply by attracting sufficient members and secondly, the precarious task of selecting who is the most capable for leadership is greatly simplified by a type of 'survival of the fittest'. See Eugene Nida, 'The Indigenous Churches', p. 99.

23. Ibid.

24. Everett A. Wilson, 'Latin American pentecostalism: challenging the stereotypes of pentecostal passivity', *Transformation: An International Evangelical Dialogue on Mission and Ethics* 11 (January/March 1994) p. 20.

25. The average Assemblies of God congregation, in Latin America, not including their *campos blancos*, has a following comprised of members and adherents of less than 100. There are several large churches in the region, with attendance that exceeds 1,000, which because of their large facilities and obvious visibility attract considerable attention when observers analyze pentecostalism. The author, who has been integrally involved with several of these 'mega-churches', would argue that certain pentecostals characteristics described in this essay, particularly those of personal militancy, community and participation, as well as discipline, are not nearly as apparent within these churches as they would be within the more numerous smaller groups.

26. Aggregate statistics taken from the Division of Foreign Missions Annual Statistics for Year Ending 12/31/96.

27. Member of the congregation of *Las Asambleas de Dios de Los Guido*, interview by author, San José, Costa Rica, June 13, 1992. Los Guido is a slum community of approximately 20,000 people on the outskirts of San José, Costa Rica.

28. This concept first put forth by Lalive d'Epinay, *Haven of the Masses*, pp. 178–9 and followed up by several, including most recently, Jean-Pierre Bastian, 'The metamorphosis of Latin American groups: a sociohistorical perspective', p. 42.
29. Wilson, 'Dynamics of Latin American pentecostalism', p. 101.
30. A most insightful and fruitful survey studying protestantism in El Salvador has been conducted by four professors of the University of North Carolina at Chapel Hill. Their research analyses the sociological and political implications of protestantism on a random sample of 1,065 respondents from five different social strata. The survey entitled *La religión para los salvadoreños* was taken between June 11 and 26, 1988. Their survey data revealed that protestants attend church on an average of 9.3 times a month, twice as frequently as practicing Catholics, and that an amazing 12.6 per cent attend daily. Further, congregational intimacy enjoyed by pentecostals was supported by the findings from the survey that showed that 77 per cent of all pentecostal followers had received a pastoral visit in their home versus only 28 per cent of practicing Catholics who had ever had a priest make a house visit. See Edwin Eloy Aguilar, et al., 'Protestantism in El Salvador: conventional wisdom versus survey evidence', *Latin American Research Review* 28 (1993) pp. 127–8.
31. For a lengthy discussion of this issue, see my article, 'The formation of popular, national, autonomous pentecostal churches in Central America', in *PNEUMA: The Journal of the Society for Pentecostal Studies* 16 (Spring 1994), pp. 23–48.
32. For a superior and comprehensive article on 'glossolalia' see, Russell Spittler, 'Glossolalia', in *DPCM*, pp. 335–41. The term 'glossolalia' is generally used by academics in reference to 'speaking in tongues'. However, two-thirds world pentecostals, almost without exception, will use the more popular phrase 'speaking in tongues', as I shall do throughout this paper.
33. A discussion between pentecostals, and especially with and among their evangelical colleagues, as to whether or not a person must speak in tongues as a sign that one has received the 'baptism of the Spirit' has carried on for decades. Other doctrinal issues often posed, such as the proverbial question, 'when does one receive the "Spirit"; at conversion or as a second work of grace after conversion?' will be left to another time.
34. Pentecostal worship is comprised of an assembly of believers that almost invariably includes a time of singing and worship, testimony sharing, the preaching of the 'Word', and an invitation for conversion followed by a corporate time of prayer for healing, or some other supernatural intervention, for the personal or collective needs of the assembly.
35. Although the subject is outside the parameters of this paper, there is a new tendency in pentecostal movements in Latin America, especially those of a neo-pentecostal variety, to escalate the emotional experience such as 'falling under the Spirit' sometimes in mass and 'being drunk in the Spirit'; actions that in one sense are similar to past spiritual ecstasies but in another sense are really very different. Though the difference is not always apparent

to the outside observer of pentecostalism, for the insider these new 'experiences' appear to be similar to current practices of certain North American televangelists. The desire or need for emotional satisfaction by Latin American pentecostals by participating in these 'exhibitions' could become destructive. Professor Quentin J. Schultze aptly notes that this type of ministry influenced by certain North American televangelists may 'transform worship into entertainment and turn congregations into audiences'. Quentin J. Schultze, 'TV religion as pagan-American missions', in *Transformation: An International Evangelical Dialogue on Mission and Ethics* 9 (October/December 1992), p. 2. The style of pentecostalism described in this note is a brand quite different from the indigenous pentecostalism being depicted in this paper.

36. Frank Macchia, 'The struggle of global witness: shifting paradigms in pentecostal theology', in *The Globalization of Pentecostalism* (Oxford, UK: Regnum Books International, forthcoming, 1998), and also 'Sighs too deep for words: toward a theology of glossolalia', *Journal of Pentecostal Theology* 1 (1992) pp. 42–73.

37. Wilson, 'Dynamics of Latin American pentecostalism', p. 102.

38. Eugene Stockwell, 'Editorial: responses to the Spirit; pt. 2: charismatics', *International Review of Mission* 75 (April 1986), p. 114.

39. Christopher Rowland, *Radical Christianity: A Rereading of Recovery* (Maryknoll, NY: Orbis Books, 1988), p. 136. The pentecostal theologian, Murray Dempster, presents a well-reasoned discussion on the moral 'significance' of glossolalia as a theological concept tied to the existential realities of life that points to a theological justification for ethical norms based upon metaethical analysis. He identifies two characteristics from the glossolalic encounter with God that could translate from theological conviction to ethical norms. First, 'an ethics of responsibility' should conform to God's moral framework (p. 24). Second, and most informative for our purposes, is that the glossolalic experience should also theologically translate to the moral norm of 'the ethics of imagination' (p. 25). Dempster posits that what is most necessary in a world of hostility, suffering and injustice is the power of the imagination. Through the empowerment of God's mighty act, pentecostals can not only 'imagine the possibility of a better world' but can take creative steps to alter the world in a radical manner (p. 28). Dempster, 'Soundings in the moral significance of glossolalia', a paper presented at the 1983 Annual meeting of the Society for Pentecostal Studies (Cleveland, Tennessee, 4 November, 1983).

40. For further discussion on the development of pentecostal social theology, see Murray Dempster, 'The church's moral witness: a study of glossolalia in Luke's theology of Acts', *Paraclete: A Journal of Pentecostal Studies* 23 (Winter 1989), pp. 1–7, and Petersen, *Not By Might*, pp. 186–226. For a popular account, see Douglas Petersen, 'Called and empowered', *Enrichment: A Journal for Pentecostal Ministry* (Winter 1998, forthcoming).

41. Many songs composed by El Salvadorans in the 1940s found in *Himnos inspirados selectos* demonstrate the above.

42. Wilson, 'Dynamics of Latin American pentecostalism', p. 102.

43. 'Joseph es sanado de sus huesos', *Noti-PIEDAD: Un Noticiero de las Escuelas de las Asambleas de Dios* (setiembre 1993). Prayer for healing and available medical help work hand in hand for many Latin American pentecostals. It would not be unusual for a pentecostal church, which offers a healing service every night, to have a medical clinic on the premises.
44. Videotape with Lucas Muñoz, *The Church Goes On* (Peru: Mandate Magazine, 1991).
45. Ibid.
46. Ibid.
47. In 1980 the *Asambleas de Peru* reported 102,000 members and adherents while in 1992 they had an aggregate membership of 204,750.
48. It would be incorrect to assume that pentecostals' non-participation in politics indicates indifference. Pentecostals consider politics to be at best futile, and at worst, dirty business. They have little hope that the political options available to them will bring meaningful change. Theories that pentecostals support the status quo are also likely misfounded. For example, a significant study among El Salvadoran pentecostals and Catholics, concluded that Catholics were more closely aligned to U.S. foreign policy than were pentecostals – hardly a position of political allies for the status quo. Aguilar, 'Protestantism in El Salvador', pp. 134–5. However, it is granted that if significant and substantial research on theological themes in the two-thirds world is still lacking, then reliable studies on emerging pentecostal political thought and practice are even less available. The few in hand are all of an introductory nature. For example, Ed Cleary, *Power, Politics, and Pentecostals*; Paul Freston, 'The protestant eruption into modern Brazilian politics', *Journal of Contemporary Religion* II (1996); and my own very tentative offering 'Toward a Latin American theological political ethic', *Transformation* 14 (January/March 1997), pp. 30–33. *Transformation* has provided a forum in their journal for the constructive contributions of two-thirds world scholars, evangelical and pentecostal, who are in process of treating this difficult theme. Of particular note are the splendid offerings and analyses in *Transformation*, especially René Padilla, vol. 9 (July/September 1992) and Ron Sider, vol. 16 (October/December 1997).
49. There is considerable research on the similarities of pentecostal movements with indigenous folk religions. Specifically, the common beliefs shared between the two usually identified are an embracing of a spirit world, acceptance of the supernatural and mysticism and an overt expression of emotionalism. In Central America, the research of Luis E. Samandú has led him to assert that pentecostalism is a restoration of some of 'the profound roots in the popular culture' such as 'demons, spirits, revelations, and divine cures'. Luis E. Samandú, 'El pentecostalismo en Nicaragua y sus raíces religiosas populares', *Pasos* 17 (May-June, 1988), pp. 1–10. Bastian goes even further when he suggests that there are grounds to consider pentecostalism as a 'syncretic religious movement'. Bastian, 'The metamorphosis of Latin American protestant groups', pp. 45, 53. For a similar notion see also Rowan Ireland, *Kingdoms Come: Religion and Politics in*

Brazil (Pittsburgh: University Press, 1991), especially chapter eight. However, it should be abundantly clear that these same pentecostal characteristics demonstrated by Latin Americans are also all found and practiced within the New Testament church. A similar critique is made of the South Korean pentecostal pastor, Cho Yonggi, and is treated in Hwa Yung, *Mangoes or Bananas? The Quest for an Authentic Asian Christian Theology* (Oxford: Regnum Books, 1997), pp. 205–13.

50. Wilson, *Dynamics of Latin American Pentecostalism*, pp. 104–5.
51. Petersen, *Not By Might*, p. 227.
52. Gordon Anderson, 'Pentecostal hermeneutics', *Paraclete: A Journal of Pentecostal Studies* 28 (Spring 1994), pp. 18–19.
53. Ibid., p. 21.
54. For further development of a pentecostal hermeneutic, see my approach in *Not By Might Nor By Power*, pp. 186–226.
55. Bryan Roberts, 'Protestant groups and coping with urban life in Guatemala', *American Journal of Sociology* 73 (1968), p. 767.
56. A detailed process of the manner in which the rules of discipline are to be applied in Assemblies of God churches in Latin America can be found in a most interesting booklet written by El Salvadoran pastors in the 1930s and still the manual used throughout Central America, *Manual de doctrinas y prácticas de las Asambleas de Dios: Reglamento local.*
57. Roger S. Greenway, 'Protestant missionary activity in Latin America', pp. 175–204. And most recently see Jorge I. Gómez V., *El crecimiento y la deserción en la iglesia evangélica costarricense* (San José, Costa Rica: Publicaciones INDEF, 1996). Both authors' understanding of the 'revolving door syndrome' seems faulty. Pentecostals would question the legitimacy of the 'loss' of those who had left the fold because they had not ascribed to the moral demands placed upon them or had neither participated in catechism, passed through the waters of baptism, or had partaken of the Lord's Supper. Insiders would consider anyone who had not fulfilled the above requirements to be a 'seeker', and not yet one who had progressed to any type of active status demonstrated by concrete and observable actions and behaviours. They would contend that you 'can't lose what you don't have'.
58. For a discussion of James Darby and the influence of dispensationalism upon pentecostalism, see *Not By Might*, pp. 19–20; 106–109.
59. Juan Sepúlveda, 'Reflections on the pentecostal contribution to the mission of the church in Latin America', *The Journal of Pentecostal Theology* 1 (October 1992), pp. 101–2.
60. Andrés Opazo Bernales, 'El movimiento protestante en Centroamérica: una aproximación cuantitativa', in *Protestantismo y Procesos Sociales en Centroamérica*, ed. Luis Samandú (San José, Costa Rica: Editorial Universitaria Centroamericana, 1991), p. 15.
61. Deborah Huntington, 'The prophet motive', *NACLA ~Report on the Americas* 18 (January/February 1984), pp. 2–11.
62. Emilio Núñez and William Taylor, *Crisis in Latin America: An Evangelical Perspective* (Chicago: Moody Press, 1989), p. 168.

63. In the sense that pentecostals hold to the continuity of God's power from the time of the New Testament through to the present, they cannot be considered to be dispensational. See Gordon Anderson, 'Pentecostal hermeneutics', p. 21. Professor Gerald Sheppard, 'Pentecostals and the hermeneutics of dispensationalism: the anatomy of an uneasy relationship', in *PNEUMA: The Journal of the Society for Pentecostal Studies* 6 (Fall 1984), pp. 5–33 argues that any pentecostal effort to embrace a dispensationalism that applies traditional dispensational notions regarding church ecclesiology (strict separation in the literal meaning of biblical texts relating to the church from those applicable to Israel) raises problems for 'the identity of pentecostals – hermeneutically, sociologically, and politically' (p. 5). Though early pentecostals gave prominence to the doctrine of eschatology, particularly with an emphasis upon premillennialism, Sheppard agrees, their designation of the Christian church was that of a 'new congregation or church' and the 'repeated naming of Israel' as 'the church of Jehovah' implies terms of continuity common to reformed theology but alien to dispensationalism (p. 12). Sheppard provides an historical survey of early pentecostal theologians who consistently shaped their ecclesiology so as not to adopt a dispensational scheme that would run contrary to their pentecostal claims.

64. I provide a descriptive analysis of the terms *alienation* and *anomie* in *The Evangelical Dictionary of World Missions*, ed. A. Scott Moreau (Grand Rapids: Baker Books, forthcoming, 1997).

65. See *Not By Might*, p. 160 for a description of the meaning of the opposition of the order of the world and the order of the kingdom – the latter as a model of new life pentecostals begin to practice in the present. I have argued that the concept of the kingdom of God, as the unifying theme for pentecostal praxis, provides the eschatological contemporary meaning and certainty to personal life often threatened by death. The kingdom motif contributes a pattern for community life that 'anticipates' the future quality of the kingdom in its consummation.

66. Though the theological concept of the kingdom of God has not been articulated clearly in Latin American pentecostal doctrines, the essence of the eschatological tension between the inbreaking of the kingdom of God in the present reality ('the now') and the consummation of the kingdom of God in the future ('the not yet') is implicit and certainly discernible in their practices.

67. The immensity of the social concern programmes instituted by two-thirds world pentecostals has until recently been ignored. Much of my research has focused on these ministries of compassion. For a specific case study, see the analysis of Latin America ChildCare, the largest unified school programme in the world, in *Not By Might*, pp. 147–226.

68. Pentecostals must take seriously the critique that, in spite of their significant contributions in areas of social concern within their communities, there has been little conscious effort to provide a horizontal linkage from their experiments in ways of coping with life in their own context to a

larger forum where they would have more direct access to the means of cultural production. If pentecostals are content to form only their own 'substitute societies', they may forfeit the opportunity to participate in radical change or structural transformation.

69. *Tongues of Fire*, p. 108.

Six

Pentecostal Mission and Social Concern
Brussels Statement April 1999

As those committed to world missions standing at the threshold of a new millenium, we are experiencing a strategic time within the Assemblies of God. There is an overwhelming sense that we have arrived at a juncture where our response to a hurting, hungry, oppressed, and lost world must be reaffirmed and expressed with clarity and conviction. The church's proclamation and demonstration of life in its fullness, available through the person of Jesus, grows ever more urgent as our world society becomes more broken and fragmented.

Throughout our history men and women called by God and anointed by the Holy Spirit expressed their call by reaching, planting, training and touching the world's people. Visible expressions of 'touching' meant feeding the hungry, clothing the needy, pouring oil on the wounded, and in general, continuing the compassionate

'Brussels Statement on evangelization and social concern' in *Transformation*, Vol. 16, No. 2, April 1999.

ministry of Jesus Christ. We have pursued these ministries broadly, long term, and with passion. However, while 'touching' is firmly embedded within our mission statement, it is felt that our actions in compassionate ministries should be clearly enunciated as part of our intentional theology and strategy.

To affirm both the historical and contemporary commitment of our missionary family to the wholistic ministry pattern of Jesus and of the early church, a multinational consultation met in Brussels, Belgium, May 27–30, 1998. Under the Spirit's leadership, and as we begin the 21st century, the time has come to reaffirm and clarify the biblical and theological grounds on which a wholistic approach to ministry and mission is supported. This affirmation will empower us to rise to the full potential the Lord of the Harvest has ordained.

Jesus and the Kingdom of God

The theme of the kingdom of God provides a fruitful starting point to begin formulating principles of a biblically based theology of church mission aimed at the integration of evangelism and social concern.

Jesus identified his mission, ministry, and message with the inauguration of the kingdom of God; the time of God's messianic salvation (Mk 1:15). In the teachings of Jesus, it is clear that he proclaimed that the kingdom of God is both a future event (Matt. 13:36–43; 47–50), and a present reality (Luke 11:20; 12:32). In the ministry of Jesus the 'signs' that the kingdom of God had already broken into the present were demonstrated when he cast out demons, healed the sick, performed miracles, brought good news to the poor, proclaimed freedom for the prisoners, recovery of sight for the blind, and the release of the oppressed (Luke 4:18–19; 7:21–23). He responded to sickness and disease with healing and wholeness, to hunger with food in abundance, and to death with hope in the resurrection. His exemplary ministry and the sacrifice of his life on the cross became a summons to service for all of his followers.

Jesus taught that the kingdom of God, while dynamically demonstrated in his ministry, is also in the future. The kingdom of God 'already' present is 'not yet' fully consummated. There remains the eschatological fulfillment when the messianic salvation will be perfectly accomplished in the age to come (Matt. 24:29–31).

To enter the kingdom requires a radical transformation in which the rule of God is established in human lives through repentance and faith (Mk. 1:15; Matt. 18:1–4). Such a response to the message of the King and the subsequent change of life means 'being saved' or 'born again' (Eph. 2:8–10; John 3:3). This entry into the blessings of the kingdom is a gift; it comes at God's initiative and depends solely on his grace. Becoming a Christian, entering the kingdom, is open only to those who are willing to deny themselves and their own selfish interests in order to acknowledge God's lordship over the totality of their lives (Mk. 8:34–37).

The Kingdom of God and The Power of the Holy Spirit in The Early Church

The Pentecostal narrative in Acts is integrally connected to the kingdom of God and mission of Jesus. The experience of the Holy Spirit and the eschatological hope in the return of Jesus Christ were the two energizing realities that inspired and shaped early church mission, and in turn, the twentieth century Pentecostal movement, with a zeal for global evangelism. The connection derived from Acts between church mission, the empowerment of the Spirit and the eschatological hope provides a theological vantage point from which to view a biblically-based integrated understanding of evangelism and social concern in action. While the gospels focused on the activity of the Holy Spirit in the life of Jesus, the Acts described the activity of the Holy Spirit in the early church. The same Holy Spirit that had anointed and empowered Jesus of Nazareth was outpoured to empower the disciples to enable the church to continue Jesus' mission, ministry and message; to do 'all that Jesus began to do and to teach' (Acts 1:1).

In the power of the Holy Spirit the early church, following the example of Jesus, proclaimed the good news of God's redemptive reign in Christ. Miracles, signs and wonders were performed and acts of compassion were practiced in response to human need. The established social and religious orders were challenged and economic, racial and cultural barriers within the community of faith were overcome in a demonstration of the reconciling power of God's reign. In the same way, Spirit-filled believers in every age and in every nation can expect to proclaim and demonstrate the transforming power of the gospel to the peoples of the world.

Life under the rule of God

Men and women are created in God's own image, each person possesses a unique value to God and therefore the freedom and dignity of all people need to be affirmed (Gen. 1:26–28). God loves everyone (Rom. 5:8) and because he loves us first we love him in return (1 John 4:19). Because God loves us first, we love him. Our love is to be shown in acts of worship, prayer, praise, service and the fulfilling of the great commandment to love our neighbour as ourselves (Matt. 22:37–40). This love for neighbour reaches across every boundary that divides people, bringing reconciliation, restoration and wholeness. Such love bears witness that those who claim to live in the kingdom are God's people who belong to him. Such unconditional love reflective of God's own character, and contrary to human nature, is to be translated into visible human deeds enabled by God's gracious gift of salvation and the empowerment of the Holy Spirit.

To enter the kingdom and come under God's rule is to be incorporated into the new order of life where love is normative. The ethical teaching of Jesus describes what life looks like when people respond to God's gracious rule. The moral imperatives that Jesus identifies in his ethics, such as love, mercy, peace, justice, respect of persons, and generosity are not prescriptions of law. They are descriptions of grace. The mission of the church is to give visible evidence of the kingdom and its ethics within its own community and in its ministry to the world.

Love is the law of the kingdom of God. Love is much more than an emotion. It must be demonstrated in an act. God the Father demonstrated love in giving his Son. Jesus demonstrated love in his acts of compassion, healing and forgiveness of sin. Finally he gave his life on the cross because of his love. He loves every single individual, not because of any merit they may have and despite their sins (Rom. 5:8). When God reigns he loves everyone, so God's people who live under his reign ought to love everyone. Because God loved us first, we also love him. Our love is demonstrated in the acts of worship, prayer and praise. But our acts of love must also be coupled with his royal law which teaches, 'Thou shalt love thy neighbour as thyself . . .' (James 2:8).

The Church Bearing Witness to God's Reign in Human History

The community of the local church is God's ordained instrument wherein his presence dwells. The local church is called to be God's visible and corporate entity bearing witness to his kingdom in mission and reconciliation between people (Eph.2:14–18). The transforming impact of this reconciliation on all dimensions of the lives of those who are part of God's redeemed community provides an observable signpost to the reign of God (Acts 2:42–47) and is a powerful witness to the world of the redemptive mission of God (2 Cor. 5:18–20).

The ministry of the church must be to all people because all have been created in the image of God (Gen. 1:26–27). Because God bestows human dignity on all people, everyone, regardless of their status in life, deserves the church's full attention. Jesus' own growth as a child (Luke 2:52), and his earthly ministry demonstrated a deep concern for every aspect of human life (Mk. 1:25–26, 29–31, 40–42, and 6:30–43). To follow Jesus' example, the community of faith must therefore address spiritual, personal, social, economic and physical situations (Mt. 25: 35–40). In such a manner the church offers a visible representation of what life in the kingdom should look like within its own community and in its ministry to the world.

In Jesus' ministry, which is our model, he used many different ways to introduce people to God's offer of salvation. Jesus ministered to people in a manner that met their needs, challenged them, and invited them to come under the rule of God. In the gospels, for children it meant dignity, for women self worth and justice in marriage, for the sick it meant healing, for the self-righteous Pharisee it was the challenge to lay down legalism, have a childlike faith and humbly ask forgiveness and accept the gift of eternal life.

The church bears the responsibility for the proclamation of the gospel. As the Spirit-empowered church extends the offer of salvation to all people, it will reflect the same diversity in methods and means as seen in the ministry of Jesus. In order to fulfill its mandate of spreading the gospel in the most effective manner, the church should involve itself with other redeemed communities and develop strategic alliances especially in areas of evangelism, discipleship and ministries of compassion.

The Return of The King and The Consummation of God's Reign

The hope of the return of the Lord makes demands on our life and service in the present. While we long for the coming of the King, we shall not be passive. The promise of his return, our blessed hope, compels us to continue our work of proclaiming the good news, engaging the powers of darkness and showing the compassion of Jesus to the suffering people. When our vision is focused upon the coming of our Lord, with its assurance of his triumph, we are given new strength to carry on even admidst difficult circumstances.

The church of Jesus Christ knows it is not home yet; it is still on the journey towards the eternal city. But the one who came preaching the kingdom of God and calling us to be his followers, will come again in power and glory to fulfill his kingdom and establish the new heaven and the new earth. In the new heaven and the new earth there will be no war, no oppression, and no poverty. There will be no sickness or people bound by demons. Until then the church is to be faithful in fulfilling the mission of the kingdom of God, for Jesus has said: 'and this gospel of the kingdom will be preached in the whole world as a testimony to all nations; and then the end will come' (Mt. 21:14). May we, the faithful servants of the King, be able truly to respond: 'Come, Lord Jesus!'

Conclusion

We celebrate the long history of ministries to the poor and needy of the world which Assemblies of God believers have pioneered and continue through ministry endeavours. We rejoice in the ever-broadening impact of our ministries of compassion and affirm them as an integral part of the gospel and our missionary mandate.

Our faith and action are rooted both in God's self-revelation in Scripture and in the value and worth of all persons because they are created in his image. These foundational truths are fulfilled in the words and deeds of Jesus Christ in his kingdom mission, carried out by the church, and evidenced by the dynamic work and empowerment of the Holy Spirit. These fundamental affirmations which inform a Pentecostal theology provide an integral framework for wholistic ministry – reaching, planting, teaching, and touching.

Seven

Models of the Kingdom: Sorting out the Practical Meaning of God's Reign

Howard Snyder

The Biblical Theme

The Kingdom of God is a central biblical theme, but it can be understood in very different ways. Cyclically the Kingdom or Reign of God has been either stressed or relatively ignored in the history of Christian thought and action. Currently we seem to be in a time of renewed interest in this biblical theme as well as debate as to the appropriateness of monarchy language in a time of democratic, participatory models of society.

In the last decade or two, both Charismatics and Evangelical social activists have found the Kingdom of God to be a helpful theme in understanding God's work in the world today and God's agenda for the future. The Kingdom is also being stressed as a prominent theme

'Models of the Kingdom' by Howard Snyder in *Transformation*, Vol. 10, No. 1, January 1993.

in other branches of the Church, most notably the Ecumenical Movement.

This article examines different conceptions of the Kingdom of God by outlining eight 'models' or basic metaphors for understanding the Kingdom. In sketching the models I will give both historical and contemporary examples.

The Use of Models

I use models as a way to dispel the vague cloud of confusion that often forms around the theme of the Kingdom of God. Rather than a biblical exposition on the Kingdom, my approach here is primarily a theological and historical discussion. The methodology is similar to that of Avery Dulles in his books, *Models of the Church* and *Models of Revelation*.[1] Like Dulles, I find models a useful methodology in clarifying theological issues.

Jesus spoke of the 'mystery' or 'secrets' of the Kingdom and gave us a number of Kingdom parables.[2] In a sense these parables are models of the Kingdom. Using models is a more formal way of elaborating various images of God's sovereign rule over all things.

It is well to keep two points in mind in any discussion of models. First, each one is 'ideal' or 'synthetic' in the sense that its 'pure' form may not actually be found in history. A model is to some degree an intentional abstraction from reality in order to clarify issues. Secondly, models are not necessarily mutually exclusive. Different models may balance or supplement each other. On the other hand, some pairs of models are virtually opposites so that to embrace one usually means rejecting the other. We may think of models as placed along a continuum, or perhaps multi-dimensional continua, with some models more complementary and others more in conflict with their opposites. This paper, however, is an attempt to be comprehensive – that is, to include all possible models of the Kingdom. It suggests a framework which at least in theory can embrace the range of possible conceptions of God's reign.

Kingdom Polarities

As Jesus himself suggested, the Kingdom of God is a 'mystery' in several senses.[3] Models may reveal the mystery. The mysterious nature of the Kingdom is evident in Jesus' teaching and throughout Scripture. For example, Scripture speaks of the Kingdom as both present and future. In fact, this is one of at least six points of tension in the biblical material concerning God's reign. Understanding the Kingdom biblically begins with recognizing these polarities.

We may identify these as follows:

1. Present *versus* future
2. Individual *versus* social
3. Spirit *versus* matter
4. Gradual *versus* climactic
5. Divine action *versus* human action
6. The Church's relation to the Kingdom

Any biblical theology of the Kingdom will need to wrestle with these polarities. In fact, I would offer the following thesis: theologies of the Kingdom which dissolve these tensions, opting wholly for one side or the other, are to that degree unbiblical. A biblically faithful and biblically useful theology of the Kingdom will in some way maintain and live with these polarities.

These six tension points may be illustrated as follows:

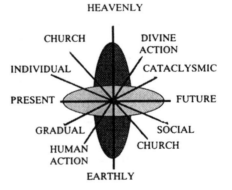

Exploring Models of the Kingdom

The eight models of the Kingdom sketched below illustrate different ways of handling or resolving these tensions. These models illustrate the way the Kingdom of God *may be* conceived as we look at the Scriptural evidence, and ways the Kingdom of God *has been* conceived historically.

1. The Future Kingdom: The Kingdom as Future Hope

Perhaps more than anything else, the Kingdom of God has been for Christians a future hope. It has been a pointer beyond this life to something more ultimate and complete – not mere spiritual survival only but a final cosmic reconciliation. This is the Future Kingdom, viewed either as that final cosmic reconciliation itself or as a millennial reign preceding the ultimate summation of all things. A primary image in this model is that of 'a new heaven and a new earth'.

Futurity is the key to this conception of God's reign. The primary present meaning of the Kingdom is the hope it offers for finally putting to rights all that is wrong in the world. This is a model of both judgment and reconciliation.

This model tends to be pessimistic about the present. Since we live in a fallen, ruined world which bears in every area the marks of the Fall there is no hope for the social order short of the second coming of Christ. The return of Christ therefore is the Church's 'blessed hope' (Tit. 2:13). For the present, Christians can at best serve as a sort of brake on the world's downhill slide.

This view of the Kingdom has been a primary one throughout much of church history. Most scholars agree that it was the commonly accepted view in the Church during the first two centuries. Other views began to emerge during the third century and especially in the fourth century when Christianity was officially recognized by the Roman Empire.

Tertullian (c.160–c.225 AD) provides an interesting study of Christian understandings of the Kingdom as Christianity progressed through the third century. Deeply concerned about what he saw as growing moral laxity in the Church, Tertullian stressed the practical meaning of the Kingdom in light of the challenges which Christians were facing in his day.

Toward the end of his life Tertullian became a part of the New Prophecy movement, later known as Montanism. Whether Montanism influenced his views of the Kingdom, or conversely whether he influenced Montanist eschatology, is a disputed question. It does seem clear, however, that Montanism saw the Kingdom of God primarily as a future hope. With their strong emphasis on prophecy and new revelations through the Spirit, however, they expected this hope to be realized soon.

This model was certainly one of the principal currents of Christian thought and expectation also in Western medieval Christendom (though often overshadowed by the model of the Kingdom as institutional church). It was especially popular during troubled or seemingly apocalyptic times, such as during times of plague. The Trinitarian dispensationalism of Joachim of Fiore (c. 1132–1202 AD) was a particularly influential and controversial form of this model.

In the United States and Europe the Future Kingdom rose to prominence in conservative Protestantism toward the end of the nineteenth century. One can trace the resurgence of this model in a somewhat apocalyptic form in the events leading up to the birth of Pentecostalism at the turn of the century. The Pentecostal Movement probably represents the most extensive embodiment of this model in the twentieth century. This is particularly significant in light of the rapid growth of the Pentecostal and Charismatic movements world-wide over the past several decades. This model is more characteristic of Pentecostalism, however, than it is of Charismatic Christianity. This in fact represents a significant point of difference between two movements which obviously have much in common. Presumably socio-economic factors are at work here. In general the Charismatic Movement has been more middle class than Pentecostalism has been. As has often been noted, apocalyptic and future-oriented visions of the Christian hope frequently occur among the poor or the nearly poor.

This raises the fascinating question of millennialism and, more broadly, social movements of the poor and possible Christian origins of social revolt. Much has been written on this question from differing perspectives.[4]

The question of the Millennium raises a host of other issues. One of these is the question of utopian visions of society. As we shall see, this actually introduces another model: the Kingdom as earthly utopia (model eight, below). In one sense the utopian model represents the farthest extreme from the vision of the Kingdom as future hope, but in another sense it is quite similar. This makes sense if one envisions the eight models in a circular fashion so that the two extremes finally meet. It would be misleading, however, to think of the model of the Future Kingdom as necessarily implying millennialism, for there can be non-millennial views of the Kingdom as future hope.

In Pentecostal and Charismatic versions of this model, future hope becomes present experience in a partial sense through the gifts and powers of the Holy Spirit. This was true as well for Montanism and other versions of this model which put particular stress on the Spirit.

A contemporary Kingdom theology worth considering at this point is represented by John Wimber and the Vineyard Movement. Wimber has put particular emphasis on the Kingdom of God in his writings.[5] The Vineyard is broadly a part of Charismatic Christianity but is developing a distinct identity and is sometimes seen as part of the 'Third Wave' of the Spirit described by Peter Wagner and others.

Does Wimber understand the Kingdom primarily as future hope? Yes and no. The element of futurity is prominent and foundational, but he also has a strong emphasis on present manifestations of Kingdom power. It would appear that Wimber's views are a composite of the Future Kingdom and the models of Mystical Communion and Counter-system (models three and five, below).

This model sees God reigning eternally over the entire cosmos, but primarily in a spiritual sense. In the future God's reign will be fully manifest and realized on earth as well as in heaven. It is God and God alone who reigns; in this model there is little place for human agency in building or manifesting the Kingdom. God (primarily as Jesus Christ or the Holy Spirit) now rules secretly in the heart of the believer whose response is to be one of faith, devotion, and obedience within the limited sphere of one's life. There is little expectation of a public, social-oriented role that contributes anything to the Kingdom of God.

2. The Inner Kingdom: The Kingdom of God as Inner Spiritual Experience

In this model, the Kingdom of God is, above all, a spiritual Kingdom. It is something to be experienced in the heart or soul of the individual believer. To enter the Kingdom is to experience the 'beatific vision' of classical Christian spirituality, at least in an anticipatory sense.

Generally this is a highly individualistic conception of the Kingdom. God reigns over all, but above all in the invisible, spiritual realm. To see and experience the Kingdom requires spiritual sight, for the Kingdom is not visible in society. Fully entering into the Kingdom is an ineffable experience that cannot really be shared with another human being. In this model of the Kingdom, fully to experience the Kingdom is to be lost in God.

A number of Christian mystics illustrate this model, such as Julian of Norwich (c.1343–1416) and Teresa of Avila's description of the 'Interior Castle'.[6] In such literature the Kingdom of God in fact rarely even appears as a specific theme, for the focus is on the immediate mystical experience of God. Practically speaking, there is little other real meaning to God's Kingdom.

This model does not deny that God does or will ultimately reign on earth, but it sees that fact as largely irrelevant to present Christian experience and the life of the Church. The primary function of the Church is to help people gain access to the spiritual Kingdom. As an image or metaphor, 'kingdom' or 'reign' has less force than do more mystical or relational images such as love and marriage, Christ's passion, or perhaps God as Mother (rather than King).[7]

3. The Heavenly Kingdom: The Kingdom as Mystical Communion

In this model the Kingdom of God is closely associated with the idea of the 'communion of saints' as it came to be understood as 'communion between the heavenly and the earthly Church and its members',[8] and so primarily in a mystical sense. This conception of the Kingdom is less individualistic than the previous model, for the Kingdom involves a spiritual communion with all believers – with those on earth and with those who have gone before. The Kingdom is an invisible corporate reality not bound by space and time which we experience now in anticipation of a fuller reality to come.

This model often centres especially in worship and liturgy. In worship one experiences the communion of the saints. Through worship believers enter into fellowship with the heavenly realm under God's sovereign rule. As in the previous model, the accent is on the heavenly, not the earthly.

Often the paradigm of this view of the Kingdom is the disciples' experience on the Mount of Transfiguration (Matthew 17:1–8 and parallels). This is especially true in some Greek Orthodox spirituality.[9] As Peter, James and John saw the glory of God on the mountain, away from everyday life, when Christ was transfigured before them, so we experience the Kingdom of God when we enter into spiritual communion with Christ and all the saints. In this model, the Kingdom now is thus a foretaste of heaven. In fact, in this model the Kingdom is essentially equivalent to heaven. Very little distinction is made between the two, so that to enter heaven is to enter the

Kingdom of God. Thus the Kingdom's ultimate reality is in the next world, beyond this life. But we may participate now in that eternal Kingdom through the communion of saints.

This is a dominant model in much Eastern and Western Christian spirituality, particularly in the mystical tradition. Good examples would be John of Damascus (c.675–749) and John Tauler (c.1300–61). It is also central to much Puritan spirituality, as in Richard Baxter's *The Saints' Everlasting Rest* (1650). Serious Christians pray that God's Kingdom may come, says Baxter; they look ahead to that 'Jerusalem which is above' while living a life of contemplation and devotion here. So Baxter writes, 'I hope you will value this heavenly life, and take one walk every day in the New Jerusalem.'[10]

Understandably, this is also the model of much revivalistic and Evangelical spirituality of the nineteenth and twentieth centuries in the United States and Great Britain, as reflected in many hymns and Gospel songs in this tradition, from 'When We All Get To Heaven' to 'We're Marching to Zion'.

In this view the Kingdom's present relevance is that it keeps before us the ideal of truth and rectitude as a pattern for our lives now so that we will finally gain heaven. The Kingdom is viewed as primarily other-worldly and future. As we shall see, however, some forms of this model may be linked with certain dispensational millennial views.

In summary, this conception of the Kingdom is similar to the previous model, but is more corporate and communal.

4. The Churchly Kingdom: The Kingdom as Institutional Church

In the centuries following Augustine (354–430), the Kingdom of God came to be increasingly associated with the institutional Church. We may think of this model therefore as the dominant view of medieval Christianity in the West from about AD 500 until the Reformation and, in the case of Roman Catholicism, until Vatican II. In the Roman Catholic tradition, this understanding of the Kingdom was embodied in the decrees of the Council of Trent (1545–63).

In the traditional Roman version of this model, the role of the pope is central. The pope is, literally, the 'vicar' of Jesus Christ; the one who at present rules on earth in Christ's stead. The Church is so closely associated with the Kingdom that very little distinction is made between the two. Thus the biblical tension between Church and Kingdom is largely dissolved.

This model of the Kingdom owes much to the influence of Augustine's *City of God*. Augustine spoke of the Church as God's 'present Kingdom', and says at one point, 'Therefore the Church even now is the Kingdom of Christ, and the Kingdom of heaven. Accordingly, even now His saints reign with Him, though otherwise than they shall reign hereafter.'[11] For Augustine the Church is much more than its visible institutional expression and God's Kingdom is much more than the Church. But his close identification of Church and Kingdom laid the foundation for a model of the Church which makes little or no practical distinction between the two. As the 'imperial papacy' developed in the centuries following Augustine, it became quite natural to conclude that the Kingdom of God had now come on earth in the form of the Church. The logic of this was bolstered as the Roman Empire collapsed and the Church became the dominant and shaping force in society.

There are also Protestant mutations of this conception of the Kingdom. The Church tends to move toward this view whenever the distinction between the Church and Kingdom is not clearly maintained. Much of Protestantism, particularly at the popular level, in fact often confuses the Church and the Kingdom with each other. The result is that Church work and Kingdom work are seen as being the same thing, and the Kingdom is reduced in its present form to the dimensions of the Church. The Kingdom may be seen as much broader, and even as being political and economic in its final, future manifestation, but the Church is seen as the present form of the Kingdom.

The question may be raised whether the modern Church Growth school, particularly in its more popular forms, holds this view. The thesis that the numerical growth of the Church is the primary cutting edge of the Kingdom of God needs careful examination. Church growth and Kingdom growth need to be distinguished. As Mortimer Arias has written, 'Church growth *per se* cannot be taken as the whole of Christian mission or the overpowering motivation for evangelization. We are not sent to preach the Church but announce the Kingdom'.[12]

5. The Subversive Kingdom: The Kingdom as Counter-system

Some people see the Kingdom of God as a 'counter-system', that is, as a way of conceiving and organizing society that is counter to the dominant forms at present. Usually this view is a protest against the previous model, which tends to associate the Church and the Kingdom too closely. Not only is the Kingdom different from the Church; it is a whole different way of living and organizing society, according to this view. Here the Church is often criticized as being unfaithful to itself, as having compromised its true identity by accommodating the spirit of the age.

Perhaps the best example of this view is St. Francis and the early Franciscans. In a radical and simple Gospel reaction to the Church of his day, Francis set out to embody a new model of the Church and of the Kingdom. He sought to model the Church in Gospel simplicity, living out the radical character of the Kingdom of God now, in this present age. Thus a key aspect of this approach is the present relevance of the Kingdom. God's reign is something to be experienced and lived out now in Christian community, in faithfulness to the example and command of Christ and in faith that God himself will eventually bring the Kingdom in its fulness.

Parallels have often been drawn between the early Franciscans and the Anabaptists, the Radical Reformers of the sixteenth century. The Anabaptists do in fact provide another historical example of this model of the Kingdom. Examples today are 'radical Christians' who see the Kingdom of God as clashing with the values and the view of society operating at present in the world and often in the Church. *Sojourners* magazine fairly consistently articulates this model of the Kingdom. It is no accident that *Sojourners* and others with similar views have been drawn to the earlier examples of the Franciscans and the Anabaptists as models, for the logic of Church and Kingdom is quite similar in all three cases.

This model tends to see the Church as a counter-culture, a counter-community living according to the values of the Kingdom of God. The Church seeks to embody visibly the new order to the Kingdom which is opposed to the old order of this present age and which is passing away. The Church is a missionary minority present in the world now as leaven, as agent of the Kingdom of God.

6. The Theocratic Kingdom: The Kingdom as Political State

The Kingdom of God may be understood as a present-day political theocracy. In this view, the Kingdom provides the values and possibly even the methodology for the social, political and economic organization of society. God is King, not an elected official. The implication, then, is that the Kingdom of God is not to be organized democratically but as a theocracy in which the righteous ones rule in the name of God and unrighteousness is not tolerated.

For obvious reasons, this model often tends to work from Old Testament examples, especially that of the Kingdom of Israel under David and Solomon.

This model gained ascendancy, understandably, after the conversion of Emperor Constantine and as the Christian Church became in effect the state religion. A good example is Byzantine Christianity, especially under Emperor Justinian (483–565). At that time it looked to many as though the Kingdom of God had truly come on earth. The Old Testament became a primary source of understanding the Church and for embodying the Kingdom.

Although Byzantine Christianity perhaps provides the closest thing to a pure instance of this model, we may cite other examples. Calvin's Geneva to some degree represents this view, with its attempt to in effect have society run by the Church. Another example, though in a more ambiguous way, is the view of the Kingdom implied in the agenda of the Moral Majority and expounded in Pat Robertson's book *The Secret Kingdom*.[13] These views tend to see the United States as 'an almost chosen people', a nation uniquely blessed by God and charged with the mission of promoting and safeguarding the Kingdom of God and free enterprise capitalism throughout the earth. These are not viewed as incompatible goals, for in this view capitalism is seen as the economic system most compatible with, and uniquely blessed by, the values of the Kingdom.[14]

The model of the Kingdom as political state is most radically articulated today by the so-called Reconstructionists, such as Cary North. Reconstructionists call for reorganizing society on the basis of Old Testament norms where crime and immorality are not tolerated but where, in effect, God's rule is enforced.[15]

Although this model is very different from the previous one, like it, it does see the Kingdom of God as present, either actually or potentially, in society today. This model tends to put a strong emphasis on law, the Kingdom being seen as more a Kingdom of law than of grace. This would be one significant point of critique.

7. The Transforming Kingdom: The Kingdom as Christianized Society

Here also the Kingdom of God is understood as providing the model for society. In fact, this model may be seen as a variant of the previous one, but with a broader range of political and economic options. In this model the Kingdom is less likely to be understood as a theocracy. It is rather a set of values and principles which Christians should live out and should work towards as citizens and participants in society (rather than as a counter-culture). The Kingdom in its fulness would be a society fully leavened and permeated by Christian values.

Postmillennialism generally views the Kingdom of God in this way – almost by definition. The grace of God and the power of the Kingdom are at present at work in society, particularly through the Church as God's people in the world. Thus society is increasingly being leavened by the gospel, more and more embodying the Kingdom of God. This was a common view among many mid-nineteenth century Evangelical Reformers in the United States. Early twentieth-century advocates of the Social Gospel represent a similar view, though in a different way. Nineteenth-century Evangelicals were hopeful about the manifestation of the Kingdom of God on earth, but never lost sight of its transcendent spiritual eschatological dimension. In the Social Gospel, the pendulum swung more fully toward a present and earthly conception of the Kingdom, losing something of the balance and the necessary biblical tension between present and future that is found in Scripture.

In general, this conception of the Kingdom sees God's reign as becoming progressively manifest in the present order, as being social and cultural as well as spiritual, and as coming by human action co-operating with God's action. In contrast, premillennial views tend to see the Kingdom as future, as coming primarily or exclusively by God's action, and as coming cataclysmically rather than gradually.

8. The Utopian Kingdom: The Kingdom as Earthly Utopia

The Kingdom of God understood as an earthly utopia may be viewed as the previous model taken to a non-biblical extreme. This view is literally utopian. It envisions a perfect society on earth, often tending to under-estimate the problem of personal sin. This view tends to see sin as primarily or exclusively environmental, so that changing the social environment in the proper way can bring a perfect society. This was the view of many nineteenth-century utopian communities, whether Christian, secular or a blending of the two, which sprang up in the United States and elsewhere. In a wide variety of ways a similar vision has recurred repeatedly down through Church history in 'the pursuit of the millennium'.[16] In yet a different way, this appears to have been the understanding of the Kingdom held by at least some of the influential 'Founding Fathers' of the United States.

The primary modern-day version of this vision has been Marxism. Marxism is perhaps best understood as a secularized, materialistic version of the Christian hope of the Kingdom. Despite its practical failures, the great appeal of Marxism is its vision of a harmonious classless society, a vision which in many of its features is clearly biblical. Conversely, Marxism's failure to achieve this vision led first to disillusionment and finally to the disintegration of Marxist political power that we are witnessing today.

Liberation theology in most of its forms generally has a conception of the Kingdom that reflects this model, the previous model, or something in between. That is, liberation theology hopes to see society transformed now into (or according to the values of) the Kingdom of God. The Christian task is to be involved in the liberating process, working to transform society now, with high realism about the social, economic and political discussions of the present order. Thus liberation theology's attraction to Marxist analysis is quite understandable.

As we noted earlier, this view of the Kingdom also has some affinities to modern premillennialism. The premillennialism of most North American Fundamentalists, for instance, combines this model with that of the Kingdom as inner spiritual experience (model two) or as heaven (model three). The Kingdom has no present-day relevance in this, the 'church age', but it will in the future, following the return of Christ, when the Kingdom comes very literally to earth in the millennial reign of Christ. The millennial reign is to be decidedly literal, political, and earthly. This will be followed, after a thousand years, by the Saints' eternal enjoyment of heaven.

Viewed from this perspective, Marxism and Fundamentalism have much in common. The vision of the Kingdom is quite similar; the main difference concerns how the Kingdom comes. In premillennialism it comes almost entirely by God's action, whereas in Marxism it comes almost exclusively through human action, or perhaps through human action co-operating with or reflecting the inexorable forces of history. Both these views dissolve the biblical tension between divine and human action and so both are to that degree unbiblical.

A curious mutation of the model of the Kingdom as earthly utopia is the so-called 'prosperity gospel' that has grown up in the United States in recent decades. In this view the Kingdom of God is ultimately future, but since we are children of the King we may even now enjoy the blessings of royalty – materially as well as spiritually. A major problem with this view, in addition to its lack of scriptural support, is that it has little or no place for the cross. The argument is that Christ suffered so that we would not have to suffer, rather than the biblical view that Christ not only suffered for us but also 'left us an example that we might follow in his steps'(1 Peter 2:21).

Conclusion

These eight models represent quite different ways of handling the six biblical polarities referred to at the beginning. Though I have not done so here, one could fairly systematically critique the strengths and weaknesses of each of these models according to how they deal with these points of tension.

If these eight models were plotted along a continuum, 'earthly utopia' might be at one extreme and 'heavenly city' at the other. The Kingdom as institutional Church would then come about in the middle, as would the model of the Kingdom as counter-system. The model of the Kingdom as political state would be closer to the 'earthly utopia' side, while the model of the Kingdom as mystical communion would be closer to the 'heavenly city' side.

In reality, however, the picture is more multi-dimensional than such a continuum would suggest.

What do these models mean for us today? Our challenge, I believe, is: first, to be clear about our models; and secondly, to critique them by Scripture. Then we can learn also from the experience of history.

No one of these models is fully biblical or fully adequate. But several of them do embody key truths of the Kingdom as taught in Scripture that need to be reflected in a usable contemporary biblical theology of the Kingdom. As we move increasingly into a one-world society, it is crucial that biblical Christians articulate and embody such a vision of the Kingdom, and accordingly an experience of the Church which is consistent with this vision.

Notes

1. Avery Dulles, *Models of the Church*, (Garden City, NY: Doubleday, 1974); *Models of Revelation*, (Garden City, NY: Doubleday, 1983).
2. Matthew 13:1–52, 20:1–16, 22:1–14, 25:1–46, and parallels.
3. Matthew 13:11, Mark 4:11, Luke 8:10. The Greek word *musterion* is usually translated as 'mystery' or 'secret'.
4. See, for example, Norman Cohn, *The Pursuit of the Millennium*, rev. ed. (New York: Oxford, 1979); William Dale Morris, *The Christian Origins of Social Revolt* (London: George Allen & Unwin, 1949).
5. See, for example, John Wimber with Kevin Springer, *Power Evangelism* (San Francisco: Harper & Row, 1966), chapter one, 'The Kingdom of God'.
6. See Kleran Kavanaugh and Olillio Rodrigues, eds. *Teresa of Avila, the Interior Castle*, (New York: Paulist, 1979).
7. For example, in Julian of Norwich, Edmund College and James Walsh, eds., *Julian of Norwich: Showings* (New York: Paulist, 1978), 8–11.
8. Wilhelm Breuning, 'Communion of Saints', in Karl Rahner, ed., *Encyclopedia of Theology: The Concise Sacramentum Mundi* (New York: Seabury, 1975), 274.
9. Jaroslav Pelikan, *The Spirit of Eastern Christendom (600–1700)*, (Chicago: University of Chicago Press, 1974), 261, 266; Colin Lulbheld and Norman Russell, trans., John Climacus: *The Ladder of Divine Ascent*, (New York: Paulist, 1982), 1–2, 56.
10. Richard Baxter, The Saints' Everlasting Rest, (New York: American Tract Society, n.d.), 442
11. Augustine, *The City of God*, trans. Marcus Dods (New York: The Modern Library, 1950), 725–26.
12. Mortimer Arias, *Announcing the Reign of God: Evangelization and the Subversive Memory of Jesus*, (Philadelphia: Fortress, 1984), 118.
13. Pat Robertson with Bob Slosser, *The Secret Kingdom*, (Nashville: Thomas Nelson, 1982). Robertson says he and many others 'are now discovering this central purpose of our Lord . . . the Kingdom of God'. Christians 'should reach from the visible into the invisible and bring that secret Kingdom into the visible through its principles – principles that can be adopted at this moment' (36,37) and which have clear socio- political implications.
14. See Robertson, 151–153.
15. See Cary North, *An Introduction to Christian Economics*, (Nutley, N.J. Craig Press, 1973); Rodney Clapp 'Democracy as Heresy', *Christianity*

Today, 31:3 (February 20, 1987), 17–23; Hal Lindsey, *The Road to Holocaust*, (New York: Bantam Books, 1989) – a premillenialist critique of Reconstructionist thought.

16. See Cohn, *The Pursuit of the Millennium*.

Eight

Eschatology and Ethics: Evangelical Views and Attitudes

Peter Kuzmic

Synopsis Dr. Kuzmič sets the stage for the discussion of history and eschatology by reminding us that the purpose of the prophetic books of Daniel and Revelation was to provide comfort, hope and strength to those facing opposition and persecution and not to encourage idle speculation on the end times.

He surveys the history and tenets of the three traditional views of the millennial reign (Rev. 20:1–6) namely, post-millennialism, amillennialism and premillennialism. He criticizes premillennialism and with it dispensationalism which dominate contemporary evangelicalism, especially in North America, for their part in the atrophy of the evangelical social conscience. At the same time he notes that premillennialists have

'Eschatology and Ethics: Evangelical Views and Attitudes' by Peter Kuzmic first published as 'History and Eschatology: Evangelical Views' by Peter Kuzmic in *In Word and Deed*, edited by Bruce Nicholls (Exeter, Paternoster, 1986).

a strong record in evangelism and in the missionary expansion of the Church. He criticizes an unhealthy preoccupation with apocalypticism and current sensational books and films on the subject. Hope, he thinks, is essential to a balanced commitment to both evangelism and social service.

Kuzmic outlines some of the tensions in relating eschatology to the Kingdom of God, such as now and not yet, continuity and discontinuity, souls and society, optimism and pessimism. He writes, 'Conservative Christian theology has an inbuilt tendency to oversimplification of complex issues. Evangelicals seem to find it hard to think in dialectical terms and can hardly endure to live with unresolved questions and amidst tensions.' He sees that belief in the total discontinuity between the present earth and 'the new heaven and earth' without understanding the continuity inherent in the standing Kingdom and in the resurrection leads to an escapist attitude and to minimising the role of culture and social involvement in the witness and service of the Church. Therefore he calls for both responsible participation in the Kingdom already arrived and watchful expectation of the Kingdom still to come.

Finally, in a section on eschatology and ethics, he decries the relegation of the ethics of Jesus to a future millennial rule and the acceptance of a present status quo. Christian ethics should be an ethic of change and Christian hope lead to Christian practice.

Introduction

Eschatology is often treated as a postscript or a kind of appendix to Christian theology. For evangelicals who take God's purposes with man and history seriously, eschatology is a very vital doctrine pointing to both the *finis* (time-end in the sense of chronos), and the *telos* (the goal) of history. One's view of eschatology determines one's views of history. And one's view of the purpose and goal of history as pointing to the eschaton definitely modifies one's attitude toward the this-worldly historical realities. It is with these views and ensuing attitudes that I am primarily concerned. I am concerned with such questions as these: How does one's eschatological view affect one's conception and practice of social responsibility and evangelism? Does one's view of eschatology determine one's behaviour? What significance does eschatology have for social ethics? How do evangelical eschatological views relate to evangelical involvement in society?

A word of caution and warning in handling such a topic is hardly necessary. Eschatology is a 'slippery word'[1] and if not clearly defined from the outset, it entails the risk of misunderstanding and confusion. There are diverse views of the future even among the most sincere and studious Bible-believing evangelicals. As a matter of fact, there is probably no other doctrine on which evangelicals are more divided and even opposed to each other as the doctrine of 'the last things'. In some Western countries, especially the USA, 'end times' are a growing brand of industry and a flourishing business. A whole apocalyptic book-market has developed (Hal Lindsey's *The Late Great Planet Earth* has sold, so I am told, more than 20 million copies), accompanied by a flood of films, specialized 'prophetic' newsletters and magazines. Much of it is marked by extravagances and speculations, exploiting both the biblical theme of the return of the Lord and the prevalent secular moods to such an extent that definite behavioural patterns are created as a result.

One of the curious and saddest features of so much of the evangelical literary output on eschatological themes is its failure to spell out the meaning and implications of the Christian hope for Christian living in the present, here and now. Some evangelicals go to great lengths to examine the 'signs of the time' and some even dare to speculate unscripturally so as even to prognosticate the actual date of the return of Christ. The average believer is overwhelmed by a plethora of controversial details about end-time events by those who claim to have *the* inside track on the future of the planet earth, and he is confused by disagreement and division among the 'experts on prophecy'. Many of these 'experts' and expositors seem to ignore the basic fact that Daniel and Revelation were written first of all for people of God who faced opposition and persecution. They overlook the fact that the purpose of these books so popular nowadays, was neither to provide ground for idle speculation and biblical arithmetic nor to show them how to escape the tribulation they had to endure. Rather biblical apocalypses in their original setting provided comfort, hope and strength to the troubled people of God. Because of a lack of this biblical emphasis and because of largely speculative concentration on some peripheral matters pertaining to the 'last things', the credibility of the evangelical witness is seriously undermined and questioned both in Christian and theological circles and in the world at large.

1. Millennial Views and Attitudes

The doctrine of the millennium has been a bone of contention through the centuries. It is one of the most divisive issues in evangelical Christianity in our century. The key scriptural passage, and the only one where a thousand-year rule of Christ is explicitly mentioned, is Rev. 20:1–6. Depending on the hermeneutical principles used in interpreting the Book of Revelation, and on the hermeneutics applied to Old Testament prophecies pointing to an era of the restoration of Israel, and an age of peace, progress and prosperity, Christians have decided for or against a millennial Kingdom and have developed elaborate theologies and schemes relating to the parousia, the second coming of Christ. By millennium is meant a distinct end-historical category of certain duration and marked by a special form of Christocracy.

A. Postmillennialism

Postmillennialists interpret Rev. 20 figuratively, and in such a way as to place the millennium within history and prior to the parousia. It is defined by one of its better known exponents as 'that view of the last things which holds that the Kingdom of God is now being extended in the world through the preaching of the gospel and the saving work of the Holy Spirit, that the world eventually is to be Christianized, and that the return of Christ will occur at the close of a long period of righteousness and peace, commonly called the millennium'..[2]

Evangelical post-millennialists should not be falsely accused and confused with those holding liberal views of human progress and social improvement by natural means and by evolutionary process. The rise of evangelical post-millennialism is usually associated with the Great Awakening (1740–1743) and with Puritan and Pietistic thinking and practice. They linked the millennial hope with the fulfilment of the Great Commission and thus were actively involved in mission and evangelization of the world.

In the eighteenth and nineteenth century Post-millennialism was the predominant evangelical view. It was first articulated as a distinct view in England in the early eighteenth-century, and became 'by far the prevalent view among American evangelicals between the Revolution and the Civil War'.[3] Some of the leading evangelical postmillennialists were: Philip Spener, Daniel Whitby, John Owen, Samuel Rutherford, John and Charles Wesley, Jonathan Edwards and among later Pietists Johann Christoph Blumhardt. These were followed by Charles Hodge, Benjamin Warfield, A.H. Strong, and James Orr.

The ultimate goal of the Puritan theology of mission and of their strong missionary consciousness was the kingdom of God, the Millennium. Jonathan Edwards (1703–1758), father of the Great Awakening and the first major post-millennial thinker, believed that revival and mission were signs of the progressive development by which the millennium would arrive. Edwards actually taught that the Kingdom of God would most probably be inaugurated in America.[4]

The Evangelical revival in the eighteenth as well as in the nineteenth century had a strong social concern.[5] Sufficient study has been done to justify the thesis that 'it was the evangelical awakening that saved England and America from the woes of the French Revolution, *not* because the revival functioned as "opiate of the people" but precisely because it spawned greater social consciousness and involvement. People such as William Wilberforce, Lord Shaftesbury, John Newton and many others whose names are associated with the abolition of slavery, the upliftment of the poor, and the war against vice, all hailed from the evangelical awakening.'[6]

Postmillennialism is optimistic in its outlook and activistic in its mission. It believes in the gradual improvement and redemption of the world. It believes in a golden age of prosperity, justice and peace as the rule of Christ is extended on this earth prior to his second coming. Postmillennialists insist that we should put greater emphasis on the demands of the Bible and those commands of Christ that require social justice, and the elimination of poverty, exploitation, and disease. Clothing of the naked and feeding of the hungry are taken as part of the mission of the church, which is to share the compassion of Christ for suffering humanity.

The evangelical postmillennialist believes in the present rule of Christ and in the transforming power of the Holy Spirit. He 'takes more seriously, or at least more literally, the socio-political aspects of the biblical prophecies' and 'expects the rule of Christ, exercised by the Holy Spirit and mediated by the word of the gospel, ultimately to transform dramatically men's social, political, and international relations'.[7] Jesus' parables of the leaven and of the mustard seed (Matt. 13:31–33) are interpreted 'as biblical evidence that the kingdom is not ushered in suddenly and cataclysmically but slowly, quietly, and almost imperceptibly'.[8] The conversion of all nations is anticipated along with the advance of civilization. Marsden, in his authoritative study *Fundamentalism and American Culture* points to this dual expectation.

> American evangelical postmillennialists saw signs of the approach of the millennial age not only in the success of revivals and missions, but also in general cultural progress. The golden age would see the culmination of current reform efforts to end slavery, oppression, and war. Moreover, in this wonderful era science, technology, and learning would advance to undreamed of accomplishments.[9]

The weakness of postmillennialism lies in its very strength – optimism. It does not seem to take seriously enough the strength of the forces of evil still operative in the world. It easily lends itself to an evolutionary understanding of history with a this-earthly hope. With its expectations for the church and the world it also undermines the expectancy of the imminent return of Christ.

B. *Amillennialism*

Amillennialism, also called the 'nonmillennial' view, is not a rejection of Rev. 20, as it is sometimes misunderstood to be. Rather it consists of a non-literal and non-temporal interpretation of this disputed passage. The millennium reign of Christ is seen in spiritual, non-earthly, and non-political terms. Amillennialists insist that the Book of Revelation be interpreted in conformity to its nature and message and that the vision of chapter 20, as G.C. Berkouwer puts it, 'is not a narrative account of a future earthly reign of peace at all, but is the apocalyptic unveiling of the reality of salvation in Christ as a backdrop to the reality of the suffering and martyrdom that still continue as long as the dominion of Christ remains hidden'.[10]

The amillennial interpretation dates back to the *Epistle of Barnabas*.[11] Augustine identified the millennial kingdom with the church and it became the prevalent prophetic view for over one thousand years until the Puritans of Old and New England modified it in the seventeenth-century and laid the foundation for postmillennial thinking.[12] All the Reformers were amillennialists.[13] Among today's evangelical theologians who accept this view we find Louis Berkhof, G.C. Berkouwer, Leon Morris, Donald Bloesch, Thomas Torrance, Anthony Hoekema, and others.

Amillennialists do not anticipate, as do the postmillennialists, a 'golden age' of widespread peace and justice on this earth, the result of the preaching of the gospel. Usually, they share the pre-millennialists' pessimistic outlook. The difference however, is that an amillennialist 'seldom bemoans the deterioration of world conditions or condemns the prevalent culture. He has noticeably less preoccupation with the details and sequence of the last things and less curiosity about "signs of the times".'[14]

Donald Bloesch, who considers that of the three views, the amillennial has the strongest exegetical support,[15] criticizes it however at four significant points, which are especially related to our considerations. Firstly, it 'too easily falls into a church imperialism', especially in cases where (as in Augustine and Calvin) the visible church is identified with the Kingdom of Christ. Secondly, Bloesch states, Amillennialism has the tendency, as we have also noted above, 'to be overpessimistic concerning the course of world history'. Some therefore look at the church 'as a remnant in the world that is still wholly under the spell of the powers of darkness, despite the fact that Revelation 20 depicts Satan as being so bound that he cannot deceive the nations any further'. Thirdly, amillennialists 'are inclined to spiritualize the kingdom and make it primarily other-worldly' thus neglecting the this-worldly dimension of the kingdom of Christ. 'Their focus of attention,' Bloesch writes, 'is usually on the life hereafter rather than the events of the last days, on immortality rather than the harvest of history, on the vision of God rather than the great commission to go into the world with the Gospel.' Fourthly, 'amillennialism tends to take away the expectancy of Christ's second coming by seeing this coming realized, at least in part, in the gift of the Holy Spirit to the church.'[16]

C. Premillennialism

As we have seen, since the time of Augustine and up to the Puritans of the seventeenth century Amillennialism was the most prevalent eschatological position. This was followed by about two centuries of postmillennial emphasis, in which the preaching of the gospel and social work went hand in hand. Premillennialist beliefs which were held by many of the church fathers in pre-Augustinian days and by some of the Anabaptists in the sixteenth century, were becoming once again widely spread in the latter part of the nineteenth century. The basic distinctive of Premillennialism as far as the sequence of expected events is concerned, is a reversal of the postmillennial view: Christ must first return, and then the millennium will follow.

Premillennialism seems to be the most prevalent, popular and aggressively advocated evangelical view in our times. Since there are varieties of premillennialism leading to significantly varied practical and behavioural consequences for both evangelism and social involvement, we have to devote more attention to it than to postmillennialism or amillennialism.

Following the Civil War in America, things instead of getting better were continually getting worse. This brought about increasing disillusionment and pessimism, which seriously undermined the credibility of Postmillennialism with its optimistic outlook for the spiritual and cultural progress of society. Such disappointing developments, preceded by the cataclysmic events at the turn of the nineteenth century and followed by two world wars in the twentieth, provide the framework for at least a partial understanding of reasons for the rapid spread and popularity of premillennial views in modern times. It is a historically observable fact that premillennialism with its apocalyptic assumptions has a special appeal and tends to flourish in times of great crisis and distress.[17] This is due to both its emphasis on the power of evil and resulting despair as far as the present age is concerned, and to the upholding hope of the dramatic inbreaking of divine intervention with its vindication of the righteous – followed by a period of justice, peace, and prosperity under the kingly rule of Christ on this earth.

There was also, however, a somewhat parallel theological development which widened the premillennialist sphere of influence and strengthened its position. It has to do with an unusual tactical alliance between premillennialists with their literalistic interpretation of Scriptures and the 'Old School' Princeton conservatives with their intellectual defence of the authority of the Bible, as they 'faced a common enemy and saw in modernism a threat to the basic assumptions of their world view'.[18] The two movements were coextensive, and the Princeton School influenced the premillennialists' view of the Scriptures.

Although we shall look at it later, we must for the reason of providing a fairly complete picture of historical development mention at this point the rise and spread of dispensationalism. Dispensationalism, though premillennial, must be distinguished from the more credible and older historical premillennialism.[19] It is a more recent development, 'invented' by one of the most formative influences among those who founded the Plymouth Brethren in Great Britain, John Nelson Darby, towards the middle of the nineteenth century. It was popularized in America through a series of prophetic conferences, the growing number of Bible institutes, and through prophetic periodicals and popular expositions. In the twentieth century it was given clear articulation, and virtual 'canonical' sanction and wide circulation through the publication of the popular Scofield Reference Bible.[20] Dispensational premillennialists have played an important role in the fundamentalist-modernist struggle in the USA.[21]

Premillennialism's underlying philosophy of history has almost inevitable negative consequences for Christian social responsibility. Not only the previously mentioned external pressures but also its own theology led to an abandonment of worldly affairs. The world is expected to grow worse and worse and there is very little or no hope of improving or reforming it by any human effort.

Within a relatively short time then, there was a significant shift from postmillennial holistic understanding of mission (Edwards and Finney saw preaching of the gospel along with political action and social reform as a means of advancing the Kingdom of Christ) to a premillennial position with its dubious effects in bringing about a *dichotomy* that is so prevalent with conservative evangelicals today.

Donald Dayton in his book *Evangelical Heritage* analyzes it as follows:

> This shift in eschatology had profound, and somewhat mixed, impact on the social involvement of evangelicals. On the one hand, the expectation of the imminent return of Christ freed many from building for the immediate future (social advancement, pension plans, etc.) to give themselves wholeheartedly to the inner cities and foreign missions fields. Resulting contact with poor and oppressed peoples often pushed these devoted souls into relief and other welfare work – and occasionally into reform.

But more characteristic was the tendency to abandon long-range social amelioration for a massive effort to preach the gospel to as many as possible before the return of Christ. The vision was now one of rescue from a fallen world. Just as Jesus was expected momentarily on the clouds to rapture His saints, so the slum worker established missions to rescue sinners out of the world to be among those to meet the Lord in the air. Evangelical effort that had once provided the impulse and troops for reform rallies was rechanneled into exegetical speculation about the timing of Christ's return and into maintenance of the expanding prophecy conference.[22]

(a) 'The Great Reversal'

The rise and spread of twentieth century American Fundamentalism then is closely tied in with the ascendance of Pre-millennialism. The attitude of the fundamentalists was essentially defensive as they saw Christian faith assaulted from various directions. Firstly it was assaulted by liberal theology which was undermining cardinal Christian doctrines; secondly by the general secular climate which was being rapidly created by the new findings and theories of the natural and social sciences. Thirdly, the fundamentalists were threatened – and this is of special connection with our topic – by the so-called 'Social Gospel' movement. The outcome of this controversy between fundamentalism and its opponents was disastrous for evangelical social concern.[23]

This 'Great Reversal' (a phrase coined by Timothy Smith), according to Marsden, had a preparatory stage from 1865–1900 consisting of a transition from the Calvinistic vision of a Christian culture, which 'saw politics as a significant means to advance the kingdom, to a "pietistic" view of political action as no more than a means to restrain evil'. This change also corresponded 'to the change from post-millennial to premillennial views of the relation of the kingdom to the present social and political order'.[24] 'The Great Reversal' actually took place from about 1900–1930 'when all progressive social concern, whether political or private, became suspect among revivalist evangelicals and was relegated to a very minor role'.[25] The stigma of the Social Gospel and its identification with theological liberalism certainly contributed to such a strong and unbalanced reaction by conservatives and to their embrace of premillennialism, and especially to the dispensationalist variety which came to dominate American fundamentalism in the 1920s.

That did not mean, however, that all evangelical premillennialists became passive in relation to social evils. We concur with Timothy Weber, however, who in *Living in the Shadow of the Second Coming: American Premillennialsim 1875–1925*,[26] came to the conclusion that Premillennialism, and especially its dispensational variety had a negative effect upon social attitudes.[27] He wrote these words:

Though not all premillennialists accepted the extreme position on the futility of reform activities, one must finally conclude that premillennialism generally broke the spirit of social concern which had played such a prominent role in earlier Evangelicalism. Its hopeless view of the present order left little room for God or for themselves to work in it. The world and the present age belonged to Satan, and lasting reform was impossible until Jesus returned to destroy Satan's power and set up the perfect kingdom. Consequently, though there were significant exceptions, premillennialists turned their backs on the movements to change social institutions. In time, the social conscience of an important part of American Evangelicalism atrophied and ceased to function. In that regard, at least, premillennialism broke faith with the evangelical spirit which it had fought so hard to preserve.[28]

(b) Saving Souls, not Societies

We have already established the fact that premillennialism is weak on social concern and mentioned some of the historical reasons for such a stance. In addition to these factors, the very pessimistic view of human history is the primary reason for its relative non-involvement when it comes to the political, social, and cultural destiny of the 'planet earth' and its inhabitants. On the one hand the premillennialists seem to take this earth seriously by refusing to spiritualize away prophecies that other views take only symbolically or as fulfilled in the church. On the other hand, however, these promises and the hope for the earth are taken to be completely future in fulfilment. They are not expected to come about by any human effort but solely by the second coming of Christ and his 1000-year rule on this earth. Evil is so deeply entrenched and interlaced in the matrix of human society that only Christ's return in power will be able to overcome it. Since the world, especially in the view of dispensationalists, is expected to grow worse and worse as part of God's programme for the last days, it makes no sense to try to improve society. It would be only a waste of time and energy. Some would even consider involvement as dangerous tampering and somehow detrimental for the Christian hope.

Premillennialists, however, have a strong record in evangelism. 'Urban revivalism and the new premillennialism developed side by side.'[29] Historians of American religion tell us that 'every major American revivalist since Dwight L. Moody has been a premillennialist'.[30]

Premillennialists see this world on a rapid course downward, awaiting judgment. They view it 'as a sinking vessel whose doomed passengers could be saved only by coming one at a time into the life-boats of personal conversion'.[31] Moody described this position in one of his sermons as follows:

> I look at this world as a wrecked vessel. God has given me a lifeboat, and said to me, 'Moody, save all you can.' God will come in judgement and burn up this world . . . The world is getting darker and darker; its ruin is coming nearer and nearer. If you have any friends on this wreck unsaved, you had better lose no time in getting them off.[32]

Premillennialism's emphasis on the imminent return of Christ provides evangelism with a certain sense of urgency. Since Christ might return at any moment, the time is short both for the evangelists in their labour and for those whom they urge not to wait with their response until it is too late. Dispensational premillennialists see their prophetic scenario fulfilled with precision in our own days in many ways and details and use this 'evidence' of the 'signs of the time' amply as an effective device to bring people to quick decisions.

Another eschatological device frequently employed in dispensational evangelistic appeals is the use of the view of the pre-tribulational rapture of the church. The present author has heard sermons and seen films[33] where this doctrine is used (and abused!) very effectively as a kind of scare-technique to press for decisions. He wonders, however, about the quality and longevity of the results obtained by such methods. The question also needs to be asked whether such presentation of salvation does not border on the betrayal of the gospel ('Good News') and of the biblical understanding of the loving nature of God. This evangelistic technique of 'apocalyptic terrorism', is intended to scare into heaven both the nominal Christian who needs to come out of his 'apostate church' (one of the signs of the last days) and the non-believer who will probably also want to escape the coming horrors he has just heard or seen described in most graphic and terrifying ways. 'Being ready' for the return of the Lord, in pre-tribulational dispensationalism seems, more often than not, to mean being ready for the secret rapture in order to avoid the horrors of the tribulation and the wrath of Antichrist. The results of such a method have negative rather than positive motivation. It is the scare of being 'left behind' more than the longing to see the Lord that underlies this eschatological scheme when applied to evangelism.

This preoccupation with apocalypticism, it seems to me, owes more to certain prevalent Western Cultural moods and fads as well as American conservative politics than to the clear teaching of Scripture. It certainly employs very dubious hermeneutic and unbelievable exegetical gymnastics in its speculative guess-work as verses of Scripture or single phrases are plucked out of their context to prove certain points about developments in modern Russia, China, the European Common Market, World Council of Churches, etc. This sensational eschatology is made attractive and popular as it is often written in the form of science-fiction. One gets the impression that in our age of renewed interest in the occult and in astrology, to many western Christians some of the popular 'last-days' writings serve as a religious substitute for astrology.

A recent edition of a popular American evangelical monthly magazine carried the theme 'Last Days'. It discloses the fact that Hal Lindsey's books sold over 30 million copies. In an interview in the same magazine Lindsey quotes with approval a radio pastor who said: 'God didn't send me down here to clean up the fish bowl but to fish in it.' Such an irresponsible statement is self-explanatory and tempts one to give it more than one interpretation. The same issue provides an annotated bibliography on 'Are We in the Last Days?' Here are some of the titles: The Coming World Crisis; Armageddon; How Close are We? The Beast System – Europe in Prophecy; The Years of the Beast; Countdown to Rapture; Christians Will Go Through the Tribulation – And How to Prepare for it; The Coming World Dictator; World War III and the Destiny of America; Latest Word on the Last Days; Armageddon, Oil, and the Middle East; The Terminal Generation; Russia Invades Israel; Prophecy in the Ring; The Two Jerusalems in Prophecy; 1980s: Decade of Shock; The Final Countdown. No comment needed![33a]

(c) The Missionary Expansion of Premillennialism

'And this *gospel* of the kingdom shall be *preached in all the world* for a witness unto all nations; and *then shall the end come*'. (Matt. 24:14). This statement of Jesus is crucial for our understanding of the premillennialists' motivation for world evangelization and their way of discerning God's time-clock. Though they do not expect any large scale results like the postmillennialists, and despite their pessimistic view regarding the future of humanity, and their strong belief in the power of evil, premillennialists are nevertheless strongly committed to evangelism and foreign missions. This involvement is at times interpreted as 'speeding up' the return of the Lord, thus making it contingent on world evangelization.

Premillennialists played an important role in the Student Volunteer Movement, and were instrumental in the founding of the 'faith missions', Missionary Training Schools and Bible Institutes.[34] By the 1920s they claimed that 'believers in the imminent second coming made up from 75 to 85 per cent of the missionary force worldwide'.[35]

Missionary expansion of the twentieth century is largely marked by the spread of the American version(s) of pre-millennialism-dispensationalism.[36] This explains at least partly, why evangelical Christianity in so many third-world countries suffers from the same and similar dichotomies and distortions as in the West, leading to withdrawal from the world, into an escapist position that awaits heaven while the world is going under. Thus they very often represent the defence of the status quo in contexts where change is imperative. By refusing to look at and live out the totality of the teaching of our Lord they seriously undermine the credibility and relevance of the gospel for poor and hungry multitudes as well as for intelligent young people and leaders to whom the mission which is void of social meaning has no meaning at all. No wonder Marxists exploit this weakness of the Christians, for we evangelicals by our behaviour do often validate their criticism of religion. Eschatological outlook that leads to passivist and fatalistic thinking has much to do with their success in certain parts of the world where evangelical Christians have laboured for long times with no great results.

2. The Tension of the Kingdom

New Testament eschatology can in no way be reduced to an apocalyptic fear syndrome. Central to the teaching of Jesus was the announcement of the Kingdom of God. In his person the Kingdom has arrived (Lk. 11:20); it was enacted by his mighty deeds as through exorcisms, healings, and in victory over forces of evil and death he defeated the 'strong man' – Satan (Matt. 12:28–29); its nature was taught in the parables and its ethics exemplified in his person and proclaimed in the Sermon on the Mount. Thus in Jesus the Old

Testament promise is fulfilled and the last days have arrived. The Kingdom has been *already inaugurated* with the arrival of the King, although it still *awaits its consummation* and fulness at the time of his second coming.

If this is the focus of the practice and teaching of Jesus, it should also be central to the teaching of evangelicals with their high regard for Scripture and the person of Jesus. In evangelical eschatology, Jesus' teaching about the kingdom, which he enacted in his first coming, should certainly be more central than the millennial debates as mentioned above and the sensational preoccupation with the events surrounding his second coming. This, unfortunately, does not seem to be so, at least when judged by the popular evangelical literary output and the treatment of eschatological themes in mass-media. The millennial question is basically the question of the Kingdom of God. Evangelicals have, by and large, unfortunately taken a limited approach to this important and complex biblical subject, focussing it one-sidedly on the differing interpretations of Rev. 20. It is only more recently that, due to the importance of this concept in modern theological debates, some evangelicals are looking at the Kingdom with greater seriousness. That has hardly, however, filtered down from the biblical theological investigations to the pulpits and has yet to produce a desired change in evangelical behaviour.

A. The Kingdom: Present and Future

Conservative Christian theology (as any conservatism) has an inbuilt tendency to oversimplification of complex issues. Evangelicals seem to find it hard to think in dialectical terms and can hardly endure to live with unresolved questions and amidst tensions. They much prefer the clear-cut answers and systematized truth and rules, which offer them assurance that they are right and boldness to communicate their convictions to others.

This may at least partly explain why conservative Christians have problems with the teaching of Jesus on the Kingdom of God. It is not easy to live with the tensions that the Kingdom 'already' brings with not only its offers but also its demands in the present age, while awaiting the 'not-yet' to simplify the issues and make an end to these tensions.

The New Testament teaching is clear. The followers of Jesus live – to use Cullman's familiar analogy – between the D-day and the

V-day, in the tension between 'already fulfilled' and 'not-yet completed'. There is both a realized *and* a future eschatology in the New Testament teaching. Not the second but the first coming of Jesus is the decisive event of the gospel teaching. The centre of gravity of Christian faith lies not in the events that come at the end of history, but in the events that have already taken place within history – in the death and resurrection of Jesus and in the outpouring of the Holy Spirit. The decisive event of redemptive history has already taken place. The end-point has been predetermined by the mid-point. The future tense is predicated on the past perfect tense of God's activity in Christ.

> The supreme sign of the *Eschaton* is the Resurrection of Jesus and the descent of the Holy Spirit on the Church. The Resurrection of Jesus is not simply a sign which God has granted in favour of His Son, but in the inauguration, the entrance into history, of *the times of the End*.[37]

With Christ then, the future has already come, or at least begun. As Erickson has said, 'The tendency of some Christians to understand Scriptural eschatology in purely futuristic terms must therefore be regarded as a mistaken, perverted view of Scriptural teaching.'[38] G.C. Berkouwer also has an important warning for many evangelical eschatologists whose emphasis borders on heresy. 'A sharp, dualistic separation between the present and future, as if the eschaton were a reality presently strange and completely unknowable, is definitely unbiblical.'[39] The keystone of the New Testament eschatology is the double advent of Christ, and there is a unique relation between the event of the first coming which predetermines the second coming and makes it inevitable, as that which has already come will be ratified and perfected by what is yet to come. Looking forward to the future coming without looking backward to the implications of the past coming of Jesus is a distortion of the biblical perspective.

The biblical understanding of the Christian faith, W. Manson wrote,

> from the beginning exhibits an essential bipolarity. The End has come! The End has not come! And neither grace nor glory, neither present proleptic fruition nor future perfection of life in God can be omitted from the picture without the reality being destroyed.[40]

This bipolarity of the biblical teaching is lost in much of the evangelical futuristic eschatology. Conservative theology is frequently framed within the 'either/or' rather than 'both/and' thinking. The modernist-fundamentalist controversy in the United States has produced a reactionary conservative ('evangelical') theology, the results of which still predetermine much of the thinking related to our topic. And, of course, such theological thinking is determinative for the kind of, or absence of, Christian involvement and action. Consciously risking some over-simplification I show this tension and differing emphasis as related to the concept of the Kingdom of God in the accompanying diagram. The scheme does assume, of course, that there are differing degrees and shades, as well as possible overlappings, present within evangelical thinking.

TENSIONS BETWEEN 'ALREADY' AND '*NOT YET*'

DOCTRINAL EMPHASIS

Immanentism	*Transcendentalism*
Creation	*Redemption*
Cosmic Redemption	*Individual Salvation*
Whole Man	*'Soul'*
'Jewish'	*'Platonic'*
Eschatology	*Apocalyptic*
Postmillennial	*Premillennial*

RELATION TO EARTH-HEAVEN

Earth	*Heaven*
This-worldly	*Other-worldly*
Present age	*Future age*
Restoration	*Annihilation*
Continuity	*Discontinuity*
Transformation	*Judgement*
'New Earth' =	*'New Earth'* =
Old Earth renewed	*totally new creation (as if* ex nihilo)

OUTLOOK/ETHICS/ACTIVITY

Optimistic	*Pessimistic*
Hope	*Despair*
Activistic	*Fatalistic*
Social Involvement	*Evangelism-Proclamation*
Penultimate (hope)	*Ultimate (hope)*

B. *Kingdom-Participation and/or Kingdom-Expectation*

The Kingdom of God has been *already inaugurated* with the first coming of Jesus, his ministry, death and resurrection and with the outpouring of the Holy Spirit upon his followers. This historico-eschatological fact stands against all attempts to overly spiritualize the Kingdom and make it primarily an other-worldly reality. As portrayed in the New Testament, the Kingdom of Christ has strong this-worldly dimensions.

The attitude of expectancy and anticipation as related to the second coming is based on an understanding of the effectiveness and implications of the first coming. It is an active and not a passive attitude; it seeks the present manifestations of the Kingdom in the full spectrum of human existence. For, as T.F. Torrance puts it:

> Through the Church . . . the new humanity in Christ is already operative among men, and it is only through the operation of that new humanity that this world of ours can be saved from its own savagery and be called into the kingdom of Christ in peace and love.[41]

Because of the victory Jesus has already achieved by his resurrection, his followers are never driven to despair even when faced with the most appalling social conditions. They are called rather to an active participation in that new movement in history which takes, God's intentions and purposes for mankind as their own. However limited or imperfect his impact may be, a Christian 'knows that every stand he takes for social righteousness and every effort he makes towards social renewal and justice and tolerance is not lost'.[42]

Much of evangelical eschatology, as I have shown earlier, is very pessimistic about the world, and thus marked by a withdrawal from the world. It emphasizes a radical break between the present earth and the awaited 'new heaven and earth'. Such teaching of total discontinuity sees the present completely unredeemable and under judgment of divine destruction, and the 'new earth' to be a kind of a new *creatio ex nihilo*.[43] This view is due to common evangelical neglect or misunderstanding of both the biblical doctrine of creation and the New Testament teaching of the present aspect of the Kingdom of God. It takes literally such apocalyptic statements as 2 Peter 3:10, while at the same time ignoring the implications of Rev. 21:24. This

neglected scripture certainly affirms that there will not be total disso-
lution and annihilation, but rather that there is some continuity
between the present and the future age. While not under-estimating
the biblical emphasis on discontinuity between this age and the next,
we must at the same time point out the biblical teaching that there is
some continuity as well. We are to work for a better world already
here and now, knowing that everything that is noble, beautiful, true
and righteous in this world will somehow be preserved and perfected
in the new world to come.[44] In this sense, indifference to culture and
social involvement, the fatalistic attitude that washes its hands of the
world letting it go to further and expected corruption is irresponsible,
and a betrayal of entrusted stewardship. This, however, is often true
of much of the popular evangelical eschatology.

Hoekema affirms the cultural continuity between the present and
the future age,[45] and quotes with approval Berkhof's reminder of
biblical figures underscoring the continuity.

> . . . the Bible . . . presents the relationship between now and later as that of
> sowing and reaping, ripening and harvest, kernel and ear. Paul states that
> a man can build upon Christ, the foundation with gold or silver, so
> that his work will remain in the consummation and he will receive his
> reward (I Cor. 3: 14). The book of Revelation mentions the works which
> will follow the believers in the consummation (14: 13), and twice it is said
> in the description of the new Jerusalem that the glory of the kings of the
> earth (21:24) and of the nations (21:26) will be brought into it. For us who
> must choose and labour in history it is of great importance to try to
> understand more clearly the meaning of this figurative language which
> speaks so plainly about a continuity between present and future.[46]

The affirmation of this neglected biblical teaching must then serve as
an incentive to social involvement. It implies that all of our present
work for a better world is of eternal significance. It also implies that
we are to appreciate and co-operate with non-Christians where in the
areas of science, art, literature, philosophy, and social work they are
producing what may well be found on the new earth. As Calvin said:
'All truth is from God; and consequently, if wicked men have said
anything that is true and just, we ought not to reject it; for it has come
from God.'[47]

Evangelicals tend at times to display not only an escapist but at
the same time a triumphalistic and judgmental attitude of superiority
over everything that is 'worldly'. They need to hear these lines from

Calvin and recognize that, 'in his redemptive activity, God does not destroy the works of his hands, but cleanses them from sin and perfects them, so that they may finally reach the goal for which he created them.'[48] Or, as the medieval theologians used to say: *Gratia non tollit sed reparat naturam.* It is interesting in this connection to note how the Jewish philosopher Martin Buber was critical of the Christian eschatology, especially of its antithesis between heaven and earth and its apocalypticism. As pointed out by Berkouwer, 'Buber seems to look on it as nothing more than a form of dualism, a visionary other-worldliness, a kind of Platonism, which makes God into nothing more than an "idea" with no real relevance for this world.'[49]

Much of the present-day evangelical other-worldly teaching and behaviour seems to justify the criticism of Christianity of both Martin Buber and Karl Marx, as well as of other secular thinkers. We can mention another Jew also who puts his critical finger on the same sore, but from a psychoanalytic perspective. Sigmund Freud in the very title of his work, *Die Zukunft einer Illusion* (The Future of an Illusion)[50] sums up his theory that religion, especially the Christian faith, is a wish-fulfilment; a self-deception by which – as if in a dream – man projects into the distant and transcendent future all the longings that are unattainable in this life. Not surprisingly, Max Warren, the great evangelical missionary statesman, came to a similar conclusion:

> The real reason for the failure of Second Adventism to win support lies in the fact that it affronts the moral conscience of the Church by its virtual abandonment of responsibility for the things of this world in deference to its preoccupation with the imminent return of the Lord and the end of history . . . On this view, salvation is salvation of the soul alone. No serious attempt is made to consider the soul's environment.[51]

Warren goes on to point out that such an attitude gains popular support in times of despair because 'its despair of the world *seems to be based on a too thorough-going dualism,*' and he responds to this perversion of Christian faith by a positive affirmation. 'This world may indeed be "enemy occupied territory," but the Enemy has got no property rights in it. He is a thief and a liar. Our responsibility as Christians is to be *good stewards* of the King's property . . . There is no room in the true dialectical process for indifference to the way this world is run.'[52]

Conservative Christians have a tendency to combat one heresy with another. They confront the 'Social Gospel' with an individualized and purely spiritual view of salvation. They oppose a 'realized eschatology' with an other-worldly, futuristic eschatological emphasis. It need not be mentioned that such 'reactionary theology' does not do justice to the complexity and richness of biblical teaching. And, on the practical level, indifference to the social problems of the day may have disastrous consequences. As D. Bosch puts it: 'Where Christianity loses its ability to recreate the world, other powers will take its place – science and technology, but also atheistic revolution.'[53] Many anti-Christian political movements in the world today are nothing but a judgment of the sin of indifference displayed by the Christians of those lands in previous times. 'To be indifferent to the way in which social life is ordered is in fact to take sides – to take sides with corruption and tyranny, graft and reaction, since these social evils feed on the indifference and inactivity of ordinary folk, and count on it for their continuing existence.'[54]

The Kingdom of God then is the redemptive activity of God in history through the person of Jesus Christ. It does not arrive by human achievement. Humans are, however, invited to repentance and faith by which they enter the Kingdom, and are invited to both the responsible *participation* in the Kingdom-already-arrived, and to the watchful *expectation* of the Kingdom-still-to-come.

Christians who emphasize Kingdom-expectation and neglect Kingdom-participation, very often reflect a sense of alienation from the world and shrink from this-worldly responsibilities. They lack the biblical emphasis on the sovereignty of God in Christ over the world and display as far as the present age is concerned, a stronger belief in the power and forces of evil than in the victory of Christ achieved by resurrection and operative in the world through the work of the Holy Spirit.

In our consideration of the Kingdom and its implications we need to agree with the summary statement of Donald Bloesch, an evangelical systematic theologian. He concluded his chapter, 'The Personal Return of Christ', with the following paragraph, which I think should be descriptive of a truly evangelical position.

Our intention has been to construct a doctrine of the millennium that includes the note of victory not only over the world powers at the end-time but also over the world powers within our present age. At the same time, we have tried to stay clear of a false church triumphalism that exempts the church from the judgment of God and from the cross of persecution. We have sought to avoid both a crippling pessimism that sees the church as only a tiny remnant besieged by the hordes of darkness and a too facile optimism that underestimates the continuing power of sin and death in the world. The messianic kingdom of Christ is already realized in the birth and life of the church, but it has yet to be consummated when the church is taken up into the eternal kingdom of God. The new age is present now, though hidden in the community of faith, but it will be manifest throughout all the earth when our Lord comes again in glory.[55]

3. Eschatology and Ethics

Part of the eschatological corrective the Apostle Paul administers in 2 Thessalonians is a warning against idleness (see 2 Thess. 3:6–14) and a withdrawal from the present-day responsibilities, which was probably due to excessive preoccupation with the future and the other-worldly as wrongly conceived in relation to the parousia. Many conceive Christian eschatology in terms of the abandonment of the world and its present sinful world-order, considering it beyond redemption and inevitably doomed for judgment. Those misguided thinkers thus substitute *for* an active involvement in the world a passive expectation of an apocalyptic inbreaking from beyond as the only hope for change, justice, peace, and order. Because of such attitudes, Christian eschatology and Christian ethics have not infrequently been considered as irreconcilable rivals. Does the expectation of the second coming of the Lord take away from the incentive for constructive Christian action in the world? Is it true that 'All the doctrines of Christian eschatology are rife with ethical content and reality, and . . . of a morally inspirational character,' – as stated by L.S. Keyser?[56] Does Christian hope lead to a passive world-denial or to a fruitful and faithful world-involvement? We have seen in our consideration of millennial views that hope gives an incentive to evangelism. Why is it, when it comes to social responsibility, that it is frequently considered a hindrance rather than an impetus? How is it that some Christians fervently and wholeheartedly evangelize the world even though they know that the results will be limited and not all the world will become Christian? How can they at the same time use a similar limitation as an excuse for non-involvement in facing social evils like poverty, sickness, racism, militarism, etc.?

We have already answered some of these questions by pointing to evangelical imbalance and heretical tendencies in relating – or, to put it more accurately, *failing* rightly to relate – history and eschatology, present and future aspects of the Kingdom of God. Constant preoccupation with apocalypticism tends to show up in evangelical theology in attempts to *de-eschatologize history* or *de-historicize eschatology*. Such a distortion of biblical truth makes it almost impossible to relate eschatology and ethics. Faithfulness to the biblical teaching makes us move beyond such unacceptable dualism. It is here that evangelical theology can be corrected and fruitfully enriched by openly and humbly, even though critically, entering into dialogue with contemporary theologians like Pannenberg, Moltmann, and many others, with their stimulating attempts to relate theology to ethics.

Eschatology has vital implications for the Christian involvement in the world. We agree with the conclusion of the British evangelical theologian Stephen Travis:

> Fortunately, the Christian does not have to choose between his personal immortality and a hope for men's future in the world. Indeed, now that 'theology of hope' and 'political theology' and 'liberation theology' have had some years of attention by theologians, a major task is the creation of a synthesis between these 'worldly hopes' and a theology of immortality in fellowship with God.[57]

A. The Ethics of Jesus

The message of the promise of the Kingdom is also a message of warning. Eschatology has unavoidable implications for present experience and action. As Jesus announces the Kingdom, he calls to repentance. 'The summons to repentance in view of the coming Kingdom is characteristic of the entire New Testament ethic . . . The impending Kingdom becomes the sanction of the entire ethical summons. The Beatitudes pronounce a moral universe that is rewarded fully and completely in the future. Main portions of the Sermon on the Mount are validated by eschatology.'[58]

The indicative of the gospel, of the Christ-event, forms an indissoluble unity with the imperative of the ethical teaching of Jesus. The parables of the mustard seed and leaven show that even before the parousia the Kingdom is present in anticipatory form. Christian ethic is an ethic of this new situation, it is the ethic of the new covenant, that does not lead to a world-denial, but rather to a self-denying and faithful discharge of our calling in this present world. In the parable of the talents (Matt. 25:14–30) Jesus commands his servants to 'do business' with the talents he has entrusted to them, and condemns the 'wicked, lazy servant' (NIV) for neglecting his duties. The parable stresses the fact that the absent Lord is still the Lord to be obeyed and served. Paul similarly reminds us that 'while we wait for the blessed hope', the second coming of Christ, we should be 'eager to do what is good' (Tit. 2:13–14).

In the parable of the sheep and the goats (Matt. 25:31–46) Jesus clearly shows that it is impossible to separate service to him from service to those who are in need among fellow human beings, and that the outcome of the future judgment will depend on whether we have recognized him in those who are hungry and naked, sick and enslaved and whether we have responded appropriately to their physical needs.

The problem with some forms of dispensationalism is that in its compartmentalization of Scripture it has to relegate to a future Millennium much of the teaching on the Kingdom that has present relevance. This is done not only with much of the Old Testament prophetic exhortation on social issues, but also with the ethical teaching of Jesus. It is true that when Jesus speaks of the Kingdom of God he uses eschatological language. But dispensational theology

> . . . in its extreme forms also evaporates the present-day relevance of much of the ethics of Jesus. Eschatology is invoked to postpone the significance of the Sermon on the Mount and other segments of New Testament moral teaching to a later Kingdom age. Dispensationalism erects a cleavage in biblical ethics in the interest of debatable eschatological theory. Dispensationalism holds that Christ's Kingdom has been postponed until the end of the Church age, and that Kingdom-ethics will become dramatically relevant again only in the future eschatological era . . . extreme Dispensationalism holds literally to both eschatology and ethics, but moves both into the future. New Testament theology will not sustain this radical repudiation of any present form of the Kingdom of heaven.[59]

Taking the ethical import of the teaching of Jesus seriously, we concur with René Padilla that:

> In the light of the biblical teaching there is no place for an 'other-worldliness' that does not result in the Christian's commitment to his neighbour, rooted in the Gospel. There is no room for 'eschatological

paralysis' nor for a 'social strike'. There is no place for statistics on 'how many souls die without Christ every minute', if they do not take into account how many of those who die, die victims of hunger. There is no place for evangelism that, as it goes by the man who was assaulted by thieves on the road from Jerusalem to Jericho, sees in him only a soul that must be saved and ignores the man.[60]

B. The Practice of Hope

Our view of the future is not only information about something we await. It is also a call to participation on the journey toward that future, and it determines the way we live in the present. Christians are called to anticipatory living that produces a proleptic life-style. Proleptic could be taken as meaning an error in chronology, referring to something that occurs before its time. The discovery of the life-style of the Kingdom of God means living in the power of the Kingdom already operative in our lives and in our world since the resurrection of Jesus the King and the giving of the Holy Spirit. It means also living anticipatorily, that is from a hope that sees that which has been inaugurated more and more realized here and now as it approaches its consummation. Proleptic living is a life by faith that takes the promises and commands of God equally seriously and honours Christ by implementing them in the present.

The future makes demands on our living in the present. God's eschatological Kingdom is a radical critique of the present state of things in the world. Christian hope does not lead to an easy acceptance of the status quo. Rather, it 'is a constant disturbance of reality as it is and a call to move ahead to the future. The God of the promise does not sacralize the present.'[61]

While Christian ethics should be an ethics of change, the evangelical ethics often suffers a serious defect in this respect whenever it is nurtured by an other-worldly distortion that conceives salvation as an escape from this world to life in another. Such a view in turn blesses the status quo due to a pessimism about this world. To be eschatologically significant we must regain the vision of both proclamation and action. Christian love that strives for the transformation of the world needs to be engendered by Christian hope, by the promise of the future. We are called to continual realization of the eschatological values that are characteristic of the Kingdom: love, joy, life, justice, peace, freedom, brotherhood, equality, harmony, unity, etc. These future realities of heaven are to be proleptically present as they are practised by the followers of Jesus, and they should motivate us to work toward their greater realization on earth.[62]

Christian ethics as an ethics of change should not be understood only in terms of individual repentance. It must also be extended to the area of social relationships and societal structures. As Christians proclaim and live out the universal values of the Kingdom and in obedience to the coming Lord actively love their neighbours, Christians surely can initiate some significant changes in the world. Even in situations where a Christian may not be able to effect a change, as Max Warren put it, 'his attitude is one of revolutionary expectancy'. When we focus our vision of faith upon the blessed return of our Lord with its assurance of his triumph, we are given new strength to carry on even amidst most hopeless situations.

Christian hope leads to Christian practice. For as Leighton Ford stated, 'The hope of Christ's return is no escapist clause. It is not an out for Christian complacency, nor an alibi for non-involvement.'[63] It is not exclusively other-worldly, but it also pertains to our historical existence as we know that the coming One is already a crucified and risen One. In view of these basic events of the redemptive history both the penultimate hopes and the ultimate hope are to be taken seriously as we pray and obey, hope, and work. We must remember also that this basic two-advent structure of the christocentric redemptive history spells out not only promise but also judgment. It allows for neither utopianism nor other-worldly detachment.

Here evangelicals face a major task to recover the fully biblical view of the future that will enable them to live truly evangelical lives in the present. This will come about only by being responsive to the grave needs for change in our world and not by becoming immobilized by subscribing to a kind of unbiblical 'latter-day fatalism'.[64]

> Contemporary evangelicalism needs (1) to reawaken to the relevance of its redemptive message to the global predicament; (2) to stress the great evangelical agreements in a common world front; (3) to discard elements of its message which cut the nerve of world compassion as contradictory to the inherent genius of Christianity; (4) to restudy eschatological convictions for a proper perspective which will not unnecessarily dissipate evangelical strength in controversy over secondary positions, in a day when the significance of the primary insistences is international.

This statement was made thirty-five years ago by Carl Henry in his evangelically epoch-making book, *The Uneasy Conscience of Modern*

Fundamentalism.[65] It is equally relevant and even more important today as we evangelicals still have a long way to go in overcoming our weaknesses, limitations and imbalances in order to discover the totality of biblical teaching and practice so that the two petitions of our daily prayer, *Thy Kingdom come,* and *Thy will be done* may equally and fully become a reality as we strive to serve our Lord while awaiting his return.

Select Bibliography

Armerding, Carl E. and Gasque W. Ward, eds: *Handbook of Biblical Prophecy* (Grand Rapids: Baker, 1980). Formerly (1977) published as *Dreams, Visions, and Oracles.*

Bass, Clarence B. *Backgrounds to Dispensationalism: Its Historical Genesis and Ecclesiastical Implications* (Grand Rapids: Eerdmans, 1960). Reprint. Grand Rapids: Baker, 1977.

Boettner, Loraine. *The Millennium* (Philadelphia: Presbyterian and Reformed, 1958).

Berkouwer, G.C. *The Return of Christ* (Grand Rapids: Eerdmans, 1972).

Bloesch, Donald G. *Essentials of Evangelical Theology, Vol. 2: Life, Ministry, and Hope* (New York: Harper and Row, 1978).

Bosch, David J. *Witness to the World: The Christian Mission in Theological Perspective* (Atlanta: John Knox Press, 1980).

Clouse, Robert G., ed. *The Meaning of the Millennium: Four Views.* Chapters by: George E. Ladd, 'Historic Premillennialism'; Herman A. Hoyt, 'Dispensational Premillennialism'; Anthony A. Hoekema, 'Amillennialism' (Downers Grove: Inter-Varsity Press, 1977).

Cullmann, Oscar. *Salvation in History* (New York: Harper and Row, 1967).

Dayton, Donald W. *Discovering an Evangelical Heritage* (New York: Harper and Row, 1976).

Erickson, Millard J. *Contemporary Options in Eschatology: A Study of the Millennium* (Grand Rapids: Baker, 1977).

Hoekema, Anthony A. *The Bible and the Future* (Grand Rapids and Exeter: Eerdmans and Paternoster), 1979.

Kik, J. Marcellus. *The Eschatology of Victory* (Philadelphia: Presbyterian and Reformed, 1971).

Ladd, George E. *The Blessed Hope* (Grand Rapids: Eerdmans, 1956).

Ladd, George E. *Crucial Questions About the Kingdom of God* (Grand Rapids: Eerdmans, 1952).

The Gospel of the Kingdom (Grand Rapids: Eerdmans, 1959).

The Presence of the Future, Grand Rapids: Eerdmans, 1974. Revised edition of *Jesus and the Kingdom* (New York: Harper and Row; London: SPCK, 1964).

Lindsey, Hal, with C.C. Carlson. *The Late Great Planet Earth* (Grand Rapids: Zondervan, 1970. 42nd. printing, 1974).

Marsden, George M. *Fundamentalism and American Culture: The Shaping of Twentieth Century Evangelicalism, 1870–1925* (New York: Oxford University Press, 1980).

Milne, Bruce. *What the Bible Teaches About the End of the World* (Wheaton: Tyndale, 1982).

Moltmann, Jurgen. *Theology of Hope: On the Ground and the Implications of a Christian Eschatology* (London: SCM; New York: Harper and Row, 1967).

Moody, Dale. *The Hope of Glory* (Grand Rapids: Eerdmans, 1964).

Pentecost, J. Dwight. *Things to Come* (Findlay, Ohio: Dunham, 1958).

Ridderbos, Herman N. *The Coming of the Kingdom* (Philadelphia: Presbyterian and Reformed, 1962).

Ryrie, Charles C. *Dispensationalism Today* (Chicago: Moody, 1965).

Sandeen, Ernest R. *The Roots of Fundamentalism: British and American Millennarianism, 1800–1930* (Chicago: University of Chicago Press, 1970).

Sine, Tom. *The Mustard Seed Conspiracy* (Waco, Texas: Word Books, 1981).

Smith, Timothy L. *Revivalism and Social Reform* (New York: Harper Torch-books 1957). Reprinted with a new afterword by the author (Baltimore and London: The Johns Hopkins University Press, 1980).

Torrance, Thomas F. *Kingdom and Church: A Study in the Theology of the Reformation* (Edinburgh and London: Oliver and Boyd, 1956).

Torrance, Thomas F. 'The Eschatology of the Reformation,' *Scottish Journal of Theology Occasional Papers*, No. 2, pp. 36–62 (Edinburgh and London: Oliver and Boyd, 1953).

Travis, Stephen. *Christian Hope and the Future of Man* (London: Inter-Varsity Press, 1980)

The Jesus Hope (London: Word Books, 1974; Downers Grove: Inter-Varsity, 1974).

Walvoord, John F. *The Blessed Hope and the Tribulation* (Grand Rapids: Zondervan, 1976).

The Millennial Kingdom (Findlay, Ohio: Dunham, 1958).

Weber, Timothy P. *Living in the Shadow of the Second Coming: American Premillennialism, 1875–1925* (New York and Oxford: Oxford University Press, 1979).

Wilson, Dwight. *Armageddon Now! The Premillennarian Response to Russia and Israel Since 1917* (Grand Rapids: Baker, 1977).

Notes

1. See I.H. Marshall, 'Slippery Words': 1. Eschatology *The Expository Times*, Vol. LXXXIX, No. 9, June 1978, pp. 264–269.
2. Loraine Boettner, *The Millennium* (Philadelphia: Presbyterian and Reformed, 1958), p. 4.
3. George M. Marsden, *Fundamentalism and American Culture* (New York: Oxford University Press, 1980), p. 49.

4. Sydney E. Ahlstrom, 'From Puritanism to Evangelicalism: A Critical Perspective,' *The Evangelicals: What They Believe, Who They are, and Where They are Changing*, ed. T.D. Woodbridge and D.F. Wells (Nashville: Abingdon) p. 276; see also David Bosch, *Witness to the World: The Christian Mission in Theological Perspective* (Atlanta: John Knox Press), pp. 142–147.

5. See Timothy L. Smith, *Revivalism and Social Reform* (New York: Harper Torchbooks, 1957).

6. Bosch, *ibid.*, p. 147.

7. James R. Ross, 'Evangelical Alternatives,' in *Handbook of Biblical Prophecy*, eds. C.E. Armerding and W.W. Gasque (Grand Rapids: Baker, 1980), p. 125.

8. *ibid.*

9. Marsden, *ibid.*, p. 49.

10. G.C. Berkouwer, *The Return of Christ* (Grand Rapids: Eerdmans, 1972), p. 307.

11. According to D.H. Kromminga, *The Millennium in the Church* (Grand Rapids: Eerdmans, 1945), p. 40: 'a very early millennial type of eschatology'.

12. Ian J. Rennie, 'Nineteenth-Century Roots,' *Handbook of Biblical Prophecy*, p. 43.

13. On the eschatological views of the Reformers see T.I. Torrance, 'The Eschatology of the Reformation,' *Scottish Journal of Theology Occasional Papers*, No. 2, pp. 36–62; and Heinrich Quistorp, *Calvin's Doctrine of the Last Things* (London: Lutterworth Press, 1955).

14. Millard J. Erickson, *Contemporary Options in Eschatology* (Grand Rapids: Baker, 1977), p. 75.

15. George E. Ladd would disagree with that as he claims: 'Sound exegesis of Revelation 20 requires a millennial interpretation; nonmillennialists usually do not appeal so much to exegesis as to theological consistency for support of their position. They interpret such passages as Revelation 20 in a nonmillennarian way because they are convinced that the totality of New Testament truth has no room for an interregnum and that there is no alternative in view of the New Testament eschatology as a whole but to interpret Revelation spiritually.' ('The Revelation of Christ's Glory', *Christianity Today*, Sept. 1, 1958, p. 13).

16. Donald G. Bloesch, *Essentials of Evangelical Theology, Vol. 2: Life, Ministry, and Hope* (New York: Harper and Row, 1978), p. 197.

17. See I.J. Rennie, *ibid.*, p. 44.

18. E.R. Sandeen, *The Roots of Fundamentalism* (Chicago: University of Chicago Press, 1970), p. xvii.

19. See the books by George E. Ladd in the bibliography; also C.B. Bass, *Backgrounds to Dispensationalism* (Grand Rapids: Eerdmans, 1960).

20. First published 1909, revised 1917. Now also available in other languages, e.g. German.

21. It is probably because of this strategic and yet coincidental alliance in their own history of struggles against liberalism that many American

evangelicals look with some suspicion at non-premillennial evangelicals in Britain and Europe.

22. Donald W. Dayton, *Discovering an Evangelical Heritage* (New York: Harper and Row, 1976), p. 127.

23. See David O. Moberg, *The Great Reversal: Evangelism Versus Social Concern* (Philadelphia and New York: J.B. Lippincott Company, 1972); and by the same author, *Inasmuch: Christian Social Responsibility* (Grand Rapids: Eerdmans, 1965).

24. Marsden, *ibid.*, p. 86 in a chapter entitled 'The Great Reversal' (pp. 85–93).

25. *ibid.*

26. A revised edition of a doctoral dissertation written at the University of Chicago. New York and Oxford: Oxford University Press, 1979.

27. Paul C. Wilt, *Premillennialism in America, 1865–1918, With Special Reference to Attitudes Toward Social Reform* (unpublished Ph.D. dissertation, The American University, 1970), focuses his study on premillennial views on temperance, the urban poor, labour-management relations, the Negro and foreign missions, and comes to a somewhat more positive conclusion than Timothy Weber: 'Given their pessimism about moral and spiritual improvement they were quite active in certain aspects of social reform.'

28. Weber, *ibid.*, p. 183.

29. *ibid.*, p. 152

30. *ibid.*

31. *ibid.*, p. 53, see also p. 71.

32. D.L. Moody, *New Sermons* (New York: Henry S. Goodspeed, 1980), p. 535; quoted by Weber, *ibid.*, p. 53.

33. Timothy Weber mentions several of such films in his article 'The Great Second Coming Alert,' *Eternity* (April 1981), pp. 19–23.

33a. Evangelical 'eschatologists' would do well to listen to John Stott's call in the exposition of *Lausanne Covenant*, 'not to go beyond the plain assertions of the Bible [but to] retain a humble agnosticism about some of the details of the Lord's return,' while affirming the fundamental truths clearly taught in Scriptures. *The Lausanne Covenant: An Exposition and Commentary*, Lausanne Occasional Papers, No. 3 (Minneapolis: World Wide Publications, 1975), p. 35.

34. See Weber, *Living in the Shadow* . . . pp. 73–81.

35. *ibid.*, p. 81.

36. Cf. Sunhee Kwak, *Eschatology and Christian Mission* (Unpublished D.Miss. dissertation written from Korean perspective at the School of World Mission, Fuller Theological Seminary, Pasadena, USA).

37. W. Manson, 'Eschatology in the New Testament,' *Scottish Journal of Theology Occasional Papers No. 2* (Edinburgh: Oliver and Boyd, 1953), p. 6.

38. Erickson, *Contemporary Options* . . ., p. 34.

39. Berkouwer, *Return*, p. 450.

40. Manson, *ibid.*, p. 14.

41. 'Foreword' to Heinrich Quistorp, *Calvin's Doctrine of the Last Things*, p. 8.

42. Bruce Milne, *What the Bible Teaches About the End of the World*, p. 146.

43. Cf. Berkouwer, *Return*, pp. 220ff.
44. 'Whatever is true, whatever is honourable, whatever is just, whatever is pure, whatever is lovely, whatever is gracious, in the whole creation, in heaven and earth, is brought together in the future city of God. But it is renewed, recreated, and developed to its greatest glory. The material for it is present in this creation.' H. Bavinck, *Gereformeerde Dogmatiek* (Kampen, 1911). Vol. IV p. 802; quoted by H. Berkhof, *Christ the Meaning of History* p. 180.
45. Cf. Anthony A. Hoekema, *The Bible and the Future* (Grand Rapids and Exeter: Eerdmans and Paternoster, 1979), pp. 39–40, 73–75, and the chapter 'The New Earth', pp. 274–287.
46. Hendrikus Berkhof, *Christ the Meaning of History* (Richmond: John Knox, 1966), p. 189.
47. *Commentary on the Epistles to Timothy, Titus and Philemon* (Grand Rapids: Eerdmans, 1948), comment on Titus 1:12, pp. 300–301.
48. Hoekema, *ibid.*, p. 73.
49. Berkouwer, *ibid.*, pp. 228–229.
50. Cf. Sigmund Freud, *The Future of an Illusion* (Garden City, NY: Double-day, 1957).
51. Max Warren, *The Truth of Vision: A Study in the Nature of the Christian Hope* (London: Canterbury Press, 1948), p. 53.
52. *ibid.*
53. Bosch, *ibid.*, p. 210.
54. Alexander Miller, *The Christian Significance of Karl Marx* (London: SCM, 1946), p. 95.
55. Bloesch, *Essentials . . . Vol. 2*, pp. 203–204.
56. *A System of Christian Ethics* (Philadelphia: The Lutheran Publication Society, 1913), p. 224.
57. *Christian Hope and the Future of Man* (London: IVP, 1980), p. 138.
58. Carl F.H. Henry, *Christian Personal Ethics* (Grand Rapids: Eerdmans, 1957), p. 553.
59. *ibid.*, p. 551.
60. 'Evangelism and the World' in *Let the Earth Hear His Voice: Official Reference Volume, Papers and Responses*/International Congress on World Evangelization, Lausanne, Switzerland, 1974; ed. J.D. Douglas (Minneapolis: World Wide Publications, 1975), p. 132.
61. J. Miguez Bonino in summarizing the argument of the J. Moltmann's *Theology of Hope* in *Doing Theology in a Revolutionary Situation* (Philadelphia: Fortress Press, 1975), p. 144.
62. Of the many evangelical books on eschatology which I read or perused I found two systematic yet popularly written treatments (both by British authors) containing some discussion about the practical significance and the motivation that Christian hope provides for responsible living and practice, including social involvement. They are: Bruce Milne, *What the Bible Teaches About the End of the World*, and Stephen Travis, *The Jesus Hope*.

Very helpful in this regard is also James R. Ross, 'Living Between Two Ages,' in *Handbook of Biblical Prophecy* pp. 231–241.

63. *One Way to Change the World* (New York: Harper and Row, 1970), p. 118. C.S. Lewis also warned that a belief in the Second Coming should not preclude '. . . sober work for the future within the limits of ordinary morality and prudence . . . For what comes is judgment: happy are those whom it finds labouring in their vocations whether they were merely going out to feed the pigs or laying good plans to deliver humanity a hundred years hence from some great evil. The curtain has indeed now fallen. Those pigs will never in fact be fed, the great campaign against white slavery or governmental tyranny will never in fact proceed to victory. No matter you were at your post when the inspection came.' 'The Christian Hope', *Eternity* (March 1954), p. 50.

64. Cf. the stimulating book by the evangelical futurologist Tom Sine, *The Mustard Seed Conspiracy* (Waco, Texas: Word Books, 1981).

65. (Grand Rapids: Eerdmans, 1947), p. 57.

Nine

God's Intention for the World

Vinay Samuel and Chris Sugden

Introduction

God's intention for the world, set forth already in creation, reaches its ultimate consummation in the return of Jesus Christ and the future he will bring to the world. The theme that relates God's intention in creation to its final fulfillment is the Kingdom of God, which will be completed with the establishment of a new heaven and a new earth in which the righteousness of God will reign through the lordship of Christ. God has not become inactive in this interim period between creation and consummation, however, so we must ask how his ultimate intention for the world – the consummated kingdom – relates to his intention for the world today, for the church, for

'God's Intention for the World' by Vinay Samuel and Chris Sugden in *The Church in Response to Human Need* edited by Vinay Samuel and Chris Sugden (Grand Rapids, Eerdmans, 1987).

human society, and for the historical process *before* the final consummation.

God's Action in History

How does the Bible relate God's work in bringing the final consummation to his work in human history? God's call to and covenant with Abraham, the Exodus, and the settlement of Canaan were each part of a historical project. Through the nation Israel and its society and laws, and through the blessing and punishment that followed obedience and disobedience, God revealed himself, his character, and his purpose to the world. The nation of Israel, its laws, and its history were God's light to the nations (Gen. 17:6; Isa. 42:6; 49:6), and so we should see God's relationship with his people Israel as a model for his intentions for all of human society.

The Old Testament makes no separation between religious history and the rest of history, between a people's relationship with God and its participation in human society, or between God's work among his own people and among other peoples. We know that God initiated the history of the Israelites and made his covenant with them, but his control over Israel is not fundamentally different from his control over the history of other nations – the Bible states that he also directed the history of the Philistines and the Syrians (Amos 9:7). While his work among his own people and that among other peoples are distinct and not to be confused, they are always integrally related.

For example, God does not always refer to his people in ways that distinguish them from other peoples – he uses the same words to refer to both. In the Psalms the Hebrew word *am* (simply, people) is used to refer to the people of Israel, but not exclusively so. The word does not designate *God's* people, for other nations may also be designated by the word *am* in this sense, as in Psalm 18:43: 'Thou didst deliver me from strife with the peoples; thou didst make me the head of the nations; people whom I had not known served me'.

In Genesis 10, where we read of the establishment of nations from the generations of the sons of Noah, we should not view the designation 'nation' as somehow distinct from the designation 'people'. One must not think that 'nation' simply refers to those groups that are estranged from God while 'people' refers to those in a relationship with him (the people of God). Psalm 82:8 declares that 'to thee belong all the nations'

– *Lagoyyim*, whether estranged or not. In Psalm 87, where the Lord calls out the register of the peoples *(ammim)*, he includes Rahab (Egypt), Babylon, Philistia, Tyre, and Ethiopia, even though these were referred to as nations in Genesis 10. And within a single psalm, Psalm 102:15, 21–22, the terms 'nations' and 'peoples' are synonymous. Kenneth Cracknell concludes that English translations of the Bible are 'misleading' in drawing a distinction between Israel as a people and others as nations.[1] While the focus is on Israel as God's chosen people, the terms 'people' and 'nations' are used interchangeably.

An examination of Old Testament covenants shows that the covenant with Abraham (Gen. 15:1–6; 17:1–21) did not abrogate those with Adam (Gen. 1:26–31) and Noah (Gen. 6:18; 9:11, 16), which were general covenants with all nations. Moreover, the covenant with Noah was not somehow incomplete – it too was a covenant of both preservation and redemption.[2] By choosing Abraham to be the father of multitudes, God did not cut himself off from the rest of humanity. In fact, the prophets insisted that any covenant with Israel was for universal benefit and significance, not exclusive blessing (Isa. 42:6; Jer. 4:2; Ps. 67). God's covenant with Abraham was particular, but again not exclusive – it took its place alongside the other covenants.

The Old Testament looks forward to Egypt and Assyria being God's people along with Israel: 'In that day Israel will be the third with Egypt and Assyria, a blessing in the midst of the earth, whom the Lord of hosts has blessed, saying, "Blessed be Egypt my people, and Assyria the work of my hands, and Israel my heritage" ' (Isa. 19:24–25). God makes plain that he will not gather the people of other nations merely as subsidiaries of Israel, but as themselves under the lordship of the Messiah. Egypt will not have to join Israel to become God's people but can maintain its identity. This is not to deny that Israel is distinct from other nations, that it does have a special covenant, and that it is already God's people; but it is important to note that God never intends by this to exclude others from being his people, unmediated by the work of Israel.

The Millennial Vision in Scripture: The Prophetic and Apocalyptic Traditions

God's activity is part of human history and calls for a human response. In the Old Testament the prophets of Israel focused sharply on this relationship and demanded that Israel respond to God. They interpreted the events of the past, called for obedience in the present, and announced hope for the future. Important to them was the meaning, not just the events, of life. To prophesy was in itself an act of demonstrating life's meaning – not only to explain, but also to call, to invite, and to condemn.[3] The prophets made no separation between religious and political history, nor between facts and their interpretation. They were convinced that God is in charge – not only of the history of his people but of all history.

In prophecy, God was active in speaking directly to his people in the present. Immediate events were decisive in that the prophets interpreted them as foreshadowing the impending end. They then related the end in turn back to the present in an attempt to motivate obedience to God. This was never a simple task, however, because it was not always apparent how God was acting in history, how his people were to respond to him and his promises, and how they could fulfill his purpose. Perhaps even more distressing, it was not always clear that God actually was in charge of history, that he really did care for his people, and that he would maintain his covenants with them. When this was unclear, God's people sometimes questioned his justice, and this doubt sometimes found its way into the Bible – in Job, for example. But God always answered his beloved people with the assertion that he was still in control, despite any appearances to the contrary.

After the fall of Jerusalem and the exile, Israel experienced a series of defeats in its attempts to rebuild the nation in obedience to what it saw as God's will. This time, however, there were no assurances that God was in charge. The heavens answered Israel's prayers with a deafening and unending silence. Prophecy faded away.

Had God really abandoned history? Apocalyptic literature, including Daniel and Zechariah in the Old Testament and the extracanonical books of Enoch and Maccabees, arose in an attempt to answer the question. It reasoned that God had acted in the past and therefore would act in the future. In an effort to appear to speak with greater validity, apocalyptic literature often put present events into the mouths of past figures as prophecy, thus 'foretelling' events that had in fact already occurred. As all that was 'foretold' had come to pass, so the next event, the end, would come as foretold. The essence of the teaching was vindication for God's people and judgment on his and their enemies. As for the present, God had abandoned it.[4] The apocalyptic writers posited the end only on the basis of past prophecy; they no longer claimed to see God's action in the present and could give their contemporaries no advice other than to wait.

In apocalyptic, any meaning was to be found behind and beyond history, not in God's activity within present human existence. God was no longer seen as an actor on stage; he was behind the scenes where the real decisions that mattered took place. It no longer made any sense for the Israelites to beg God to defeat their enemies and so prove that he was Lord. It did not make sense to pray to God to send fire from heaven to prove to the unbelievers that he was the true God, as Elijah did. It did not make sense because Israel no longer believed that God was active in their lives and history. Further, they did not see in present events the image of the end. In fact, the present really did not have any meaning in the life of Israel. True, it would eventually be invested with meaning, but that would happen only in the end, in the final conclusion: God's victory over all evil people and powers, and the establishment of his reign of peace with justice. The only relation that this end ever had to present events was that it brought the present to a conclusion. The line between the present and the end had no significance in itself: it merely led up to the end.

Though such a view of history may seem terribly pessimistic, it was in fact a great foundation for faith. Any present setbacks could be turned aside with the assurance that things would change in the future. The pagan empires could win all the battles, but Israel could live in the knowledge that they would not conquer in the end. Evil could take over the world, but it would be defeated finally. There was no need for despair or fatalism because God would win in the end. Meanwhile, his people must remain faithful and loyal to him and must patiently endure.

Is apocalyptic a retreat from history? Richard Bauckham suggests that it did not begin with the idea that God cannot act in history but with the observation of God's relative absence from history since the fall of Jerusalem.[5] Although apocalyptists were negative about this period, they did not view history in general in such a negative light.[6] In fact, their belief and desire was just the contrary; they longed for God to intervene on behalf of the faithful and expected that he would vindicate his people and his justice on the stage of history, by transcending it. So they spoke of a 'new creation': they affirmed the prophetic faith in their declaration that though God was now absent, he would eventually return in a total transformation of history.

Israel, then, no longer needed to look for daily evidence that God was in control, that virtue was rewarded and vice punished. But as things seemed only to worsen and suggest the absence of God, the Israelites began to wonder how God would win. Some attempted to resolve this problem by proposing that God was indeed active in the world in the exercise of his judgment, that God's activity was in allowing evil to pervade the world, and that he exercises his judgment by allowing it to bring destruction to the world and its inhabitants.

The New Testament Perspective

The New Testament does not share this negative evaluation of history because in Jesus Christ the expectations of the apocalyptic tradition began to be fulfilled. The coming of Jesus showed that God *was* active in the world, and even more, that he was active not only to judge but also to save, to establish his victory, to bring the firstfruits of the final destruction of evil, and to introduce his kingdom to bind the strong man and set the captives free. In Jesus the kingdom was like the mustard seed growing: its ultimate power and influence were out of all proportion to its beginnings. The kingdom was to be conceived as a present reality attacking evil, driving out demons, healing the sick, and forging new relationships of trust between alienated groups. Jesus also affirmed the apocalyptic tradition in speaking of the consummation of the kingdom as a future event that would include the vindication of his mission and the judgment of those who rejected it. The kingdom knows no final consummation in this world as it stands. It did not take its origins in this world, nor is it bound by the limitations of what is possible in it.[7] So pervasive is the disease of sin that the final consummation of the kingdom can mean nothing less than a new heaven and a new earth.

The hope in the triumph of the kingdom at the end is validated by the resurrection of Jesus. Thus Christians in New Testament times and ever since then have believed that what can be tasted now of the kingdom is but the firstfruits of the final harvest. The final harvest is not yet, but the fruits are apparent now. In the struggle against the dominion of evil, in the fruits of judgment and redemption, New Testament Christians experienced the true shalom, the true peace, that one day would prevail everywhere. They knew that not only did present events image the end but also that in Christ they tasted a firstfruit of the final end event.

Paul's letters stress that in Christ the dividing wall between Jews and Gentiles is broken down and that one new humanity is *already* formed (Eph. 2:11–12; Gal. 3:23–29; Rom. 15:7). One significance of Pentecost was that the Holy Spirit was poured out on *all* nations (Acts 2:7–8, 17; 10:47). While God made it clear that his message and promise were for all people, Paul still had to resist those who attempted to argue that God's Spirit was mediated only by the nation of Israel (Gal. 3:1–9). He asserted that all the nations receive the Spirit through their faith; and the Gentiles are inserted in the olive tree of Israel through Christ the Messiah (Rom. 11:17–27; Eph. 2:11–13). Israel's obstruction of God's purposes and his plans for the nation did not totally thwart God's intentions; he was able to fulfill them through other means related to but not dependent on Israel (Rom. 11:25–27). The great vision of the end sees all the nations bringing glory and honor into the new Jerusalem (Rev. 21:24–27).

Does the presence of the kingdom through Christ and its triumph at his return cancel the significance of the history of the Old Testament and of present history? In order to answer these questions it is critical to understand the relation between the history of Israel and the history of other nations. In the Old Testament, the history of Israel was demonstrably God's history. Divine and human activity were integrated as God ruled over and interacted with his people. It is clear that we can draw some distinctions between the story of God and his people on the one hand and the story of God and other nations on the other. But at the same time we must challenge, as the prophets always did, any *separation* between God's relationship with Israel and his relation with other peoples. Both relationships took place within *one* history, and there was always interaction between the two. God was equally concerned with all nations. His people were blessed in order that they might be a blessing to other nations, which God also used and for which he also had a purpose. This concern and purpose was not denied but was confirmed as the Gentiles entered the new Israel proclaimed by Jesus.

The invitation to the Gentiles took place despite their histories. That is, even though the Gentiles were 'aliens from the commonwealth of Israel' and entrance into the people of God was not a logical or necessary outcome of their history, they were invited nonetheless. And they came with their histories as nations intact, for they were not considered agglomerations of private and separate individuals but rather public, corporate bodies. As nations, they will lay the tribute of all of their members at the feet of Jesus, while the Jews also keep their national identity within the new Israel.

The new Israel affirms the ethnic identity of the Gentile Christians without dispensing with the old Israel. The old Israel will one day enter into the full inheritance of God's promises, but these promises are not exclusive. The Gentiles will enjoy those promises as well, because what in the Old Testament was particular to God's relationship with the old Israel is in the New Testament opened by Christ to all peoples. The Gentiles enter into covenant history and share the final fulfillment with the remnant of the old Israel as they bring their histories, the wealth of the nations, as tribute to the feet of Jesus.

We must never equate this covenant history with some sort of spiritual history. To say that when the Gentiles entered the church God was no longer concerned with their history in human society but only with their spiritual history, as some would do, is not at all biblical. The New Testament never spiritualized or individualized history. When the Gentiles entered the church they were incorporated into the people of God and took the history of Israel and the Messiah as theirs also, not as a replacement for but as an addition to their own national history.[8] So the history of Israel was the history of God's promise to all the nations, and the promise to Abraham was likewise a promise for blessing to all peoples.[9] Now in Christ all nations must relate their own histories to Israel's history and must incorporate themselves into it.[10] All nations must be grafted into the olive tree of Israel to participate in the blessings of redemption vouchsafed to it and through it. For Paul, the faithfulness of God in keeping his promises to Israel is the key issue on which the certainty of faith depends. If God does not keep his promises to Israel, how can he be trusted to keep his promises to anyone? Consequently, the final salvation of Israel (Rom. 9–11) is central to the argument of Paul's letter to the Romans: 'The consummation cannot come unless Israel is saved.'[11]

God's faithfulness depends on the fulfillment of his promises to Israel and, by implication, the promises to the other nations as well. The double historical reference into which all Gentile Christians are called to enter is crucial. The temptation is to neglect it and opt for a monohistorical approach. Some Indian Christians, for example, in seeking an authentic identity, tend to take their Indian history as an absolute and see the Old Testament as a mere example, as only a pattern for how God may act in Indian history. If we absolutize our own history in this way, however, we lock ourselves into the ghetto of an ethnocentric church that has no necessary relationships with other 'churches' as part of the body of Christ. It would be sufficient unto itself in terms of its own historical identity and self-understanding, but it would not meet the demands of Christ. No matter what nationality we may be, the Old Testament does not say to us 'this is akin to how God acted in your history' but rather 'this *is* your history.' Old Testament history is a formative part of all Christian history,[12] and so we might say that all Christians participate in two histories – both Judeo-Christian and ethnic. The former is a history for all nations, the bearer of God's promise to the world, and it is only when we see this in balance with a particular ethnic history that we can truly understand the nature of the church.

Evangelicals sometimes fall into one of two traps here. Either they so identify with the new Israel that they forget about their own national history and lose their context in concrete existence, or they make the history of the new Israel subordinate to their own history and produce a national religion. Both the tendency to allow Jewish Christian history to obliterate all other history and the temptation to ignore it are monohistorical. The solution is, as always, to return to Jesus Christ. If we take him seriously, we will recognize that we do live within two histories, neither of which denies the other. Indeed, we cannot live a fully human existence wholly within one to the exclusion of the other. This dual history is united under the umbrella of the kingdom of God, which fulfills God's promise to the nations mediated through the history of his people. People from all races with their histories find their fulfillment in the consummated kingdom, when the wealth of the nations is brought into the new Jerusalem.

With a heritage of hundreds of years of Christian history, the Western church has tended to neglect the task of relating God's particular activity in the history of his church and his people to his more general activity in all human society. The Western church has tended to see Western cultural history and Christian history as one and the same, and it has consequently lost at times the ability to distinguish Christianity from non-Christian civil religion. In the Two-Thirds World it is much more difficult to do this simply because Christianity has not been a formative cultural and historical force here as it has been in the West – the situation here is more akin to that in Europe before Christianity became the dominant and accepted religion. Christianity in the Two-Thirds World does not have the inertia that it has in the First World, and consequently believers here are constantly seeking to define for the first time the place Christianity must play within and in distinction to culture. The situation in the non-Western world makes it impossible for believers to accept unthinkingly Western ideas about the relation of God's activity among his people to that throughout history – even if those ideas are valid in the context of the West.

The history of mission in Africa, Asia, and Latin America has often been written as if it were little more than the expansion of the Protestant churches of Europe and America. African churches have been pushed to perceive their histories as part of Western Christianity and to submerge their relationship to their own African histories. As we mentioned before, a biblical perspective encourages us to relate the history of Africa to that of Israel, and to draw the continuity between God's action in Israelite and African history. African churches are unified with Western churches not in their acceptance of Western forms of Christianity but in their acceptance along with the churches of the Western forms of Christianity but in their acceptance along with the churches of the West of the entire stream of Judeo-Christian history – even as they retain their own cultural history. This process is crucial for the discovery of African, Asian, or Latin American Christian identity.[13] We shall see that it is also crucial for accounting for the influence our historical and cultural contexts have on the way we perceive God at work in history.

The Messiah and History

Jesus the Messiah is the fulcrum on which the continuity and discontinuity of the Old and New Testaments turns. As David Bosch writes, ' "Geographically" Jesus journeys to the temple, to Jerusalem and his death; "theologically" he is bound for the nations. In the final analysis he himself would take the place of Jerusalem and the temple (John 2:19–21). As the "New Jerusalem" he himself becomes the place of encounter with the nations.'[14] Thus Jesus is not the Messiah of Israel alone, or of the new Israel alone. His kingdom is not to be identified with the church. Much more than that, it is the establishment of God's rule over the cosmos, the whole creation (Eph. 1:21–22). Even though the church is a sign of God's rule, his plan to govern all things established in the Old Testament is not fulfilled in the church alone. Its fulfillment is a universal one, as his rule extends over all creation and all nations. God's present activity in the world, in part demonstrated by his care for the church, gives us reason to see his kingdom building activity in the history of all the nations and human society.

The sense that history was now the scene of God's activity impelled the mission of the New Testament Christians and marked them off from other groups who still believed that God had deserted history. David Bosch writes that

> if the present is empty, as the Pharisees, Essenes, and Zealots believed, then you can only flee into the memory of a glorious past recorded in codes (Pharisees), or you can with folded arms sit and wait for God's vengeance upon your enemies (Essenes), or you can play God yourself by violently liquidating the empty the present, thus trying to make the utopian future a present reality (Zealots), or you can enter into an uncomfortable compromise with the status quo (Sadducees). But if the present is filled; . . . if 'the kingdom of God has already come upon you' (Luke 11:20) . . . those who partake of this new history . . . can only let themselves be taken along by Christ into the future, not as soldiers fighting in the vanguard, but as 'captives in Christ's triumphal procession' (2 Cor. 2:14).[15]

Some views of the relation between the kingdom and history make a sharp distinction between the mission of Jesus and that of his church. Some theologians believe that early Christians and Jesus himself thought that the apocalypse was imminent. But when the expected apocalypse did not come, the church found itself with a task unforeseen by Jesus. Arthur Johnston took such a position in 1982 when he wrote that there is 'a basic discontinuity between the Old and New Testaments, and the kingdom mission of Jesus is largely unrelated to the visible church which possesses an interim mission until the restoration of the historical Israel by the second coming of Jesus.'[16]

For Johnston, 'the kingdom of God was present in a unique way in history by the incarnation,' and this is not continued in the mission of the church and present historical experience.[17] If this view of the discontinuity of Jesus' mission with that of the church is correct, then history would once again be empty: it could not be filled with the presence of the kingdom as the Gospels record. Bosch notes, however, that this position is made untenable by certain pivotal events in New Testament times. The resurrection of Christ and the coming of the Holy Spirit assured the early Christians that the present was still filled with the power and activity of God. These events prevented them from attempting either to retreat into the golden past of the unrepeatable experience of Jesus' ministry or to escape into another world with eyes only on the parousia. God made it clear to his people that they were irrevocably involved with the world and therefore with mission, so it made sense to live – still within this world – according to the standards of the 'coming age.'[18]

Does our refusal to segregate God's work among his own and other peoples into 'sacred' and 'secular' history mean that we deny any difference between special revelation and general revelation? God works in many different ways in different histories, but always with the same goal. If we used a distinction between sacred and secular history to define the difference between special revelation and general revelation we would be assuming that God's special revelation is confined to his activities with either Israel or the church. Such an assumption is not biblical. In the Bible God used historical events at Sodom and Gomorrah, Nineveh, Babylon, Assyria, and Rome to reveal himself. His special revelation does not create a sacred history of his own. God identifies certain normal human histories as revelatory of himself in a special, privileged, and authoritative way. He reveals himself in all history, but some revelation is special in that it helps us to understand that historical revelation and see it more clearly. Although it was directed to Israel and the church and was proclaimed by them, special revelation is never confined to them – it does not create a sacred history in contradistinction to profane history. To separate sacred from profane history and to state that special revelation is the only place that God acts is to propose that God has a plan for one people that is wholly different from his plan for the rest of humanity.

While it is true that the destiny of the nations in God's purpose is linked with that of Israel (Rom. 9–11), we must emphasize again that it is not mediated through that people. Instead, all nations have equal access to God through the Messiah, who is Lord of both Israel and the nations. We cannot state that God's activity with Israel is revelation while that with the other nations is mere providence. There is no such distinction between revelation and the rest of history, because God was involved with Israel, Assyria, and Philistia all at once, in both their political and religious histories, and he will rule them all directly through his Messiah.

The Millennial Vision in Relation to Creation and Fall

Obviously the kingdom is not yet, however. It is not complete; evil still exerts its power in the world; and humans are still fallen from the position of honor granted them at the creation. How does God deal with the fall of humanity and the power of evil? Is it merely wishful thinking to believe that he is still at work in human history to restore humanity to the stewardship of creation? Not at all. The New Testament tells us that God's activity in history is now focused on the Messiah to whom Israel and the nations owe allegiance. God *is* back on the stage of history in Jesus Christ, in the Holy Spirit, and in the church. The rift between sacred and profane history is healed. God does not deny that the struggle continues, that his people are still awaiting the final victory, but at the same time he proclaims that victory has already begun – in our world – in Christ the Messiah. In the process of judgment and redemption, God has already established the foundations of his kingdom.

God's activity in the world provokes ever more virulent opposition from the forces of antichrist and evil as they see the hour of their banishment coming. The devil roams around 'like a roaring lion, seeking some one to devour' (1 Pet. 5:8), and Paul warns of 'the prince of the power of the air, the spirit that is now at work in the sons of disobedience' (Eph. 2:2). How do we reconcile this with his affirmation that Christ now rules above all heavenly rulers, authorities, powers, and dominions (Eph. 1:21)? It may be helpful to say that Christ is center stage while the lion roars offstage trying to get on. Christ has become the central element of history, and Satan has been thrown aside. Though we may not see Christ at center stage, we know from the Scriptures that he is there. The New Testament confirms that Jesus, not Caesar, is Lord of history, a confession by the power of the Holy Spirit (1 Cor. 12:3). If we only let Christ be de jure and not de facto ruler now, it may be that we are looking too much at the problems of the context and taking the roar of the lion for substance. Those problems are only evidence of the lion's roar and not of his rule. This is the paradox of the kingdom: the devil still roars even while Christ is already Lord.

After the Resurrection, the disciples asked Jesus whether he would 'at this time restore the kingdom to Israel' (Acts 1:6–7). He answered them and said, 'It is not for you to know times or seasons which the Father has fixed by his own authority. But you shall receive power

when the Holy Spirit has come upon you; and you shall be my witnesses in Jerusalem and in all Judea and Samaria and to the end of the
earth' (Acts 1:7–8). His answer was not an evasion, nor an indication
that he was not invested by God with dominion over the world.
Rather, it was an attempt to change the disciples' expectations for the
kingdom of God. The disciples thought that the kingdom would consist in the restoration of the Davidic kingdom to Israel. Jesus' reply
was that his kingdom was not an ethnic kingdom, limited in scope,
but the rule of the Lord extended 'to the end of the earth.' He promised that the Holy Spirit would come so that the disciples would
witness to that kingdom and its presence in Judea, Samaria, and the
end of the earth.

Different biblical traditions about the fulfillment of God's work in
the world are in tension with each other. Prophetic themes stress
God's action within history that leads to a final consummation. These
themes do not necessarily tie God to historical processes but see his
activity as charging history with significance. Apocalyptic themes on
the other hand stress God's work behind the scenes, so to speak, in
another realm beyond human history. What we experience in this
world are consequences of decisions and activities that take place elsewhere. While neither tradition is wrong, neither tells the whole story;
and to concentrate on one to the exclusion of the other can lead to an
inaccurate view of the way God really acts. An overemphasis on the
prophetic tradition can produce the optimistic idea that history holds
God within its process and keeps him ever present. On the other hand,
an overemphasis on apocalyptic can lead to a very pessimistic view of
the present – and of the future until the eschaton. Apocalyptic can
become so concerned with God's judgment and so taken up with a
higher realm that it reduces this world to a mere waiting room for the
end to come. Our job is to be aware of this tension between valid biblical themes and to show what both traditions at their best are trying to
affirm.

In our analysis of the relation of the kingdom of God to the historical process, as elsewhere, we must be careful to keep these two
traditions in balance. If we do not, we may fall into a view that is
overly pessimistic – for example, the view that the historical process
is in a continual state of deterioration that will continue until some
future time when God will intervene to bring dramatic and final
change. According to this view, the world today bears few signs of
the kingdom – and to know the kingdom as it is represented in the

world now is not to know it as it will be. The real kingdom is a new heaven wholly beyond our knowledge. What matters is the arrival of this kingdom, and consequently everything else becomes a lesser concern.

The Activity of God in History

Those who hold this view affirm God's work in human history only when his sovereignty, grace, and perfection can be clearly seen: in experiences of new birth, deliverance, or guidance. For the rest, they consider God to be absent; and they hold that God excludes humans from participating in his kingdom work. By instituting the kingdom in the incarnation of Christ, they say, God seemed to say that those who hope to contribute to this divine-human work must follow Christ's example of perfection. But God does not ask us to model ourselves on Jesus' divine nature. Rather, we are to focus on his mission, with all its ambiguities, misunderstandings, and apparent imperfections. Jesus knows that we will all fail him in the end, but that does not mean that we cannot participate with him in the building of the kingdom. Indeed, he chose to include among his disciples a leader who denied him – not to mention a traitor who handed him over to those who would kill him. Jesus knows that we are children of Adam; but through our adoption as sons and daughters, through our union with the New Adam, we are called to take part in his mission. Though the church often seems rife with quarrels, disagreements, and backslidings, it is still through this body – Christ's body – that his mission is continued in history, guided by the Holy Spirit. In this mission God, by his sovereignty, grace, and perfection, takes and uses our human imperfections and ambiguities to fulfill his purpose.

The Perfect and the Imperfect

To assume that everything 'spiritual' must be perfect is to imply that an experience of redemption cannot be mingled with imperfection. However, the Scriptures do not imply that redeemed people will be perfect in the world. God will judge our response to him: have we built with gold, silver, wood, grass, or straw on the foundation of Christ (1 Cor. 3:10–15)? We cannot take salvation for granted; the parables of the talents and the separation of sheep and goats and the teaching on grace, sin, and righteousness (Rom. 5–7) all show that God will judge our response to his gifts. So redemption is not a mystical experience that is perfect and cannot be removed. Instead, it comes only in a relationship of forgiveness, love, and obedience to God that is subject to his judgment.

We cannot separate our spiritual experiences or our relationship with God from our life in the world and our human relationships. The individual is called as God forms a community and a people.[19] His forgiveness depends on our forgiveness of others (Matt. 18:35): if we do not love our brother we cannot love God (1 John 4:12, 20), and we forfeit our inheritance. Love of God and love of neighbor explain each other and give the meaning of the law.[20] No law of God enjoins us to relate to him independently of a relationship with other people.[21] His laws demand rather that we live in union with other people even as we live in union with him. Life in union with Christ is life in union with others in Christ (Gal. 3:26–28).

This union is made visible in the world in the church, where true relationships in Christ are characterized by love, forgiveness, compassion, generosity, and patience. These values are 'heavenly' in contrast to 'earthly', because they will last (Col. 3:1–17). Even though these relationships are imperfect and will be judged, God can still use them in their present state to mediate his redemption and demonstrate his concern for us. God's grace in redemption takes these imperfect human relationships, redeems them, and uses them in care and love. Relationships redeemed in the church will be fully transformed only when the bride is reunited with the bridegroom; but now, while we are still in this world, these relationships are a real experience of the future kingdom. Heavenly values of the kingdom are shown in earthly bonds – between husband and wife, parent and child, and master and slave (Col. 3:18–22).

Heaven and Earth

Just as imperfect relationships in the church can provide some real experience of the kingdom, other imperfect experiences in society outside the church can also demonstrate some signs of the kingdom.[22] 'If the kingdom is limited to the spiritual relation of men to God,' writes George Eldon Ladd, 'the consummation of the kingdom would be achieved by the final inclusion of all men in the kingdom when every last individual on earth has accepted God's rule.'[23] To view the kingdom as wholly spiritual is to separate what God has joined together in his creation. As Andrew Lincoln points out, heaven and earth must not be separated, for they are one structure in God's creation.[24] Not only were both created by the same God, but both were affected by the Fall: 'For in him all the fulness of God was pleased to dwell, and through him to reconcile to himself all things, whether on earth or in heaven, making peace by the blood of his cross' (Col. 1:19–20). The heavenly world is populated now by spiritual forces of wickedness that believers are to fight against (Eph. 3:10; 6:12). Heaven too is involved in the battles of the present age, and war in heaven will go on until victory brings in the fullness of the new age with its reconciled cosmos. 'Above all,' Lincoln writes, 'heaven and earth are shown to be inseparably connected by the redemption which God has accomplished in Christ'[25] (cf. Col. 1:19–20; Eph. 1:9–10, 22ff.; 4:10). The important point is that heaven is not the place of perfection that will one day replace earth. Heaven is not set over against earth. Both form one structure of created reality, partake in the results of human sin, and will experience redemption in Christ.

Humanity can respond in two different ways to what God has made. 'The sinful response brought about disunity in the cosmos, and this direction of disobedience can be called "earthly."'... In Philippians 3:19 and Colossians 3:2, 5, "earthly" is contrasted to heavenly and takes on the connotation of sinful, with the earth being viewed as the primary setting of fallen creation.'[26] In Colossians, the things of the earth include the practices of the old human nature (3:5–9), the indulgence of the flesh (2:23), and life in the world with its bondage to elemental spirits (2:20). The direction of obedience, exemplified by the obedience of Christ (Rom. 5:19), is linked with the heavenly (1 Cor. 15:47). Insofar as believers continue to live in Christ in response to God's offer of salvation, they are blessed with spiritual blessings in the heavenly places (Eph. 1:3), can be called 'heavenly' themselves (1 Cor. 15:48), and are encouraged to seek the things that are above (Col. 3:1).

Now in union with Christ we experience the substantial restoration of the unity of the whole cosmos, which expresses the restoration of all things under the rule of God. Lincoln adds that

> because they belong to Christ, all things belong to believers, including the world (1 Cor. 3:22). Colossians demonstrates that it is because believers

participate in the triumph of the exalted Christ over the powers that they have been set free to use this world and its structures. . . . Since their Lord is in heaven their life is to be governed by the heavenly commonwealth (Phil. 3:20). . . . Paul does not believe that real life is in this other world and that as a consequence life on earth has relatively little significance (Col. 3). . . . The apostle can insist both on the necessity of heavenly-mindedness and on the fulness he expects to see in the personal, domestic, communal and social aspects of Christian living. The quality of the concentration on the things above where Christ is will ensure that the present sphere of his rule will not remain simply in heaven but will be demonstrated in the lives of his people on earth.[27]

When Paul writes of the heavenly things, he is expressing humanity's restored relationship of obedience to and reconciliation with the Creator, which is part of the total reconciliation of the whole creation. He is describing a relationship with God that embraces and affects life in both this world and the next. He is not speaking of a sphere of existence that sometime in the future will invade this world but of a relationship with God that is both possible now and will last forever. This relationship is expressed in a lifestyle that gives precedence to the values that Jesus demonstrated in his life and taught in the Sermon on the Mount. God vindicated these values, the ethics of the kingdom, in the Resurrection, and he promises they will last forever.

The Conscious Confession of Christ

To limit God's work to an inner, individual experience and to relate only our spiritual life to the future kingdom is to assert that we experience now a lesser Christ than the one who does and will reign in glory. This 'two kingdoms view' – the kingdom of the world as wholly separate from the kingdom of God – falls down on its Christology and thus its doctrine of God by suggesting that what we experience of Christ and his kingdom now is but a pale imitation that has little continuity with the future reality. The kingdom, as it exists even now, is not an individual spiritual entity. It is corporate, and it permeates with its influence all of historical life. There are many activities, structures, and movements in the world that already share in God's saving work by his grace. God's salvation has redeemed the human race, broken the power of evil, and created a new humanity – already, though the process is not yet complete. The world is already changed by Christ's victory on the cross and the Resurrection, which exalts him as Lord of all.

One need not submit personally to the lordship of Christ to be able to experience this grace and this transformation in one's life. For example, in India many women who do not confess Christ may experience the fruit of the kingdom in the transformation of their status in society. Yet this transformation is still part of God's work of breaking down the dividing wall of hostility between separated groups, of creating in himself one new humanity in Christ in which there is neither male nor female. God has used the church in India in its witness to Christ to change the status of women and other oppressed groups in society. Those who benefit from this work live transformed lives to some extent – they are no longer the same people they would have been. Transformation is not salvation, though. Those who do not confess Christ are not saved by the kingdom in this world; only obedience to and faith in the King can provide salvation.[28] But even without that confession of faith, many still participate in the transformation that the kingdom brings. Christ healed ten lepers, all of whom participated in the blessings of the kingdom; yet only one demonstrated any faith and returned to thank him (Luke 17:11–19).

In the confession of Jesus as Lord, which is the heart of the kingdom experience inspired by the Holy Spirit, there is freedom for Christ's lordship to operate, to be expressed, and to be experienced in its fullness. On the other hand, Christ's lordship may be evident in many other areas of life – in the struggle for economic justice, for example – though it cannot be confined to any one of them. The Holy Spirit's activity of applying the lordship of Christ may begin with economic justice, but it breaks through to infuse all of life with the lordship of Christ so that all people will profess his name and bow to him as Lord of all.

The Spiritualization of History

Because God desires to rule over history in this world, we have to seek a statement of the relation of the kingdom to history that does not spiritualize history or relegate it to insignificance. The spiritualization of history is a fundamentally Hindu idea, based on a monistic view of the cosmos in which the only reality is God. Everything else, including humanity, is nonreality or illusion until it achieves the desired goal of union with God. History, too, is unreality, and thus God cannot be experienced within history. Consequently, any desire to approach God must be furthered by the denial of history in the attempt to depart the plane of unreality for that of reality. The Hindu desire is to spiritualize history and make it and human life ahistorical (in the Western sense) and mythological. God and human history are and remain separate.

Any attempt to spiritualize the history of Jesus and the kingdom – isolating it from the Old Testament, from secular society, or from the church – by creating a 'sacred' history devalues human history because it is regarded as no longer truly real. This sacred history then becomes ever more divorced from humanity, and Jesus himself becomes a wholly mythological character akin to the deities of Hinduism. As David Jenkins writes, 'If worshippers of God do not really believe that he is to be encountered in and through the actualities of daily living and contemporary history, then he is indeed merely a cultic object sustained by a "myth" which works effectively only as long as the myth dominates culture, but which is simply a mere story maintained by "believers" against the realities of the world, once culture changes.'[29]

Those who affirm that only Jesus and his kingdom are truly real remove him from ordinary history, spiritualize his history, and so make him a 'myth.' By asserting that Jesus and his kingdom are truly real by virtue of being removed from ordinary history, they directly deny the message of the Bible, which states that the 'Word became flesh' and 'in him dwelt the fulness of God bodily.'[30]

It is interesting to note that when this 'mythologized' Jesus is the subject of evangelical preaching in India, he elicits little response. For the Hindus he is little different from the thirty-three million other gods in their pantheon, so they place him there along with the rest. But when Christians proclaim that Jesus and the kingdom are at work now, in human history, through healing miracles, social change, and social development then there is significant response.[31]

The anthropologist Paul Hiebert suggests there are three levels in anyone's worldview. First is the level of cosmic gods and forces that are involved in the origin of the universe and are at the heart of the questions that permeate all of life: What happens at death? What is our fate and destiny? The second level is concerned with intermediate forces – demons, witches, and saints. The third level is the level of interaction between persons and of interaction between people and nature through science. The second level – the level of the intermediate powers and forces – is very powerful among poor communities whose life is often dominated by religion.[32] No area of life is secular in the strictest sense; all things are under the control and influence of these intermediate powers. People in these cultures see life as a constant interaction between the human and the level just above. Though this level may be considered the domain of forces both good and evil, in many cultures it is dominated by the evil forces. Day to day life is then lived in fear. People attempt to manipulate these forces to their benefit or to propitiate them when they have been offended. Sin, as a rebellion against the cosmic God above all, has little significance.[33]

In Christian mission, it is necessary that the rule of the one true God be proclaimed in all areas and levels of life. If God is proclaimed as being high above the world and human concerns, those to whom the mission is directed may hold on to their existing beliefs about intermediate deities and the need to propitiate them to get pragmatic results in the healing of worldly ills. For example, Christian mission has often preached a cosmic God and practiced medical science for healing. But if the level of principalities and powers is not addressed adequately, if God is not continually proclaimed as the author of all healing, then the new believers may ascribe that healing to the influence of those intermediary deities. As far as they are concerned, the propitiation of a local deity or demon to heal a sick child does not contradict at all adherence to the transcendent God of Christianity.

Both the process of demythologization advocated by some Christians and the spiritualization of history practiced by others demonstrate the effects of the Enlightenment on Christian mission worldwide. The first proposes that the supernatural cannot be real simply because science and rationality can tell us nothing about it. The only reality there is is the cosmos, which we must deal with as we can. The second process, the spiritualization of history, states on the contrary that a supernatural God is real but the world is not. Each process results in a secularism that denies the interaction of God with human history.

To push God out of our human history is to accept the rise of paganization and totalitarianism. It also turns realism about human sin into pessimism about the human condition. Jenkins states that

a properly Christian doctrine of sin must be placed firmly within a Christian understanding of creation and redemption. We are to perceive what sin is in relation to the Glory of God, his commitment to the fulfillment of creation and saving work in Christ to redeem, restore and sum up all things. Realism concerning evil distortion and failure is demanded but pessimism is exorcized. Pessimism arises out of the basic theological mistake of pushing God out of history and out of the mistake in discipleship which will not share in God's risk of getting close to men and women in their actual struggles, sufferings and hopes.[34]

How Far Is the Kingdom Continuous with History?

The biblical understanding of the new earth depends on the belief in God's continuing action in the world. An indispensable part of the new reality, of the new order, is a consummated and perfected human history. The work of God in creation, and the work of humanity as his steward in history, will be taken up and completed in the new earth. Furthermore, the Old Testament clearly proclaims that our earth, not some other place, is to be the site of the consummation of history. Because Christ affirmed the continuity of the Old Testament and the New, we as his followers must include in our eschatology the hope of the transformed earth. The New Testament continues the Old Testament view of one history by universalizing the history of Israel and making it the olive tree into which all Gentile nations are grafted in order to participate in redemption.

While we may see this earth as the site for the future consummation, what continuity is there in the New Testament between present history and the kingdom? We have seen the dangers of asserting that there is none: religion becomes otherworldly and believers seek either merely to endure or to escape this world. But does this allow us to move in the opposite direction to say that certain historical events have some sort of 'kingdom value'? Do historical happenings help to bring the kingdom that God prepares and will establish in the parousia? In discussing this question, José Míguez Bonino argues that we must seek an answer in terms of causality. He fears that too often the desire to protect God's initiative – and the fear of claiming initiative for ourselves – reduces our view of historical action to a minimum. We may see in history images that remind us of the kingdom, but we do not claim that they have any actual significance for its coming among us. This fear of regarding any human action as an activity of the kingdom means that historical action of both right and left are equally valuable – or invaluable – as far as the coming of the kingdom is concerned. Neither is effective, we might say, so there is nothing to distinguish between them.

Is there some way for us to move beyond this fear while still recognizing the danger of absolutizing our human action? Can we map out a conception of the relationship between the kingdom of God and human history that is biblical and that enables us to commit ourselves to pragmatic action in history as a project of the coming kingdom?[35]

Key to a biblical answer is the resurrection of the body. The body is resurrected so that who we are in our present historical life will be recognizable in the next. Our identities as physical human beings are vitally important in the coming kingdom. Yet at the same time, we will be totally transformed – not to disfigure or weaken our bodily life, but to fulfill and perfect it by eliminating all corruptibility and weakness. This is in great contrast to Eastern mysticism. God does not propose to 'rescue' our spiritual elements from the bodily experience and personal identity of physical life. Rather, in the resurrection of the body God proclaims the total redemption of humanity, the fulfillment of bodily life cleansed from self-deception and self-seeking (Matt. 22:29–32; Phil. 3:20–21; 1 John 3:2; Rev. 7:13–17).

According to Paul, what we do in our bodies in everyday life is vitally important. We will be perfected only after our resurrection. Yet before that we are to live in Christ; that is, we are to mirror his bodily perfection, putting off all things of the flesh and donning the fruits of the Spirit, above all 'love, which binds everything together in perfect harmony' (Col. 3:14). We must attempt to model the life of the kingdom within the structures of history, as masters, slaves, wives, husbands, parents, and children (Col. 3–4). Because Christ has risen and brought in a new realm of love, deeds of love bear the marks of the new age and will find lasting fulfillment when that age is fully with us at the return of Christ.

This new age does not deny history but eliminates its corruption, frustration, and sin in order to bring to fulfillment the communal life of humanity. Any deed in any sphere of life, be it social, political, economic, or religious, will remain if it is marked by the love of the new order. This fulfillment is not a matter of gradual evolution, however. We do not see in society a continual progression to a state of perfection. The pathway by which history finds its consummation in the kingdom is paved with suffering, conflict, and judgment. The kingdom at its consummation will redeem and transform deeds of love done in history. Though these deeds will be fulfilled only in the total transformation at the return of Christ, now in the present they are not mere reflections or foreshadowings of the kingdom within history but the actual presence and operation of the kingdom already begun, however imperfect and partial. The kingdom is present now, but its fulfillment is still not yet.

Protests against expressions such as 'building the kingdom' are valid as a protection against a naive optimism and as a validation of the sovereignty of the divine initiative. But they are usually cast in an unbiblical view of God as a preprogrammed force who produces certain events like the Incarnation and the return of Christ without reference to what is going on in human history. We must remember that God is also active *within* our history – he does not just impinge on it at widely separated intervals – and he calls us to act with him. So the parables that serve to illuminate the growth of the kingdom, those of the sower, the mustard seed, and the leaven, for example, have biblical and theological warrant.

If we adopt this perspective, the main question is not the whereabouts or signs of the kingdom in today's history, but, 'How can I take part in, express, and produce the quality of personal and corporate life that will be fulfilled in God's kingdom?' Such action will involve both proclamation and deeds. Both the announcement of the kingdom and action in keeping with its quality are eschatologically significant, and neither can be reduced to the other. There is a tension between them, between what names this future and what corresponds to its reality, that cannot be reduced this side of the full realization of the kingdom. To avoid absolutizing any of our human action in the name of the kingdom, we must have recourse neither to idealism nor divine politics, but to the best human politics possible – and that will always be open to debate.

The Christian faith stimulates us to look for the actualization of the kingdom in history in terms of justice, equal access to the creation that God intended for all, and the creation of human community through love, worship, work, and play. In the light of the present and coming kingdom, Christians can invest their lives in the building of a historical order in the certainty that neither they nor their efforts are meaningless or lost. The confession of the resurrection of believers is not a selfish desire for immortality, a recompense for sufferings, or a wish-fulfillment, but rather the affirmation of the triumph of God's love, of the fulfillment of humanity's stewardship of creation, and of the vindication of all struggles against evil.[36]

The Option of Suffering

In seeking options for historical engagement, the clear Christian option set forth in the Scriptures demands a life of suffering. In his life, on the cross, and in his resurrection, Jesus' suffering was God's way of bringing change and God's instrument of redemption. While salvation comes only through Christ's suffering, as we share in that suffering we may serve as vehicles of God's change and reconciliation in the world. But this is not to say that we must idealize suffering. Indeed, nothing indicates more clearly the imperfection and corruption of human society than the sufferings we experience as its members and the persecution we endure as the church. The New Testament does not regard these sufferings as apocalyptic messianic woes that have to be endured before the end comes. Instead, the presence of the kingdom in history impels Christians to address the injustices caused by humanity and, as far as possible, to remove the sicknesses of the sick and the poverty of the poor.

Views that see the presence of suffering as confirmation that this world is bound for destruction tend to cut off any impulse toward addressing personal and social evil. By no means is all suffering to be endured as we await the final consummation. Some suffering will be irremovable, such as deformities, psychological hurts, and incurable diseases. But we can only identify the irremovable ones in the process of trying to remove them. Far from being an experience of imperfection and evil that cuts us off from the love of God (see Rom. 8, esp. vv. 38–39), suffering is experienced with Christ (Phil. 3:10–11); it is a channel of his resurrection life (2 Cor. 4:7–18); and it is the means of overcoming the powers of evil (Rev. 12:11). Sufferings in union with Christ are by God's grace both a real *experience* of redemption and a *means* of redemption.

Jesus changed history through his suffering – much more than through his miracles, which stood as signs of the presence of the kingdom. His message was 'Take up your cross and follow me.' In response to that, the church's witness to redemption must not be to escape from the world, nor to resort to an isolated mystical experience that cannot be touched by the world and suffering. Rather, believers must attempt to witness in the sufferings involved in living out redemption. Redemption, then, can be a present reality; it can be mingled with imperfection and known in imperfect suffering relationships. It can even mediate redemption to others.

The experience of suffering always reminds us that the kingdom cannot be consummated in this world as it stands, nor even in the perfection of the 'spiritual.' We know this because the consummation promises a world from which all suffering has been removed (Rev. 21). The continuing experience of suffering in this world thus prevents us from the triumphalism of both 'super-spirituality' and utopian expectations.

Suffering implies and presupposes conflict: it resides in injustice, and we bring it on ourselves as we challenge those situations of injustice and so unearth the conflict within them. Yet such sufferings are 'in Christ.' God is at work in them bringing his change to the heart of their imperfection. As we engage in the struggle for justice, as we undergo suffering for God's sake, we are not constructing the kingdom of God here on earth by seeking to create perfect structures and model situations that can be proclaimed 'foretastes of heaven.' The sign of Christian development and social change is not the New Jerusalem but the cross.

The struggle may make us weary, but the suffering of the cross is victory, not defeat. Bound up in this suffering is the reality of the Resurrection and its promise of life (2 Cor. 4). While the Resurrection does not promise that the angels will come to open our prison gates in a miraculous deliverance, it is a sign that all suffering is to be borne in the promise of ultimate vindication and triumph. Such experiences of suffering and resurrection in the conflict involved in social change are, in their ambiguities and imperfections, true experiences of the kingdom of God at work in human history.

It is not easy to see God at work in the midst of suffering and conflict. It is not always easy for those who suffer to feel his presence. It is easier to say that he is not at work here now but that he will triumph over suffering sometime in the future. We are tempted to project all change into the future, to wait passively for God's powerful solution, and in the meantime to rejoice in the 'spiritual' aspect of 'heaven' here. Isn't it easier to see blessings and success as signs of belonging to that final kingdom? Isn't it easier to see demonstrations of the kingdom's presence in miracles and other events beyond our control? Isn't it easier to identify right entirely with our cause and to go forward in an uncompromising crusade? It is much more difficult to see God at work in suffering, in a situation that is ambiguous and provisional because of our involvement. Yet we have the promise that just because God is in it this work is not ultimately futile.

Our survey of the relationship between the kingdom and history shows that our vision of the future molds and determines the content of our mission. Our different contexts and commitments in the world give different emphases and meanings to the same biblical material. Our vision of the future sometimes leads us either to put God's spiritual work in a plane wholly and eternally above history or to see the kingdom restricted to certain actions within history. Some put the spiritual above the historical and others seem to lose sight of the spiritual completely and find the kingdom wholly of the world.

Perhaps it is best to view the kingdom as a higher plane that intersects the imperfections of the historical order. The ambiguities and provisionalities of history do not stop God acting through them; yet we cannot absolutize these imperfections and sufferings because we know that there is much more to this plane than what intersects our history. This higher plane of the kingdom gives meaning and hope to the impermanence of history without making it permanent. It affirms the reality of our personal relationship with God and our future glorious inheritance and consummation in the future. It reminds us of the personal dimension of history and of the incompleteness of the historical experience. By establishing the presence of his kingdom not just in the church but in history, God commits himself to work through history to bring change, the results of which will be incorporated into his future kingdom. With this assurance, the option for involvement in society is chiefly one of suffering to bring change.

We are not simply following a predetermined countdown to a final destruction. However ominous the signs of the times, they are not just of judgment and destruction. The judgment of the old age is always in conjunction with the foundation of the new age that breaks into it. The interim and imperfect nature of our work in the world is not a mark of the corruption of a world that will be destroyed but a sign of the new day to come, an indication of the new earth prepared for us by God that is already active within imperfect human history and will one day come in all its glory.

This view of the future saves us from both unalloyed optimism and unrelieved pessimism. Our works of reconciliation will all be judged and found lacking. But once they go through the sieve of God's judgment and grace, they will participate in his final kingdom. Historical events do not make up the building blocks of the kingdom: they are provisional. The world situation that looks so hopeless at times will be renewed and perfected by God. Our view of our action in the world should be neither a utopian dream nor a mere holding operation, waiting for the King to come. We should see ourselves as going about on the King's business in his world, caring for his property with the aid of his Counselor, and preparing for his arrival when he will evaluate and perfect everything.

Implications for Development

How then will we be able to detect where God works and involves himself in the ambiguities of human history? One clear guideline is where we see the values of the kingdom replacing values not of God in persons, movements, and structures. God is thus at work in every corner of the world and history.

Where we see *human dignity* being affirmed and people discovering a sense of self-worth, self-acceptance, and a sense of having something to contribute to the world and others, there God is at work.

Where we see that people have the *freedom* to act according to their conscience without threat from others who control their actions and thus their attitudes, there God is at work.

Where people are able to make their own contribution to the life of society, especially in *participation in decisions* that affect them in the family, in the community, in religious matters, and in political structures, there God is at work.

Where people can live in *hope*, a sense that it is possible and worthwhile to plan for the future, where they can experience the *respect* of the community, and where there is *sharing* that enhances, not reduces, the humanity of the community, there God is at work.

Where people are committed to the *struggle against evil and injustice,* and where there is a sense of *equity*, there God is at work.

Where women, the weak, and the handicapped find roles that give them dignity and *equality*, and where their needs get priority and power is shared to benefit all and dehumanize none, there God is at work.

Where we find a *sense of God's presence, a recognition of the power of evil* without and within, and true *humility* about the limitations of our knowledge in the face of God's wisdom, there God is at work.

We should also look for God's work and influence as people make decisions, share information, help each other in emergencies, look for and work at jobs, attend social functions, direct the course of their families, help the under-privileged and marginalized, use resources, and worship. We should see the expression of God's work in social and family structures, in the political and government sphere, and in religious institutions. The temptation is to see God at work only in values, but he also works to transform structures to promote the values of the kingdom. While it is possible to be content with the expression of the values of the kingdom in the lives of individuals or small groups, if these values do not find structural expression they cannot bring lasting change. So development work must also focus on structures, both to transform them and to bring to light those that already reflect the values of the kingdom.

Appendix

The Vision of the Kingdom in the History of the Church

A strong tradition in the early church (linked with Montanus, Tertullian, and Irenaeus) stressed that Christ would come to reign on this earth. But from the time of Constantine to that of Augustine, this vision was progressively spiritualized. Gradually, many came to believe that the kingdom of God was a matter of faith that had nothing to do with society. They believed that God's activity and kingdom were locked in the church. Closely related to this was the acceptance of the church by some of the later emperors of the Roman Empire. The culture of the late empire and afterwards became identified as Christian and was considered to be superior to all others. This decisively changed the mission of the church. Christianity was originally an outsider religion: it had worked among people who had no place in society, it was despised itself, and it had taken other religions seriously. But now Christianity had become an insider religion – the religion in power.[1]

The Reformers protested against equating the kingdom of God with the divinized authoritarian institution of the church. Protestants saw God at work outside and beyond the structures of the church. Anabaptists saw him as judging both the world and the institutional church. And Lutherans detached God's work in the church from that outside it: within the church Christians were judged by the laws of God, but outside the church they could take part in society, as ordinary citizens, according to the laws of the land and the demands of society, not as church members. Calvin focused on the current rule of the ascended Christ over the whole of human history. He did not believe that secular bodies were necessarily in opposition to the spiritual kingdom nor separate from it, rather that they were complementary – 'that a public form of religion might exist among Christians and humanity among men.' He saw the kingdom of God as penetrating and transforming the political realm, and he believed that to be involved in this process, to be involved in the political realm, was part of the witness and mission of the church.

The European Enlightenment secularized God's work in the world and the coming of the kingdom. Even while many Enlightenment thinkers denied the direct action of God in the world, they still tried to maintain the idea of the coming kingdom – *a* coming kingdom – that would bring perfection to the world after a long period of progress. They tried to remove the promise of the kingdom from the church and to wrest its ultimate fulfillment from a far-off transhistorical future because they wanted the new age of humanity to take place in the here and now, or at least in a historical time in direct continuity with the present. Kant sought in human reason and moral strength a basis for continuity between human history and the kingdom of God. It was on this rock that the Enlightenment tradition was to founder, for it proved too optimistic about the goodness of human reason and the altruism of human moral choice.

The child of this tradition was the social gospel movement in the United States. This saw God working as a spirit in history directing it towards its final goal, an idea in consonance with the evolutionary optimism and the doctrine of progress of the day. But not all its supporters saw the coming of the kingdom as the inevitable result of uninterrupted human progress. Some believed that humanity could never perfect itself, so they tried to reserve the initiative in bringing the kingdom for the divine and to maintain an awareness of the power of evil over humanity. A major question about others in the social gospel tradition, however, is whether they saw the kingdom as the result of human historical processes, which may have been under the control of God, or whether they even saw the kingdom as a wholly human construct.

The first expression of the vision of the kingdom in the United States was permeated by an optimism similar to that of the social gospel. Up to the time of the Civil War, many people believed that the kingdom would be established on earth before the return of Christ.

The great outburst of revival and mission, the sense of destiny about the growth of the United States, and the apocalyptic terrors of the French Revolution and Napoleonic Wars were all taken as signs of the approaching end. In Britain, by contrast, upper-class Christians who feared the loss of their privileges by revolts among the lower orders took the French Revolution as a sign of approaching catastrophe. Drawing from the same signs on which the North Americans based their optimism, they pessimistically believed that the kingdom would not be established before Christ returned.

This latter view – that only Christ could bring in the kingdom – came to dominate evangelical circles as the nineteenth century progressed. Slowly there took place what Timothy Smith and David Moberg call the Great Reversal: the social concern of evangelicals in the nineteenth century gave way to a distinct antipathy to social involvement by evangelicals in the twentieth century. Moberg traces this change to a way of interpreting the Bible that precluded guidance for social concern and to a preoccupation with the supernatural facets of faith that, in combination with a pessimistic vision of the future, cut off this world from the other.[2]

Moberg also links this reversal with the shifting social basis of the evangelical community. Old cultural values of the frontier did not fit the inner city, and evangelicals withdrew to the suburbs. I.J. Rennie noted some of the social factors surrounding the two kingdoms view: 'Following the Civil War in America, things instead of getting better were continually getting worse. This brought about increasing disillusionment and pessimism, which seriously undermined the . . . optimistic outlook for spiritual and cultural progress of society.'[3] In addition, 'the cataclysmic events at the turn of the nineteenth century' and 'two world wars in the twentieth' contributed greatly to the rapid spread of the two kingdoms view. Its 'apocalyptic assumptions' give it 'a special appeal . . . in times of great crisis and distress.'

The tension between prophetic and apocalyptic traditions of eschatology runs throughout Christian history. There is also tension between the desire to make the kingdom relevant to all history, and the conflicting desire to root it in the experience of the church. Obviously, how one resolves this tension has a direct influence on what one believes to be the proper relation of the church and society and the kingdom and history. Believers' views are also influenced by the cultural values of their time and their relationship to the cultural main-stream. For example, when the church settled into society under Constantine, it took on a spiritualized vision of the future. Socially marginalized people are sometimes drawn to revolutionary apocalypticism and the hope it provides for a radically changed future. In the social and cultural optimism of early America many saw the French Revolution as a sign of the fulfillment of the kingdom; but in Britain the upper classes viewed it as a threat[4] and a sign of the deterioration that would continue until the return of Christ.

While the two kingdoms view expects the world to get worse and worse, holding out little hope for human reform, those who hold such a view often (but by no means always) resist change and strongly support existing structures and patterns of life. For them, the more the present is radically separated from the future hope, the more the existing order loses realistic reference points for criticism – and the less reason there is to worry about change. Any social or political option is equally good or bad. When Christians lose hope about the efficacy – or necessity – of action in history, they merely reproduce the dominant cultural values of their society. Some supported Hitler in the Third Reich, and some support today's oppressive regimes.

While in the twentieth century many see the kingdom as an escape from a doomed history, in the nineteenth century, by contrast, evolutionary optimism reigned and the hope of the kingdom was identified with the doctrine of progress by those whose experience of the world was of situations that were getting better and better. Though both views claim to take the Bible literally, they each lack a sound method of interpretation. Many who hold limited views of the kingdom are socially concerned, but on the face of it their views are not theologically integrated. The internal logic of the two kingdoms view cannot criticize or direct Christian social responsibility. Adherents who want to demonstrate Christian faith in a socially responsible way must do so in obedience to other scriptural themes such as the love commandment, not in response to the demands of the kingdom.

But social action, to make the impact the kingdom demands, must be motivated by a kingdom vision of God's intention for society, history, and the world – not just by a desire to show the fruits of our spirituality. There are two poles to Christian social involvement: personal obedience to God and God's activity and purpose for all history. Those who take the first pole alone, who see their relationship to God as a wholly personal matter, do not orient social action within the historical context of God's plan. They may address the needs of communities and even the problems of structures, but they are not motivated then by the God of history. We must heed the warning of Christian leaders in Marxist countries who point out that social action without a Christian vision of the kingdom will give place in the end to the Marxist alternative, which is rooted in a vision of history. Furthermore, Christian social action, which is based on a vision of the kingdom that sees the present only in negative terms, is not as effective as it could be.

The close link between historical context and views on eschatology does not mean that we must try to – or can – divorce ourselves from our context to get an objective, neutral, biblical view. Nor should we regard most eschatology since New Testament times as declensions from an obvious and clear biblical position on the matter. Each was a pilgrimage to discover the meaning of the biblical material in the readers' own context. Each has a claim to be rooted in the biblical tension between different qualities of the kingdom. Yet although there is no one viewpoint from which to judge all the various views, this does not mean that all views are equally valid.

The main evangelical view today has its roots in the premillennial tradition of the nineteenth century. It strongly distinguishes between the consummated kingdom and present experience. No experience of the kingdom now can connect with the consummated kingdom or share any of its qualities. All that we can know of the future in the present is spiritual and limited to the church. Any material dimension of the kingdom that seems to be revealed in the biblical records is therefore not part of the human task in history but is to be isolated in the mission of Jesus, which was unique, or to be located in the millennial future. We have already examined in the main article above some of the theological questions and practical consequences that this view raises.

God's Work outside the Church

One further question, however, is whether the kingdom's connection with this world is limited to the church or whether it has to do with the whole of human history. What is the future of God's work outside the church? Some describe this as the work of God's left hand and believe it is not connected with his work within the church. The kingdom, in their view, is manifest in history only in the church, in the spiritual realm. Such a view, however, demands certain untenable theological assumptions, so we must examine the possibility and the nature of God's work outside the church, and its relationship with the presence and consummation of the kingdom.

Can we use the term *redemption* for God's activity outside the church? If we define redemption as God's activity in fulfilling his intention for the world, the focal point of which is the lordship of Christ in the present working toward the consummation of his purpose, then we can see some evidence of redemption outside the church. Within this overarching understanding of redemption, one may speak of the experience of regeneration, forgiveness, and new life. But the experience of regeneration itself cannot be the defining category for redemption. The defining category can only be Jesus' lordship, not the individual experience of that.

The church's own experience of redemption is based on the lordship of Christ over creation. Jesus as the resurrected Lord is exalted now as Lord over all creation, from which he derives his lordship over the church. Paul writes that God 'has put all things under his feet and has made him the head over all things for the church, which is his body, the fulness of him who fills all in all' (Eph. 1:22–23). God has given Christ full authority in heaven and earth, that is, throughout the unified creation (Matt. 28:18). So we may boldly pray, "Thy kingdom come, thy will be done on *earth* as in heaven" – and not just "in the church as in heaven." David Bosch notes in this context that "the Kingdom comes wherever Jesus overcomes the evil one. This happens (or ought to happen) in fullest measure in the church. But it also happens in society." [5]

According to Alfred Krass, the rediscovery of a vision of the future that affirmed Christ's present lordship in the world came in the struggle of the German churches with Hitler, for Nazism challenged all that the Reformed tradition had stood for. The issue was joined, according to W.A. Visser't Hooft, with the Barmen Declaration of 1933: 'In the light of the Kingship of Christ, it is a priori to be explained that the state stands under the Lordship of Christ, all power has been given to him.' [6] Krass adds that 'Reformed theologians had been tempted to operate with a "history of salvation" separate from the natural order, but they discovered under pressure that "the New Testament does not know a general providence apart from the history of salvation. . . ." When Hitler sought to turn the course of world history against what the church knew was God's plan, the church was pushed to exercise its proper, positive, prophetic vocation, to speak out on behalf of all efforts contributing to the intra-historical realization of God's promises.'[7]

After this experience, the Netherlands Reformed Church published 'Foundation and Perspectives of Confession' in 1950 and 1954. It stated 'We can take our place in history without fear. History is the total event, directed from Christ's first coming toward his second coming . . . . History manifests itself in a series of crises. There is no evolution, but a continuing advance of Christ's work and consequently an increasing raging of anti-Christian forces.'[8]

One author of this document was Hendrikus Berkhof, who held the tension between the kingdom's work both beyond and within history. 'The kingdom of God,' he wrote,

> is the work of God himself. This is the truth of the orthodox position. The error is to believe that it must therefore be sudden, even entirely from without. God is active in the world. The kingdom of God grows. This is the truth of the liberal position. The error is to believe that it is therefore man's labour, and that it is identical with moral and social progress. . . .
>
> In the struggle for a genuine human existence, for the deliverance of the suffering, for the elevation of the underdeveloped, for the redemption of the captives, for the settlement of race and class differences, for opposition to chaos, crime, suffering, sickness and ignorance . . . an activity is taking place throughout the world to the honour of Christ. It is sometimes performed by people who know and desire it; it is more often performed by those who have no concern for it, but whose labour proves that Christ truly received – in full objectivity – all power on earth.

He concludes: 'The new world does not fall into the old like a bomb, nor does it take the place of the old which is destroyed, but is born through the old in which it had been active.'[9]

The kingdom does not act only in the church. The church always exists in a historical context, and there is thus much interaction between the two.[10] Sometimes the church interacts with secular history almost 'unintentionally,' as when converted individuals cause positive change in society merely by example. At other times the interaction is more overt and intentional. The influences of the church may be tragic, as in the case of the Crusades and the Inquisition, or it may be creditable, as in the vast expansion of the church in parallel with the growth of mercantile colonialism. Even when the church is faithless to its inheritance, God can work through and around it to spread the gospel outside its original confines. This only supports our contention that the experience of redemption cannot be limited to the action and body of the church.

The Fear of Absolutization

In a justified effort to maintain the sovereignty of God, some are afraid to identify any historical project with the kingdom of God. To stop us from identifying our own projects with the work of the kingdom, they prefer to see history only as an image, foreshadowing, or reflection of the kingdom. Westerners are particularly sensitive to anything that seems to make history absolute, in part, we think, because they live against a background of movements and institutions that tried to do just that. Many of them believe that liberation theologians have fallen into the trap of identifying acts of liberation with the bringing of the kingdom, for liberation theologians are in dialogue with Marxism, which represents an absolutist tradition.

Oddly enough, both those who attack Marxism and the Marxists themselves – both those who spiritualize the significance of history and those who endorse life in this world completely – are children of the Enlightenment. This tradition attempted to bring religion into the realm of rational discourse and scientific examination. Some reacted against Enlightenment thinking merely by denying the validity of reason and science in this field – they spiritualized religion and history. If history is not really 'real' they can only turn their eyes to the transcendent. But the religion they find there is not grounded in any sort of concrete reality, and the life of the world is left devoid of any Christian perspective and influence. The Marxist tradition, on the other hand, accepted the critique of the Enlightenment that made human experience and reason absolute. Human experience and reason are in turn directed by the collective life of classes and the means of production. The only arena for the fulfillment of human aspirations is within earthly history understood as a conflict between classes.

The social gospel of the nineteenth century was also a child of the Enlightenment, which, as we noted, was an attempt in part to make real the Christian millennial vision of the world. The social gospel movement sought to reclaim this heritage for Christianity. So we can represent these offspring of the Enlightenment as follows.

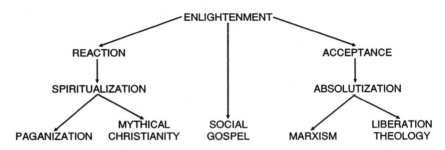

We must beware of both spiritualizing and absolutizing history, and of the fear of doing so, as we seek an open space for other options for Christian historical engagement.

Western theologians are particularly sensitive to anything that seems to absolutize history. The West experienced the growth of freedom and human rights only through desacralizing institutions that tried to make history absolute. The early church condemned the emperor cult and replaced it with prayer on the emperor's behalf, so setting a limit to his power. In the Reformation, freedom got a boost through the desacralization of political orders. These orders gained strength even as the church lost it, but they were restricted to serving the welfare of the people, not providing salvation. In the English-speaking world, Puritanism replaced the divine right of kings, a sacred institution, with a constitution or political contract, a wholly secular institution. Demands for freedom of religion and conscience led to demands for free assembly, freedom of the press, and civil liberties. Jürgen Moltmann concludes that in the long run this is to the benefit of Christianity, which indeed must stay on the path of secularizing, desacralizing, and democratizing political rule if it wants to keep true to its faith and hope.[11]

The experience of the Two-Thirds World is somewhat different. In Asia there is little absolutization of history because the predominant view is that history is unreal. The only reality recognized is the transcendent – God – but God can never be experienced in history and there is little chance of seeing him at work there. There is in Asia, then, much less hope – or even concern – for history than there is in the West. But when Asians are converted to Christianity, the news they hear is good news indeed. They are only too glad to see and know of God at work in history because that restores meaning to what they see around them; there is now reason to work for the betterment of society because not only is God here but he is working for the same things that they are. This is a great revelation for non-Westerners because their society is not based on Christian assumptions of justice and rights, as much of the West is at this point, but instead on the naked exercise of power in relationships at all levels. In this context, to see God at work for justice in their own situation is their great desire.

One's context always shapes one's response to God's work in history. When Europeans hear theologians from the Two-Thirds World speaking enthusiastically about God bringing the mighty low, they fear that those theologians have absolutized history and lost sight of the transcendent. And when those from the Two-Thirds World hear the warnings from the West about absolutization, they fear that the Westerners have spiritualized history and have lost sight of the importance of this world – something that those in the Two-Thirds World know well from their own context.

Obviously we must keep a partnership and balance between these two perspectives. To make any category absolute is the wrong road. Neither justice through social action nor a faith that looks only to the transcendent can be absolute. To absolutize or spiritualize is to ask for a perfect new earth or a perfect new birth here. It is to demand that whatever God does now must be perfect, complete, and final. David Jenkins writes that 'idolatry has always been a besetting sin which leads again and again to dreadful destructions and inhumanities. Idols are not always just false gods. They may be the promotion by absolutization of a provisional and ambiguous good to the level of a god, and this particularly in politics.' He concludes that 'to redeem and renew the distortions and destructions arising from false absolutizations of valuable insights, we need a clear worship of the Presence, Power and Promise who relativizes every human activity and every created fact. We also need the hope that comes from beyond us and makes provisional every definition we make or every expectation we entertain.'[12]

That we reject absolutization does not mean that we deny God's present work in bringing either the new birth or the new earth. We should not let the fear of absolutization blind us to seeing where God is at work in the imperfect and ambiguous. The reaction of spiritualization and the fear of absolutization can so convince people that they will never see God at work in history that it becomes a self-fulfilling prophecy. Such paralysis may be infecting many Western Christians. They do not expect to see God at work in normal human history but look for him only in the supernormal dimension of healing and tongues. What they are left with is a God-of-the-gaps: a God defined by humanity that can exist only in the few gaps between the areas from which the Western worldview has 'conclusively' eliminated him. In the Two-Thirds World, believers are more ready to see God at work in human history, which may also be a self-fulfilling prophecy.

Notes to God's Intention for the World

1. Kenneth Cracknell, 'God and the Nations,' in *Dialogue in Community*, ed. C.D. Jathanna (Mangalore: Karnataka Theological Research Institute, 1982), pp. 2–3.
2. See Karl Barth, *Church Dogmatics* (Edinburgh: T. & T. Clark, 1956), IV, 1, pp. 26ff.
3. See José Míguez Bonino, *Revolutionary Theology Comes of Age* (London: SPCK, 1975), pp. 134–35.
4. See Stephen Travis's discussion of this in *Christian Hope and the Future* (Downers Grove, Ill.: Inter-Varsity Press, 1980).
5. See Richard Bauckham, 'The Rise of Apocalyptic,' *Themelios*, vol. 3, no. 2, pp. 19–23. See also K. Koch, *The Rediscovery of Apocalyptic* (London: Allenson, 1970; Naperville, Ill.: Allenson, 1972), pp. 28–33.
6. Bauckham argues that Daniel's four world empires embrace only the period after the fall of Jerusalem, not the whole of history. And, since temporal dualism did not arise until the first century A.D., apocalyptic did not begin from a dualistic dogma but from an experience of history. See also Travis, *Christian Hope*, pp. 37–38.
7. Vinay Samuel and Chris Sugden, 'Evangelism and Social Responsibility: A Biblical Study on Priorities,' a paper presented at the Consultation on the Relationship Between Evangelism and Social Responsibility (CRESR), held in Grand Rapids in 1982, and published in *In Word and Deed*, ed. Bruce, J. Nicholls (Exeter: Paternoster, 1985; Grand Rapids: Eerdmans, 1986).
8. See Bonino, *Revolutionary Theology Comes of Age*, pp. 135–36.
9. David Bosch notes that 'the history of Israel is a continuation of God's dealings with the nations. Precisely as the elect, the patriarch, and with him Israel, is called into the world of the nations.' *Witness to the World* (Atlanta: John Knox; London: Marshall, Morgan & Scott, 1980), pp. 61–62.
10. Andrew Walls of Aberdeen University emphasizes this.
11. J. Christiaan Beker, *Paul the Apostle* (Edinburgh: T. & T. Clark; Philadelphia: Fortress, 1980), p. 337.
12. The tendency here to absolutize Indian history arises from an evolutionary understanding of history that rejects the authority of biblical revelation.
13. The necessity of this process was affirmed by the First Conference of Evangelical Mission Theologians from the Two-Thirds World, held in Bangkok

in March 1982. Papers from this conference were published in *Sharing Jesus in the Two-Thirds World* (Bangalore: Partnership in Mission – Asia, P.O. Box 544, Bangalore-5, 1983; Grand Rapids: Eerdmans, 1984).

14. On this see Bosch, *Witness to the World*, p. 63.

15. Ibid., pp. 64–65.

16. This quote is from the manuscript of 'The Kingdom in Relation to the Church and the World,' a paper presented by Arthur P. Johnston at the Consultation on the Relationship between Evangelism and Social Responsibility. This paper was later revised and published in *In Word and Deed*, ed. Bruce Nicholls, but without the section containing the quote.

17. Ibid. See Nicholls, *In Word and Deed*, p. 117.

18. See Bosch, *Witness to the World,* pp. 65–66.

19. See G.E. Wright, *The Biblical Doctrine of Man in Society* (London: SCM, 1954), pp. 18–19.

20. See Victor Paul Furnish, *The Love Command in the New Testament* (London: SCM, 1973), ch. 1.

21. See Vinay Samuel and Chris Sugden, 'Evangelism and Social Responsibility,' pp. 193ff.

22. See further Jürgen Moltmann, *The Church in the Power of the Spirit* (London: SCM; New York: Harper & Row, 1977), p. 196.

23. George Eldon Ladd, *Jesus and the Kingdom* (New York: Harper and Row, 1964; London: SPCK, 1966), p. 179. This book has been revised and updated and is now published under the title *The Presence of the Future* (Grand Rapids: Eerdmans, 1980).

24. Andrew Lincoln, *Paradise Now and Not Yet* (New York: Cambridge University Press, 1981), pp. 191–92.

25. Ibid., p. 192

26. Ibid.

27. Ibid., p. 193

28. See John Howard Yoder, *The Politics of Jesus* (Grand Rapids: Eerdmans, 1972).

29. David Jenkins, 'Doctrines which Drive One to Politics,' in *Christian Faith and Political Hopes*, ed. Haddon Willmer (London: Epworth, 1979), p. 145.

30. Many Christians affirm the Incarnation in theory – that the Word became flesh – but still maintain in practice a docetic soteriology. They betray their similarity to the Docetists – early Christian heretics who proposed that Christ only *seemed* to have a human body and to die on the cross – in that even as they pay lip service to the idea of God become man they hold to a salvation out of the world and out of history, which maintains the removal of God from the world.

31. For case studies that demonstrate the importance that preaching the historical Jesus has for social development projects, consult the following: (for Bombay and Madras) Graham Houghton and Ezra Sargunam, 'The Role of Theological Education in Church Planting Among the Urban Poor,' *TRACI Journal* 19 (April 1981); (for Jamkhed) Vinay Samuel and Chris Sugden, 'Dialogue with Other Religions – An Evangelical View,' in

Sharing Jesus in the Two-Thirds World (Bangalore: Partnership in Mission – Asia, 1983; Grand Rapids: Eerdmans, 1984); and (for Bangalore) Vinay Samuel and Chris Sugden, eds., *Evangelism and the Poor – A Third World Study Guide*, ed. Vinay Samuel and Chris Sugden, rev. ed. (Bangalore: Partnership in Mission – Asia, 1983).

32. See Paul Hiebert, 'Folk Religion in Andhra Pradesh: Some Missiological Implications,' in *Evangelism and the Poor – A Third World Study Guide*, ed. Vinay Samuel and Chris Sugden, rev. ed. (Bangalore: Partnership in Mission – Asia, 1983).

33. We contend that the effects of the Fall are seen predominantly at the second level, which controls and deforms humanity. The effects of the atonement and resurrection of Christ also have their most significant impact at this level, leading captivity captive.

34. Jenkins, 'Doctrines which Drive One to Politics,' p. 149.

35. See Bonino, *Revolutionary Theology Comes of Age*, pp. 139–40.

36. Ibid., pp. 140–42, 152.

Notes to the Appendix

1. See Arthur P. Johnston, 'The Kingdom in Relation to the Church and the World,' the manuscript of a paper presented at the Consultation on the Relationship between Evangelism and Social Responsibility, p. 18. This paper was later revised and published in *In Word and Deed*, ed. Bruce Nicholls (Exeter: Paternoster, 1985; Grand Rapids: Eerdmans, 1986).

2. See David Moberg, *The Great Reversal* (Philadelphia: Lippincott, 1973), p. 33.

3. I.J. Rennie, 'Nineteenth Century Roots,' in *Handbook of Biblical Prophecy*, ed. Carl E. Amerding and W. Ward Gasque (Grand Rapids: Baker, 1980), p. 44.

4. D.N. Hempton formulates this conclusion about the situation in England in an unpublished paper, '*Evangelicalism and Eschatology,*' University of St. Andrews, Scotland, 1977, pp. 15–16.

5. David Bosch, *Witness to the World* (Atlanta: John Knox; London: Marshall, Morgan & Scott, 1980), p. 209.

6. W.A. Visser't Hooft, *The Kingship of Christ*, The Stone Lectures, Princeton University, 1947 (New York: Harper, 1948), p. 136.

7. Alfred Krass, *Five Lanterns at Sundown* (Grand Rapids: Eerdmans, 1978), p. 140.

8. Quoted in *ibid.*, pp. 142–43.

9. Hendrikus Berkhof, *Christ the Meaning of History* (Richmond: John Knox, 1966), pp. 169, 173.

10. See José Míguez Bonino, *Revolutionary Theology Comes of Age* (London: SPCK, 1975), p. 137.

11. Jürgen Moltmann, *The Church in the Power of the Spirit* (London: SCM; New York: Harper & Row, 1977), p. 179.
12. David Jenkins, 'Doctrines which Drive One to Politics,' in *Christian Faith and Political Hopes*, ed. Haddon Willmer (London: Epworth, 1979), p. 153.

Ten

A Presentation of the Concern for Kingdom Ethics

Chris Sugden

For 20 years I have debated with Oliver Barclay our common concern to overcome the hesitancy of some western evangelicals to engage in significant bible-based social witness. I stress *westerners*, for such hesitancy is not shared in many parts of the Two-Thirds World where evangelicals have developed their own theology and practice. My own experience leads me tentatively to conclude that one factor underlying this hesitancy is the individual and dualistic categories learned from their culture with which some westerners read the bible. The way forward is therefore not to trade texts, but to examine theologically the framework in which they are understood.

'A Presentation of the Concern for Kindgom Ethics' in *Kingdom and Creation in Social Ethics* by Chris Sugden and Oliver Barclay (Nottingham, Grove Books, 1990).

The Kingdom Position

There has been a concern to relate Christian social ethics to the Kingdom of God for the following reasons; practical, theological and biblical.

1. Practical Reasons

If the church is called to invite people to acknowledge the Lordship of Christ personally, it must also exhort them to live out that Lordship in their total life, personal and social. How are personal conversion and social responsibility related? Without a link people become guilty or ineffective, or allow their social involvement to be determined by forces inimical to their faith. Our contention is that personal conversion and social responsibility can only be related through Jesus' Lordship, of which the content is the Kingdom of God.

2. Theological Reasons

a) Concern for Unity in God's will and activity

God acts in history and creates a people of God. But human history has been separated into sacred – where God is at work among his people – and secular. The key to uniting them is to regard human history from the perspective of the final Kingdom in which God will fulfil his purpose by the renewal of all creation. In Romans 8.20–21 this renewal is linked with the redemption of the people of God. The completion of God's work in creation is when creation shares in the glorious freedom of God's children.

Therefore the history of God's people is not separate from that of creation. Their freedom anticipates and defines the freedom all creation will enjoy; their history interprets all history, not because God is at work only there, but because there he defines how he works everywhere. And secondly the redemption of God's people must express itself in the renewal of the world, as they demonstrate that their freedom is not for themselves alone, but is a firstfruit of the world's freedom.

b) Concern to discover God's will for Society

How does God intend people to live together in society? What are
Christian ethics for human community living, and how should Christians witness to those communities? Many of the issues facing the
world and Christians today are social – the role of women in society,
sexuality, abortion, race relations, economics, . . .

Some categories by which God's work has been understood
divorce God's work in the whole of history from his work among his
people, so preventing the development of such ethics. E.g. the use of
individualistic categories to describe God's work restricts to within
individual believers any true change towards God's purposes for
people in society arising from Christ's death and resurrection. From
this comes a concern to prove Christians do things best, and that the
only way to tackle social evils is to convert people. Hence the world
outside the church is viewed as impersonal nature, and the world of
persons is focused on the church, for 'God can only work through
redeemed persons.' A dualism arises focusing on individual redemption in the spiritual sphere, and as a result some evangelicals are
unable to develop a theology for social involvement, which is
reduced to changing individuals in their inner lives.

c) Evil overcome through the Cross

Wherever evil is overcome in society it is due to Christ's work on the
cross.[1] God's action against evil in any sphere must be related to that
victory. Some expressions of evangelical social ethics imply that in
some cases God overcomes evil without reference to the cross. This
can lead to triumphalism and worldly use of power. But Jesus established the righteousness of God through resisting evil, suffering,
death and resurrection. These are the gospel themes of how God
redeems the world.

3. Biblical Reasons

God's will is uniquely and supremely expressed in Jesus. Through
and for him all things were created, and in him they have their
proper place.[2] He is the expression of the Creator, and will bring
creation to fulfilment. The focus of Jesus' ministry was the

announcement of the Kingdom of God, and that theme gives an overall description of Jesus' work and preaching, and of the work to which he commissioned his disciples.[3]

God's purpose for creation will be fulfilled in his Kingdom, the new age at the end of the world. The life and power of this Kingdom has invaded this age through Jesus. The Kingdom is here in quality, though not yet in its full expression. It is God's gift, and cannot be built by people. In Jesus it fulfils his will for his creation. Its content is rooted in the Old Testament expectation that God would establish his will for Creation – 'Your kingdom come, your will be done . . .' – forgiveness of sins, new relationships between people, justice for all, a renewed creation and the outpouring of God's Spirit.[4]

Jesus declared that the Kingdom's quality of life was already operative through his ministry; people could now call God 'Abba', Father; a new relationship existed (in his healings) between people and creation, and between Jew and gentile, slave and free, . . . while the forgiven should also forgive. That ministry continues God's Old Testament revelation, for God's will in Old and New Testaments is one. His will for creation must be understood with reference to its fulfilment in the Kingdom, and to how Jesus demonstrated its life in a world where it conflicted with the kingdom of darkness.

This Kingdom activity is founded in the death and resurrection of Christ: his atonement enables repentant sinners to enter the Kingdom; Calvary defeated evil, enabling people to experience the powers of the Kingdom; the resurrection vindicates Jesus as the one who brought the Kingdom and its newness of life into human history now; it exalts him as Lord, enabling him to give the Spirit. This Kingdom activity is linked with judgment on sin and grace, which is God's activity in opening people to repentance and salvation.

St. Paul does not often use the term 'Kingdom of God'[5], but the concept is there in his theme of the new age, marked by new relationships and the Spirit, invading the old. He focuses on the Lordship of Christ. The Kingdom is about the Lordship of Christ – its key person – and makes no sense without it. The Kingdom centres on Jesus' Lordship and his activity through his people, but it is a fact, dependent not on people's acknowledgement of Jesus. Otherwise if no one acknowledged Jesus, the Kingdom would cease to exist.

Jesus' Lordship is the content of the Kingdom, not Kingdom ethics. Kingdom ethics arise from the acknowledgement of Jesus as Lord of everything. They are not about behaviour in a Kingdom society, nor a blueprint to be imposed legalistically, but are about how people behave who live out Jesus' teaching of the rule of God. They are a response of love to Jesus' Lordship.

A Christian social ethic must be rooted in grace, and related to the good news of the Kingdom announced by Jesus. The proclamation of its forgiveness and new life must be related to the demonstration of that life in new relationships which witness to people's need to give Jesus their allegiance.

When non-Christians express values approximating to Christian values these must be related to the revealed will of God. This preserves the unity of God's actions; his activity inside the church is not separable form his activity outside. Any separation would tend to make church activity irrelevant to the needs God would have his people address in the world. His concern is that all enter his Kingdom; this is the goal of all his activity in the world; all his activity is salvific in intent if not in itself.

The Kingdom integrates the calls to follow Jesus and to steward creation. Paul integrates the two themes by identifying Jesus as the true image of God, the second Adam who fulfils the role of God's image and steward of creation.[6] In the Kingdom of God we follow Jesus in building relationships of Justice between people and with creation, fulfilling the call to be stewards.[7]

Argument from the Biblical Material

Is the Lordship of Christ, and the activity of his Kingdom confined to where he is consciously acknowledged? Surely not! but his activity where his people are is normative. He does not act in a Kingdom way among his people and in a non-Kingdom way among others. As first-born both of creation and the new creation he has loved the world, not just as his people, and has died to take away the sin of the world. Wherever he acts in the world it is as redeemer and Lord, not just creator. We cannot divide the world into areas where the Kingdom activity is real, and where it is absent. That would undermine Jesus' Lordship over all.

This activity is qualified in a number of ways; first by human sinfulness. Humans do not respond to God's activity. Evil has no future, but continues to exist. Christians are to act in society knowing that evil is dead. Therefore in a sense there is no compromise with evil.

Redemption is where the Kingdom is acknowledged and Jesus worshipped, but his Lordship and Kingdom activity also continues beyond those who consciously accept Jesus' rule.

Amidst human sinfulness the only ethics a Christian knows are the ethics of the Lordship of Christ, for Christians have to respond to the absolute. Expediency can always distort because we can never identify how far sin is at work in the pragmatic . If we advocate the pragmatic in a mixed society we say 'the absolute cannot work, so a mixture of absolute and non-absolute can!' How can we know we have the right mixture, leading society up to the absolute good and not down from it?

Amidst sinfulness human society is dynamic, moving up or down. The Kingdom ethic approach recognizes that evil is not static; humanity is involved in a perpetual fall. Even in the best of societies evil remains active. Left to themselves people spiral perpetually downwards. Evil grows inexorably; the counter-activity is Kingdom activity which conserves and lifts creation.

Our Kingdom activity will not convert present society into the Kingdom of God. That will only come when Jesus returns. We simply *witness* to the reality of the Kingdom and the possibility of the absolute – God's intention for humanity – against the distorting witness of evil.

Kingdom activity *empowers* society as Christians and others willing to follow it move in the direction of the Kingdom, counteracting the moral disablement evil brings in society. The Holy Spirit works in society strengthening the wills of people who may not be Christians to turn to God's way.[8] Such empowerment does not guarantee that all will be able to live out the Christian ethic, but it enables them to see the possibilities and make the choice. Kingdom activity unblinds the masking activity of the evil one, and convicts people, strengthening their wills to act.[9] It conserves society and clarifies people's choice. This makes the invitation of the gospel relevant in every situation.

Without such empowerment society will destroy itself. The world has two options; forwards to God's way, or backwards. Without Kingdom activity what would it look like? Mission fields are replete with examples where Kingdom activity has not just conserved but advanced society. Without it, what would they be like? That is the question to ask, not why everything has not been transformed despite the presence of the Kingdom through Jesus' ministry. Left to itself the world degenerates. Talk of a sense of creation order that God has written into humanity, conserving it and enabling it to acknowledge God and exercise choice, presupposes evil to be other than the dynamic force in people's lives which must needs to be addressed by God's activity in Christ which keeps the choice alive for God. Both evil and Jesus' Lordship are at work in the world; the creation ethics view can become hostage to the view that God is helpless. The Kingdom approach addresses this issue.

Kingdom activity produces *hope*. Its vital eschatological perspective enables active and absolute ideals. Though fulfilment comes when the King comes, the hope is for the present, not just the future. Unlike the intertestamental apocalypses the New Testament does not consign the present to hopelessness. The content of eschatology is the Kingdom – the total Lordship of God, consummating the Lordship of Jesus, and vindicating him, thus fulfilling God's intention for humanity. We can continue in service here because we know we shall be vindicated; we witness to the Kingdom because it will vindicate us. We act, not out of idealism or pragmatic calculation, but because we are convinced that the future will vindicate us. The New Testament people lived convinced that not history but Jesus would vindicate them when he came. We live in the same hope. This is the basis of Paul's argument in Colossians 3; the values Jesus demonstrated, the resurrection vindicated, and which express a risen life hidden in Christ, are eternal; compassion, kindness, humility, gentleness, patience, tolerance and forgiveness.

The Discussion with Non-Christians

We do not impose Christian ethics on a mixed society but converse with people, knowing that the Holy Spirit works to conserve society and enable people to test all laws by these standards and move towards them. No laws are static. They must have a goal. They recognize pragmatic realities but there is a measure and a movement to them. Ethics are relational. They must have movement as well as measure. While we cannot have a perfect society we can move towards one that is closer to a good than an evil one. Without movement forwards we move backwards because of sin. The movement of static rules, which are the lowest common denominator, is always downwards unless an ideal pushes them forwards. Thus some societies have positive discrimination. Equality is not just written into the statute book, but continually maintained.

In discussion with non-Christians the Christian is shaped by all that makes him/her a Christian. Only Kingdom ethics shapes a Christian, for no other represents the Lordship of Christ.[10] When Kingdom ethics is abandoned so is the Lordship of Christ over all aspects of life. That is the beginning of a secularization which declares independence in moral decision-making from external authority, and thus affirms the autonomy of human rule-making. A Christian society and Christian individuals cannot afford to abandon Kingdom ethics as the governing factor in their lives, for this reduces their faith to personal and internal belief.

The motivation for social ethics in Jesus' teaching of the Kingdom is love of the neighbour, integrally linked with love of God. Because of this motivation, Kingdom ethics has no choice but to be available to all neighbours. That is the witness of Christians as they dialogue with non-Christians about how love of neighbour becomes a reality in any society.[11]

If in a mixed society action is based on the lowest common moral denominator, the gospel has no chance. It needs a Kingdom ethic. Anything lower is a secular argument deriving from nineteenth Century liberals who allowed for a general morality in society, and particular moralities belonging to interest groups. At the heart of their argument was acceptance of a lower level of morality for society. Such pragmatism is secular and 'creation ethics' displays such a stance.

The underlying concept of the renewed creation, the Kingdom, and the new age relating God's will and redemption to History is fundamental.

Both Paul and Peter, writing to Gentile churches, use such Old Testament images as the new Israel or the holy nation to describe the church, showing that they thought its Jewish heritage important. To argue from a lack of Old Testament background in some readers of scripture is therefore beside the point. What matters is how a Christian social ethic is rooted in the bible, and in Paul's writings Christ's Lordship/the new age is to the fore; this is tantamount to the Kingdom.

I agree with ORB that the Kingdom is over against people in rebellion against God. People have to enter it, and only believers can see it. I do not deny ORB's affirmation that Christian Ethics are rooted in creation, but the Kingdom is the fulfilment of the rule of God the Creator.[12] I do deny that Kingdom ethics are voluntarist or arbitrary, and have never held that view.

ORB suggests that, taken on its own, a Kingdom approach 'all too easily seems based on God's arbitrary commands, or to be voluntarist.' I myself do not take Kingdom ethics on its own in that way. I agree with him about the difference between deriving and defining Christian ethics and promoting and defending them to non-Christians. They are derived from God's will revealed in scripture. I contend that this will is the fulfilment of God's purpose in Creation, expressed in the Kingdom of God.

How we justify Christian ethics to non-Christians will vary depending on what categories they respond to; some cultures appreciate natural laws, or social order; others respond to family issues, and other fundamental relationships.

All find some support in scripture; all derive from a shadowy awareness of God's will, but none is definitive for the nature of Christian ethics. That depends on the definition most adequate to the biblical evidence, and also (as ORB acknowledges) which is most adequate to the fallen state of the world. I suggested the value of Kingdom ethics in this regard above.

I am glad that ORB agrees that 'the Kingdom is one way in which the outworking of the creation nature of ethics is expressed in some NT passages,' and thus affirms the continuity between the two concepts. I should clarify that 'the Kingdom' is not a social programme, nor a set of rules, nor purely about social justice. Nor is it primarily about people's response to God; it is the content of the Lordship of Christ, and its ethics are the behaviour of those who have responded in love to Jesus the Lord.

Kingdom ethics may seem vague, but this charge may be levelled at any other biblical material, since we cannot expect to read precise information about every present-day situation direct from scripture. For instance, Christians give the straightforward command not to kill various interpretations in the areas of punishment and war. 'The Kingdom' is not the only biblical concept which is used to support contradictory practical policies; witness the applications of biblical teaching on wealth. The value of 'the Kingdom' is that it draws together the work of God as Creator and as Saviour; his work in persons and in society; the response of faith to Christ and the obedience of faith in discipleship; God's work in the world now and its fulfilment when Jesus returns. It helps counteract the unbiblical separation of these concepts lying behind western evangelical hesitancy about involvement in social responsibility.

I see a distinction in scripture between God's Kingdom activity in the world and people entering the Kingdom. From God's perspective, his Kingdom activity is not limited to leading people to faith in Christ, but can include and use non-believers in so far as their activity promotes his will. Paul appears to affirm this in I Timothy 2.1–6, where he links prayer for kings, proper conduct, and God's will for all to be saved through Christ. The proper activities of rulers can promote God's work of salvation.

ORB argues that if non-Christians can be used in Kingdom activity it is hard to see the new and distinctively Christ-centred dimension of the Kingdom which he stresses. I suggest that he is confusing the objective reality of Christ's Lordship with people's subjective response to it. The Kingdom is new and Christ centred as God acts in history bringing salvation, but all God's people before and after Christ are his people because of Christ. Abraham experienced salvation before Christ; there are signs of the Kingdom apart from God's people and acknowledgement of Christ, but it is still God's acts in Christ which define the Kingdom and have brought it into history.

From the perspective of human response only those who put their faith in Jesus enter the Kingdom. So can God use in his Kingdom activity those who have not yet entered it? ORB properly observes that the Kingdom is Christological. It is Christological because it is the Kingdom of God who is Christ. To deduce that it cannot therefore work through those who do not enter it through Christ is to confuse the objective fact of God's Kingdom and Christ's Lordship with subjective response to it.

How can God's will for mankind be wider than the Kingdom? The Kingdom fulfils God's will in creation. God's blessings of sun and rain do fall on just and unjust, so how do they relate to the Kingdom which people can enter? The classic answer is to divide God's blessings into those of creation (which all share) and those of redemption (forgiveness and eternal life . . .), thus separating these blessings. But in scripture these blessings of redemption are blessings precisely because they transform the blessings of creation – thus in Christ hardness of heart leading to divorce can be cured so that marriage may be fully enjoyed. Blessings of creation do not stand on their own; God's purpose is not that people remain content with temporal blessings, or misuse them, but that they come to worship him.[13] There is a continuity between creation and redemption. As people experience common blessings they may experience them more fully and properly in God's Kingdom.

The confusion may lie in the term 'wider.' In what sense is God's will wider than a Kingdom which is both historical and eschatological? Perhaps people do not enter the Kingdom, or God's blessings for all humanity affect more people than the blessings of the Kingdom which fulfils them, but that does not determine the nature of God's will.

Unbelievers and Kingdom Activity

Is it unbiblical to suggest that social good done by those who have neither repented nor centre their activity on Christ is 'Kingdom activity?' The state of the agents is irrelevant; what matters is that the Redeemer Jesus Christ is Lord over the created order. Biblical evidence is as follows:

a: The New Testament links God's rule in history with that of Christ the ascended Lord.[14] Where just relationships such as characterize Christ's Lordship are established it is appropriate to read them as signs of that rule.

b: Jesus' action and rule are cosmic. He has disarmed the principalities of evil which create division in society.[15] Where we see barriers broken down, can we divorce this from God's will seen in Christ's victory over the powers on the cross?[16] To credit any diminution of evil in the world to any source other than Christ's victory on the cross is to say that some force other than the cross can defeat evil, and thus to undermine the centrality of the cross to God's activity in the world.

c: The 'world' in which the Kingdom is active is both humanity-in-society in rebellion against God, and also a world loved by God. By the cross God overcomes the power of this rebellion; by his love it is not destined for final abandonment but for transformation into a new heaven and earth at Christ's return. In either sense His work is the key to overcoming and transforming 'the world.'

d: Moving from Old to New Testaments we move from law to promise. Redemption, expressed in God's Kingdom, is in fulfilment of his promise and to establish his law. The promise fulfils the law which implied it; they are not separate. The law itself was a gift of grace, fulfilling God's promise of deliverance and of a land where they could serve him. Christ, supremely in his atoning death, fulfils both. Old Testament law, intended to prevent structures from exploiting the poor and to protect and relieve them, offered hope not condemnation. It sought to change the status quo, not preserve it, opening it to acceptance of God's promise.[17] Even judgment in society is an expression of grace, as is the Kingdom, pointing people to salvation in the Kingdom and as ORB says a prelude to its coming.

Similarly in the New Testament judgment points towards grace. Judgment separate from grace is condemnation, which must await the last judgment.[18] God works in the political structures in judgment and grace, opening society to conscious acknowledgement of Christ and thus the fulfilment of his purpose for humanity. The goal of this work is always to bring people into the Kingdom. To quote the writer with Vinay Samuel:

> We must not identify the action of God's grace in the world outside the church with the conscious acknowledgement of the Lordship of Christ by his believing body. But we do claim that the Lordship of Christ is exercised beyond the church as God acts in judgment and (unacknowledged) grace in the world. The difference between unacknowledged and acknowledged grace lies not in the manner of God's activity but in the nature of man's response. Where men respond to judgment and grace they receive Christ; where men do not respond they incur judgment on themselves.
>
> Paul is confident that God works through kings and rulers and the political structures of society to open society up to the conscious acknowledgement of Christ, by judgment on its unjust structures and grace in moving it towards God's purpose for human life. This is the effective operation of the Lordship of Christ in the world beyond the church, to bring creation to its God-ordained goal.
>
> This understanding gives a basis for seeing that God is at work in society beyond the church applying the effects of Christ's victory in society through social changes.[19]

The Will of God in a Mixed Society

By the nature of revelation the will of God for a mixed society is found through the reading of scripture by those who accept it, but that will is not for his church only, but for them as the exemplar of what all humanity should be like, as it was with his will for Israel. And his will is not arbritrary, for it is the will of the God who made the created order.

Application of the Sermon on the Mount in a mixed society is not as impractical as some have suggested.

a. We cannot separate Jesus' ethics into ethics for individual obedience and ethics for a mixed society. This separates individual and corporate existence in a way foreign to Hebrew thought.
b. To take specific examples; 'Do not resist evil' is not a command for absolute acquiescence, but must be interpreted by Jesus' own practice. He resisted evil by challenging current attitudes to *Torah*, Samaritans, or table fellowship with the ʿam ha'arets; he denounced the Pharisees' hypocrisy, etc.[20]

How does Jesus' renunciation of the sword sit with the teaching that the magistrate does not bear it in vain? After detailed study of Christian pacifism and its alternatives I believe that the nature of Christian love which gives worth to people, founded on God's grace, implies a legitimate form of self-defense applicable in society to the use of force in police action. The nature of Christian love is not self-sacrifice tout simple.[21] Niebuhr's argument that Kingdom love is necessarily self-sacrificial and unworkable in a mixed society has been well refuted by Outka and others.[22]

Notes

1. See 'Towards a theology of social change,'in R.J. Sider (ed.) *Evangelicals and Development*, (Paternoster, Exeter, 1981).
2. Mark 1.14; Matt. 4.23; Luke 8.1; 11.20. Matthew uses the phrase 'Kingdom of Heaven.'
3. Jer. 31.31; Isaiah 35; Joel 2.28–32.
4. But see Col. 1.12–13; Also Col. 3; 1 Thess. 5.4–6; Rom. 6.5–11; Rom. 8.
5. In the Genesis account of creation 'image' refers to the human role of dominion over creation. David Clines (*op. cit.*) argues that the image refers to the role of the tenant of an absentee landlord.
6. Rev. 21.24 speaks about the fulfilment of this role.
7. Rev. 21.24 speaks about the fulfilment of this role.

8. This trinitarian perspective encompasses the Spirit's work in human community and moves beyond a binitarian perspective involving God and Christ alone.
9. This is the argument against the concentration camp guard's line that he is only doing his job.
10. Acceptance of dualistic ethics – a Two Kingdoms view – leads to the abandonment of Christian ethics, whereas a Christian cannot abandon Kingdom ethics which is acknowledgement of Jesus' lordship. Two Kingdoms theory allows different laws to apply in the church and the world, and is associated particularly with Luther's approach to social ethics. See *Social Gospel or No Gospel*, (Grove, Nottingham, 1975) p. 7.
11. Take for example the work of the gospel and secular civil servants in India. The gospel enhanced the position of women. Early missionaries such as Charles Grant, motivated by Kingdom ethics talked about gospel standards. Their high Christian vision of the human shaped their values.

    They dialogued with non-Christian leaders, lifted people to Kingdom ethics, and prompted reform movements in Hinduism. By contrast the civil servants with a deistic view of God insisted that in a mixed society there can be no appeal to Kingdom 'rules'. This witness to Kingdom values resulted in two things; gratitude in Indian society for the willingness to witness and refusal to compromise over what men like Grant saw as God's intention for all societies; and Hindu reforms energized by the support of such a movement.

    A high Christian viewpoint was being offered, not a pragmatic one. Had they accepted a lowest common denominator, what would that have meant *vis-à-vis* the caste system, or the low place of women? Similarly in South Africa today what denominator can a Christian accept with apartheid, or in Britain with racism?
12. I agree with Oliver O'Donovan that the 'very act of God which ushers in his kingdom is the resurrection of Christ from the dead – the reaffirmation of Creation', in *Resurrection and the Moral Order*, (IVP, Leicester, 1980) p. 15.
13. Rom. 2.4
14. Eph. 1.23
15. E.g. through the misuse of Jewish law, seen as an elemental spirit in Gal. 4.9
16. E.g. between Jew and Gentile, slave and free . . . in Gal. 3.28
17. See especially V. Samuel and C. Sugden, 'Towards a Theology of Social Change' in (ed.) R. J Sider, *Evangelicals and Development*, (Paternoster Press, Exeter, 1981). A number of issues in the formulation of the views shared in this presentation and response owe a debt to continued discussions with Vinay Samuel.
18. In Rom. 10 judgment operates on Israel so that Gentiles and Jews may be saved. In 1 Tim. 2.1–4 secular justice provides tranquillity for men to enter God's kingdom.
19. *op. cit.* p. 37
20. Matt. 5.39. The alternative Jesus describes is retaliation 'eye for eye.' David Hill in his commentary (*Matthew*, Oliphants 1972) pp. 127–128 identifies

the context as seeking reparation through the courts. For a fuller treatment see C. Sugden, *A Christian Approach to Violence and Revolution*, (M. Phil. thesis presented to the University of Nottingham, 1974) p. 207ff.

21. See my M. Phil. thesis which was a refutation of this Niebuhrian position, partly on the grounds of the lack of eschatology in Niebuhr's theology.

22. Gene Outka, *Agape, an Ethical Analysis*, (Yale, 1972).

Part II

Missiological Expressions

Introduction

Transformation as a concept was adopted in the 1983 Wheaton Statement on the Church in Response to Human Need, reproduced here in chapter thirteen. But the concept required further elucidation which is given first in the opening two chapters of Part Two to introduce the concept of Transformation. Vinay Samuel in chapter eleven, 'Mission as Transformation', expounds Transformation as it had developed to 1998. One aspect of Mission as Transformation is the central place of the poor in the Mission of God. In chapter twelve Chris Sugden in 'What is Good about Good News to the Poor?' expounds how good news to the poor and a bias to the poor faithfully express and expand the meaning of the biblical gospel of grace.

But how is evangelism located in wholistic mission? Stephen Neill said that if everything is mission then nothing is mission. Having laid a clear foundation for their biblical social involvement, evangelicals felt confident enough by 1987 to request a meeting with the World Council of Churches to explore together what was meant by evangelism in the context of wholistic mission. The late David Bosch and Bishop Michael Nazir Ali were among those who drafted the

Stuttgart Statement on Evangelism, here reproduced in chapter fourteen which John Stott identified as representing an overlap and convergence between evangelical and ecumenical concerns at that time.

People began to be hopeful for some rapprochement and co-operation between traditions of mission that had taken divergent paths since the merger over twenty-five years previously of the International Missionary Council with the World Council of Churches in 1961. But such hopes did not come to fruition because of the new reality of post-modernity. This was first identified internationally among evangelicals by Os Guinness at the 1989 Manila Congress on World Evangelisation in his presentation 'Mission Modernity: Seven Checkpoints on Mission in the Modern World' reproduced as chapter 15. Dr Guinness identified the forces of modernity, the engines of modernity, and the late stages of modernity in post-modernity. Modernity noticed that what was significant about humanity was how everyone was the same. This had driven the search for a universal gospel message and the unity of institutional Christian expressions of the gospel. Modernity's late stages in post-modernity noticed how everyone was different. This undermined the search for one global expression of the gospel and one global method of evangelism. Significantly the Manila congress was the last global congress of the Lausanne Committee for World Evangelisation. The social and economic expression of modernity and post-modernity in globalisation, the integration of all aspects of human life in one global market, sets new agendas for the expression of Christian mission and of the Christian gospel, primarily around the question of human identity.

Eleven

Mission as Transformation

Vinay Samuel

One of the most significant responses to mission today is to see Mission as Transformation. The tension between justice and love shapes all contemporary missiological reflection and action. Reinhold Niebuhr has said a rational ethic aims at justice whereas a religious ethic is the ideal. Love is always more important. In that sense, the overarching response should be love. Every vital religion has a millenial hope for society in which the ideal of love and equity is to be fully realised. Every religion has a hope for society – impulses and aspirations that love will be fulfilled and equity established.

The mystical emphasis makes the individual withdraw from the world – wihtout attending to one's neighbour. The prophetic dimension involves one in bringing justice and change in the world. This can be illustrated from Christian choruses. Compare for example the

Mission as Transformation by Vinay Samuel (Unpublished Lecture given at Oxford Centre for Mission Studies, 1998).

songs 'This world is not my home, I am just passing through', and 'Heaven is a Wonderful Place', with the song 'Lord of the Dance' which places its emphasis on the love of God for the poor and marginalised. Here are the tensions of faith, between the mystical desire to withdraw from the world and the desire to serve the neighbour.

How have Christians addressed this tension? They have seen them as two different commissions. The terms used were the evangelism mandate and the creation mandate. John Stott spoke in these terms, at least in the seventies. I do not think he uses such language today. The terms represent the struggle to relate making a response to society and enabling individuals to experience a spiritual transformation in their lives. Some spoke of them as two wings of the same bird, or parallel tracks of the same railway.

This was the approach of the document on Evangelism and Social Responsibility produced by the Consultation on Evangelism and Social Responsibility (CRESR) held in June 1982 and published as 'In Word and Deed' edited by Bruce Nicholls (Paternoster 1986). Those who majored on evangelism claimed that the spiritual mandate for evangelism was primary, the creation mandate for social justice was secondary or was only the fruit of evangelism.

Missiologists put forward many statements and formulations to relate the two together. But practitioners were saying that in practice they could not be separated. For example, a number of people leading mission agencies and projects in India never separated them in practice. But when they attended conferences, especially those which were attended by white people from the West, the same practitioners insisted on separating them, and speaking in public terms of church planting as their primary mission. However, the reality was that direct evangelism took 10% or less or less of their time while 90% of their time was devoted to changing people and the circumstances in which they lived. But in their minds the activists said that evangelism was their priority. In such ways were schizophrenic Christian workers produced.

This struggle to get our priorities right was to some extent resolved by the Consultation on the Church in Response to Human Need in Wheaton in 1983. This produced the document called 'Transformation – the Church in Response to Human Need', which I think would be better subtitled 'The Church's Call to Mission' as it is not limited to a response to need through development and should probably now be revised as a mission text. A year earlier in 1982 the WCC produced an

Ecumenical Affirmation of Mission. They are very similar in a number of concerns and commitments to relate evangelism and social responsibility in an integral way. Of course Evangelii Nuntiandi from the Roman Catholic Church had already defined the relation much earlier. These three statements produced a tremendous impact.

What Are The Components of Mission as Transformation?

1. To see the integral relation between evangelism and social change. Can each component (of evangelism and social change) have a life on its own? Bosch[1] criticises evangelicals and John Stott for saying that evangelism could have a life on its own. But we can criticise Bosch in turn, for while he criticises evangelicals for having evangelism stand on its own, he does not criticise people committed to social involvement for having that stand on its own. How can you have social change without relation to Christ? Wherever social change is attempted it cannot be done without relation to God in Christ – without reference to and relation to what Christ offers to people. Thus one component of transformation is the integral relation of evangelism to social action and not to allow either evangelism or social action to stand on their own.

2. Mission as witness and a journey within the world, not a judgement made from outside it. Mission is not itself an act of judgement. So much of mission gives the impression of being an act of judgement rather than a journey with people and communities towards God's intention. Mission is more of a jounrey than event. Mission is mission on the way – inviting people to take part in a journey. An event on the other hand is a critical judgement. There are critical events that take place on the journey.

3. Mission in Context. A foundational element of transformation is mission in context. Mission as transformation should show that Christian faith is translatable. Faith itself is shaped by the context. The process of the objective truth of the bible applied to personal life was one particular process developed in the West. Different concepts and issues of context came in from the third world, which reminded us again that there were socio-political dimensions to all the theological battles in the early church. Context shapes the very understanding of the Bible. Every text is an interpreted text.

4. Practice and theory: Praxis. Praxis says there is no neutral

relationship to the world. It is a commitment to change it in the direction of abundant life, equity and love. How should we be involved in the world and at the same time maintain our identity in Christ? If Christians have no involvement in the world they become cardboard figures. The question of identity relates not just to who I am, but also to my praxis as well.

5. Context is always local. Context says that theology, Christian mission and understanding is always local. Theological systems claim to explain most things we need to know. But most Two-Thirds World contextual theologians do not write systematic theologies. Systematic theologies are of little use to help change a local church. They help people to write exams. A systematic theology however wonderful has to be localised to a local community.

There are three particular aspects in the context noted by David Bosch[2]: theory, praxis, poiesis. We need all three: Truth; Commitment to Change; Imagination. This is how the Spirit acts. What God will bring out of all that is Faith, Hope and Love.

One of the problems we face is to understand any action historically as the action of God and yet refrain from making it an absolute. The local experience, our way of dealing with the poor, often becomes absolutised, and the universal gets relativised. The gospel is universal. It is truth for all people. Yet, to relate it to my context I relativise the gospel.

6. Freedom and Power. 'If the son shall make you free you shall be free indeed'. This represents the liberating and the empowering dimension of the gospel. The liberating refers to the personal and the social. In the personal sense everyone needs liberation and empowerment – rich and poor alike. In the social sense who needs the liberating dimension of the gospel most? It is then we should talk about the preferential option for the poor.

Liberation theology focused on the poor not because it was trying to undermine the personal dimension of the gospel but when you take the social dimension the poor need it most. When you take the bible and the way it looks at the poor, the youth and the homeless, these become particular objects of the gospel. That is what the bias to the poor is about.

The Gospel is power and freedom – for whom? Who needs it most, who deserves it most?

7. Reconciliation and Solidarity. The Gospel is that which

reconciles God and humanity. The moment we broaden the scope of the gospel from the personal to the social, reconciliation as mission becomes the focus. We are called to address the violence that is endemic to society. This is the mystery hidden for ages (Ephesians 3). In Christ Jew and Gentile become one new humanity. Reconciliation is not just the reconciliation of individuals to God but of people to people. Even angels rejoice in this and evil shudders at it. Paul as a Jew could not quite get over this marvellous reality. What is the most powerful demonstration of the gospel? For Paul that reconciliation was the most powerful expression. Who are we in solidarity with? Where do you see your own solidarity?

8. Building up communities of change. The emphasis of the gospel as transformation is on change and hope. The book of Acts for example is not about merely the calling of individuals to Christ.

Models of Wholistic Mission

The process of entering communities is not the matter of a few days mission. Taking a trip to other places to do mission may be symbolic but it often undermines transformation. Can reconciliation automatically flow out of it? Reconciliation has to be a commitment from the beginning.

In the whole enterprise of mission it has to be noted that those with money are not wholistic. Their local agents may produce a few converts for the bunch of young people to go back to their own context reinforced by this in their unidimensional view of Christianity. When you accept and experience Christ there has to be a transformation of your relationships. Without that commitment to community building there is no transformation in the long haul.

What is Community Building?

1. It is total commitment to the social community, to build communities, to build and bring change. It does not begin with an individual gospel which you then project on to a group of people. People then believe that going to heaven is more important than their commitment to the community. Where is the commitment to the community? My experience is that when people with a unidimensional theology

actually experienced the context, they got changed. There should be a commitment first. Pastors and ministers should be committed to push their church to be involved in the community. If they throw you out so much the worse for them.

2. It is discovering where God is already at work and who is God using already. God is already ahead of me. Who is he working with? Where is the evidence of his work?

3. It is inviting people to join a church, not just to change allegiances. It is inviting people to join a journey with you during which you witness to them of your Lord. You are not there to bring transformation yourself. You are on a journey yourself of self transformation, of community transformation, and you are inviting the people to join a journey, and witness to them of your Lord and your experience.

4. It is inviting people to recognise and respond to the presence of Christ. It is not a journey which you as an individual are taking on your own. What makes the difference is the presence and the reality of Christ with you: not Christ as an idea or Christ described in propositions. The problem is that the gospel is often reduced to a few statements. We then reduce that to a week of mission where statements are bandied about and spoken and everything else is forgotten. My daughter went to Cambridge three years ago, where she first experienced 'Mission'. For her the shock was that here were these wonderful Christian Union kids who were sharing these wonderful words during the week, but their lives afterwards did not reflect anything of all the wonderful happiness they shared. They were not committed to her. They made tremendous efforts to be committed to her to try and get her to that mission week. But there was no commitment beyond that; they do not even know you after that – not even a hi! That is mission for a lot of people. But it is a caricature of mission. Mission should be a willingness of the young people to be committed and say we are here for the long haul. We are here because Christ is with us and we point to that Christ who transforms my life in this journey and we enable people to work together to address their context. It is not to shove the gospel at them but to show them constantly how the gospel relates to their context. That takes time.

It takes time to show how the gospel relates to an undergraduate bewildered, uncertain about the future – understanding and struggling with that and sharing that rather than producing a formula and shoving it at them. I am not talking about preachers, but about young people being trained only to produce formulas. This process was tried by another university Christian organisation in certain contexts but has not really worked. It is essential that people are committed to help them to understand their context, and their struggles where there is no longer ethics only aesthetics, where is no longer real understanding of truth or text.

It is important to centre the whole process on what God has done in Christ by opening individuals and communities to the transcendant and to the intervention of God in contemporary life. One of the contexts where transformation takes place is where you enable communities and individuals to see God intervene and be present personally and directly, not just in words, but enabling reconciliation to shape community life, so that the relationships of the group that is involved are shaped by reconciliation. This process of entering, involvement and change has been documented in actual practice and case studies. If you want the theology of it there is plenty of theology, all the biblical verses for every action you want, in the document 'Transformation'. But I am not just talking about theology – it is important to get involved and start the costly process in the long haul, but that is the only way the gospel's ability to empower can ever be demonstrated.

Issues in Discussion following Lecture

The crucial concept is integration. When I said that 90% of the time people were involved in social action and 10% of the time in direct evangelism, I was not saying that social change was a parallel thing separate from evangelism. Constantly relating the social change they are involved in to Christ is evangelism. When they treat a patient, when they are involved in a project they are sharing about the reality of Christ. You articulate why you do it. If people ask you why are you doing this, that is evangelism. When the same missionary goes back to the West he gives the impression he is doing primary evangelism and the other activities are only secondary and derivative activities, thus short-changing his own western church from understanding how to do wholistic mission in their own context.

The question is that they are trapped by the context that supports them. The context does not accept the integration as legitimate and therefore delegitimises their own mission contexts. Large churches in the UK/US are not involved in their own cities while their own missionaries are involved in some fabulous wholistic work in the

Two-Thirds World. But when the missionaries come back they have to delegitimise their work and put it in this unidimensional context. This undermines their own ability to do transforming mission in their own context.

But a vast number of evangelical churches have integrated and see themselves as taking part in integral evangelism and mission. A lot of Pentecostal churches are good examples of this. Many evangelical churches that are growing are expressing integration but are hampered by the suspicion it is not quite legitimate and you cannot go deeper into it. So while it grows in comparison to its recent past, its sheer impact on society continues to be negligible in cultural and social change.

Where there is no church, efforts from outside are not rejected. But so much local mission has been undermined by those who have not got a calling but just the money. Because they have resources to enter a local context they think they have the calling. If there is a local church elsewhere, however weak or inward looking it may be, it is right for any outside church to see its calling also to be involved in strengthening, enabling and equipping it for the long haul. But such partnership has always been one-sided because of the lopsidedness of resources.The history of this kind of involvement has been where there is a need, we will respond; having the resources generates a calling. But whatever language it is dressed up in, the resources generate the calling. So I want to be suspicious of that. Therefore Christian reconcilation, brotherhood and partnership demands those with resources do not automatically believe they have a calling. They should question their calling vigorously, and ask where is God at work? Who is he working with?

People cannot be unidimensional as people. They are part of a culture. But they are part of a religious culture that has already separated theory from practice; that you can have a theory of truth and take it to outsiders so that they can then practice it. This undermines the very validity of that gospel. It is a cultural issue. That missiological culture is what I am questioning. When those missionaries from that culture who go and do wholistic mission come back here they delegitimise their wholistic mission and act as unwholistic people. They do not bring the fruits of their mission context back home. How many people who have worked in India or Africa come back and their churches cannot use them? But to imagine they can not be used here except for their stories is a myth.

I use evangelism as a journey, saying come alongside, and relate involvement with Christ with involvement in life. How do you relate this to involvement with other religions? We cannot separate our religious commitment from our transforming involvement. What happens to other communities which have other religious commitments? There are some common grounds and starting points. For us in our involvement it is that religion is important for life. Respect for religion is important. But the whole tradition of the West was of Christians not respecting other religions, seeing religions as full of untruth, and temples as abodes of evil spirits. In India, temples were regarded by Christians as abodes of evil spirits. But when I first went into a temple it was not of a fear of evil spirits which I had grown up with from childhood, it was an experience of discovery, the presence of peace, and presence of God, my Jesus weeping over, crying over, drawing people to himself. I found it a place of peace, where thousands of people who over generations have cried out and waited for God. My cry was, did you ever hear their prayers Jesus? They were people with genuine cries. Did you hear them Jesus? You are the only true God. No Hindu who hears me say this would misunderstand my respect for religion or my commitment to Christ or my commitment to religion. The tradition of the Christian faith that has gone beyond falsification to the demonisation of other religions has been the biggest stumbling block for Christian mission in the context of other religions.

Notes

1. David Bosch, *Transforming Mission* (Maryknoll, Orbis, 1992), p. 405.
2. *Ibidem*, p. 431–2.

Twelve

What is Good about Good News to the Poor?

Chris Sugden

John Stott has been passionately concerned with and dedicated to the cause of evangelical Christians in the Two-Thirds World. He gives priority to support for Two-Thirds World evangelical scholars, makes visits to the Two-Thirds World, and is committed to providing literature for their needs in different ways. He holds that the 'mission to which we put our hand must be a wholistic mission that combines the evangelistic and the social and does so unashamedly, and believes that good news and good works belong together and that without good works the good news lacks credibility'.[1]

It is worth asking whether John Stott sacrificed his once preeminent role among English Anglican Evangelicals because of this commitment. For, in 1967 and 1977 John Stott was the acknowledged intellectual leader and arbiter of Anglican Evangelicals at the

'What is Good about Good News to the Poor?' by Chris Sugden in *AD 2000* and Beyond edited by Vinay Samuel and Chris Sugden (Oxford, Regnum, 1991).

two National Evangelical Anglican Congresses at Keele and Nottingham. Yet at the third NEAC at Caister in 1988, though he chaired the listening team and presented the final report one of the features of the congress was the way in which some conservative Anglican evangelicals dissented from positions that John espoused. At a private conference in 1989, John was asked how he handled criticism and misunderstandings of his views. His dignified response showed a person who was vulnerable and able to be hurt by those who appeared to question the integrity with which he bound himself to the word of God.

This essay in tribute seeks to expand our understanding of the glory of the gospel of Jesus Christ by articulating some of the themes that make the good news good to the poor in the Two-Thirds World to which John Stott has devoted his attention. The essay will examine in particular the work and thought of the first scholar to benefit under John Stott's Langham Trust Scholarship Programme Canon Dr Vinay Samuel, who may be dubbed a 'theologian of human dignity'. His thought has opened new paths for theological reflection on the good news to the poor. Such a study of Samuel's thought represents an important fruit of John Stott's work in facilitating and encouraging the development of Two-Thirds World evangelical theologians.

In What Sense is the Good News Good News to the Poor?

The gospel was defined by Jesus as good news to the poor. This is to the materially and socially poor.[2] What the good news means to them is to define what it is to mean to all. It is important then that we discover what is good about the good news to the poor who receive it.

The report of the social concern track at Lausanne II at Manila says:

> The good news is that God has established his Kingdom of righteousness and peace through the incarnation, ministry, atoning death and resurrection of his Son Jesus Christ. The Kingdom fulfils God's purpose in creation by bringing wholeness to humanity and the whole creation. In the Kingdom, people receive by grace alone a new status before God and people, a new dignity and worth as his daughters and sons, and empowerment by his Spirit to be stewards of creation and servants of one another in a new community. The Kingdom will come in its fulness in a new heaven and earth only when Jesus returns.

Those who respond to this good news who are poor in the material sense or powerless are empowered by the Spirit and served by other members of the Kingdom community to experience full humanity as stewards of God's creation. The non-poor who become poor-in-spirit receive a true dignity replacing false pride in riches and are liberated to be truly human with a passion for justice for the poor. They are to trust in the power of God's Spirit which enables them to serve rather than control. They enter a new family that accepts them for who they are rather than for their achievements – in material prosperity or status. The task of evangelisation among the majority of the unreached who are poor will be carried out primarily by those who are poor, with appropriate support from those economically advantaged who are poor in spirit.[3]

A major category for understanding what is good about the good news to the poor is the category of dignity or identity. This is a new category for evangelicals to express the gospel in. It bears further exploration.

Definitions

Dignity literally means a sense of worth. In a Christian view dignity assumes identity. Identity answers the question 'Who am I?' while dignity answers the question 'What am I worth?' The Bible makes the question of identity the prior question. It stresses that both the creation of humanity and redemption are acts of God's grace. Humanity's worth or merit contributes nothing to their creation, and humanity's redemption is despite its demerits. Grace confers identity.

Such a perspective depends on a Christian anthropology which sees humanity as the creation of God, redeemed by Christ and destined for eternal life through the resurrection. If this perspective is removed, for example in a secular world view, then identity tends to be grounded in worth. For example, doctors in the West have to make medical decisions on allocating scarce resources for medical work. The grounds for their choice tend to be the contribution an individual makes to society. Thus a 28 year old married man with two children is considered more eligible for scarce resources than a 68 year old widow. The decisions are grounded not in people's existence as inviolable creatures and children of God, but in their contribution to society evaluated on a certain scale. In such cases people's identity is based on their worth.

True dignity is a sense of self-worth. It requires a sense of identity (a sense of self, of who one is) and a sense of worth (or value) which could come from within oneself or from affirmation by another. Vinay Samuel gives the following definition of human dignity.

> Where we see human dignity being affirmed and people discovering a sense of self-worth, self-acceptance and a sense of having something to contribute to the world and others, we can see God at work.
>
> Where we see people free to be able to act according to their conscience without threat from others who control their actions and thus their attitudes, we can see God at work.
>
> We can see God at work as people are able to make their own contribution to the life of the community, especially as participants in decisions which affect them in the family, the community, in religious matters and the political structures.
>
> We can see God at work as people develop . . . *self-respect* and a sense of worth that they believe the community sets on them; as people *share* in such a way that it enhances the humanity of those they share with rather than reduces it; as people are committed to *struggle against evil* and injustice and as people have a sense of equity and justice.
>
> We can see God at work when women, the weak and the handicapped have a role which accords them dignity and equality, and when their needs receive a priority. We can see God at work when power is shared in such a way that all benefit from its exercise and none are dehumanised.[4]

Human dignity is not the same as human rights in the West which are the rights of the individual before the law. In the Two-Thirds World they are more the rights to basic necessities of life, and set in a more communal framework. Samuel prefers to speak of the right to be human. What counts as human dignity is related to what counts as the right to be human.

Identity, Status and Worth in the Gospels

The concept of dignity is a biblical theme. People are called to find their true human worth and dignity in the context of the call of God to give their allegiance to him. This theme can be seen in the following texts: Deut. 7.7–8; Hos.2.2–3; 1 Cor. 1.26; Eph.2.12–19; 1 Pet. 2.10.

In the New Testament Jesus calls in question the status differentials of his society and gives people a new identity as children of God in his new people of God, starting with those judged to be of least worth according to the values of the day. In the New Testament, status is the key to social ethics.[5]

Jesus crossed status boundaries – he included and ate with 'sinners', people 'characterised by an observable lifestyle or economic activity which has been ethically condemned'.[6] Jesus mixed in public with women. He taught that to enter his kingdom, all had to become as children and servants.

Vinay Samuel points out that the term 'sinner' in the gospels was an identity imposed by the Pharisees on those whom they wished to exclude:

> It was a technical term referring to those who were marginalised by others . . . because their activities and occupations separated them from the life of purity of the Jewish community . . . They were alienated from the life of the Jewish community, from its temple and its religious life.[7]

They were the tax collectors, the prostitutes and the drunkards.

The gospels show that Jesus makes it clear that a person should have an identity that is not imposed, arbitrary or denied. For, as Mott continues:

> Jesus names as 'the lost' those whom his objectors call 'sinners' (cf. also Luke 15:6–7). The redefinition is significant. They are not sinners to be hated and driven away. They are lost, needing to be found and rejoiced over. 'Lost' implies a different status; there is something to be recovered. 'He is a son of Abraham' (v.9). He is neither a devil, nor less than human. He is a lost child of Abraham, the very criterion of membership in the community. (In the Pauline mission, the equivalent criterion is replaced by the universal 'one for whom Christ died'.) Jesus' mission is to find and locate those lost persons and bring them back into the community of God's people. . . . I omit here other groups to which Jesus extended his mission who were also hurt by their social relationships; the sick, women, children, Samaritans. But the same factors of status are present. The status boundaries that Jesus crossed are crucial to the stability of a society. That is why he provoked hostility. Status is one of the most basic elements of a social system. It is a way of controlling people . . . To those who claim that Jesus' ministry was merely personal, we reply that he could not have done anything more basic to challenge institutions and social structures.[8]

Identity and Worth in Paul

Paul keeps identity and worth linked yet separate. Identity includes a sense of having gifts. 'Worth' includes the opportunity to use those in service to others. The understanding of the gifts of the Spirit in the body of Christ is central to Paul's teaching about the new community in Christ. This suggests that human dignity is in part defined by the ability of everyone to contribute their gift to the good of the whole.

Yet Paul's teaching on grace in Ephesians 2:8–9 keeps identity and worth separate. He stresses that our identity is based on being 'saved through grace' and 'not of works'. In Western culture, there is less of a danger of people thinking they can find identity through religious observances, than that they find their identity through the symbols of the standard of living they enjoy. Once the perspective of grace is lost, people's identity is made coterminous with their role, and identity and worth are then confused. Those whose role is judged to be of low value or worth very easily assume that their identity is in question.

Dignity Among Marginalised People

How is human dignity affirmed among those whose dignity has been rubbed out, for example by poverty and the caste system in India? Vinay Samuel includes the social dimension of the gospel in close conjunction with the spiritual dimension to affirm human identity and self-worth.

The detrimental aspects of caste are addressed by making the perceived inequalities between people relative rather than absolute. Christianity relativises the inequalities between people by stressing their common calling as stewards of creation (as the image of God [see below p. 253f.]), their unity in the first Adam as rebels against God, and their common calling as equal creatures of God in a new society. The New Testament gives a basis for mutuality in giving and receiving by stressing that all people and groups have gifts to contribute to the whole body and community which others need. Thus everyone is to be affirmed as a child of God with a gift to share.

Identity and dignity have been key categories in India for interpreting and applying Christianity. M.M. Thomas writes:

Considering the fact that the Christian Missions were the first in many parts of India to treat the untouchables as human beings, and to bring them the gospel of their dignity in Christ as well as education, Christianity has played a part in arousing and strengthening Anti-Brahminism. Further, the climate created by Anti-Brahminism about the necessity of the depressed classes to leave the Hindu fold, for the sake of their human dignity, paved the path of Christian evangelism and the mass movement of conversion among them. And this in turn awoke the Brahmin and other caste Hindu leadership to the need of putting the Hindu household itself in order by social and religious reform . . . fear of Christianity has been the beginning of social wisdom for Hinduism.[9]

We see here the stress on human dignity as the category which made Christianity both attractive to the depressed classes and a threat to Hinduism. Thomas writes 'The search for self-identity by oppressed groups is an essential part of the struggle for human dignity'.[10]

It is the considered judgement of Duncan Forrester and M.M. Thomas among Christian leaders that the major change in the caste system in India in the last one hundred years has come about as the result of Christianity. Forrester concludes:

The most significant achievement of the Protestant critique of caste was undoubtedly its major contribution towards a radical transformation of educated opinion in India. Egalitarian ideas first introduced to India by Protestant missionaries have shown themselves strikingly attractive to the depressed and transformingly challenging to educated opinion. Views on caste which were at the start of our period held and expressed by hardly anyone except Protestant missionaries have now become part of the conventional wisdom.[11]

M.M. Thomas writes:

The outcastes, the poor and the orphans saw Christian faith as the source of a new humanising influence and the foundation of a human community. Where conversion was genuine, whether of individuals or of groups, the converts saw salvation in Christ not only in terms of individual salvation, of heaven after death, but also as the spiritual source of a new community on earth in which their human dignity and status were recognised. It was the promise of humanisation inherent in the gospel of salvation which led to the influx of the oppressed into the church.[12]

Lesslie Newbigin writes:

> The fundamental need was not just the transfer of land but a change of
> consciousness. And this was happening in the communities of Christians
> who lived in the outcaste quarter of hundreds of villages. People who had
> lived for untold centuries as serfs were learning to think of themselves as
> children of God.

Newbigin also writes: 'The Gospel was doing what it has always
done, making it possible for those who were formerly "no people" to
become God's people.'[13]

Godwin Shiri notes how dignity is a crucial category in
contemporary Indian Christian thinking:

> The significance of human dignity, and the Christian responsibility to
> ensure it, is one of the major subjects of discussion in Indian Christian
> social thought. The human is the crown and criterion of creation. The
> human has finite spiritual freedom. Each individual is accorded with dig-
> nity, full personhood, freedom and justice . . . It is argued that within a
> widely dehumanised situation like that of India, the only course of action
> left is humanisation, which can restore human dignity and freedom. The
> concern for human dignity has also motivated Indian Christian social
> thinkers to attempt dialogues with people of other faiths and ideologies.
> It is now recognised that different faiths, ideologies and the state are also
> grappling with the question of human dignity and trying to eradicate the
> sub-human conditions created by the traditional, feudal and colonial
> past and continued by present unjust structures.[14]

In 1981 C.B. Samuel, now director of EFICOR India, Ron Sider and
the writer met in the grounds of Delhi Cathedral with Christian workers among poor communities. We asked them what signs they had
seen of the gospel making an impact on their communities. Luke
Samson talked of a group of garbage workers they had got to know.
These people made their living by scavenging off the open tubs of rubbish on street corners. When they first met these people and struck up
conversation they asked what group they belonged to. They replied
they were ' "konjars", nobodies for no one notices us, they just look
through us'. Luke and his colleagues spent a year visiting them, and
providing a small school for their children. When asked what sign he
saw of the impact of the gospel on their lives, he replied that they no
longer called themselves nobodies.

Christian Lalive D'Epinay in *Haven of the Masses*[15] notes that the reason for the phenomenal growth of Pentecostal churches in Chile was that the churches gave dignity, worth and a role for slum-dwellers who had been made to feel worse than rubbish.

In April 1989 the writer was with an international team of evangelical visitors to South Africa. We had been invited to make a presentation to a mixed audience in Cape Town by Graham Cyster. Donn Thomas, a black pastor and gospel artist from Georgia USA shared passionately that to people whose identity had been taken from them the gospel of God's grace proclaimed: 'You are somebody'.[16]

H. Malcolm Newton speaks of the role that Christianity played in the black community in the USA.

> Religion was not used as a cover up of oppression or the struggle black people encountered throughout America. Instead, it was a source of power, identity and survival. The faith of the church was that factor which sustained people when everything else failed, that is because the Black church and the Black community were one. Black people knew that they were somebody because they could turn to God who gave them identity and worth in the existing social, political and economic structure that said they were nobody. That was why they called each other Mr and Mrs, or brother and sister. The value structures in the society were completely reversed in the church. The last became first in that the janitor became the chairman of the Steward Board and the maid became the president of the Stewardess Board. Everybody became somebody, and there were no second class people in the Black church.[17]

Contemporary Christian reflection on relief and development notes that economic projects do not of themselves enable people to develop this crucial sense of self-worth. Rather the development of self-worth is the foundation for every other human growth. This makes the gospel so vital for any form of change. For change requires that the poor and oppressed change from a perception of themselves as those who are told by the prevailing values in society that they are worthless failures, to a perception that they are people who in Christ have a strong sense of their own and other people's worth. This insight on identity and dignity delivers us from an instrumental view whereby we seek change solely through new rules or rulers, or through programmes brought in from outside or any economic development on its own.

For example, in India some suggest an economic solution to the problem of caste. They argue that craftsmen and peasants should be organized into strong guilds so that they cannot exploited. Others looking for a political solution point out that the people below the poverty line need to gain power by asserting their own rights. But V.T.Rajshekar, a non-Christian leader of the harijans, asserts that the only solution is for the harijans to convert to another religion such as Christianity. He argues that both the economic and political solution require the cooperation of high caste people. But in religious conversion which is a personal matter, cooperation with the high castes is unnecessary. So Rajshekar writes:

> The social degradation of the Untouchables has had religious sanction under Hinduism. So they seek fresh air under other liberating religions . . . conversion to other religions has become popular among the Untouchables, not because after conversion to Christianity and Islam the problem of poverty is solved. To them poverty is not the number one problem. People cannot live by bread alone. They want the self-respect which is denied under Hinduism. They will get it the moment they get out of Hinduism and convert to other religions.[18]

Identity is also an important category for sharing the gospel with the non-poor as the gospel calls them to renounce false pride and security. Extensive sections of Jesus' teaching are devoted to this. First, mammon is a rival divinity to God, which leads people to get their priorities wrong and prevents people entering God's kingdom where they would find the fulfilment of their humanity. To enter the kingdom, people need to renounce wealth (Mark 10:27); love for riches is a major obstacle to spiritual growth (Mark 4:19), and fields, oxen and marriage arrangements lead people to refuse God's invitation (Luke 14:15–24). In the parable of the rich fool, Jesus teaches that riches blind people to God's kingdom. For rich people tend to seek their security in wealth. Jesus encourages people to seek their security in God's kingdom, for in God's kingdom, God will provide the basic necessities of life for his subjects. So they have no need to use up energy and attention worrying about their own food, drink, clothing, length of life, the future, persecution or death. Instead, free of self-concern they can give time and attention to God's kingdom standards of just relationships. Since God will provide their necessities, members of the kingdom can give to the poor. Giving money to the poor is saving treasures in heaven (Luke 12:33) and enables trust in God to be expressed. When people give to the poor, they find security in trusting that God will provide enough for their needs. Saving riches on earth expresses no trust in God, because the riches are being laid up for the self. People then do not give money time or attention to the needs of the poor because they need everything to bolster their own sense of security which can never be satisfied.

This is good news for the rich. Jesus sets them free from rebelling against God by seeking security in their wealth. He sets them free to devote their attention and wealth to the concerns of God's kingdom, God's right relationships and especially the poor.

Identity as the Source of Dignity

People cannot fulfil God's purpose for them if they have no sense of worth or of identity. Without identity or worth they will be prey to the idea (often fostered by others) that they deserve no more than the poverty and suffering that is their lot. They will have no hope for anything better.

A sense of identity gives people a sense of worth, and the idea that they should not be treated as less than human. Identity which is a gift of grace from God contradicts the middle-class value which tends to seek identity through works and effort, and the value (to which Jesus thought that religious leaders were particularly prone) to seek identity through approbation by people (Matt.23:5–7).

An example of how a sense of identity was a crucial dimension of the gospel is the story of Christian mission in Jamkhed in Maharashtra state, near Bombay. Two Christian doctors, man and wife, identified that the people with the greatest need were the children. Many died before they reached five years old. This group of villages had been evangelised fifty years before but the people had rejected the gospel. Now the doctors began to address the needs of the children. That was their starting point. To do that they trained some women to give the nursing mothers some information about child-rearing. The women they chose were the women of the lowest status – the widows of outcastes. Their starting point with the women was to give them dignity, a role and status. They taught them how Jesus gave equality to women. This process gave them a dignity and equality their society had denied them. The process took twenty years, but as a result seventeen villages have accepted Jesus as their Lord, child mortality has been greatly reduced, women have been given equality and Jesus is accepted as the village God.

Vinay Samuel sees that in calling people to himself, God gives them identity and worth by giving them worth through a new set of values by which to evaluate worth. He enables them to have worth through stewarding creation and through mutual sharing with one another in the body of Christ. We identify four major components of Samuel's thought. Identity is a gift of grace. It is to be found in the family of God. Dignity and identity depend on a truly biblical doctrine of humanity, and dignity is affirmed as people develop their theology in context.

Identity is a Gift of Grace

The basic identity given in Christ is a matter of grace. Vinay Samuel writes:

> In the New Testament we also see a focus on the restoration of the true relationship between the community, people's gifts and their access to resources. Paul focused on the gifts which people had in themselves and on just relationships. This was to enable people's gifts to be used and developed in community to benefit everyone. There was a clear separation between the development of people's gifts and their personal fulfilment on the one hand, and the meeting of their needs on the other. This was because people's worth was found neither in their gifts, nor in their role, but in Christ. In the world at large the incentive to develop one's gifts is in order to meet needs. This assumes that people's needs will only be met if their talents are developed. It closely ties people's worth to their gifts and their role.[19]

Here Samuel asserts that people's identity is established in Christ as a matter of grace, and expressed and affirmed as they discover and exercise their gifts.

The gospel of grace gives people identity independently of their role, status or works. In the Indian context low valuation is given in society to certain groups of people (outcastes, the poor, women). There is no worth for them in the social system. Economic development will not change this. But Christianity offers a new identity. A major reason for the mass movements of conversion to Christianity in the early part of this century in India was so that people could escape the low valuation given them in Hindu society. The new identity of being a creature of God, and in Christ a son/daughter of God, came from outside the system. The gospel brought a new identity and dignity measured by a new set of values. The identity was to be a son of God. The new dignity was given through the new set of values from God: that to be a son of God was to be in his family; that God's purpose was that people should be whole and healthy, that there should be equality between men and women, and that poverty was not his will for them.

The dignity (worth) of this new identity (self) is to be expressed in tasks that affirm the new dignity; thus men and women worship together, outcastes and higher castes share the same Lord's table, and women receive medical treatment and education. But this new dignity does not find its source in the tasks. Thus Christians can be called on to take on the role of a servant, itself of low value, without their identity being threatened. Samuel writes:

> This feudal pattern (in India) only survives because it creates dependency in others. The leaders can create dependency because they act as gate-keepers to the Aladdin's cave of scarce resources and coveted positions. For the masses such dependency is often a vital factor for survival. People remain dependent because they know that to get the 'goodies' they must support the dominant and prominent. . . . One reason why the church has not provided servant leadership is that the vast majority of her members have come originally from the servant castes in society where insecurity is the norm . . . Conversion from Islam may remove the stigma and status of servanthood. But it is unlikely to produce the kind of people who are willing to be servants of the country. Only in the gospel of Christ can sons be sent out to be servants.[20]

Grace confers identity before we have the opportunity to acquire merit, and in spite of our demerits. Eugene Outka stresses this in his discussion of agape.[21] Agape is the love of God which confers dignity and identity.

Many discussions of agape polarise agape as either a virtue resident in the agent alone (in this case a hermit can be as loving as Mother Teresa) or as enlightened self-interest seeking a relationship that in fact benefits the agent. Outka argues that God's love is revealed as a love that bestows value on people. God's love is spontaneous and unmotivated by the particular worth of particular people. Jesus' own action is that he seeks out the lost and consorts with publicans and sinners.

God's love is indifferent to value. One cannot understand what grace is until one abandons all thought of the worth of the particular human object of that love.

God's love creates value. What gives a person value is precisely the fact that God loves him/her. God's love initiates fellowship with God.

On such a view, agape bestows worth. Any worth people have is not their's intrinsically but is bestowed by God. This is no creative fiction because a person's ultimate status does not depend on others acting as though he had this status, but is a status conferred by God.

This love of God is revealed. People do not know of it by themselves because our knowledge of good and evil is obscured by sin. This revealed love of God entails equal regard for the neighbour. For this status of value before God is shared by all people in relation to each other. Therefore one person's well-being is as valuable as another's. If God bestows value on people, people ought to appraise other people as of equal value in the light of God's bestowal and not because of any supposed intrinsic worth.

God is able to love those who have obvious demerits because of the cross where Jesus took the penalty of God's judgement on all our demerits. The cross is the heart of grace which confers worth. To urge that the good news of the gospel is that God gives a new identity to people freely as his sons and daughters is to expound the meaning of the grace that is at the heart of the cross of Jesus.

The cross gives a further important link between identity and the liberation of poor people. In a study of John Perkins' ministry in the USA Stephen Berk notes:

> A new sense of spiritual power and self-worth gave Mendenhall's blacks the impetus to challenge their white oppressors politically. As the civil rights movement mounted, Voice of Calvary (John Perkins' organisation) led a voter registration drive which marked the turning point away from codependent accommodation. Newly emergent blacks campaigned for a highway commissioner candidate who had promised them jobs . . . Victims always need to come to a place of such self assertion in order to overcome powerlessness and fully experience their indignation. But once such self-affirmation occurs, forgiveness and healing reconciliation must take place in order for community to grow.[22]

This love and grace is not in tension with God's justice. For this grace is not experienced by the individual in isolation. Philip Wogaman writes:

> God's grace is what defines his justice – His grace is what reveals the deep moral reality lying at the foundations of a Christian conception of justice.

In answer to Aristotle's implied question about justice, the Christian responds that what is 'due' to everyone has already been given in Christ: God's total acceptance in grace. We are, as Ephesians puts it, 'no longer strangers and sojourners' (2:19). By God's grace what is due to us is to belong. In the first instance it is to belong to God, the Creator and Sustainer of all. But derivatively, it is also to belong to one another. No-one who is loved by God may any longer be rejected by us – which is a minimal way to put it. A stronger way to say this is that God's love has made us all family. . . . God's gracious purposes are to be implemented by his creative purposes. Concretely, this means that our belonging to one another in community must be undergirded by the physical, legal and institutional conditions making our participation possible.[23]

Identity is to be Found in the Family of God

Identity is not first of all a question of individual identity. Identity is affirmed through relationships in the new community of God's family. Samuel writes:

> In calling people to join him and his community, Jesus established people's new identity, as people of God. The emphasis in the New Testament on Christian's (sic) identity as children of God is on the community first. The 'children of God' was a phrase for Israel. The 'children of God are a family and a community, not just an aggregate of the sons of God. Just as individuals gained their identity by belonging to the covenant community of Israel, so followers of Jesus gain their identity by allegiance to him and incorporation into his community.'[24]
>
> God's covenant with the community is the basis for the identity of the individual, and a vital community life in obedience to God requires members who are personally loyal to the community's Lord and to one another. Thus the very basis for personal change is the establishment of a new society which is in itself an element of social change.[25]

When people are alienated from their true identity, the gospel reconciles them with their true selves as God intends them to be, stewards of creation and children of God. In the same moment the gospel also reconciles people with others as God gives them a new identity in his family in which divisions are broken down. The gospel of a new identity in Christ is thus the gospel of reconciliation. Samuel writes:

> The Christian gospel is about breaking down barriers between God and man and between man and man and so addresses issues such as the

barriers between rich and poor, caste and outcaste. So the Christian witness cannot be the witness of an individual alone testifying to his own personal religious experience. It must be the witness of the life of a Christian community in which the new life of reconciliation is being expressed.[26]

Samuel consistently refuses to consider the individual apart from the context of the community. He argues that the gospel is addressed to groups and communities first, and within that the individual is addressed. Christopher Wright affirms this insight from the Bible:

Westerners like myself have to undergo a certain reorientation in our habitual pattern of ethical thought in this matter if we are to see things from a biblical perspective. We tend to begin at the personal level and work outwards . . . However, the Bible tends to place the emphasis the other way round: Here is the kind of society that God wants . . . what kind of person must you be to be worthy of your inclusion within it, and what must be your contribution to the furthering of these overall social objectives.[27]

The new identity given to the poor is not therefore a new individual self-image attained in a spiritual sphere divorced from other relationships or received on one's own apart from the world.

Jesus did not call people to have a transcendental or inward relationship with himself, to which their social relationships of wealth, fraud, lust of lack of forgiveness were to a greater or lesser extent hindrances which had to be taken care of . . . . Jesus' call to his disciples was totally bound up with his view of what the community of disciples and Israel should be and do.[28]

Again:

Many Christians speak of receiving eternal life as though it was a gift of transcendental bliss or inward peace, which comes to people to be received in totality in complete isolation from their context . . . (The Biblical) call to discipleship was a call to follow Jesus and join a community who took a stance in a context.[29]

Identity in a new family has practical implications. For this new identity is found in a new community of Jews and Gentiles, rich and poor, reconciled in one body. So, first, if people are to gain this new identity in full, the interelationship between those who have formerly been divided must be restored; for example the relationship between Western and Two-Thirds Worlds[30] and between rich and poor. This is not a new individual identity, or an identity over against others. It is an identity of persons in a new community, men and women, black and white, Western and Two-Thirds World together where the precious gift of those from another culture is to help us, even painfully, to find our true selves.

The identity of the poor is not to be found in suffering, in being endlessly the victim. It is found in God's grace, God's victory, that before the revolution, apart from any prediction about change in structures, people can have a new identity as sons and daughters of God.

People's identity is not to be found in conflict over against others – as in a pale reflection of a Marxist dialectic – or in building up strength in worldly terms. That ignores the need for the cross which calls *both* rich and poor to repentance and God's forgiveness of their sins.

It is crucial that people in separated groups experience this new identity together because both have been accepted in grace at the cross of Christ. When this understanding is lacking, a process begins of blaming others and ignoring the sins of our own societies which contribute to the problem.

In 1990 the writer attended an international Christian conference where a large number of people from suffering groups in the Two-Thirds World were telling their stories. They identified that the the pain and hurt their communities were suffering was caused by the activities of economies originating from 'the north'. Representatives of countries from the north were at the conference. Many of them thoroughly supported the cause of the suffering communities in the Two-Thirds World. However, the cross of Christ was not central in the discussions. Thus the south kept blaming the north, and became oblivious to sins in the south, such as the corruption of one party state dictators in Africa. The north was not heard except as it punished itself.[31]

Christ's atoning death needs to be central as the basis of forgiveness. God has forgiven all an unpayable debt, so that we may forgive each other the debts we owe one another. If a sense of Christ's death is not present, people cannot easily let go of the sense of the wrongs they have suffered or been party to inflicting. Victims continuously present themselves as victims. They take on a heroic, even messianic role. A competition emerges to demonstrate that one particular group is undergoing the worst suffering – depending on the situation contenders may be inner city blacks in western cities; Indian outcaste women; South African blacks; youths sent to war and prostitution. The guilty have continually to express their guilt and atone for it by keeping silent or by a self-righteous posturing on behalf of the oppressed.

Secondly, the proclamation among the poor of a gospel that affirms a new identity and dignity requires relationships within the church which affirm people's dignity, equality and their contribution. The local church has a very important role in this respect. Here Samuel's concern for leadership which affirms and builds people up is most important.[32]

Dignity and identity depend on a truly biblical doctrine of humanity

What counts as human dignity for Samuel is related to what counts as the right to be human. He defines humanity functionally and biblically through the concepts of community and stewardship.

Samuel analyses his own context of India as a context in which production, employment and economics curtails people's ability to be stewards. 'Dispossession of power over resources through unjust distribution of wealth or through exclusion from decision making procedures in a common undertaking leads to false dependence, lack of responsibility and powerlessness.'[33] His activities in setting up employment projects in Lingarajapuram slum in the north of Bangalore City, South India are to enable people to become what God means them to be – stewards and managers of creation.

Samuel understands the image of God to mean the dominion that God gives to men and women together over creation. He does not discuss image in the classical Western categories of 'Godlike', 'able to communicate with God' or 'reflect his character'. Following the view taken by Old Testament scholar, David Clines,[34] Samuel writes:

The term (image) referred to the statue in the temple, or the king on the throne who represented an invisible god who lived on the mountain. The king was the substitute for the god, and accountable to him for the way he ruled. The image was the regent, agent or overseer for God. He was responsible for God's territory in that area. He was the tenant of his property, responsible to him for its management. This concept of management on behalf of another comes across clearly in Genesis 1.27–28, the verse which describes man and woman being made in the image of God.[35]

Samuel therefore argues:

> The doctrine of the image of God is about man's role as steward of creation . . . about man's relationships . . . the image is to be understood in terms of personal relationships, rather than in terms of man's individual psychological make-up. Man is to exercise his role of dominion together with women over the creation as the steward of God. Thus people are not isolated individuals, but persons in relationship to God, one another and the material world.[36]

Samuel uses the concept of stewardship to analyse humanity's fall theologically. He wants to address and correct a view of humanity that divorces God's restoration of humanity from life on earth. He notes that some views see the corruption of the relationship with God as prior to all other relationships. He develops the theme of stewardship and its spoiling through the fall to demonstrate that:

> the fall was the corruption of all humanity's relationships. . . . the corruption of the relationship with God is integral to the corrupting of the relationships with other people . . . We are sometimes given the impression that the only relationship which matters which is corrupted is the relationship with God and that the rest are just consequences of that. The fall would tell us that all those relationships together are corrupted. The corruption of the relationship between people is an expression of the corruption of the relationship with God. The corruption of the relationships with the environment are an expression of the corruption of the relationships with people and with God.[37]

He sets this call to be stewards as a framework for the restoration of humanity:

> If the image of God is stewardship and if Christ is enabling the true image of God to be formed in us (a reference to Romans 8.29) then Christians

should now express a better ability to be stewards. The working out of our salvation should include the demonstration of the recovery of our responsibility for creation. The image of God will only be truly recreated in us when we are rightly related not only in our personal relationships, but to nature as well.[38]

Samuel notes the misuse of stewardship when humanity exercises its proper dominion over creation improperly over other people and so usurps the place of God. The correction is that Christians are to be servants. Samuel argues that in the parable of the talents, talents are to be stewarded by being used in the service of the master who, in the next block of teaching, tells his followers that they serve him when they serve the poor, the sick, the naked, the prisoner.[40]

Neither the New Testament nor Samuel in his interpretation sees stewardship of creation as a manipulation of the earth's resources purely for humanity's benefit. Stewardship is to be exercised in servanthood to Jesus and to those he calls his brothers, the poor.[41] In this framework he harnesses the resources of the wealthy in building clinics and financing loan schemes. He calls and enables them to be servants with their resources.

The dignity of being stewards, of being managers of creation also speaks to those who are entrusted with resources to facilitate people in business and other enterprises. Their calling is not to be dispensers of charity or funds to address the 'needs' of others which are endless. Their calling is to enable others to be stewards also. Samuel is co-chairman of the Oxford Conference on Christian Faith and Economics which published a three year study by Professor Joe Remenyi on income generation programmes. Remenyi found that:

> there is sufficient evidence to indicate that investment in the enterprises of the poor is well below socially desirable levels . . . The overwhelming importance of private enterprise in the informal poverty economy gives non-government organisations a special place and a special opportunity to take the lead in income and employment generation initiatives among the poor.[42]

Samuel encourages dignity by promoting a view of humanity, deriving from his biblical understanding, which involves promoting a just stewardship of resources, either through giving people access to resources or through calling people to servanthood in using them.

Dignity and the Theological Enterprise

Samuel makes activity in history to affirm and promote human dignity the basis of dialogue with Hindus in India. He points out that in the Hindu context the oppressive dimensions of casteism which treats twenty per cent of the Indian population as less than human is reinforced by the religious world view of the Brahmin. This world view says that the wealth of the oppressor and the suffering of the oppressed are both caused by fate. The poor have no grounds for claiming that their situation is objectively unjust. 'The gospel . . . enables the questions of the marginalised Hindus to be affirmed and addressed by the gospel and it addresses those questions to the socially elite leader.'[41] The gospel proclaims that it is not the will of God for people to be other than his stewards, sons and daughters and servants.

Christian activity in history must be in line with the activity of God in the context of scripture. In scripture, history is the context of the claim that Jesus was unique and that he is the Messiah, the one who announced the Kingdom of God and brought it through his death and resurrection and so fulfils God's purposes given through the prophets for Israel and the creation.

Christian activity which affirms the worth of poor people, calls them to be sons and daughters of God, and enables them in practical ways to be stewards of the creation is a witness to the activity of God through Jesus Christ in history enabling people to be human. The challenge is to those of other religious faiths to demonstrate similar activity which also witnesses to a similar understanding of humanity and to such activity of God through their community. Dialogue on issues of the place of the poor and the denial of their human rights is how Jesus dialogued with the religious leaders of his time and is a powerful form of dialogue today.

Evangelical mission theologians in and from the Two-Thirds World articulate the category of dignity as an important category for expressing the gospel in contexts of poverty. They are sensitive to this category from their own experience. For they perceived their relationship with Western churches and agencies that control so much of the resources for world mission as paralleling the experiences of poor people. Many such theologians have been facilitated by John Stott.

Such theologians desire to make their own contribution to the theological enterprise. Bishop Michael Nazir-Ali, a former Langham Scholar, points out that the Western church was often content to refer to Michael and his colleagues for examples and case-studies of mission, but not for input on fundamental matters of theology. But as Gustavo Gutierrez pointed out in Oxford, the logical corollary of describing a theology as 'Latin American theology' is to describe other theology as 'English' or 'North American theology'.

Evangelical mission theologians from the Two-Thirds World hold that their being and dignity as Two-Thirds World Christians is undermined if they have to accept as determinative a gospel formulated in a different context than their's. If the church is to be genuinely a home for affirming human dignity among the poor communities they work among, its own international relationships must affirm and express that dignity.

So the nineteen eighties were marked by a series of conferences in which Two-Thirds World evangelical mission theologians articulated their own theologies.[43] John Stott himself supported these conferences of mission theologians from the Two-Thirds World in different ways. He responded to the papers presented at the first conference by writing these words in commending the conference book: 'I welcomed the decision to hold this first conference of evangelical mission theologians from the Two-Thirds World; those of us who belong to the remaining One Third World not only need to listen respectfully to them, but will undoubtedly be enriched in the process.'[44]

The Lambeth Conference of Anglican Bishops particularly demonstrated this contribution as the African bishops brought their agendas, their stories, and their evangelistic theology to the fore in a process which launched the Anglican Communion on a decade of evangelism.[45] At a crucial stage in the planning of this conference, a Two-Thirds World theological process was injected which enabled the request 'To bring your diocese with you' to bring the grassroots experiences of the churches in mission into the processes of theological formulation. This is a major contribution of the theological insights and inputs from the Two-Thirds World.

Summary

God's grace is the source of identity, and humanity in relationships is the context for affirming dignity. Grace gives a new identity in the family of God. This identity is expressed in the stewardship of gifts and servanthood.

To the poor the gospel affirms that they are equals in the family of God, have gifts to share, and need access to resources in order to fulfil their calling as stewards and servants.

The category of identity gives a criteria for analysing and identifying oppression. Oppression is when people are prevented from being stewards and from fulfilling God's purpose of being truly human.

Identity cannot be provided by relief, welfare, or development projects. Identity is provided in the gospel. That is why the gospel is so fundamental to Christian involvement in any social change.

This identity is not contentless, nor to be left in the abstract. It is to be expressed in a new community where old barriers are broken down; it is to be expressed in fulfilling God's calling to humanity to subdue the earth as stewards of earth's resources.

Only in Christ can people be given that new identity as sons and daughters of God the father. This identity empowers them to believe that God's purpose for them is that they be stewards and that all the power of God is available to them to overcome the forces of evil that prevent them from exercising and fulfilling stewardship.

Notes

1. In a speech made on the occasion of his retirement as president of the Evangelical Fellowship in the Anglican Communion.
2. The biblical discussion of this point can be followed in *Evangelism and the Poor* edited by Vinay Samuel and Chris Sugden (Paternoster, 1986). The Lausanne publication *Christian Witness to the Urban Poor* found that 'The poor refers to the manual worker who struggles to survive on a day to day basis, the destitute cowering as a beggar; the one reduced to meekness, the one brought low . . . those weak and tired from carrying heavy burdens, the leper and very often "the common people" . . . the majority of references indicate that the poor are the mercilessly oppressed, the powerless, the destitute, the downtrodden.'
3. 'Report of the Social Concern Track at Lausanne II' in *Transformation* July 1990.
4. 'God's Intention for the World: Tensions between Eschatology and History' in *The Church in Response to Human Need* edited by Vinay Samuel and Chris Sugden (Eerdmans, 1987) p. 149.
5. Stephen Mott, *Jesus and Social Ethics* (Nottingham, Grove Books, 1984) p. 11.
6. Mott op. cit. p. 12.
7. Mott op. cit. p. 13.

8. *The Gospel of Transformation* unpublished paper chapter 4 p. 11.
9. M.M. Thomas *The Secular Ideologies of India and the Secular Meaning of the Gospel* (Madras, Christian Literature Society, 1976) p. 152.
10. M.M. Thomas op. cit., p. 156
11. Duncan Forrester, *Caste and Christianity* (London, Curzon Press, 1980) p. 201.
12. M.M. Thomas, *Salvation and Humanisation* (Madras, Christian Literature Society, 1971) p. 14
13. Lesslie Newbigin, *Unfinished Agenda* (London, S.P.C.K., 1985), p 142.
14. Godwin Shiri, *Christian Social Thought in India 1962–1977* (Bangalore, Christian Institute for the Study of Religion in Society, 1982) pp. 149–150.
15. Christian Lalive D'Epinay, *Haven of the Masses* (Lutterworth, 1969).
16. The Report of this visit is reproduced in *Transformation* October 1989.
17. H. Malcolm Newton, 'Missiology from a Black Perspective' Thesis presented to Dallas Theological Seminary 1984 pp. 8–9.
18. V.T. Rajshekar in *The Gospel among our Hindu Neighbours* edited by Vinay Samuel and Chris Sugden (Bangalore, 1982) p. 131–2.
19. Vinay Samuel, *The Gospel of Transformation* op. cit. chapter 2 p. 12.
20. Vinay Samuel and Chris Sugden 'Sons and Servants' in *Third Way* October 1981 p. 9.
21. Gene Outka, *Agape, an Ethical Analysis* (Yale, 1982) p. 154–169.
22. 'From Proclamation to Community – The Work of John Perkins' Stephen E Berk *Transformation* Vol. 6 No. 4 October 1989 p. 5.
23. Philip Wogaman 'Toward a Christian Definition of Justice' *Transformation* Vol. 7 No. 2 April 1990 p. 18.
24. 'Evangelism and Social Responsibility' by Vinay Samuel and Chris Sugden in *In Word and Deed* edited by Bruce Nicholls (Exeter, Paternoster Press, 1985) p. 193.
25. 'Evangelism and Social Responsibility' op. cit. p. 211.
26. 'Dialogue with Other Religions' by Vinay Samuel and Chris Sugden in *The Gospel among our Hindu Neighbours* edited by Vinay Samuel and Chris Sugden (Bangalore, 1982) p. 208.
27. Christopher Wright 'The Use of the Bible in Social Ethics' in *Transformation* Vol. 1 No. 1 January 1984 p. 14. See also Grove Books on Ethics, No. 51 Nottingham 1983.
28. Vinay Samuel, *The Meaning and Cost of Discipleship* (Bombay, BUILD, 1981) p. 55.
29. Vinay Samuel, *The Meaning and Cost of Discipleship* op. cit., p. 56.
30. See for example Vinay Samuel and Chris Sugden *Partnership for Mission – a Third World View* (Bangalore, Partnership in Mission Asia, 1983) and *Christian Mission in the Eighties – A Third World Perspective* (Bangalore, PIM Asia, 1981).
31. See Christopher Sugden 'The Poor are the Losers' in *Transformation* Vol. 7 No. 3 July 1990.
32. Vinay Samuel 'Leadership' in *Transformation* Vol. 3 No. 4 October 1986 p. 26.

33. 'A Just and Responsible Lifestyle' in *Lifestyle in the Eighties* edited by Ronald J Sider (Exeter, Paternoster Press, 1981) p. 51.
34. See David Clines 'The Image of God in Man' in *Tyndale Bulletin* (1968) p. 57.
35. Vinay Samuel in *The Gospel of Transformation* op. cit. p. 6.
36. 'Evangelism and Social Responsibility' op. cit. p. 198–9.
37. Samuel, *The Gospel of Transformation* op. cit. p. 8–9.
38. Samuel, *The Gospel of Transformation* op. cit. p. 7.
39. See *The Gospel of Transformation* op. cit. p. 7–8 and 'Sons and Servants' *Third Way* October 1981 p. 9.
40. Vinay Samuel, *The Meaning and Cost of Discipleship* op. cit. p. 26–28.
41. See Joe Remenyi, 'Income Generation Programmes for Poverty Alleviation' in *Transformation* Vol. 7 No. 2 April 1990.
42. Vinay Samuel and Christopher Sugden, *The Gospel among our Hindu Neighbours* (Bangalore, Partnership in Mission-Asia, 1982) p. 207–208.
43. See *Sharing Jesus in the Two-Thirds World* edited by Vinay Samuel and Chris Sugden, (Eerdmans, 1984); *The Living God*, edited by David Gitari and Patrick Benson, (Nairobi, Uzima, 1987); 'Witnessing to the Living God' in *Transformation* 1988.
44. See *Sharing Jesus in the Two-Thirds World* edited by Vinay Samuel and Chris Sugden, (Eerdmans, 1984)
45. See Vinay Samuel and Chris Sugden, *Lambeth – a View from the Two-Thirds World* (London, S.P.C.K., 1989).

Thirteen

Transformation:
The Church in Response to Human Need
Wheaton Consultation June 1983

Introduction

For two weeks during June 1983 we have come together from local churches and Christian mission and aid agencies at Wheaton College in the USA from 30 nations to pray about and reflect upon the church's task in response to human need. Some of us belong to churches which are situated among marginalized peoples who live in situations of poverty, powerlessness, and oppression. Others come from churches situated in affluent areas of the world. We are deeply grateful to our heavenly Father for allowing us the privilege of

'Transformation – the Church in Response to Human Need' in *The Church in Response to Human Need* edited by Vinay Samuel and Chris Sugden (Grand Rapids, Eerdmans, 1987).

sharing our lives with one another, studying the Scriptures in small groups, considering papers on aspects of human development and transformation, and looking closely at the implications of case studies and histories which describe different responses to human need. Because God hears the cries of the poor, we have sought each other's help to respond (Exod. 3:7–9; James 5:1–6). We rejoice at what we believe the Holy Spirit has been teaching us concerning God's specific purpose and plans for His distressed world and the part the church has to play in them.

As we have faced the enormous challenge before God's people everywhere to alleviate suffering and, in partnership together, to eliminate its causes, we are more than ever aware of the liberating and healing power of the Good News of Jesus. We gladly reaffirm, therefore, our conviction that Jesus Christ alone is the world's peace, for He alone can reconcile people to God and bring all hostilities to an end (Eph. 2:14–17).

We acknowledge, furthermore, that only by spreading the Gospel can the most basic need of human beings be met: to have fellowship with God. In what follows we do not emphasize evangelism as a separate theme, because we see it as an integral part of our total Christian response to human need (Matt. 28:18–21). In addition, it is not necessary simply to repeat what the Lausanne Covenant and the Report of the Consultation on the Relationship between Evangelism and Social Responsibility (CRESR, Grand Rapids, 1982) have already expressed.

What we have discovered we would like to share with our brothers and sisters throughout the world. We offer this statement, not as an attempt to produce a final word, but as a summary of our reflections.

Both Scripture and experience, informed by the Spirit, emphasize that God's people are dependent upon His wisdom in confronting human need. Local churches and mission agencies, then, should act wisely, if they are to be both pastoral and prophetic. Indeed the whole human family with its illusions and divisions needs Christ to be its Wisdom as well as its Savior and King.

Conscious of our struggle to find a biblical view of transformation that relates its working in the heart of believers to its multiplying effects in society, we pray that the Spirit will give us the discernment we need. We believe that the wisdom the Spirit inspires is practical rather than academic, and the possession of the faithful rather than the preserve of the elite. Because we write as part of a world full of conflict and a church easily torn by strife we desire that the convictions expressed in this document be further refined by God's pure and peaceable wisdom.

Some may find our words hard. We pray, however, that many will find them a help to their own thinking and an encouragement to 'continue steadfast, immovable, always abounding in the work of the Lord, knowing that in the Lord your labor is not in vain' (1 Cor. 15:58).

I. Christian Social Involvement

1. As Christians reflect on God's intention for the world they are often tempted to be either naively optimistic or darkly pessimistic. Some, inspired by a utopian vision seem to suggest that God's Kingdom, in all its fullness, can be built on earth. We do not subscribe to this view, since Scripture informs us of the reality and pervasiveness of both personal and societal sin (Isa. 1:10–26; Amos 2:6–8; Mic. 2:1–10; Rom. 1:28–32). Thus we recognize that utopianism is nothing but a false dream (see the CRESR Report, IV. A).

2. Other Christians become pessimistic because they are faced with the reality of increasing poverty and misery, of rampant oppression and exploitation by powers of the right and the left, of spiralling violence coupled with the threat of nuclear warfare. They are concerned, too, about the increasing possibility that planet earth will not be able to sustain its population for long because of the wanton squandering of its resources. As a result, they are tempted to turn their eyes away from this world and fix them so exclusively on the return of Christ that their involvement in the here and now is paralyzed. We do not wish to disregard or minimize the extensive contribution made by a succession of Christians who have held this view of eschatology, through more than one hundred years, to medical and educational work in many countries up to the present day. Nevertheless, some of us feel that these men and women have tended to see the task of the church as merely picking up survivors from a shipwreck in a hostile sea. We do not endorse this view either, since it denies the biblical injunctions to defend the cause of the weak, maintain the rights of the poor and oppressed (Ps. 82:3), and practice justice and love (Mic. 6:8).

3. We affirm, moreover, that, even though we may believe that our calling is only to proclaim the Gospel and not get involved in political

and other actions, our very non-involvement lends tacit support to the existing order. There is no escape: either we challenge the evil structures of society or we support them.

4. There have been many occasions in the history of the church – and some exist today – where Christians, faced with persecution and oppression, have *appeared* to be disengaged from society and thus to support the status quo. We suggest, however, that even under conditions of the most severe repression, such Christians may in fact be challenging society and even be transforming it, through their lifestyle, their selfless love, their quiet joy, their inner peace, and their patient suffering (1 Pet. 2:21–25).

5. Christ's followers, therefore, are called, in one way or another, not to conform to the values of society but to transform them (Rom. 12:1–2; Eph. 5:8–14). This calling flows from our confession that God loves the world and that the earth belongs to Him. It is true that Satan *is* active in this world, even claiming it to be his (Luke 4:5–7). He is, however, a usurper, having no property rights here. All authority in heaven and on earth has been given to Christ Jesus (Matt. 28:18; Col. 1:15–20). Although His Lordship is not yet acknowledged by all (Heb. 2:8) He is the ruler of the kings of the earth (Rev. 1:5), King of kings and Lord of lords (Rev. 19:16). In faith we confess that the old order is passing away; the new order has already begun (2 Cor. 5:17; Eph. 2:7–10; Matt. 12:18; Luke 7:21–23).

II. Not only Development but Transformation

6. The participants at this conference have entered into the current discussions concerning development. For many Western political and business leaders development describes the process by which nations and peoples become part of the existing international economic order. For many people of the Two-Thirds World it is identified with an ideologically motivated process of change, called 'developmentalism.' This process is intrinsically related to a mechanistic pursuit of economic growth that tends to ignore the structural context of poverty and injustice and which increases dependency and inequality.

7. Some of us still believe, however, that 'development,' when reinterpreted in the light of the whole message of the Bible, is a concept

that should be retained by Christians. Part of the reason for this choice is that the word is so widely used. A change of term, therefore, would cause unnecessary confusion.

8. Others in our Consultation, because of difficulty in relating it to biblical categories of thought and its negative overtones, would like to replace 'development' with another word. An alternative we suggest is 'transformation,' as it can be applied in different ways to every situation. Western nations, for example, who have generally assumed that development does not apply to them, are, nevertheless, in need of transformation in many areas. In particular, the unspoken assumption that societies operate best when individuals are most free to pursue their own self-interests needs to be challenged on the basis of the biblical teaching on stewardship (Luke 12:13–21; 16:13–15; Phil. 2:1–4). People living in groups based on community solidarity may help these kinds of societies see the poverty of their existence.

9. Moreover, the term 'transformation,' unlike 'development,' does not have a suspect past. It points to a number of changes that have to take place in many societies if poor people are to enjoy their rightful heritage in creation.

10. We are concerned, however, that both the goals and the process of transformation should be seen in the light of the Good News about Jesus, the Messiah. We commit ourselves and urge other Christian believers to reject the cultural and social forces of secularism which so often shape our idea of a good society. We believe that notions alien to God's plan for human living are often more powerful in forming our opinions about what is right for a nation than the message of Scripture itself.

11. According to the biblical view of human life, then, transformation is the change from a condition of human existence contrary to God's purposes to one in which people are able to enjoy fullness of life in harmony with God (John 10:10; Col. 3:8–15; Eph. 4:13). This transformation can only take place through the obedience of individuals and communities to the Gospel of Jesus Christ, whose power changes the lives of men and women by releasing them from the guilt, power, and consequences of sin, enabling them to respond with love toward God and toward others (Rom. 5:5), and making them 'new creatures in Christ' (2 Cor. 5:17).

12. There are a number of themes in the Bible which help us focus on the way we understand transformation. The doctrine of creation

speaks of the worth of every man, woman, and child, of the responsibility of human beings to look after the resources of nature (Gen.
1:26–30) and to share them equitably with their neighbors. The doctrine of the Fall highlights the innate tendency of human beings to
serve their own interests, with the consequences of greed, insecurity,
violence, and the lust for power. 'God's judgment rightly falls upon
those who do such things' (Rom. 2:2). The doctrine of redemption
proclaims God's forgiveness of sins and the freedom Christ gives for a
way of life dedicated to serving others by telling them about the Good
News of Salvation, bringing reconciliation between enemies, and
losing one's life to see justice established for all exploited people.

13. We have come to see that the goal of transformation is best
described by the biblical vision of the Kingdom of God. This new way
of being human in submission to the Lord of all has many facets. In
particular, it means striving to bring peace among individuals, races,
and nations by overcoming prejudices, fears, and preconceived ideas
about others. It means sharing basic resources like food, water, the
means of healing, and knowledge. It also means working for a greater
participation of people in the decisions which affect their lives, making possible an equal receiving from others and giving of themselves.
Finally, it means growing up into Christ in all things as a body of
people dependent upon the work of the Holy Spirit and upon each
other.

III. The Stewardship of Creation

14. 'The earth is the Lord's and all that is in it' (Ps. 24:1); 'The land is
mine' (Lev. 25:23). All human beings are God's creatures. As made in
His image they are His representatives, given the responsibility of caring wisely for His creation. We have to confess, however, that God's
people have been slow to recognize the full implications of their
responsibility. As His stewards, we do not own the earth but we
manage and enhance it in anticipation of Christ's return. Too often,
however, we have assumed a right to use His natural resources indiscriminately. We have frequently been indifferent, or even hostile, to
those committed to the conservation of non-renewable sources of
energy and minerals, of animal life in danger of extinction, and of the
precarious ecological balance of many natural habitats. The earth is

God's gift to all generations. An African proverb says that parents have borrowed the present from their children. Both our present life and our children's future depends upon our wise and peaceful treatment of the whole earth.

15. We have also assumed that only a small portion of our income and wealth, the 'tithe,' belongs to the Lord, the rest being ours to dispose of as we like. This impoverishes other people and denies our identity and role as stewards. We believe that Christians everywhere, but especially those who are enjoying in abundance 'the good things of life' (Luke 16:25), must faithfully obey the command to ensure that others have their basic needs met. In this way those who are poor now will also be able to enjoy the blessing of giving to others.

16. Through salvation, Jesus lifts us out of our isolation from God and other people and establishes us within the worldwide community of the Body of Christ. Belonging to one Body involves sharing all God's gifts to us, so that there might be equality among all members (2 Cor. 8:14–15). To the extent that this standard is obeyed, dire poverty will be eliminated (Acts 2:42–47).

17. When either individuals or states claim an absolute right of ownership, that is rebellion against God. The meaning of stewardship is that the poor have equal rights to God's resources (Deut. 15:8–9). The meaning of transformation is that, as stewards of God's bountiful gifts, we do justice, striving together through prayer, example, representation, and protest to have resources redistributed and the consequences of greed limited (Acts 4:32–5:11).

18. We are perturbed by the perverse misuse of huge amounts of resources in the present arms race. While millions starve to death, resources are wasted on the research and production of increasingly sophisticated nuclear weapon systems. Moreover, the constantly escalating global trade in conventional arms accompanies the proliferation of oppressive governments which disregard people's elementary needs. As Christians we condemn these new expressions of injustice and aggression, affirming our commitment to seek peace with justice. In the light of the issues of the stewardship of creation we have discussed here, we call on the worldwide evangelical community to make the nuclear and arms trade questions a matter of prayerful concern and to place it on their agenda for study and action.

IV. Culture and Transformation

19. Culture includes world-views, beliefs, values, art forms, customs, laws, socioeconomic structures, social relationships, and material things shared by a population over time in a specific area or context.

20. Culture is God's gift to human beings. God has made people everywhere in His image. As Creator, He has made us creative. This creativity produces cultures. Furthermore, God has commissioned us to be stewards of His creation (Ps. 8; Heb. 2:5–11). Since every good gift is from above and since all wisdom and knowledge comes from Jesus Christ, whatever is good and beautiful in cultures may be seen as a gift of God (James 1: 16–18). Moreover, where the Gospel has been heard and obeyed, cultures have become further ennobled and enriched.

21. However, people have sinned by rebelling against God. Therefore the cultures we produce are infected with evil. Different aspects of our culture show plainly our separation from God. Social structures and relationships, art forms and laws often reflect our violence, our sense of lostness, and our loss of coherent moral values. Scripture challenges us not to be 'conformed to this world' (Rom. 12:2) insofar as it is alienated from its Creator. We need to be transformed so that cultures may display again what is 'good and acceptable and perfect' (Rom. 12:2).

22. Cultures, then, bear the marks of God's common grace, demonic influences, and mechanisms of human exploitation. In our cultural creativity, God and Satan clash. The Lord used Greek culture to give us the New Testament, while at the same time He subjected that culture to the judgment of the Gospel. We too should make thankful use of cultures and yet, at the same time, examine them in the light of the Gospel to expose the evil in them (1 Cor. 9:19–23).

23. Social structures that exploit and dehumanize constitute a pervasive sin which is not confronted adequately by the church. Many churches, mission societies, and Christian relief and development agencies support the sociopolitical status quo, and by silence give their tacit support.

24. Through application of the Scriptures, in the power of the Spirit, we seek to discern the true reality of all sociocultural situations. We need to learn critically from both functionalist and conflict approaches to human culture. The 'functionalist socio-anthropology'

approach emphasizes the harmonious aspects of different cultures and champions a tolerant attitude to the existing structures. This position is often adopted in the name of 'scientific objectivity.' By contrast, the 'conflict' approach exposes the contradictory nature of social structures and makes us aware of the underlying conflicts of interests. We must remember that both approaches come under the judgment of God.

25. Given the conflicting ethical tendencies in our nature, which find expression in our cultural systems, we must be neither naively optimistic nor wrongly judgmental. We are called to be a new community that seeks to work with God in the transformation of our societies, men and women of God in society, salt of the earth and light of the world (Matt. 5:13–16). We seek to bring people and their cultures under the Lordship of Christ. In spite of our failures, we move toward that freedom and wholeness in a more just community that persons will enjoy when our Lord returns to consummate His Kingdom (Rev. 21:1–22:6).

V. Social Justice and Mercy

26. Our time together enabled us to see that poverty is not a necessary evil but often the result of social, economic, political, and religious systems marked by injustice, exploitation, and oppression. Approximately eight hundred million people in the world are destitute, and their plight is often maintained by the rich and the powerful. Evil is not only in the human heart but also in social structures. Because God is just and merciful, hating evil and loving righteousness, there is an urgent need for Christians in the present circumstances to commit ourselves to acting in mercy and seeking justice. The mission of the church includes both the proclamation of the Gospel and its demonstration. We must therefore evangelize, respond to immediate human needs, and press for social transformation. The means we use, however, must be consistent with the end we desire.

27. As we thought of the task before us, we considered Jesus' attitude toward the power structures of His time. He was neither a Zealot nor a passive spectator of the oppression of His people. Rather, moved by compassion, He identified Himself with the poor, whom He saw as 'harassed and helpless, like sheep without a shepherd' (Matt. 9:36). Through His acts of mercy, teaching, and lifestyle, He exposed

the injustices in society and condemned the self-righteousness of its leaders (Matt. 23:25; Luke 6:37–42). His was a prophetic compassion and it resulted in the formation of community which accepted the values of the Kingdom of God and stood in contrast to the Roman and Jewish establishment. We were challenged to follow Jesus' footsteps, remembering that His compassion led Him to death (John 13:12–17; Phil. 2:6–8; 1 John 3:11–18).

28. We are aware that a Christlike identification with the poor, whether at home or abroad, in the North, South, East, or West, is always costly and may lead us also to persecution and even death. Therefore, we humbly ask God to make us willing to risk our comfort, even our lives, for the sake of the Gospel, knowing that 'everyone who wants to live a godly life in Christ Jesus will be persecuted' (2 Tim. 3:12).

29. Sometimes in our ministry among the poor we face a serious dilemma: to limit ourselves to acts of mercy to improve their lot, or to go beyond that and seek to rectify the injustice that makes such acts of mercy necessary. This step in turn may put at risk the freedom we need to continue our ministry. No rule of thumb can be given, but from a biblical perspective it is clear that justice and mercy belong together (Isa. 11:1–5; Ps. 113:5–9). We must therefore make every possible effort to combine both in our ministry and be willing to suffer the consequences. We must also remember that acts of mercy highlight the injustices of the social, economic, and political structures and relationships; whether we like it or not, they may therefore lead us into confrontation with those who hold power (Acts 4:5–22). For the same reason, we must stand together with those who suffer for the sake of justice (Heb. 13:3).

30. Our ministry of justice and healing is not limited to fellow Christians. Our love and commitment must extend to the stranger (Matt. 5:43–48). Our involvement with strangers is not only through charity, but also through economic and political action. Justice must characterize the government's laws and policies toward the poor. Our economic and political action is inseparable from evangelism.

31. Injustice in the modern world has reached global proportions. Many of us come from countries dominated by international business corporations, and some from those whose political systems are not accountable to the people. We witness to the damaging effects that these economic and political institutions are having on people, especially on the poorest of the poor. We call on our brothers and sisters in

Jesus Christ to study seriously this situation and to seek ways to bring about change in favor of the oppressed. 'The righteous care about justice for the poor, but the wicked have no such concern' (Prov. 29:7).

VI. The Local Church and Transformation

32. The local church is the basic unit of Christian society. The churches in the New Testament were made up of men and women who had experienced transformation through receiving Jesus Christ as Savior, acknowledging Him as Lord, and incarnating His servant ministry by demonstrating the values of the Kingdom both personally and in community (Mark 10:35–45; 1 Pet. 2:5; 4:10). Today similar examples of transformed lives abound in churches worldwide.

33. We recognize that across the generations local churches have been the vehicle for the transmission of the Gospel of Jesus Christ, and that their primary, though not their only, role is a threefold ministry: the worship and praise of God, the proclamation in word and deed of the Gospel of the grace of God, and the nurture, instruction, and discipleship of those who have received Jesus Christ into their lives. In this way transformation takes place in the lives of Christians as individuals, families, and communities; through their words and deeds they demonstrate both the need and reality of ethical, moral, and social transformation.

34. All churches are faced at times with the choice between speaking openly against social evils and not speaking out publicly. The purpose for the particular choice should be obedience to the Lord of the church to fulfill its ministry. Wisdom will be needed so that the church will neither speak rashly and make its witness ineffective nor remain silent when to do so would deny its prophetic calling (1 Pet. 3:13–17). If we are sensitive to the Holy Spirit and are socially aware, we will always be ready to reassess our attitude toward social issues (Lk. 18:24–30).

35. Integrity, leadership, and information are essential for the transformation of attitudes and lifestyles of members of local churches. Churches are made up of people whose lives are pressured by the way their neighbors spend their money. They are often more aware of this than of the suffering and human need in their own and other countries. Often, too, they are reluctant to expose themselves to

the traumas of global need and to information which would challenge their comfort. If church leadership fails adequately to stress the social dimensions of the Gospel, church members may often overlook these issues (1 Tim. 3:1–7; Heb. 13:17).

36. We should be sensitive and responsive to need within the local church. Widows, prisoners, the poor, and strangers are people who are particularly the responsibility of the local church (Gal. 6:10). We should attempt to be well informed about local human need and to seek God's will for us in meeting those needs. We should seek to minister to the poor in our local area who are not members of the church (James 1:27; Rom. 12:17).

37. Our churches must also address issues of evil and of social injustice in the local community and the wider society. Our methodology should involve study, earnest prayer, and action within the normative, ethical guidelines for Christian conduct set out in Scripture. Within these guidelines there are times, no matter the political system, when protest can be effective. Christians should carefully consider the issues and the manner in which they protest so that the identity and message of the church is neither blurred nor drowned.

38. The local church has however to be understood as being a part of the universal church. There is therefore a genuine need for help and sharing (*diakonia*) built on fellowship (*koinonia*) between churches of different localities and contexts. In this connection we considered a model for relating churches in different areas of the world. In such 'church twinnings' the relationship should be genuinely reciprocal with giving and receiving at both ends, free from paternalism of any kind (Rom. 15:1–7).

39. Such reciprocal relationships in a spirit of true mutuality are particularly needed in view of the fact that every local church always lives on the edge of compromise with its context (Rom. 12:3–18). Some churches are immersed in the problems of materialism and racism, others in those of oppression and the option of violence. We may help each other by seeking to see the world through the eyes of our brothers and sisters.

40. With regard to the wider world community, Christian churches characteristics, training, and Christian maturity to work across cultures in the name of Christ and of the sending church. These men and women would go as servants and stewards characterized by

humility and meekness; and they would work together with members of the Body of Christ in the countries to which they go.

VII. Christian Aid Agencies and Transformation

41. In reflecting upon the Christian response to human need, we have recognized the central place of the local church as the vehicle for communicating the Gospel of Jesus Christ both in word and deed. Churches around the world have throughout history displayed active concern for the needs around them and continue to serve the needy. We call upon the aid agencies to see their role as one of facilitating the churches in the fulfillment of their mission.

42. We recognize the progress which in recent years has been made in our understanding of the Gospel and its social and political implications. We also recognize, however, the deficiencies in our witness and affirm our desire for a fuller understanding of the biblical basis for our ministry.

43. We acknowledge that the constituency of the aid agencies is generally concerned with human suffering, hunger, and need. However, we recognize that this concern is not consistently expressed with integrity. In efforts to raise funds, the plight of the poor is often exploited in order to meet donor needs and expectations. Fund-raising activities must be in accordance with the Gospel. A stewardship responsibility of agencies is to reduce significantly their overheads in order to maximize the resources for the ministry.

44. We are challenged to implement in our organizations a positive transformation demonstrating the values of Christ and His Kingdom which we wish to share with others. We must, for example, avoid competition with others involved in the same ministry and a success mentality that forgets God's special concern for the weak and 'unsuccessful' (Gal. 2:10; Ps. 147:6). We should continually review our actions to ensure biblical integrity and genuine partnership with churches and other agencies. Decisions on ministry policy, including how resources are to be used, need to be made in consultation with the people to be served.

45. We need to ensure that our promotional efforts described what we are actually doing. We accept the responsibility of educating our donors in the full implications of the way Christian transformation is

experienced in the field. The Holy Spirit has led us to this ministry. In accepting the responsibility of education we recognize the process may cause some to question our approach. We will strive to educate with a sense of humility, patience, and courage.

46. In all of our programs and actions we should remember that God in His sovereignty and love is already active in the communities we seek to serve (Acts 14:17; 17:23; Rom. 2:9–15). Agencies, therefore, should give adequate priority to listening sensitively to the concerns of these communities, facilitating a two-way process in communication and local ownership of programs.

The guiding principle is equitable partnership in which local people and Western agencies cooperate together. Many models for development have originated in the Two-Thirds World. Christian aid agencies should in every way encourage these local initiatives to succeed. In this way the redeemed community of the Kingdom will be able to experiment with a number of models of transformation.

47. The agencies' legitimate need for accountability to donors often results in the imposition of Western management systems on local communities. This assumes that Western planning and control systems are the only ones which can ensure accountability. Since the communities these agencies seek to serve are often part of a different culture, this imposition can restrict and inhibit the sensitive processes of social transformation. We call on development agencies to establish a dialogue with those they serve in order to permit the creation of systems of accountability with respect to both cultures. Our ministry must always reflect our mutual interdependence in the Kingdom (Rom. 14:17–18; 1 Cor. 12).

48. In focusing on the apparently conflicting requirements of our action as Christian agencies, we are conscious of our sin and compromise. In a call to repentance we include a renunciation of inconsistency and extravagance in our personal and institutional lifestyle. We ask the Spirit of truth to lead us and make us true agents of transformation (Acts 1:8).

VIII. The Coming of the Kingdom and the Church's Mission

49. We affirm that the Kingdom of God is both present and future, both societal and individual, both physical and spiritual. If others have over-emphasized the present, the societal, and the physical, we

ought to confess that we have tended to neglect those dimensions of the biblical message. We therefore joyfully proclaim that the Kingdom has broken into human history in the Resurrection of Christ. It grows like a mustard seed, both judging and transforming the present age.

50. Even if God's activity in history is focused on the church, it is not confined to the church. God's particular focus on the church – as on Israel in the Old Testament – has as its purpose the blessing of the nations (Gen. 12:1–3; 15; 17; Isa. 42:6). Thus the church is called to exist for the sake of its Lord and for the sake of humankind (Matt. 22:32–40).

51. The church is called to infuse the world with hope, for both this age and the next. Our hope does not flow from despair: it is not because the present is empty that we hope for a new future (Rom. 5:1–11). Rather, we hope for that future because of what God has already done and because of what He has promised yet to do. We have already been given the Holy Spirit as the guarantee of our full redemption and of the coming of the day when God will be all in all (1 Cor. 15:28). As we witness to the Gospel of present salvation and future hope, we identify with the awesome birthpangs of God's new creation (Rom. 8:22). As the community of the end time anticipating the End, we prepare for the ultimate by getting involved in the penultimate (Matt. 24:36 –25:46).

52. For this reason we are challenged to commit ourselves to a truly vigorous and full-orbed mission in the world, combining explosive creativity with painstaking faithfulness in small things. Our mission and vision are to be nurtured by the whole counsel of God (2 Tim. 3:16). A repentant, revived, and vigorous church will call people to true repentance and faith and at the same time equip them to challenge the forces of evil and injustice (2 Tim. 3:17). We thus move forward, without either relegating salvation merely to an eternal future or making it synonymous with a political or social dispensation to be achieved in the here and now. The Holy Spirit empowers us to serve and proclaim Him who has been raised from the dead, seated at the right hand of the Father, and given to the church as Head over all things in heaven and on earth (Eph. 1:10, 20–22).

53. Finally, we confess our utter dependence on God. We affirm that transformation is, in the final analysis, His work, but work in which He engages us. To this end He has given us His Spirit, the Transformer *par excellence*, to enlighten us and be our Counselor (John 16:7), to impart His many. gifts to us (Rom. 12; 1 Cor. 12), to

equip us to face and conquer the enemy (2 Cor. 10:3–5; Gal. 5:22–23). We are reminded that our unconfessed sins and lack of love for others grieve the Spirit (Eph. 4:30; Gal. 5:13–16). We therefore fervently pray for our sins to be pardoned, for our spirit to be renewed, and for the privilege of being enlisted in the joyous task of enabling God's Kingdom to come: the Kingdom 'of . . . justice, peace, and joy in the Holy Spirit' (Rom. 14: 17).

Fourteen

Statement of The Stuttgart Consultation on Evangelism March 1987

Introduction

We have gathered here at Stuttgart from different parts of the world to consider the place of Evangelism in the programme of the World Council of Churches and of our respective Churches and organisations. Of the many who are evangelicals here, some belong to Churches which are members of the WCC, while others belong to Churches which are not. Some of us are particularly involved in the work of promoting evangelism in our own denomination, local church or area. We have come with varying degrees of ecumenical experience.

'Statement of the Stuttgart Consultation on Evangelism' in *Proclaiming Christ in Christ's Way* edited by Vinay Samuel and Albrecht Hauser (Oxford, Regnum, 1989).

Coming from very different theological and ecclesial backgrounds, we have become deeply conscious of our fellowship in the Gospel and of our common desire to carry out mission in Christ's way so that God's will may be done. We acknowledge humbly that mission is God's mission and that the Evangel is God's good news for humankind. We are unworthy servants, earthenware vessels, who have been entrusted with a priceless treasure (2 Cor 4:7). This treasure we seek to share with all, grateful that this sharing brings a blessing to us as well as to those with whom we share (1 Cor. 9:23).

We have heard different emphases on how the Gospel is to be shared. Some emphasized the sharing of the Gospel through resisting oppression and exploitation of the poor and by identifying with the marginalized. Others, while not denying the necessity for such an attitude on the part of the churches, have, nevertheless, emphasized the necessity for an explicit invitation to faith in Jesus Christ. While recognizing these different emphases, we have come to a common mind on certain matters which are set out below. We offer this statement to the CWME in the hope that it will stimulate reflection on the place of evangelism in the conciliar movement, especially in the planning of the 1989 Conference on World Mission and Evangelism.

The Nature of Evangelism

1. In our reflections we were reminded of the following statements in *Mission and Evangelism: An Ecumenical Affirmation*:

> The Church is sent into the world to call people and nations to repentance, to announce forgiveness of sin and a new beginning in relations with God and with neighbours through Jesus Christ. This evangelistic calling has a new urgency today. (Preface)

> The proclamation of the Gospel includes an invitation to recognize and accept in a personal decision the saving lordship of Christ. It is the announcement of a personal encounter, mediated by the Holy Spirit, with the living Christ, receiving his forgiveness and making a personal acceptance of the call to discipleship and a new life of service. (para. 10)

We did not spend much time on trying to define evangelism. Even so, there is broad agreement between us that evangelism always means that – in one way or another – people are to be called to faith in Christ. We therefore endorse the *Ecumenical Affirmation* when it states: 'Each person is entitled to hear the Good News' (par. 10). The essence of this Good News is that God was in Christ reconciling the world unto himself and has now called us to a ministry of reconciliation. This ministry pertains both to reconciliation between God and humans, as well as to reconciliation between individuals and groups alienated from each other. The Gospel is the good news of the possibility of a new beginning.

2. This ministry of reconciliation has, however, to be exercised within the specific context of every person or groups. There are different entry points for the love of God into the lives of people, both as individuals and as communities. It is only in dependence upon God's Spirit that we can develop a sensitivity toward these and thus become able to minister authentically to people's deepest needs.

3. In view of the above, it has to be emphasized that we can only communicate the gospel to people if we open ourselves to them and enable them to open themselves to us. This means that listening to them is crucial in the sharing of the gospel with them; we cannot share the gospel without sharing ourselves. We live by the gospel of an incarnate Lord; this implies that the gospel has to become incarnated in ourselves, the 'evangelists'. This is not to suggest that, in our evangelism, we proclaim ourselves, but that those whom we wish to invite to faith in Christ will invariably look for signs of that faith in us. And what will happen if they do not find these? Does not the credibility of our evangelism, to some extent at least, depend on the authenticity of our own lives? Can we evangelize others without becoming vulnerable ourselves?

4. Radio and television have contributed greatly to the spread of the Gospel in many cases. They penetrate areas where they are the only means of putting people in touch with the gospel and extend information about the witness of the Church well beyond its membership. However we have grave reservations about uses of the media in evangelism which are not related to or point to local Christian communities. When evangelists and audience cannot experience mutual sharing together or engage in processes of reconciliation with others we have to ask whether such evangelism does full justice to the ministry of reconciliation with which the Church is entrusted. We should do all we can to encourage uses of the media that are responsible and consonant with the nature of the gospel itself.

5. We are agreed that evangelism always includes the explication of the gospel. We recognize, however, that we cannot generalize about the way this should be done. We realize that there are places and situations where the public, verbal witness to the gospel is virtually impossible. A 'silent' Christian life-style is, in itself, profoundly evangelistic. Even a radiant and sacrificial life-style, however, is not in itself sufficiently explicit. We should always be prepared – under the guidance of the Holy Spirit – 'to give an account of the hope that is within us' (1 Peter 3:15).

6. The Church's evangelistic ministry can never be detached from its other ministries. If the Church chooses to remain silent in the face of injustice and oppression, both in society at large and in the Church itself, it jeopardises its entire evangelistic ministry. These concerns – which Scripture consistently summarizes as the plight of the widow, the orphan, the alien and the poor – are inseparably related to evangelism and every effort to drive a wedge between these is to be rejected as the proclamation of a spurious gospel.

We were told of situations where Christians are involved in such integral evangelism, by challenging unjust structures and mobilizing themselves and their neighbours in the struggle for justice and peace. Their actions are motivated by their joint study of the scriptures and such often lead to a profound conversion of those who join hands against oppression. This experience of incarnational evangelism in which *kerygma* and *diakonia* are integrated, usually transcends denominational and confessional barriers. We see here a new form of contextual evangelism.

7. We have been reminded of the fact that 'the blood of the martyrs is the seed of the Church' and that, in God's mysterious ways, it is often a persecuted Church that grows, both in numbers and in maturity. We have, however, also been reminded that the issue is not martyrdom as such but faithfulness and that it is precisely our faithful witness (*martyria*) to the gospel that may lead the Church into situations where it is ostracized, marginalized or even persecuted. But we also know that martyrdom has always been one of the lesser threats to the life and survival of the Church; lesser, certainly, than complacency and pride in who we are and what we have achieved. Since no authentic evangelism can issue from a complacent Church we solemnly pledge constantly and prayerfully to challenge ourselves, and examine our own lives and the lives of our Churches in the light of our high calling. We recognize that such an attitude of humble

self-examination will also imply that we judge ourselves before we judge others.

8. We were told of countries and situations where whole communities of Christians boldly and courageously witness to Christ with the result that people in their thousands turn to faith in Him. We rejoice with our brothers and sisters in those situations. We are challenged to ascertain whether such evangelistic efforts might not be appropriate also in other contexts. At the same time we sadly ask whether the absence of these bold, widespread evangelism activities might be attributable, in some cases, to timidity and failure of nerve, or to lack of confidence in the power of Christ through the Gospel, or even to not affirming the necessity of inviting others to faith in Christ.

9. We recognize, however, that there may be situations where people have lost confidence in the Church and have become impervious to the gospel and its claims. We do not believe that such situations spell the end of all evangelism, but simply that they may call for another evangelistic style and approach. We have been reminded of the profound impact and influence music has, particularly on the youth, and been given examples of how music, drama and other forms of the arts may be used to present the gospel to people. Christians who are sensitive to the promptings of the Spirit will be inventive and will always discover new ways of presenting the Word of Life to those who have not yet made a commitment to Christ. The dissemination of Scripture and of other appropriate literature also remains a powerful means of reaching such people.

10. In our evangelism we are challenged to be sensitive to people's cultures. This means, *inter alia*, that we cannot simply export models of evangelism from one culture to another. Some of us are particularly concerned about the highly individualistic approach in evangelism in the West which is often conducted in exactly the same way in other parts of the world, with the result that converts are often isolated and even alienated from their families and communities. We were reminded of the fact that, in some cultures, important decisions – and is not the decision to become a disciple of Jesus Christ an eminently important one? – are never taken individually but always corporately. We must respect such values in these cultures, not least because they help us become more sensitive to the biblical understanding of our humanity, and also challenge the excessive individualism in some cultures.

11. We acknowledge that we can never wholly determine, in advance, the road our evangelistic ministry will take, nor the way the

gospel will come alive in the life and culture of a community. The outcome of our evangelistic ministry may often surprise and sometimes even perplex us, but it belongs to the authenticity of our evangelism and the trust we have in both the gospel and the people to whom we go, that we shall desist from any attempt at manipulation. The outcome of Peter's first evangelistic encounter with somebody outside the Jewish nation was a surprise to him (Acts 10:14, 34) and precipitated a fundamental crisis in the Jerusalem church (Acts 11:2, 3). This has happened before and the same may happen today.

12. The Christian faith is by its very nature a missionary faith. It is therefore intrinsic to the Christian Church to always wish to cross frontiers and share the gospel with others. Even so, it is not the church or the individual Christian who converts people but God. It is not we who bring people to faith but the grace of God which works through us. Evangelism is therefore, ultimately, not dependent on our technology, resources or expertise but on the mysterious and unfathomable workings of the Holy Spirit in the human heart. There is, therefore, a strange and wonderful paradox here: On the one hand we are to give our all to the evangelization of God's world and yet, on the other hand, we are given the assurance that it is God's work and that God will do it. The awareness of this paradox makes us bold and committed to the task of evangelism yet at the same time relaxed in the knowledge that God's Spirit is the supreme Evangelist.

Local Christian Communities and Evangelism

13. Jesus Christ, our Lord, gave the missionary mandate 'Go therefore, and make disciples of all nations' not to a believer in isolation but to believers in community. The disciples to whom he addressed this command constituted the nucleus of the early Christian Church. Scripturally and ideally, therefore, evangelism should be centred in a local church – enhancing its life, strengthening its vision and extending its influence.

Though there is validity in discussing the theologies, strategies and programmes of evangelism at national and international consultations, we believe that the experiences and concerns of local churches and groups should not only be reported in these meetings, but should feature prominently in the agenda of such meetings.

14. In God's rich and gracious provision, believers are endowed with different gifts (Rom. 12:3–8, 1 Cor. 12). These gifts are ennobling and enabling means of presenting a winsome, saving and reconciling God in Jesus Christ. Thus evangelism, insofar as the diversity of gifts is concerned, cannot be limited to one or even a series of activities. As believers become faithful in expressing their particular gifts, the Holy Spirit defines for them their avenues of service.

God calls all believers to participate in the evangelistic task. Men and women, clergy and laity, young and old – all are one in Christ, one in the Spirit (Gal. 3:28; 1 Cor. 12:13), all are proclaimers, in word and act, of the Good News they together share.

We are aware that there are still structures which inhibit the full participation of all believers in evangelism, particularly women and youth.

15. The local churches are highly diverse in location, history, culture, socio-political situation and religious ethos. Therefore there cannot be the same evangelism agenda for all Churches everywhere.

Local churches should take seriously the need to develop incarnational models as part of their evangelistic obedience to God. They should be given ample creative space to evolve these models based on much prayer and reflection on God's Word and their personal and communal experiences with God.

Evangelism and the Renewal of the Church

16. Authentic evangelism renews the Church; a renewed Church evangelizes. Believers appropriate in their own lives – individually and corporately – the transforming grace and power of the Good News as they proclaim it to others. Such manifestations, of growing Christ-likeness before the world, commend the evangelistic message which in turn is used by the Holy Spirit to draw others. The early churches in the book of Acts showed this life-giving, life-changing dynamism. So do many local churches today.

As we have already seen, the Holy Spirit is the Great Evangelist. The Spirit's role in evangelism is often ignored, though lip-service may be paid to it. Churches are in danger of centring their evangelistic efforts only on personnel, denominations, programmes and money. The local church must learn to be still, to wait upon the wind of the Spirit's stirring which often comes in quietness, worship and prayer; to listen carefully to the Spirit's voice in humble obedience. A reflective local church will be effective in its evangelism.

17. Commitment to other brothers and sisters in Christ is an aspect of Church renewal which in itself has evangelistic dimensions. People everywhere are searching for meaningful human relationships that will help them weather many of the storms of life. Such relationships do not exploit or discriminate; they help people define their identity; they help them to share in the struggles of others; and to rejoice with them. Sadly however, relationships in many Church circles can be superficial and artificial. Authentic relationships are nurtured when we submit to each other in obedience to the Lord (Phil 2:1–8; Eph. 5:21).

18. A corporate commitment to worship, prayer, fellowship and celebration of the Good News is another aspect of Church renewal and evangelism. Such a commitment characterised the churches mentioned in the book of Acts. These churches grew (Acts 2:21, 5:14). In times of persecution and danger their solidarity in Christ and with each other helped them stand, even to the point of death.

Evangelism and the Unity of the Church

19. 'God was in Christ reconciling the world to himself' (2 Cor. 5:19). We are called to be ambassadors of and for our reconciling God; ambassadors who bear, individually and corporately, the signs of reconciliation – at one with each other as Christ is at one with the Father.

The nature of evangelism will rise out of our understanding of the good news that is being proclaimed and will colour the nature of the good news that is received.

Salvation brings spiritual and total wholeness to the individual at one with God in Jesus Christ. Such wholeness gives people a new identity not by affirming them in their self-centredness but by calling them to give themselves to others in Christ's way. The New Testament communities of faith were rebuked when they divided to suit the taste, preference or personal loyalties of individuals (1 Cor. 1:10–13).

20. Our Lord Jesus Christ in John 17 prayed for the unity of his followers. Forms of evangelism which cater primarily to denominational aggrandizement fail to affirm the indivisibility of the one body of Christ. Authentic evangelism calls people into a community with all

Christian people, a community which – in spite of denominational and other barriers – lives under the sign of at-one-ment under the cross.

21. We have discerned two related circumstances which jeopardise the unity and the evangelistic effectiveness of the Church.

a) In some places, churches which have been present for a long time consider that the unity of Christ's people is not helped by the activities of groups undertaking direct evangelism towards persons who have a traditional relationship to those churches.

b) In the opinion of others, some of these churches appear defensive about 'their' nominal members but unable or perhaps even uninterested in active evangelism towards them. They believe there is an imperative to evangelize in such circumstances.

We need to address these issues with care and creative sensitivity.

22. Any evangelism which does not build up good relationships with other Christians in the community must inevitably come under question. Local churches therefore should be encouraged to pray and work together in a co-operative and loving spirit as a sign of witness and of the attractiveness of the face of Jesus Christ: 'See how they love one another'.

23. We affirm that Christian unity, important as it is, must never be a unity for its own sake. It is a unity so that all may believe, and in harmony with a mission in Christ's way on behalf of, and in identification with, the poor, the lost and the least in God's creation.

The Role of Para-Church Organizations in Evangelism

24. We give thanks for the dedicated individuals and the stewardship of resources in organisations and agencies which work to support the churches and serve the world in the name of Christ. We greatly value the work done by these bodies when they act after consultation, and in conjunction with the churches and communities of Christ's people in local areas, in such a way as to build up the sign of Christ's unifying love, and to empower the actions of Christ's people there.

25. We hear the cries of pain of churches and communities of Christ's people in local areas when some outside agencies, driven by the ardour of their convictions, have acted – in the opinion of some local churches – without consultation, to the detriment of the work and vision of these churches. Such action does not strengthen, but weakens the credibility and witness of the Church.

Evangelism in the Context of Other Faiths

26. We acknowledge and affirm that authentic witness to Jesus Christ should be carried out in a spirit of respect for the beliefs and devotion of others. It can never be simply a 'telling' but must also be a sensitive 'listening'. It must, furthermore, always respect the freedom of others and should not be coercive or seductive in any way. We acknowledge that God has not left himself without witness anywhere (Acts 16:17) and we joyfully recognize a knowledge of God, a sense of the transcendent, among many human communities including many faith-communities. At the same time, it needs to be pointed out that humankind's knowledge of God is vitiated by sin and God's gracious revelation in Christ is needed to call us all back to an authentic vision of God. We agree with the *Ecumenical Affirmation* (para. 43) that the Spirit of God is at work in the world convincing humankind of God's righteousness and convicting them of their own sin (John 16:8). As we enter into dialogue with those other faiths we should keep in mind both the knowledge of God which is available to all and the work of the Spirit ahead of our own witness. We recognize also the figure of Christ in the poor, the needy, the ill and the oppressed (Matt. 25:31–46).

27. Christians, nevertheless, owe the message of God's salvation in Jesus Christ to every person and to every people (Ecumenical Affirmation para. 41). As we have already, said, the proclamation of the Gospel includes an invitation to each person to recognize and accept in a personal decision the saving Lordship of Christ (para. 10). This might be seen as a fulfilment of the aspirations of humankind expressed sometimes in religious traditions but at other times in non-religious movements and even at times in counter-religious movements. Such proclamation may also be understood as a making explicit of an implicit knowledge; or as bringing assurance and certainty of salvation to all those who, without prior explicit knowledge of Jesus Christ, the only Saviour and Lord, have nevertheless realized their own inadequacy and sin and have thrown themselves on the mercy of God. While the proclamation of the Gospel will affirm and confirm certain aspects of a person's or a people's previous religious experience. It is always, therefore, a call to repentance and new life. We recognize that dialogue is not to be used for cheap proselytism but we believe that it can be a medium of authentic witness, though we are aware that there are other reasons for the necessity of dialogue with

those of other faiths. Such reasons would include the building up of community, common witness about the dignity and rights of human beings and addressing human need.

28. As Christians we welcome the fact that many societies are moving towards greater openness and pluralism. In some cases the emergence of a plural society makes the existence of Christian Churches, in a predominantly non-Christian culture, possible. In others, societies, which have hitherto been largely 'Christian', become increasingly plural with many different old and new faiths represented in them. We recognize both phenomena as within God's providence and as giving Christians fresh opportunities to love, serve and witness to their neighbours. We are concerned that some societies remain closed and continue to deny freedom of belief, of conscience and of free expression to their members. As Christians, we are committed to the promotion of these freedoms in our respective societies.

Programmes for Evangelism in the WCC

29. We welcome the stimulus to evangelism which the 'Evangelism Desk' at CWME has been in recent years and we feel that a more comprehensive programme would be beneficial for the task of evangelism among the member-Churches of the WCC and beyond. Such a programme should enable, equip and strengthen the Churches for the task of evangelism. The programme could include within it the following elements:

i) Sharing: This would include the sharing of news and views and models of evangelism among the different Churches but would also seek to bring evangelists, pastors, theologians, church administrators and lay Christians witnessing in their daily tasks together for consultation and planning. Such consultations would be learning experiences and could lead to a sharing of resources between different Churches.
ii) Education and Training:
a) The programme would stimulate theological reflection on the nature of evangelism and its relationship to the nature of the Church.
b) The programme would seek to educate Christians regarding the importance of evangelism. It would promote the production

of materials which could be used by local churches, facilitate locally and regionally based seminars and encourage such cross-cultural exchanges as promote and stimulate evangelism.

c) The programme would encourage the development of training programmes for evangelists and would seek to integrate missiology, especially as it relates to evangelism, into the curricula of theological studies. It would disseminate information on these matters to a wider constituency.

d) The programmes would promote workshops for members of different denominations where they can share their evangelistic experience, where they can reflect on their community, and where they can urge new and appropriate methods of evangelistic action.

iii) Relating to other Christian organisations on matters of evangelistic concern: This would include not only relating to Roman Catholic initiatives in evangelism but also to non-conciliar bodies such as the Lausanne Committee for World Evangelization, the World Evangelical Fellowship, the Billy Graham Evangelistic Association and other organisations as and when they come to be identified.

iv) It would be useful if the desk could stimulate, directly or indirectly, programmes which address the following:

a) The circumstances of Churches from all traditions with large numbers of 'nominal' members, whereby there can be a renewal of the spiritual life of the faith community that will again set forth Christ as the one who calls to newness of life and to unity – not as one who divides his own.

b) The circumstances where the surrounding society encourages people to think of the gospel as a commodity to be chosen and rejected like any other product in a market economy. How can the WCC enable us to help each other as Churches and individual Christians to repent of preaching and living the gospel in such a way as to encourage people to believe that the Gospel is something which can be divided into parts some will like, and other parts preferred by others, placed in a range of packages for marketing purposes.

c) The circumstances where decline in church membership and influence subtly affects the motivation for evangelism, with the danger that subconsciously the desire is for survival of the church (denomination – even congregation) rather than the formation of

Christ-centred, reconciled and reconciling communities where all Christians accept, affirm and support each other as brothers and sisters in the one Lord, fully welcome in common worship.

v) We encourage CWME to do everything possible to stimulate, throughout the various WCC sub-units, an analysis and awareness of the mission and evangelism implications of their various programmes.

List of Participants:

Oberkirchenrat Walter Arnold
Rev. Dr. Kwame Bediako
Prof. Dr. David Bosch
Rev. Clayton L. Berg
Mr. Marlin VanElderen
Rev. Hamish Christie-Johnston
Mrs. Hilary Christie-Johnston
Col. William Clark
Rev. Juan Damian
Mrs. Jill Dann
Mr. Raymond Fung
Rev. Vasi Gadiki
Rev. Rainer Gerhardt
The Right Rev. Dr. David M. Gitari
Rev. Per Harling
Mr. Albrecht Hauser
Mrs. Rosmarie Hauser
Mr. Graeme Irvine
Rev. Goran Janzon
Rev. Dr. Emmett V. Johnson
Rev. David W. Kerr
Mrs. Marsha A. Kerr
Rev. Dr. Peter Kuzmič
Bishop Lavrentije

Rev. Kevin Livingston
Rev. Dr. Denton Lotz
Rev. Isabelo F. Magalit
Mrs. Evelyn Miranda-Feliciano
The Right Rev. J. Michael Nazir-Ali
Ms. Iris Odoi
Prof. Dr. Chun Chae Ok
Rev. Dr. William Pannell
Rev. Dr. Rene Padilla
Mrs. Catherine Padilla
Rev. Sang-Hyuk Park
Rev. Dr. Vinay Samuel
Prof. Dr. Ronald Sider
Rev. Dr. Eugene L. Stockwell
Mrs. Margaret S. Stockwell
Father Tom Stransky
Mrs. Jean Stromberg
Rev. Chris Sugden
Rev. Klaus Teschner
Rev. Inge Tranholm-Mikkelsen
Rev. Dr. Gordon Bruce Turner

Stuttgart 27 March 1987

Fifteen

Mission Modernity: Seven Checkpoints on Mission in the Modern World

Os Guinness

Introduction: The Promise and the Threat

Modernity, or the world civilization that the forces of modernization is now producing, represents the greatest single opportunity and the greatest single threat the Christian church has faced since Apostolic times. Yet no great theme concerning Christian discipleship and mission has been more overlooked by more Christians with more consequences, than this one. For evangelicals at large, modernity is still an unconfronted problem.

'Mission Modernity: Seven Checkpoints on Mission in the Modern World', Os Guinness in *Faith and Modernity* edited by Philip Sampson, Vinay Samuel and Chris Sugden (Oxford, Regnum, 1995).

Let me open this momentous subject in a simple way with a story, an observation, a thesis, and a quotation.

First, the story. Soviet leader Nikita Kruschev used to tell of a time when a wave of petty thefts hit the former USSR, and so the authorities put guards at all the factories. At one of the timberworks in Leningrad the guard knew the workers well. The first evening, out came Pyotr Petrovich with a wheelbarrow and, on the wheelbarrow, a great bulky sack with a suspicious-looking shape.

'Come on, Petrovich,' said the guard. 'What have you got there?'

'Just sawdust and shavings,' Petrovich replied.

'Come on,' the guard said, 'I wasn't born yesterday. Tip it out.'

And out it came nothing but sawdust and shavings. So he was allowed to put it all back again and go home.

The same thing happened every night all week, and the guard was getting extremely frustrated. Finally, his curiosity overcame his frustration.

'Petrovich,' he said, 'I know you. Tell me what you're smuggling out of here, and I'll let you go.'

'Wheelbarrows, my friend,' said Petrovich. 'Wheelbarrows.'

We may laugh, but we must remember that in the area where the church and modernity meet, the laugh is on us. Modernity is a new kind of worldliness that has sneaked up on us without our realizing it. We have tried to use the forces of modernization to serve us, but unwittingly we ourselves have been shaped by them. We have set up endless patrols to detect the dangers of the world in our societies, but the devil has trundled this new worldliness right past our eyes and into the church. As Peter Berger warns, whoever sups with the devil of modernity had better have a very long spoon.

Second, the observation. Back in the early seventies, a renowned social scientist at Oxford University turned to me, knowing I was a Christian, and said, 'By the end of the seventies, who will be the worldliest Christians in America?' I must have looked a little puzzled, because he continued, 'I guarantee it will be the fundamentalists.'

At the time such an idea was startling. Worldliest? Fundamentalism had always been world-denying by definition. But now, as we meet to discuss the task of world mission and look at the impact of modernization two decades later, that impact confronts us bluntly: World-denying conservatism has become virtually impossible. And Christendom's ultimate worldling today is not the Christian liberal but the Christian conservative. The contemporary church's proto-typical charlatan is not the mediaeval priest but the modern evangelist. The Tetzels of history and the Elmer Gantrys of fiction pale beside the real-life examples of evangelical and evangelistic worldliness in our own time. In its sweatless, disincarnate, electronic form, modern evangelism has created the ultimate parody of the incarnation.

Third, the thesis. A full account of the relationship of modernity and the church is probably beyond any of us, and certainly beyond the scope of this paper. But just compare the church's position in 1993 with her prospects in AD 993 on the eve of the first millennium. In 993 she held only a tiny segment of the globe and had made only a limited impact on the deep paganism that underlay the official layer of 'Christian civilization'. A millennium later she is the world's leading faith and lays the strongest claim to be a truly global religion. And while the Christian faith is currently in recession in Europe, which was once its heartland, it still experiences the most massive worldwide expansion in its history.

At first sight, then, the close relationship between the church and modernity appears to have been overwhelmingly advantageous. The Christian faith has been tied intimately to the most successful, the most nearly global, the most consciously copied of all civilizations in history. Once due allowance has been made for 'Western imperialism' and 'Eurocentrism', the balance sheet from the church's partnership with modernity seems unquestionably positive.

But to anyone who looks more closely, and who examines the con-trast between the state of the church in the more modernized and the less modernized parts of the world, a far more sober interpretation is suggested. No persecutor or foe in two thousand years has wreaked such havoc on the church as has modernity. And the strongest theory that explains this analysis is one that was used as a tool by Marx and Engels but which is rooted in Puritanism and the Bible – the 'grave-digger thesis.' Stated briefly, *The Christian church contributed to the rise of the modern world; the modern world, in turn, has undermined the Christian church. Thus, to the degree that the church enters, engages and employs the modern world uncritically, the church becomes her own gravedigger.*

This theme of the church warring against herself in her own worldliness becomes most focused in the discussion of mission and modernity. For if modernity represents the most powerful, the most all-embracing, and the most seductive setting in human history, then 'contextualization' in the setting of modernity is both amplified promise and amplified threat. The desire to witness and the danger of worldliness are enhanced simultaneously and exponentially.

Lastly, the quotation. One hundred years ago, the German philosopher and self-styled Anti-Christ, Friedrich Nietzsche, remarked that when there was 'the death of God' in a culture, that culture became increasingly hollowed out, or 'weightless'. Karl Marx, in his *Communist Manifesto*, had noted the same effect earlier 'All that is solid melts into air, all that is holy is profaned.' But he blamed it on the corrosive acid of modern capitalism, which dissolved the ties and bonds of traditional society.

Today we would place both their insights into the wider framework of modernization, for modern unbelief and modern market economics are simply two related aspects of modernity. But Nietzsche's insight into 'weightlessness' is a telling description of the hollowing out of reality which is characteristic of modernity even upon truths as powerful and precious as the gospel. And it also points in the direction of the sole, ultimate answer to modernity, for the biblical opposite of, and antidote to, 'weightlessness' is 'glory'.

Far more than his renown or radiance, God's glory is his own inexpressible reality, a reality so real that it alone has gravity and weight – the only 'really real reality' in the entire universe. Therefore, when things move away from God, they become hollow and weightless. It can accurately be said of them, '*Ichabod*', 'The glory has departed', or '*Mene, mene, tekel, upharsin*', 'You are weighed in the balance and found weightless or wanting'. That is why idols, by contrast with God, are literally 'nothings'. That is why revival is the refilling of a nation with 'the knowledge of the glory of the Lord, as the waters cover the sea'.

In sum, the civilization of modernity is a world system and spirit that today both encompasses us as individuals and encircles the globe. It therefore raises ultimate questions and requires ultimate responses. We cannot tackle the character and predicament of modernization if we simply summarize trends, marshal statistics, devise strategies, and assess prospects. To do that is to limit things to 'technique', and thus to fall victim to the mesmerizing spell of modernity itself, and to fail to see that modernity's real questions and impact go far deeper.

Modernity is a profound challenge to the church precisely because its menace is not merely to how we communicate, but to what we communicate and who we are to the very character of the gospel and the church itself. At a time when the church is on the threshold of 'reaching the world,' modernity calls into question what it means to reach anyone. We may indeed 'win the whole world, but lose our own soul'. As Jacques Ellul says, those who understand modernity know that it raises the ultimate question – Christ's: 'When the Son of Man comes, will he find faith on the earth?'

This paper was therefore deliberately different from most others presented at Lausanne II in Manila for several reasons. First, it is unashamedly theoretical, but only so that mission can be truly practical and effective in the end. Second, it is undoubtedly difficult because of the sociological terms, but partly because some people have not experienced modernity, many who have have not reflected on it, and even for those who have it is notoriously difficult. And third, its chief focus is a critical view of the character of modernity, but simply because modernity represents a danger of worldliness as strong as any desire to witness. In tempting us with its distinctive secularity, modernity becomes a test of what we believe is ultimately real. Its challenge is to our character and integrity, not simply to our communication and cultural adaptability.

This paper, then, is a call to repentance, prayer, spiritual warfare, and hard thinking as much as to planning and new enterprise. It is a call to a deeper, tougher response to a challenge far greater than most Christians have realized. If we are to engage modernity and 'plunder the Egyptians' without 'setting up a golden calf', we shall have to understand more deeply both modernity and an incarnational theology that alone can overcome it.

Definition and Description

But what exactly is 'modernization' or 'modernity'? At a rudimentary level, we all have answers to that question, because all of us are to some extent accustomed to many of the components of 'modern society'. For example, think of the fact that those of us born before the end of World War II (1945) actually have preceded many of the advances modern people take for granted: television, penicillin, credit cards, frozen foods, satellites, copying machines, contact lenses, word processors, artificial hearts, tape decks, split atoms, ballpoint pens, fax machines, men walking on the moon, and so on. Such discoveries underscore how far and fast we have come. But this view of modernity remains impressionistic. A far harder and more important task is to move beyond impressions to define what modernization is, and to describe how it arose and what its consequences are.

It is simple to see that the term *modernization* is derived from the Latin word *modo*, 'contemporary' or 'just now'. But modernization and modernity remain widely misunderstood today. Some people, for example, turn them into a kind of 'rich man's Marxism', a deterministic movement that will inevitably sweep the world with prosperity, progress, and democratic revolutions. Christians, however, tend to fall foul of a simpler misunderstanding. Many use the word modernity as if it were a fancy word for 'change' or simply a matter of being 'up to date'. They therefore treat it as something simple and straightforward, as if one can understand it through monitoring the latest trends and statistics and put it to use simply like a new fax machine or laser printer.

But modernity is much more than that. It refers to the character and system of the world produced by the forces of modernization and development centered above all on the premise that the 'bottom up' causation of human designs and products has now decisively replaced the 'top down' causation of God and the supernatural.

Modernity is therefore not a fancy word for 'change' and little of it can be understood merely by watching trends and keeping up with the latest technologies. To grasp modernity is a challenge: it requires an understanding of the whole, not simply just the parts. Ironically, when we wrestle with a tough-minded overview of modernity, it turns out to be far from modern.

Modernity's replacement of 'top down' God-centered living with 'bottom up' human-centered living represents a titanic revolution in human history and experience. We can trace its origins in two main ways. One way is to focus on human beings and the impact of their ideas. Thus, the road to modernity traces from the revolutionary changes in ideas to the way they have affected society throughout the centuries. This mode of analysis goes back at least to the seventeenth-century scientific revolution and follows the story through the eighteenth-century Enlightenment and the nineteenth-century romantic movement to the modernist and postmodernist movements in the twentieth century.

The rarer but even more important way to analyze modernity and face the challenge is to focus on society and social change. The line is traced in reverse as the story is followed from the revolutionary changes in society to the way they have affected ideas. This mode of analysis goes back to major structural and institutional developments – supremely those that resulted from the capitalist revolution in the fifteenth century, the technological and industrial revolution in the eighteenth century, and the communications revolution in the twentieth century.

This general statement can be made a little sharper by underscoring some of the components that make up the challenge of modernity. The following twelve statements summarize this challenge from the standpoint of North American evangelicals (who are currently and perhaps unenviably on the leading edge of modernity as British evangelicals were a century ago).

1. *Modernity is the central fact of human life today*: Modernity is the first truly global culture in the world and the most powerful culture in history so far. Thus the empire of modernity is the great alternative to the kingdom of God. Extensively, it encircles the planet; intensively, it encompasses more and more of each individual's life. The massiveness and seeming permanence of its imperial systems and ideology threaten us with captivity as surely as the empire of Egypt did Moses and the empires of Assyria and Babylon did exiled Israel.

2. *Modernity is double-edged for human beings*: Modernity simultaneously represents the greatest human advances in history in such benefits as health, speed, power, and convenience and the greatest assaults on humanness in history in such areas as the crisis of identity and the crisis of the family.

3. *Modernity is double-edged for followers of Christ*: Modernity represents the crux of the contemporary challenge to the gospel because it is the greatest single opportunity and the greatest single challenge the church has faced since the apostles. In the first case, it is equivalent of Roman roads in the first century and printing presses in the sixteenth. In the second, it is our equivalent of the challenges of persecution and gnosticism rolled into one.

4. *Modernity is foundational for the character and identity of both Americans and American evangelicals*: The United States as the world's 'first new nation' and American evangelicalism as Protestantism's 'first new tradition' both have features of modernity that are constitutive of their very character and identity (for example, pluralism in the case of America and a reliance on technique in the case of evangelicalism). This close affinity is an advantage because America and American

evangelicalism have prospered at the growing edge of modernity. But it is also a disadvantage in a double sense: those most blessed by modernity are most blind to it, and those first hit by modernity are often the worst hurt by modernity. This is one reason why non-Westerners in relation to Americans, and Roman Catholics and Orthodox in relation to evangelicals, consider themselves superior to, and immune from, either the crises facing America or American evangelicals.

5. *Modernity's central challenge to America is focused in America's crisis of cultural authority*: Modernity creates problems far deeper than drugs, crime, illiteracy, AIDS, broken families, or the plight of the inner cities. It creates a crisis of cultural authority in which America's beliefs, ideals, and traditions are losing their compelling power in society. What people believe no longer makes much difference to how they behave. Unless reversed, this hollowing out of beliefs will finally be America's undoing.

6. *Modernity's central challenge to evangelicals is focused in the crisis of the authority of faith*: Modernity undermines the churches' capacity both to demonstrate the integrity and effectiveness of faith and to provide an answer to America's crisis. Their captivity to modernity is the reason why faith's influence on the culture has decreased while culture's influence on faith has increased.

7. *Modernity is a monumental paradox to the everyday practice of faith*: Modernity simultaneously makes evangelism easier – more people at more times in their lives are more open to the gospel – yet makes discipleship harder, because practicing the lordship of Christ runs counter to the fragmentation and specialization of modern life.

8. *Modernity pressures the church toward polarized responses*: Ever since the early days of modernity in the eighteenth century, a pattern of response to modernity has grown strong. Liberals have generally tended to surrender to modernity without criticizing it; conservatives have tended to defy modernity without understanding it. This tendency has been reversed in the last generation as more progressive evangelicals now court the 'affluent consumers' of the gospel as ardently as liberals once courted the 'cultured despisers' of the gospel. The two main examples today are the megachurch leaders marrying the managerial, as we shall see, and the Christian publishers romancing the therapeutic.

9. *Modernity's challenge cannot be escaped by the common responses to which Christians typically resort*: Those who recognize the deficiencies of the extreme liberal and conservative responses

often go onto two further deficient responses. One is a resort to premodernism – looking to the Third World to refresh the West, not realizing that Third World Christians have yet to face the inevitable challenge of modernization. This is true too of our brothers and sisters in Eastern Europe and Russia, who face a greater challenge from modernity than they previously faced from Marxism. The other is the resort to postmodernism – failing to see that though modernism as a set of ideas built on the Enlightenment has collapsed, modernity, as the fruit of capitalism and industrialized technology, is stronger than ever.

10. *Modernity represents a special challenge to the church*: The three strongest national challenges to the gospel in the modern world are Japan, Western Europe, and the United States. Japan has never been won to Christ; Western Europe has been won twice and lost twice; and America, though having the strongest and wealthiest churches, is now experiencing the severest crisis, so represents the clearest test case of Christian responses to modernity.

11. *Modernity represents a special challenge to reformation*: The reason for this special challenge is its central dismissal of the place of words. On the one hand, the overwhelming thrust of modernity has been to replace words with images and reading with viewing. On the other hand, the words that remain have been weakened because they have become technical, specialized, and abstract to most people. At the same time, postmodernism further devalues words by using them to create a pastiche of effect regardless of their original meaning (for example, the multiple cultural uses of 'born-again' in advertising or news programs).

12. *Modernity represents a special challenge to revival*: Quite simply, it is a fact of history that the church of Christ has not experienced any major nationwide revival under the conditions of advanced modernity. On the one hand, modernity undercuts true dependence on God's sovereign awakening by fostering the notion that we can effect revival by human means. On the other hand, modernity makes many people satisfied with privatized, individualistic, and subjective experiences that are pale counterfeits of true revival. While many Christians no longer have a practical expectation of revival, those who count on God's sovereignty over modernity have every reason to look to God for revival once again.

In sum, modernization is not something simple, local, transient or inconsequential. At its most developed level, it confronts us with such relentless power and pervasiveness that it has been aptly described as an 'iron cage' around human life (Max Weber) and 'a gigantic steel hammer' that smashes traditional institutions and traditional communities of faith (Peter Berger). This darker side of modernity raises two fundamental questions. The first is the human question: How can human beings live in a tolerably human way in a world created by modernization? The second is the religious question: How can faith in the modern world retain its traditional authority and integrity and remain the deepest source of a sense of human meaning and belonging? The answers to both questions are vital, of course, to the church in itself as well as to the church in mission. We turn now to a series of fundamental checkpoints to help us engage critically with the opportunity and challenge of modernity to our mission for Christ.

Exploiting Modernity: Two Opportunities

The main accent in this paper is on the challenge of modernity, its threat to the Christian faith and to the humanness of life as traditionally understood. But that of course is only half of the picture, if the most neglected half, and I would like to begin more positively. The fact is that even the sternest critics of modernity would be reluctant to return to the premodern world. And even beyond the undoubtedly positive aspects of modernity, such as its freedoms and conveniences, there are still further aspects of modernization that represent extraordinary opportunities for mission.

Cultural Openness

The first, and most obvious opportunity grows from the fact that certain features of modernity prompt *cultural openness*. As modernization spreads further and further, particularly in the form of decentralized modern media, the totally closed society is made more and more difficult. The success of the 'second Russian revolution' is the most dramatic example, but even the failure of the Chinese revolution in Tiananmen Square illustrates the same point. Modernization opens up not only traditional closed societies, but even centralized totalitarian states.

No societies are finally immune to modernization. And to any society that would hope to benefit from modernization, centralization is a recognized handicap. Thus, for example, when the decision came down to a choice between Marxist equality and modern efficiency, death by obsolescence or freedom for new ideas, modernity was impossible to resist. So the modernizing trend moves inevitably, if unevenly and against considerable resistance, toward the opening of societies and nations to a myriad of outside influences to which they would once have been impervious. Raisa Gorbachev uses American Express cards and 'Big Macs' have entered the world of the 'Big Brother'.

This point needs to be guarded against distortion, partly because all sin and all sinful cultures are in part a form of 'closure' designed to exclude God, and partly because we should never forget those countries that are still closed and those three hundred thousand brothers and sisters who each year seal their witness to Christ with their own blood. Yet the point itself requires little elaboration. This dramatic cultural openness is partly why the most explosive missionary growth has been outside the influence of missionaries, such as the indigenous working-class movements among people feeling their 'homelessness' in the face of the gale-force winds of modernization (for example, Latin American Pentecostalism in its self-supporting, self-propagating form).

In addition, this extraordinary openness is behind the fact that in the last century and a half, Christians have used every last means, medium, and methodology to reach the unreached in an enterprise in creative ingenuity unrivalled in history. And no Christian tradition has been richer in such ingenuity, enterprise, and pragmatic organization than evangelicalism. What Greek and Roman roads were to the explosion of the gospel in the first century, and the printing presses were to the Reformation in the sixteenth century, everything from steamships in the nineteenth century to radio, television, and satellites are to missionary enterprise in the openness of the modern world. What this openness means overall, then, is that the church faces the greatest opportunity for missionary expansion since the days of the Apostles.

Cultural Rebounds

The second opportunity is less obvious and only becomes apparent on the far side of the dislocations of modernity. This opportunity stems from the fact that modernization breeds its own distinctive *cultural rebounds*.

The general possibility of these rebounds is grounded in the dynamics of human sin. No one should have a better appreciation of irony, comedy, and unintended consequences than the Christian. Theologically speaking, sin means holding 'the truth in unrighteousness', which means in turn that neither sin nor its philosophies and institutions is ever stable. But our concern here is with the practical consequence. For modernity reinforces the instability so that every rebound contains some speeded-up disillusionment with some false faith or idol, and therefore presents a moment of spiritual openness – that moment which forms the 'today' in which the Gospel addresses every human being.

The list of such cultural rebounds and their ironies is unending. 'God is dead,' people say. 'The modern world has come of age and outgrown the tutelage of faith.' But its prodigal descent has been swift. Modern cities make people closer yet more alienated at once; powerful modern weapons bring their makers to the point of impotence and destruction simultaneously; modern media promise facts but deliver fantasies; modern education introduces mass schooling but fosters subliteracy; modern technologies of communication encourage people to speak more and say less and to hear more and listen less; modern life styles offer do-it-yourself freedom but slavishly follow fads and end often in addictions; modern conveniences, being disposable and ephemeral, bring people closer to happiness but further from joy; modern and styles of communication make people hungry for intimacy and authenticity but more fearful than ever of being prey to phoniness, manipulation, and power games. And so on.

Prior to modernity the corruptions of Christendom tended to rebound into anti-Christian hostility. 'I am not a Christian,' Voltaire is supposed to have prayed to Christ, 'but that is so that I can love thee the better.' Today, the shoe is on the other foot. 'Modern people have come of age,' did someone say? Hardly. Modern people are less often humanists, but only so they can be more human. The very *reductio ad absurdum* of modernity is the open door for orthodoxy. Into the ultimate homelessness of our modernized existence breaks in the way to the ultimate home. The shelf life of modern idols is brief. The very openness of modernity is a destroyer even of its own unbeliefs.

Reading the Signs of the Times: Two Pitfalls

Raymond Aron's remark that very few people are contemporaries of their own generation has been made even more apt by the modern explosion of knowledge and the capacity-cum-anxiety that comes with it. As more and more is known and communication becomes faster and better, the lag between information and comprehension grows greater and more frustrating at once. The result does more than divide people between the 'knows and the know-nots.' It lures even those who do know toward two pitfalls that are deepened by the knowledge explosion.

The Unknowing

One pitfall of the information age is summed up in the common mentality, 'Happiness is a small circle'. Life is more tolerable, they suggest, if we know as little as we need and care as little as we can. Yet this attitude is the result of knowing too much rather than too little, and in particular the result of an avalanche of 'news' that leaves people blindingly aware of the last twenty-four hours but ignorant of the last twenty-four years, let alone of history.

The resulting state of mind is a form of information without wisdom and of knowing severed from doing. Christians who react to the knowledge explosion by saying, in effect, 'I'm happy with my small world,' grow irresponsible. Their attitude becomes a serious factor in undermining the missionary initiative of the modernized sectors of the church. From that point on, instead of the whole church reaching the whole world, mission becomes a specialized concern of a dedicated minority.

The All-Knowing

The other pitfall is not found in society at large, but in those for whom thinking is a profession. Summed up in an attitude that David Boorstin mocks as 'Homo-up-to-datum,' this pitfall grows from the belief that harnessing the knowledge explosion offers the key to instant, total information. Its goal is to know every thing in order to predict everything in order to control everything. If the first pitfall ends in irresponsibility, the second can end in an idolatry of information that becomes more of a handicap than a help to mission. It pushes mission and mission studies in the direction of the modern specialization and 'professionalization' of knowledge, and eventually toward the creation of a missionary version of the new 'knowledge class'.

The growing numbers and importance of a 'new thinking class' is one of the most distinctive features of the information society, and some of its unhappy consequences for Christians can be noted: (1) Christian thinkers often become closer to the 'cultured despisers' of the faith than to their fellow Christians, (2) expert knowledge is pursued as an end in itself, (3) specialized knowledge (which can be understood only by other specialists) creates a gap between experts and ordinary people, (4) originality and development are so prized that a fallacy is fostered that the newer-is-the-truer and the latest-is-the-greatest, (5) specialization fosters an expertise and professionalism that creates dependency and becomes disabling for anyone but the professional, (6) it is forgotten that ignorance is a constant in human affairs, and the capacity to act is often greatest when the clarity of understanding is smallest (and vice versa), and (7) members of the new 'knowledge class' become slowly adapted to the language and logic of the expanding world of seminars, forums, consultations, and Congresses (like this one) and thus further and further from other (Christianly more important) such styles of discourse as preaching and prayer.

Advocates of modern mission studies who scoff at such a caution should ponder the fate of most university disciplines today and especially the fate of Christian apologetics, liberal theology, evangelical higher education, and seminary training over the past century. Similarly, we can be sure that sophisticated missiology and 'evangelology' without the love of Christ, compassion for the lost, concern for our neighbor, and utter reliance on the Holy Spirit could quickly develop its own élitism, arrogance, and impracticability. If you asked me to search my own heart and choose between the 'simplicity' of mission as I have seen it lived out by my own missionary parents and the 'sophistication' of much of its equivalent today, I would choose my parents' way without hesitating.

Perhaps the most telling evidence for this point is the style of discourse at Lausanne II itself compared with that of Lausanne I. Under the influence of the 'terrible trio' (advertising, television, and pop-culture), modernization has caused profound changes in public discourse: above all in the shift from word to image, action to spectacle, exposition to entertainment, truth to feeling, conviction to sentiment, and authoritative utterance to discussion and sharing. Most of these wider cultural shifts have been well exemplified here, and the general diminishing of any sense of 'Thus saith the Lord' has been marked.

If we are to be unriddlers of our time and, like David's followers to be 'skilled in reading the signs of the times', we need to immerse our studies and strategic thinking in humility, responsibility, and a deep sense of the sovereignty of God and the sinfulness and smallness of our human projects. Just because we are modern does not mean that we have modernity by the scruff of the neck or that any of us knows definitively what our modern context is. We are all always more shortsighted than we realize. Modern culture can never be an exotic subject studied by outside observers, such as a group of anthropologists on a South Sea island. It is the mould in which we are all cast and that we can only recognize, resist, and change by God's outside perspective in the midst of our ignorance, an ignorance in some ways deepened by the overload of modern information.

Assessing the Damage to Persisting Religion: Two Trends

In earlier days, when secularization was exaggerated as progressive and irreversible, religion was widely thought to have no future. It was pronounced fated to disappear. So today's revised assessment of secularization means a revised prognosis for religion: Religion, it is now said more humbly and more accurately, has not so much disappeared in modern society as changed its character and location. What then are the trends that have effected this change, and continue to shape the religion that still persists in the modern world?

Privatization

The first trend, which in many ways is the reverse side of secularization, is *privatization*. By privatization I mean *the process by which modernization produces a cleavage between the public and private spheres of life and focuses the private sphere as the special area for the expression of individual freedom and fulfillment.* There has always been a distinction between the more personal and the more public areas of life, but until recently the relationship between them was marked by a continuum rather than a cleavage. Today in many modern cities, it might as well be the Pacific Ocean. One one side of the cleavage is the public sphere, the macroworld of giant institutions (such government departments as Britain's Whitehall, such large corporations as Japan's Mitsubishi and Korea's Hyundai, and such military complexes as America's Pentagon). On the other side of the cleavage is the private sphere, the microworld of the family and private associations, the world of personal tastes, sports, hobbies, clubs, and leisure pursuits.

Privatization has its undoubted benefits supremely because it does ensure authentic freedom in the private sphere. Compared with the situation in the past, it permits more people to do more, buy more, and travel more than ever before, free of the constraints of community, tradition, and other people. But for religions such as the Christian faith, the disadvantages outweigh the advantages. Above all, privatization is limited and limiting. Modern society spells freedom for religion, but only so long as it is confined to the private sphere. Far from being an area of true choice and creativity, the modern private sphere is all too often a sort of harmless play area, a sort of spiritual 'Indian reservation' or 'Bantustan', a homeland for separate spiritual development set up obligingly by the architects of secular society's apartheid.

A classic illustration of privatization came in an interview with the founder of McDonald's hamburgers by the New York Times. Asked what he (a Christian) believed in, he replied: 'I speak of faith in McDonald's as if it were a religion. I believe in God, family, and McDonald's and in the office that order is reversed.' The record of the interview gave no indication whether the reply was facetious or not. But whatever the case, the response was a perfect expression of privatized faith that millions of modern Christians practice daily without realizing it.

Pluralization

The second modernizing trend that shapes all persisting religion is *pluralization*. By pluralization is meant *the process by which the number of options in the private sphere rapidly multiplies at all levels, especially at the level of worldviews, faiths, and ideologies.*

Unlike secularism, pluralism is by no means new. The church was born in a period of similar pluralism, and modern pluralism even has its roots partly in the Protestant conviction of freedom of conscience.

But modernization represents a stupendous enhancement of pluralism that in turn has set off a tidal wave of choice and change. Urban crowding, the knowledge explosion, modern travel, mass media, enormous dispersions of Third World people across the modern West . . . these are only the most obvious of the factors behind the heightened modern sense of 'all those others' and 'all those options'. We have now reached the stage where it can almost be said that 'everyone is now everywhere' and choice is not just a state of affairs, but a state of mind. Choice has become a value in itself, even a priority. Choice and change have become the very essence of modern life.

The side effects of pluralization on religion have been varied. One is that pluralization creates in modern believers a high degree of self-consciousness. Confronted constantly by 'all those others', modern people are constant question marks to each other, and modern faith is rarely as assured as it sounds.

Another effect is that religious believers in the modern world have become conversion-prone. Whereas faith was once rock-like and the turn-around of conversion was radical, complete, and lasting, modern believers are prone to being reconverted and reconverted and reconverted (or 'born again and born again. . . and again'). Multiple conversions are now common, being 'born again' is easily trivialized, and even testimonies are reduced to the status of a spiritual visiting card in constant need of updating in a spiritually mobile society.

Yet another effect is that pluralism reduces the necessity of choosing at all. The very extension of choice increases the likelihood of the evasion of choice. But the overall direction is clear. Pluralization means an increase in choice and change that is almost automatically a decrease in commitment, continuity, and conviction. Pluralization now creates as many tensions within each church, denomination, or religion as there once were between them. With picking, choosing, and selectiveness the order of the day, the result of pluralization is a general increase in shallowness, transience, and heresy. Few challenges to Christian discipleship and mission are so subtle yet so corrosive.

Sizing Up The Competition: Two Rivals

A common consequence of exaggerating secularization is to jump to the conclusion that modernity is hostile to all religion. Nothing could be further than the truth. Modernity is directly opposed to two defining features of some traditional religions that the Christian faith shares with only a few others – the absoluteness of its notion of *transcendence* and its notion of *totality*. But partly for that reason, modernity is very welcoming to religions without such angular features and such ornery insistence. Indeed, modernity provides an almost perfect setting for reinforcing two potent rivals to the Christian faith. What is common to both rivals, and in strong contrast with the Christian faith, is the implicit relativism in their truth claims and the evolutionary optimism in their view of history, though one tends to be in favor of modernity and the other, at least quietly, against it.

Generalized Secularism

The first rival to the Christian faith is a *generalized secularism*, which combines relativism and evolutionary optimism in various types of naturalism that are favorable to modernity. The leading examples today are liberal humanism and Marxism, both being Western in origin, though ironically the second has outgrown its origins and appeals especially to those repudiating the 'West'.

What needs underscoring is that *secularism* is not the same thing as *secularization*. *Secularism* is a philosophy, with all the strengths and weaknesses of one, not least that it is commonly unemotional and that to subscribe to it demands a considerable effort of mind or will. *Secularization*, by contrast (as we defined it earlier), is not a philosophy; it is a process. Its roots are not in an intellectual concept but in institutional change. It is a process that has actually taken place in the structures of society and cannot be avoided or simply wished away.

Secularization (the process) therefore provides the perfect setting for secularism (the philosophy). Modernity is the new context which enhances the old concept, making the latter seem natural, even necessary. Secularization, therefore, has a double thrust: *it constricts religion, thereby decreasing its power, but it also reinforces secularism, thereby increasing its power.*

Modernity's reinforcement of secularism is the context for a sobering fact. Since 1900, the percentage of the world's atheistic and non-religious peoples (agnostics, secularists, communists, and so on) has grown from 0.2 percent to 21.3 percent – in other words from less than one-fifth of one percent to over one fifth of the world's population. This is the most dramatic change on the entire religious map of the twentieth century. Secularists, or people with no religious commitment, now form the second largest bloc in the world, second only to Christians, and catching up fast (at the rate of 8.5 million 'converts' a year).

Generalized Syncretism

But this is only half the story. Modernization also provides natural reinforcement to a second potent rival to the Christian faith: *generalized syncretism*. Like secularism, modern syncretism in its varied forms often pivots on a relativism and evolutionary optimism that is conducive to modernity. But it takes them in a religious or semi-religious (rather than naturalistic) direction, and one that is often countermodernizing (rather than promodern) in tendency, and collectivist (rather than purely individualistic) in concern.

The leading examples in the West are the science-based mysticisms, such as the New Age movement, as well as socialism and environmentalism, in their more mythic form. But elsewhere in the developing world, where resistance to modernization and resistance to Westernization often overlap, the appeal of, and potential for, such syncretisms is even greater. Such are the blandishments of modernity that few religious leaders will have the obstinacy of an Ayatollah Khomeini to reject it outright. Far more are likely to seek to control modernity and cushion its full impact on their society by some variety of local, national, or religious syncretism. Its religion then becomes a key part of any society's selective adaptation to modernity.

Among examples of this trend are the Umbanda movement in Brazil (with its Christian rites and pagan content) and the recent movement in Japan to revitalize State Shinto as a conscious civil religion that will replace 'post-war democratic Japan' and fill the vacuum of values created by modernity. Similar syncretistic movements were Japan's way of adapting to earlier waves of outside, influence, such as the introduction of Confucianism from China, Buddhism from India and, in the nineteenth century, the Christian faith from the West.

And, of course, this reinforcement of syncretism by modernity is one reason for the persistence of certain kinds of religion even in highly 'secular' societies. Because of their substratum of magic, superstition, and fatalism at a popular level, modern nations like France and Britain are not so much 'post-Christian' as pre-Christian and pagan. Similarly in Japan, animistic worship of sun, mountains, trees, and rocks was always just below the surface of official State Shinto, so the revitalization of State Shinto will mean a reinforcement of popular animism.

Engaging Modernity: Two Master Principles

All engagement in the modern world requires or reveals an answer to the question: How do we view modernity theologically? Modernity is only one more form of human culture, and the view of culture we find in the Scriptures is a bifocal vision. Always and everywhere at once, human, culture and therefore modernity is two things: God's gift to us, and the devil's challenge to us to worship him and not Christ.

Two great master principles have characterized the church at its most penetrating, and both are essential today.

Protagonist Principle

The first is the *protagonist principle*, which flows from the theme 'Christ *over* all' and has as its key word *total*. The story of the exodus provides an Old Testament example. The whole issue with the Egyptian pharaoh was lordship. He who can liberate is he who is lord. As the bargaining went on, Pharaoh relented enough to let the Israelite men go, at least for worship. Moses said no. 'Let my people go' meant not just the men and not just for worship. Men, women, and children must go, and go for good. Then a remarkable little phrase was added: 'Not a hoof is to be left behind.'

A New Testament example can be found in Luke. Peter, as a fisherman, was glad to allow Jesus to preach from his boat. But Jesus said to Peter, 'Put out into the deep water, and let down the nets for a catch.' And we can almost hear Peter reply, 'Look, Lord, I'll listen to you as my teacher all day long, but when it comes to fishing, that's my job.'

We know the result. Peter found that Jesus was Lord of nature, too, and he could only respond, 'Go away from me, Lord; I am a sinful man!' Christ was Lord of nature as well as truth. He is the Alpha and the Omega. He is the source, guide, and goal of all there is. That is why every eye will one day see him, every tongue will be stopped, and every knee will bow. After all, as Abraham Kuyper said, expressing the protagonist principle perfectly, 'There is not an inch of any sphere of life of which Jesus Christ the Lord does not say, "Mine." '

This protagonist principle is indispensable today because modernity renders earlier forms of Christian separatism impossible and many newer forms of activism ineffective. So our engagement, whether in work, politics, art, voluntary action, recreation, or mission, will only be faithful and effective to the degree that Christ remains lord of every part of our lives.

Antagonist Principle

The second master principle is the *antagonist principle*. It flows from the theme 'Christ *over against* all that which does not bow to him', and the key word here is *tension*. The Lord himself puts the point unmistakably in Exodus 20: 'I am the Lord you God . . . You shall have no other gods before [to set against] me' (verses 2 and 3). Over forty times in Leviticus 18 and the following chapters is the recurring assertion, 'I am the Lord.' Each time it accompanies a strict instruction not to do as the Egyptians or the Canaanites did, neither worshipping their idols nor copying their ideas and institutions.

The reason? The Lord is the jealous one, the one who brooks no rivals. Since he is our 'decisive Other', he demands of us a decisive contrast with everything that is over against him and his ways, his ideals, and his institutions. Most wonderful of all, the deepest reason is personal. It is 'that you may belong to me'.

In short, God and the world stand crosswise. We are in the world but not of it. To be faithful to him we have to be foreign to the world. We are not to be conformed but transformed by the renewing of our minds. Even the much vaunted critical analysis of Marxists should pale beside the obedience-rooted critical commitment of Christians. But Marxist hardliners and Muslim fundamentalists are often wiser than we are in their deep suspicion of modernity. It is the 'Great Satan' to their cause. It does contain 'spiritual pollution', as they say, and Christians should be wary too.

Modernity, in other words, is not 'the holy ground' some urban theologians proclaim. Modernity is the devil's challenge to us. But that is not because we are the innocents and the modern world is so tempting. Rather it is because we are the temptable ones. The modern world is simply our hearts writ large. Our hearts are simply the modern world writ small. So our view of modernity needs to be theologically realistic. God pronounces the no of his judgment over all our human works before he pronounces the yes of his grace. But while his yes transcends his no, it is not because his no is merely temporary or apparent. God's no is his total, radical, continual, and final judgment of all our works that are born of sin and are moving toward death.

Of course, the protagonist principle and the antagonist principle must never be separated. They go hand in hand. Without the former, the latter would create a 'we/they' division that is Manichean and not biblical. The Protagonist principle means there must be no hatred of the world or false asceticism with us. Yes, the world is passing away, and we are passing through the world. But the responsible realism of that bifocal vision should shape our perspective. Holding these two truths together, we are to be, in Peter Berger's memorable phrase, 'against the world for the world'.

Engaging Modernity: Two Special Prerequisites

It is characteristic of modernity that its challenges to faith are fundamental. It calls faith into question in a 'do or die' form. Again and again its pressure is so unrelenting that only the deepest truth, only the real thing, is sufficient. Everything less is exposed as shallow, weak, insubstantial, and ineffectual.

Among many of the taken-for-granted strengths from the church's two-thousand-year history, two are special prerequisites for engaging modernity today.

Plausibility

In an ideal world, untouched by the effects of the Fall, the credibility of any belief would be determined simply by whether it were true or false. It would be believed if, and only if, it were objectively true; and if it were false, it would be quite literally incredible.

Needless to say, such a state of affairs is not our situation after the Fall. It doesn't take a cynic to see how the truth requirement has weakened to the vanishing point. Thus in the fallen world flagrant nonsense or complete error can be believed, and incontrovertible truth can be disbelieved without the question of their being objectively true or false being raised at all. In short, plausibility, or a thing's seeming to be true, is often mistaken for credibility, or its being true.

The Freudian concept of 'rationalizing' is the best-known application of the essentially biblical theme. But a more fruitful application is Peter Berger's concept of 'plausibility structure'. The degree to which a belief (or disbelief) seems convincing is directly related to its 'plausibility structure' that is, the group or community that provides the social and psychological support for the belief. Seen this way, only a genius or a madman can believe by himself or herself. For most human beings, it is easy to believe if the socially constructed support group is strong, but difficult to believe if it is weak.

The importance of plausibility can easily be defended biblically either through such recurring emphases as the practice of truth or through such statements as the Apostle Paul's description of the church as 'the pillar and bulwark of the truth'. Needless to say, Paul did not mean that the Christian faith was true because the church was strong. But since the church is the plausibility structure of the Christian faith, its strength or weakness critically determines the plausibility of the faith at any particular moment.

Modernity has multiple implications for Christian plausibility in the modern world . Well-publicized incidents, such as the sexual scandals of the American televangelists or the bitter controversies of the U.S. Southern Baptist Convention, are the least part of the problem. The effects of such subtle influences as 'privatization' and 'weightlessness' are subtler but far more damaging – the former making the faith 'privately engaging but publicly irrelevant', the latter creating a sort of *'Christian Lite'*. At the end of the day, the gospel of Jesus Christ stands or falls by whether or not it is true and therefore credible. But modernity makes the practice of truth absolutely critical. Only through the gravely endangered practice of truth will the gospel become plausible to modern people.

Persuasion

Evangelicals have characteristically been a people of persuasion; modernity puts a high premium on the place of persuasion; yet many modern evangelicals are strikingly persuasionless. This blatant contradiction lies at the heart of evangelical ineffectiveness in communications today.

One way to gauge this dilemma is through evangelical responses to pluralism, a crucial feature of modernity to the integrity of the gospel as well as to Christian mission. Evangelicals can trace a long and mostly fruitful relationship to pluralism in Christian history. Was it not in the highly pluralistic setting of the first century AD that the early Christians experienced explosive growth without compromise to their exclusive allegiance? Was it not the Protestant principle of freedom of conscience that became the greatest generator of choice and dissent in history, and thus a reinforcement of pluralism? Did not nineteenth-century evangelicals make their greatest headway when they showed themselves ready and able to exploit the 'free market' opportunities for enterprising faiths that were opened up by the First Amendment's separation of church and state?

The full story of the relationship of faith and pluralism is not all positive, of course. But no one who knows it can be other than shocked at the sea change in evangelical attitudes to pluralism today. Pluralism has been confused with relativism and become the evangelical 'P word'. Thus at the very moment when modern pluralism reinforces the grand overall shift from coercion (as in state churches where the state's sword and purse are behind the church) to persuasion, many Christians have abandoned persuasion for non-persuasive styles of communication, such as preaching, pronouncements, protest, and picketing.

A second way to gauge the dilemma of persuasionlessness is through evangelical attitudes to apologetics. Apologetics has usually held an honored, if controversial, place in Christian history. So much so that B.B. Warfield said that the Christian faith 'stands out among all religions as distinctively "the Apologetick religion" '. Today, however, ignorance of apologetics, and unease with it, are widespread.

On the one hand, the liberal tendency has been to say, 'Don't defend, dialogue!' A declining rational certainty in argument has coincided with a declining historical certainty in evidence and a declining cultural certainty in style. As one Oxford professor said to me in my application interview, 'Don't mention apologetics here. It's a dirty word in Oxford!'

Many would therefore agree with Dietrich Bonhoeffer: 'The attack by Christian apologetics upon the adulthood of the world I consider to be in the first place pointless, in the second ignoble, and in the third unChristian.' Others would agree with Jacques Ellul's equation: 'To suppose that it is still possible to have a crusade or an apologetic is to be out of your mind.'

On the other hand, the equally mistaken though opposite conservative tendency has been to say, 'Don't persuade, proclaim!' Apologetics, they fear, diminishes biblical authority by relying on human wisdom. It dries up spontaneity and spirituality by relying on reason. 'I am not sure,' wrote Martyn Lloyd-Jones in 1958, 'that apologetics has not been the curse of evangelical Christianity for the last twenty to thirty years.' The result is that apologetics needs its own apology. As secularist philosopher Antony Flew says, with some regret, 'Belief cannot argue with unbelief: It can only preach to it.'

Ironically, evangelicals are growing persuasionless at a time of extraordinary apologetic opportunity. After centuries of relentless skepticism and hostility to the gospel, many of the great, post-Christian intellectual rivals to the faith are in deep disarray. But there are all too few evangelicals with the convictions, courage, compassion, and imagination to exploit the vacuum. Yet when all is said and done, the Christian faith is a persuading faith. As Peter Berger says, 'The Christian community consists of those people who keep on telling the story to each other, some of whom climb up on various boxes to tell the story to others.' Today, more than ever, modernity has created a world in which persuasion has to be central to proclamation.

Overcoming modernity: two points of reliance

Additional checkpoints that might be included here are legion. But let me conclude with one last checkpoint that concerns our practical faith and two grounds of our confidence as we seek to wrestle with and overcome modernity.

Prayer and Fasting

First, looking at things in terms of our part, we must acknowledge that modernity poses a challenge that can be overcome '*only by prayer and fasting*'. This, for me, is not something that comes naturally. It would be far easier to speak of requirements such as 'thinking Christianly'. For at the very least modernity requires a degree of thoughtful wrestling that is on the level of the prophet Daniel: 'Though this word was true, it cost him much toil to understand it.' But precisely because it is even more difficult, commitment to the spiritual disciplines in general and to prayer and fasting in particular is more than a pious truism. It is an emphatic repudiation of modern technique and an open acknowledgement that when we wrestle with modernity, we do not wrestle with flesh and blood. And to link fasting with prayer is even to press beyond the admirable emphasis on prayer demonstrated in modern missions since the Moravian movement. I think of heroic of exemplars from Count von Zinzendorf down through Hudson Taylor to the Dorothea Mission and national movements for intercession in our own time such as Intercessors for Britain.

We have the example and the teaching of our Lord himself as he engaged with the enemy at his deadliest, and taught us how to do the same. We can see that prayer and fasting are singularly appropriate for unmasking modernity because the heart of their spiritual purpose is a direct challenge to the heart of the grand lie of modernity.

Modernity, of course, tries to turn even fasting into a technique. Thus for modern people, fasting has lost its spiritual purpose and become a form of weight control or political protest (such as 'hunger strikes'). Even for many Christians it is either neglected or left at the level of the ascetic, the legalistic, or the purely nominal. All of which are a form of reductionism precisely because they have lost their spiritual point.

But when the spiritual is restored and prayer and fasting are rejoined, they form an indispensable weapon without which we could not unmask or disarm modernity. The reason is theological and can be seen in the contrast between Adam and Jesus. Adam, in eating the forbidden fruit, disobeyed God's Word and 'broke his fast'; whereas the second Adam, overcoming the temptation, sustained both his obedience and his fast and thus demonstrated his repudiation of living on bread alone and his dependency on every word that proceeds out of the mouth of God.

Prayer with fasting is therefore both a statement and a stand – a statement about the ultimate meaning of life and a stand against the ultimate lie and its source. What does life mean? In creating 'a world without windows' (Peter Berger), modernity is history's greatest reinforcement of sin's cosmic lie about life-as-bread-alone (purely biological, naturalistic, secular). But, like Adam, modern people who live their lives eating, working, playing, sleeping 'autonomously' for the sake of these things alone, apart from God, find out that such autonomous life is impossible and such an autonomous culture turns out to be death-producing.

How are prayer and fasting an effective stand against this lie? Fasting quickly brings us to the point of hunger, which is the state when our dependency on something outside ourselves is inescapable. In knowing how much we need food, we know we do not have life in ourselves. But when we encounter the test that only prayer and fasting overcomes: on what, then, do we depend? Bread alone, says the evil one, so Adam believed him and ate. God and his Word alone, said Jesus, so he refused the devil's lie and shifted the principle of life back to its source.

This pivotal victory in the war against evil and its lie shows that prayer and fasting are practical rather than theoretical, yet profound spiritual warfare rather than a facile 'how-to' technique. Decisive victory comes only through severe testing. Christ met and overcame Satan in praying and fasting, and he later told his disciples that the 'Prince of this world' can be overcome only by prayer and fasting. Do we think modernity, with all its strengths and seductions, will be different? Unless we recover the practice of prayer and fasting, our best intentioned use of modern media and methods will end only in assisting the triumph of technique and hastening a new Babylonian captivity, albeit with air-conditioned cells and spiritual Muzak to divert us.

Word and Spirit

Second, looking at things in terms of God's part, we must acknowledge that modernity poses a challenge that can be overcome *only by God's Word and Spirit*. This reminder, too, is more than a truism, because once again it addresses the heart of the challenge of modernity. In producing Nietzsche's 'last men', Weber's 'iron cage', and Berger's 'world without windows', modernity does more than spawn a crowd of problems. It is a deliberate locking-out of genuine transcendence that constructs a suffocating, air-tight world filled with problems that admit of no internal solution.

Nietzsche saw clearly what this loss of transcendence would mean.

'Alas,' he wrote, 'he wrote, 'the time of the most despicable man is coming, he that is no longer able to despise himself. Behold, I show you the *last man*'.

But modernity's repression of transcendence explains not only the triumph of triviality in the 'last men' of Western consumer societies, but the flawed enterprise of spurious forms of transcendence, such as Promethean Marxism. Anyone prepared to believe with Karl Marx that the revolutionary will of history can be incarnate in any human political party is bound to be disillusioned. Addressing this lack of transcendence in Marxism, David Martin points out, 'It is a paradox that a system which claimed that the beginning of all criticism was the criticism of religion should have ended up with a form of religion which was the end of criticism.'

But how is the Christian faith different? As we survey the deepening captivity of the church, is there any lasting escape from modernity? What are the grounds for our confidence? After all, is not our very understanding of God and our listening to his Word dependent on the closed circle of our modern context?

No! A thousand times no, the church cries, because the gospel itself contains the secret of why the Christian faith can survive repeated periods of cultural containment and contamination. On the one hand, it has in God's Word and Spirit an authority that stands higher than history, a judgment that is irreducible to any generation and culture. Which is why, when God speaks, not even the worst or best of our hermeneutics can hold him down. On the other hand, the gospel has in its notion of sin and repentance a doctrine of the church's failure, which can be the wellspring of its ongoing self-criticism and renewal.

Like an eternal jack-in-the-box, Christian truth will always spring back. No power on earth can finally keep it down, not even modernity's power of Babylonian confusion and captivity. 'At least five times,' noted G.K. Chesterton earlier, 'the faith has to all appearances gone to the dogs. In each of these five cases, it was the dog that died.'

To write these things is not to whistle in the dark, but to grapple with modernity with hope and direction. We do not 'put our trust in princes', nor in management-streamlined missions, television evangelism, and computer-planned church growth. Even as we use the best modern media, our reliance from beginning to end must be on God's Word and Spirit and on their grave-opening, jail-breaking power in preaching, revival, reformation, and mission. Only so will modernity be restrained and overcome.

Conclusion: The Reality and the Glory

We should all be encouraged that many of the most penetrating observers of modernity are Christians – for example, Peter Berger, Jacques Ellul and George Grant. But when all is said and done, we would be foolish to pretend that modernization and modernity are easy either to understand or to engage. Little wonder that first reactions to the 'big picture' are often pessimistic. We feel overwhelmed. Which of us is equal to the challenge? 'Winning the World by 2000,' like John R. Mott's earlier 'The Evangelization of the World in This Generation,' is easier to handle as a rhetorical rallying cry than as a job actually to be accomplished before the clock strikes twelve on a certain day in a certain year.

What are my objectives in presenting this burden? Some of the simplest are as follows: As followers of Christ concerned to know him and make him known, we need, first, to put the topic of modernity high on our agendas for our concern, study, and prayer; second, to analyze the local and specific impact of modernization on our own country, region, city, church, ministry, and audience; third, to reform those areas of the church's doctrine and life that modernity has rendered weak or non-existent (for example, the place of truth and the importance of the incarnation in a day of electronic evangelism); fourth, to forswear facile excuses and false evasions (modernization may have hit the West first and worst, but modernity is now a world problem and not simply 'a Western problem'. Besides, the real test of 'Third World spiritual vitality' is not the first modernized generation but the third); and fifth, to deepen the 'reality' of our own faith in both knowledge and experience in order to be able to combat modernity.

The extraordinary burden of mission in the face of modernity makes me think of two men under titanic pressure. One was the great German thinker, Max Weber. He never shut his eyes to the modern world. He wrestled with it, but the more he wrestled, the more pessimistic he became. One day, a friend saw him pacing up and down, nearing the verge of a second breakdown.

'Max,' he said, 'why do you go on thinking like this when your conclusions leave you so depressed?'

Weber's reply has become a classic of intellectual commitment and courage, 'I want to know how much I can stand.'

Admirable in many respects, that is not the way for followers of Christ. If we are not called to be Promethean entrepreneurs of the gospel, we are certainly not called to be stoics or tragic heroes.

A very different response under pressure was that of Moses. Faced with enemies behind, around, and ahead, and finding discontent not only among his own people but within his own family he suddenly met the ultimate threat to his people and to his task as their leader: God himself. The Lord declared that, because of their sin, he would destroy the Israelites.

His very life and trust in God called into question, Moses countered the challenge daringly by putting God on the line (arguing the covenant), the people on the line (calling for a consecration to the Lord even against families and friends), and finally himself on the line (asking to be blotted out himself, rather than the people).

Then, when the Lord had listened to his prayers, agreeing first to forgive the people and then to come with them in person rather than by an angel, Moses made his supreme request, surely the most audacious prayer in all the Scriptures: 'Show me your glory.' He wanted to know all of God that a fallen sinner could be allowed to know, for nothing less would be enough to see him through the crisis of his calling.

In that prayer, we have our ultimate answer to modernity and to its keenest observers, such as Nietzsche and Weber. When 'God is dead' for a nation, a church, a movement, or an individual, a weightlessness results for which there is only one remedy – ultimate reality, the glory of God refilling them as the waters fill the sea. Wasn't that Jeremiah's message to his generation? To a people who had exchanged their glory for a god who was altogether nothing, he warned, 'Ascribe glory to the Lord your God before the darkness falls.'

If in mission today we stress the spiritual aspects of the gospel without the social, we lose all relevance in modern society. But if we stress the social without the spiritual, we lose our reality altogether. The ultimate factor in the church's engagement with modernity is the church's engagement with God.

Are we still tempted today to believe that we or anyone else can pull off the task of evangelizing the world? We must forget it. On the other hand, are we overwhelmed by the thought of the task, overburdened by the state of modernity and the world? Let us forget modernity and ourselves and turn from the what and where of our calling to the Whom. Then we can follow Moses to the source of the only reality that counts, the one power sufficient for facing up to the Colossus of modernity.

'*Lord, show me your glory*'.

Part III

Transformation and Praxis: Practical Issues from the Perspective of Wholistic Mission

Introduction

As evangelicals gained more experience and confidence in the field of development involvement, they began to explore the nature of economic policies and systems that expressed or contributed to poverty. The fruit of a three year study begun in 1987 was the Oxford Declaration on Christian Faith and Economics of 1990 included as chapter sixteen. The most significant aspect of this declaration was the agreement across the ideological divides of right and left. The end of the Cold War had made possible a much more careful definition of economic positions because the economic and political polarisation had been removed. Doug Bandow, a participant in the conference wrote in the Wall Street Journal on April 24th 1990 'Although not perfect, the Oxford document is far better than anything that would have come from most any other recent international religious gathering.'

The Oxford Centre for Mission Studies hosted this conference, and along with INFEMIT hosted from 1984 onwards a series of annual international consultations on matters on the cutting edge of mission. The objective of these consultations was not to bring evangelicals up to speed on technical issues. Rather, drawing on the experience of Christian professionals in these fields, the consultations related biblical concerns and themes to the practice of mission in these contexts so that the mission should be genuinely Christian. Subjects covered in consultations included Refugees, Theological Education, the City, the Local Church and Cross Cultural Mission, Base Christian Communities, Business and Christian Mission, Inter-Faith Dialogue, the Living God in Contemporary Life, and Fund-Raising for Christian Mission. Materials from these consultations were reproduced in the journal *Transformation*, which has been the journal of record of the consultations and also of the research theses carried out at the Oxford Centre for Mission Studies. It also developed a series on Models of Wholistic Mission.Those consultations which produced statements which are reproduced here are Evangelical Christianity and the Environment (chapter seventeen); Population Growth (chapter eighteen); the Future of Development Agencies (chapter nineteen), Children at High Risk (chapter twenty), and Disability (chapter twenty-one).

The issue of Church–State relationships was given significant attention. Rene Padilla's article on 'The Politics of the Kingdom of God and the Political Mission of the Church' (chapter twenty-two) was a seminal contribution to the thinking and practice of a number of key evangelical leaders in different parts of the world as they explored the field. Consultations on the topic took place in Hong Kong in 1989 on 'Church and State and Nation-Building' (chapter twenty-three), in Yugoslavia on 'Freedom and Justice in Church State Relationships' (chapter twenty-four) in 1991, weeks before the outbreak of the Serbian Bosnian War, and most recently in Croatia in 1998 on 'The Kingdom and the kingdoms' (chapter twenty-five). Thus the Kingdom of God has continued to inform the theological and missiological reflection of the movement for wholistic mission through the collapse and rebirth of nations throughout Europe during this period.

Sixteen

The Oxford Declaration on Christian Faith and Economics
January 1990

Preamble

This **Oxford Declaration on Christian Faith and Economics** of January, 1990 is issued jointly by over one hundred theologians and economists, ethicists and development practitioners, church leaders and business managers who come from various parts of the world. We live in diverse cultures and subcultures, are steeped in differing traditions of theological and economic thinking, and therefore have diverse notions as to how Christian faith and economic realities should intersect.[1] We have

---

'The Oxford Declaration on Christian Faith and Economics' in *Transformation*, Vol. 7, No. 2, April 1990.

found this diversity enriching even when we could not reach agreement. At the same time we rejoice over the extent of unanimity on the complex economics of today made possible by our common profession of faith in our Lord Jesus Christ.

We affirm that through his life, death, resurrection, and ascension to glory, Christ has made us one people (Galatians 3:28). Though living in different cultures, we acknowledge together that there is one body and one Spirit, just as we are called to the one hope, one Lord, one faith, one baptism, and one God and Father of us all (Ephesians 4:4).

We acknowledge that a Christian search for truth is both a communal and also an individual effort. As part of the one people in Christ, each of us wants to comprehend the relevance of Christ to the great issues facing humanity today together 'with all the saints' (Ephesians 3:18). All our individual insights need to be corrected by the perspectives of the global Christian community as well as Christians through the centuries.

We affirm that Scripture, the word of the living and true God, is our supreme authority in all matters of faith and conduct. Hence we turn to Scripture as our reliable guide in reflection on issues concerning economic, social, and political life. As economists and theologians we desire to submit both theory and practice to the bar of Scripture.

Together we profess that God, the sovereign of life, in love made a perfect world for human beings created to live in fellowship with God. Although our greatest duty is to honour and glorify God, we rebelled against God, fell from our previous harmonious relationship with God, and brought evil upon ourselves and God's world. But God did not give up on the creation. As Creator, God continues patiently working to overcome the evil which was perverting the creation. The central act of God's redemptive new creation is the death, resurrection and reign in glory of Jesus Christ, the Son of God, and the sending of the Holy Spirit. This restoration will only be completed at the end of human history and the reconciliation of all things. Justice is basic to Christian perspectives on economic life.

Justice is rooted in the character of God. 'For the Lord is righteous, he loves justice.' (Psalm 11:7) Justice expresses God's actions to restore God's provision to those who have been deprived and to punish those who have violated God's standards.

A. Creation and Stewardship

God the Creator

1. From God and through God and to God are all things (Romans 11:36). In the freedom of God's eternal love, by the word of God's omnipotent power, and through the Creator Spirit, the Triune God gave being to the world and to human beings which live in it. God pronounced the whole creation good. For its continuing existence creation is dependent on God. The same God who created it is present in it, sustaining it and giving it bountiful life (Psalm 104:29). In Christ, 'all things were created . . . and all things hold together'(Colossians 1:15–20). Though creation owes its being to God, it is itself not divine. The greatness of creation – both human and non-human – exists to glorify its Creator. The divine origin of the creation, its continued existence through God, redemption through Christ, and its purpose to glorify God are fundamental truths which must guide all Christian reflection on creation and stewardship.

Stewardship of Creation

2. God the Creator and Redeemer is the ultimate owner. 'The earth is the Lord's and the fullness thereof' (Psalm 24:1). But God has entrusted the earth to human beings to be responsible for it on God's behalf. They should work as God's stewards in the creative, faithful management of the world, recognizing that they are responsible to God for all they do with the world and to the world.

3. God created the world and pronounced it 'very good' (Genesis 1:31). Because of the Fall and the resulting curse, creation 'groans in travail' (Romans 8:22). The thoughtlessness, greed, and violence of sinful human beings have damaged God's good creation and produced a variety of ecological problems and conflicts. When we abuse and pollute creation, as we are doing in many instances, we are poor stewards and invite disaster in both local and global ecosystems.

4. Much of human aggression toward creation stems from a false understanding of the nature of creation and the human role in it. Humanity has constantly been confronted by the two challenges of selfish individualism, which neglects human community, and rigid collectivism, which stifles human freedom. Christians and others

have often pointed out both dangers. But only recently have we realised that both ideologies have a view of the world with humanity at the centre which reduces material creation to a mere instrument.

5. Biblical life and world view is not centred on humanity. It is God-centred. Non-human creation was not made exclusively for human beings. We are repeatedly told in the Scripture that all things – human beings and the environment in which they live – were 'for God' (Romans 11:36; 1 Corinthians 8:6; Colossians 1:16). Correspondingly, nature is not merely the raw material for human activity. Though only human beings have been made in the image of God, non-human creation too has a dignity of its own, so much so that after the flood God established a covenant not only with Noah and his descendants, but also 'with every living creature that is with you' (Genesis 9:9). Similarly, the Christian hope for the future also includes creation. 'The creation itself will be set free from its bondage to decay and obtain the glorious liberty of the children of God' (Romans 8:21).

6. The dominion which God gave human beings over creation (Genesis 1:30) does not give them licence to abuse creation. First, they are responsible to God, in whose image they were made, not to ravish creation but to sustain it, as God sustains it in divine providential care. Second, since human beings are created in the image of God for community and not simply as isolated individuals (Genesis 1:28), they are to exercise dominion in a way that is responsible to the needs of the total human family, including future generations.

7. Human beings are both part of creation and also unique. Only human beings are created in the image of God. God thus grants human beings dominion over the non-human creation (Genesis 1:28–30). But dominion is not domination. According to Genesis 2:15, human dominion over creation consists in the twofold task of 'tilling and taking care' of the garden. Therefore all work must have not only a productive but also a protective aspect. Economic systems must be shaped so that a healthy ecological system is maintained over time. All responsible human work done by the stewards of God the Sustainer must contain an element of cooperation with the environment.

Stewardship and Economic Production

8. Economic production results from the stewardship of the earth which God assigned to humanity. While materialism, injustice, and

greed are in fundamental conflict with the teaching of the whole scripture, there is nothing in Christian faith that suggests that the production of new goods and services is undesirable. Indeed, we are explicitly told that God 'richly furnishes us with everything to enjoy' (1 Timothy 6:17). Production is not only necessary to sustain life and make it enjoyable; it also provides an opportunity for human beings to express their creativity in the service of others. In assessing economic systems from a Christian perspective, we must consider their ability both to generate and to distribute wealth and income justly.

Technology and its Limitations

9. Technology mirrors the basic paradox of the sinfulness and goodness of human nature. Many current ecological problems result from the extensive use of technology after the onset of industrialization. Though technology has liberated human beings from some debasing forms of work, it has also often dehumanised other forms of work. Powerful nations and corporations that control modern technology are regularly tempted to use it to dominate the weak for their own narrow self-interest. As we vigorously criticise the negative effects of technology, we should, however, not forget its positive effects. Human creativity is expressed in the designing of tools for celebration and work. Technology helps us meet the basic needs of the world population and to do so in ways which develop the creative potential of individuals and societies. Technology can also help us reverse environmental devastation. A radical rejection of modern technology is unrealistic. Instead we must search for ways to use appropriate technology responsibly according to every cultural context.

10. What is technologically possible is not necessarily morally permissible. We must not allow technological development to follow its own inner logic, but must direct it to serve moral ends. We acknowledge our limits in foreseeing the impact of technological change and encourage an attitude of humility with respect to technological innovation. Therefore continuing evaluation of the impact of technological change is essential. Four criteria derived from Christian faith help us to evaluate the development and use of technology. First, technology should not foster disintegration of family or community, or function as an instrument of social domination. Second, persons created in the image of God must not become mere accessories of machines. Third, as God's

stewards, we must not allow technology to abuse creation. If human work is to be done in cooperation with creation then the instruments of work must cooperate with it too. Finally, we should not allow technological advancements to become objects of false worship or seduce us away from dependence on God (Genesis 11:1–9). We may differ in what weight we ascribe to individual criteria in concrete situations and therefore our assessment of particular technologies may differ. But we believe that these criteria need to be taken into consideration as we reflect theologically on technological progress.

11. We urge individuals, private institutions, and governments everywhere to consider both the local, immediate, and the global, long term ecological consequences of their actions. We encourage corporate action to make products which are more 'environmentally friendly'. And we call on governments to create and enforce just frameworks of incentives and penalties which will encourage both individuals and corporations to adopt ecologically sound practices.

12. We need greater international cooperation between individuals, private organisations, and nations to promote environmentally responsible action. Since political action usually serves the self-interest of the powerful, it will be especially important to guarantee that international environmental agreements are particularly concerned to protect the needs of the poor. We call on Christians everywhere to place high priority on restoring and maintaining the integrity of creation.

B. Work and Leisure

Work and Human Nature

13. Work involves all those activities done, not for their own sake, but to satisfy human needs. Work belongs to the very purpose for which God originally made human beings. In Genesis 1:26–28, we read that God created human beings in his image 'in order to have dominion over . . . all the earth'. Similarly, Genesis 2:15 tells us that God created Adam and placed him in the garden of Eden to work in it, to 'till it and keep it'. As human beings fulfil this mandate, they glorify God. Though fallen, as human beings 'go forth to their work' (Psalm 104:23) they fulfil an original purpose of the Creator for human existence.

14. Because work is central to the Creator's intention for humanity, work has intrinsic value. Thus work is not solely a means to an end. It is not simply a chore to be endured for the sake of satisfying human desires or needs, especially the consumption of goods. At the same time, we have to guard against over-valuation of work. The essence of human beings consists in that they are made in the image of God. Their ultimate, but not exclusive, source of meaning and identity does not lie in work, but in becoming children of God by one Spirit through faith in Jesus Christ.

15. For Christians, work acquires a new dimension. God calls all Christians to employ through work the various gifts that God has given them. God calls people to enter the kingdom of God and to live a life in accordance with its demands. When people respond to the call of God, God enables them to bear the fruit of the Spirit and endows them individually with multiple gifts of the Spirit. As those who are gifted by the Spirit and whose actions are guided by the demands of love, Christians should do their work in the service of God and humanity.

The Purpose of Work

16. In the Bible and in the first centuries of the Christian tradition, meeting one's needs and the needs of one's community (especially its underprivileged members) was an essential purpose of work (Psalm 128:2; 2 Thessalonians 3:8; 1 Thessalonians 4:9–12; Ephesians 4:28; Acts 20:33–35). The first thing at issue in all fields of human work is the need of human beings to earn their daily bread and a little more.

17. The deepest meaning of human work is that the almighty God established human work as a means to accomplish God's work in the world. Human beings remain dependent on God, for 'unless the Lord builds the house, those who build it labour in vain' (Psalm 127:1a). As Genesis 2:5 suggests, God and human beings are co-labourers in the task of preserving creation.

18. Human work has consequences that go beyond the preservation of creation to the anticipation of the eschatological transformation of the world. They are, of course, not ushering in the kingdom of God, building the 'new heavens and a new earth.' Only God can do that. Yet their work makes a small and imperfect contribution to it – for example, by shaping the personalities of the citizens of the eternal kingdom which will come through God's action alone.

19. However, work is not only a means through which the glory of human beings as God's stewards shines forth. It is also a place where the misery of human beings as impeders of God's purposes becomes visible. Like the test of fire, God's judgment will bring to light the work which has ultimate significance because it was done in cooperation with God. But it will also manifest the ultimate insignificance of work done in cooperation with those evil powers which scheme to ruin God's good creation (1 Corinthians 3:12–15).

Alienation in Work

20. Sin makes work an ambiguous reality. It is both a noble expression of human creation in the image of God, and, because of the curse, a painful testimony to human estrangement from God. Whether human beings are tilling the soil in agrarian societies, or operating high-tech machinery in information societies, they work under the shadow of death, and experience struggle and frustration in work (Genesis 3:17–19).

21. Human beings are created by God as persons endowed with gifts which God calls them to exercise freely. As a fundamental dimension of human existence, work is a personal activity. People should never be treated in their work as mere means. We must resist the tendency to treat workers merely as costs or labour inputs, a tendency evident in both rural and urban societies, but especially where industrial and post-industrial methods of production are applied. We encourage efforts to establish managerial and technological conditions that enable workers to participate meaningfully in significant decision-making processes, and to create opportunities for individual development by designing positions that challenge them to develop their potential and by instituting educational programmes.

22. God gives talents to individuals for the benefit of the whole community. Human work should be a contribution to the common good (Ephesians 4:28). The modern drift from concern for community to preoccupation with self, supported by powerful structural and cultural forces, shapes the way we work. Individual self-interest can legitimately be pursued, but only in a context marked by the pursuit of the good of others. These two pursuits are complementary. In

order to make the pursuit of the common good possible, Christians need to seek to change both the attitudes of workers and the structures in which they work.

23. Discrimination in work continues to oppress people, especially women and marginalised groups. Because of race and gender, people are often pushed into a narrow range of occupations which are often underpaid, offer little status or security, and provide few promotional opportunities and fringe benefits. Women and men and people of all races are equal before God and should, therefore, be recognised and treated with equal justice and dignity in social and economic life.

24. For most people work is an arduous good. Many workers suffer greatly under the burden of work. In some situations people work long hours for low pay, working conditions are appalling, contracts are non-existent, sexual harassment occurs, trade union representation is not allowed, health and safety regulations are flouted. These things occur throughout the world whatever the economic system. The word 'exploitation' has a strong and immediate meaning in such situations. The God of the Bible condemns exploitation and oppression. God's liberation of the Israelites from their oppression served as a paradigm of how God's people should behave towards workers in their midst (Leviticus 25:39–55).

25. Since work is central to God's purpose for humanity, people everywhere have both the obligation and the right to work. Given the broad definition of work suggested above (cf. para 13), the right to work here should be understood as part of the freedom of the individual to contribute to the satisfaction of the needs of the community. It is a freedom right, since work in its widest sense is a form of self-expression. The right involved is the right of the worker to work unhindered. The obligation is on every human being to contribute to the community. It is in this sense that Paul says, 'if a man will not work, let him not eat.'

26. The right to earn a living would be a positive or sustenance right. Such a right implies the obligation of the community to provide employment opportunities. Employment cannot be guaranteed where rights conflict and resources may be inadequate. However the fact that such a right cannot be enforced does not detract in any way from the obligation to seek the highest level of employment which is consistent with justice and the availability of resources.

Rest and Leisure

27. As the Sabbath commandment indicates, the Biblical concept of rest should not be confused with the modern concept of leisure. Leisure consists of activities that are ends in themselves and therefore intrinsically enjoyable. In many parts of the world for many people, life is 'all work and no play'. While masses of people are unemployed and thus have only 'leisure', millions of people – including children – are often overworked simply to meet their basic survival needs. Meanwhile, especially in economically developed nations, many overwork to satisfy their desire for status.

28. The first pages of the Bible tell us that God rested after creating the universe (Genesis 2:2–3). The sequence of work and rest that we see in God's activity is a pattern for human beings. In that the Sabbath commandment interrupted work with regular periods of rest, it liberates human beings from enslavement to work. The Sabbath erects a fence around human productive activity and serves to protect both human and non-human creation. Human beings have, therefore, both a right and an obligation to rest.

29. Corresponding to the four basic relations in which all people stand (in relationship to non-human creation, to themselves, to other human beings, and to God), there are four activities which we should cultivate in leisure time. Rest consists in the enjoyment of nature as God's creation, in the free exercise and development of abilities which God has given to each person, in the cultivation of fellowship with one another, and above all, in delight in communion with God.

30. Worship is central to the Biblical concept of rest. In order to be truly who they are, human beings need periodic moments of time in which God's commands concerning their work will recede from the forefront of their consciousness as they adore the God of loving holiness and thank the God of holy love.

31. Those who cannot meet their basic needs without having to forego leisure can be encouraged by the reality of their right to rest. The right to rest implies the corresponding right to sustenance for all those who are willing to work 'six days a week' (Exodus 20:9). Modern workaholics whose infatuation with status relegates leisure to insignificance must be challenged by the liberating obligation to rest. What does it profit them to 'gain the whole world' if they 'forfeit their life' (Mark 8:36).

C. Poverty and Justice

God and the Poor

32. Poverty was not part of God's original creation, nor will poverty be part of God's restored creation when Christ returns. Involuntary poverty in all its forms and manifestations is a result of the fall and its consequences. Today one of every five human beings lives in poverty so extreme that their survival is daily in doubt. We believe this is offensive and heart breaking to God.

33. We understand that the God of the Bible is one who in mercy extends love to all. At the same time, we believe that when the poor are oppressed, God is the 'defender of the poor' (Psalm 146:7–9). Again and again in every part of scripture, the Bible expresses God's concern for justice for the poor. Faithful obedience requires that we share God's concern and act on it. 'He who oppresses a poor man insults his maker, but he who is kind to the needy honours Him' (Proverbs 14:31). Indeed it is only when we right such injustices that God promises to hear our prayers and worship (Isaiah 58: 1–9).

34. Neglect of the poor often flows from greed. Furthermore, the obsessive or careless pursuit of material goods is one of the most destructive idolatries in human history (Ephesians 5:5). It distracts individuals from their duties before God, and corrupts personal and social relationships.

Causes of Poverty

35. The causes of poverty are many and complex. They include the evil that people do to each other, to themselves, and to their environment. The causes of poverty also include the cultural attitudes and actions taken by social, economic, political and religious institutions, that either devalue or waste resources, that erect barriers to economic production, or that fail to reward work fairly. Furthermore, the forces that cause and perpetuate poverty operate at global, national, local and personal levels. It is also true that a person may be poor because of sickness, mental or physical handicap, childhood, or old age. Poverty is also caused by natural disasters such as earthquakes, hurricanes, floods, and famines.

36. We recognise that poverty results from and is sustained by both constraints on the production of wealth and on the inequitable distribution of wealth and income. We acknowledge the tendency we have had to reduce the causes of poverty to one at the expense of the other. We affirm the need to analyse and explain the conditions that promote the creation of wealth, as well as those that determine the distribution of wealth.

37. We believe it is the responsibility of every society to provide people with the means to live at a level consistent with their standing as persons created in the image of God.

Justice and Poverty

38. Biblical justice means impartially rendering to everyone their due in conformity with the standards of God's moral law. Paul uses justice (or righteousness) in its most comprehensive sense as a metaphor to describe God's creative and powerful redemptive love. Christ, solely in grace, brought us, into God's commonwealth, who were strangers to it and because of sin cut off from it. (Romans 1: 17–18; 3:21–26; Ephesians 2:4–22) In Biblical passages which deal with the distribution of the benefits of social life in the context of social conflict and social wrong, justice is related particularly to what is due to groups such as the poor, widows, orphans, resident aliens, wage earners and slaves. The common link among these groups is powerlessness by virtue of economic and social needs. The justice called forth is to restore these groups to the provision God intends for them. God's law expresses this justice and indicates its demands. Further, God's intention is for people to live, not in isolation, but in society. The poor are described as those who are weak with respect to the rest of the community; the responsibility of the community is stated as 'to make them strong' so that they can continue to take their place in the community (Leviticus 25:35–36). One of the dilemmas of the poor is their loss of community (Job 22:5; Psalm 107:4–9, 33–36). Indeed their various needs are those that tend to prevent people from being secure and contributing members of society. One essential characteristic of Biblical justice is the meeting of basic needs that have been denied in contradiction to the standards of scripture; but further, the Bible gives indication of how to identify which needs are basic. They are those essential, not just for life, but for life in society.

39. Justice requires special attention to the weak members of the community because of their greater vulnerability. In this sense, justice is partial. Nevertheless, the civil arrangements in rendering justice are not to go beyond what is due to the poor or to the rich (Deuteronomy 1:17; Leviticus 19:15) In this sense justice is ultimately impartial. Justice is so fundamental that it characterises the personal virtues and personal relationships of individuals as they faithfully follow God's standards. Those who violate God's standards, however, receive God's retributive justice, which often removes the offender from society or from the divine community.

40. Justice requires conditions such that each person is able to participate in society in a way compatible with human dignity. Absolute poverty, where people lack even minimal food and housing, basic education, health care, and employment, denies people the basic economic resources necessary for just participation in the community. Corrective action with and on behalf of the poor is a necessary act of justice. This entails responsibilities for individuals, families, churches, and governments.

41. Justice may also require socio-political actions that enable the poor to help themselves and be the subjects of their own development and the development of their communities. We believe that we and the institutions in which we participate are responsible to create an environment of law, economic activity, and spiritual nurture which creates these conditions.

Some Urgent Contemporary Issues

42. Inequitable international economic relations aggravate poverty in poor countries. Many of these countries suffer under a burden of debt service which could only be repaid at an unacceptable price to the poor, unless there is a radical restructuring both of national economic policies and international economic relations. The combination of increasing interest rates and falling commodity prices in the early 1980s has increased this debt service burden. Both lenders and borrowers shared in creating this debt. The result has been increasing impoverishment of the people. Both lenders and borrowers must share responsibility for finding solutions. We urgently encourage governments and international financial institutions to redouble their efforts to find ways to reduce the international indebtedness of the

Third World, and to ensure the flow of both private and public productive capital where appropriate.

43. Government barriers to the flow of goods and services often work to the disadvantage of the poor. We particularly abhor the protectionist policies of the wealthy nations which are detrimental to developing countries. Greater freedom and trade between nations is an important part of reducing poverty worldwide.

44. Justice requires that the value of money be reliably known and stable, thus inflation represents poor stewardship and defrauds the nations' citizens. It wastes resources and is particularly harmful to the poor and the powerless. The wealthier members of society find it much easier to protect themselves against inflation than do the poor. Rapid changes in prices drastically affect the ability of the poor to purchase basic goods.

45. Annual global military expenditures equal the annual income of the poorest one-half of the world's people. These vast, excessive military expenditures detract from the task of meeting basic human needs, such as food, health care, and education. We are encouraged by the possibilities represented by the changes in the USSR and Eastern Europe, and improving relations between East and West. We urge that a major part of the resulting 'peace dividend' be used to provide sustainable solutions to the problems of the world's poor.

46. Drug use and trafficking destroys both rich and poor nations. Drug consumption reflects spiritual poverty among the people and societies in which drug use is apparent. Drug trafficking undermines the national economies of those who produce drugs. The economic, social, and spiritual costs of drug use are unacceptable. The two key agents involved in this problem must change: the rich markets which consume drugs and the poorer countries which produce them. Therefore both must urgently work to find solutions. The rich markets which consume drugs must end their demand. And the poorer countries which produce them must switch to other products.

47. We deplore economic systems based on policies, laws and regulations whose effect is to favour privileged minorities and to exclude the poor from fully legitimate activities. Such systems are not only inefficient, but are immoral as well in that participating in and benefitting from the formal economy depends on conferred privilege of those who have access and influence to public and private institutions rather than on inventiveness and hard work. Actions need to be taken by public and private institutions to reduce and

simplify the requirements and costs of participating in the national economy.

48. There is abundant evidence that investment in small scale enterprises run by and for the poor can have a positive impact upon income and job creation for the poor. Contrary to the myths upheld by traditional financial institutions, the poor are often good entrepreneurs and excellent credit risks. We deplore the lack of credit available to the poor in the informal sector. We strongly encourage governments, financial institutions, and Non Governmental Organisation's to redouble their efforts to significantly increase credit to the poor. We feel so strongly about this that a separate statement dedicated to credit-based, income generation programmes has been issued by the conference.

D. Freedom, Government and Economics

The Language of Human Rights

49. With the United Nations Declaration of Human Rights, the language of human rights has become pervasive throughout the world. It expresses the urgent plight of suffering people whose humanity is daily being denied them by their oppressors. In some cases rights language has been misused by those who claim that anything they want is theirs 'by right'. This breadth of application has led some to reject rights as a concept, stating that if everything becomes a right then nothing will be a right, since all rights imply corresponding responsibilities. Therefore it is important to have clear criteria for what defines rights.

Christian Distinctives

50. All human interaction is judged by God and is accountable to God. In seeking human rights we search for an authority or norm which transcends our situation. God is that authority; God's character constitutes that norm. Since human rights are a priori rights, they are not conferred by the society or the state. Rather, human rights are rooted in the fact that every human being is made in the image of God. The deepest ground of human dignity is that while we were yet sinners, Christ died for us (Romans 5:8).

51. In affirmation of the dignity of God's creatures, God's justice for them requires life, freedom, and sustenance. The divine requirements of justice establish corresponding rights for human beings to whom justice is due. The right to life is the most basic human right. God created human beings as free moral agents. As such, they have the right to freedom – e.g. freedom of religion, speech, and assembly. Their freedom, however, is properly used only in dependence on God. It is a requirement of justice that human beings, including refugees and stateless persons, are able to live in society with dignity. Human beings therefore have a claim on other human beings for social arrangements that ensure that they have access to the sustenance that makes life in society possible.

52. The fact that in becoming Christians we may choose to forego our rights out of love for others and in trust of God's providential care does not mean that such rights cease to exist. Christians may endure the violation of their rights with great courage but work vigorously for the identical rights of others in similar circumstances. However it may not be appropriate to do so in some circumstances. Indeed this disparity between Christian contentment and campaigning on behalf of others in adverse situations is a witness to the work and love of God.

53. All of us share the same aspirations as human beings to have our rights protected – whether the right to life, freedom, or sustenance. Yet the fact of sin and the conflict of competing human rights means that our aspirations are never completely fulfilled in this life. Through Christ, sin and evil have been conquered. They will remain a destructive force until the consummation of all things. But that in no way reduces our horror at the widespread violation of human rights today.

Democracy

54. As a model, modern political democracy is characterised by limited government of a temporary character, by the division of power within the government, the distinction between state and society, pluralism, the rule of law, institutionalisation of freedom rights (including free and regular elections), and a significant amount of non-governmental control of property. We recognise that no political system is directly prescribed by scripture, but we believe that biblical values and historical experience call Christians to work for the

adequate participation of all people in the decision-making processes on questions that affect their lives.

55. We also recognise that simply to vote periodically is not a sufficient expression of democracy. For a society to be truly democratic economic power must be shared widely and class and status distinctions must not be barriers preventing access to economic and social institutions. Democracies are also open to abuse through the very channels which make them democratic. Small, economically powerful groups sometimes dominate the political process. Democratic majorities can be swayed by materialistic, racist, or nationalistic sentiments to engage in unjust policies. The fact that all human institutions are fallen means that the people must be constantly alert to and critical of all that is wrong.

56. We recognise that no particular economic system is directly prescribed by scripture. Recent history suggests that a dispersion of ownership of the means of production is a significant component of democracy. Monopolistic ownership, either by the state, large economic institutions, or oligarchies is dangerous. Widespread ownership, either in a market economy or a mixed system tends to decentralise power and prevent totalitarianism.

The Concentration of Economic Power

57. Economic power can be concentrated in the hands of a few people in a market economy. When that occurs political decisions tend to be made for economic reasons and the average member of society is politically and economically marginalised. Control over economic life may thus be far removed from a large part of the population. Transnational corporations can also wield enormous influence on some economies. Despite these problems, economic power is diffused within market-oriented economies to a greater extent than in other systems.

58. In centrally planned economies, economic decisions are made for political reasons, people's economic choices are curtailed, and the economy falters. Heavy state involvement and regulation within market economies can also result in concentrations of power that effectively marginalise poorer members of the society. Corruption almost inevitably follows from concentrated economic power. Widespread corruption so undermines society that there is a virtual breakdown of legitimate order.

Capitalism and Culture

59. As non-capitalist countries increasingly turn away from central planning and towards the market, the question of capitalism's effect on culture assumes more and more importance. The market system can be an effective means of economic growth, but can, in the process, cause people to think that ultimate meaning is found in the accumulation of more goods. The overwhelming consumerism of Western societies is testimony to the fact that the material success of capitalism encourages forces and attitudes that are decidedly non-Christian. One such attitude is the treatment of workers as simply costs or productive inputs, without recognition of their humanity. There is also the danger that the model of the market, which may work well in economic transactions, will be assumed to be relevant to other areas of life, and people may consequently believe that what the market encourages is therefore best or most true.

The Role of Government

60. Government is designed to serve the purposes of God to foster community, particularly in response to our rebellious nature (Romans 13:1, 4; Psalm 72:1). As an institution administered by human beings, government can exacerbate problems of power, greed, and envy. However, it can, where properly constructed and constrained, serve to limit some of these sinful tendencies. Therefore, it is the responsibility of Christians to work for governmental structures that serve justice. Such structures must respect the principle that significant decisions about local human communities are usually best made at a level of government most directly responsible to the people affected.

61. At a minimum, government must establish a rule of law that protects life, secures freedom, and provides basic security. Special care must be taken to make sure the protection of fundamental rights is extended to all members of society, especially the poor and oppressed (Proverbs 31:8–9; Daniel 4:27). Too often government institutions are captured by the economically or socially powerful. Thus, equality before the law fails to exist for those without power. Government must also have regard for economic efficiency and appropriately limit its own scope and action.

62. The provision of sustenance rights is also an appropriate function of government. Such rights must be carefully defined so

that government's involvement will not encourage irresponsible behaviour and the breakdown of families and communities. In a healthy society, this fulfilment of rights will be provided through a diversity of institutions so that the government's role will be that of last resort.

Mediating Structures

63. One of the phenomena associated with the modern world is the increasing divide between private and public sectors. The need for a bridge between these two sectors has led to an emphasis on mediating institutions. The neighbourhood, the family, the church and other voluntary associations are all such institutions. As the early church did in its context, these institutions provide citizens with many opportunities for participation and leadership. They also provide other opportunities for loyalty in addition to the state and the family. Their role in meeting the needs of members of the community decreases the need for centralised government. They also provide a channel for individuals to influence government, business, and other large institutions. Therefore Christians should encourage governments everywhere to foster vigorous voluntary associations.

64. The future of poverty alleviation is likely to involve expanded microeconomic income generation programmes and entrepreneurial development of the so-called 'informal sector' as it becomes part of the transformed formal economy. In this context, there will most likely be an even greater role for Non-Governmental Organizations. In particular, church bodies will be able to make a significant and creative contribution in partnership with the poor, acting as mediating institutions by virtue of the churches' longstanding grass-roots involvement in local communities.

Conclusion

65. As we conclude, we thank God for the opportunity God has given us to participate in this conference. Through our time together we have been challenged to express our faith in the area of economic life in practical ways. We acknowledge that all too often we have allowed society to shape our views and actions and have failed to apply scriptural teaching in this crucial area of our lives, and we repent.

We now encourage one another to uphold Christian economic values in the face of unjust and subhuman circumstances. We realise, however, that ethical demands are often ineffective because they are reinforced only by individual conscience and that the proclamation of Christian values needs to be accompanied by action to encourage institutional and structural changes which would foster these values in our communities. We will therefore endeavour to seek every opportunity to work for the implementation of the principles outlined in this **Declaration**, in faithfulness to God's calling.

We urge all people, and especially Christians, to adopt stewardship and justice as the guiding principles for all aspects of economic life, particularly for the sake of those who are most vulnerable. These principles must be applied in all spheres of life. They have to do with our use of material resources and lifestyle as well as with the way people and nations relate to one another. With girded loins and burning lamps we wait for the return of our Lord Jesus Christ when justice and peace shall embrace.

Seventeen

Evangelical Christianity and the Environment

World Evangelical Fellowship Theological Commission
Unit on Ethics and Society/Au Sable Forum 1992

SUMMARIZING COMMITTEE REPORT

This report seeks to summarize the substance of the discussions at the
Au Sable Forum, 26–31 August 1992. The Forum comprised 60 individuals from 8 countries and 5 continents. They had a wide variety of
expertise, academic disciplines, and current professions, but all were
closely concerned in different ways with the natural environment.

The report identifies the many points on which there was substantial
agreement between the participants. A few points are however identified separately either because it was agreed that further consideration
was desirable or because there was substantive disagreement within the
group (these areas of disagreement are noted in the text below).

'Evangelical Christianity and the Environment' in *Transformation*, Vol. 9,
No. 4, 1994.

The points are grouped in three sections:

I.   The Biblical theological framework
II.   The *praxis* of sustainable development
III. Tasks for the Christian community and individuals.

The discussion was undertaken against the background of the creation in northern part of the lower Michigan peninsula and instruction on the flora, fauna, geography of the area, and on seven specific degradations to which creation is currently subject:

(1) *alteration of Earth's energy exchange* with the sun that results in *global warming and destruction of the Earth's protective ozone shield.* A **specific example:** Ozone loss each spring over Antarctica, based upon 25 years of nearly continuous measurements by the British Antarctic Survey station at Halley Bay detected slight ozone decline n the late 1970s, greater declines in the 1980s, with 30% depletion by 1984 and 70% of the total column ozone content in 1989. [Anderson, J., D. Toohey and W. Brune, 1991, 'Free Radicals Within the Antarctic Vortex: The Role of CFCs in Antarctic Ozone Loss.' Science, 251:39–46.]

(2) *land degradation* that reduces available land for creatures and crops by 'adding house to house and field to field' and destroys land by erosion, salinzation and desertification. **A specific example:** Infiltration of rain water in eroded soils may be reduced by over 90%; in Zimbabwe water runoff is 20% to 30% greater than on non-eroded soil, with resulting water shortages even during years with good rainfall. [Pimentel, D., et al. 1987. 'World Agriculture and Soil Erosion.' BioScience, 37:277–283.]

(3) *water quality degradation* that defiles groundwater, lakes, rivers and oceans. **A specific example:** In Europe and the U.S. between 5% and 10% of all wells examined have nitrate levels higher than the recommended maximum of 45 milligrams per litre. [Maurits la Riviere, J. 1989. 'Threats to the World's Water,' Scientific American, September 1989:80–94.]

(4) *deforestation* that each year removes 100,000 square kilometres of primary forest and degrades an equal amount by over-use. **A specific**

example: In Thailand forest cover declined from 29 to 19 percent of the land area between 1985 and 1988. In the Philippines undisturbed forests have been reduced from 16 million hectares in 1960 to less than a million hectares left at present. [Repetto, R. 1990. 'Deforestation in the Tropics.' Scientific American. April 1990:36–42.]

(5) *species extinction* that finds more than 3 species of plants and animals eliminated from Earth *each day*. **A specific example:** In Ecuador since 1960 the original rainforest has been almost totally eliminated and converted to cash crops; a small remnant at Rio Palenque of less than one square kilometre is the only remaining site for 43 plant species and the adjacent Centinella Ridge that once supported 100 endemic plant species was cleared between 1980 and 1984. [Given, D. 1990. 'Conserving Botanical Diversity on a Global Scale.' Annals of the Missouri Botanical Gardens, 77:48–62.]

(6) *waste generation and global toxification* that results in distribution of troublesome materials worldwide by atmospheric and oceanic circulations. **A specific example:** DDT is found in the fatty tissue of penguins in Antarctica and pesticides are found in a remote lake on Isle Royale in Lake Superior between the United States and Canada.

(7) *human and cultural degradation* that threatens and eliminates long-standing knowledge of native and some Christian communities on living sustainably and cooperatively with Creation, together with the loss of long-standing garden varieties of food plants. **A specific example:** A 1975 study of the Hanunoo tribe of the Philippine Islands found that an average adult could identify 1,600 different species – some 400 more than previously recorded in a systematic botanical survey; for Nigeria and elsewhere in the Two-Thirds World there are similar findings. [Awa, N. 1989, 'Participation and Indigenous Knowledge in Rural Development.' Knowledge, 10:304–316.]

1. The Biblical Theological Framework

God in creation

1.1 All creatures are deeply intertwined with and dependent on each other, and humans have no right to destroy or despoil other species.

However, since Evangelical Christians have affirmed that God is distinct from Creation, and has given humans unique status among creatures, some environmentally conscious people have felt that Christianity has given humans licence to exploit other creatures. Some such people feel that the earth ought rather to be identified directly with divine powers (symbolized by Gaia, the earth goddess) or regarded as God's 'body'. We affirm that God is indeed distinct from creation, yet deeply involved in it. This involvement arises not from natural necessity (as though the earth were God or part of God) but from the triune God's free love and grace. God the Son, as the eternal Word, gives form to all creatures, and became human flesh, with which all creatures are interconnected; while God the Spirit breathes energy into all.

1.2 We affirm the value of the Gaia hypothesis (that the earth, or its living creatures, form one interconnected system) for scientific research. While we reject the religious implication sometimes drawn – that the earth is a divine being – we recognize that many are attracted to it as a result of the spiritual hunger prevalent in secularized industrial societies and of the church's failure adequately to proclaim its living, triune God as both clearly distinct from and intimately involved with the creation.

1.3 Some critics of Evangelical Christianity feel that its frequent use of masculine God-imagery, in contrast to feminine imagery, heightens a sense of God's distance from the world. At the same, many feel that feminine imagery implies an identity between God and creation. While we did not discuss specific constructive responses to these concerns, we recognize their importance. We also affirm that adequate imagery for expressing God's 'masculine' and 'feminine' characteristics are to be found in Scripture, and that the Bible's main concern in this area is to communicate that God is *personal*.

The Goodness of Creation

1.4 We wholeheartedly affirm that the universe, as created by God, is good.

1.4.1 We experienced some uncertainty and disagreement as to the nature and presence of evil in relation to creation. We did not attain clarity as to whether death as experienced before humankind's fall should be regarded as natural or evil, or as to exactly what the 'curse' brought with this fall, or how it operates.

The Fulfillment of Creation

1.5 In the Old Testament, the creation account begins by showing the threefold relationship between God, creation, and humanity. This relationship is later exemplified in the covenant with Israel, which includes the people of Israel, the gift of the land of Israel and their responsibility for it to God. The well-being or despoilation of the land was connected with their obedience or disobedience. In the New Testament, this triadic relationship of God, people of Israel, and land of Israel is reaffirmed and extended as the triad of God, the new people of God and the liberation of all creation. God's call to faith in Jesus Christ includes the call to care for and work towards the transformation of all creation.

1.6 God's purposes for creation include the development of urban areas. Concern for creation should not compete with, but should include and enhance, the development of healthy urban environments.

1.7 God draws all creatures towards a final fulfilment, the bodily resurrection of redeemed humanity and the liberation of all creation. The resurrected Jesus is the 'first fruit' of this liberation. The resurrection enlivens our responsibility for involvement in environmental matters, since it indicates how highly God values material reality, and arouses our hope, giving energy for the task.

1.8 The Sabbath rest is both a replication of God's rest in creation and an anticipation of creation's final perfection when it participates with the people of God in their rest. In both cases humanity is to trust that God will provide what is needed for life.

Humanity and creation

1.9 Although all creatures receive life ultimately from God, human beings are intertwined with all other creatures, and in this sense dependent upon them for life. Yet humans are also called to a special task of caring for creation in a shepherdly manner, since they reflect God's image in a unique way. Many felt that the traditional term 'stewardship' adequately describes this task. Others cautioned that it can convey the mistaken notions that God is an absentee landlord, and humans may therefore manage creation in any way that they see fit.

1.10 We affirm that all God's creations are valuable in and of themselves, apart from any usefulness to humans. Though humans may at times use other creatures in the attainment of legitimate purposes, they are (so far as possible) to support the well-being of other creatures.

1.11 Where mankind has significantly damaged creation, the motivation for its restoration comes from our stewardship responsibilities, our hope for the liberation of creation, and the sufferings inflicted on particular groups of people, especially the poor (in the context of the fact that Jesus shared humanity's sufferings and proclaimed good news, especially to the poor).

Spiritual dimensions

1.12 Humans participate most fully in God's purposes for creation through personal appropriation of the benefits of Jesus Christ's life, death and resurrection, which become present, participatory realities through the Holy Spirit. Essential for this participation is spirituality focused on Jesus's teaching and his cross, enlivened by the Spirit who moves throughout creation and connects our yearnings with those of all other creatures.

1.13 While we do not entirely understand how they operate, we affirm that supernatural forces of evil seek to block the accomplishment of God's purposes for creation. We therefore expect our participation in these purposes to involve struggle with these forces, and sometimes to involve suffering, which we will overcome through reliance on the triune God.

Sections 2 and 3 below assemble points for consideration and action by the Christian and wider communities. They should not be read as a complete manifesto, but as points which arose in the course of inevitably time-limited discussions: there were many relevant matters which were not touched upon.

2. The *Praxis* of Sustainable Development

2.1 We affirm the concept of sustainable development, as that which seeks to provide an environment that promotes a life of dignity and well-being compatible with the continuation and integrity of supporting ecosystems.[1] The concept includes the concern that material blessings should be available to successive generations as a fundamental God-given right. We note that beneath this concern lie absolutes of justice, equity and human responsibility which are not always expressed. Sustainable development cannot depend on the changing values and aspirations of succeeding generations, which may be in conflict with each other and with the divine will.

Population

2.2 We noted the importance of the issue of population as part of care for the environment. This is an issue of culture rather than technology. Current methods of assessing the value of the environment fail to make adequate allowance for the value of the environment where it provides livelihoods. We would urge a culture specific approach of promoting child-spacing, with due regard for the sanctity of human life, rather than the one-solution approach (of contraceptive techniques or abortion) advocated by some. We welcome the suggestion of providing for new parents non-contributory old age pensions, or life insurance for their progeny, to remove the incentive to have many children to provide for old age.

Over-consumption

2.3 Over-consumption in the North can have a debilitating impact on countries of the South. Consumption of non-renewable resources in the North should be significantly reduced, by increasing recycling and reuse of materials, and by encouraging transition to less material-intensive technologies.

Poverty and degradation of creation

2.4 The evidence of growing numbers of poor people in the world is unmistakable, as is the evidence of the worsening condition of the creation contributing to and in part caused by poverty. We recognize that a fundamental cause of poverty is the sinful nature of humankind which manifests itself through violence, greed and self-interest overriding the God-given mandate to meet the needs of both the human and natural creation, and specifically of the poor. Human beings are interdependent with the rest of creation but distinctly unique in that they are made in the image of God. We believe that it is of equal importance when addressing the needs of creation to deal adequately with needs of the poor, and specifically to address world hunger.

2.5 In poor countries, sustainable development requires first and foremost addressing the following interrelated tasks: the establishment of a just and stable political power; economic development to provide jobs and alleviate poverty; capital investments in human development to stabilize populations and enable people to improve their well-being and their livelihoods: protection of God's creation, in large part by providing poor and landless peoples with alternatives to the over-exploitation of marginal lands; and support for improved development practices that are both appropriate within the culture and to the task.

Development assistance

2.6 We recognize the need of low-income countries, communities, and economies in transition to receive technological, educational and financial assistance to meet the incremental costs of caring for the creation while promoting economic development.

Women

2.7 The enormous disparities that exist between opportunities and rewards for men and women, and the disproportionate burden, on women, of poverty and the degradation of creation, mean that expanded opportunities for women can result in substantial gains for them, their families and their communities. Increases in the status of women's education and earnings, along with the availability of maternity and child health care, are also significant factors in improving child nutrition and health, as well as tending to reduce family size and its impact on creation (see Population, 2.2).

Mission and culture

2.8 Christianity is distinctive in not being bound to a particular cultural context. Both Christian mission and development work need to be properly sensitive to the cultural context, while affirming the active role of Christians within all cultures whether representing minority or majority viewpoints. Churches must be aware of and sensitive to existing sustainable patterns of development and indigenous stewardship practices in terms of self-reliance and equity, since Christianity is not an expression of any one cultural pattern. Where there have been situations of dependence and cultural imperialism, steps need to be taken redress the wrongs of these situations. There needs to be reciprocity and respect between all Christians and cultures. Cultures interact and change. Missions and development activities are agents of change, and should work with national churches where they exist. The impact of these changes on the environment – positive and negative, intended and unintended – cannot be ignored, and are of great concern.

2.9 Lessons for the care of creation and methods or practices of Christian stewardship were drawn from the practices of Christians worldwide. An example was given from recent mission history where the outcome of Christian compassionate mission was to remove the hindrances to child survival, without compensating activity to relieve subsequent pressure on the environment. A more positive model is the church in Bali, a Christian community formed in the context of a community with a lively relationship to the surrounding creation. The revelation and love of Christ has been expressed in the context of this concern for creation by building churches amid gardens and water, establishing experimental farms, and setting up credit unions and employment-creation unions and employment-creation programmes. These innovations have been made without either compromising the uniqueness of Christ's revelation, or obliterating the many positive aspects of the Balinese culture.

Technology and Culture

2.10 Technological possibilities must be in a framework of Christian understanding the socio-cultural context, and the natural environment. Uncontrolled development of technologies can ultimately threaten the very existence of humanity.

Farming

2.11 **Agriculture**. Modern methods of agriculture with inputs of chemical fertilizers and pesticides may lead to pollution of groundwater and other problems. Such pollution can produce health problems for human and animal populations. Chemical fertilizers fail to sustain the natural nutrients in the soil, resulting in reduction of crop productivity and cutrophication of surface waters. Often, in past agriculture, pests were controlled and nutrient status of the soil was maintained by practices such as crop rotation, inter-cropping, multiple cropping, etc. However, in some cases, as in Ethiopia, traditional practices have resulted in loss of soil fertility and soil erosion. It is necessary to identify successful traditional practices and upgrade them as appropriate in order to develop (or recover) appropriate site-specific technologies which enhance crop productivity without degrading the environment.

2.12 **Livestock**. When animals or birds are domesticated to provide food or other products or services, attention should be paid to ensure their proper care and welfare. Modern biotechnology techniques have made it possible to introduce changes in animals and birds to enhance the quality and/or productivity or products derived from them like milk, meat, leather, etc., but such changes affect their natural lifestyles and may sometimes cause them considerable discomfort. The ethics of introducing such changes in living creatures needs to be examined in the light of scriptural teachings.

2.13 **Wildlife**. When animals in the wild are affected or used for human purposes, attention should be paid to ensure their proper care and welfare. Animals in the wild must be recognized as having certain needs for maintaining their life, their 'creatureliness' as willed by their Creator, their habitats, and their kinds. Destroying the animal world upsets not only the animals but also the ecological balance. Such destruction results from poaching, abusive use in entertainment, animal sacrifices, and pollution and destruction of their homes and habitat. Abusive use always takes place when cruelty is involved, and/or the species is over-exploited. Trade in animals and animal parts must always be done in accordance with strict ethical criteria.

Industry

2.14 The principle that the 'Polluter pays' and that 'one person cannot exploit or pollute another person's source of living' must take account of who the polluter is – he/she is often the actual consumer on whose behalf the producer acts. Shaping technology so as to prevent pollution and or reduce it at source can often be much cheaper than cleaning it up later.

Military preparations and war

2.15 Wars (including terrorist activities, military preparations, and some forms of training) degrade the environment. The Bible insists that the environment be protected in case of conflict (for example, olive trees may not be destroyed). If even a small percentage of the resources devoted to armaments research and development were diverted to environmental conservation, substantial improvement could be achieved in the state of creation.

3. Tasks for the Christian Community and Individuals

The kingdom community

3.1 The church's task is to take part in and give expression to the present and future kingdom of Christ. When the kingdom arrives in its fullness, creation will be set free from its bondage to decay.

Care for Creation and Evangelism

3.2 Many people in the environmental movement are in an intense religious search even though they explicitly reject Christianity. As Christians articulate a Biblical view of creation and model loving care for its wellbeing, they will have significant evangelistic opportunities. Christian environmentalists should take eagerly these opportunities to point people to Christ.

3.3 When people come to Christ and churches are formed, then in the process of obedient discipleship, care for creation frequently emerges. This care needs to be more consciously and systematically taught and sought as a mark of Christian discipleship, both for the individual Christian and for the Christian community, in place of expressions of discipleship which are limited to the life of the individual. Caring treatment of non-human creation will enhance our care for the crown of creation, men and women.

Youth

3.4 Because they will be around the longest, young people should (and often do) have a special interest in the care of creation. This special interest of the young requires the development of a robust environmental apologetic to be made available to youth and youth ministries. A commitment to evangelism is integral to efforts to care for creation and vice versa. Young Christians need not only to be equipped with evangelistic materials, but to be given practical teaching on issues of lifestyle, as well as opportunities to express their care of creation in a meaningful way. 'Whose Earth', the Spring Harvest initiative in association with TEAR Fund, is a model which has attempted to meet these goals in the United Kingdom.

The Sabbath Rest

3.5 God rested at the end of the Creation week, he exemplified for us what 'sabbath' should mean. In addition, the fourth commandment requires us to honour the sabbath. Observation of the sabbath may take many forms; however, it should fulfil the purposes of worship, rest, and recreation. More thought is needed, to develop ways in which Christians in differing cultures should observe the sabbath, for the sabbath is for creation.

Political engagement and Education

3.6 The Christian community, who follows the one who is the Truth, must dare to proclaim the full truth about the environmental crisis in the face of powerful persons, pressures and institutions which profit from concealing the truth. Such recognition of hard truths is a first step towards the freedom for which creation waits.

3.7 The Christian community needs to develop practical policy approaches to the environment and environmental issues, based on Biblical principles and sound analysis.

3.8 Christians need to form and join environmental organizations that apply explicitly Christian principles to environmental problems. In addition, they have an important witness as participants in secular organizations.

3.9 The Christian community must be willing to identify and condemn social and institutionalized evil, especially when it becomes embedded in systems. It should purpose solutions which both seek to reform and (if necessary) replace creation-harming institutions and practices.

3.10 Churches should seek to develop as creation-awareness centres in order to exemplify principles of stewardship for their members and communities, and to express both delight in and care for creation in their worship and celebration. They should particularly aim to produce curricula and programmes which encourage knowledge and care of creation.

3.11 The Christian community must initiate and support the process of education (for all its members) on the Christian approach to environmental ethics. In particular, Christian colleges and seminaries should provide teaching in this area. The church's goal should be the growth of earthkeepers, both in the habits of everyday life, and in the provision of leadership for the care of creation.

3.12 Many other issues which may be the root cause of proximate cause of environmental problems, may require similar political and educational initiatives, such as those identified in paragraphs 2.2 to 2.7 above (population pressure, over-consumption, poverty, international financial transfers, and the status and role of women).

We welcome dialogue with all who are concerned with preserving and enhancing our environment (which is God's creation). We pray that these reflections may provide a positive contribution towards achieving the goals which we share.[2]

The Earth Is the Lord's He [Christ] is before all things, and in him all things hold together

Participants by Location

ARGENTINA: Adriana Powell, Kairos Community, Tucuman. Wilfredo Weigandt, Municipalidad de Embalse, Cordoba. **CANADA:** Dianne MacTavish, Outdoor Christian Education Centre, Beaverton, Ontario. Loren Wilkinson, Regent College, Vancouver, British Columbia. Brian MacTavish, Outdoor Christian Education Centre, Beaverton, Ontario. **INDIA:** Bruce Nicholls, Evangelical Review of Theology, New Delhi. Jesudason Jeyaraj, Tamilnadu Theological Seminary, Madurai, Tamilnadu. Jeyakar Chelleraj, Bishop Heber College, Tiruchirapalli. Johnson David, World Wide Fund for Nature, Bangalore. **INDONESIA:** Wayan Mastra, Protestant Christian Church, Denpasar, Bali. **KENYA:** Praveen Kapur, Nairobi. **UNITED KINGDOM:** Chris Sugden, Oxford Centre for Mission Studies, Oxford. Greg Valerio, Whose Earth?/Tear Fund, Chichester, Sussex. Chris Scalon, Whose Earth?/Tear Fund, Bognor Regis, Sussex. Neil Summerton, Department of the Environment, London. Deryke Belshaw, University of

East Anglia, Norwich. Christopher Wright, All Nations Christian College, Easneye, Ware. **ROMANIA:** Lorelai Gavrila, University of Bucharest, Bucharesti. Valeria Gavrila, University of Bucharest, Bucharesti. Irina Rebedea, University of Bucharest, Bucharest. **U.S.A. CALIFORNIA:** Tara Cahill, Au Sable Alumna, Pasadena. Robbie Cahill, Fuller Theological Seminary, Pasadena, Paul Thompson, World Vision, Monrovia. **LOUISIANA:** Krista Clements, Baylor University, Shreveport. **MINNESOTA:** Paul Menthe, Christian Environmental Alliance, Minneapolis. **NEW HAMPSHIRE:** Christine Marklin, Nashua. **OHIO:** Arnold Fritz, Malone College, Canton. **PENNSYLVANIA:** Patrick Adams, Hookstown. Ron Sider, Evangelicals for Social Action, Wynnewood. Beth Adams, Hookstown. **VIRGINIA:** Frieda Redekop, Harrisonburg. **WISCONSIN:** Ruth DeWitt, Au Sable Institute, Oregon. Dick Blomker, Lake Edge Lutheran Church, Madison. Peter Bakken, Outreach Coordinator, Au Sable Institute, Martha Nack, Evangelical Lutheran Church in America, Madison. Martin Evers, University of Wisconsin, Madison. Jill Lyons, Outreach officer, Au Sable Institute. Vern Visick, Madison Campus Ministry, Madison. Mark Thomas, Au Sable Senior Research Fellow, Madison. **VIRGINIA:** Cal Redekop, Conrad Grebel College, Harrisonburg. Tom Finger, Eastern Mennonite Seminary, Harrisonville. **IOWA:** Fred Van Dyke, Northwestern College, Orange City. **MASSACHUSETTS:** Andy Fritz, Au Sable Alumnus, South Hamilton. **MICHIGAN:** Bud Watson, Michigan State University, East Lansing. John Olmstead, Au Sable Trustee, Linden. Gloria Whelan, Author, Mancelona. **ILLINOIS:** Linda Vick, North Park College, Chicago. Job Ebenezer, Evangelical Lutheran Church in America, Chicago. Steve Bouma-Prediger, North Park College & Seminary, Chicago. **CONNECTICUT:** Paul Santmire, Grace Lutheran Church, Hartford. **MICHIGAN:** Roxanne Ewert, Mennonite Central Committee, Marcellus. Greg Wilson-Youngchild, Western Michigan G.R.E.E.N., Montague. Bob Barr, Coordinator of Support Services, Au Sable Institute. Dan Denk, Inter Varsity Christian Fellowship, Grand Rapids. Joan Huyser-Honig, Christianity Today, Grand Rapids. Leon Watson, Michigan State University, East Lansing. Rolf Bouma, Eastern Ave Chr Ref Church, Grand Rapids. Becky Barr, Au Sable Institute, Mancelona. **WASHINGTON, D.C.:** Susan Drake, United States Department of State, Washington. **AU SABLE STAFF:** Dave Mahan, Associate Director, Au Sable Institute. Bill

Note

1. We recognised that there are many different definitions of sustainable development and The Forum considered a paper which referred in greater detail to the question.
2. Papers from the consultation are published in *Transformation*, April 1993 and *Evangelical Review of Theology*, April 1993.

Eighteen

A Christian Response to Population Issues – An Oxford Statement January 1996

No more shall there be in (the land) an infant that lives but a few days, or an old person who does not live out a lifetime; for one who dies at a hundred will be considered a youth, and one who falls short of a hundred will be considered accursed. They shall build houses and inhabit them; they shall plant vineyards and eat their fruit. They shall not build and another inhabit, they shall not plant and another eat; for like the days of a tree shall the days of my people be, and my chosen shall long enjoy the work of their hands. They shall not labour in vain, or bear children for calamity; for they shall be offspring blessed by the Lord – and their descendants as well. Isaiah 66:20–23.

'A Christian Response to Population Issues – An Oxford Statement Resource Document' in *Transformation*, Vol. 13, No. 2, April 1996.

Introduction

The Oxford Consultation on **A Christian response to population issues** met from 8–20 January 1996 in Oxford, England. The consultation was sponsored by the Oxford Centre for Mission Studies and Tear Fund. Thirty five experts on demography, community development, theology, ethics, economics, family planning, health care and missiology met from fifteen countries. The range of subjects covered at the consultation included: mother and child health; community development; gender issues; international institutions and policy; demographic analysis; fertility and family planning; environmental issues; employment; ethical frameworks; human rights; AIDS care and prevention; displaced persons; interfaith perspectives; economic development. Consultation members also shared case studies from their own cultures. Each of these subjects was examined in the light of theological and ethical teaching and conclusions drawn for Christian reflection and action.

The consultation issued the following report of its findings.

1. The Consultation's Purpose

The purpose of the consultation was to examine a wide range of inter-related population issues from a specifically Christian perspective. We debated technical, demographic, economic and social issues but our focus was on the relevance and authority of biblical theology and ethics to the issues we are facing, and the possibilities for action together through local churches and Christian organizations. We heard several presentations on global trends and took careful note of these as the widest context in which we think and work. However, we were aware that discussion of global population trends can quickly become discussion of ideologies. This was not our emphasis, which from the outset of the consultation, focused instead on community development, human relationships and family life to enable people working at the grass roots to develop tools and perspectives. We were concerned to develop a Christian approach to population issues which has the person, together with their family, community and cultural contexts, at its heart.

2. Report

Population Challenges

World population is 5.7 billion and rising. The UN forecast for the year 2050, which assumes that current levels of fertility will continue to decline, predicts a world population of 9.8 billion. There is wide disparity between population patterns in the north and south. The north has ageing populations and rapidly declining birth rates, whereas the south has young and rapidly growing populations.

Population projections

Population projections are important tools in understanding possible scenarios for our global future. When they are used to portray an apocalyptic scenario they create confusion and alarm. This is meant to motivate us into taking unprecedented action. More often people feel a sense of powerlessness and anxiety. This in turn can produce inertia which works against positive action. Love and justice are the prime motivators of human social action. Love needs to replace fear, for what love desires, justice demands.

Population Control

There is a major difference between culturally sensitive family planning which enables people to put their own decisions into operation, and coercive policies of population control with their targets, incentives and constraints. All too often state programmes have been inadequate and instead of serving the needs and desires of the family have coerced families to fit into patterns of behaviour shaped by government policy. Where state coercion is used to force families to reduce fertility and to conform to a state-imposed family size this is a violent abrogation of human rights. It is reported that the 'one-child policy' in China has had the effect of distorting the sex differentials in the population as a whole. For every 100 baby boys who die 118 baby girls die since boy babies are preferred.

Family Decisions

The place for informed and responsible decision-making about having children is the family, with the couple making a mutual decision within their own cultural context. We note the call at the Cairo conference to move from an approach based on targets to one based on needs and preferences, and hope that this might lead to high quality family planning programmes which are genuinely person-centred.

Secularization

Where population programmes idolize low fertility, secularization and modernization can be seen as essential tools to make this possible. Where low fertility is made the highest virtue, religious belief and custom, moral codes, and traditional family values are frequently disregarded. Definitions of freedom of choice derived from market economics are imported into cultures which until then have seen voluntary moral restraint and the promotion of virtue as an essential component of freedom. Secularization has not served the industrialized societies well and the individualistic and hedonistic definitions of freedom combined with consumerism have led to the breakdown of public and private morality.

Employment

Between 1995 and 2000 AD the UN estimates that 100 million additional people will be added to the global population. This presents a challenge to policy makers and planners to create opportunities for employment for the 40% of them who will make up the labour force. Structural adjustment policies in the third world have resulted in a reduction in employment. The impact of these policies has been felt most by lower-skilled men and women who are the easiest to remove from the labour force in times of resource constraint. International debt repayments also hamper the ability of governments to use resources for internal development.

Rural-urban Migration

Rural-urban migration often threatens the integrity of the family. Poverty in the rural areas forces people to leave their homes to seek employment in the city. Such poverty can be the result of government funding being focused on urban areas to the detriment of rural areas. The lack of employment can bring about a sense of desperation and insecurity. Removed from their traditional values people can succumb to alcohol and drug addictions, prostitution and theft. Those who remain at home bear the burden of providing food and other resources for their children and extended family. This migration also places kinship structures, local management systems, extended families and traditional support structures under great strain. Furthermore it reinforces an individualistic approach to life, found in the city, which rests uneasily with indigenous and traditional values. Despite these problems the migration to the cities in search of a better life continues. Cities are expanding at an enormous rate. Lack of proper housing, sanitation and the basic amenities of life leads to the growth of slum dwellings which are often illegal and constantly threatened with removal. The conditions in the slums are so poor that children frequently die from diarrhoeal and respiratory infections. This is not a dilemma of the 21st century: it is a harsh reality of the 20th century to which we are called urgently to respond.

Human Rights

Population pressures and programmes have a direct relationship with the way human rights are implemented: the rights of displaced peoples and the rights of families vis-à-vis the state. The rights of individuals, unborn children and of existing populations are issues of serious ethical concern to which Christians must respond.

Theological Responses

Stewardship

God made the world and pronounced it good. He made men and women in the image of God. This is the primary source of identity for all human beings and precedes economic, sexual or cultural bases for human identity. God made us stewards over creation. This means that we are to nurture, maintain and develop creation's resources rather than destroy them. Our responsibility for the creation derives from our accountability to God who provides enough for all in justice, but not for everything that human profligacy may demand.

Children as a Blessing

Having children is a blessing and an expression of the fruitfulness with which God has endowed his creation. Children, regardless of gender, are to be welcomed into a world which God has endowed with abundant resources so that all may experience fulness of life. The number of children is not by itself a blessing, but those children must be able to enjoy the blessing of life and its fulness. Sadly, many children are unwanted and girl children are tragically aborted in many societies because they are not valued as highly as boy children. In other cases children struggle against disease or malnutrition because although the resources exist to feed them, their families cannot afford to buy them or need education to know how to prevent disease.

The Results of the Fall

In the story of the fall child-bearing and parenting as well as economic development of the world's resources through work, became a painful struggle. The possibility of scarcity and an unjust distribution of resources appeared. The mutual partnership between men and women became a relationship characterized by power. In population issues both these struggles play their part. Integrated development requires economic and social justice, fair trade, and attention to human rights issues. It also requires access to family planning and spacing, health care and education so that people might have life characterized by security and sufficiency.

Shalom

Even in a world which is distorted and fallen God desires that we should live in shalom. This describes a harmony of right relationship between people and God, with each other and with the world's resources. Living in shalom requires accountability to God, stewardship of the environment, distributive and retributive justice, love for our neighbour, and personal and social holiness. This vision of peace and wholeness is a multidimensional and holistic picture of the goal of integrated development when it is viewed within a Christian context.

The Future

In the population debate the future is often used to make decisions about the present. While we listen as carefully as possible to the projections of demographers and historians we recognize that the vision of the future that shapes our contemporary decisions is the Kingdom of God and the shalom which sees its fulfilment in the new world. The resurrection of Jesus Christ is the affirmation that Jesus inaugurated the Kingdom of God which will be consummated on his return when God will reveal a new heaven and a new earth as the climax of world history. Human projections of the future must be related to God's intentions for the world and not force us into ethical pragmatism. We should avoid panic and immoral decisions which disrespect human life. Since God is the God of the future, obeying him in the present will never undermine that future.

The Family

The life of the family is at the heart of the community. Family life derives its identity from God who is the father (Eph. 3:14–5; Hos. 11:1–4). Families provide a context in which love, respect and mutual support combine with the commitments of men and women to permanent and faithful relationships to provide a stable and nurturing environment in which children can flourish. Such families can include others who through bereavement, divorce or exclusion of other kinds have become separated from their original families. In this way families can be a healing presence in communities in which the pain of grief, loneliness and rejection can threaten to overcome people.

Christians are called to reflect biblical realism about the family. Life becomes a tragedy for people when the family becomes the very place where they are most abused. Children are particularly vulnerable to abuse, not only through physical and sexual violence and emotional abuse, but also through underage employment and in war. The Church as the people of God the Father is the primary definition of the family (Mark 3:35 and par.) and thus the Christian community is called to be the larger family in which people suffering the pains and hurts of human families can be supported and in which their healing can begin.

Christians must not idolize the family. Families are to be in the service of the Kingdom, not in the service of nurturing individual consciences. On the one hand, the Kingdom paradigm provides a warning to families where family life has become an idol. Families live for their security, welfare and fulfilment. Family life becomes an end. Jesus' teaching on the conflict of interest between family obligation and Kingdom service is clear. 'No one', said Jesus, 'who puts his hand to the plough and looks back is fit for service in the Kingdom of God' (Luke 10:62). The service of the Kingdom is to be the goal of family life. Self-fulfilment and family wholeness and happiness are to be fruits of such service. On the other hand, in the Protestant West, the responsibility of nurturing and teaching individual consciences was assigned primarily to the family with support from the local church. This model of family places the emphasis on individual responsibility which a family must nurture and support. The individual's needs take priority over family needs. The social vitality of the family is neglected in the commitment to promote individual fulfilment and responsibility.

We note with great concern the growing incidence of sexual activity and childbearing outside a marriage and against biblical norms. The church should teach biblical chastity and responsible parenthood and affirm that it is wrong to engage in sexual relations and childbearing outside a marriage. Single parents should not be stigmatized.

Mother and Child Health

Mother and child health is an important part of shalom. Maternal mortality is the leading cause of death among women of reproductive age (15–44). Half a million women die every year as a result of pregnancy complications. 99 percent of those deaths are in the Two-Thirds World. The risk of a woman dying as a result of pregnancy is 200 times higher in the developing world than in the west. The vast majority of these deaths are entirely preventable through improved access to maternal and child health resources. Spacing children has dramatic impact on the health of mother and child. A child born within two years of a previous birth has twice the risk of dying than one born over two years later. Providing maternal health care means healthy mothers and healthy babies and also affirms the dignity and value of women. The emphasis on women's childbearing role has led to a concomitant emphasis on reproductive health. But other areas of their health have been neglected.

Women in Society

In societies where women are undervalued, a woman can only become powerful as the mother of a son through whom she can exert influence in the home. A woman's identity is tied up with the number of sons she produces, and in a society where women are not a part of the labour market it is seen as necessary for them to produce sons as labour inputs in order to contribute to the family income. From the time a girl is born she is regarded as a drain on resources. The practice of dowry is seen as an indicator of a woman's status, and is almost always linked to the lack of inheritance rights. In Asian societies where dowries are common parents are under pressure to go into debt to pay for a girl's wedding. Many women are made to feel guilty for causing debts and in some cases they are harassed to the extent that they either commit suicide or are burned by their in-laws. Girls are often not regarded as part of the family. A daughter is regarded as a guest in her father's home. It is necessary to change all laws which oppress women, including inheritance laws, and promote female education and employment in order to facilitate a reduction in fertility. Women need to be affirmed because together with men they bear the image of God and intrinsically have equal worth in God's eyes. They need to be valued, not only for the fruit of their womb but for the fruit of their labour. Those women who suffer domestic violence, who have childbearing imposed upon them, who are regarded as sex objects or who are only valued for procreation need to have their dignity restored.

AIDS Care and Prevention

AIDS is a pandemic problem which has serious consequences for people, their families and communities, the church and the nations. It causes intense suffering to those who contract it and always results in death. Christians as a healing community are called to respond to HIV/AIDS tragedy with acts of compassion. However, the church community is also a source of values which result in permanent personal and social transformation. Churches can help to prevent the further spread of HIV infection:

- through effective and appropriate HIV/AIDS awareness campaigns.
- by addressing the socio-economic, cultural and other behavioural factors that put people at the risk of infection, such as the culture of premarital and extramarital sex, widow inheritance, unfair economic systems, AIDS orphans, inappropriate sex education proposals and gender disparities.

- by being involved in practical medical help, home care and counselling.
- by building appropriate coping mechanisms in their communities to support affected families.

In our world we have to live with the consequences of our behaviour and take responsibility for behaviour which may be intrinsically wrong whether it has negative consequences or not. The link between HIV/AIDS and sexual behaviour has led some to see AIDS as a personal curse of God on someone who is sexually immoral. We do not accept this. If it were so it would be easy to continue the behaviour but avoid the curse by using 'safer sex' methods in acts which are still sinful if outside the marriage context. Also, many people contract HIV/AIDS who have not been involved in immoral sexual behaviour: spouses may contract it through unprotected sexual contact with their partners, infants through breast milk and haemophiliacs through infected blood transfusions. However, when societies depart from God's norms for communities in socio-economic, political and spiritual relationships, then they have to take the consequences (Amos 1 and 2, Ezek. 16:48–52, Rom. 1:18–32, 1 Cor. 11:27–33). This is not only true of immoral sexual behaviour but also of the poverty which drives so many women into prostitution as the only means of providing for themselves and their children. God suffers with people in their distress, so Christians should be compassionate and sensitive to the needs of people living with HIV/AIDS and aim to be a source of healing love to them.

A Christian Response to Population Issues – An Oxford Statement Resource Document

Introduction

The Oxford Consultation on **A Christian response to population issues** met from 8–20 January 1996 in Oxford, England. The consultation was sponsored by the Oxford Centre for Mission Studies and Tear Fund. Thirty five experts on demography, community development, theology, ethics, economics, family planning, health care and missiology met from fifteen countries. The range of subjects covered at the consultation included: mother and child health; community development; gender issues; international institutions and policy; demographic analysis; fertility and family planning; environmental issues; employment; ethical frameworks; human rights; AIDS care and prevention; displaced persons; interfaith perspectives; economic development. Consultation members also shared case studies from their own cultures. Each of these subjects was examined in the light of theological and ethical teaching and conclusions drawn for Christian reflection and action.

The following materials represent notes, papers, discussions and outcomes from small group and plenary discussions held throughout the consultation. They are offered as a resource for others working in the field.

1. The Consultation's purpose

The purpose of the consultation was to examine a wide range of inter-related population issues from a specifically Christian perspective. We debated technical, demographic, economic and social issues but our focus was on the relevance and authority of biblical theology and ethics to the issues we are facing, and the possibilities for action together through local churches and Christian organizations. We heard several presentations on global trends and took careful note of these as the widest context in which we think and work. However, we were aware that discussion of global population trends can quickly become discussion of ideologies. This was not our emphasis, which from the outset of the consultation, focused instead on community development, human relationships and family life to enable people working at the grass roots to develop tools and perspectives. We were concerned to develop a Christian approach to population issues which has the person, together with their family, community and cultural contexts, at its heart.

2. The nature of population challenges and responses

The focus of the consultation was on populations of the south. (The needs of declining and ageing populations in the north were not our theme.) Some perceive the problem to be that populations of the south are growing so much that they threaten the finite resources of the world. For others the issues relate primarily to the needs and rights of populations: identity, health care, the allocation of resources, and issues of justice since the populations of the north consume far more of the earth's resources per capita than the populations of the south. Our approach was to develop a global perspective, examine the effect of relationships between nations of the south and the north with respect to the challenges of population and speak to the whole church with a global Christian response.

Many countries of the south face challenges of rapid population growth and policies of population control. The roots of these policies go back to theoretical frameworks defined earlier in the north.

Population growth does not provide the drama of a financial crisis or political upheaval, but it has received more than its fair share of attention over the last fifty to sixty years from academics, policymakers and activists. Many people believe that what governments and their peoples do today to influence their demographic future will set the terms for a development strategy well into the next century.

There is a need to view the population issue from other perspectives than those formed from classical demographic transition theory which appears to be the dominant influence on responses to population issues. There is also a need to avoid perspectives which are premised on finite resources since statistics show that food supplies are increasing and may still increase further.

By the end of the nineteenth century it was common knowledge that the birth rates were falling in many if not all of the industrialized countries of the north. The classical demographic transition theory was born in 1945 when Notestein offered a twofold explanation for why western fertility had begun to decline. Fertility was kept high in premodern societies through the maintenance of a whole series of support structures: 'religious doctrines, moral codes, laws, education, community customs, marriage habits and family organizations . . . all focused towards maintaining high fertility' (Notestein 1945). High fertility was necessary for the survival of families in the face of high infant mortality that would otherwise have led to population decline and extinction. Notestein (1945), Davis (1945) and Thompson (1929) put forward the view that the initial trigger of change was a decline in mortality, to which fertility responded by declining after some time-lag. Furthermore, fundamental to the understanding and application of the demographic transition theory was the idea that the development of industrialized and urban societies dissolved the largely corporate family based traditional societies and replaced them with an individualism marked above all by the increasing secularization of urban societies. Therefore economic development and subsequent urbanization necessarily undermine traditional values that support high fertility in premodern societies. In 1953 the 'father of modern demography' Nostestein pointed out the 'urban industrial society,' was the 'crucible of the demographic transition theory.'

These notions have been widely employed by policymakers and politicians and, until recently, largely accepted without significant modification. In 1972 Paul Demeny stated that the '. . . demographic transition theory has become the central preoccupation of modern demography because of the light it claims to shed on the rapid population growth in the developing countries.' In the last twenty years, the improved availability of historical and contemporary data has revealed that there are considerable weaknesses in the classical formulation. More specifically, John Knodel and Eitteene van de Walle (1979) point out that there is no simple association between economic development and population growth. Furthermore, the French transition demonstrated a widespread decline in fertility whilst the country was still at a low level of industrial, urban and social development. Also, there was a simultaneous reduction in both mortality and fertility in the population as a whole. Demographers have begun to understand that within individual countries regional cultural factors, such as language and religion, seem to be more important sources of variation in fertility in many cases than economic variables.

Nevertheless, the central tradition of the demographic transition theory: that modernization is the route to lower population growth, is still an integral element in population policies in the Two-Thirds World. Proponents of radical action to reduce population growth see humans facing a new problem. Rapid and exponential population growth in this 'closed system' will inevitably cause a systemic strain on resources. Poorer nations of the south will become 'demographically entrapped' as the weight of current and projected numbers of people overcome the carrying capacity of the environment. Authors of this view (King, Elliot, Hellberg) argue that to avert a crisis, extreme measures are necessary. The provision of family planning methods are therefore a pragmatic response to an increasingly global environmental catastrophe. King *et al* have advocated the case for a 'one child world.' Despite the obvious ethical implications of the Chinese experiments, proponents of population control believe that since the tension between human demography and ecological limits is unprecedented so too must be the solution.

At the heart of the demographic transition theory and subsequent population policies is the need to do away with traditions, cultures, ideologies, ethics, gender sensitivities and religious implacabilities that are seen to promote and support high fertility in nations of the south. Radical proponents of control like King *et al* urge us to steel ourselves for a taboo-free discussion of radical solutions. However, it is the extent to which governments and individuals agree with this view of population growth that will determine the future action for population policies and programmes in the different cultures and contexts of the Two-Thirds World.

2. Theological Themes Relevant to Population Issues

Whatever our perception of the population issue, in order to identify the appropriate contribution of Christian communities, in particular their role in shaping the policy of governments, we need a theology of populations. The understanding of populations must be understood in the light of God's purpose in creation as seen in the Genesis record and God's plans for the future as revealed in the images of the consummation of the kingdom of God.

Responsible Stewardship of God's Provision

God created the earth and its resources and proclaimed that they were good. He placed human beings as stewards on this good earth. Humanity is given dominion over the earth, and is to image and represent God the king. So humanity is to mirror God's kingly rule of the earth, which the Bible describes in such terms as the rule of a shepherd, a husband, a beneficent ruler, and a father (Ps. 23; Hos. 2:16; Ps. 16; Ps. 10:16–18; Luke 11:2; Hos. 11:1–4). God is actively involved in enabling us to fulfil that stewardship.

God enabled the creation to multiply and promised to provide for that fruitfulness. God's blessing of creation was to provide 'every seed-bearing plant . . . every green plant for food' (Genesis 1:30). Humans are called to justice and love in stewarding God's provision.

Our stewardship includes our relationships with God, one another and the environment. The Genesis material calls for development of God's resources through work, just distribution, caring relationships between men and women, and parenthood. All these are to be undertaken in accountability to the God who provides enough for all in justice. They therefore are to be exercised with responsibility since God's provision is not at the whim of human excess and irresponsibility. The transcendent dimension which requires responsible use of earth's resources is humanity's accountability to God, not necessarily to the transcendent notion of non-existent unborn generations in the future.

God created humanity in grace and free-will to be his image and representative. God's undeserved love for all humans he created and their calling to present him in the task of developing the creation is the basis for the intrinsic value of persons, prior to their membership of a community or their economic role. It is the reason why people are ends and not means.

The Fall impacted both God's provision and humanity's stewardship. The task of securing food now from God's provision required real effort (Gen. 3:17–19). God's provision is no less. The failure is in the capacity of humans to steward God's resources so that they are able to feed themselves with abundance. The forces of unjust power, lust and greed frustrate relationships between men and women resulting in much of the suffering women experience. They also spoil the proper use and sharing of resources and create the poverty which puts pressure on human ability to support a rising population. In such situations stewardship has not been exercised responsibly or shaped by justice, and so some have consumed more at the expense of others.

The Fall has also affected women's role in being fruitful. The fruitfulness which characterizes women now has an extra cost in increased pain while bearing children. Men have the extra burden of providing for their families through harder toil, women experience extra pain in the bearing of children. 'To the woman God said: "I will greatly increase your pangs in childbearing; in pain you shall bring forth children, yet your desire shall be for your husband, and he shall rule over you.' And to the man he said: 'Because you have listened to the voice of your wife . . . cursed is the ground because of you; in toil you shall eat of it . . . by the sweat of your face you shall eat bread" ' (Gen. 3:16–18).

For men and women, excessive pain in work or lack of work both express the pain of the Fall and threaten their identity and self-esteem. The economic and emotional support of the family is to be shared by a male and female. In situations of unemployment, when men have no paid work, women can still bear children but men are further oppressed if they are denied a role in the support of the woman and her child.

In a Christian relationship, men and women are to support each other in bearing one another's pain whether that be the pain associated with childbearing, the pain of infertility, painful work or lack of work.

Shalom and Responsible Relationships

Humanity is still accountable to God after the Fall, and if we live responsibly in the light of that accountability we can still build shalom; just relationships in human communities. Shalom is experienced in justice, compassion and mercy, and needs to be expressed in law, covenant and regulated commitments (Jer. 32:38–41).

Children are not the product of the curse of the Fall, they are a blessing from the Lord. God's blessing to Abraham was the promise of many descendants, in particular through a barren wife, even when there was no human capacity to fulfil his promise. God also blessed Abraham's first son Ishmael and his mother, Hagar. She was a single mother by the decision of others. While Hagar and Ishmael were a reminder to Abraham and his descendants of Abraham and Sarah's failure and unfaithfulness, God did not reject her but blessed her, promised her many descendants, and provided for her (Gen. 16).

The Hebrew slaves who had become numerous and were subjected to an enforced programme of population limitation (Exodus 1:8–22) became more populous. The Hebrew midwives who feared God and protected the babies were given families, and the Hebrews were promised a land flowing with milk and honey (Exodus 13:5). God's promise to Abraham was fulfilled even through conditions of slavery and oppression.

The Future, Freedom and Choice

In the population debate projections about the future are important tools in understanding possible scenarios in our global future. They are often used to make decisions about the present. When they are used to portray an apocalyptic scenario, they create confusion and alarm. This is meant to motivate us into taking unprecedented action. More often people feel a sense of powerlessness and anxiety which can in turn produce the inertia which works against positive action.

While we listen as carefully as possible to the advocacy of demographers and historians, we ought to recognize that the final vision of the future that shapes our contemporary decision making is the vision of Kingdom of God in Christ and the right relationships, the shalom, it demands. Jesus was the one who brought the Kingdom of God, which is new relationships between people and God, between people, and between people and the whole of creation (Luke 11:2–4:20). His resurrection is the affirmation that the Kingdom of God has entered world history (Rev. 11:15; 21:1–4), and that Christ's return to consummate the Kingdom will bring a new heaven and a new earth as the climax and fulfilment of world history (Rom. 8:23). As we await his return, we live in the Kingdom in the power of God's Holy Spirit, which is the first fruits of the Kingdom.

The argument about accountability to future generations has in many debates tended to replace the transcendent accountability to God. The Kingdom of God is the only future reality to which we are finally accountable. Human projections must be related to God's revealed purposes of the consummation of the Kingdom and not force us into ethical pragmatism or ambiguity. We should therefore avoid panic, and making pragmatic and immoral decisions which do not respect human life and choice. The price we pay for God's moral choices will never undermine the future God has planned. Our goal is to build a community which practices and promotes Christian virtues of virginity and faithfulness (1 Cor. 6:16–20; Col. 3:12–17).

The Kingdom of God sets the context for our moral action and choices which express Christian virtues. The Kingdom of God is righteousness, peace and joy in the Holy Spirit (Rom. 14:17). In this Kingdom, the Son of God makes us truly free (John 8:36). The freedom which is presupposed by the exercise of choice is not an anarchic freedom to choose any action we may please. Freedom means we are not hindered from fulfilling our calling to be the human beings God wills us to be, whatever the constraint. There are many obstacles to fulfilling this calling, many of which are expressions of human sin and selfishness. The activity of the Kingdom in the world empowers society. Christians and others who accept this activity of Kingdom move society in the direction of the life of the final Kingdom of God, countering the moral disablement that evil brings in society, strengthening the good and restraining evil. The Holy Spirit, the gift of the Kingdom, works in society strengthening the wills of people who may not be Christians to turn God's way. Such empowerment does not guarantee that all will be able to live out the Christian ethic, but it enables them to see the possibilities and make their choices. Kingdom activity unmasks the activity of the evil one, convicts people and strengthens their wills to act (John 18:8–11). It conserves society and clarifies people's choice. This makes the invitation of the gospel of the Kingdom relevant in every situation.

We act therefore, not out of panic or pragmatism, but because we are convinced that God's future for the world will vindicate biblical obedience. New Testament Christians lived in the conviction that not history but Jesus would vindicate them when he came. We live in the same hope. In Colossians 3:1–4 and 12:15 Paul argues that the values and virtues that Jesus demonstrated are eternal. The resurrection vindicated these values and virtues which express the risen life hidden in Jesus until he comes: compassion, kindness, humility, gentleness, patience, tolerance and forgiveness. These virtues must direct our action, inform our choices, and support the choices that people make in the light of the life of the Kingdom.

In our commitment to enable people to exercise the choice which is fundamental to being human, we both recognize the 'right to be wrong' and also the need to provide the context of the Kingdom which is necessary to enable people to make the choices which are 'in the way' of the Kingdom and which express the life of virtue. This will require both information and support for individuals, and in the wider context of society, processes and structures which support and enable those choices to be sustained. It will also require teaching and sharing of the life of the Kingdom and the lifestyle that represents it. People do not make choices as isolated, independent, rational decisions, but in relation to a whole series of cultural, religious, traditional, and relational factors. In order to enable people to make informed and Christian choices in reproduction, we need Christian input to address all these areas.

The Family

God is revealed in the New Testament as the Father. Parents not only receive children as a gift from God but see their parenting as being representative of God's care for his children. Marriage is at the heart of family life in that men and women together represent the image of God and in their permanent, faithful and public commitment to one another provide a stable and loving context in which children can flourish. Families provide a context in which mutual support, respect and love combine, and this can be the basis for including others who through bereavement, divorce, or exclusion of other kinds have become separated from the loving support of their original families. This inclusiveness means that families may have many members who may or may not be blood-related but who see themselves as belonging to a family group with whom they have made their home. Such inclusiveness provides the basis for a critique of the view of the nuclear family which is seen as complete when only parents and children are included. It also means that although marriage is at the heart of the family it is possible for people to become family together who share that mutual support, love and respect. The church is called the family of God and Christians see each other as brothers and sisters in Christ.

Christians are called to reflect biblical realism about the family. In a fallen world the family is threatened and becomes a place where there is pain. The work and employment which provide for the family's needs may be scarce or if available may be arduous toil. Unemployment becomes not only associated with low personal self-worth but also becomes a threat to the sustainability of the family. Reproduction and child-rearing, which should reflect fruitfulness and blessing become intermingled with pain and frustration. Maternal morbidity, infant mortality, adolescent waywardness or other tragedy provide a context in which men and women are to share in each other's pain.

Sadly many families' relationships are not loving and respectful. Life becomes a tragedy for people when the life of the family becomes the very place where they are most abused. Children are particularly vulnerable to abuse not only through physical and sexual violence and emotional abuse, but also through underage employment and in war. The church as the people of God the Father is the primary definition of the family (Mark 3:35 and par..) and thus the Christian community is called to be the larger family in which people suffering the pains and hurts of human families can be supported and in which their healing can begin.

Christians must not idolize the family. Families are to be in the service of the Kingdom, not in the service of nurturing individual consciences. On the one hand, the Kingdom paradigm provides a warning to families where family life has become an idol. Families live for their security, welfare and fulfilment. Family life becomes an end. Jesus' teaching on the conflict of interest between family obligation and Kingdom service is clear. 'No one,' said Jesus, 'who puts his hand to the plough and looks back is fit for service in the Kingdom of God' (Luke 10:62). The service of the Kingdom is to be the goal of family life. Self-fulfilment and family wholeness and happiness are to be fruits of such service. On the other hand, in the Protestant west, the responsibility of nurturing and teaching individual consciences was assigned primarily to the family with support from the local church. This model of family places the emphasis on individual responsibility which a family must nurture and support. The individual needs take priority over family needs. The social vitality of the family is neglected in the commitment to promote individual fulfilment and responsibility.

Marriage and Singleness

While marriage is the norm for most people, the church in many places is too directed to those who are married and neglects the single. In some cultures, there is a tendency (even amongst Christians) to disparage those (especially women) who have never married or who have been widowed or divorced. Paul sees singleness as a desirable state for Christians (1 Cor. 7:8). There is a widespread need for the church and individual Christians to give full acceptance to those who are single for whatever reason. The church must not be allowed to marginalize or exclude the single (for example by activities directed solely to the married and their families), and positively must ensure that singles have an equal place in the church, that their gifts are identified and fully used in the church.

Sex and Sexuality

Sex and sexuality is God's good gift to us, but can be misused. God's will is that the exercise of our sexuality should be restricted to the marriage relationship. Scripture says little about the procreational purpose for sex. Sex in scripture is primarily relational. In Matthew 19:4–5 Jesus quotes from Genesis 1:27 and 2:24 that God made humanity as male and female, and that therefore a man leaves his father and mother to be joined to his wife and become one flesh with her. Here, sexuality has its role within the one-flesh relationship of marriage. In 1 Cor. 7:1–5, Paul responds to those Corinthians who proposed that it is better for a man not to 'touch,' i.e. have sexual intercourse with, his wife: 'Because of temptations to immoralities, each man should have his own wife, and each wife her own husband.' He shows that each partner has a responsibility towards the sexual needs of the spouse, and that the body of the husband belongs to the wife and that of the wife to the husband. They may not deprive each other of a sexual relationship except by agreement for a short time for prayer. In Paul's discussion, there is evenhandedness between the sexual needs and responsibilities of both husbands and wives, and there is no reference to procreation. For Paul, sex has an important role in marriage apart from procreation.

We note with great concern the growing incidence of sexual activity and childbearing outside a marriage against biblical norms. The church should teach biblical chastity and responsible parenthood and affirm that it is wrong to engage in sexual relations and childbearing outside a marriage. The story of Hagar and Ishmael indicates that single parents should not be stigmatized. God entered into a covenantal relationship with them (Gen. 16 and 21). Such people must also be welcomed into and experience God's blessings in the covenant as families.

Marriage and in vitro Fertilization

We recognize the strength of the desire of couples to have a child and to use IVF if pregnancy is not possible by other means. There is no inherent Christian objection to IVF for married couples, but it is open to grave abuse, particularly where fertilized ova are frozen and later used for experimentation. But we also hold two views about the use of IVF. One view, based on the belief that life begins at fertilization, is that a fertilized ovum is a human being. This view objects to freezing ova, keeping them alive as ova, implanting them, and throwing them away if not needed. It would be preferable to take ova for their immediate fertilization and implantation without freezing them. The other view is that there is no Christian basis for rejecting the freezing of ova, or their implantation in the mother at a suitable later time, or to the destruction of fertilized ova that are not needed for implantation, so long as abuses are avoided. There is room for Christian discussion of what is and is not acceptable.

Marriage and Polygamy

The Bible neither condemns nor prohibits polygamy, and sets forth monogamy as God's perfect will. The Old Testament has numerous instances of polygamous marriages, and though accompanied by problems of suffering, they are recognized as valid marriages. The scripture provides for the protection of second and other wives from exploitation. When missionaries brought the gospels to polygamous cultures, they usually made no attempt to explore the reasons for polygamy in that culture. Missionaries usually required converted husbands to have only one wife. In some areas the husband was required to put away all except his first wife; in other areas the husband was permitted to choose which wife to keep. Both policies were contrary to the Bible's teaching against separation and divorce and assumed, contrary to scripture, that polygamous marriages were invalid marriages. These policies caused great anguish through the break up of loving, caring polygamous families, and brought great deprivation to polygamous wives and their children through forcing them out of their marital homes.

Some churches accept polygamous families in their midst, but do not allow the husband or his wives to be the communicants or be baptized. Christians are to adhere to the biblical ideal of marriage as a union of one man and one woman, but equally

a) the church must recognize polygamous marriages entered into prior to conversion as valid marriages, even if less than the Christian ideal.
b) policies adopted by the church in relation to the parties of polygamous marriages must take account of the biblical teaching noted above
c) the church must seek to change or remove the cultural, economic and other factors that have led to the practice of polygamy in a society.

Mother and Child Health

Mother and child health is an important part of shalom. Maternal mortality is the leading cause of death among women of reproductive age (15–44 years). Half a million women die every year as a result of pregnancy complications. 99 percent of those deaths are in the two-thirds world. The risk of a woman dying as a result of pregnancy is 200 times higher in the developing world than in the west. The vast majority of these deaths are entirely preventable through improved access to maternal and child health resources. Spacing children has dramatic impact on the health of mother and child. A child born within two years of a previous birth has twice the risk of dying than one born over two years later. Providing maternal healthcare means healthy mothers and healthy babies and also affirms the dignity and value of women. The emphasis on women's childbearing role has led to a concomitant emphasis on reproductive health. But other areas of their health have been neglected.

Women in Society

The education of women is a task which is inherently significant and important. This is not because of its consequences but because women are equal with men before God and should have access to wisdom and knowledge about the world they live in and which God has placed them in. This educational provision does not refer to health education alone but to all sectors of general education including primary education for girl children. In terms of fertility it has been repeatedly shown that every year of female education has the impact of lowering fertility. When women are educated they start having children later, space them further apart and finish having them sooner which is good for both mother and child health.

Women may suffer domestic violence, have the decision to have children imposed on them, be regarded as sexual objects or only valued for procreation. Infertility may bring disgrace and rejection, and widowhood may bring loss of status and even home. In such a society the woman become powerful as the mother of a son through whom she can exert power. A woman's identity can be tied up with the number of sons she produces and in society where women are not part of the labour market can only add to the income of the family through producing sons. Daughters have to be paid for and are not themselves part of the income of the family but are seen as a drain on its resources. This has implications for the need to change inheritance laws and to promote access to education and employment for women so that they may provide for their families. Women need access to the opportunities which men enjoy not because the education and employment of women lowers fertility, but because they are human and intrinsically have equal worth in God's eyes. Children may be forced to work as child labour or thrown out of home and having to eke out an existence as a 'street kid'. In countries where there is a boy preference, girl children may be aborted, given names which express dismay, lack adequate nutrition, or have their humanity disregarded in other ways.

Family Planning

Is it ethically desirable to limit the potential size of our families? There seems to be widespread agreement that where couples desire to limit the size of their families this is an appropriate stewardship of resources and callings. However Christians also often celebrate larger families and some feel that family size should be left to the providence of God. We recognize that Catholics reject modern contraceptive methods in favour of natural methods of fertility postponement; but we affirm that people should have the opportunity of access to and informed choice from the full range of available methods of contraception. A person's view as to whether human life begins at fertilization or at implantation is likely to affect their decision concerning which methods of contraception are ethically acceptable. We endorse the statement of the Cairo conference that abortion is not acceptable as a means of family planning.

Across the world family planning is overwhelmingly the responsibility of women. The proportion of couples who rely on male methods – the condom, withdrawal and vasectomy is 1–12% in most countries. The debate on family planning therefore usually focuses on the needs and preferences of women. Family planning is important where couples want to have smaller families, or where they wish to space their children. Where they do not family planning will not be effective. We see a difference between family planning and the use of contraception in population control. All too often state programmes or those of international agencies have had as their objective the lowering of fertility levels rather than enabling couples to plan their own families. Such programmes have been accompanied by population targets through which the success of the programme can be monitored. From the standpoint of the needs of women all too often the quality of these programmes has been low. There has been inadequate information, counselling and follow-up associated with them.

AIDS Care and Prevention

HIV/AIDS is a pandemic problem which has serious consequences for people, their families and communities, the church and the nations. It causes intense suffering to those who contract it and always results in death. Christians as a healing community are called to respond to the HIV/AIDS tragedy with acts of compassion. However the church community is also a source of values which result in permanent personal and social transformation. Churches can help to prevent the further spread of HIV infection . . .

* through effective and appropriate HIV/AIDS awareness campaigns.
* by addressing the socio-economic, cultural and other behavioural factors that put people at the risk of infection. For example, the culture of premarital and extramarital sex, widow inheritance, unfair economic systems, HIV/AIDS orphans, inappropriate sex education proposals and gender disparities.
* by being involved in practical medical help, homecare and counselling.
* by building appropriate coping mechanisms in their communities to support the affected families.

In our world we have to live with the consequences of our behaviour and take responsibility for behaviour which may be intrinsically wrong whether it has negative consequences or not. The link between HIV/AIDS and sexual behaviour has led some to see HIV/AIDS as a personal curse of God on someone who is sexually immoral. We do not accept this. If this were so it would be easy to continue the behaviour but avoid the curse by using 'safer sex' methods which are still sinful if outside the marriage context. Also many people contract HIV/AIDS who have not been involved in immoral sexual behaviour. Spouses may contract it through unprotected sexual contact with their partners, infants through breast milk and haemophiliacs through infected blood transfusions. However, when societies depart from God's norms for communities in socio-economic, political and spiritual relationships, then they have to take the consequences. This is not only true of immoral sexual behaviour but also of the poverty which drives so many women into prostitution as the only means of providing for themselves and their children. God suffers with people in their distress, so Christians should be compassionate and sensitive to the needs of people living with HIV/AIDS and aim to be a source of healing love to them.

Human Rights

Rapid population growth is either left for future generations to address or tackled with the blunt instrument of economic and social policies which ignore the humanitarian aspects of the problem. Public policies designed to reduce poverty, urban growth or unemployment may violate the basic right to life and liberty and so aggravate rather than alleviate the problem.

'Human Rights' – the idea that individuals possess certain fundamental rights – have been enshrined in national law and international treaty. The legal instruments attempt to define human rights and to argue for their universality. This framework is used as a starting point for the development of public policy.

But there is a tension between the legal provisions and practical experience. Policy makers are sometimes unaware of the humanitarian implications of their actions. Rampant individualism (the western pre-occupation with 'self-determination' and 'self-fulfilment') can ignore responsibility for the neighbour and respect for the world. Human beings must always be the subject and never the object. From this perspective we need to go behind the legal instruments to recognize that human rights derive from the essential nature of the human being. They reside in the answer to the question 'What is the right for human?'

It is therefore difficult to separate the question of rights from a discussion of the origin and destiny of humankind. Made in God's image, spoiled by sin and yet reconciled and set free by Christ, the human being is destined to conform to the image of God's Son (Rom. 8:29). Whatever else may be intended by this idea, the image of God (sometimes understood statically as the possession of some inherent characteristic) is changed into a dynamic concept (being transformed into the image of Christ). To be human is to be 'on the way' to this identity. Human experience (including suffering and death) is a means to this end.

This suggests a positive, transforming Christian view of human rights. The present legal instruments are often inadequate in the numerous particularities of human life. Action is needed inside the claims of those who life in pain and desperation. The reality of human life must be grasped as concretely as possible. Only then can despair be transformed into hope.

Life is a gift: ('I have come to bring life in all its abundance:' Jesus said) and is protected by God. Not even a sparrow falls to the ground without the Father's knowledge. (Matt. 10:29). The right to life is in his hands. (Gen. 9:5–6).

The most basic human right, after the right to life itself, is to speech: the freedom to process pain in words. Suffering people will not receive help if they remain silent. The Biblical records shows how human suffering, when articulated, calls upon God to act, and releases his power into the human situation. Barthimaeus was insistent in his cry for help (Mk. 10:47). Moses knew that silence leads to brick quotas. Words of pain or protest begin the transformation.

So, too, do honest words of confession. 'I am a man of unclean lips', set Isaiah on his path to fulfilment. Until pain or sin is articulated, the human lot is not a happy one. When it is, human life is transformed in accordance with its purpose and people begin to discover 'what is right for humans'.

Thus we affirm that

• Human beings, both male and female, are created in the image of God and are loved unconditionally by him. From this they derive rights and responsibilities.
• God has granted freedom of choice, which does not mean unlimited freedom to encroach on the rights and freedoms of others.
• Life is a gift from God, and all couples have the right responsibly to choose the number, spacing and timing of their children.
• God-given life is sacred and no one has the right to terminate life from conception on until God decides to recall that life.
• God intended that every human being has a right to life in all its fulness (Jn. 10:10).

The implications of this for population issues are for us as follows:

• The compulsory use of sterilization and abortion (also a means of contraception) should be condemned, and its unqualified prohibition, as a serious violation of human rights.
• We disapprove of all forms of incentives and disincentives for pro-choice behaviours as these could be of disproportionate value to the poor; this is an infringement of their freedom of rights.

- We believe that institutions, be it the state, church or NGOs should not formulate and implement policies that interfere with and impinge on the conjugal life and rights of couples.
- We affirm the right of the people and the church to participate in the formulation and implementation of state policies and programmes in relation to population and reproductive health.
- We affirm that people have a right of access to full information and also the means of planning the welfare of their families. We should strive to spread awareness of an increase access to such information.
- We caution that experiments both in positive and negative eugenics should be monitored for human rights violation.
- We categorically condemn infanticide and use of medical technology for sex determination leading to foeticide, and see this as an infringement on the rights of unborn children.

Rights should go hand in hand with responsibility and should be discussed in the contexts of God's purposes for creation. Programmes on human rights should go hand in hand with empowerment.

Economic Development, Urbanization and Employment

Economic Development

There is no simple relationship between growth and economic development. Economic development is essential when one is focusing on the wider issues associated with population needs. Healthcare, housing, education and employment are all components of economic development. Countries such as Sri Lanka and Taiwan have succeeded in lowering fertility without being seen as economically 'developed' nations. Despite this, the world's majority especially in the Two-Thirds World are increasingly being trapped on the grim realities of poverty.

Out of the biblical mandate to pursue and promote justice in society, the church is called to take her prophetic role and critically analyze and challenge inappropriate and insensitive population and economic policies. World peace and development will depend more on individual and corporate repentance at all levels and on the willingness to act justly. Unconditional love for neighbour should permeate all levels of policy formulation and implementation.

Urbanization

When urbanization is handled appropriately, it is possible for it to be managed in such a way that it can result in the celebration of family life. But the way urbanization is taking place in the Two-Thirds World and produces increasing pollution, displacement of people, the phenomenon of street children, prostitution, unemployment and the disintegration of families are aspects which we Christians cannot ignore.

Rural-urban migration often threatens the integrity of the family. Poverty in the rural areas forces people to leave their homes to seek employment in the city. Such poverty can be the result of government funding being focused on urban areas to the detriment of rural areas. The lack of employment can bring about a sense of desperation and insecurity. Removed from their traditional values people can succumb to alcohol and drug addictions, prostitution and theft. Those who remain at home bear the burden of providing food and other resources for their children and extended family. This migration also places kinship structures, local management systems, extended families and traditional support structures under great strain. Furthermore it reinforces an individualistic approach to life, found in the city, which rests uneasily with indigenous and traditional values. Despite these problems the migration to the cities in search of a better life, continues. Cities are expanding at an enormous rate. Lack of proper housing, sanitation and the basic amenities of life leads to the growth of slum dwellings which are often illegal and constantly threatened with removal. The conditions in the slums are so poor that children frequently die from diarrhoeal and respiratory infections.

This is not a dilemma of the 21st century. This is a harsh reality of the 20th century to which we are called urgently to respond in a ministry of bringing wholeness of life.

Secularization

Where population programmes idolize low fertility, secularization and modernization can be seen as essential tools to make this possible. Though modernization brings some comforts of life, in many instances it has not enriched the spiritual life of many urban dwellers.

Where low fertility is made the highest virtue, religious belief and custom, moral codes, and traditional family values are frequently disregarded. Definitions of freedom of choice derived from market economics are imported into cultures which see voluntary moral restraint and the promotion of virtue as an essential component of freedom. Secularization has not served the industrialized societies well and the individualistic and hedonistic definitions of freedom combined with consumerism have led to the breakdown of public and private morality.

Therefore as we participate in improving people's welfare, we should constantly remind ourselves about the duty we have of bringing people to Christ. We also recommend that the church sets the example of tackling urbanization by decentralizing more her services by taking more part in developing the rural areas of the south.

Employment

Between 1995 and 2000 AD the UN estimates that 100 million additional people will be added to the global population. This presents a challenge to policy makers and planners to create opportunities for employment for 40% of them that will make up the labour force. Structural adjustment policies in the third world have resulted in a reduction in employment. The impact of these policies have been felt most by lower skilled men and women who are the easiest to remove from the labour force in times of resource constraint. International debt repayments also hamper the ability of governments to use resources for internal development.

As we proclaim 'shalom' and wholeness of life to the world, we should remember that work is central to self-actualization and fulfilment. The lives of many people today are miserable because they cannot access meaningful and fulfilling work. We are particularly concerned that if the gospel is to be a fulfilling gospel, the churches should:

i) examine the level and nature of unemployment in their particular communities;
ii) identify the factors responsible for this problem, and
iii) design and implement appropriate measures for dealing with this problem as part of the gospel.

Also work has been taken by many people as a curse contrary to the original biblical value of stewardship. The church should reconstruct an appropriate theology of work and encourage people to value and appreciate every type of work available to them, mindful of the fact that there is a divine duty of maximizing the productivity of whatever resources that have been available to each of us as the parable of the talents teach us.

Environmental Issues

Though some environmentalists worship the creation in place of the creator, we are concerned that creation is being plundered and polluted at a rate that will make human life impossible in the near future. God called us to be stewards of earth, to develop, use and protect it.

We therefore call upon governments, the churches and all people to:

i) review the present environmental situation in their country or communities;
ii) identify the factors that are causing degradation of the environment and the extinction of species;
iii) review the existing policies that protect the environment, and
iv) develop appropriate measures for addressing the problem of environmental destruction and degradation.

These measures should stand against irreversible choices and harm; favour sustainable rather than one-off benefits and pay special attention to those groups of people, plants and animal species that will be especially vulnerable to policy choices and decisions.

Interfaith Co-operation

We approve and support the move to understanding other faiths in order to find a base for dialogue and for positive action on global issues that affect our practice of the religion we follow. We are conscious however that witnessing to our faith should not be lost on account of dialogue and tolerance and that witness should not only be in word but also in action.

Appendix

Further Resources

On issues of development, see *Transformation – The Church in Response to Human Need* (EFICOR Training Unit, India, Grove Booklets on Ethics) 1986 (available from Ridley Hall, Cambridge)

On wider aspects of Economic Policies see 'The Oxford Declaration on Christian Faith and Economics' *Transformation Journal*, (April 1990), pp. 325–344 in this volume and 'The Market Economy and the Poor,' *Transformation Journal* (July 1995). (Available from OCMS, P.O. Box 70, Oxford OX2 6HB.)

On issues of Church and State see 'Osijek Statement on Church and State,' *Transformation Journal* (July 1991).

On wider aspects of environment, see 'International Evangelical Statement on Environment,' *Transformation Journal* (October 1993 and January 1994).

On issues of migrant populations see 'Refugees and Ethnic Identity,' *Transformation Journal* (April 1995).

On the Kingdom of God, see 'Word, Kingdom and Spirit' (available from OCMS, P O Box 70, Oxford OX2 6HB), and 'Kingdom Affirmations' in *Transformation Journal* (July 1994), pp. 11–25 in this volume.

Nineteen

Christian Relief and Development Agencies in the Twenty First Century: Consultation Report June 1996

We met in Oxford from June 20–23, 1996 – thirty-five chief executives of Christian Relief and Development Agencies from sixteen nations. We were invited by the Evangelical Fellowship of India Commission on Relief (EFICOR), Fieldstead and Company, California, Tear Fund Holland and Tear Fund UK, the International Fellowship of Evangelical Mission Theologians (INFEMIT), Opportunity Foundation, Australia and Opportunity International, the Stewardship Foundation, Tacoma, USA, The Association of Evangelicals in Africa, Latin American Child Care, World Vision International and the Oxford Centre for Mission Studies. Our purpose was to consider Christian Relief and Development Organizations in the twenty-first century. In our discussions, the terms relief and development agency (RDA) and non-governmental organization (NGO) were used

'Christian Relief and Development Agencies in the 21st Century' in *Transformation*, Vol. 13, No. 4, October 1996.

interchangeably. We would like to address our findings to the leaders of Christian relief and development agencies and through them to the leaders of churches.

A. Trends and the Future

Any Christian vision of the future must trace trends of the future, new areas of concern and a positive Christian response. But, in addition, in viewing the future itself as Christians we must see the way in which God acts in the present leading to the future. We must not only discern trends in the world but far more importantly the acts of God in the world in contemporary and future history. This is the role played by the prophets of the Old Testament and gifted to the church in the New Testament. The prophetic concern is also with how we should deal with the present so that certain things that are likely to happen do not happen. To do this with authenticity we need to be rooted in the word of God and to think as Christians biblically and theologically in understanding God's action in the world.

Contemporary views of the future with different orientations, such as the Marxist view, no longer have the dominance they once had. The increasingly dominant view of the future is shaped by the market economy and culture. The Bible contains apocalyptic and prophetic views of the future, and also the view of the future from the tradition of wisdom. Some dispensational apocalyptic views of the future have been shaped by the apocalyptic literature which sees the future more in terms of crisis and restoration. The prophetic view of the future sees the rule of God in terms of the process and fulfilment of history. A wisdom approach to the future stresses the practicality of God's plans both for the present and for the future. We can view wisdom as stressing an approach of managing the future; the prophetic can be viewed as facilitating a confident march to shape the future; the apocalyptic prayerfully waits for the future to happen.

The three views come together in the kingdom of God. The kingdom is the presence in history of the fulfilment of God's purposes which will bring an apocalyptic climax to human history. In the present world it belongs to the poor and the meek who will inherit the earth. It is in our meekness and humility, as we see God at work, and can partner with him and his people in sharing whatever gifts we have, that we see the best Christian way of shaping the future.

Global Trends

We will look first at global trends over which few people have any
control, and then we will examine in later sections the expression and
impact of those trends.

We identify the following global trends:

- Global integration of economy.
- Breakdown of political machinery.
- Emergence of global communication and information network.
- Growth in modern technological innovations and related knowledge.
- Increase in cases of AIDS, development of new clones of viruses,
  drug-resistant bacteria and parasites.
- Environmental degradation.

The consequences of the above are:

- A widening gap between the rich and the poor.
- Movements of people for security and economic reasons.
- Diminishing sovereignty of the nation state.
- Marginalization of peoples and nations.
- Raised expectations which have no real hope of fulfilment.
- Major economic decisions which affect a majority of people are
  made by the emerging global economic community which is not
  accountable to governments or the people.
- Increase in internal conflict and disintegration of communities and
  nations.
- The high cost and unavailability of health care.

In many of the marginalised countries, Christianity is also growing
apace. However, such growth has not always been accompanied by
the expression of integral kingdom values.

Arising out of these trends and consequences are the following
questions which require our attention.

- Have we accepted a model of poverty that is exclusively material
  and economic rather than a model that includes social, intellectual
  and spiritual dimensions as well?
- What are the roles of Christian RDAs in relation to the contemporary trends?

- How can churches and Christians become truly salt and light?
- How can churches in the West become better educated in the issues that have contributed to the marginalization of communities?
- How can believers exercise advocacy on behalf of the marginalised?

B. Issues for Christian Relief and Development Agencies

2. Spirituality, Religion, Culture and Development

Most of world's poor are in the Two-Thirds World's unreached communities. They are people of other faiths. These poor live in nations where there is growing religious fundamentalism and resurgence of traditional religions. Today the important place of spirituality in human development is being acknowledged. Secular groups involved in development are beginning to take seriously the religions of the communities with whom they work. People are seeking for ethics and morality in development strategies. Therefore true development, be it Christian or non-Christian, requires addressing the spiritual, because it is not possible to get to the ethical without the spiritual.

Current trends very clearly show that development is incomplete without the spiritual component. This, though it seems to be a healthy move, is also causing problems for Christian RDAs. After the Second World War the focus was on government and government agencies working to reconstruct Germany and Japan. This led to a major focus on secular development and modernity as the driving force in the sixties. The combination of the right people and the right resources were thought to produce an accelerated process of change. For a long time Christian development agencies were the sole representatives of religion in the field. The focus has changed. Christianity is now only one religion among many involved in development. Government aid, in a desire to be tolerant and even-handed, often requires participation of those of all religions together. The world trend, therefore, is toward pluralism. Any spirituality is acceptable from whatever religion. The world sees nothing special about Christianity.

Christian RDAs begin from a different starting point from that of secular agencies. Development is not an accelerated process of change but obedience to the Lord in stewardship of creation and love for neighbour empowered by the Holy Spirit. In Christian R and D programmes the centrality of Jesus' experience is the key to human development. Since the world does not accept exclusivity, we will be encouraged to downplay our faith or else be excluded from funding or involvement in various projects. Tolerance will be a requirement for resource mobilization. Christian R and D agencies should, therefore, develop clear policies for cooperation with other religions and even for use of other religions and even for use of other religious experience to bring in value changes necessary for development. Often we will need to cooperate with other religious groups in advocacy actions.

In some situations, however, compassionate concern for the poor by certain religious groups is primary and an effective tool to protect their people from being attracted away to other religions – especially Christianity which is sometimes accused of proselytism. In such situations it may not be possible to work in cooperation. We distinguish a legitimate desire to share and witness to Christ from proselytism which is not confined to religious organizations but is practised by movements which actively work to impose their secular, materialistic and modern value systems on people with whom they work.

The advent of post-modernity has led to an emphasis on the uniqueness of cultures and a recovery of ethnicity. Relief and development organizations are having to focus on cultural issues which include religious values. Strongly related to religion is the culture of the people in many parts of Two-Thirds World. Many of the keys for the communication of the gospel are found in a culture. Development agencies need to see that many of the solutions to problems may be

---

Strategies: issues and questions for Christian involvement

Christian RDAs cannot carry out the whole ministry of God without partnership with local churches.

How should we respond and educate our donors to respond to requirements of government funding support that involve participation with those of non-Christian religions?

Can we use such support without losing our Christian integrity? How does a definition of Christian integrity involving belief and lifestyle relate to this?

Can Christian witness with integrity be sustained apart from the involvement and participation of the local church?

Should we actively promote the resurgence of culture? In some cases traditional values run against other religions and are complementary to Christianity. In other cases the situation is reversed.

found in the indigenous culture. The problem is that culture is usually tied to religion and it is difficult to separate the two. In working with culture we must always ensure that cultural traits and practices should be judged on the grounds of biblical truth and values. Christian RDAs are generally seen as representing a western culture both in their style and programme. In the future NGOs will have to consider seriously culturally appropriate process of change. Ethnicity too will demand special attention in development programmes.

3. Church and Development

The gospel is the most significant force for social transformation and the Church is one of the most effective grassroots organizations in the world. This cannot be explained without the spirit of God. The growth of the church in Africa, Asia and Latin America has important implications for the development of these continents.

The Church, which includes Christian RDAs, is called to be a visible expression of the holistic mission of Christ to a broken world, displaying his love, compassion and justice among the poor and socially deprived. Christian RDAs often have a language of holism, but a practice of dualism. In many places, they work in good and fruitful relationship with the churches: denominations, local congregations. Elsewhere, they ignore or underestimate the importance of the churches for sustainable relief and development. In other cases RDAs have unintentionally marginalised the churches and even gone so far in their involvement in society that the churches cannot follow. At the same time the churches lack a knowledge, understanding and commitment to relief and development. The only way they can be united is through fully developed biblical teaching to show that relief and development is an essential part of the Christian message.

The critical issue is how RDAs and the church can develop stronger and more fruitful partnerships, especially when we note that the Gospel is the most significant force for social transformation in the world.

A future exploration of the following will enhance the role of church in development:

Global and Local

Because western cultures, agencies and churches have networks that span the world, they often present their concerns as spanning the

---

Strategies: issues to enhance the role of the Church in development

Christian RDAs recognize the fact that churches, evangelical alliances and councils of churches are involved in relief and development. They should strive to support and cooperate with one another.

National churches and evangelical alliances should ensure that relief and development departments should operate with the involvement of the local churches.

Appropriate concepts of relief and development among churches needs to be developed. Like the local churches, relief and development is involved in the biblical change of lives and cultures. We must work together in holistic change.

Christian RDAs must set up appropriate forms of accountability to the churches in the context in which they operate, which involves communication, consultation and transparency.

Christian RDAs should make clear to local churches the nature of the expertise they have and can offer. Christian RDAs should also make time and people available, where possible, to address the local churches in order to make their work known through visits, printed and audio-visual material and networking etc. They should also make clear where they lack input and support from the Church.

The Church should seek to learn how it can carry out its pastoral and supportive role in teaching and counselling those under stress in society and people working in RDAs.

Relief to people in distress is an area of special concern for RDAs and churches.

---

globe, and are perceived by others to be globe, and are perceived by others to be global agencies. This can produce a defensive reaction in Two-Thirds World people or minority groups in the North. They protect their own identity and contribution from being subsumed under other powerful agendas and co-opted into a global operation over which they have no control by stressing the integrity of their own national identity. This can become a token nationalism in the face of a dominant supposed internationalism. It can misinterpret the present and misprescribe for the future on the basis of an idealized picture of a past that never was; it can pit the traditional against the modern.

Thus, for example, local theologies are emphasized over allegedly global theologies. The contextual is seen as local and anti-global. However, western agencies and churches are just as local and contextual as Two-Thirds World agencies and are just as shaped by their own social cultures. The global is not the preserve of one culture or agency. In the Christian sense the global is all kinds of local comprising a family together. The global takes place at the intersection of two or more equally local cultures.

While a vision may be global, its application is always local. If any one local context sets itself up as global and claims to present a global content, then the local contexts are weakened, and the content itself lacks substance. The colonial process continues when the forces of modernity globalise all problems. This undermines the contextual shape of problems in each situation.

In every context the global and the local intersect. We need to look at the intersection of the global and the local rather than see them always as opposites. We need to see how the intersection of the global and local is also at the heart of a Christian understanding of the world where the gospel is universally valid and at the same time does not homogenize local cultures but rather transforms them and where necessary recovers them. We need to question whether the global is only owned by those who have economic power or whether a Christian understanding reinterprets the global in the light of spiritual realities of the existence and growth of the church globally, where God's work in power is discernible. Otherwise the definition of the global and the local will be shaped only by socio-political and economic understandings. There is an urgent need to reinterpret these terms from biblical and theological viewpoints.

In these changing circumstances and especially in the face of the tendency of modernity to globalise, the role and level of partnership will need to be redefined:

Partnerships can exist in a number of ways:

1. Between northern and southern NGOs in the context of resourcing.
2. Between donors and implementing NGOs.
3. Between NGOs and beneficiaries.
4. Between implementing the NGOs in the context of cooperative ventures.

The nature of our partnership must reflect the new realities of changes and challenges, of new players in the scene, and of our understanding of the appropriate relationship between local cultures as an expression of the global. The issues of cooperative partnership will become increasingly important. The tasks are too great and complex for any single group to handle alone. The aim is not to compete with each other in resourcing and implementation but to complement each other's strength. The need to be big and small, global and local at the same time, will require new expressions of partnership. NGOs will need to be more aware of each other's activities and abilities and look for ways to work together for the benefit of the developing world.

Yet the call for partnership will also create tough choices. Christian agencies will be challenged to work with other faith-based or secular NGOs which may have different value systems and objectives. As Christian NGOs we should be careful to preserve our kingdom values and not compromise our standards so that our opportunity for ministry is not lost.

C. Issues in Development

5. The Future of Relief

The world of relief response is changing in fundamental ways. Increasingly, relief needs are resulting from ethnic and religious violence in contexts where governments and rule by law are no longer effective. Somalia, Rwanda and Bosnia are cases in point. Responses often mean closer, sometimes delicate, connections between military operations and relief and development agencies. Many military structures maintain some form of liaison for the commander with civilian agencies and authorities. These will need to be identified and NGO personnel equipped in order to relate effectively to the military systems and thus accomplish common objectives for divergent purposes. These 'complex humanitarian emergencies' often become perpetual relief situations because no government or civil society is in place to exercise governance when the disaster phase is over. These situations are making demands upon RDAs which go beyond their current competencies, such as human rights, negotiation, conflict resolution, reconciliation, infrastructure repair, political competency in issues of governance to build up civil society, and in the north, advocacy and lobbying.

NGOs will need to respond by:

1. Carefully thinking through how they maintain their identity and unique contribution when working closely with local and multilateral missions, including peace keeping, peace-making, and nation-building.
2. Deciding which new competencies they should develop and which they should decline as being divergent to their mission.
3. Reading the signs of the times to intervene at an early enough stage to prevent a crisis. Rwanda is an example where the church did not 'read the signs' as had been done so successfully in the Philippines in 1986.

6. Family and Development

Strong Christian families provide stability in the community which contributes to sustainable development. The development of strong Christian families which recognize the individual within the context of communities must be on a biblical basis. This provides a context where there is commitment, where love is shared and where people feel accepted and appreciated. In this environment, children grow up with a sense of worth that helps to accomplish their best in the world.

There has been a shift in the perception of the family as a necessary unit of society. There is a continual demand to re-define the institution. The focus is changing to incorporate single parent families, homosexual families, separated families, etc. Challenges too are faced by traditional societies which on one hand want modern education for their children and yet end up pulling them back to traditional practices which curtail full expression of their potential.

More factors are on the rise that continuously threaten the family structure. How will RDAs and churches respond to the following?

a. Economic Aspirations

Economic development and the resultant increasing pressure on the family to maintain particular expensive lifestyles. Individuals and families, anxious to keep up these standards, are pressurized into multiple incomes where more and more women have to take up demanding jobs with the sole motive of generating income. The family equilibrium gives way resulting in anxiety, hostility, physical illness, depression, child abuse, youth rebellion, drug use and alcohol abuse. Finally, apathy sets in and the family disintegrates.

b. Family Separation
Separated families due to civil war and strife, rural-urban migration, migrant workers and bonded labour. Issues brought to bear in this trend are human degradation, single parent homes, sexual immorality, polygamy and the spread of STDs and HIV/AIDS among others. RDAs and churches should take up advocacy where prevention of these negative trends can help to strengthen the family. There will be need to explore creation of employment in rural communities to cut back on rural-urban migration.

c. Poverty
The pressures of shifting economies, unplanned families, widowhood all impact on family resources and the way they are shared.

d. The Impact of AIDS
Family resources will be used in seeking for cures and providing for numerous funerals. More and more children will be orphaned at a time when community structures of foster parenting are crumbling. Can RDAs and churches motivate community-based care for orphaned children?

e. Gender Issues
Gender related programmes involving empowerment of women through exclusive funding of women's projects. Men and their sons are alienated, a trend that directly impacts the family through divorce, separation, alcoholism, polygamy, and communication breakdown. How can gender balance be restored? The challenge will be to lay a biblical basis of gender expression so that the family unit is not undermined.

f. Youth
i. **Hopelessness, pessimism and identity crisis** will increase among the youth. Confusing messages of 'safe sex' and the right to abortion from the secular world require practice biblical solutions. These are urgently needed to address issues of youth culture, adolescent sexuality, careers, job creation and income generation. Youth also needs to

be given time and space to grow up towards responsible adulthood. In education programmes, care should be taken to avoid programmes that give young people false hope through academic preparation without a future in the world of work. The great potential of young people is recognized. Their idealism and energy may provide further stimulus for Christian relief and development initiatives and ministry in churches in the twenty-first century. For example, currently, many RDAs and churches in the Two-Thirds World are in fact youth movements.

　　ii. **Youth in difficult circumstances** for example, those in refugee camps and war zones. These often become victims of exploiters who capitalize on youth idealism and their disillusionment for the further-ance of fundamentalist causes. How will RDAs and churches respond to this challenge?

　　iii. **Among the marginalized, children are among the most vulnerable.** More and more RDAs and churches are called upon to respond to needs of children in a wholistic manner. Advocacy is necessary too to ensure legal rights for orphaned children who cannot reclaim their parents' property on their own.

g. External stresses

With increasing urbanization, economic pressures, people mobility, civil wars and ethnic conflict, many are stressed and emotionally wounded. These adversely impact on the family. How can Christian counselling be incorporated as a ministry in the work place, church and community?

Strategies: sound management of natural resources

- Agroforestry and silvo-pastoral systems to produce food, cash crops and multibple purpose wood.
- Environmental education, management and conservation of eco-systems.
- Waste disposal management.
- Health education to slow down population growth.
- Soil and water conservation.
- Watershed management and conservation.
- Use of recycling systems.

Environment

Overpopulation, lack of stewardship in the use of management of natural resources, and pollution of the air, land and water are having consequences on the increase of poverty, abuse of the human rights of minority groups of indigenous societies, and reduction of biodiversity.

RDAs face the enormous challenge to establish cultivation systems that will reverse this situation. This will include.

8. Health and development

The health care need of the impoverished impose both a monumental burden as well as an opportunity upon the church and RDAs. Decreased spending by local governments, international strategies, ethnic unrest and civil wars have exacted a toll on marginalized people.

Adequate health care must demonstrate integrative and holistic approaches. Specific emphasis should be placed upon education for children, especially girls, primary health care and intervention and treatment for diseases such as HIV/AIDS, TB and malaria. The mental health of those who have been afflicted by sexual or physical abuse, displaced by migration or participation and victims of war must not be neglected.

Efforts should be concentrated upon the transfer of skills and knowledge related to health care rather than the established process of viewing health care as a commodity.

Low-income groups will be unable to generate sufficient resources needed for sustainable primary health care. The trend toward market economies raises the risk that the poorest will be cut off from adequate medical attention. In such a context, the church and their related RDAs province the best grassroots network for health care in all its aspects.

9. Assets for development

There is an urgent need for a radical rethink on assets for development. The traditional focus derived from western business culture has identified assets as capital assets. However, it is now recognized that the assets that help to develop business are human assets utilizing knowledge, wisdom and opportunity. The twenty-first century definitely belongs to those who have knowledge and the access to the means to use it. Realization of the abilities of the marginalised is only possible, therefore, with the motivation, opportunity and means to use and enhance the marginalised's own knowledge. To date, the focus in RDAs has been on the transfer of funds, resources, and services between donors and RDAs and between RDAs and local people.

However, RDAs are in fact knowledge organizations and the implications of this for agencies and for grass roots communities needs further exploration. Critical to this change of focus are appropriate methods and systems of transfer of pertinent knowledge. For, even programmes related to knowledge have been flawed with transfer of 'non-consequence-knowledge,' inappropriate and/or often destructive knowledge, and disregard of local knowledge. Furthermore, the methods of transfer are often inappropriate, often making the marginalised dependent on NGOs. Care must be taken to ensure that cultural changes are not inappropriately imposed by the type of knowledge transferred or the methods of transfer, especially in technical fields. Effort must be made to make knowledge cross-cultural.

NGOs must focus on:

1. Facilitating collection of local knowledge and wisdom.
2. Dialogue with local communities to identify information needs, assess problems, and enhance the local capacity to effect solutions.
3. Equipping local communities for knowledge acquisition and application.
4. Facilitating the communication of local knowledge to the larger world.
5. Facilitating an exchange of knowledge among the marginalised.
6. Adding and enhancing highly capable systems of bottom-up, lateral, and external exchange of information flow to replace or complement the traditional top-down systems now working.

It is also recognized that knowledge without wisdom and experience in its application is deficient. Priority must be given to adequate mentoring and coaching of new leaders, especially the young, in order that the emphasis on the leadership role is in servanthood and not status. Skills of resourcing in the local and international environment will be essential in the coming years as well as skills of research, problem solving and implementation. NGOs will need to provide significant resources of education and mentoring to facilitate future leaders' participation in programmes. Education models already exist. However, the shift necessary requires a firm hand from the top down to change the systemic focus. Inertia is monumental. All education must be supported by frequent sustainment training coupled with aggressive systemic accountability checks and balances.

10. Funding for Relief and Development Agencies

Funding possibilities will cause some NGOs to grow and others to shrink. As far as fund-raising in concerned, Christian RDAs operate in an open market.

Christians as the target group for fund-raising by Christian RDAs tend to give more emotionally than thoughtfully. As Christian RDAs operate in an open market, they have a responsibility to encourage Christians to give to Christian organizations.

Christian RDAs are challenged to communicate complex issues in short periods of time and to build contextual relationships with their donors. Some mass media approaches to fund-raising are increasingly losing their effectiveness. Cost-benefit analysis is important in fund-raising campaigns.

In thinking about alternatives, Christian RDAs need to maintain their distinctive Christian character. They should pay much attention to accountability and authenticity. Ethical presentation of an agency message is vital. The use of images of people, particularly women and children, that are degrading must always be avoided: all people are made in the image of God.

11. Ethnicity and Identity

With the growth of market cultures which integrate and homogenize cultures and nations the quest both for identity and for security are enhanced. Since the poor will never attain economic security, they invest increasingly in their ethnicity as their source of identity. The ethnic identity of the group is sometimes at the expense of other groups and so inter-ethnic conflict increases. The twenty-first century will be marked by increasing ethnicity, often rooted in religious commitment and fundamentalism, even Christian in origin.

12. Civil Society

In this context a commitment to the stability of a civil society will be increasingly important. Civil society is a three-legged stool supported by the ways in which leaders are to be held accountable, ways ordinary people can take part in decision-making, and ways conflicts can be resolved. If one of these three is lacking, the ability of NGOs to undertake development is hindered. Famines, forced migrations, and the criminalization of politics with its attendant corruption, to name but a few causes of suffering are often traceable to the lack of a significant civil society in a community to promote education, the rule of law and community responsibility. In such situations governments may request NGOs to provide some of the services which are properly the government's responsibility. NGOs should be cautious about such requests, since unless the government itself shoulders the responsibility, the very possibility of other agencies to bring development is frustrated.

13. Rights of Entitlement

There is also a need for a commitment to rights of entitlement. Many countries in the Two-Thirds World have long traditions of authoritarianism and militarization, national security bureaus and laws, strict control of the legislature and judiciary, censorship of information, land dispossession, significant gaps between rich and poor people, repressive and greedy leaders, and other violations of fundamental human rights.

The term 'human rights' is subject to misunderstanding. In the past decades many states often in the context of pro-or anti-communist propaganda, stressed the need for national security to justify authoritarian or military dictatorships and strong anti-subversion measures that restrict civil liberties. In more recent times some newly industrialized countries attempt to justify authoritarian and closed forms of government as necessary for the development of their economies – even at the price of curtailing personal freedom and human rights.

Sometimes a comparison is made between the 'eastern' emphasis on productivity, cooperation and discipline, and the 'western' focus on individualism, rights and freedom. But there is an interdependence rather than a distinction between communal and personal rights, liberty and security, democracy and discipline, fair distribution and economic prosperity. Human rights are universal although they may be applied in varying ways according to cultural context. There are rights to which all are entitled, including the right to live with adequate water, food and housing, the right to live with dignity and with proper access to participate in economic, political, social and cultural activity and the right to the pursuit of happiness and the search for spiritual wholeness. Participatory community requires people to be subjects of decisions that shape their lives. Too often, models of development favour the powerful, the violent, the greedy and the few. Any 'new world order' should emphasize a fair social order which respects the poor, the marginalised, the peacemaker and the many. There is a need to promote human rights and the values of justice, compassion, respect and trust. The spiritual and ethical principles of Christianity emphasize the sacredness of human life, the importance of generosity, non-exploitation of sentient life and natural resources, as well as the development of a person's full and best potential, right relationships and the value of diversity.

The challenge is now how NGOs should carry out advocacy on these issues from the conceptual viewpoint – policy reform, empowering indigenous people and raising issues and cases to be settled in an equitable and civilized way. For this purpose, study programmes, research, network development cooperation, organizing of policy dialogues with governments and with entrepreneurs, empowerment programmes for indigenous people in organizing their community and economy, advocacy on their rights, network cooperation and so forth constitute a most urgent agenda.

14. The Growth and Future of Ngos

NGOs are private organizations, many of which grew out of Christian churches and missions involved in health, education and relief. Global trends will impact both their growth and future. As western governments withdraw from bilateral provisions, they will be increasingly contracting NGOs to fill this gap. Additionally, the expansion of poverty in the South, the privatization of care in the North, and the tendency of local governments to diminish social expenditures will lead to further proliferation of NGOs.

Though the global economy can provide jobs and opportunities, it is also recognized that the resultant market economies and cultures have a tendency to marginalize many groups including children, women, and families. NGOs, from a Christo-centric perspective, should play a critical and significant role in specifically addressing the sectors 'left by the side of the road.'

As NGOs approach the twenty-first century, they will be confronted with the complexities inherent within the reality of market economies, the increasing competition for funds designated for relief and development, and the challenge to develop further an ethical and biblical strategy for acquiring necessary resources and assets.

Twenty

Children at Risk
Statement of an International Consultation at Oxford, January 1997

From January 6–10, 1997, 51 representatives of 38 different ministries to children at high risk from Africa, Asia, Europe and North and South America came together to an international consultation on Children at Risk at Oxford, England. As a product of this conference the following declaration has been drafted and agreed upon.

Background

We feel it necessary to draw attention to the increasingly vulnerable position of our world's children. We affirm that all children are at risk from their very moment of conception. Even within our own families, we are aware of the destructive effects that the rough edge of society can inflict on our children.

'Children at Risk: Statement of an International Consultation' in *Transformation*, Vol. 14, No. 2, April 1997.

However, it is for the neglected and exploited children of our generation that our hearts cry out. We can no longer stand by and watch them suffer and die in their millions while their enemies are left free to stalk them on every side. The issues that face children at high risk today are not their problem, but our problem. We therefore identify the following areas of concern and shall commit our sweat and tears to addressing them:

Malnutrition: 35,000 children (under the age of 5) die every day as a result of malnutrition or starvation [World Vision].

Abortion: Every year 40,000,000 children lose their lives through parental consent [UN]. This means that 29% of all children are never born.

Family Disintegration & Abandonment: There are at least 100,000,000 children who live or work on the streets of our cities [UNICEF, 1994]. Most of these children are confronting the dangers of life in this hostile environment as a result of family breakdown.

Sex-exploitation, Rape and Abuse: There are at least 1,000,000 children currently suffering the oppression of forced prostitution and another 1,000,000 join this industry every year [World Vision, UNICEF].

War: During the period 1984–1994, more than 1,500,000 children were killed in wars, over 4,000,000 were disabled, maimed, blinded or brain damaged by wars and 12,000,000 lost their homes as the result of war. During this period, 35 nations are known to have conscripted children into their armed forces [Save the Children, 1994].

Slavery and Abusive Child Labour: Between 100 and 200,000,000 children are currently involved in child labour [UN Children's Fund]

Drug and Alcohol Abuse: 75% of British 15–16 year old school children report that they have used cannabis, and 3% have taken heroin [(1) Health Education Association 1987, (2) Manchester University research project]

Disease: 1,500,000 children are currently infected with AIDS [WHO/UNICEF, 1995]. 2,000,000 children die every year through lack of immunisation against preventable diseases [World Vision].

Disability: Over 500,000 children go blind every year, mostly as a result of Vitamin A deficiency. Only one in every 60 of those has access to education. [Christoffel-Blindemission].

Suicide: Today's children face a level of psychological pressure totally unknown to previous generations. Faced with unattainable goals and a culture with few answers, many see suicide as the logical way out.

We are compelled to challenge anyone who feels able to continue with business as usual in full knowledge of these facts. This generation of children is the future of our societies, and too many of them are dying. If there is no hope for these children, then our societies have no future. It is through the eternal hope of God's Kingdom planted in our hearts that we are able to seek solutions to such overwhelming issues. With this hope, there is a future for the children currently at risk in our generation.

The fruit of this hope can already be seen in the work of those who have relinquished personal ambition to devote themselves to the needs of children at risk. These people are the silent workers who through their daily commitment are addressing the great needs of children at risk. Like the children they serve, these people are also

---

Children at risk: Prevention of disability

'**Children at Risk**' means to Christoffel Blindenmisson children losing their sight, their hearing or their physical and mental health. Although education and rehabilitation of disabled children constitutes an important part of our ministry, our main focus is on the prevention of disability in the community.

However, we do know that in the least developed parts of the third world, the major causes of childhood disabilities are vitamin deficiencies, malnutrition, infectious diseases, and, to a lesser extent, accidents. Basically, we have the knowledge and technology to eliminate these conditions. They are relatively cheap but there are considerable logistical problems.

Successful vitamin distribution programmes, public education and immunisation programmes require efficient and well managed health infrastructures – not always the case in the least developed countries. They also require an acceptance by the community.

CBM has been very successful in preventing blindness and other disabilities at the grass root level. However, the number of disabled children is still increasing. We have the technology, we have the knowledge – it is the dissemination of that knowledge and the changing of attitudes and increased awareness in the population about intervention that is our greatest challenge.

suffering. They are under-resourced. They are tired. They are scared. They experience continual stress. They need support. A key to the future rests in the continued commitment of these people.

2.0 Issues

2.1 Violations of the Rights of the Child

The gross violation of the rights of children is appalling. Millions are denied the right to be born, denied the right to live, deprived of a family, deprived of opportunity, deprived of the right to know God, and are exploited and abused in unimaginable ways. The UN Convention on the Rights of the Child (CRC) drafted in 1989 provides a very useful and comprehensive account of rights which we commend for study in relation to this document. Children, along with all humanity, have

---

Cape Town City Mission

Defining Children at Risk: Children without adequate protection against exploitation, abuse, manipulation, abandonment and without basic living standards in order to maintain health, both physical and emotional.

Addressing Children at Risk: Cape Town City Mission endeavours to provide holistic care in the form of physical, emotional and spiritual help to the poor and needy of South Africa. Cape Town City Mission believes in the God-given potential of each child and seeks to enable them to become self-reliant, but Godly dependent members of the community. The aim is to present each child perfect in Christ. (Colossians 1:28).

A 3-phase project has been developed, whereby the child can make the choice to move from one phase to the other, ultimately being reunited with either their parent/s, relatives or foster families.

Street workers start the process, visiting the children on the streets, building relationships, advocating for them, accompanying them to hospital, etc. The street workers encourage the children to attend the first phase.

Phase 1 is a day centre, open 5 days a week. Children come for meals, wash their clothes, shower and then attend workshops, creative activities, numeracy and literacy classes, drama classes, recreational outings, etc. to build self-esteem and relationships. Devotions are taken for and by the children daily. Workshop topics include drug rehabilitation, violence, sexuality, prostitution etc. The programme is for 3 months, after which the children can choose to enter Phase II. Street workers make attempts to trace the relatives of the children from the start and if reunion is possible it is preferred, if decided by the children.

Phase II is a series of cottages, each accommodating a maximum of 8 children with a house mother/father. Lifeskills are again part of the programme, the child re-enters school and becomes more involved with the community life once more. Home visits occur where possible. If no family reunion is possible, the child moves to Phase III after one year.

Phase III is a further extension of Phase II and prepares the child for family life. All phases have appropriate programmes to the felt and real needs of the child. All programmes are biblically founded. Each project is situated in the communities the children originally ran from.

The child is usually the symptom of family breakdown and the hub of many complicated and interwoven relationships so the Family Life Department of Cape Town City Mission and the street workers work alongside the families of the children to restore the family so that the child can be reunited safely and happily.

The Combat Child Abuse Department offers training to the child care workers on how to approach and facilitate healing to children suffering from effects of abuse.

Cape Town City Mission believes each child belongs with a family and the gospel is central to all care given.

inalienable God-given rights which must be protected so that each child can grow up wholistically as Jesus did. Each child has the right to grow in wisdom and stature, and in favour with God and man. (Luke 2:52). This access to growth is also impaired wherever religious liberties are restricted.

2.2 Family disintegration

God's intention is that children be nurtured within the family. However, the breakdown of families through separation, divorce, mobility and self-centredness has wounded and destabilized the child. This is worsened by changing values that give priority to material possessions above human life and development. Children are at risk when families are at risk. We grieve at how pervasive is the failure of the family today around the world. Many children are sexually abused by family members. Tragically, for many children, the home and family have become hostile, rather than nurturing environments. The family structure has been devastated by the violence of war, the dislocation of forced migration, and the blatant exploitation and abuse of children.

2.3 Poverty and Malnutrition

The largest cause of death amongst children is malnutrition. Tens of thousands die every day as a result of curable diseases caused by simple nutritional deficiencies. This malnutrition is the inevitable outcome of a poverty cycle which neither family nor child is able to escape.

2.4 Urbanisation

Due to rural poverty, the family members, especially young people, migrate to cities in search of jobs and better living conditions to end up in overcrowded slum communities. Rural poverty and urban growth has thrust millions of helpless children onto the streets, overstretching the meagre resources available in the cities and exposing the children to disease, abuse and exploitation. It is very difficult to trace the roots or families of these resultant street children populations.

2.5 War and Ethnic Conflict

In many countries destabilized by ethnic conflict and political turmoil, repression and authoritarianism are growing. This results in poor investment climate, loss of revenue, disruption of an already delicate trade and economic system, and undermines health and education services. Remaining resources are diverted for emergencies and military spending. Consequently more and more children die, are displaced, orphaned and become refugees internally and internationally. More appalling is the number of child soldiers recruited in many nations to fight in conflicts that they do not understand.

Youth with a Mission Brazil

Isabel Zwahlen – YWAM Brazil Children's Ministry Director, Contagem

In any part of the world today, especially in the developing counties where the one third of the total population is under 18, children are at risk. For example, in health; from infant mortality, abortion, lack of primary health care. In education; from illiteracy or where education is forbidden to girls or when due to the need to work children/young people do not attend school. They are at risk when they do not hear about Jesus. They are at risk in societies that give high value to materialism, sex (along with abuse, prostitution and pornography) and no value to the eternal soul. They are at risk where there is war for political, religious or ideological reasons.

YWAM Brasil is addressing seriously the situation of our children. We visualise the education of children with pre-schools, elementary schools, student centres and day-care centres. The street children ministry is responding to the needs of the children in the urban areas, in the slums, in the street; seeking to rescue them from the street and restore them to their families, where possible, or to a foster home. We also have a ministry focus to children with AIDS, providing a home with healthcare, and preparing them for eternal life.

We are convinced that we need to focus our efforts on prevention. By working with families, and helping them to apply and live by God's principles for marriage and parenting we believe we are diminishing the risks. Training children and teens to have a relationship with God through Jesus, to take care of their bodies, to say NO to drugs and premarital sex and teaching them are also important aspects of prevention.

Children at risk is an important issue on God's heart. We need to listen to him for new strategies to meet the needs of the emerging generation. So that the words of the prophet may come true in our days: "They will neither harm nor destroy on all my holy mountain, for the earth will be full of the knowledge of the Lord as the waters cover the sea".

2.6 Disability

Children with disabilities are among the most neglected and abused by both families and society. Adults are often embarrassed by malformed children. Families hide them away believing that disablement is a form of curse. These children often have less access to facilities and thus have less than full participation and equality in the social and economic life of the community. Very few initiatives address the

---

Church Mission Society

Martyn Payne
Children's work Co-ordinator

CMS is a two-hundred year-old mission agency in partnerships with churches in Asia, Africa and Eastern Europe. In my role, I am involved with helping to relate news and issues concerning the church and children worldwide to Christians in the UK. The aim is both to introduce children to the wider Christian Family to which they belong and also to help them learn from that wider church which faces many issues in its local situations. Through leadership training, special events for children and publications, it is our hope to inspire churches to share the Christian message effectively with the coming generation and to encourage them for mission as they hear stories from the church around the world.

The children, with whom I am in contact, are not obviously at risk as the vast majority of children in the 2/3 world. They are not refugees, not traumatised by war, not shot at in the streets, not dismembered by land mines, not child labourers (on the whole) nor forced to sell their bodies. They are however at risk in other ways. At risk, because, in a materialistic and market-dominated society, they are being denied their childhood; at risk, because they are unloved and abused in broken homes; at risk, because, still sadly, they are unwelcome and unvalued by many churches and are not able in other contexts to hear the story of Jesus; at risk, because they are exposed to ideas, influences and pressures that force them to grow old before their time. My work in the UK seeks to address and be aware of these issues and to help churches work out appropriate strategies for mission and compassion toward such children.

special needs of disabled children whose condition in many cases is preventable or curable.

2.7 Abusive Child Labour

We recognize that child labour is not necessarily unjust and that in many cultures family relationships are strengthened when children work alongside their parents. However, poverty has meant that an increasing number of young children are being pressured into finding work so that millions of children are currently involved in forced labour which denies basic human rights. In extreme cases children have become trapped in total bondage to individuals who have no concern for their welfare.

2.8 Sex Tourism

In many countries, tourism has become the greatest source of foreign exchange. However, the depravity of humankind has eroded our respect for the dignity of children to the extent that paedophilia is almost an institutionalized practice in certain tourist-spots of the world. Sexually exploited children are particularly susceptible to long-term trauma, usually well into adulthood.

2.9 Government Complicity and Corruption

The promotion of the welfare of every citizen is a responsibility of government. However, we note with great dismay that many governments have left much of the care of children at risk to NGOs and religious groups. Many governments formulate socio-economic policies which in the long term work against the promotion of children's welfare. Corruption in governments has also led to child trafficking, sexual exploitation of children and child labour.

2.10 Lack of Accountability

We are saddened that while children at risk cry out for help certain individuals have chosen to divert resources gained for the benefit of children into their own pockets, and established organizations for selfish gain. There is a need to promote a sense of accountability to God in all ministries for children at risk. At the same time mutual trust and accountability between donor and recipient organizations based upon integrity are foundational to any successful ministry.

2.11 Lack of Training of Care-givers

Appropriately equipped workers are foundational to successful ministry for children at risk. We are alarmed to note that many Christian workers in certain areas of ministry amongst children at risk do not have adequate skills, lack access to training needed, or are not encouraged to acquire the basic skills needed to work effectively with the children. Short and long-term training is required in health care, nutrition, counselling, socialization, education, vocational training, evangelism, discipleship, management and administration. Organizations should provide opportunity and structure for personnel development and in so doing contribute to building up the body of Christ.

2.12 Care for the Care-givers

Persons who commit their efforts and lives to the service of children at risk often experience a sense of aloneness, discouragement and pain. Such wounded healers are vulnerable to burnout and to the destructive effects of oppressive pressures. Their immediate family and dependants are equally vulnerable.

2.13 Despair and Lack of Hope

While poverty has always been with us, and children have always been at risk, children today are growing up in a different context from previous generations. Today's post-modern paradigm has caused adults and children not only to abandon hope but to embrace despair. The context of child poverty and crisis has always been spiritual as well as physical, and today is no exception.

3.0 Theological Foundations for Ministry to Children at Risk

3.1 The Biblical Significance of the Child

Scripture clearly shows that God is outraged about what is happening to children. Our own anger is but a pale reflection of God's fury and indignation. Our compassion for hurting children and the righteous anger that arises within us reflects nothing less than the jealous love and righteous anger of our Heavenly Father. Our anger is predicated upon God's anger, and our actions on His actions. Over and over again God's warning throughout the Bible is 'Don't touch my precious children!' (Ex 22:22–24; Psalm 68:5, Ezekiel 16:4–14, Deuteronomy 24:17 etc.) He indicates terrible consequences for anyone harming his children: '. . . it would be better that a millstone be hung around his neck and [he] be drowned in the depths of the sea' (Mt. 18:6).

Nowhere do we learn more of the loving and jealous character of God than in His protection and defence of His children. (Deuteronomy 24:17, 27:19). Indeed, God entrusting His own Son to humankind as a vulverable child, requiring that Son to be nurtured by a frail but able family and community, symbolically provides a model of trust and responsibility which sets an example for His interaction with all humanity, and which shouts to us about the significance of children.

Thus we find ample justification for special possessive and protective guardianship of children at risk clearly demonstrated and mandated throughout the Scriptures. Moreover, Jesus uses the simple faith and courage which marks the heart of children as a model for adults seeking to be a part of His Kingdom:

> Let the little children come to me, and do not hinder them, for the kingdom of God belongs to such as these. I tell you the truth, anyone who will not receive the kingdom of God like a little child will never enter it (Mk. 10: 14b–15 NIV).

As Christians then, we gladly acknowledge that our profound concern for children at risk flows from God himself and our commitment to Jesus Christ. Most fundamentally, we affirm that children, born and unborn, along with the rest of humanity, are created in the image of God and therefore have intrinsic worth. (Gen. 1:27, Psalm 139:13–14) Any actions that demean, devalue or otherwise diminish children are sinful. Unfortunately, we live in a world where an attitude of cynicism towards the dignity of human life has resulted in a tragic loss of respect for humankind. Children are increasingly the underserving victims of human and demonic forces. The criminal waste of children's lives is an indictment upon all societies which cries out to God for vengeance.

3.2 Children to be Nurtured Through the Family . . .

We affirm that God's basic societal unit is the family (Gen 2:24; 5:21–6:4) which God has ordained as based upon a man and a woman living in faithfulness to one another and the offspring with which He blesses that union (Psalm 127:3–5). The family which nurtures children is to be characterized by faithfulness, responsibility and obedience, and mutual submission. It is God's intention that the primary responsibility for the nurture and discipline of children belongs to the family. (Ephesians 6:1–4).

The family has been undermined by the sin and pride of individualism and by the desire for human autonomy and self-fulfilment rather than obedience to God. Moreover, consumerism and materialism, which places more value on acquisition rather than relationships, has further subverted the family. Family disintegration and dysfunction invariably results in children at risk.

In such a situation, the body of Christ must intervene. The repeated injunctions in both Old and New Testament to 'defend the cause of the weak and fatherless' (i.e. Psalms 82, 103:6, I Tim 5:16, James 1:27, 5:1–6) are explicit directives for every believer within the church family to be active ambassadors of God's grace, especially to at risk children.

. . . Through the Church . . .

The church, represented by and including its institutions, the local believing community, and Christian agencies involved in specialized ministries, is also expected to provide support, protection, and nurture to all its children. The community of faith, empowered by the Spirit, constitutes a wider family. This wider family serves as God's agent with responsibility to provide protection and nurture alongside of, or where it fails or abdicates, in place of the family. Children who have made a confession of faith, and who represent the church of both today and tomorrow, are full members of the household of faith and enjoy all the privileges of this family.

Children, like all church members, need mentoring to bring them to maturity in Christ.

. . . and Through the Community

Moreover, children are also part of the society as a whole, and are to be protected and nurtured by its cultural structures, including its schools, local societies, and public and private agencies. These entities too have a moral obligation to care for the children within their sphere of influence. The culture of a community has a great impact on the culture of the family and its ability to provide such care. Christians should seek that these cultures and their corporate expressions protect children as far as possible.

3.3 A Call for Christian Ethics in Care-giving

It is not enough simply to rescue those at risk; they must also be offered the fullness and wholeness of life in the kingdom.

But we humbly confess that in our efforts to share the good news of the Kingdom of God to these 'little ones', we have at times been manipulative or exploitative. This is never acceptable. God's own model of transparency, unconditional love, and patience in relating to us should be our guide.

The Ethics and Support of Care-givers

We acknowledge that the actions of care givers, while well intentioned, may themselves do harm rather than good. We must ensure that our own ministries do not, through lack of awareness and planning, inadvertently permit harm to children. Procedures and guidelines must protect children from harm from staff, volunteers and donors.

Marketing activities should seek to present the needs of children in ways which maintain their dignity and worth as individual human beings. Project planning should include assessment of potential areas of risk so that activities to protect children can be implemented.

We are called by God to a ministry that is motivated and sustained by Him. Those who minister in Christ's name amongst those at risk are themselves at risk. We need to draw upon the full resources that God supplies by His Spirit through such means as prayer, worship, the sacraments, praise, the study of the Scriptures and time away from stressful environments.

3.4 A Call to Prayer

From the Scriptures we understand that the destructive powers making for dislocation and disintegration in human affairs are both temporal

Alay Pag Asa

Manila

All children are at risk to begin with because of their vulnerability/helplessness. They are dependent on others for their survival, protection and development. But there are children at greater risk, those in especially difficult circumstances whose survival, protection and developmental needs are hardly or not being met at all. In the Philippines, they are the following:

1. disabled children
2. children in situations of armed conflict
3. children who work
4. children of indigenous cultural communities
5. children of the urban poor who are either working children or street children
6. children trapped in sexual exploitation and drug abuse and in conflict with the law
7. children from areas affected by natural calamities/disasters

Most of them are symptoms of families that have been in crisis for some length of time. Their families are unable to support them because in themselves they are in dire need of support. Given this perspective the problem of children at risk can be approached in 2 ways:

(1) directly helping the children meet their survival, protection and developmental needs, and
(2) empowering the families, particularly the parents, because in doing so, the children will be empowered as well.

Alay-Pag-Asa is reaching the street children and urban poor families in Metro Manila for Christ to help them become followers of Christ and productive, useful members of society. Our street-and centre-based programs and services are helping street and urban working children while the community-based programs and services are seeking to empower families in several urban poor communities.

and spiritual (Ephesians 6). In as far as nations, cultures, religions, communities, families, and individuals fail to foster the well-being of the children for whom they are responsible, they are under the judgement of God. We are called both to promote that which makes for the total well being of children and to combat that which makes for their oppression. We are also called to engage the spiritual dimensions of these realities with prayer.

The cry in Lamentations to 'pour our hearts out like water for the lives of the children who faint from hunger at the head of every street' (Lamentations 2:19) is an image that calls us to fervent intercession on behalf of children at risk around the world. We must encourage the whole church to seek understanding, compassion and brokenness in order to lift the needs of the children to the Lord.

The whole church includes children and scripture would suggest that they have a particular role in intercession. Hence we do not only pray on their behalf, but also invite them into this process of intercession (Psalm 8:2).

Malachi 4:6 informs us however that 'unless the hearts of the fathers are turned to the children and the hearts of the children turned to the fathers, God will strike the land with a curse.' The effects of 'the curse' are seen throughout Biblical history. However, God in his mercy and love for humankind has used the birth of a child as redemption amidst 'the curse'. After humanity's fall into sin, Shem became the hope for the future of God's created world, Moses was the hope of redemption for the captive nation of Israel, and Jesus is our hope for salvation from sin. Hence the child represents hope to the nations.

3.5 Understanding Cultural Diversity

Our interpretations of God's word on children at risk, as with our interpretations of any scriptural truth, must be understood in the light of our cultural backgrounds and biases. The identity of children is shaped by cultural values and there are aspects of all cultures which enhance the dignity of children and aspects which destroy this dignity and even their lives. We affirm our intent to be sensitive and responsive to cultural differences while always seeking to 'correctly handle the word of truth' (2 Timothy 2:15). This will be achieved by sharing between each context the ways in which Scripture affirms and challenges the cultural values ascribed to the child.

The Viva Network

An International Network for Children at Risk Ministries

The Viva Network links together Christians working with children at risk and through this network they are provided with services. By bringing together every ministry and agency active in this field the Viva Network is able to act as a voice for those ministering to children at risk. Many of those working with children in situations of risk do so in great isolation, often unable to access the resources they need. A network provides the context in which they can share fellowship, information and contacts to resources.

Children's ministries form the Viva Network through becoming members of a network in their nation. There are currently 18 national networks working in conjunction with the International Coordination Office in Oxford. The International Coordination Office is the central hub of the network. All the information received from member ministries via the national networks is used to provide services including prayer support, research into resources and training, introduction to potential volunteers, publications to encourage and edify Christian Child care workers and access to a wider audience for the voice of those ministering to children at risk.

The national networks provide fora for fellowship between those in ministry to children at risk. Through conferences, prayer events, social events and visiting ministries the National Networks ensure that members are benefiting from the services and advice available through the network. Members share prayer and resource requests through the network, nationally and internationally. In this way they can be voiced to a much larger audience.

4.0 Present Action

The depth and variety of work undertaken on behalf of children is extensive.

While what is being done by Christians and others is but a small portion of what needs to be done, we nevertheless celebrate the fact that so many Christians around the world are responding to the needs of children at risk.

Current interventions include:

- Rehabilitation programmes for children who have suffered from exploitation and forced prostitution or who have become addicted to drugs or alcohol.
- Counselling for children who have been traumatised by war, abuse, or natural disasters.
- Outreach to children on the streets in the form of feeding programmes, education, evangelism, and first aid.
- Long term residential care for orphans and children who are unable to live with their remaining family. Adoption and foster care.
- Primary health care for children with medical needs, and dignified care for children suffering from disabilities and terminal illness such as AIDS.
- Schooling and vocational training for children. Equipping of community leaders and child care workers. Training of parents.
- Fund-raising on behalf of individual children, and the ministries that support them through sponsorships, and grants and self sustainability programmes. Micro-enterprise and small business projects for poor children.
- Community and environmental improvements.
- General community development programmes, and wholistic community development with a focus on preventative action to help avert family disintegration.
- Reunification of street children, and children caught up in war with their families.
- Media services including awareness raising publications, tapes and videos for the general public, and radio for children.
- Intercession on behalf of children and by children for children.
- Advocacy and lobbying on behalf of those who have no influence over government policy, and empowering of grassroots communities.
- Partnerships between ministries with common goals.

5.0 Recommendations for the Future

1. **All Churches** have a responsibility to search for and implement tangible structures by which they can effectively minister to children at risk both locally and globally. We recommend that they:

a) be aware of the crisis;

b) be aware of what other people and ministries are currently doing;

c) set aside resources, financial and persons, in order to link with and participate in a specific ministry programme;

d) regularly pray within the congregational worship service for children at risk;

e) ensure that children at risk and their families are welcomed into the church community;

f) encourage children to participate in worship and ministry;

g) provide a sense of significance, emotional acceptance and support for care givers.

2. **All Grass-Roots Ministries** (whether run by local churches or particular organisations) should seek to reinforce forms of interconnectedness in their common endeavours to minister effectively to children in their community. We recommend that local regional and international networks be encouraged by the development of facilitators and networkers in a servant hearted capacity. These various networks could serve the body of Christ by identifying those who are involved in doing creative ministries, though often isolated and unknown, so that these smaller groups have access to shared information, resources and encouragement. Mutual support and mutually shared resources should be encouraged at all levels.

3. **All Christian Agencies** supporting work with children at risk should be committed to improving the quality of existing efforts through the sharing of ideas, information and resources, as well as through training and the development of meaningful structures of accountability.

4. **The Christian Community** must raise a voice for and along with children to call to account those in positions of economic and government power who make and implement laws and policies that abuse, ignore, or take advantage of children at risk. This will involve increased participation in fora recommending and implementing social policy toward children at risk.

The above statement was produced and is sent out by the following persons:

Jasmine Adaickalam	Carl Armerding	Saheb John Borgall
Centre for	OCMS, UK	Tribal
Community Studies,	Arkle Bell	Transformation,
Malaysia	Frontier Youth Trust, UK	India

Renita Boyle
  Viva Network,
  Scotland
Edward Bradley
  Oakseed Ministries
  International, USA
Dan Brewster
  Compassion
  International, USA
David Bueno
  International Child
  Care, El Salvador
Lonah Cheptoo
  Christian Community
  Services, Kenya
Judi Coles
  Oasis Trust, UK
Michael Eastman
  Frontier Youth Trust,
  UK
Sonya Elliot
  Viva Network, UK
David Erasmus
  Viva Network, UK
Paul Freston
  OCMS, UK
Yolanda Freston
  CAISN University of
  Campinas, Brazil
Judy Fondren
  Alliance for Children,
  USA
Sheila Gethaiga, Kibuka,
  Kenya
Sara Glover
  Viva Network, UK
Josefina Guttierez
  Philippines
Axel Hardenberg
  Christoffel-
  Blindenmission,
  Germany

Albert Hengelaar
  The Netherlands
Karen Hinder
  Cape Town City
  Mission, South Africa
Joel Holme
  Pathfinders Education
  Foundation USA
Martin Hull
  Viva Network, UK
Pam Kerr
  World Vision
  International, USA
Byron Klaus
  Latin American Child
  Care, USA
Isaac Kumar
  Help a Child India,
  India
Margaret Kwanga
  Daystar University,
  Kenya
Emily & Patrick
  MacDonald
  Viva Network, UK
Yvonne Mildred
  SIM
Aaron Mokobane
  The Evangelical
  Alliance, South
  Africa
John Morley
  Viva Network, UK
Gladys Mwiti
  Oasis Counselling
  Centre, Kenya
Emmanuel Oladipo
  Scripture Union
  International, UK
Martyn Payne
  Church Mission
  Society, UK

Doug Petersen
  Latin American Child
  Care, Costa Rica
McDaniel Phillips
  Next Generation
  Network, USA
Amber & Ripley
  Robinson
  Viva Network, UK
Colleen Samuel
  Divya Shanti
  Christian Association
  India
Vinay Samuel
  INFEMIT, UK
Tereza Dos Santos
  Comunidade Central
  Batisto de Brasilia
  Brazil
Christopher Sugden
  OCMS, UK
Isaac Sutherson
  Florence Swainson
  Centre for the Deaf
  India
Liya Tegengnework
  SIM, Ethiopia
Robin & Nancy
  Wainwright
  Caltin Foundation,
  USA
David Westwood
  World Vision, UK
Heddwyn Williams
  Children of Hope,
  UK
Richard
  Worthing-Davies
  Mercy Corps Europe,
  UK
Isabel Zwahlen
  YWAM, Brazil

Twenty-One

Biblical and Theological Reflections on Disability
Oxford Consultation February 1998

Target Audience

We direct our findings to a range of people in the church, leaders of
various kinds as well as lay people, in the various parts of the world
which we represent. We hope our document might be useful to disabled people themselves in various positions of responsibility in the
church. We do not assume that the disabled are to be merely
the passive beneficiaries of the strategies we recommend. For those
strategies to be truly suited to the particular needs of disabled people
in different contexts, disabled people will have to take the lead. This is
a biblical principle: when the Greek Christians were not fully included
in the early church community, leaders among this neglected group
were appointed and empowered to take primary responsibility that

'Biblical and Theological Reflections on Disability' in *Transformation*,
Vol. 15, No. 4, October 1998.

the problem would be remedied (Acts 6:1–7). They were not made the recipients of charity handed out by others.

Summary of findings

We want our disabilities to be perceived as part of the rich diversity that God has created in creation, and we want to be accorded the dignity that God has given us in our difference.

- It is a calling of all people, dis-abled and non-disabled, to reach beyond our limits to explore the possibilities of our lives.
- The claims of persons with disabilities should be addressed under the category of human rights, understood as dignitarian rights rooted in the intrinsic goodness and dignity of bodily human life, created and given by God.
- While disability is not the result of sin, all disabled people are still sinners like everyone else and need spiritual ministry and nurture.
- Jesus Christ reveals the dis-abled God in being willing to empty himself of his glory to become human, becoming a part of a community of people with disabilities healing people with different disabilities as a sign of hope and transformation of all human beings when God makes all things new, allowing himself to be dis-abled by the disabling community of his day, bearing the marks of the crucifixion in his resurrection body, transforming all people, disabled and non-disabled into a new humanity defined by the kingdom of God, not being able-bodied.
- The church is to demonstrate the reconciliation between able-bodied and disabled just as much as it is to demonstrate the reconciliation between races, genders and classes.
- Spiritual access is the foundation for total access. What practically can be done to ensure that disabled people are not just treated the same as people with physical needs but as spiritual beings deserving the same spiritual access and nurture as everyone else? We make some suggestions in our strategy section.

Biblical and theological reflections

1. People who have impairments are also dis-abled by societies which exist for the non-disabled. They have problems of physical access to

buildings, but also face barriers consisting of oppressive attitudes, inappropriate language, inappropriate expectations and false stereotypes. Disability is not a medical matter of primary concern to the individual who is impaired. It is a social injustice which needs to be challenged and overcome. Dis-ability will only disappear if societies change.

2. In many countries, particularly those in the Two-Thirds World, disability can be a threat to survival. Some cultures neglect people with disability. It is estimated that there are 600 million people in the world with disabilities. Of these 20 per cent have problems caused by malnutrition. Disability is therefore inextricably linked with poverty, with disabled people making up the poorest and most powerless of the poor. Some children are blinded to make them more effective beggars. Young women in Asia may have acid thrown in their faces because their dowry is too small, they are infertile or their prospective partner wants to marry someone else and needs a good excuse.

3. It may surprise some to know that Christians with disabilities believe in the goodness of God's creation. We are all 'fearfully and wonderfully made' and though we may struggle in life we give thanks to God for his goodness to us.

4. People with disabilities often need help from others. Adam himself was help-less before Eve was made. We all need others. We are created not for isolated independence but for interdependence in mutually supportive human relationships. Needing help is not a sin, it is an expression of what it means to be truly human.

5. We are all created with a rich diversity of gifts and talents which we wish to develop and use. But all too often people with disabilities face such low expectations of what they can do or contribute to others that they are given little opportunity to develop their gifts which God has given them to enrich the lives of others. People with disabilities are often thought of as a group with common characteristics rather than as unique people in whom we can see God and from whom we receive God's love and grace. The Bible says that we are made in the image of God but some are never allowed to show the many ways in which we can uniquely express that great truth.

6. Some people confuse the limitations of being human with disability. This leads to statements such as 'we are all disabled'. This is emphatically not the case. All human beings have limitations on who we can be and what we can do. But this is positive. It is through understanding our limitations as well as our aspirations that we discover

who we are. All human beings have limitations but only some are disabled and own the identity of a disabled person. Whatever our human experience we all want to be encouraged by others to grow as human beings and explore new possibilities. Some disabled people are never offered that encouragement because it is assumed that they can do nothing.

7. Because disability is personal, social and economic, it is also a political issue. Disabled people are not a high priority when it comes to the application of government resources. It is a human rights issue. Human rights are founded on equal human dignity. Being human should be a sufficient reason for being treated with dignity. Sadly, some people, far from being respected are considered to be living lives which are considered to be not worth sustaining. We need to fight for the basic right to dignity for each person whatever their situation.

8. Though God's creation is good we all live in a fallen and compromised world. All of us have bodies prone to illness, decay and ultimately death. Yet discrimination is borne most heavily by those who have the most overt impairments. How unjust this is. In many cases they are made to feel that they have done something to 'deserve' that impairment, or lack faith for healing. Discrimination occurs in the church as well as outside as outside it. Many people with disabilities who have found no reason to doubt the love of God because of their impairment, have found reason to doubt his love because of their treatment by the church. The church must repent of these attitudes if it is to live what it preaches – good news for all.

9. Not all disabled people suffer bodily because of their impairment, but many do. We support the role of medicine in enabling people to be more fully themselves. However, people must be respected, consulted, and empowered by the medical professional who invariably treat the 'condition' rather than relate to the person. We are implacably hostile to eugenics and all forms of medical and scientific research which share its values and goals.

10. *Jesus Christ – The 'disabled' God.* Jesus shows God's attitudes to people with disabilities in five ways:

Firstly, Jesus himself is willing to empty himself of his glory (Phil. 2) to share our common limitations and to be open to all those problems and struggles to which human beings are vulnerable. He rejected any power or privilege which might give him a degree of protection which others did not share.

Secondly, he became part of the community of people with disabilities, eating, befriending, teaching and drawing them into the circle of his followers. He cut across the social norms of his day by putting people thought of as outcasts at the heart of the kingdom of God.

Thirdly, he healed people as a sign of hope for all, but also as an act of renewal and transformation. All people will one day be transformed when God makes 'all things new'. Jesus heals not by magical power, but by being willing to take illness and disability on himself, taking into himself the experience of disability along with other human experience. By healing people he restored them to family and community; primarily he restored them to shalom, that wholeness which speaks of the kingdom of God.

Fourthly, Jesus allowed himself to be disempowered by the dis-abling community of his day. This is particularly apparent after the last supper. He allowed people to have power over him and rejected the possibility of regaining control over his own life knowing that his calling to live like us and to die for us, could not be accomplished if he did so. On the cross his broken, disabled body, nailed to the cross, was helpless, allowing people to abuse him, despise him and reject him. On the cross he not only identifies with us in our suffering but reconciles us to God. By taking on himself our personal sin, structural evil and environmental decay he opens the way for new life in God, a new community of God's people and a new world.

Fifthly, the risen Christ appears to the disciples inviting them to touch him to verify that his is a physical body ('flesh and blood'). Even though he has dealt with sin he still bears the marks of the crucifixion. He is whole, he is risen, he has fulfilled his vocation, but he is disabled. He invites Thomas to put his hand into his side showing the extent of the continuity between the broken body of Christ and the risen body of Christ. Since Christ is whole, disabled people cannot be said to live a reduced life. They too are whole human beings.

11. Jesus ascends into heaven having experienced disability, powerlessness, and brokenness as well as joy, friendship and celebration. In doing so, human experience is revealed at the heart of Trinity. Disabled people are not made in the image of God despite their disabilities but with their disabilities. Christ in heaven remains with the scars in his hands interceding for us in our weakness. Although we shall all be transformed into the image of Christ and shall be like him, this transformation does not consist of people with disabilities becoming able-bodied. All human beings belong to a world which is

groaning under the extent of its decay. We all are waiting for transformation and renewal into a world in which there will be no more suffering. However this is not the negation of our earthly experience but the liberation of the people God intended us to be. Christ's scars indicate that we will carry appropriate signs which witness to our earthly lives whether disabled or able-bodied. There is both continuity and discontinuity in the new world. We know that we shall all be transformed but we do 'not yet know what we shall be'. We do not know what our new bodies will be like or in what way we shall be changed. It is very important that we do not know these things. The new humanity is the normative humanity. Everybody who lives is implicated in a fallen world and therefore non-disabled people cannot be used as a norm by which disabled people are compared. Our full humanity will be restored when 'we shall see him as he is' and 'we shall be like him'. The fullness of Christ's humanity was founded on his relationship with the father. In the same way God's relationship with us defines our humanity and completes it when that relationship is perfected.

12. *Healing*

All healing that is rooted in Christ must start from the biblical concept of shalom, the life of the kingdom of God which is wholeness and completeness in fellowship with God, other people and creation. The healing ministry of Christ was to enable people to gain shalom.

We also note that Jesus did not heal everyone in Galilee, and often deliberately withdrew himself from those pressing on him to heal them. Those miracles of healing which he did carry out were unique and specific occasions to each person he encountered. From those encounters we can derive a Christian approach to a ministry of healing which have high standards of integrity and respect for human dignity at its heart.

13. *The Holy Spirit and the disabled*

The Holy Spirit brooded over the creation, groans with the fallen creation, and is the first fruits of the new creation. In Christ, the Spirit is given to all. All should expect to bear his fruit and manifest whatever gift of the Spirit they are given. The Holy Spirit is no discriminator of persons. The Holy Spirit brings all the people of God into one united body. The inclusion of all into the inclusive community of the people of God is the work of the Spirit. We should expect the Spirit to gift and empower disabled people. The purpose of the Spirit is to make us like Christ, not to enable us to see or to walk. A church composed only of non-disabled people is ironic especially as the church is a witness to the body of Christ crucified and risen. Both disabled and non-disabled people must worship together in a community of struggle and a community of celebration.

14. *The church – The inclusive community*

In his body on the cross, Christ broke down the walls of division that had been created out of human differences. Through his cross, those differences are brought into harmony. The church is to demonstrate that reconciliation between non-disabled and disabled just as much as it is to demonstrate the reconciliation between races, genders and classes. In as much as much of the disabling that disabled people experience is as a sinful result of the fall, the church as the new community should demonstrate the victory of Christ over sin and evil as expressed in the ignorance, prejudice and discrimination which disabled people experience, sadly many times in the church itself.

15. *Hope – more truly ourselves*

Our hope is set on the resurrection and the new heavens and the new earth which God will bring at the return of Christ. Our hope, along with the hope of all God's people, is for new and transformed bodies, not that we shall become 'normal'. We do not know what we shall be. But we shall be like Jesus. Just as his resurrection body contained the healed wounds of his spear-scars, our resurrection bodies may well express the healed wounds of our disabilities. Could someone imagine their daughter with Down's Syndrome as being her true self in the new heaven and new earth without some manifestation of her condition?

Texts Relevant For Reflection

Old Testament

'Do not curse the deaf or put a stumbling-block in front of the blind, but fear your God. I am the Lord' (Leviticus 19:14).

'The Lord said to Moses, "Say to Aaron: 'For the generations to come none of your descendants who has a defect may come near to offer the food of his God. No man who has any defect may come near: no man who is blind or lame, disfigured or deformed; no man with a crippled foot or hand, or who is hunch-backed or dwarfed, or who has any eye defect, or who has festering or running sores or damaged testicles. No descendant of Aaron the priest who has any defect is to come near to present the offering made to the Lord by fire. He has a defect; he must not come near to offer the food of his God. He may eat the most holy food of his God, as well as the holy food; yet because of his defect, he must not go near the curtain or approach the altar, and so desecrate my sanctuary. I am the Lord, who makes them holy' " ' (Leviticus 21:16–23).

'For this is what the Lord says: "To the eunuchs who keep my Sabbaths, who choose what pleases me and hold fast to my covenant – to them I will give within my temple and its walls a memorial and a name better than sons and daughters; I will give them an everlasting name that will not be cut off" ' (Isaiah 56:4–5).

New Testament

'One Sabbath, when Jesus went to eat in the house of a prominent Pharisee, he was being carefully watched. There in front of him was a man suffering from dropsy. Jesus asked the Pharisees and experts in the law, "Is it lawful to heal on the Sabbath or not?" But they remained silent. So taking hold of the man, he healed him and sent him away. Then he asked them, "If one of you has a son or an ox that falls into a well on the Sabbath day, will you not immediately pull him out?" And they had nothing to say' (Luke 14:1–6).

'Then Jesus said to his host, "When you give a luncheon or dinner, do not invite your friends, your brothers or relatives, or your rich neighbours; if you do, they may invite you back and so you will be repaid. But when you give a banquet, invite the poor, the crippled, the lame, the blind, and you will be blessed. Although they cannot repay you, you will be repaid at the resurrection of the righteous" ' (Luke 14:12–14).

'There are different kinds of gifts, but the same Spirit' (1 Cor. 12:4).

'Now to each one the manifestation of the Spirit is given for the common good' (1 Cor. 12:7).

'But in fact God has arranged the parts in the body, every one of them, just as he wanted them to be' (1 Cor. 12:18).

'Now you are the body of Christ, and each one of you is a part of it' (1 Cor. 12:27).

'For we are God's workmanship, created in Christ Jesus to do good works, which God prepared in advance for us to do' (Eph. 2:10).

'Is any one of you in trouble? He should pray. Is anyone happy? Let him sing songs of praise. Is any one of you sick? He should call the elders of the church to pray over him and anoint him with oil in the name of the Lord. And the prayer offered in faith will make the sick person well; the Lord will raise him up. If he has sinned, he will be forgiven. Therefore confess yours sins to each other and pray for each other so that you may be healed. The prayer of a righteous man is powerful and effective. Elijah was a man just like us. He prayed earnestly that it would not rain, and it did not rain on the land for three and a half years. Again he prayed, and the heavens gave rain, and the earth produced its crops' (James 5:13–18).

'The Word became flesh and made his dwelling among us. We have seen his glory, the glory of the Only Begotten Son who came from the Father, full of grace and truth' (John 1:14).

'He bent over and looked in at the strips of linen lying there but did not go in. Then Simon Peter, who was behind him, arrived and went into the tomb. He saw the strips of linen lying there, as well as the burial cloth that had been around Jesus' head. The cloth was folded up by itself, separate from the linen' (John 20:5–7).

'Jesus said, "Do not hold on to me, for I have not yet returned to the Father. Go instead to my brothers and tell them, 'I am returning to my Father and your Father, to my God and your God" ' (John 20:17).

'On the evening of that first day of the week, when the disciples were together, with the doors locked for fear of the Jews, Jesus came and stood among them and said, "Peace be with you!" After he said this, he showed them his hands and side. The disciples were overjoyed when they saw the Lord' (John 20:19–20).

'Then he said to Thomas, "Put your finger here; see my hands. Reach out your hand and put it into my side. Stop doubting and believe" ' (John 20:27).

'Jesus said to them, "Come and have breakfast." None of the disciples dared ask him, "Who are you?" They knew it was the Lord. Jesus came, took the bread and gave it to them, and did the same with the fish. This was now the third time Jesus appeared to his disciples after he was raised from the dead' (John 21:12–14).

Twenty-Two

The Politics of the Kingdom of God and the Political Mission of the Church

C. Rene Padilla

Two thousand years ago, according to an ancient report, Jesus went into the province of Galilee proclaiming the good news of God. 'The time has come,' he said. 'The kingdom of God is near. Repent and believe the good news' (Mk. 1.14–25). Ever since those words were pronounced, Christians have struggled to unfold their meaning. What was the 'kingdom of God' that Jesus had in mind? What was its nature? In what sense was it 'near'? Did it actually arrive or was it postponed? If it did arrive, where is it? How can it be recognized? And what is its significance for human life and history here and now?

It is not my intention to discuss all these questions in this paper. My topic here is restricted to the *political* dimension of the kingdom of God

'The Politics of the Kingdom of God and the Political Mission of the Church' by C. Rene Padilla in *Proclaiming Christ in Christ's Way* edited by Vinay Samuel and Albrecht Hauser (Oxford, Regnum, 1989).

and its implications for the *political* mission of the church. Elsewhere I have dealt with other aspects of the biblical teaching on the subject of the kingdom;[1] my objective now is to explore the significance of this teaching for the role of the church in the public arena.

In 1972 a book was published whose purpose was to testify to 'the conviction that, well beyond the questions of formal orientation, there is a bulk of specific and concrete content in Jesus' vision of the divine order, which can speak to our age as it seldom has been free to do so before, if it can be unleashed from the bounds of inappropriate a prioris'.[2] I am referring to John Howard Yoder's *The Politics of Jesus*, a landmark in biblical social ethics. The study began by claiming that, although New Testament scholarship today widely recognizes that Jesus is 'a model of radical political action,' people concerned with social ethics ('the mainstream consensus') assume that Jesus is not relevant to social questions and to problems of power and revolution. [3] Some regard the ethic of Jesus as an ethic for an 'interim' which in his view would be very brief, others as an ethic of a simple rural society, others as an ethic of a small minority unable to influence society, others as an ethic exclusively concerned with spiritual matters, others as an ethic of a radical monotheist that relativized all human values, while others claim that Jesus came to give his life for sin but had no interest in ethics. From any of these points of view, said Yoder, Jesus cannot be seen as intending to provide guidance in the field of ethics. But if Jesus is not normative for ethics, he added, then 'there must be some kind of bridge of transition into another realm or into another mode of thought when we begin to think about ethics . . . the substance of ethics must be reconstructed on our side of the bridge',[4] and that is what the mainstream consensus attempts to do. Finally, 'the reconstruction of a social ethic on this side of the transition will derive its guidance from common sense and the nature of things,' according to what is 'fitting' or 'adequate', 'relevant' or 'effective', 'realistic' and 'responsible'.[5] The study of the realities around us thus takes the place of hearing the proclamation of the Word of God. It was over against this majority consensus that Yoder proposed the task of reading the gospel narrative asking whether in fact there could be an understanding of Jesus that would be 'of direct significance for social ethics' and whether that understanding would be 'not only relevant but also normative for a contemporary Christian social ethic'.[6]

Since Yoder published his book, the religious New Right has emerged on the political scene in the United States, with unprecedented assertiveness and vigor, ready to 'turn America around'. Also in various Latin American countries, especially where Pentecostalism has lately gained an impressive numerical weight (notably Chile, Brazil and Guatemala), Protestant Christians have become involved in politics, no longer believing that 'religion and politics do not mix.' This phenomenon has thrown into relief in a very forceful way, perhaps as never before, the question of the basis, nature, limits and means of political action on the part of Christians. It is at this point that the reflection upon the subject matter of this paper is particularly relevant.

If the gospel of Jesus Christ is good news of the Kingdom of God, and if the Kingdom of God is a political reality, then it is only to be expected that the citizens of that Kingdom raise questions regarding its implications for the political mission of the church. On the other hand, Christians cannot afford to become involved in politics without raising the question as to how their action relates to the Kingdom of God. What is at stake is nothing less than faithfulness to the gospel of Jesus Christ. With this in mind, in the first part of this paper I will consider the political significance of the Kingdom which was inaugurated by Jesus Christ, and in the second part I will attempt to show its implications for the political mission of the church.

I. The Politics of the Kingdom

The Old Testament Background

Christians representing a wide variety of theological positions have openly objected to, or simply assumed, the impracticality of using the New Testament for the ordering of social relations. All too often it is taken for granted that, in contrast with the Old Testament, the New Testament is not concerned with social matters and structures but exclusively with spiritual issues.

The least that must be said in response to that assumption is that the New Testament has to be read together with the Old. After all, the Old Testament *was* the Bible of Jesus and the early church, and that means that the ethical teaching contained in the New Testament does not represent the totality of the ethical instruction given in the first-century Christian communities. The early Christians believed with Paul that Old Testament Scripture was 'God-breathed' and 'useful for teaching, rebuking, correcting and training in righteous-ness [justice]' (2 Tim. 3.16). Therefore, it is quite safe to assume that the deep concern for justice and peace present in the Old Testament was part and parcel of the 'didache' given to believers so that they might be 'thoroughly equipped for every good work' (2 Tim. 3.17). The study of the use that the New Testament makes of the Old to interpret the life and ministry of Jesus and to articulate the meaning of Christian discipleship would go a long way to substantiate that assumption but it lies outside the scope of this paper.

Furthermore, the Old Testament provides the basis for a proper understanding of the New Testament concept of the Kingdom of God. Although the expression 'Kingdom of God' as such does not appear in the Old Testament, the hope of God's intervention in his-tory to establish a new order of justice and peace is one of its basic themes. Beasley-Murray is probably right in suggesting that the absence of the expression could simply be an accident.[7] Quite early in the history of the people Israel, God is acknowledged as the King and the manifestations of his sovereign action call forth their worship. God's kingship is related not only to the past, but also to the present and the future. The hope of the Kingdom reaches full density in the prophets, particularly in the utterances of the preexilic prophets con-cerning the messianic Kingdom. They view the future Kingdom as an unprecedented display of God's power to establish justice and peace in all the earth. From their perspective, history will reach its goal when Yahweh's sovereign rule is universally acknowledged and justice and peace reign.[8]

The peace (*shalom*) of which the prophets speak is not merely absence of war. The term is used as a synonym for salvation and is all-embracing. The prophetic vision of a world of peace foresees a new order in which men and women live in full harmony with God, with one another and with creation. *Shalom* is wellbeing, wholeness, abundance of life. It points to the fulfilment of God's loving purpose for human-kind. And it is inseparable from justice (*tzedakā*); in fact, according to Isaiah 32.17, it is the fruit of justice. It is not surprising, therefore, that a number of Old Testament texts coincide in this emphasis so beautifully expressed in Psalm 85.10: 'Love and faithfulness meet together; justice and peace kiss each other.'

The centrality of justice in the Old Testament can hardly be exag-gerated. Justice is not merely a social convention or a human value but God's passionate concern for the oppressed and the powerless, the marginalized and the weak, the needy and the disenfranchized. To say that God reigns is not to make an abstract affirmation of his sovereignty but to confess him as the living God who, in contrast with the 'gods' of the nations, is moved by and acts in active compassion for the disinherited of the earth. This is why time after time, especially in the Psalms, the affirmation that 'He reigns' or that 'He is King' is coupled with the affirmation that he does what is just and right, that he loves justice and establishes equity, that he judges the world in righteousness (see, for instance, Ps. 89.9–18; 96.10–13; 99.4; 101.12–20; 113.4–9). A good illustration of the very close relationship between God's kingship and his concern for the poor and oppressed is Psalm 146:

> Blessed is he whose help is the God of Jacob,
> whose hope is in the Lord God,
> the Maker of heaven and earth
> the sea and everything in them –
> the Lord, who remains faithful forever.
> He upholds the cause of the oppressed
> and gives food to the hungry.
> The Lord sets the prisoner free,
> The Lord gives sight to the blind
> The Lord lifts up those who are bound down,
> The Lord loves the righteous.
> The Lord watches over the alien
> and sustains the fatherless and the widow,
> but frustrates the ways of the wicked.
> The Lord reigns forever,
> your God, O Zion, for all generations.
> Praise the Lord.

According to many prophetic texts, the Messiah plays a significant role in bringing this Kingdom of justice and peace to consummation. He is 'the representative of Yahweh in his kingdom, in whom Yahweh is present and through whom he acts'.[9] He is the 'anointed one' through whom Yahweh rules over his people and by whom the people are represented before Yahweh. He is thus 'uniquely related to God and man, and as the representative of Yahweh he is the instrument of his rule'.[10] It must be noted, however, that in the new age that he is to usher in there will be not only a new relationship to God and the assurance of heavenly bliss but a new social order of justice and peace.

As Beasley-Murray puts it, 'The hope of Israel is not for a home in heaven but for the revelation of the glory of God in this world, when "the earth shall be full of the knowledge of the glory of the Lord as the waters fill the sea" (Hab. 2:14). As God's claim on man encompasses the totality of his life, so God's salvation for man encompasses the totality of human existence, including our historical existence'.[11]

Jesus and the Kingdom

The central thrust of the New Testament is that Jesus Christ has come to fulfil Old Testament prophecy and that in his person and work the Kingdom of God – the messianic Kingdom of justice and peace – has become a present reality. God has acted definitely in order to fulfil his all-embracing redemptive purpose. In anticipation of the end of 'this age', God's Messiah has appeared in history, and 'the new age' of Jewish eschatological hope has been ushered in.

The centrality of the Kingdom of God in Jesus' proclamation has been recognized by scholars representing a wide theological spectrum. Bultmann, for instance, affirms that 'the heart of the preaching of Jesus Christ is the Kingdom of God',[12] and Jeremias states that 'our starting point is the fact that the central theme of the public proclamation of Jesus is the kingly reign of God'.[13] We must be reminded, however, that Jesus' proclamation was made not only in words but also in terms of his entire life and mission. Behind the various portraits of Jesus in the Gospels stood Jesus of Nazareth, a messianic prophet or prophetic king, 'powerful in word and deed before God and all the people' (Lk. 24.19), in whom and through whom God was acting in a definite way to establish his kingdom.

To be sure, the oldest tradition of Jesus' preaching combines the affirmation of the coming Kingdom as a present reality with the expectation of the future completion of God's redemptive purpose. This simultaneous affirmation of the present and the future gives rise to the eschatological tension which permeates the entire New Testament, and undoubtedly represents a rediscovery of the Old Testament 'prophetic-apocalyptic' eschatology which Judaism had lost.[14] Yet the basic premise of Jesus' mission and the central theme of his preaching is not the hope of the coming of the Kingdom at some predictable date in the future, but the fact that in his own person and work the Kingdom is already present among men and women in great power. He affirms that no one knows the day and the hour at which the eschatological drama will come to its conclusion, 'not even the angels in heaven, nor the Son, but only the Father' (Mk. 13.32). But he also affirms that the beginning of the last act of the drama ('the last days') has already begun in him. The Kingdom is God's dynamic power made visible through concrete signs pointing to him as the Messiah: 'The blind receive sight, the lame walk, those who have leprosy are cured, the deaf hear, the dead are raised, and the good news is preached to the poor' (Lk. 7.22). In other words, God in Christ is showing his passionate concern for the poor; a new eschatological reality is present in human history affecting human life not only morally and spiritually but also physically and psychologically, materially and socially. The promised Kingdom of God is already active among people, although it can only be discerned from the perspective of faith (Lk. 17.20–21; cf. Mt. 12.28; Lk. 11.22). The completion of God's purpose still lies in the future, but a foretaste of the eschaton is already possible.

The way Jesus went about his ministry was such that it could not but puzzle people in general, provoke suspicion in many, and infuriate those who held positions of privilege in the Jewish religious-political establishment. A brief listing of the main features of his work will make that clear:

He speaks with authority despite his lack of theological study, regarded as the essential requirement for the profession of a scribe. He sees himself as a prophet and claims to have the authority of a prophet.

He claims to be related to God in a unique way and addresses him as *'abba,* 'my Father.'

He is 'a friend of publicans and sinners' and eats with them. As a result, he surrounds himself with people who, according to the common convictions of the time, are rejected by God and have no hope of salvation.

He affirms that the Kingdom of God is present in history and being manifest in the healing of the sick, the raising of the dead, the deliverance of the demon-possessed, and the preaching of the gospel to the poor. According to him, the Kingdom of God is not coming by the power of the sword, nor is it intended to satisfy nationalistic Jewish aspirations, nor is it associated with material success and wealth. It is the Kingdom of *God*, and it brings a total inversion of values. Its blessings belong to the poor, to the hungry, to those who weep, and to those who are hated. By contrast, those who are rich, those who are well fed, those who laugh and those who are socially accepted lack its blessings. All of Jesus' ministry throws into relief his special concern for the poor and oppressed. He sees himself as the one that has been anointed by the Spirit of the Lord to preach good news to the poor, to proclaim freedom for the prisoners and recovery of sight to the blind, to release the oppressed, to proclaim the year of the Lord's favour. He interprets his mission in light of God's purpose to establish justice and peace on the earth.

He concentrates his ministry on the uneducated, the downtrodden, the disreputable. He spends much of his time going through all the towns and villages of the underdeveloped province of Galilee, preaching, teaching, and healing. He looks at the harrassed and helpless multitudes with compassionate eyes, for they lack leaders who care for them and therefore have no sense of direction and peoplehood.

He attacks religious oppression and rejects empty religious ceremonies, self-assured piety, and the idea that one's relationship to God is dependent on merit. He is critical of the priests, the teachers of the law, and the Pharisees, and he vividly expresses God's judgment on the religious-political establishment of his day by driving out of the temple those who are selling. He claims that justice and mercy are the objectives of the law.

He condemns wealth and regards greed as idolatry. He himself is poor and lives simply, but his poverty has been freely chosen, not imposed on him by social conditions. He can therefore eat with the rich while at the same time regarding wealth as dishonest and opposed to God. Taking into account the Old Testament prescriptions for the jubilee year, he calls his disciples to redistribute their capital and orders a wealthy man to sell his possessions and give to the poor.

He defines power in terms of sacrificial service and affirms nonviolent resistance as the social stance in full harmony with the Kingdom.

He summons his disciples to social nonconformity patterned on his own and to a community of love and justice, forgiveness and sharing.

The total impression derived from these facts is that Jesus of Nazareth took upon himself a prophetic role in the tradition of the old prophets of Israel. It is not surprising that the most common verdict on him on the part of his contemporaries was that he was a prophet, as suggested by the apostles' answer to his question regarding who people said he was: 'Some say John the Baptist; others say Elijah; and still others, Jeremiah or one of the prophets' (Mt. 16.14; cf. Mk. 6.15; 8.28; Mt. 21.11, 46; Lk. 7.16; Jn. 4.19; 6.14; 7.40, 52; 9.17). Nor is it surprising that when the conflict with the Jewish religious-political establishment came to a head, he was arrested and brought to Pilate under the charge of stirring up the people and inciting them to rebellion (Lk. 23.2, 5, 13). Quite clearly, he had become a public figure, and his words and action were interpreted as a real political threat that had to be countered.

No justice is done to the evidence provided by the Gospels in any reconstruction of Jesus' death that disregards the political charge implied in the *titulus* written on the cross: 'This is the king of the Jews'. He did not die as a religious teacher who had become an unbearable annoyance to the members of the Sanhedrin but as a political rebel whose prophetic public activity could be interpreted as a subversion deserving the penalty that the Romans reserved for seditious provincials at that time: crucifixion.

Yet the cross is not only the logical conclusion of the dramatic conflict between Jesus and the religious-political establishment. It is also the most eloquent expression of the politics of the Kingdom. The giving of himself in death is at the heart of gospel and defines God's method to accomplish his purpose. God's Messiah is 'a crucified Messiah,' the Servant-King who 'did not come to be served, but to serve, and to give his life as a ransom for many' (Mk. 10.45). God's Kingdom of justice and peace is not wrought by the love of power but by power of love. Through the resurrection God has definitely confirmed that the way of Jesus is the way of victory – the victory not of worldly dominion and arrogance but of sacrificial love and service.

The Messianic Community

The Kingdom of God does not merely point to a spiritual reality but to a new order that has been inaugurated in Jesus Christ. Through his life, death and resurrection the powers of the new age have been released in history. God's new creation is taking shape in the world, in the lives of those who acknowledge Jesus as Lord and submit to his rule. The Church is the messianic community, the community of the King.

'Messiah' and 'messianic community' are correlative terms. If Jesus was the Messiah, then it is not at all strange that among other things he should surround himself with a community that recognized him as such. Even a superficial analysis of the evidence leads us to conclude that this is in fact what he did. In his ministry he calls men and women to leave everything to follow him (cf. Lk. 9.57–62; 14.25–33; Mt. 10.34–38). Those who respond to his call become his 'little flock' to whom God desires to give the Kingdom (cf. Mt. 26.31;

Lk. 12.32). They are the ones whom he will acknowledge before his Father who is in heaven (cf. Mt. 10.32ff). They are his family, closer to him than his own brothers and sisters and mother in the flesh (cf. Mt. 12.50).

Jesus is the Messiah through whom the Kingdom of God has become a present reality; his church is the community that comes into existence as a result of his kingly power. That being the case, it is quite clear that the church must not be equated with the Kingdom. As G.E. Ladd has put it, 'If the dynamic concept of the Kingdom is correct, it is never to be identified with the church . . . In the biblical idiom, the Kingdom is not identified with its subjects. They are the people of God's rule who enter it, live under it, and are governed by it. The church is the community of the Kingdom but never the Kingdom itself . . . The Kingdom is the rule of God, the church is a society of men [and women]'.[15]

In God's purpose, after Pentecost the Kingdom of God continues to be a present reality through the gift of the Holy Spirit. He is the agent of eschatology in the process of fulfilment. The church as the body of Christ, on the other hand, is the sphere where the life of the new age initiated in Jesus Christ operates by the power of the Spirit. The importance of this relationship between the Holy Spirit and the church for the correct understanding of the relationship between the Kingdom of God and the church can hardly be exaggerated. The church is dependent on the Spirit for her very existence. So its words and deeds are meant to be the means for the present manifestation of the Kingdom not to be explained as merely human deeds and words. The Kingdom of God does not belong exclusively to the future. It is also a present reality manifested in the Christian community which is 'a dwelling place of God in the Spirit' (Eph. 2.22). The church is not the Kingdom but is called to be the concrete result of the Kingdom. It still bears the marks of its historical existence, the marks of the 'not yet' which characterizes the present time. But here and now it participates in the 'already' of the Kingdom of God that Jesus has inaugurated.

As the community of the Kingdom indwelt by the Holy Spirit, the church is certainly called to be 'a new society' which stands alongside Jews and Gentiles (cf. 1 Cor. 10.31). The church must not be identified with the Kingdom, but it must not be separated from it either. Here and now it is intended to reflect the justice and peace of the Kingdom by the power of the Holy Spirit. This is not to claim that the church is already victorious, but to recognize that the church is 'the Israel of God' (Gal. 6.16), the people of God called to confess Jesus Christ as Lord and to live out that confession. As Lesslie Newbigin has put it, 'It is the community which has begun to taste (even only in foretaste) the reality of the Kingdom which alone can provide the hermeneutic of the message . . . Without the hermeneutic of such living community, the message of the Kingdom can only become an ideology and a program; it will not be a gospel'.[16]

The result of Pentecost was not only power to preach the gospel, but also 'many wonders and miraculous signs' done by the apostles, and a community of people who 'devoted themselves to the apostles' teaching and to the fellowship, to the breaking of bread and to prayer', who 'were together and had everything in common' (Acts 2.42–44; cf. 4.32–37). Pentecost, therefore, meant power for a new lifestyle, including a new economy. The powers of the new age, released by Jesus Christ, were present through his Spirit among God's people, enabling them to be a credible sign of the Kingdom of justice and peace.

II. The Political Mission of the Church

If the Christ of faith is the Jesus of history, then it is possible to speak of Kingdom politics for disciples who seek to fashion their lives on God's purpose of justice and peace concretely revealed in his Messiah. If the risen and exalted Lord is Jesus of Nazareth, then it is possible to speak of a community that seeks to manifest the justice and peace of the Kingdom in the public square.

To be sure, Jesus' example cannot simply be transported to the modern world. The incarnation took place in a particular time and place, and we live in totally different situation. The point here, however, is that because of the life and teaching of Jesus of Nazareth we are not free to understand Christian involvement in politics as if his life and teaching were completely irrelevant. On the contrary, the starting point for *Christian* political involvement is the fact that God has revealed his purpose for human life in a unique man: Jesus of Nazareth. The basic question for Christians today, therefore, relates to the way in which faith is to be lived out in their concrete historical situation. Because the Word became flesh, they cannot but affirm history as the context in which God is fulfilling his redemptive will.

The historicity of Jesus leaves no room for a dualism in which the soul is separated from the body, or for a message exclusively concerned with salvation beyond death, or for a church that isolates herself from society to become a ghetto.

Jesus' prophetic ministry had a shape and colour that corresponded to the historical circumstances in which he lived. Nevertheless, the church today cannot claim to be rooted and built up in Christ unless it both takes due account of Jesus' role and is itself prophetic in its life, teaching, and action. One can hardly exaggerate the urgency that a serious consideration of questions related to religious oppression and legalism, injustice and poverty, wealth and power has for the political mission of the church.

In light of the foregoing discussion, I would propose that what the Kingdom demands at this critical moment of history is nothing less than a revolution of values for the fostering of justice and peace; a restructuring of the Church as the community that exists for sacrificial service to the gospel of Jesus Christ, and a renewed spirituality that brings together worship and public life, evangelism and social responsibility, personal faith and kingdom service.

A Revolution of Values

The church today urgently needs to experience the cross as far more than the cultic symbol of a privatized faith. It needs to experience it as God's victory over the powers of darkness and therefore as a basis to challenge every dehumanizing power that is destroying life in the modern world, be it militarism or consumerism, statism or materialism, individualism or hedonism. From a Kingdom perspective, these 'fundamental principles' of a godless society *must* be questioned for the sake of justice and peace. And they must be questioned wherever they appear, in the North or in the South, in the East or in the West. The real threat to modern civilization is not Soviet expansionism but a system of institutionalized injustice which benefits the wealthy and oppresses the poor. In Costas' words, 'the poor's rights to life must be defended and the machinery of socio-economic oppression and repression that contributes to poverty must be fought'.[17]

If peace is the fruit of justice, then peace and injustice cannot coexist. In the absence of justice only a counterfeit peace is possible: the false security of the oppressors, based on coercion, or the slumber of the oppressed, based on fear, but not real peace; the peace of a cemetery, a concentration camp, or a country under military occupation, but not genuine, lasting peace. *Shalom* can never be the experience of a corrupt society, of a materialistic society obsessed with wealth and indifferent to the plight of the poor; of a hedonistic society oriented towards the satisfaction of artificially-created needs and blind to the suffering of the masses; of a consumer society committed to the idolatry of the fashionable and callous to the misery of the underprivileged; or of a wasteful society given to the ideology of unrestrained economic growth and heartless in the face of the hungry multitudes.

Nor can *shalom* be a reality in a world characterized by international injustice; a world dominated by the lust of political power and oblivious of human rights; a world in which bread is taken out of the mouth of the deprived masses in order to fatten an already overfed elite; a world in which the future generations of the poor nations are economically mortgaged by the rich. The only peace possible in this kind of world is the peace imposed by the 'national security state' a peace totally dependent on persecution and exile, arbitrary arrest and torture, forced disappearances, mutilations and assassinations; a peace built upon bloodshed; a sham peace especially designed for the wealthy, privileged elite, but bought with the lives of the oppressed; a false peace that the poor abhor and the rich cannot fully enjoy; a peace that threatens to blow up modern civilization.

If the fruit of justice is peace, the fruit of injustice is violence and social chaos, enmity and insecurity, hatred and fear. Every injustice committed against the poor carries with it the seeds of subversion. Justice leads to life, injustice ends in death. Injustice not merely violates human rights, but it is a sin against the living God, who loves justice. Therefore, those who persist in injustice place themselves under the judgment of God. 'He who mocks the poor shows contempt for their Maker; whoever gloats over disaster will not go unpunished' (Prov. 17.5).

It follows that the most efficient way to work against peace is to work for injustice, and the most efficient way to work for peace is to work for justice. Sow injustice and you will reap violence; sow justice and you will reap peace. As someone has put it, 'Those who make peaceful revolution impossible, make violent revolution inevitable.' The real choice for the poor today is definitely *not* between freedom and capitalism, on the one hand, and totalitarianism and Marxism, on the other, as if capitalism and Marxism were ultimate realities. The real choice is, rather, between justice and peace, on the one hand, and injustice and violence, on the other.

From this point of view, *the first Kingdom priority today is a revolution of values that places justice above security and peace above economic growth.* The passive accommodation to the 'American Way' of life is cooperation with the 'international dictatorship of economic power' (Helder Camara) and a sad enslavement to the principalities and powers of this world. The acquiescence with the arms race and violence in the name of national security is inimical to faith in the Prince of Peace. The support of a foreign policy that favours vested interests in the name of economic development is contrary to God's will, for he requires 'to act justly and to love mercy and to walk humbly' before him (Micah 6.8).

The prophetic denunciation of every form of injustice and exploitation is an essential aspect of the political mission of the church. Where that denunciation is absent from the Christian witness, the church is unfaithful to God and lacks the authority to proclaim the good news to the poor. 'Woe to Christianity on the day the eyes of the masses are opened, if they believe themselves to have been abandoned to the great and powerful with the connivance of the Church'.[18]

In practical terms, this revolution requires, in the first place, *a process of 'conscientization'* of Christians of both the ethical demands of the Kingdom and the socioeconomic and political situation in the world today. All those who confess Jesus Christ as their Lord have been given the possibility to experience the reality of the Kingdom of justice and peace that he inaugurated in his coming. All of them should perceive the possibility to live out that reality in the midst of a world of injustice and oppression. The need is for a contextual exposition of Scripture to open up these possibilities before the People of God with prophetic passion and pastoral concern.

Conscientization is required by both the rich and the poor. The rich need to see their relation to the poor from a totally different angle. 'As long as the developed world thinks in terms of aid, as long as it is not persuaded that what is at stake is universal justice, there will be no understanding among the peoples of the world, no peace on earth; for peace without justice is a delusion'.[19] The poor need to be liberated from fatalism and to recover a sense of their own human dignity and the possibilities of creative participation in changing their own situation.

The revolution of values requires, in the second place, a *process of cross-fertilization* between Christians from various nations, cultures, and social strata. In Jesus Christ, all the barriers that separate human beings have been broken down. Christians should, therefore, avail themselves of every opportunity to establish meaningful relationships with people (especially the poor and marginalized) who will help them experience the reality of the Kingdom from a different angle and to see things 'from the underside of history'.

The revolution of values requires, finally, a *process of transformation*, both personal and communal, by the power of the Spirit. The new humanity created in Christ is being shaped in history as the humanity that reflects his character and embodies the values of the Kingdom. Christians should be open to the action of the life-giving Spirit and obedient to his leading.

In the final analysis, the revolution of values is the work of the Spirit through his Word and the Christian community. Although it finds its nucleus in the church as the community of the Kingdom, it points beyond the church to God's intention to create a new world of justice and peace. And no one can guess what God may do through a minority that confesses Jesus Christ as Lord and lives by the power of that confession.

A Restructuring of the Church

If the church is to be used by the Spirit as God's witness to justice and peace, however, she must restructure herself for the mission of the Kingdom. Like Christ, the Servant-King, she does not exist for herself but for others; she has been sent 'to preach good news to the poor', 'to proclaim freedom for the prisoners and recovery of sight to the blind, to release the oppressed, to proclaim the year of the Lord's favour' (Lk. 4.18–19). Her life and mission derive their meaning from this over-arching purpose, and her structures are in place when they facilitate its fulfilment.

Accordingly, the church in the Two-Thirds World cannot simply adapt herself to the oppressive colonial structures of society. Nor can the church in the North Atlantic allow herself to become a corporation that accepts the logic of death of the military-industrial complex. Nor can her missionary agencies simply be modeled on the transnational corporations with their criteria for productivity, efficiency and success.

Orlando Costas did well in insisting that if the church is to be faithful to her call, she has to learn to go with Christ, 'Outside the Gate' and to engage herself in 'Mission Beyond Christendom'. In other words, she has to renounce every temptation to become established, accepted, and acceptable to the power holders; she has to take the side of the powerless and marginalized; and she has to organize herself accordingly.

One of the most encouraging signs of the church's renewal in Latin America is the growth of the *comunidades eclesiales de base* ('grass-roots ecclesial communities'). This is not the place to elaborate on the subject, but a few comments on it are unavoidable in relation to the restructuring of the Church for mission. As a matter of fact, these communities that have emerged as the new model for the church in several countries, especially in Brazil, are fundamentally a new articulation of the church for the mission of the Kingdom in a context of poverty and oppression. Defined as 'the church of the poor and from the poor', they function side by side with other popular organizations involved in the struggle for justice. Perhaps more significant from the point of view of the Christian mission, however, is the fact that they have rediscovered the meaning of the priesthood of all believers. In contrast with traditional Roman Catholic theology, they view all Christians as equal members in the body of Christ and, in line with this, believe that they all have a part in the Christian mission. In Leonardo Boff's words, 'The mission of the People of God is not entrusted only to a few but is given to all; sacred power is, initially, held by everyone and only later is held by sacred ministers. All are sent to proclaim the good news about the bright future of history and about the meaning of the world already won and anticipated by the resurrection that makes Jesus' utopia about the Kingdom concrete and real'.[20]

The question remains as to how wealthy churches can release all their potential for the mission of the Kingdom. The answer is that they cannot unless they are willing to disinvest themselves and to break free from the modern military-industrial complex for the service of the hungry, the thirsty, the stranger, the naked, the sick, the imprisoned. Without that, they reflect earthly power but fall far short of the demands of Kingdom.

A Renewed Spirituality

At the very heart of the gospel of the Kingdom is God's intention to create a new world where people are reconciled to him and to one another through Jesus Christ. A gospel that conveys the idea that salvation is a subjective experience of isolated individuals is not the Christian gospel. This is not to deny the importance of conversion and the need for personal commitment. Rather, it is to affirm that being 'born again' is far more than an individualistic religious experience. If anyone is in Christ, there and then God's new world becomes visible, a new creation encompassing heaven and earth is manifest. Forgiveness of sin and God's call to become his 'fellow workers' go together; worship and public life are inseparable.

Orlando Costas saw in this area one of the basic problems of the Christian mission today. In the face of 'an amorphous community with very shallow rootage in the gospel of Christ,' he called for 'healthy growth' – 'a process of holistic development in which the community of faith is fed by new *members*, expands the participation of its members within its *organic* life, deepens *understanding* of the faith, and becomes an *incarnated* servant in its social situation'.[21] This was his way of saying that the church does not exist to promote a private religious experience but to enlist people for the service of the Kingdom of justice and peace.

If the fruits of the gospel are to be made evident in the today's world, far more attention will have to be given to the need for a new spirituality that brings together worship and public life, evangelism and social responsibility, faith and service, prayer and praxis, and enables Christians to be in the world the salt, the light and the leaven of the Kingdom. This kind of spirituality is not merely for 'the chosen few' who are willing to dedicate themselves to 'full-time Christian service', but for all the people of God, regardless of their occupation or station in life.

The third Kingdom priority for the missionary agenda of the church is a renewed spirituality that will help Christians to draw on the resources provided by the Spirit of God to become agents of justice and peace in every area of life.

There is deep crisis in the world today. The imbalance of power between the wealthy countries and the poor, in combination with the internal problems that afflict the latter, has produced a situation of injustice and poverty which is no longer sustainable. In the final analysis, there is here an ethical and spiritual problem. That being the case, the Christian mission today calls for a creative minority that embodies the ethics of the Kingdom, lives by the power of the age to come, and invites people to leave their old ways and to believe that in

Jesus Christ the new creation has broken into history for the healing of the nations.

Notes

1. C. Rene Padilla, *Mission Between the Times*, (Grand Rapids, Wm. B. Eerdmans, 1985).
2. John Howard Yoder, *The Politics of Jesus*, (Grand Rapids, Wm. B. Eerdmans, 1972), p. 6.
3. Yoder, *op. cit.*, pp. 11–12.
4. Yoder, *op. cit.*, p. 19.
5. Yoder, *op. cit.*, p. 20.
6. Yoder, *op. cit.*, p. 23.
7. G.R. Beasley-Murray, *Jesus and the Kingdom of God*, (Grand Rapids, Wm. B. Eerdmans, 1986), p. 17.
8. Beasley-Murray, *op. cit.*, p. 20
9. Beasley-Murray, *op. cit.*, p. 22.
10. Beasley-Murray, *op. cit.*, p. 23.
11. Beasley-Murray, *op. cit.*, p. 25.
12. Rudolph Bultmann, *Jesus Christ and Mythology*, (New York, Scribner's, 1958), p. 11.
13. Joachim Jeremias, *New Testament Theology*, vol. 1: *The Proclamation of Jesus*, (London, SCM Press, 1971), p. 96.
14. George Eldon Ladd, *A Theology of the New Testament*, (Grand Rapids, Wm. B. Eerdmans, 1974b), p. 318ff.
15. Ladd, *op. cit.*, p. 11.
16. Lesslie Newbiggin, *Sign of the Kingdom* (Grand Rapids, Wm. B. Eerdmans, 1980), p. 19.
17. Orlando Costas, *Christ Outside the Gate: Mission Beyond Christendom*, (Maryknoll, Orbis Press 1982).
18. Dom Helder Camara, *Revolution Through Peace*, (New York, Harper and Row, 1971), p. 104.
19. Camara, *op. cit.*, p. 108.
20. Leonardo Boff, *Church, Charisma and Power*, (Maryknoll, Orbis, 1985), p. 155.
21. Costas, *op. cit.*, p. 86.

Twenty-Three

Church And State And Nation Building:
A Conference Report
Hong Kong 1988

Participants

This statement was agreed in principle by the participants in the consultation who entrusted their final revisions to a small editorial team.

Sr Pedro Arana Q. (Peru)
Mr. Mac Bradshaw (Philippines)
Dr. Jonathan Chao (Hong Kong)
Dr. Wilson Chow (Hong Kong)
Ms. Evelyn Miranda-Feliciano (Philippines)

'Church and State and Nation Building' in *Transformation*, Vol. 6, No. 3, July 1989.

Mr. David Fitzstevens (Thailand)
Mr. Keat-Peng Goh (Malaysia)
Dr. Phu Xuan Ho (Vietnam)
Mr. Denison Jayasooria (Malaysia)
Mr. Silawech Kanjanamukda (Thailand)
Mr Somboun Khaopaseuth (Laos)
Rev. Andrew Kirk (UK)
Mr. Tony Lambert (Hong Kong)
Mr. Anand Layraman (Thailand)
Dr. David Lim (Philippines)
Ms. Arlette Laduguie (UK)
Dr. Isabelo F. Magalit (Philippines)
Ms. Melba Maggay (Philippines)
Dr. Dorothy Marx (Indonesia)
Dr. Wayan Mastra (Indonesia)
Evangelist Nana Mensah-Amponsah (Nigeria)
Bishop Michael Nazir-Ali (Pakistan)
Dr. S.B. Pardede (Indonesia)
Mr. Ed Rumberger (Philippines)
Mr. C.B. Samuel (India)
Dr. Herbert Schlossberg (USA)
Dr. Philip Shen (Hong Kong)
Dr. Bong-Ho Son (Korea)
Rev. Dr. Chris Sugden (UK)
Dr. Miroslav Volf (Yugoslavia)
Rev. Dr. Chris Wright (UK)
Rev. Washio Yamazaki (Japan)
Gideon Yung (Hong Kong)

Introduction

We gathered as 33 participants from 15 nations to consult together from October 17–21, 1988 at the Maryknoll Retreat Centre, Stanley, Hong Kong, invited by Partnership in Mission Asia and the Church and State Task Force of the Unit of Ethics and society of the Theological Commission of the World Evangelical Fellowship.

We came together as those with an evangelical commitment who find themselves in a wide variety of Christian traditions, both in evangelical and conciliar denominations. We came to realize we had much to learn on the matter of church and state from Christians beyond our own traditions.

We heard 17 formal presentations on the issues of Church and State from Asia, Africa, Latin America and East and West Europe. We shared with one another testimonies and reports of the experiences of Christians and Churches, especially in situations where they experience pressure.

Participants from Hong Kong shared the emerging concern of their church, not only for religious freedom but also for the protection of human rights under the Basic Law which will be the mini-constitution for Hong Kong after 1997. We also heard of the long experience of faithful witness amidst suffering of the church in China since 1949. Participants told of the difficulties Christians experience in countries where fundamental Islam holds sway, and of the use of the Internal Security Act against Christians in Malaysia. We record our solidarity with them and assure them of our prayers.

We were encouraged to hear of the participation of evangelical Christians along with Roman Catholics and others in the February 1986 revolution in the Philippines and of the continuance and growth of the church in Vietnam and Laos.

We were encouraged to hear of the resources and developments within ideologies and religions with which the church often finds itself in conflict in our nations on matters of church and state. We heard of the emerging understanding of the positive social function of religion in some Marxist states giving greater appreciation of the role of Christians in the building of their societies, and of the resources within Islam for understanding and granting religious freedom to minorities. We give thanks to God for these developments.

We wish to share the privilege we had of meeting together and learning from each other with the wider church by sharing through this report some of our concerns and tentative conclusions.

Freedom of Religion

We became aware that Christian concern for freedom of religion can take many forms. In some cases, regrettably, it can be no more than a concern for the vested interests of a minority group to enjoy freedom for cultic activity. In other cases it can be a concern for all peoples to experience the freedom to choose their beliefs and courses of action, which is God's will for all. In some cases there is disagreement whether a concern for freedom of religion includes freedom to preach the Gospel publicly without hindrance, or whether such concern is adequately met by operating within the limits set by the state power. We became aware that a Christian concern for freedom of religion cannot be at the expense of, but must be set in the framework of a concern for the human rights of all. Religious freedom should be equated more with the ability to develop a culturally relevant, locally led, and spiritually powerful church rather than the freedom to receive input of resources and personnel from Christians from overseas.

Definitions

In order to clarify Biblical principles of nation building, it is necessary first to define the terms used in this report.

(i) *Nation*, for the limited purposes of this report, refers to a people with a geographical boundary and self-government, enjoying the recognition of other nations. We recognize that there are peoples who regard themselves as nations but do not presently enjoy independence. However the subject of church and state limits us to considering nations which also currently exist as states.

We believe that Scripture affirms ethnicity as part of God's creative intention for humanity. Ethnic diversity is not in itself evil, though it is a major contributor to human problems (Babel, Gen. 11). The final kingdom of God will include, not eliminate all ethnic distinctives of humanity (Rev. 7:9, 21:24ff., 22:2). But ethnicity itself is not helpful in defining nations, since nations are fluid and sometimes transient, geographically and historically, a fact recognized in the Bible (Acts 17:26). Several ethnic groups may constitute one nation (e.g. Yugoslavia) or one ethnic group may exist as several nations (e.g. China). Nation building is therefore not to be confused with ethnocentricity, or racism.

(ii) *State* is the political organization of the nation in terms of the exercise of power through government. Government refers to those who rule at a given time. It is necessary to distinguish between state/government and nation. The purpose of the state is not only to make organized life in society possible, but above all, in biblical terms, to promote justice and restrain evil among the people (Rom. 13:1–5, 1 Pet. 2:13). Ideally, then, the state exists for the good of the nation. In reality, it is often the case that the state acts against the best interests of the people and in the interests of those who wield actual power (which may or may not be those who govern politically). Nation building is therefore not to be confused with the glorification of the state.

(iii) *Nation building* means the articulation and promotion of a just social order for the nation as a whole, in which human life, rights and dignities are respected.

(iv) *Human rights* are inherent to human beings as made in the image of God. They include both the freedom rights (e.g. freedom of expression, religion, association, etc.) and rights of sustenance (such as food and shelter).

Biblical and Theological Reflections

Reading the Bible

Historical and cultural contexts often condition responses to the text of scripture. For example a Marxist understanding of social change influences the way scripture is read by some in Latin America; in cultures especially receptive to materialism and the idea of success a prosperity gospel is emerging. We certainly need to respond sensitively to issues that confront a Christian concern for justice. For example in Malaysia, Protestants are working together with Roman Catholics and those of other faiths to secure fair legislation on religious policy.

To protect our commitment to the authority of scripture in such situations we need to

a) read the scriptural text carefully to take into account the tradition of interpretation and insights developed by the churches through the centuries.
b) consult together with other Christians; the extent of the consultation should depend on the significance of the issue at stake.

Church and State

In considering issues of church and state we are tempted to regard the two entities as being exhaustive or ultimate in themselves and therefore to confine ourselves to the relation between the two. It is essential to resist this temptation and to recognize that both church and state – as indeed all human institutions – are subject to Christ who is King of kings and Lord of lords. Thus we insist that neither church nor state be permitted to think of itself as ultimate, but rather be recalled from this idolatry and reminded that it is subject to the will of God.

Biblical resources on the subject of church and state are so vast that we could not adequately handle them all.

In the OT, Israel was the people of God, but their history comprises a wide diversity of modes of existence. It is misleading simply to say that the people of God was identical or co-extensive with the state. They developed through stages, from pilgrim family, to a liberated, theocratic federation of tribes, to an enslaved remnant in a hostile empire, finally to a distinctive ethno-religious community of faith. Each period provides insights and models for discerning the relationship of the people of God to the state. But the controlling paradigm for both, in the historical and the prophetic literature, was the law of God with its demand for justice, equality, brotherhood, compassion and human rights and dignity. We recognize the need for further reflection on how the diversity of models in the OT can function normatively for church-state relations today.

From the OT it seems possible to affirm that whatever form of government a nation may choose, there are certain irreducible elements that are required to conform to God's pattern. Such elements would include the following points, which should be taken into consideration particularly in theological reflection on democracy.

(i) Israel as a people stood before God as covenant partner, not merely as his subjects. It is the interests of the people that forms the beginning and end of all forms of government.

(ii) Under God's rule, Israel was placed under the rule of law. God's personal freedom and will was manifested in objective and concrete rules for all to obey. The rule of law is fundamental to social order.

(iii) The people of Israel stood before God not only as a community but also as individuals. Each individual stood within the covenant and shared its obligations. Each individual likewise was challenged to choose whether or not to follow Yahweh (Josh. 24).

(iv) The right of the people to choose their own form of government was respected by God, even when it conflicted with his best will for them. God acceded to Israel's demand for monarchy, when they persisted in it in spite of warning about its consequences.

(v) The institutional and recognized social role of the prophets in Israel clearly affirms the validity of the voice of criticism and opposition to those who wield political power. The right to appeal to higher authority than that of the state itself and to hold it accountable to God's authority is fundamental.

(vi) In Israel participation in the political process was directly linked to the right of families to have access to the benefits of the land and to enjoy the fruit of their own labour. The jubilee and other OT economic institutions underline the importance of economic viability and freedom to social and political freedom. The economically poor were thereby also politically powerless and the purpose of the restorative measures was not just relief, but to return them to meaningful participation in the community.

The OT points to the *messiah*, The messiah, when he came embodied Israel in all its dimensions. Further, he passed on to his followers the messianic mission (Jn. 20:21). In specifying the content of the messianic mission of the church in relation to the state, we can therefore make use of both the OT 'input' into the messiah, and the NT 'output' of the messiah himself.

In OT Israel, there was recognition of the distinct roles of king, prophet, priest, and wisdom-teacher. These roles are found in Christ also. The church as the body of Christ exercises not only a prophetic role, as is often pointed out, but also has kingly, priestly and wisdom functions in relation to the nation.

The king was executively responsible to do justice in the nation. The social order (or disorder) flowed from him. To say that Christians have a 'kingly' role is not to endorse the church controlling the state, or Christian political parties in government. Rather, it is to highlight our responsibility to see that justice is done. Where Christians live in a democracy (*rule* of the people), they share with all citizens the privilege of political power (in theory), and therefore have the greater responsibility to ensure that it is characterized by justice. The OT model of kingship, however, was servanthood (Deut. 17:14–20; Ps. 72:12–14; Prov. 31:4–9; Jer. 22:1–5; Ezek. 34:1–4).

So the church needs to exemplify, as well as call for, a style of leadership which actually serves.

The prophet was the voice of critique and evaluation of the actions of the king. Prophets were not responsible for administration and executive political action, but they subjected all political action to the standards of God's law, in particular in defence of the weak. The social role of prophets was recognized in Israel inasmuch as they were

consulted and expected to inject the voice of God into the deliberations of the political leaders, though this was not always welcomed.
For the church to be prophetic implies loyal (i.e. non-traitorous)
opposition to, or responsible (i.e. non-sycophantic) approval of, the
actions of the state, on behalf of the people. It also means being prepared to be unpopular and to suffer for speaking up for God's
demands as the moral conscience of the nation.

The separation of king and prophet in Israel has implications for
the church in relation to the state. The two roles require the gifts and
resources of the whole church. The church as an *institution* does not
exhaust the meaning or scope of the *visible church*. So, while a local
church or a denomination in its prophetic moral critique may not
become political in the sense of clerics telling rulers precisely how to
manage state affairs, politically gifted and informed Christians may
corporately exercise visible Christian presence in political life by
forming pressure groups, or individually accepting public office (the
'kingly role') and other such means as are available within a given
political system.

The priest mediated between God and the rest of the nation. On
the one hand he represented God to them through teaching the law,
and on the other, he represented them to God through sacrificial
atonement and intercession. God gave Israel the role of being his
priesthood in the midst of the nations (Ex. 19:4–6), and the same role
belongs to the church (1 Pet. 2:9). The church therefore, has the
priestly role of making God known to the nation (which means, his
character, demands and purposes), and to bring the nation to God
(in prayer and evangelism, cf. 1 Tim. 2:1–4; Rom. 15:16).

The Wisdom literature both holds up ideals (Proverbs) and also
faces fallen realities (Eccles., Job). It is full of reflection and comment on the ambiguities of political social and economic life, both as
God intends it and as humanity experiences it. The church is called
to bring godly wisdom to the nation, both exalting his standards,
and wrestling with realities.

In the New Testament, the messiah inaugurated the *Kingdom of
God*, already defined in its moral and social dimensions in the OT. In
terms of its relevance to the state, we noted the following points.

(i) The Kingdom of God relativizes all human power and authority.
For the disciple and the church, it alone has ultimate allegiance and
receives highest priority (Matt. 6:33). Jesus was not known for excessive deference to those who exercised political authority: the religious
authorities of the nation of Israel, Herod, and the Roman state. He

called the nation of Israel to fulfil its God-given mandate to be the servant of God to the nations. He rebuked its leaders, broke its codified rabbinical laws (the sabbath), and formed a new community within it to carry out its calling. The nation's leaders understood and identified him as a mortal threat to its life. But he claimed that the destruction of Jerusalem, which would be the end of Israel's national life, would vindicate his ministry. He called Herod, king of Israel and client of Rome, 'that fox'. He recognized the imperial might of Rome as accountable to God, even while it had claim to taxation (Matt. 22:21). Before its chief executive in Israel, he declared the invasion of a kingdom which would change the world but did not owe its power and authority to this-worldly sources (John 18:36). Such was the power of this kingdom that its servants had no need to fight to extend it. Within the economy of this kingdom, non-retaliation may transform enemies and even dying is ultimately productive.

The early church indirectly continued Jesus' challenge to the state to fulfil its high calling under God. Both Peter and Paul disobeyed or resisted human political power when used wrongly. Yet Paul also identified the state as being God's servant for good, and he personally demonstrated what his view of revelation required, namely that the church witness to the state the nature of the good it should uphold (Romans 13:4; Acts 22:25). The early Christian confession, 'Jesus is Lord', relativized all claims of the state to ultimate allegiance, since it was articulated in contradistinction to the claim of the Roman emperor to be lord. And for this confession Christians were prepared to die labelled as political subversives.

(ii) The Kingdom of God invades the kingdom of satan and evil. The NT teaching on the principalities and powers perceives the reality of spiritual, potentially demonic, power behind political authorities. When the state claimed ultimate allegiance, or systematically regarded evil instead of good, it could be portrayed through the OT picture of a beast, oppressing and deforming God's creation and God's people. We recognize therefore that if nation building involves promoting justice in the midst of the world's evil, then this will entail not only social struggle but also spiritual warfare. Christian nationalism and participation in nation building must therefore be as much centred on the power of the cross and the victory of resurrection as any other dimension of Christian life in the world.

(iii) The Kingdom of God is the affirmation of life (in all its fulness) against death (in all its forms). The role of the Holy Spirit in the ministry and teaching of Jesus is crucial here, for the Holy Spirit is the giver of life and of freedom (2 Cor. 3:6, 17), which coincide markedly with the objectives of true nation building. The Holy Spirit is also the creator of the new humanity, which is the desire of many nation building efforts. Further, it is the Holy Spirit who enables Christians to 'put all things to the test and hold fast to that which is good', so that we may be 'whole in body, mind and spirit', which is the nature of true *shalom*, peace (1 Thess. 5: 19–23; 2 Thess. 3:16). It is the Kingdom of God which provides the true values, objectives, and dynamic for participation in nation building.

Nation Building

As Christians, we participate in nation building as an affirmation of the lordship of Christ over the whole of human life and our need to make a holistic obedient response to it. Since nation building means promoting the welfare of the people, physically, mentally, spiritually and socially, it must include evangelism as the sharing of the gospel in its wholeness and applying it to every perceived need in the community.

Preaching the Gospel and challenging people to conversion are an essential task of the church. We affirm that the process of conversion can contribute positively to the education of citizens in their humanity, dignity and rights, and thus can have beneficial consequences for nation building. However, nation building in the above sense does not depend upon a majority in the nation being converted. Regrettably we have to admit that experience shows that even large scale conversion does not necessarily or automatically lead to nation building or a just social order. Our involvement is on the basis of God's creation of all human beings in his own image, and our appeal to fellow citizens presupposes that they are accountable to him and are subject to his moral law, simply as human beings. Christian participation in nation building on this basis and for these objectives can exist when Christians are a tiny minority.

Nationalism

Nation building requires healthy nationalism (or, as some would prefer to call it, patriotism). For many Christians this has often been undesirable because of its negative and quasi-religious aspect, and this has been one reason among many that has led them to opt out of nation building altogether. However, nation building in the positive sense described requires a responsible nationalism consistent with Christian loyalty to God alone and submission to the lordship of Christ. We therefore tried to identify criteria for distinguishing true from false nationalism.

A fundamental guide for Christian conduct in any sphere is the twin commandment (both OT and NT) to love God totally and to love the neighbour as oneself. Put negatively, this means no idolatry and no chauvinism.

(i) *The Christian cannot identify with a nationalism which is idolatrous, that is, which treats the state or nation as ultimate in any sense, or glorifies them as virtually divine.* Where nationalism has become idolatrous, the Christian must resist it and refuse to participate (e.g. Shadrach, Meshach, Abednego, Dan. 3). In such a case, nation building may actually involve denying idolatrous nationalism as part of the 'tearing down' that must accompany or precede 'building up' (Jer. 1:10). Jeremiah, though a fervent nationalist in desiring the welfare of his people, was branded a traitor because he resisted the policies of the state. Subject to that, however, the Bible affirms that the people of God may serve the secular state (Joseph and Daniel), and are obliged to honour and submit to it, under God and for Christ's sake (Rom. 13; 1 Pet. 2). There is, therefore, a godly nationalism, short of idolatry, to which Christians can subscribe.

(ii) *The Christian cannot identify with a nationalism which ignores the needs of the neighbour.* Because Christians readily assent to the rejection of idolatry, this criterion needs to be emphasized more strongly, since there is the danger of subscribing to a nationalism which does not appear to be idolatrous (and may even be professedly Christian), but which fails in the criterion of neighbour-need. In biblical terms, the neighbour is primarily anyone in need. Special concern is commanded for the vulnerable, the powerless, the poor, the marginalized and victims of racial discrimination. Godly nationalism is concerned for such groups – *inside and outside one's own nation*. It therefore rejects nationalism that promotes the glory of the nation in ways that either ignore or worsen the plight of the poor within the nation (e.g. through the prestige of high profile weaponry, superfluous and expensive technology which does not benefit the poor, etc.), or depends upon the external exploitation of the poor in other countries (e.g. through economic imperialism, unfair trading, protectionism, etc.). Subject to this, true nationalism implies, and the Scripture affirms, love for one's own people and passionate desire for their welfare.

Paul exemplifies both criteria. He professed such love for his own people that he would exchange his personal salvation for theirs (Rom. 9: 1–5, 10:1). But he subordinated every aspect of his national heritage and personal cultural identity to the supremacy of knowing and serving Christ as Lord (Phil. 3:4–8). Similarly, the OT is a testimony to Jewish nationalism in both positive and negative senses. As a nation, they were chosen to be witnesses to the uniqueness, power and redemptive acts of God in the midst of the nations. In contrast, their repeated idolatry was not merely religious but put the state and its policies in the place of faith in the sovereignty of Yahweh. Nationalism easily became chauvinism, which Jonah, the man, illustrated, and Jonah, the book, was probably written to counter. Equally, Israel was chosen, in Abraham, to bring blessing to all the nations. A major feature of this was to be by modelling the righteousness and justice of God in their social order (Gen. 18:19). In contrast, they succumbed to injustice and oppression, especially at the high points of their national pride and power (e.g. Solomon, the 8th. century) and became 'like the nations'. The church has often failed in the same way by exercising or endorsing idolatrous national arrogance or participating in systems of state power which oppress the neighbour.

Further Resources for Study and Issues for Reflection Include:

Moses, and the work of national construction: his modelling, the laws and institutions of Sinai.

The jubilee, as a model of holistic concern for people – economic viability, social dignity and power, spiritual response to the sovereignty of God, and future hope,

Nehemiah and Ezra, and the work of national reconstruction.

Daniel, serving God *and* the state, with integrity to both.

Acts, and the resistance to authorities, but use of citizenship.

The Bible affirms that God can and does use secular nations as agents of his purposes, in judgement and in deliverance. This raises the question of whether or not other nations, then or now, participate in salvation history, and what implications our view of this will have on church-state relations.

What methods are legitimate and appropriate for Christians in participating in nation building with others?

To what extent Christians can join with people of other faiths in nation building, if it includes participating in multi-faith religious events?

The ways in which the state makes use of religious power.

A Christian Vision for Society

A Christian concern for society holds up a vision of a just social order. Such an order has the following marks:

1) The preservation, promotion and defence by the state of the right to life for every person.
2) A political constitution which sets limits to the scope of political action so that the basic rights of the people, such as freedom of speech, of religion, of thought and of assembly are not infringed, and which is upheld by an independent strong judiciary.
3) Equal protection for all under the law.
4) Access to enjoy the benefits of one's own labour.
5) The right of people to decide who shall govern them, and to be able to hold such a government accountable with regard to its competence and honesty.
6) The biblical testimony clearly expresses the spirit of democracy. Israel as a people is regarded as a covenantal partner with God, not just as his subjects. God ceded to Israel the choice of its own forms of government (1 Sam. 8). It was even given the freedom to renew or not to renew the covenant with God (Joshua 24).

We now consider the issues of church-state relations as they are presented in three types of government under which the church lives in the world.

Parliamentary Democracies

To express Christian values about humanity, democracy must embrace social, political and economic democracy. It must express the Christian concern for equality and for the dignity of each person; one person should not rule over another without freely given consent and each person should have the right to take part in the making of those decisions which affect his/her life.

Democratic systems cannot guarantee just and fair results. Democracies are vulnerable to influence by other means of power. The temptation of power can influence the media and public officials to use their office for private gain. Parties in power can use their executive authority to manipulate the process of representation in their favour, or if they have large enough majorities in some cases to change written constitutions where they exist.

The reliance on majority rule must not be taken in a democratic system to justify the oppression of minorities. Therefore decision-making in democracies which fulfils the concern for protection of minorities, freedom and democracy is better based on a process of consensus which for example in some cases is obtained through discussion and, in some, by processes of voting through proportional representation.

Christians corporately and individually have a vital role in protecting some of the processes on which democracies depend for their just functioning.

1. To engage in moral and political education so that people know their rights and the working of the democratic process, and are instilled with a respect for their country's democratic constitution and institutions. This enables them to want what is just and fair.
2. To encourage just and fair elections; where appropriate, by campaigning for an election commission which is independent of the executive power; by engaging in the monitoring of election.
3. To encourage active participation in the political system and the nation building process.
4. To encourage and defend a free press.
5. To do research and study which will provide the information necessary for suggesting and formulating policy initiatives. Research Institutions and informal networks of Christian thinkers, to monitor policy developments and set out just and equitable proposals, can make an important contribution.
6. To protest and suggest changes when unjust policies are proposed and implemented.

For Christians to carry out this role with integrity,

1. they have to ensure that in their relationships and functioning as individuals and groups they model the values that they expect the state to demonstrate.;
2. they need to accept with humility that there are others outside the Christian faith who are also concerned about the same values and participate in cooperative actions with them without compromising a basic commitment to the gospel.

These are six processes for Christians to defend in a parliamentary democracy, which we believe is the system that has best protected human rights. These processes should also be pursued where possible by Christians living under other systems of government.

Socialist Societies

Introduction

We understand socialist societies to be nation-states in Marxist-Leninist tradition in which the Communist Party has the monopoly of power.

Since we are concerned for the well-being of all peoples of the world, we want to encourage processes of democratization within socialist societies which obtain in 40% of the world's population. And since the churches that live in these societies are a part of the world-wide body of Christ of which we too are members, we want to challenge the governments of these societies to guarantee the churches constitutional and legal rights to live freely all aspects of their Christian faith.

Democratization and Human Rights

We recognize and value the processes of increased democratization currently occurring in many socialist societies. We would want to encourage these socialist societies which exhibit all characteristics of totalitarian societies to follow the best examples of democratic opening in the socialist societies. In order to foster the processes of democratization in all socialist societies we encourage freedom of the press, free access to information, independence of the judiciary, secrecy of balloting, nomination of the candidates by the people, and complete freedom of movement for all members of the society.

Socialist societies have highly valued and striven to implement such important human rights as the right to work and the right to a free education. Christian faith leads us to appreciate those rights and we want to encourage the socialist societies not to allow these rights to be eroded (as they are in some countries) under pressure of economic crisis. We are also concerned that other fundamental human rights are not being attended to and sometimes blatantly violated in socialist societies, such as the freedom of expression, thought, conscience, religion, association, and assembly.

We encourage churches throughout the world to raise their voices with due sensitivity to local situations, in order to bring international pressure on oppressive governments to respect all human rights (including freedom of religion of all religious groups). We recognize that churches within socialist societies will often not have the luxury of raising issues of human rights and would encourage churches abroad not to interfere with the response of domestic churches to human rights issues. Yet as the circumstances allow them, churches in socialist societies too should express their concern for human rights in their countries. Since the concern for human rights is an important aspect of the prophetic role of the church, churches in socialist societies should begin the human rights conscientization process within their own ranks and not succumb to false spiritualization of their faith.

The Church in Socialist Societies

Both constitutional and legal provisions about the relation between church and state, and the vigour with which these provisions are practically implemented, differ from one country to another, ranging from the more liberal policies of countries like Laos and Yugoslavia to the very restrictive policies of countries like North Korea and Albania. In general, however, socialist societies perceive the relation of their governments to the churches in the following ways:

(1) citizens are constitutionally guaranteed freedom of religion;
(2) church is separated from the state;
(3) religion is exclusively a private affair of individuals;
(4) churches are free to conduct religious activities within the constraints prescribed by the government;
(5) one of the tasks of the Communist Party is to actively promote the 'inevitable' fading away of religion.

In general, our concern about church-state relations in socialist societies is twofold: the actual behaviour of the state toward the church in socialist societies should not lag behind some of these stated policies and the stated policies should be consistent with the universal declaration of human rights (which most of these states affirm). In particular we want to raise the following issues in church-state relations in socialist societies:

1. We urge the governments to ensure that there are no abuses of authority in the interpretation and implementation of existing laws (in particular at the local level), which result in the mistreatment of individuals and intimidation of communities.
2. We urge that the principle of separation of church and state be consistently observed and that governments of socialist societies cease intruding into the life of the church and attempting to manipulate it to serve their domestic or international purposes.
3. We would encourage socialist societies to distinguish in theory and practice between *state* (the formal organization of the society for purposes of government) and *society* (the sum-total of citizens and their non-governmental organizations and activities) as some Marxist philosophers have done and hence acknowledge that there is a sphere of responsible action that can be social without necessarily infringing on the political realm. From a Christian perspective such a distinction is essential for the life of the church in socialist societies because of the inherent social-public dimension of the Christian faith. While we are critical of the tendency to manipulate religion for political purposes, we are at the same time encouraged to see some Marxists recognizing that biblical values (such as justice, peace, dignity of human personhood, etc.) can contribute to the well-being of the society. To the extent that socialist governments distinguish in practice between state and society, the domestic and foreign churches will be able to make the same distinction; which would enable them to see more clearly how they can make a positive contribution to the building of their societies.
4. Instead of relegating Christian faith to be a private affair of individuals, we urge the governments of socialist societies to provide opportunities for the church's active involvement in the resolution of social problems (such as alcoholism, drug addiction, homelessness, etc.).

5. We urge that more just and/or adequate laws be passed in relation to religious communities (e.g. abolition of the prohibition to educate young people in religious belief).
6. We urge that all religion be not indiscriminately viewed as a socially detrimental superstition and Christian believers be not treated as alien elements in the society, with the result that they are barred from full participation in the economic, social, and political life of the nation at all levels.
7. We urge socialist governments not to repeat unreflectingly the classical Marxist critique of religion. Though we recognize that in many respects Marx's critique of religion was and is accurate, we encourage honest sociological and psychological research of the *actual* function of Christian faith in society. We believe that such research would prove that the critique of religion both as opiate *of* the people and opiate *for* the people does not apply to authentic Christianity.

In order to facilitate a better relation between church and state in socialist societies we make the following recommendations to churches living in these societies:

1. We recommend that in socialist societies wherever possible believers participate in and encourage Marxist-Christian dialogue in order to build mutual understanding and trust, without compromising their Christian faith.
2. We appreciate the opportunities Christians and churches within socialist societies have, to exchange information and resources among themselves and encourage their increased networking in order to expose the believers to other Christian responses in similar situations.
3. We encourage the churches to reflect not only upon their relation to the state but also upon their relation to the society in which they live. This will enable them to be more ready to make positive contributions to nation-building.

Foreign Churches and Churches in Socialist Societies

We consider it essential for the worldwide Body of Christ outside of socialist societies (the church abroad) to nurture relations of equality and mutual respect with the churches in socialist societies. The church abroad should listen and learn from the domestic churches and make every effort to avoid paternalistic attitudes. It should be aware that the degree of liberty a church enjoys is not the measure of its spiritual health. Reliable research centres should be established and used by those wanting to help churches in socialist societies. Groups concerned abroad should prayerfully and cooperatively work together, share information for the benefit of Christ's church within socialist societies and recognize the legitimacy of different approaches to cooperating with Christians in socialist societies.

The church abroad should encourage the production and use of printed materials, radio and TV programmes by Christians in socialist societies. Those involved in the production of such materials abroad should humbly work in response to the needs and directives of the domestic churches. Churches abroad should use discretion when describing the situation of socialist societies and in particular the situation of the church in these societies, especially when raising funds.

Christians from abroad should be encouraged to go to live in socialist societies and assist in nation-building where needed and desired. They may consider involvement in the modernization programmes, and present projects of such programmes to policy-makers and develop them. Christians from abroad should encourage the exchange between their home countries and socialist societies at all levels, and in particular get involved in dialogue with intellectuals and political leaders of socialist societies.

The churches abroad should take pains to prevent abuses of church relationships by foreign governments.

Authoritarian States

Authoritarianism defined

An authoritarian state is usually characterized by (a) the use of power beyond its original purpose, (b) the resort to one-man rule and the exclusion of people from the decision-making process, (c) self-perpetuation through the use of the military as a coercive force, the guises of formal democratic procedure, such as rewriting the constitution and a curtailed judicial process, the suppression of dissent and an appeal to national security and economic stability; for example in a benevolent dictatorship.

The Content of Religious Freedom in An Authoritarian Situation

Is religious freedom a Western concept that has its roots in a human-istic understanding of inalienable rights? The habit of making a conceptual divide between 'Western' and 'non-Western' understand-ings of religious freedom may be counter-productive in that it tends to legitimize authoritarianism, e.g. strongman rule as consistent with indigenous political tradition in Asiatic and Latin cultures. It is worth noting that rights now considered 'inalienable' – human rights and religious freedom – are themselves products of a long history of struggle in the West against autocratic monarchies and the dubious synthesis of church and state in medieval culture.

Religious freedom is better located in the concept of biblical jus-tice, of people made in the image of God, and therefore intrinsically gifted with dignity and freedom of choice. The liberty to choose one's religion, to worship and bear witness are inalienable rights that proceed from this premise. Ultimately, the freedom to preach and worship is not something a government gives or takes away. The Word of God is unfettered.

Are our expectations regarding the minimum content of religious freedom disproportionate to what the church historically has been prepared to live with? The Early Church suffered restraints in a con-text of absolute despotism. In the same way, present legal constraints in religiously hostile environments need not deter efforts at faithful and persevering witness, although acceptance of curtailed movement may sometimes lead to stagnation in the church, as has happened in Islamic countries.

Persecution as both a hindrance and opportunity for growth calls for a transforming vision as well as the acceptance of restraint and suffering. While the Early Church laboured under a social structure where racism, female inferiority, and the terrible institution of slavery were regarded as natural and necessary, it nevertheless held out a vision of a transformed society where privilege and prejudice no lon-ger exist between men and women, Jew and Gentile, slave and free (Gal. 3:28).

How the Church Can Operate in An Authoritarian Context

The church must assist societies that have only learned the form but not the substance of democratic procedure to move towards a consciousness which is critical of the traditional autocratic strain in the culture.

Even in a situation where the church is a minority and operates under severe political restraint, it has a duty to critique the abuse of power and infringements of both political and religious rights.

Wisdom should discern when to push an advantage or test the limits of what is allowable, and when to be discreet when conditions signal retreat. Respect and tolerance are due both to brethren who see public witness as essential to maintaining loyalty and those engaged in disciplined witness within legal constraints.

Appeal can be made to formal provisions in the legal structures, e.g. the principle of equality under Islamic law in cases where the church needs to assert its cultic rights, and the universal declaration of human rights.

Help from the outside could take the form of the world-wide body of Christ assisting beseiged churches in authoritarian regimes by putting pressure on their respective governments to use economic and other sanctions that would soften hard-line restrictions and oppression. This would serve as a complement or an alternative to direct missionary input where such external resource is either unwanted or unhelpful.

The church must make its suffering known to the outside world.

Conclusion

In many of the situations from which we have come there is a threat to freedom of expression. It is possible that along with members of our churches we may be called on to suffer for speaking the truth in love in our contexts. So we make a commitment to each other to stand together in solidarity ready to suffer with each other. On the basis of our unity in the one universal church of Jesus Christ, which is his body throughout the world, we call the church in whatever situation it finds itself to stand with us in the concerns we have identified and to pray for our common witness.

Twenty-Four

Freedom and Justice in Church State Relationships
Osijek, Yugoslavia, April 1991

1. Preamble

We 85 participants representing the continental bodies in Africa, Asia and Latin America which form the International Fellowship of Evangelical Mission Theologians – with associates from North America and Europe – met at Osijek, Yugoslavia from April 10–16 1991 in the 4th Conference of this Fellowship (following Bangkok, Thailand 1982; Tlayacapan, Mexico, 1984; and Kabare, Kenya, 1987).

Among our number were professional theologians, missiologists, pastors, including two bishops representing large dioceses in Africa, sociologists, politicians, lawyers and social activists. We came together as persons with an evangelical commitment from our contexts of mission. We learned together, shared insights and encouraged

'Freedom and Justice in Church State Relationships' in *Transformation*, Vol. 8, No. 3, July 1991.

one another in our common witness to the relevance of the Gospel of Jesus Christ to the struggles for freedom and justice in the world.

We had with us the Second Vice-President of Peru, an evangelical Christian who participated in all the sessions. His presence made us vividly aware that in several countries around the world, particularly in Africa and Latin America, evangelical Christians are beginning to be actively involved in the political life of their nations. This underlined the significance of our theme. We have reflected on the theme: 'Freedom and Justice in Church–State Relations', with special emphasis on the new found political freedom of the peoples of Eastern Europe, the rights of ethnic minorities to exist and express their own identities, and the problems facing religious minorities.

We visited Orthodox, Roman Catholic, Lutheran, Baptist and Pentecostal churches, met their leaders and experienced the complex relationship between religion, ethnic identity and state organisation in a historical moment of great fluidity.

In this context we reflected on the following issues:

2. The Missiological Implications of the Collapse of Bureaucratic Socialism in Eastern Europe

The invitation to meet in Osijek, Yugoslavia was extended at our third consultation in Kabare, Kenya in August 1987. We could not have envisaged at that time that as part of this conference we would be welcomed to a civic reception by the first democratically elected mayor of Osijek in nearly 50 years, that public prayer would be said in the City Chambers at the conclusion of the reception, nor that our proceedings would attract the attention of the press, radio and television.

We rejoice at the increased freedom enjoyed by our sisters and brothers in Yugoslavia. We realize that there have been many sides to the witness of the church in Eastern Europe. Some churches of different traditions in Eastern Europe were at the forefront of the changes in 1989. Other churches were more hesitant to take part in the changes. We also wish to pay tribute to the churches which suffered in Eastern Europe and recognize this witness of the servant church to the cross of Christ as authentic discipleship.

It is also remarkable that the historic changes in the region took place for the most part relatively peacefully and in the eyes of many Christians this was directly related to sustained prayers. There is an urgent and continuing need for a revival of prayer and spirituality, not only among Christians in Eastern Europe, but wherever Christians have to cope with oppressive political or religious regimes.

In the new situation the Eastern European churches are facing new challenges. They need not only to adapt their commitment to evangelism in creative ways that respond to the new conditions, but also to rediscover their responsibility for socio-economic realities. They need to place their 'theology of martyrdom' within the broader concept of uncompromising Christian discipleship in all the spheres of life.

The challenge to churches in the West is to collaborate as servant-partners with their Eastern sisters in a fashion that is supportive and not religiously imperialistic. Another concern for the Western Church is to be careful to refrain from introducing uncritically Western values and ways which may be culturally inappropriate for others. Nevertheless, material and personal resources and visions of faith may be shared in a way that glorifies God.

While recognizing the urgent opportunity for involvement in Eastern Europe, this must not be at the expense of continued partnership with Two-Thirds World churches. We urge Western churches to protest against the tendency of their governments to divert aid from the third world to Eastern Europe rather than increase their overall aid budgets. We continue to affirm that aid alone should not be seen as a substitute for needed global structural economic changes.

Not only has the barrier fallen between the so-called first and second worlds, but also between the second and third worlds, inasmuch as the countries of Eastern Europe are increasingly facing similar economic and social problems as are plaguing the third world. While we celebrate the breaking down of totalitarian regimes and the attempts at democratization in Eastern Europe, we are deeply concerned with the simplistic proclamation of the victory of capitalism which, when coupled with unjust political systems, has had such a devastating effect in the Two-Thirds World. The collapse of state socialism in Eastern Europe cannot be regarded by Christians as a simple legitimation of capitalism, but on the contrary has shattered dreams in parts of the world where communism provided an alternative idealistic vision. It has also led to a vacuum of economic alternatives to capitalism as a global project. It is all the more urgent for Christians to develop Christian principles and advocate economic models such as are presented in the Oxford Declaration on Christian Faith and Economics of January, 1990. (See Transformation April 1990)

At the same time, these recent events in Eastern Europe have strengthened the movement for freedom and democracy in other parts of the world, especially in Africa. While the movement for more participatory forms of government in Africa predates *perestroika*, it has received significant encouragement from it, thus enabling a Christian view of persons in society to find a fuller expression in the political order.

The missiological implications also need careful discernment. The European collapse of bureaucratic socialism does not invalidate the concern for justice in a holistic understanding of Christian mission. Liberation theology has often been castigated for dependence on Marxist analysis and social objectives. But its concern for the poor and for the earthing of theology in practical engagement on their behalf has biblical roots which do not depend on Marx.

There is a long tradition of Christian social criticism before Marx and Christian theologians need not be beholden to Marx for their social vision. Many questions about the negative social consequences of capitalism were raised by Christians before Marx proposed a systematic critique of it. Totalitarian state socialism's failed answers do not invalidate those questions or release us from the task of finding biblical responses.

Bureaucratic socialism sought at some points to enshrine values which have independent validity in biblical revelation, especially justice in the distribution of goods and services in society. It behoves those committed to such values as a dimension of biblical mission to find more appropriate ways of expressing them in the changed economic, social and political directions of increased freedom. Neither freedom nor justice should be at each other's expense.

3. Religious Freedom in the Context of a Dominant Religion

In creation God has granted to men and women the freedom to respond to his love in obedience or not. Coercion has no place in the opening story of the world until humanity has made its own response to the Creator's world. Following from this aspect of the biblical doctrine of humanity, Christians must be prepared to allow for genuine religious pluralism in society. It is unacceptable for state systems to espouse any one religious expression in such a way that other religious groups find that their God-given rights to life, participation in society, and to believe and propagate their faith are politically or socially denied.

In whatever way the relation of church and state be understood, whether as complete separation, or where religion has a formal place in the life of the civil society, what is required of the state is religious neutrality. This means that if religious conflict arises, the state must ensure that the dominant religion is not allowed to oppress minority religions. The state must not favour one religion or allow its own apparatus to be co-opted by dominant religious control, or interfere with the religious freedoms of any group. In short, the state must provide the social and political framework which guarantees the unhindered exercise of religious freedom. Countries which are signatories to the United Nations Universal Declaration of Human Rights should enforce it in order to make this a reality.

Religions also have self-limiting responsibilities in relation to the state. The conference received papers from different contexts where religious domination of the state leads to oppression. In several Latin American countries, Roman Catholicism, with state permission, has severely restricted the religious freedom of other minority religious communities. In some Islamic contexts, Islamic dominance has continued to be exercised over religious minorities through the application of the historical *dhimma* system, in varying degrees in different Islamic states, from very severe restrictions on religious freedom and human rights to rather milder practices. We have also heard concern from several East European countries where the predominant 'national' Orthodox churches claim monopoly on the religious lives of their nations and discriminate against Protestant minorities. And it must not be overlooked that Protestantism, sometimes with clear evangelical orientation, with clear evangelical orientation, has served in some contexts as legitimisation for oppression.

Nevertheless, movements based on Protestant theology and ethics have sometimes contributed to the break-up of the dominance of religiously totalitarian regimes and traditions. When this has occurred, the resulting situation imposes limits on government. It can no longer impose particular world views or social projects against the will of the people. Yet clearly evangelicals cannot agree with a relativization of *moral* values which we believe to be grounded in biblical revelation. How are the values of Christian faith to be brought to bear on public policy? Another important area which illustrates the clash between the desire for social pluralism and the ejection of ethical or religious relativism is the matter of religious education in public (state) schools.

In the interests of freedom and justice, Christians must apply the Golden Rule to do to others what they would like others to do to them and ensure religious freedom to others. As Christians we confess that we have not always granted religious freedom to other religious groups living among us. We resolve to change and to defend religious freedom for all in the spirit of the Lord's injunction to servanthood.

4. Biblical Faith and the Desacralisation of Power

The recognition that all authority comes from God relativises all human use of power. Political arrangements have a tendency to sacralise human power, that is, to claim a divine status or sanction which is idolatrous but which achieves the self-legitimation of those who wield it.

However, the biblical tradition points to a quite different notion of power. In the Old Testament, the centrality of the teaching that Yahweh alone is king, landowner and commander, relativises all human power, political, economic and military. In the social system that God established in Israel, power was diffused in a plurality of elders and the kinship network. Centralized kingship was at first resisted, and when it came, was clearly set under the authority of covenant law (Deut. 17: 14–20). Kings were held accountable by the prophets to God's requirement that they should exercise justice and defend the powerless. It was the abuse of power, socially and economically, by the ruling elite in Israel which led to the sustained prophetic indictment and to God's wrath and judgement.

In the New Testament Jesus reaffirmed the Old Testament teaching in his own attitude and actions in relation to earthly power. He was not intimidated by earthly rulers (Lk. 13:31–2). He held a notion of power which was in explicit contrast to what he saw in the world (Lk. 22:24–27). He contrasted his own kingdom with that of Pilate's (Jn. 18:16). His cross was the defeat of the demonic forces which masquerade behind the destructive exercise of power in the world (Col. 2:15). The followers of Jesus must take the cross seriously in their political involvement as they overcome the love of power by the power of love and are empowered by him in their powerlessness. Such a view of Christian political involvement cuts across all authoritarian personality cults of the strong.

For the industrial nations of the North, democratic forms of government appear at present to be the best way of preventing the sacralization of power. Further investigation is needed into how existing 'democracies' could become more truly democratic by allowing more effectively for the participation of the marginalized. At the same time, we need to examine what other forms of political arrangements would be appropriate instruments of preventing the sacralization of power in other cultures and socio-economic contexts.

5. Ethnic Identities and Christian Peoplehood

Ethnic diversity is part of God's creativity and it is God's plan for all creation to glorify him. Therefore the riches of ethnic variety can be affirmed where it gives glory to God.

God's creative and redemptive intention is for all peoples to become part of the people of God. This purpose, however, is hindered by human fallenness, as a result of which ethnicity tends to be absolutized and thereby is distorted into idolatrous ethno-centrism. God's redemptive work dethrones all idolatries and therefore when a person becomes a member of the people of God through Christ, a new identity is received. This new identity in Christ relativises every ethnic identity, but does not efface it or invalidate its cultural expression. Citizenship in the Kingdom of God is the only absolute, non-negotiable identity for the Christian, besides which all other levels of identity are mobile and may be freely affirmed or freely laid aside for the sake of the Gospel. Paul could affirm or set aside his Jewish identity according to the missionary demands of his context (1 Cor. 9:19–23) and in any case counted it as wholly secondary compared to his new identity in Christ (Phil. 3:4–9).

The Gospel affirms ethnic identity by enabling the Christian to rejoice in it for its intrinsic created goodness, to subordinate it to the Lordship of Christ, and to use it for the service of God and the neighbour. The church, therefore, which includes all ethnic groups, is a sign of God's multi-ethnic people and kingdom. It should affirm healthy ethnicity and the positive values of nationhood where these do not either become idolatrous towards God or oppressive towards fellow human beings. In the fallen world, however, the church has the duty to challenge states which manipulate ethnicity, by exalting it into a national idolatry, or by using it as a criterion for denial of human rights, and states which marginalise ethnic minorities by tolerating discriminatory and exploitative forces in society. Such action for freedom and justice in relation to ethnicity can only come from a church which is not itself captive to ethnic idolatry theologically, culturally or politically.

There exist in our world many submerged ethnic identities which have resulted from the artificial drawing of state boundaries after conquest, colonisation and wars. Part of Christian mission must include working for the protection, recovery and re-emergence of such groups to the human rights and dignity, including the right to homeland and statehood, to which their ethnicity is as entitled as any others. However, we recognize painfully that in some parts of the world separate ethnicity has been spuriously promoted as a tool of oppression. In such contexts it is superficial to deal with ethnicity questions without regard to issues of social, economic and political freedom and justice.

The mixing of ethnic groups is not in itself wrong, theologically or culturally. In the course of history, however, many ethnically mixed populations have *resulted* from processes which were fundamentally unjust and oppressive. Many examples of this are found in American (North and South) and Caribbean nations through centuries of conquest, exploitation of native populations, and plantation slavery. Missiologically, however such populations of mixed ethnicity often function positively as vehicles for the trans-cultural spread of the Gospel. Biblical examples of this include the role of Galileans, Samaritans and Hellenistic Jews (all ethnic mixtures) in the missionary expansion of NT Christianity.

Furthermore, God's incarnation in the person of Jesus of Nazareth in Galilee indicates his option to identify with and minister among a mixed and marginalized population.

We celebrate the fact that the Gospel and the Christian community has from the beginning proved able to cross ethnic boundaries to share the message of God's love. This points beyond merely peaceful toleration towards genuine ethnic reconciliation and shalom which Paul, in Ephesians 2, saw as the heart of the Gospel. Christians need to face up to the existence of real wounds to be healed between Christians of different ethnicity living in the same context, even when they share the same commitment to mission.

There is also a need to be willing to speak the truth about the past. Christians must encourage fellow Christians, and also wider ethnically divided communities, to re-examine their history, with a willingness to look at it from the point of view of the other group. There must be a healing of historical memories by a commitment to acknowledge the truth, to seek forgiveness for historical wrongs, to seek to correct those wrongs as far as possible, and to repent of the perpetuation of unbiblical attitudes based on ancient ethnic hostilities.

6. The Need for Evangelical Political Theology

We note with joy the increasing degree of more active political engagement on the part of evangelicals, in Latin America and elsewhere. For the first time in the history of several nations, evangelicals are being elected to high government office. The Second Vice-President of Peru was among our number at the conference. The President and Vice-President of Guatemala are also evangelical believers.

Recognizing, however, the need for Christians in politics to be guided by biblically based political theology and ethics, there is an urgent need to develop such resources. Evangelical political praxis must be based on and critiqued by deep reflection on the social dimensions of biblical revelation. This is a task not merely for theologians but for the whole people of God.

A political theology provides answers to questions such as: what is the purpose of government? What is the role of force in government and how should it be used? What moral values should be legislated and what should not, and what are the criteria for distinguishing? How is power used and controlled? Is there a transcendant norm above the state? Without a political theology that answers such questions, political engagement is superficial, often misguided and counterproductive.

Many Christian traditions have an extensive history of systematic reflection on the relationship between Christian faith and public life and have developed sophisticated political theologies. If the recent worldwide evangelical involvement in politics is to be biblical, substantial and of more than passing significance, we must interact with the political theologies from these other Christian traditions and ground our own political activity in a political theology that flows from evangelical faith. And we need to work at that task in ways that both emerge from our unique social contexts and are accountable to the worldwide body of Christ.

The following affirmations illustrate the kind of claims that such a political theology might make:

1. It is God's will that there should be governing authorities within nations. The purpose of government is to promote social wholeness and well-being for its citizens and to prevent anarchy. To this end those in authority should be reminded that they are servants of God whose duty is to work for the good of citizens and to promote good relations with other nations. It is their duty to restrain evil by punishing evil-doers and by upholding justice.

2. Basic human rights (e.g. the right to life, religious and political freedoms and the right to share fairly in society's material goods) come from God, not the state, which can only recognise and nurture them.

3. The church must be free of state interference, but the church as an institution must not dominate government. At the same time, the church must exercise its prophetic role and religious values should have free reign in evaluating and critiquing public life.

4. Since God measures every society by how it treats the poorest and weakest, the voiceless and marginalized (Prov. 31:1–9), it is an important responsibility of government to create just conditions within which the welfare of such groups can be actively promoted.

5. 'As a model, modern political democracy is characterised by limited government of a temporary character, by the division of power within the government, the distinction between state and society, pluralism, the rule of law, institutionalisation of freedom rights (including free and regular elections), and a significant amount of non-governmental control of property. We recognize that no political system is directly prescribed by scripture, but we believe that biblical values and historical experience call Christians to work for the adequate participation of all people in the decision making processes on questions that affect their lives.' (Oxford Declaration, para. 54).

6. 'We recognize that no particular economic system is directly prescribed by scripture. Recent history suggests that a dispersion of ownership of the means of production is a significant component of democracy. Monopolistic ownership, either by the state, large

economic institutions, or oligarchies is dangerous. Widespread ownership, either in a market economy or a mixed system tends to decentralise power and prevent totalitarianism.' (Oxford Declaration, para. 56).

7. The results of political engagement are significant but limited. Political activity does not bring the kingdom of God, nor is it the only way to change society. Nevertheless, it is a vital activity by which Christians can bring the values of the kingdom of God in our nations.

7. Conclusion: A Call to Prayer

We recognize that in our engagement in struggles for freedom and justice in the world, we fight 'not against flesh and blood, but against the rulers, authorities and powers of this dark world, against the spiritual forces of evil in the heavenly realms' (Eph. 6:12). Hence prayer becomes a necessary dimension of our engagement. Freedom and justice are signs of the kingdom of God; through prayer we receive strength and hope in believing that God's kingdom will come. Through fervent intercessory prayer, we are enabled to participate in the struggles of those for whom we thus seek divine help.

In the light of our findings at our conference, therefore, we urge fervent prayer on behalf of the following.

1. Evangelical Christians and all those who suffer any form of persecution as a result of seeking to be bridge people and peacemakers in the ethnic conflicts in Yugoslavia.
2. Evangelical Christians and all who suffer any form of deprivation and oppression in contexts of dominating Islam in parts of Africa and Asia.
3. Evangelical Christians and all those who suffer under the conditions of repressive Roman Catholicism in several countries of Latin America.
4. Evangelical Christian leaders and all those who endure hardship and persecution as a consequence of seeking to promote those conditions in which freedom and justice will flourish in the lives of their nations. In the expectant hope of the coming of God's kingdom of freedom and justice promised in the Gospel of our Lord Jesus Christ, we pray, 'THY KINGDOM COME'.

Appendix One: Catholicism and Society in Latin America

The Roman Catholic Church was very influential in the formation of the Latin American nations because her missionary work was closely linked to the Spanish and Portuguese conquest in the 16th century. During three centuries of colonial domination, this church dominated society because she had control of culture through education, and was also powerful in economic and political life. The commitment of Spain and Portugal to build in the Americas a new Christendom free from the inroads of Protestantism led to the establishment of the Inquisition which controlled religious and social life.

In the process of Independence, between 1810 and 1850, the church identified with the Spanish crown and became a conservative institution in society. All through the 19th century, though the new nations kept a place of privilege for the Catholic Church, a tension between church and state developed, especially with the initiatives of liberal governments to curb the power of the church.

Protestantism came to Latin America taking advantage of the space created by liberal governments and established a *de facto* alliance with them. The growth of Protestantism was an evidence of the spiritual hunger of the Latin American masses that could not be satisfied by a declining church that suffered from a chronic shortage of clergy and falling popularity among the masses because of her alliance with the ruling classes.

During the 20th century, slowly but steadily, the church ceased to be the state church. This process was first successful in Mexico, Uruguay, Chile and Brazil. The Protestant minorities, however, were discriminated against and persecuted bloodily in Peru, Bolivia and Colombia, but in the 1960s religious freedom was increasingly achieved due to the rapid growth of Protestantism, the liberalization of governments and the liberalizing trends after the Vatican II Council.

Contemporary studies have proved that the Catholic missionary work of the 16th century was not completed. In many places it was superficial. This explains the need of the Catholic church to depend on the protection of the state for her survival and maintenance of her privileges. The gigantic migration to the cities has been a significant factor, among others, of the modernization process. In face of it, Protestant churches have offered better pastoral alternatives to the masses, and they continue to grow. Protestants hope that the Catholic

Church will adapt to life in a pluralistic society, but restrictions on religious minorities continue in several countries. However, the doctrine of the church about her position in society as well as her relationship to the state is based upon her self-understanding as the only true church and the deep-rooted tradition of domination in Spain and Portugal, and these two elements continue to be determinative for her attitudes.

Appendix Two: Freedom and Justice in Islamic States

Historically, Islam as a whole was never prepared, either in theory or practice, to accord full equality to those of another faith. The *dhimma* or *melet* system formulated in the 1st century of the Islamic era and defined in the so-called 'Pact of Umar', in its various versions places severe restrictions and handicaps on non-Muslim minorities. In the modern world these are applied in varying degrees in different Islamic nations. Islamic fundamentalists, on the one hand, demand a total return is the Shari'ah and all other restrictions of the *dhimma*; while moderates, on the other, are willing to lessen these restrictions, if not do away with them altogether.

Thus, for example, in Saudi Arabia no non-Islamic worship services outside embassy grounds are allowed. In Iran, since the 1979 revolution, thousands of Bahais have been executed for religious apostasy from Islam, and both Jews and Christians have been harassed, jailed and in some cases, killed. In Sudan, the efforts of the Islamic majority to impose the Shari'ah on all have led to an on-going civil war which began decades ago. The Egyptian Church which dates back to the 1st century A.D., continues to live today under a series of legal and social restrictions. Even in Turkey, there are continuing reports of discriminations against non-Muslims, a hangover from its Ottoman past, although these are prohibited by a fully secular constitution. Finally, in almost all Islamic states, non-Muslims are not given the freedom to change their faith. Many more examples could be given.

The world Islamic community is rightly concerned with the rights of Muslim minorities in non-Islamic lands. Again it must be noted that Islam is often concerned to instill the highest ideals of justice and tolerance. We would therefore like to ask the Muslim community to recognise more adequately the logic of their concerns. If they are concerned with the freedom to practice and propagate their faith and to ensure that Muslim minorities in non-Islamic lands are not treated as second-class citizens, they must be prepared to grant non-Muslims in Islamic states the same freedom and equality. No Muslim living in non-Islamic lands would happily live under the *dhimma* system applied in reverse. Therefore Muslims must be helped to understand that they cannot ask for what they are not prepared to concede.

At the same time it is recognised that Christians have often failed to provide adequately for the freedom and justice of religious minorities, including Muslims, in our societies. In recognition of these concerns, we propose:

1. That Christians must make a diligent effort to understand the historical grievances and present-day concerns of Muslims and initiate a dialogic process aimed at seeking greater reconciliation between the two communities.
2. That all members of the world community be challenged to make a genuine attempt to implement fully the United Nations Declaration of Human Rights (ratified by all Islamic states except for Saudi Arabia and Yemen) which provides fully for religious freedom and equality of all, irrespective of religious affiliation.
3. That non-Islamic nations (especially those in the West) should initiate an international consultation with the Organisation of Islamic Countries with the view of working toward an accord similar to the Helsinki Accords, as the best means to safeguard the rights and freedoms of both Muslims and non-Muslims.

Participants

The Osijek Conference was attended by the following participants.

They took part in drawing up the declaration but did not sign the declaration individually.

Africa

Rev Dr Robert Aboagye-Mensah
 (Ghana)
Deaconess Eugenia Adoyo (Kenya)
Rev Dr Kwame Bediako (Ghana)
Rt Rev Dr D M Gitari (Kenya)

Rev Graham Kings (Kenya/UK)
Rt Rev Godfrey Mdimi Mhogolo
 (Tanzania)
Caesar Molebatsi (South Africa)
Kalambo Mutambo
 (Yugoslavia/Ghana)
Moss Ntlha (South Africa)

Rev Dr Cyril Okorocha (Nigeria)
Rev Jeremy Pemberton (Zaire/UK)
Dr Daniel Wambudta (Nigeria)

Asia

David Bussau (Australia)
Rev Dr Wilson Chow (Hong Kong)
Dr David Lim (Philippines)
Ms Melba Maggay (Philippines)
Goh Keat Peng (Malaysia)
Dr Bong Rin Ro (Korea)
Canon Dr Vinay Samuel (India)
C B Samuel (India)
Rev Hwa Yung (Malaysia)

Europe

David Adeney (UK)
ThDr Jaraj Bandy (Czechoslovakia)
Dr Aleksander Birvis (Yugoslavia)
Rev Dr Tim Dearborn (UK/USA)
Dr Hans-Christian Diedrich
    (Germany)
David Dorusek (Yugoslavia)
Mark Jantzen (Germany/USA)
Dr Goran Janzon (Sweden)
Paul Jarosz (Poland)
Ms Maria Kaissling (Germany)
Rev Andrew Kirk (UK)
Dusan Kljic (Yugoslavia)
Zelko Krivic (Yugoslavia)
Dr Henryk Krol (Poland)
Magda Ksenija (Yugoslavia)
Rev Dr Peter Kuzmic (Yugoslavia)
Walter Lang (Germany)
Angela Ludwig (Germany)
Anatoli Mamalat (USSR)
Hovan Martin (Yugoslavia)
Jovan Nikolic (Yugoslavia)
Ms Pia Haase-Leh (Germany)
Beniamin Octavian Poplacean
    (Romania)
John Victor Selle (Norway)

Rev Dr Christopher Sugden (UK)
Karel Taschner (Czechoslovakia)
Rev Istvan Thuroczy (Hungary)
Dr Hans Visser (Netherlands)
Dr Miroslav Volf (Yugoslavia)
Dr Judith Volf (Yugoslavia/USA)
Rev Dr Joachim Wietzke (Germany)
Heinz Wollesky (Germany)
Rev Dr Christopher Wright (UK)
Peter Zimmerling (Germany)
Rev Rolf Zwick (Germany)

Latin America

Ms Carmen Perez Camargo (Mexico)
Dr Guillermo Cook (Costa Rica)
Ms Elsie De Powell (Argentina)
Dr Samuel Escobar (Peru)
Dr Carlos Garcia (Peru)
Humberto Lagos-Schuffeneger (Chile)
Dr Enio Mueller (Brazil)
Las Newman (Jamaica)
Rev Dr C Rene Padilla (Argentina)
Dr Ruben Tito Paredes (Peru)
Dr Pablo Perez (Mexico)
Dr Pedro Arana Quiroz (Peru)
Victor Rey (Chile)
Juan D Rogers (Argentina)
Dr Edesio Sanchez (Costa Rica)
Dr Valdir Steuernagel (Brazil)

North America

Jonathan J Bonk (Canada)
Joel Carpenter (USA)
Dr William Dyrness (USA)
Dr Ward Gasque (USA)
Mrs Laurel Gasque (USA)
Dr Daniel Sanchez (USA)
Dr Walter Sawatsky (USA)
Dr Gerald Shenk (USA)
Rev Dr Ronald Sider (USA)
Dr Darryl Trimiew (USA)
Robin Wainwright (USA)

Twenty-Five

The Kingdom and The Kingdoms
Osijek, Croatia 1998

Introduction

1. We gathered as 170 educators, theologians and church leaders at the Evandeoski Teoloski Fakultet, Osijek, Croatia from thirty countries from September 1–5 1998 to share in a cross cultural global reflection on theological education for Christian mission. We had a particular focus on the Kingdom of God and the kingdoms of the world in the current situation in Central and Eastern Europe. We intentionally drew on the experience of participants from South Africa, Malaysia, Myanmar, India, Indonesia, Brazil, Chile, United States, United Kingdom, Canada and Germany.

We were generously received by the deputy governor of Eastern Slovenia and the Mayor of Osijek. The Croatian national press, radio and television were present throughout the conference.

'The Kingdom of God and the Kingdoms of the World' in *Transformation*, Vol. 16, No. 1, January 1999.

We also visited the nearby city of Vukovar. This took the form of a pilgrimage to a place where massive evil had been done and suffering borne. It brought to mind other places of destruction around the world. We were greatly encouraged to hear from the District President of the area of their commitment to engage in a process of education that would combine religion and morality (separated in the communist era with such devastating consequences) and especially focus on the sanctity of human life. We were humbled to meet in his ruined church, which still stands after bombardment by more than 600 shells, the Abbott of the Franciscan Priory Church of St Philip and St James Church. His testimony was living proof that the gates of hell shall not prevail against Christ's church. We can only offer our sympathy and prayers for the Vukovar community in the death of 12,000 (20 per cent) of their population, and in their determined efforts to rebuild their community and city. Our visit vividly presented to us the challenge of ministry to people who have experienced such devastation.

An Analysis of The Context of Post-Communist Central and Eastern Europe

2. Central and Eastern Europe is home for a rich and diverse family of nations who live in a variety of very differing contexts. We all share a recent past under communist rule, and a far longer history of Christianity, stretching in some cases right back to the earliest years of the church. We have growing reservations about describing our current context in the phrase 'post-communist' which is essentially a backward looking phrase. Some of its characteristics are characteristics of all totalitarian regimes, not just communist ones. The phrase can mask many of the current realities of our situation on the periphery of the dominant capitalist world economy and give a superficial air of 'sameness' to very differing economic, social, religious and political situations in our countries. We seek a more adequate phrase to describe our region in future.

3. The current uni-polar world of the global market economy is not always beneficial to the weak. We all now experience increasing globalization, understood as the homogenizing of society by market economics and technology. The consequences of globalization are both good and bad. It is reducing the time lag between the West and Eastern Europe. More and more people have access to increased information, the same questions, and the same needs, prompted by

the same global media and global marketing processes. Consumer greed distorts individual choice and undermines all political restraints and moral norms. Lawlessness and a lack of a legal society hinders healthy economic development. Our family, community and church life is under increasing stress as life gets busier and busier. Those who feel the fullest effects of globalization and are most vulnerable to its onslaught on ethical values are our children and young people.

4. We are all shaped by the recent communist mind-set in the context of Central and Eastern European societies. This has often resulted in a lack of personal responsibility in favour of unquestioned authority of the state. This was and still is often accepted in our societies at large and in Christian circles. For example, in a church the pastor may assume the responsibility for the spiritual fulfilment of their members who in turn become passive. This reflects a fatalism that is also evident in political, economic and social terms.

5. This fatalism has been realised in relationships of failed trust, which has arisen from the long history of oppression, predating communism, and expressed in manipulation and conflict. In these situations reconciliation must become a high priority especially because such reconciliation yields qualitative and quantitative growth of the church.

6. The decline of communism as the ascendant political philosophy removed the basis from a strong sense of direction and purpose (albeit mistaken) in the history of our cultures. Some have interpreted the processes of history to their own advantage; and many have become cynical about history, impacted by the marginalization of history through globalization. In addition, many countries now struggle to recover a sense of continuity with their national past of the pre-communist era, albeit in a very changed world. The combination of lack of responsibility for public life, low levels of trust, and disillusion with history reinforces those tendencies in the churches to keep Christianity in the private sphere of life.

7. For these reasons we are convinced that we must witness that Jesus Christ is the Lord of history; that history is moving to its final fulfilment in the Kingdom of God; that in the course of human history the other globalizing force has been the universal spread of the gospel and church of Jesus Christ to all peoples and to all areas of life. Acknowledging Christ's lordship is the same as submitting to his

kingship and is thus the point of entrance into the Kingdom of God. Our Christian mission is to witness to the work of the Kingdom of God in history and take our part in it, all the while realising that we are fallen human beings and that the work of the Kingdom is ultimately the work of God.

The calling of the church to witness to the triune God

8. We witness to God the Father, God the Son and God the Holy Spirit, the triune God. Our faith in the Trinity is very important for our being as churches and our relationships with other churches. The church is above all both a human and divine organization. God calls the church to be in relationship with the Trinity and with those who obey God's call. The structure of the church must reflect the freedom in relationship of each believer with the Trinity and with all other believers. Thus the church is more than a fellowship or a corporation run according to a managerial model. In Central and Eastern Europe, we are heirs to models of the church's order patterned either after the collectivism of the Roman empire, the European nation states, and the Bolshevik Revolution, or individualism patterned after the Enlightenment, and American Protestantism. All of these are inadequate. Further, the difficulties facing Christians who try to work together in our countries and the fragmentation of churches owe much to these competing non-trinitarian models of the church's life as institutions or fellowships. We cannot separate our relationship with the triune God from relationships with others who follow Christ.

9. The church is a sign of the Kingdom, points to the Kingdom, and is the community of the King. Its mission can be rightly understood, lived and practiced only in right relation to its founder and head, Jesus Christ, and in accordance with his central message about the Kingdom of God. In different contexts there will be different priorities for its mission and its expression. In all cases the understanding of our role as servants of the King is important, especially as an antidote to the temptation of secular models of leadership. The understanding that the church is the sign and community of the Kingdom, but not the Kingdom itself, is an important preventative of the renaissance of religious nationalism and neo-Constantinianism.

Christian witness in the public sphere

10. We must therefore call for a public witness to the Christian faith in all areas of life. We must encourage our churches to see that their very lives as congregations are expressions of civil society, of those voluntary organizations committed to social good.

Our churches under communism were marginalized and persecuted. In this situation, the range of possibilities for action in society was extremely limited, and, consequently, the range of expertise needed by the church was relatively narrow. Our experience in some situations of being a minority fighting for survival and for our rights is, rightly, expressed in testimony which must continue to be a resource for our theology. However, in the 'post-communist' situation, we need to change our 'minority complex' in order to address concerns of the wider society. Our communities have the possibility of being present in a wider range of societal activities, and for this we need a wider range of expertise from amongst our members. We need to be able to ask questions we have never answered before and carry out tasks that are completely new. This should be reflected in a broader conception of the educational task of the church, as well as in the encouragement of some members to seek necessary training in both theological and non-theological disciplines.

11. We reject as inadequate for the public square the secularism which precludes any religious contribution, and the religious exclusivism which insists that social engagement must be based on terms defined only in terms of one religion alone. Nation-building and community consensus presupposes goodwill and the contribution of all citizens regardless of their own religious faith. Plurality is a reality in the religious field and the public sphere. We recognise that common morality is a reality, but also allows for different religious and ethical commitment.

12. In some Christian circles, it is customary to bring in outside experts to prime thinking regarding the context (social, political, etc) in which the church is situated. This can give false leads, especially when the analysis is assumed to be 'neutral' and unaffected by the absence of Christian commitment and by knowledge of the church context. On the other hand, common practice in Christian circles is virtually to dispense with analysis of the situation and talk directly of theological perspectives and proposals for mission. Often, these proposals get bogged down because they are unrealistic with regard to

the potentialities of the situation. One way to avoid both of the above weaknesses is to train (and encourage the training of) members of the churches who can describe and analyse their context, all the while informed by an evangelical faith commitment and familiarity with theological discussions.

13. The 'context' which must be analysed refers not only to the economic, social, political and cultural dimensions, but also includes the church context. Many proposals for Christian action in the public realm are unrealistic because they do not take into account the reality of the church in a specific country or region. The church is embedded in society and is not separate from it; the sociological study of the Christian community is thus vital if we wish to have a broader presence in our societies.

14. In considering context, we must beware of nostalgia for 'Christian Europe'. In some countries of Western Europe and North America, this nostalgia can have a strongly evangelical component, but in Central and Eastern Europe it is almost inevitably Orthodox or Roman Catholic. We from Central and Eastern Europe can warn our foreign brethren of the dangers of this nostalgia. But we ourselves must be sure that opposition to such Orthodox or Roman Catholic pretensions is a principled opposition, and not merely an opposition based on current powerlessness. In some contexts, such as Latin America, such merely 'contextual' opposition has been transformed into similar pretensions once the evangelical community has started to gain numerical and political power. In many parts of the world, the dominant model of how religion relates to power and the state (whether Islamic, Orthodox, Roman Catholic, etc) has been unconsciously assimilated by Protestants, who have failed to provide their societies with an alternative model of the relationship between religion and the state.

Christian witness of reconciliation

15. The God whom we serve, the Father, the Son and the Holy Spirit, is the God who lives in the eternal communion of love and who created humanity to have fellowship in that love. In the cross of Christ, that same love of God has come to humanity that has through sin estranged itself from God – and thus fallen into injustice, deception and violence – to redeem it by grace and receive it back into the communion of divine love.

The triune God calls the church to participate in God's mission in the world to reconcile humanity with himself and with one another. The apostle Paul tells us to receive one another as we – sinful and godless human beings – have been received by God in Christ. Just as grace, which overcomes godlessness, stands at the heart of the gospel we proclaim, so grace, which overcomes injustice, deception and violence, stands at the heart of our social responsibility.

We must be concerned with justice within society and the freedom of persons, but our goal must be the creation of a community of love. In this community persons are respected, their cultural differences are affirmed, the needs of the poor are satisfied, power is given to the weak, and enemies are made into friends.

We cannot always expect a mutual reciprocation of our reaching out in reconciliation. In this we must mirror the action of God, who is always reconciling the world to himself. We must develop attitudes of reconciliation and sow seeds of reconciliation which will bear fruit in due season.

16. Churches will be able to promote a community of love in society only if they model such communal life for the world. This is why the challenge of reconciliation extends to the relationships between Roman Catholic, Orthodox, mainstream Protestant and evangelical faith traditions. We have much to offer as well as receive in such a process. We can be a resource to them in our countries as we seek to meet the needs of young people and address the public sphere with the gospel. In dialogue with the Orthodox we may offer the recovery of personal faith and personhood in the context of the family. We may be intentional about seeking fellowship and common cause with them so that we may be seen as colleagues in Christian leadership. We must model reconciliation and go beyond our own self-interest and rights and seek the rights of all religious and minority groups. The social dimension of reconciliation should extend to areas of historic alienation in our region, including ethnic, political, economic, gender and religious divisions.

17. We recognise that the sudden openness between Eastern and Central Europe and and the West has in some cases been traumatic for the churches in the East. The uncritical acceptance of Western methodologies has on the whole not been helpful to the maturation of the church. On the other hand, help and support arising out of a sensitive understanding of the needs of the suffering church is highly appreciated.

East and West, South and North have much to learn from one another. The grace of suffering that the Eastern and Central European churches have experienced is a gift that can enrich the world church when we learn to listen in mutuality. Genuine partnership is reciprocal and builds up the whole body of Christ. The basis of effective help lies in understanding each other's needs and generous sharing with one another. That is the atmosphere we have experienced during this conference.

Implications for The Church's Membership and Leadership

18. Given our new awareness and understanding of the social, political, and cultural changes in our context and in the world at large, we conclude that there are new challenges and problems that the church must face in order to be a relevant, credible and reconciling presence of Christ.

These new challenges and problems create a need for a new kind of church leader and marketplace witness. We must recognise we have been shaped by a totalitarian style of leadership. We can be tempted to repeat this pattern in our churches and exercise a high degree of control. We must develop a pattern of team leadership and a style that creates space for all Christians to exercise their gifts. We need a wider range of specialists to address the expanding range of opportunities for ministry in the new context of freedom we enjoy. We need to encourage church members to play their role in civil society in local voluntary and civic organizations. Congregation leaders and pastors will especially need to understand and address the challenges faced by children and young people in order to pass on the gospel to the next generation.

We affirm the Protestant distinctive of the priesthood of all believers to ensure as wide as possible inclusion of all members in the ministry of the church and the exercise of their gifts as servants of one another. So we need a style of leadership that will create space for all people of God to exercise their gifts and enable them to use biblical resources to inform their ministries.

Implications for Theological Education

19. The character, content, curricula and goals of theological education must reflect and engage the new missiological realities and challenges described above. This means that each theological discipline must work out its own missiological dimension and how the

missiological imperative of the church affects its academic content, instructional approach and educational goals.

We must encourage Protestants to engage with our national myths, which often exclude them, rework these myths and make creative use of Protestant history and sociological characteristics in our countries. We must encourage Christians to produce intellectually sound arguments for a pluralist model of national religious life. The battle for legitimacy is vital for defending and enlarging the space for everyday religious activities and for greater involvement in public life.

We must have a vision for equiping the whole people of God with theological education for ministry. Theological education can no longer afford to ignore its responsibilities for leadership development in every task of the church (theologians, denominational leaders, pastors, evangelists, youth workers, health workers, and teachers) and for those in the public arena (businesspeople, journalists, politicians, and intellectuals).

We must educate such people in ministry with the biblical resources for ministry. We must encourage seminaries and training institutes to focus on the new opportunities for ministry opening up in our cultures and provide all Christians in ministry with the biblical resources they need to address and fulfil these opportunities.

20. We commit ourselves to the vision that 'every church will have national leaders who manifest a Christian style of leadership in terms not of domination but of service' and that 'in every nation and culture there should be an effective training programme for pastors and laity in doctrine, discipleship evangelism, nurture and service' (Lausanne Covenant para. 11).

The task we face in theological education and leadership development for the church's witness to the lordship of Christ in the whole of society is too big for one denomination and group. Therefore we all, with the Council for East European Theological Education, reaffirm the commitment made in the Oradea Declaration in 1994: 'By God's grace alone, we intend to move forward with shared faith in the triune God, shared fellowship in Christian ministry and service, shared understanding of the task of true theological education, shared cognisance of what this means in post-communist Europe, shared vision for co-operative and collaborative action in nurturing Christian leaders, and shared hope for the impact that our churches might have . . . because of godly, willing and capable leaders' (Oradea 26).

Appendix A

The Chicago Declaration
United States 1973

The Chicago Declaration of Evangelical Social Concern was produced at the Thanksgiving Workshop on Evangelicals and Social Concern held in Chicago 1973, November 23–25. The declaration and its related papers are published in The Chicago Declaration *edited by Ronald J. Sider (Creation House, 499 Gundersen Drive, Carol Stream, Illinois 60187, USA, 1974).*

As evangelical Christians committed to the Lord Jesus Christ and the full authority of the Word of God, we affirm that God lays total claim upon the lives of his people. We cannot, therefore, separate our lives in Christ from the situation in which God has placed us in the United States and the world.

We confess that we have not acknowledged the complete claims of God on our lives.

We acknowledge that God requires love. But we have not demonstrated the love of God to those suffering social abuses.

We acknowledge that God requires justice. But we have not proclaimed or demonstrated his justice to an unjust American society.

Although the Lord calls us to defend the social and economic rights of the poor and the oppressed, we have mostly remained silent. We deplore the historic involvement of the church in America with racism and the conspicuous responsiblity of the evangelical community for perpetuating the personal attitudes and institutional structures that have divided the body of Christ along colour lines. Further, we have failed to condemn the exploitation of racism at home and abroad by our economic system.

We affirm that God abounds in mercy and that he forgives all who repent and turn from their sins. So we call our fellow evangelical Christians to demonstrate repentance in a Christian discipleship that confronts the social and political injustice of our nation.

We must attack the materialism of our culture and the maldistribution of the nation's wealth and services. We recognize that as a nation we play a crucial role in the imbalance and injustice of international trade and development. Before God and a billion hungry neighbours, we must rethink our values regarding our present standard of living a promote more just acquisition and distribution of the world's resources.

We acknowledge our Christian responsibilities of citizenship. Therefore, we must challenge the misplaced trust of the nation in economic and military might – a proud trust that promoted a national pathology of war and violence which victimizes our neighbours at home and abroad. We must resist the temptation to make the nation and its institutions objects of near-religious loyalty.

We acknowledge that we have encouraged men to prideful domination and women to irresponsible passivity. So we call both men and women to mutual submission and active discipleship.

We proclaim no new gospel, but the gospel of our Lord Jesus Christ, who, through the power of the Holy Spirit, frees people from sin so that they might praise God through works of righteousness.

By this declaration, we endorse no political ideology or party, but call our nation's leaders and people to that righteousness which exalts a nation.

We make this declaration in the biblical hope that Christ is coming to consummate the Kingdom and we accept his claim on our total discipleship till he comes.

Appendix B

The Lausanne Covenant

The Lausanne Covenant was produced by the International Congress on World Evangelism, Lausanne, Switzerland, July 16–25, 1974.

Introduction

We, members of the Church of Jesus Christ, from more than 150 nations, participants in the International Congress On World Evangelization at Lausanne, praise God for his great salvation and rejoice in the fellowship he has given us with himself and with each other. We are deeply stirred by what God is doing in our day, moved to penitence by our failures and challenged by the unfinished task of evangelization. We believe the gospel is God's good news for the whole world, and we are determined by his grace to obey Christ's commission to proclaim it to all mankind and to make disciples of every nation. We desire, therefore, to affirm our faith and our resolve and to make public our covenant.

1. The Purpose of God

We affirm our belief in the one eternal God, Creator and Lord of the world, Father, Son and Holy Spirit, who governs all things according to the purpose of his will. He has been calling out from the world a people for himself, and sending his people back into the world to be his servants and his witnesses, for the extension of his kingdom, the building up of Christ's body, and the glory of his name. We confess with shame that we have often denied our calling and failed in our mission, by becoming conformed to the world or by withdrawing from it. Yet we rejoice that even when borne by earthen vessels the gospel is still a precious treasure. To the task of making the treasure known in the power of the Holy Spirit we desire to dedicate ourselves anew (Isa. 40:28; Matt. 28:19; Eph. 1:11; Acts 15:14; John 17:6, 18; Eph. 4:12; 1 Cor. 54:10; Rom. 12:2; 2 Cor. 4:7).

2. The Authority and Power of the Bible

We affirm the divine inspiration, truthfulness and authority of both Old and New Testament Scriptures in their entirety as the only written word of God, without error in all that it affirms, and the only infallible rule of faith and practice. We also affirm the power of God's word to accomplish his purpose of salvation. The message of the Bible is addressed to all mankind. For God's revelation in Christ and in Scripture is unchangeable. Through it the Holy Spirit speaks today. He illumines the minds of God's people in every culture to perceive its truth freshly through their own eyes and thus discloses to the whole church ever more of the many coloured wisdom of God. (2 Tim. 3:16; 2 Pet. 1:21: John 10:35; Isa. 55:11; 1 Cor. 1:21; Rom. 1:16; Matt. 5:17, 18; Jude 3; Eph. 1:17, 18; 3:10.18).

3. The uniqueness and Universality of Christ

We affirm that there is only one Saviour and only one gospel, although there is a wide diversity of evangelistic approaches. We recognize that all men have some knowledge of God through his general revelation in nature. But we deny that this can save, for men suppress the truth by their unrighteousness. We also reject as derogatory to

Christ and the gospel every kind of syncretism and dialogue which implies that Christ speaks equally through all religions and ideologies. Jesus Christ being himself the only Godman, who gave himself as the only ransom for sinners, is the only mediator between God and man. There is no other name by which we must be saved. All men are perishing because of sin, but God loves all men, not wishing that any should perish but that all should repent. Yet those who reject Christ repudiate the joy of salvation and condemn themselves to eternal separation from God. To proclaim Jesus as 'the Saviour of the world' is not to affirm that all religions offer salvation in Christ. Rather it is to proclaim God's love for a world of sinners and to invite all men to respond to him as Saviour and Lord in the wholehearted personal commitment of repentance and faith. Jesus Christ has been exalted above every other name; we long for the day when every knee shall bow to him and every tongue shall confess him Lord. (Gal. 1:6–9; Rom. 1:18–32; 1 Tim. 2:5, 6; Acts 4:12; John 3:16–19; II Pet. 3:9 II Thes. 1:7–9; John 4:42; Matt. 11:28; Eph. 1:20.21; Phil. 2:9–11).

4. The Nature of Evangelism

To evangelize is to spread the good news that Jesus Christ died for our sins and was raised from the dead according to the Scriptures, and that as the reigning Lord he now offers the forgiveness of sins and the liberating gift of the Spirit to all who repent and believe. Our Christian presence in the world is indispensable to evangelism, and so is that kind of dialogue whose purpose is to listen sensitively in order to understand. But evangelism itself is the proclamation of the historical biblical Christ as Saviour and Lord, with a view to persuading people to come to him personally and so be reconciled to God. In issuing the gospel invitation we have no liberty to conceal the cost of discipleship. Jesus still calls all who would follow him to deny themselves, take up their cross, and identify themselves with his new community. The results of evangelism include obedience in the world. (II Cor. 15:3, 4: Acts 2:22–24; John 20:21; 1 Cor. 2:40, 47; Mark 10:43–45).

5. Christian Social Responsibility

We affirm that God is both the Creator and the Judge of all men. We therefore should share his concern for justice and reconciliation throughout human society and for the liberation of men from every kind of oppression. Because mankind is made in the image of God, every person, regardless of race, religion, colour, culture, class, sex or age, has an intrinsic dignity because of which he should be respected and served, not exploited. Here too we express penitence both for our neglect and for having sometimes regarded evangelism and social concern as mutually exclusive. Although reconciliation with man is not reconciliation with God, nor is social action evangelism, nor is political liberation salvation, nevertheless we affirm that evangelism and socio-political involvement are both part of our Christian duty. For both are necessary expressions of our doctrines of God and man, our love for our neighbour and our obedience to Jesus Christ. The message of salvation implies also a message of judgment upon every form of alienation, oppression and discrimination, and we should not be afraid to denounce evil and injustice wherever they exist. When people receive Christ they are born again into his kingdom and must seek not only to exhibit but also to spread its righteousness in the midst of an unrighteous world. The salvation we claim should be transforming us in the totality of our personal and social responsibilities. Faith without works is dead. (Acts 17:26, 31; Gen. 18:25; Isa. 1:17; Psa. 45:7; Gen. 1:26, 27; Jas 3:9; Lev. 19:18 Luke 6:27, 35; Jas. 2:14–16; John 3:3,5; Matt. 5:20; 6:33; II Cor. 3:18; Jas 2:20).

6. The Church and Evangelism

We affirm that Christ sends his redeemed people into the world as the Father sent him, and that this calls for a similar deep and costly penetration of the world. We need to break out of our ecclesiastical ghettos and permeate non-Christian society. In the church's mission of sacrificial service evangelism is primary. World evangelization requires the whole church to take the whole gospel to the whole world. The church is at the very centre of God's cosmic purpose and is his appointed means of spreading the gospel. But a church which preaches the cross must itself be marked by the cross. It becomes a stumbling block to evangelism when it betrays the gospel or lacks a living faith in God, a genuine love for people, or scrupulous honesty in all things including promotion and finance. The church is the community of God's people rather than an institution, and must not be identified with any particular culture, social or political system, or human ideology. (John 17:18:20–21; Matt. 28:19, 20; Acts 1:8: 20:27; Eph. 1:9, 10:3:9–11; Gal. 6:14: 17:2; II Cor. 6:3, 4; II Tim. 2:19–21; Phil. 1:27).

7. Cooperation in Evangelism

We affirm that the church's visible unity in truth is God's purpose. Evangelism also summons us to unity, because our oneness strengthens our witness, just as our disunity undermines our gospel of reconciliation. We recognize, however, that organizational unity may take forms and does not necessarily forward evangelism. Yet we who share the same biblical faith should be closely united in fellowship, work and witness. We confess that our testimony has sometimes been marred by sinful individualism and needless duplication. We pledge ourselves to seek a deeper unity in truth, worship, holiness and mission. We urge the development of regional and functional cooperation for the furtherance of the church's mission, for strategic planning, for mutual encouragement, and for the sharing of resources and experience. (John 17:21, 23; Eph. 4:3, 4; John 13:35; Phil. 1:27; John 17:11–25).

8. Churches in Evangelistic Partnerships

We rejoice that a new missionary era has dawned. The dominant role of western missions is fast disappearing. God is raising up from younger churches a great new resource for world evangelization, and is thus demonstrating that the responsibility to evangelize belongs to the whole body of Christ. All churches should therefore be asking God and themselves what they should be doing both to reach their own area and to send missionaries to other parts of the world. A re-evaluation of our missionary responsibility and role should be continuous. Thus a growing partnership of churches will develop and the universal character of Christ's church will be more clearly exhibited. We also thank God for agencies which labour in Bible translation, theological education, the mass media, Christian literature, evangelism, missions, church renewal and other specialist fields. They too should engage in constant self-examination to evaluate their effectiveness as part of the Church's mission. (Rom. 1:8; Phil 1:5; 4:5; Acts 13:1–3: I Thes. 1:6–8).

9. The Urgency of the Evangelistic Task

More than 2,700 million people, which is more than two-thirds of mankind, have yet to be evangelized. We are ashamed that so many have been neglected; it is a standing rebuke to us and to the whole church. There is now, however, in many parts of the world an unprecented receptivity to the Lord Jesus Christ. We are convinced that this is the time for churches and para-church agencies to pray earnestly for the salvation of the unreached and to launch new efforts to achieve world evangelization. A reduction of foreign missionaries and money in an evangelized country may sometimes be necessary to facilitate the national church's growth in self-reliance and to release resources for unevangelized areas. Missionaries should flow ever more freely from and to all six continents in a spirit of humble service. The goal should be, by all available means and at the earliest possible time, that every person will have the opportunity to hear, understand and receive the good news. We cannot hope to attain this goal without sacrifices. All of us are shocked by the poverty of millions and disturbed by the injustices which cause it. Those of us who live in affluent circumstances accept our duty to develop a simple life-style in order to contribute more generously to both relief and evangelism. (John 9:4; Matt. 9:35–38; Rom. 9:1–3; I Cor. 9:19–23; Mark 15:15; Isa. 58:6, 7; Jas. 1:27; 2:1–9; Matt. 25:31–46; Acts 2:44, 45; 4:34, 35).

10. Evangelism and Culture

The development of strategies for world evangelization calls for imaginative pioneering methods. Under God, the result will be the rise of churches deeply rooted in Christ and closely related to their culture. Culture must always be tested and judged by Scripture. Because man is God's creature, some of his culture is rich in beauty and goodness. Because he has fallen, all of it is tainted with sin and some of it is demonic. The gospel does not presuppose the superiority of any culture to another, but evaluates all cultures according to its own criteria of truth and righteousness, and insists on moral absolutes in every culture. Missions have all too frequently exported with the gospel an alien culture, and churches have sometimes been in bondage to culture rather than to the Scripture. Christ's evangelists must humbly seek to empty themselves of all but their personal authenticity in order to become the servants of others, and churches must seek to transform and enrich culture, all for the glory of God. (Mark 7:8, 9, 13; Gen. 4:21, 22; I Cor. 19–23; Phil. 2:5–7; I Cor. 4:5).

11. Education and Leadership

We confess that we have sometimes pursued church growth at the expense of Church depth, and divorced evangelism from Christian nurture. We also acknowledge that some of our missions have been too slow to equip and encourage national leaders to assume their rightful responsibilities. Yet we are committed to indigenous principles, and long that every church will have national leaders who manifest a Christian style of leadership in terms not of domination but of service. We recognize that there is a great need to improve theological education, especially for church leaders. In every nation and culture there should be an effective training programme for pastors, laymen in doctrine, discipleship, evangelism, nurture and service. Such training programmes should not rely on any stereotyped methodology but should be developed by creative local initiative according to biblical standards. (Col. 1:27, 28; Acts 14:23; Tit. 1:5–9; Mark 10:42–45; Eph. 4:11, 12).

12. Spiritual Conflict

We believe that we are engaged in constant spiritual warfare with the principalities and powers of evil who are seeking to overthrow the church and frustrate its task of world evangelization. We know our need to equip ourselves with God's armour and to fight this battle with the spiritual weapons of truth and prayer. For we detect the activity of our enemy, not only in false ideologies outside the church, but also inside it in false gospels which twist Scripture and put man in the place of God. We need both watchfulness and discernment to safeguard the biblical gospel. We acknowledge that we ourselves are not immune to worldliness of thought and action that is to a surrender to secularism. For example, although careful studies of the church growth, both numerical and spiritual, are right and valuable, we have sometimes neglected them. At other times, desirous to ensure a response to the gospel, we have compromised our message, manipulated our hearers through pressure techniques, and become unduly preoccupied with statistics or even dishonest in our use of them. All this is worldly. The church must be in the world; the world must not be in the church. (Eph. 6:12; II Cor. 4:3, 4; Eph. 6:11, 13–18; II Cor. 10:3–5; 1 John 2:18–26; 4:1–3; Gal. 1:6–9; II Cor. 2:17; 4:2; John 17:15).

13. Freedom and Persecution

It is the God-appointed duty of every government to secure condi-tions of peace, justice and liberty in which the church may obey God, serve the Lord Christ, and preach the gospel without interference. We therefore pray for the leaders of the nations and call upon them to guarantee freedom of thought and conscience, and freedom to prac-tise and propagate religion in accordance with the will of God and as set forth in the Universal Declaration of Human Rights. We also express our deep concern for all who have been unjustly imprisoned, and especially for our brethren who are suffering for their testimony to the Lord Jesus. We promise to pray and work for their freedom. At the same time we refuse to be intimidated by their fate. God helping us, we too will seek to stand against injustice and to remain faithful to the gospel, whatever the cost. We do not forget the warnings of Jesus that persecution is inevitable. (1 Tim. 1:1–4; Acts 4:19:5–29; Col. 3:24; Heb. 13:1–3; Luke 4:18; Gal. 5:11: 6:12; Matt. 5:10–12; John 15:18–21).

14. The Power of the Holy Spirit

We believe in the power of the Holy Spirit. The Father sent his Spirit to bear witness to his Son; without his witness ours is futile. Convic-tion of sin, faith in Christ, new birth and Christian growth are all his work. Further, the Holy Spirit is a missionary spirit; thus evangelism should arise spontaneously from a spirit-filled church. A church that is not a missionary church is contradicting itself and quenching the Spirit. Worldwide evangelization will become a realistic possibility only when the Spirit renews the church in truth and wisdom, faith, holiness, love and power. We therefore call upon all Christians to pray for such a visitation of the sovereign Spirit of God and that all his fruit may appear in all his people and that all his gifts may enrich the body of Christ. Only then will the whole church become a instrument in his hands, that the whole earth may hear his voice. (I Cor. 2:4; John 15:26, 27; 16:8–11; I Cor. 12:3; John 3:6–8; II Cor. 3:18; John 7:37–39, I Thes. 5:19; Acts 1:8; Psa. 85:4–7: 67:1–3; Gal. 5:22, 23; I Cor. 12:4–31: Rom. 12:3–8).

15. The Return of Christ

We believe that Jesus Christ will return personally and visibly, in power and glory, to consummate his salvation and his judgment. This promise of his coming is a further spur to our evangelism, for we remember his words that the gospel must first be preached to all nation. We believe that the interim period between Christ's ascension and return is to be filled with the mission of the people of God, who have no liberty to stop before the End. We also remember his warning that false Christs and false prophets will arise as precursors of the final Antichrist. We therefore reject as a proud, self-confident dream the notion that man can ever build a utopia on earth. Our Christian confidence is that God will perfect his kingdom, and we look forward with eager anticipation to that day, and to the new heaven and earth in which righteousness will dwell and God will reign forever. Meanwhile, we rededicate ourselves to the service of Christ and of men in joyful submission to his authority over the whole of our lives. (Mark 14:62; Heb. 9:28; Mark 13:10; Acts 1:8–11; Matt. 28–20; Mark 13:21–23; John 2:18; 4:1–3; Luke 12:32; Rev. 21:1–5; II Pet. 3:13; Matt. 28:18).

Conclusion

Therefore, in the light of this our faith and our resolve, we enter into a solemn covenant with God and with each other, to pray, to plan and to work together for the evangelization of the whole world. We call upon others to join us. May God help us by his grace and for his glory to be faithful to his our covenant! Amen.

Annotated Bibliography

A number of key texts expound the biblical basis and missiology of Transformation. In addition to those that have been mentioned and excerpted in this collection, especially at the conclusion of chapters five and eight there are:

Primary Documents

The Lausanne Covenant 1974 Reproduced in Appendix B
Ecumenical Affirmations on Mission and Evangelism (Geneva, WCC, 1982) The statement of mission produced by the CWME, which many evangelicals found to be the best of recent WCC statements on mission.
Evangelism and Social Responsibility – an Evangelical Commitment, The Grand Rapids Report of the Consultation on the Relationship between Evangelism and Social Responsibility (Exeter, Paternoster, 1982).
Texts on Evangelical Social Ethics 1974–1983 edited by Rene Padilla and Chris Sugden (Cambridge, Grove Booklets, 1985) Contains excerpts of significant documents including 'The Madras Declaration' of 1979 by evangelicals in India.

'Mission and Ministry' in *The Truth Shall Make You Free – documents of the Lambeth Conference* 1988 edited by Michael Nazir-Ali and Derek Pattinson (London, Church Information Office, 1989).
'The Bible, Truth and Modernity' in *Transformation*, Volume 10, No. 4 October 1993. A statement from 150 evangelical Anglicans from 29 countries, described as 'A ringing statement of mainstream Anglican Evangelical Attitudes to the Bible' by the Church Times (London).

Biblical Studies

David Gitari, *In Season and Out of Season* (Oxford, Regnum, 1995) Biblical preaching in the context of prophetic ministry to the Kenyan state.
Ken Gnanakan, *Kingdom Concerns* (Bangalore, Theological Book Trust, 1989)
George Eldon Ladd, *Jesus and the Kingdom* (SPCK, London, 1966).
A Theology of the New Testament (Lutterworth, 1974) especially chapters 3–8.
I Believe in the Resurrection of the Jesus (Hodder).
John Mason, 'Biblical Teaching and Assisting the Poor' in *Transformation* Vol 4 No 2 April 1987. An exhaustive study of the biblical material on practical assistance to the poor which maintains their dignity.
Ronald J Sider, 'Christian Ethics and the Good News of the Kingdom' in *Proclaiming Christ in Christ's Way* edited by Vinay Samuel and Albrecht Hauser (Regnum, Oxford, 1989).
Ronald J Sider, 'What is the Gospel?' in *Transformation* Volume 16 No. 1 January 1999.

Missiology

Kwame Bediako, *Theology and Identity – the impact of culture on Christian Thought in the second century and modern Africa* (Oxford, Regnum, 1992).
David Bosch, *Transforming Mission* (Maryknoll, Orbis, 1992) A major text which covers the biblical material admirably but unfortunately neglects some aspects of evangelical missiology from the Two-Thirds World in the last 25 years. Discussed and critiqued in William Saayman and Klippies Kritzinger *Mission in Bold Humility* (Maryknoll, Orbis, 1996).
David Bussau and Vinay Samuel, *How Then Should We Lend?* (Oxford, Opportunity International, 1998)
David Bussau and Vinay Samuel, *Reflections on Christian Microenterprise Development* (Oxford, Opportunity International, 1998)
Tim Chester, *Awakening to a World of Need* (Leicester, Inter-Varsity Press, 1993) An account of the growth of and theological basis for evangelical involvement in development ministries.

Orlando Costas, 'Proclaiming Christ in the Two-Thirds World' in *Sharing Jesus in the Two-Thirds World* edited by Vinay Samuel and Chris Sugden (Grand Rapids, Eerdmans, 1986) The keynote address from the first consultation of Evangelical Mission Theologians from the Two-Thirds World (later INFEMIT).

Orlando Costas, *Christ Outside the Gate* (Maryknoll, Orbis, 1984) Latin American missiologist responding to the challenge of liberation theology from an evangelical commitment.

Orlando Costas, *Liberating News* (Grand Rapids, Eerdmans, 1989) The last work from this pioneering Latin American missiologist of wholistic mission.

Peter Cotterell, *Mission and Meaninglessness* (London, SPCK, 1990) An exposition of mission in the context of Marxism, poverty and religious pluralism.

Samuel Escobar, 'Missiology in the Lausanne Movement' *Transformation* Volume 8 No. 4 October 1991.

Raymond Fung, 'Good News to the Poor – a Case for a Missionary Movement' in *Your Kingdom Come* (WCC 1980) A major study on the place of the poor in the mission of the church.

Raymong Fung, *The Isaianic Agenda* (Risk Books, WCC, Geneva) A practical strategy based on making Isaiah 65 a reality in the lives of communities.

Tom Houston, 'Good News for the Poor' in *Transformation* Vol. 7 No 1 January 1990.

Peter Kuzmic, in Bruce Nicholls ed. *The Church-God's Agent for Change* (Exeter, Paternoster, 1986).

Melba Maggay, *Transforming Society* (Oxford, Regnum, 1995) A biblical and practical exposition of wholistic mission in the Philippines.

Thomas McAlpine, *By Word, Work and Wonder* (Monrovia, MARC, 1995) A collection of case-studies selected from issues of Transformation Journal since 1984.

Bryant Myers, *Walking with the Poor: Principles and Practice of Transformational Development* (Maryknoll, NY and Monrovia, CA: Orbis and World Vision, 1999)

Michael Nazir Ali, *From Everywhere to Everywhere* (London, Collins, 1990). A Two-Thirds World missiology of global partnership.

Michael Nazir Ali, *Mission and Dialogue* (London, SPCK, 1995).

Bruce Nicholls (ed.), *In Word and Deed* (Exeter, Paternoster Press, 1986) The papers presented at the Grand Rapids Consultation on the Relation between Evangelism and Social Responsibility.

Bruce Nicholls and Beulah Wood (eds.), *Sharing Good News with the Poor* (Carlisle, Paternoster Press, 1996) Papers from a World Evangelical Fellowship Consultation.

Rene Padilla, *Mission between the Times* (Eerdmans, Grand Rapids, 1985) An important collection of studies relating the Kingdom of God and mission.

Douglas Petersen, *Not by Might nor by Power* (Oxford, Regnum, 1996) A powerful statement of the social concern of Latin American Pentecostalism.

Philip Sampson, Vinay Samuel, and Chris Sugden, (eds.), *Faith and Modernity* (Oxford, Regnum, 1994).

Vinay Samuel, Herbert Schlossberg and Ronald J Sider, *Christian Faith and Economics in the Post-Cold War Era* (Grand Rapids, Eerdmans, 1994).

Vinay Samuel and Albrecht Hauser (eds.), *Proclaiming Christ in Christ's Way* (Oxford, Regnum, 1989) A collection of essays on mission seeking to express the overlap that had developed between the WCC and evangelicals on mission in the late 1980's.

Vinay Samuel and Chris Sugden (eds.), *AD 2000 and Beyond: A Mission Agenda* (Oxford, Regnum, 1990) A collection of essays on missiology from the Two-Thirds World.

Vinay Samuel and Chris Sugden (eds.), *The Church in Response to Human Need* (Oxford, Regnum, 1987). The papers and report of the Wheaton 1983 consultation.

Vinay Samuel and Chris Sugden (eds.), *Evangelism and the Poor* (Exeter, Paternoster, 1983) A collection of essays from the Two-Thirds World.

Vinay Samuel, 'Gospel and Culture' in *Proclaiming Christ in Christ's Way* (Oxford, Regnum, 1989).

Vinay Samuel, 'The Development Movement – an Overview and an Appraisal' in *Transformation* Volume 13 No 4 October 1996.

Ronald J Sider ed., *Evangelicals and Development* (Exeter, Paternoster, 1981) Papers from an international consultation.

Ronald J Sider, *One Sided Christianity – Evangelism and Social Action* (London, Harper Collins 1993).

Ronald J Sider, *Rich Christians in an Age of Hunger* (London, Hodder, 1978 and reprints) A classic text.

Ronald J Sider, *Cup of Water, Bread of Life* (Grand Rapids, Zondervan, 1994) A series of case studies of wholistic mission.

Chris Sugden, 'Evangelicals and Wholistic Evangelism' in Vinay Samuel and Albrecht Hauser *Proclaiming Christ in Christ's Way* (Oxford, Regnum, 1989). Traces the development of evangelical thinking on evangelism and social concern from Lausanne 1974 to 1988.

Chris Sugden, *Fair Trade as Christian Mission* (Cambridge, Grove Books, 1999).

Chris Sugden, *Seeking the Asian Face of Jesus: the Practice and Theology of Christian Social Witness in Indonesia and India 1974–1996* (Oxford, Regnum, 1997) A unique account of the development of Evangelical Wholistic Mission in Asia.

Chris Sugden, *The Right to be Human* (Cambridge, Grove Booklets, 1997).

Chris Sugden and Oliver Barclay, *Kingdom and Creation in Social Ethics* (Cambridge, Grove Books, 1990)

Paul Vallely, *Bad Samaritans* (London, Harper, 1986).

Andrew Walls, *The Missionary Movement in Christian History* (Edinburgh T and T Clark, 1996) A brilliant exposition of the relation of gospel and culture throughout history.

Miroslav Volf, *Exclusion and Embrace* (Grand Rapids, Eerdmans, 1998).

Chris Wright and Chris Sugden (eds.), *One Gospel, Many Clothes* (Oxford, Regnum, 1990) Case studies in wholistic mission from the Anglican Communion.

Tetsunao Yamamori et al. *Serving with the Poor in Africa: Cases in Wholistic Ministry* (Monrovia, MARC, 1996)

Tetsunao Yamamori et al. *Serving with the Poor in Asia: Cases in Wholistic Ministry* (Monrovia, MARC, 1996)

Tetsunao Yamamori et al. *Serving with the Poor in Latin America: Cases in Wholistic Ministry* (Monrovia, MARC, 1997)

Hwa Yung, *Mangoes and Bananas* (Oxford, Regnum, 1997) A critique of western theology and missiology and an examination of a number of significant Asian missiologists.

Journals

The journal *Transformation, an international evangelical dialogue on mission and ethics*, published by the Oxford Centre for Mission Studies, and begun in 1984 has acted as the journal of record of the Transformation movement in missiology. Many documents of consultations held on missiological topics have been published in its pages. Published by Oxford Centre for Mission Studies, PO Box 70, Oxford, OX2 6HB. E-mail OCMS@ocms.ac.uk web site regnumbooks.com

The journal *Mision*, Jose Marmol 1734, 1602 Florida, Buenos Aires, Argentina. Edited by C. Rene Padilla. E-mail admin@kairos.cci.org.ar

The journal *Prism*, published by Evangelicals for Social Action, 10 East Lancaster Avenue, Wynnewood, PA 19606, USA. E-mail prism@esa-online.org. Publisher Ronald J. Sider.

Index

266
M6784